Fresh from the Garden

Also Published by the University of Minnesota Press

Growing Perennials in Cold Climates
   Mike Heger, Debbie Lonnee, and John Whitman

Growing Roses in Cold Climates
   Richard Hass, Jerry Olson, and John Whitman

Growing Shrubs and Small Trees in Cold Climates
   Debbie Lonnee, Nancy Rose, Don Selinger, and John Whitman

Fresh
from the
Garden

⬩•◆•⬩

An Organic Guide to Growing
Vegetables, Berries, and Herbs
in Cold Climates

⬩•◆•⬩

John Whitman

University of Minnesota Press

Minneapolis

London

The University of Minnesota Press gratefully acknowledges the financial support for the publication of this book from Whole Foods Market Minnesota.

All photographs were taken by John Whitman with the exception of those on pages 46, 102, 106, and 118, which were taken by Donna Whitman.

Published by the University of Minnesota Press
111 Third Avenue South, Suite 290
Minneapolis, MN 55401-2520
http://www.upress.umn.edu

Printed in China

The University of Minnesota is an equal-opportunity educator and employer.

22 21 20 19 18 17 16   10 9 8 7 6 5 4 3 2 1

Library of Congress Cataloging-in-Publication Data
Names: Whitman, John, author.
Title: Fresh from the garden : an organic guide to growing vegetables, berries, and herbs in cold climates / John Whitman.
Description: Minneapolis, MN : University of Minnesota Press, 2017. | Includes index.
Identifiers: LCCN 2016027971 | ISBN 978-0-8166-9839-4 (hc) | ISBN 978-0-8166-9841-7 (pb)
Subjects: LCSH: Organic gardening—Snowbelt States. | Organic gardening—Canada. | Vegetable gardening—Snowbelt States. | Vegetable
    gardening—Canada. | Berries—Snowbelt States. | Berries—Canada. | Herb gardening—Snowbelt States. | Herb gardening—Canada.
Classification: LCC SB453.5 .W52 2017 | DDC 635.9/87—dc23
LC record available at https://lccn.loc.gov/2016027971

CONTENTS

INTRODUCTION

I have been growing vegetables, berries, and herbs in cold climates for more than half a century. This growing guide is based primarily on personal experience. I have experimented with various gardening techniques and will share my opinions on these throughout the book. The use of chemicals in a garden is highly controversial. This guide is intended for organic gardeners but will certainly be useful to those who have not yet converted to this way of thinking. I try to keep the format easy to use, the writing simple and clear, the information concise and precise, and the advice as opinionated as possible. Some of the advice I offer is essentially heresy in the gardening world. It is simply a point of view; eat the chicken and throw away the bones. As for eating, the book provides information on each plant's nutritional value and tips on cooking, from harvesting to preparation—just an added bonus for those who don't have the slightest idea what to do with burdock.

Why I began growing vegetables at an early age is hard to explain. The simplest reason is that I liked it. I also made extra money selling the produce, but it was not enough to explain my fascination with gardening. I was very lucky: we lived on a four-acre hobby farm with an assortment of animals that gave me an endless supply of manure. I had no idea what organic gardening was—I simply used what I had at hand, didn't have enough money to buy chemicals, and was too ignorant to know that disease and insects were hovering

over my shoulder waiting to devastate my crops. I encountered a few problems . . . it took me a few years to associate little white butterflies with green worms on the cabbage, but those problems really didn't make that much difference, which is why I believe that in the home garden you can do just fine without chemical intervention. If you move up to mini-farming to earn extra money, you may begin to use organic pesticides, but many mini-farmers do not.

As I have become older, I have recognized that my passion for gardening increasingly comes from an aesthetic, almost mystical place, similar to the feeling associated with art and religion. Creating something special from the soil brings us into the circle of life with full recognition that from death springs life. I feel like Thomas Jefferson, who said, "Though I'm an old man, I am but a young gardener." Gardening keeps you fit, always looking forward with hope, surrounded by beauty, and in a peaceful state of mind. It just feels good. I like it. I hope you will, too.

Fresh from the Garden

To get the very best, most nutritious, freshest-tasting vegetables, you have to grow your own. Here's why: vegetables sold commercially are picked days or weeks before being sold, and every day that passes means loss of flavor. If you have ever eaten fresh peas straight from the garden, you already know how true this is. Many vegetables are picked too late because produce is sold by size or weight. There is no comparison between overly mature vegetables and ones that have been picked at just the right moment. It's possible that you have never experienced the true taste of lima beans, peas, pattypan or summer squash, new potatoes, and many other fresh vegetables.

Some unusual vegetables are not available in stores. Commercial growers appeal to the major demands and skip the minor ones, which means that interesting and delicious foods are not for sale simply because the demand for them is limited. In this guide you will find offbeat vegetables that you may end up liking more than ones you are already familiar with. Stores must carry specific varieties of vegetables suited to shipping and storage, many of which are far inferior in taste to varieties that you can grow at home. For example, some of the very best tomatoes ship poorly because of their ultrathin skins; these are incredibly delicious, but it is only practical to grow them in the home garden.

Vegetables start to lose their nutritional value as soon as they are picked, but for the most part even more is lost in processing. The vegetables you grow at home are rich in vitamins, and if properly prepared as soon as possible after picking, they lose very little of their health benefits. All of this adds up to one thing: if you want the best, you have to grow your own.

Doing this in cold climates can be tricky. As Mark Twain might have put it, "The coldest winter I ever spent was a summer in Duluth." In colder areas we have to do odd things to get the most out of our gardens, and that's what this growing guide is all about: helping you get the most and best vegetables, herbs, and berries in cold climates whether you are a home gardener or moving into mini-farming. You don't have to be a magician to have a bountiful garden, but it helps to have basic information about the needs of the plants you are growing, an understanding of how to work in a cold climate, and basic gardening know-how that applies to plants generally. The three blend together, with experts often disagreeing on the finer points. You will end up disagreeing, too, sometimes, with this guide, but that's not the point. A beautiful, satisfying garden filled with ripe vegetables and berries—that's what counts. How you get there is going to be a personal trip, and the tips in this guide could help make this trip one of the best you have ever taken.

Organic Gardening

Organic gardening is a general concept, with many dis-agreements about what it is. It entails working with nature to get the most out of the garden while keeping the soil and surrounding environment healthy. The two key factors most commonly advocated are the use of natural fertilizers and avoidance of synthetic pesticides. It's actually more complicated than that, since really good organic gardens minimize outside resources while replenishing anything that is taken from the garden at the same time. In this way, organic gardens are systems, of which there are many types. The system advocated in this growing guide reveals itself as varied gardening techniques that are combined in a coordinated manner. The goal is a good yield of vegetables, berries, and herbs that not only taste great but are nutritious and safe. If you follow the steps described throughout this book, you will reach this goal—with a few bumps along the way. There is an old saying that "gardening is not a destination, it's a path."

Myths about Gardening

It's a myth that certain people are born with a green thumb. Your interest in gardening may come early in life or be inspired later. Good gardening comes from hard work (patience), knowledge (logic and know-how), and love of gardening (faith, joy, and passion). Some books and articles tell you that you can do it all in a few minutes a day. This makes for a good sales pitch, the get-rich-quick appeal, but it's the no-maintenance myth. Good gardeners work hard, but since they enjoy gardening, it doesn't seem like work. Good gardening takes time and energy. Many experts try to impose their way of thinking on you, but there is no right or wrong way to garden. There are many ways to be a good gardener, and these can seem quite contradictory. Some people have gardens that are meticulous, with no weeds in sight; other people believe that weeds can be beneficial to gardens and use them to encourage growth in the vegetable patch (strange but true). The only thing that counts is that your gardening method works for you.

You are in control of your garden—another myth. You can help your garden grow, but other forces are outside your control. You simply react to these forces by making the best choices you can. Letting go of the need to control and replacing it with working with nature are important. That's why gardening is both a science and an art. And that's part of the reason it's so much fun—it's full of surprises. Another misconception is that you will have a great garden the first year. Even the best gardeners, ones with years of experience, have off years. So you shrug your shoulders and start again, just like farmers do. Yes, you could have a really good garden the first year, but don't expect to; most gardens take three years or longer to peak. Unless you are extremely lucky, your soil will require a couple of years or longer to become the rich loam that all gardeners learn to recognize by its color (black) and feel (moist, loose, crumbly). It takes a year or two or longer to figure out how to control marauders and insects, and a year or two to master most gardening techniques. This guide will help you with this and will save you effort, time, and money.

Gardening in Cold Climates

A cold climate is defined in this guide as any area where temperatures can dip below −20°F during the winter. This temperature threshold is important for any perennial plant exposed at that time. Some plants die back and are extremely hardy, coming back to life in spring; others die back but are less likely to survive without winter protection; and still others stay standing with woody canes or stems that can be killed by extremely low or fluctuating temperatures.

The majority of plants in the home garden are grown as annuals. For them, a cold climate is defined by a shorter growing season and longer day length. The abbreviated season means that special measures must be taken to get a good yield or any yield at all. Exactly how to do this is explained in detail throughout the guide. Day length also affects the productivity and choice of specific groups and varieties within those groups. This growing guide deals with all of these concerns. Throughout Part II, specific plants are starred with five asterisks (*****): these plants grow well in cold climates. This does not mean they are the best plants in any given plant group, but they are an excellent place to start for comparison. Many gardeners grow more than one

plant in a plant group, and over a period of years they replace the poorer performers with new choices. New plants are constantly being offered. The goal of the companies selling them is to pique your curiosity and get you to try them. In any given year several of these will shine and become five-asterisk plants in future editions—the plants to beat, so to speak.

Using the Growing Guide

Read through Part I of this guide before starting to grow individual plants. This is especially important for anyone new to gardening. Even if you are experienced, there likely will be information new to you there. The chapters are as succinct as possible; getting to the point quickly is one of the goals of this growing guide. Reading Part I will not take a lot of time, and you can skip information already familiar to you.

The section on mail-order sources in chapter 2 includes an explanation about how to find specific varieties. These may be offered by many companies or by only one. Every variety listed in this book was checked for availability at the time of writing, but varieties come and go. That is one reason why a number of plants are included in each section. If one variety is no longer available, several others could take its place.

The glossary at the end of the book lists many terms, some of which may be new to you. Like all activities, gardening has its own language, and understanding it from the start will be helpful.

PART I

The Basics of Growing Vegetables, Berries, and Herbs

CHAPTER 1

WHERE TO PLANT

Where you plant your garden is determined by a number of factors, many of which you can't control. Each plant description in Part II includes simple guidelines on where that plant will do well under the headings "Site and Light" and "Soil and Moisture."

Choosing a Garden Site

For the most part the plants in this guide thrive in full sun with at least six to eight hours of direct light a day. Without the energy provided by sunlight, plants cannot combine the hydrogen in water with the carbon in carbon dioxide to make carbohydrates (food for plants) through the process known as photosynthesis. Full sun may be available in different parts of your yard, so a garden does not have to be all in one place. Spaces with good light often vary in size and shape. You can grow a lot more than you might think in very little space.

Sun affects temperature. Warmth-loving plants will do poorly unless they get enough light and heat. Even plants that thrive in cool weather need sun but can get by in cooler weather or cooler locations. However, no plants do well in frost pockets, areas at the base of hills where cool air accumulates. Temperatures may be lower or higher by lakes depending on their size and location, higher by buildings and walls, and higher in cities than zone maps indicate. These areas are often referred to as microclimates.

All plants need ample amounts of water. The amount varies by plant. Having a garden or gardens by a water source is important.

The quality of soil is one of the most important factors in growing plants. Plants thrive in nutrient-rich soil that drains freely and is neither too alkaline nor too acidic. This is one thing within your control. A number of gardening methods are described later in this chapter. All of these deal with improving or importing healthy soil into whatever area you intend to use for growing plants.

Wind can affect the growth of plants. A gentle wind is fine, but gusty areas can cause some serious problems. You may not be able to find a calm spot in your yard, but you can provide protection from wind with either plantings or structures such as trellises and solid fences.

In cold climates a gentle, south-facing slope is ideal,

Herbs and vegetables grow well in beds and borders.

These are the best characteristics of the popular methods. If you are new to gardening, start small. There's an old saying: Plant only the size of garden your partner can take care of.

Beds and Borders

Intermingle plants into flower beds and borders. Parsley makes a lovely edging plant, herbs are easy to mix in with flowering plants, and some plants, such as okra, have gorgeous hibiscus-like flowers and bright pods. Numerous plants included in this guide can be mixed into such a setting.

Compost Gardening

The heading explains it all. Make compost piles in different areas of the garden. Or make one large, elongated pile over a period of years if you have the space. This is nicknamed a "walking compost pile." One end will be almost completely decomposed while the other is almost entirely fresh. Let the piles or oldest portion of a long pile decompose for at least one year, dig holes into the pile and fill with topsoil, plant seeds or transplants, and let them grow. This works especially well for vining plants such as pumpkins and winter squash. I use this method every year on the edges of a level garden where vines can spread out freely.

You can also dig pits and toss organic matter into them. Make sure that they are covered so that children, friends, and neighbors do not fall into these "traps." Keep adding material throughout the gardening season. Once the material has broken down, you can plant in these humus-rich holes. The only advantage to this is that the compost pile is hidden from view; otherwise, I would stick to raised compost piles. You can also dig smaller holes. Dump kitchen scraps into these, and cover with soil. This sounds simple in theory, but animals have an uncanny ability to find and dig these up even when the holes are quite deep. I prefer burying kitchen scraps deep into a raised compost pile before covering them with a thick layer of organic debris. See more detailed information on composting later in this chapter.

Community and Guerilla Gardens

If you do not have space for a garden where you live, check into the availability of a community garden plot. A number of city dwellers have found these to be a good replacement for the home garden. Gardening does not have to be in a designated community garden. It can be almost anywhere with available space. This is often referred to as "guerilla gardening," which roughly translates into gardening wherever you can even though you may not legally own the land. This has become a nationwide trend. Few people complain; most people applaud this kind of inventive thinking. One warn-

but steep slopes should be terraced. Relatively few gardeners have to deal with this problem, but it is one that can be solved.

Do not grow plants under gutters, under trees, too close to large shrubs, or in areas that remain wet for any length of time. Overflowing gutters crush plants. Trees prevent light from getting to plants. Their roots and those of large shrubs rob essential water from plants growing under or near them. Wet areas stop oxygen from getting to plant roots, which results in root rot.

Types of Gardens

There is no one right way to grow plants. Many methods have evolved over the years and often have their roots in practices dating back centuries or even millennia. The three most popular ways to grow vegetables in the home garden are in containers, level gardens, and raised beds. All methods of gardening have strengths and weaknesses. I like gardens with extremely loose soil to a depth of at least 12 inches and free of rocks and debris, and laid out in a way that it makes it easy for me to care for and harvest any produce.

Squash and other vining plants thrive in active compost piles, which are both moist and hot.

ing: Some of these areas may contain heavy metals that can cause health problems. More about this later.

Container Gardening

It is amazing how many plants grow well in containers placed on balconies, decks, patios, or rooftops. In fact, this is now a popular way to grow vegetables where people once believed they couldn't grow anything at all. While certain crops are clearly not suited to this type of growing, many do extremely well. Container gardening is addressed throughout this guide, and specific varieties are often recommended for this method.

Container gardening is most popular in cities where traditional gardens are at a premium or virtually nonexistent, but if you have space and a more traditional garden, it is still a smart way to grow herbs and leafy greens. If containers are on a deck, you can enjoy both their color and scent. Some herbs are not hardy and need to be brought indoors during the winter. These include French thyme, Greek oregano, lavender (in many areas), lemon verbena, and rosemary. When brought indoors, pots are typically placed on saucers filled with pebbles or small rocks. Water that accumulates in the saucers is usually dumped out by the end of the day,

and the soil in the pot allowed to dry out somewhat before the next watering.

Container gardening is an intensive form of gardening. Small spaces, meticulously cared for, can be very productive. It requires few tools. Anything that will hold soil can be used as a container for growing fresh vegetables. You can use household odds and ends or construct more elaborate containers from scratch. Good containers are barrels, baskets, buckets, gallon cans, garbage cans, plastic milk jugs, clay pots, plastic pots, sinks, strawberry jars, troughs, tubs, wheelbarrows—you name it. You might even try black plastic bags filled with soil. Admittedly, the most beautiful containers can be expensive. I prefer clay pots because they "breathe" freely. Soak them in water before using them for the first time in the season. If containers have been used before, it takes only a few minutes to wash them out with soap and water. Wiping them off with vinegar kills some pathogens. Cleaning pots with a solution containing one part bleach to nine parts water definitely kills pathogens; however, some organic gardeners will not use bleach, since it is quite toxic. Since you rinse the pots off after treating them in this way, I do not see this as a problem.

Fill appropriately sized containers with potting soil, and provide feet under the pot for good drainage.

Make your own potting soil by mixing loam, perlite, and sphagnum peat moss in roughly equal parts.

Containers can be extremely heavy if filled with garden soil. Don't use it, since it tends to compact badly, especially if it is clay based. Use a soilless mix. These mixes are light and sterile, drain freely, but hold moisture for a reasonable period of time. Mixes are expensive but widely available. Sun Gro Horticulture makes some organic OMRI (Organic Materials Review Institute)–approved soilless mixes. Miracle-Gro® makes an excellent soilless potting mix that is relatively inexpensive if purchased in 2-cubic-foot bags when on sale. Pro Mix® is a superb soilless mix but extremely expensive. Bags or bales of Miracle-Gro® or Pro Mix® are technically not organic, since they contain minimal amounts of synthetic fertilizers. Miracle-Gro® does make an organic soilless mix, but it doesn't stack up to its synthetic cousin.

Alternatively, use potting soil. Note that potting soil is a vague term and can contain different or almost identical ingredients to soilless mixes. If bags are heavy, use the soilless mixes. Of course, you can make your own potting mix, and many gardeners do using a variety of ingredients including bark (aged for several years), coir (shredded coconut husks), compost, manure (well aged), perlite, leaf mold, sand (for special plants), soil (preferably sterilized by baking or pouring boiling water through it and used sparingly), sphagnum peat moss, and vermiculite. They may also add alfalfa meal, blood meal, bonemeal, charcoal, Epsom salt, fish meal, greensand, limestone, rock phosphate, and soybean meal according to "personal formulas." If possible, make potting soils well in advance, and keep warm and moist for several weeks to allow for the release of ammonia and breakdown of organic acids. Note: Some gardeners place a few squashed pop cans or milk jugs in the bottom of large pots, not to help with drainage, but to reduce the amount of potting mix needed to fill up the pot. You do not need to put broken pieces of pot, pebbles, or rocks into the bottom of pots. This was once advised to help drainage but now is considered unnecessary.

The size of the container should match the potential size of the plant. Large plants require large pots. As the plants grow, they create an extensive root system demanding space. And the tops of the plants get heavy and will tip over if the pots are too small. Container-grown plants often require staking, especially if they bear heavy fruit. Staking should be done simultaneously with planting, or plants can be tied to supports such as rails on decks.

Pots can get really hot in direct sun. The color or material a pot is made of can make a difference. For example, black and metal pots get hotter than others. You can soften the effect of heat and drying sun by double potting. Place a smaller pot inside a larger one. Rest the smaller pot on a frog, a little metal support available at most floral shops. Fill the space between the two pots with sphagnum moss or coir, and keep it moist at all times. (Sphagnum moss is long and stringy and should not be confused with sphagnum peat moss. It may contain the fungus *Sporotrichum (Sporothrix) schenckii,* which is the cause of a disease called sporotrichosis. This skin infection can be painful and often takes months and even years to heal. For this reason, sphagnum moss is being replaced in many instances by coir [coconut husk fibers].)

You must water container plants frequently, sometimes twice daily during a summer heat wave. Vegetables require lots of water to grow rapidly. The faster they grow, the better

Push soil back into place, and water immediately if it pulls away from the side of a pot.

they produce. Test the soil by pushing your finger several inches down. If it comes up dry, water the plant immediately. If soil pulls away from the edge of a pot, push it back in place. This is a sign of underwatering. Water the pot to the brim until it pours out the drain holes. Then water again. If containers do not have drain holes, watering must be done so that water does not pool up in the bottom of the pot, causing root rot. For this reason, drain holes are highly recommended, as are supports, such as small feet, placed under the containers to keep the drain holes open. Place mulch on the soil surface to keep soil moist and cool. Cocoa bean husks are attractive and have a chocolate smell, but pulverized leaves look nice and cost nothing.

Frequent watering means loss of nutrients. You may have to fertilize consistently to keep plants growing well. Use of diluted fertilizers is highly recommended. Apply the fertilizer to the soil or foliage by misting leaves with the diluted solution.

You can move containers easily from one spot to another to take advantage of different locations. Simply move the pot into bright sun for warmth-loving plants or into a shady location for leafy vegetables that prefer cool, moist areas. You may want to have a board with casters or a dolly to help you with this process since containers can be heavy.

Lasagna (Lasagne) Gardening

Lasagna gardening is an offshoot of no-till gardening, described later. Choose a sunny location in any level area, including one covered with grass or previously used as a garden. You do not have to remove grass or weeds. Just mow them over, rake up, and set aside. Now cover the proposed garden area with cardboard (not coated) or thick sections of newspaper (not colored). The size of the garden is up to you, but a 4-feet-by-12-feet area is a good size for your first garden. Scrounge up whatever organic material you can find to place in layers over the paper. The layered garden can be open or enclosed. Compost, kitchen scraps, grass clippings, leaves, manure, sphagnum peat moss, weeds, and so on are added regularly in layers over a period of months or years. Place any available topsoil in holes in the debris. Plant only in that soil. You are essentially growing plants in a marginally active compost pile. Until the material breaks down, this type of gardening is suited to a limited number of plants. It is essentially an offshoot of "sheet composting," where organic debris is spread out in gardens to decompose. Note that animals get into kitchen scraps far more easily in lasagna gardens than if buried in deep mounds of compost.

In my opinion, the best time to start this garden is in the fall when leaves are available by the bagful. Try to build the garden up to a height of 24 inches or so. Moisten mate-

Flat gardens tilled each year are popular, even though tilling can affect soil structure.

rial lightly each time you add it as a layer to the pile. Over the winter the material will sink somewhat and will begin decomposing once the weather warms up in spring.

Level Gardens

Most gardeners grow vegetables in level gardens, an area on their property that is level and in full sun. So-called level gardens may be gently sloped. If the slope is too intense, the area can be terraced into a series of truly level gardens. If you are lucky, there may already be a garden in place. If not, you have to prepare it. You can grow vegetables, herbs, and berries wherever there are weeds, brush, or trees growing. You just have to clear the area.

Removing trees is difficult, both physically and emotionally—unless the tree is in bad shape. Cutting down a large tree requires experience, so if you have not done this before and know little about chain saws, hire a professional. Tree removal is expensive. And the debris has to be chipped and hauled away. Or it can be burned if zoning laws allow it in your area. It can also be chipped and used as a cover for pathways.

Stump removal is also difficult. Hire someone with a stump grinder to do this job for you. It is back-breaking work, and a professional with an appropriate machine can

Steep slopes can be terraced to provide flat beds for planting, as in this lush and large garden.

remove a stump in about half an hour. Do not rent a stump remover. The kind professionals use is not available for rent, and the ones you can rent are usually next to worthless. A good stump remover costs thousands of dollars.

Most home gardeners can remove smaller trees and shrubs by themselves. A chain saw makes the job easier, but you can use an ax for the trunk and lopping shears for the branches. A pickax helps in removing the stumps of smaller trees and shrubs. Wear eye protection during this kind of work—brush goes down fighting! Also wear gloves and a long-sleeved shirt. Buckthorn and wild blackberries have vicious spines.

What you need to do aboveground is obvious; underground, not so clear. Root removal on larger trees is a real chore; on smaller ones, comparatively easy. The diameter of roots is largest near the stump. Dig around the root, and follow it out as far as you can. As you get to the end of the root, it gets narrower. Cut it with loppers. Then pull up as hard as you can. All along the root there may be other roots that angle off the main root, either sideways or deep into the ground. Keep cutting these and lifting up. By the time you get close to the stump, you may be able to pull the larger end of the root out. You will have to repeat this process many times since root systems can be extensive and widespread. Using a rototiller to dig up the soil surface helps a lot. The tines hang up on the roots, pinpointing where they are.

The next step is weed removal. There are annual, biennial, and perennial weeds. Weeding is covered in detail in chapter 4.

Sodded areas pose a different kind of challenge. If you rototill sod, you just spread roots (stolons) throughout the soil. They will resprout and become a nightmare. Do it the right way from the start. Remove the sod. There are many ways to do this. With an edger, a tool with a curved blade, scoop out a little sod around the perimeter of your proposed garden. With a sharp spade dig deep enough under the sod

to get the stolons. You don't have to dig deep into the soil, but deep enough so that your spade can slide under the roots. With practice you can remove a spadeful of sod at a time. A pickax also works well. Toss the sod into a wheelbarrow, and whack each piece against the inside of the wheelbarrow. Most of the soil will fall off, leaving grass and roots in your hand. Pick out any pieces of root or debris that drop into the soil. Put the sod and any pieces of root into a bucket. Keep doing this until all of the grass and stolons have been separated from the soil. This is much easier to do than it sounds.

Hopefully, you will have no more to do than just remove sod and weeds. Now that the garden is cleared, move on to soil preparation. Dig into the ground with a spade. Make a deep cut, and flip the soil over. If you have good soil, it will be dark and crumbly the full depth of the spade. Unfortunately, this dark topsoil may be covering a subsoil that is less desirable. You can tell by the color change from the upper soil surface to the subsoil. Your goal is to have at least 12 inches of good soil. If you only have a thin layer of topsoil, the two main ways of dealing with this problem are to loosen it and add soil or to build a raised bed. In both cases you may have to purchase soil—more about that later. If you have a deep layer of topsoil, till, spade, or plow it until it is loose. While doing this, remove all debris, especially rocks. Tilling the soil brings these to the surface and locates larger rocks in the subsoil. Dig out the larger rocks. If really large, roll them out of the hole onto a tarp or strong piece of cloth. Dragging large rocks along the soil surface and out of the garden is much easier than lifting them. Use a pronged garden rake to run through the soil. Rocks of any size make a distinctive sound as the metal hits them. Pick up and toss them into a large pail to remove them from the garden soil. Avoid mixing the subsoil with the topsoil. Ideally, it is best to till and separate the topsoil from the subsoil, loosen the subsoil, and then place the topsoil back in place, a process often labeled "double digging." This is incredibly hard work in most instances, suggested by many, done by few. The technique is described in more detail later.

Like so many things in organic gardening, tilling is controversial. Few people disagree with the idea that tilling may be necessary as a starting point for gardening, since it loosens often compacted topsoil. It's a quick and easy way to get things going. However, detractors claim that tilling loosens soil only to have soil compact again later in heavy rains, that the tiller blades (tines) stir subsoil into the topsoil, that the blades disturb worm "tunnels" and decrease the worm population, that microbes die off as they are brought up and out of their natural state, that fungal strands are broken, that a hardpan is created at the base of the blades, that tilling brings thousands of weed seeds to the soil surface, that the soil structure is harmed, damaging the delicate balance of air space (pores) between soil particles, that organic material breaks down rapidly when soil is tilled, and so on. In short, tilling disturbs the unique natural balance of interrelated organisms often referred to as the "soil food web," described simply but in depth in the USDA's *Soil Biology Primer,* an old but well-written and illustrated booklet. These organisms include arthropods, bacteria, fungi, mites, nematodes, protozoa, slime molds, and numerous other soil organisms that interact in fascinating ways to enrich the soil with nutrients, control pests, break down pesticides, and reduce disease while protecting the quality of air, soil, and water (stop nutrients from leaching into underground water). In brief, they create a soil that is vibrant and alive. The points against tilling are well made, especially in the lengthy book *Teaming with Microbes,* coauthored by Jeff Lowenfels and Wayne Lewis. Tilling probably does everything for which it is criticized. However, the alternatives are few. By applying compost, green manures, and soil amendments and employing only limited shallow tilling, the structure and living soil can be renewed—in my opinion. So I continue limited tilling as part of an overall system of gardening and willingly except the fact that others find this "unacceptable." I augment level gardening with raised beds, another gardening style I strongly endorse.

The best time to create a level garden is in the fall. The plowing, spading, or tilling kicks up insects and exposes disease organisms, and many of these die. In the fall you can add organic matter and anything else required by the soil. These blend into the soil over the winter. Just leave the soil in a rough form. Don't rake it smooth. Now cover the garden with a thick layer of mulch kept nice and moist, so the worms will go to work for you until cold temperatures force them underground. The soil will be richer and easier to work in the spring thanks to these allies. While starting a garden in the fall is best, you may not have the luxury of choice and will have to start your gardens in the spring. And that's fine.

Most gardeners enclose level and other types of gardens with fences to keep marauders at bay.

Mulched and No-Till Gardens

Mulched and no-till gardens are variations of the level garden. A flat space, usually a rectangle, is left "as is" without any tilling at all. You plant seeds and plants into the ground in furrows or holes and then surround them with mulch. This method may be called "natural" or "do-nothing farming." Fukuoka, a Japanese farmer, made the method famous by creating a gardening philosophy around it. A pragmatic pursuit took on spiritual overtones. Few people follow this method to the letter, since most organic gardeners disturb the soil, compost, and weed—all seen as unnatural by Fukuoka. Ruth Stout is also famous for her success with mulched gardens, which she often tended "au naturel." She took natural gardening to the limit.

An obvious advantage of these gardens is that you don't have to plow or till the garden. You don't have to create any raised beds. These gardens are the least expensive and easiest to start up *if you have a good source of mulch* (see chapter 4 for information on mulches). In the no-till garden thick mulching is absolutely essential. The mulch creates an ideal environment for worms, which come into the area and work through the soil like underground tillers. Gardeners who use these methods firmly believe that they create a much better soil structure than do traditional garden methods, which rely on tilling, whose disadvantages have already been described. Mulching takes time, however, and the amounts of mulch required can be difficult and expensive to obtain.

The no-till method requires skill, garden know-how, and patience. It does work, but it may take two to three years or much longer for the garden to peak depending on the original quality of the soil. For some people, the trade-off between light labor and longer time is worth it. But this can be a difficult method for the beginning gardener, who has more immediate success with transplants and seeds planted in soil that has been worked thoroughly and enriched properly. The advanced gardener has the know-how and instinct to do this where it counts—where plants and seed will be planted and nowhere else.

The no-till method doesn't work everywhere. It's fine in areas with good drainage and a noncompacted layer of topsoil. It's fine in climates where summer temperatures soar, but in areas that tend to stay cool and moist, it can cause problems. The section on mulch in chapter 4 explains why.

Whether you make a no-till garden in spring or fall makes little difference. The key is when mulch is available—you need lots of it to be effective. Some people equate this method somewhat with lasagna gardening because you are building up layer after layer of any available organic matter in the garden. So when you add the layers is far less important than the need to keep adding it whenever you can. There is in my opinion a compromise, which is to till compacted or poor soil lightly once, plant, mulch, and never till again. The no-till method is often said to be the best way to garden for people who are busy, ill, lazy, old, or tired. I disagree—it's not *that* easy.

Raised-Bed Gardens

Raised beds are commonly built in areas with little topsoil or compacted subsoil with poor drainage—areas otherwise

Peanuts grow vigorously in this short raised bed filled with soil enriched with organic amendments.

If there is fieldstone on your site, use it to build raised beds. Make sure the first row of rocks is level.

worthless for gardening since good drainage is essential for healthy root growth. Growing vegetables in soil mounded into an 8- to 12-inch bed has been going on for centuries. It is just a variation of the ancient Chinese mound system or the French intensive system. A raised bed can be temporary, a mound of soil sloped down on both sides with a flat top, or permanent, an area enclosed by nontoxic boards, cement blocks, stones, or timbers. You can make permanent beds as high, wide, and as long as you want. Many gardeners make a series of raised beds.

Raised beds have many things going for them. By covering permanent raised beds with plastic in fall, you get a jump on the season in spring, as the plastic traps heat at that time. Permanent raised beds are easy to cover with row covers to prevent insects from attacking young plants. Permanent raised beds contain the growth of plants that spread, such as the runners of strawberries or the roots of meandering mint. Tacking fencing on the sides of these raised beds keeps rabbits out. Different beds can be prepared for differing needs of specific plants. This can be as exact as creating soil that is either more or less acidic, more or less sandy, more or less fertile, and so on, so that the bed is geared to a specific plant or group of plants. Raised beds dry out quickly after a rain

and warm up faster in spring, both an advantage—you can work in the beds sooner—and disadvantage—the soil dries out quickly in warm, hot periods. Raised beds are easy to care for. Weeding and watering these contained areas can be done easily from the sides of the bed. Soaking a contained area cuts down on water waste.

Raised beds have some disadvantages. Constructing permanent beds takes time, and although the carpentry work is basic, it's still work. Permanent raised beds are hard to move. If you prepare certain beds for specific plants or groups of plants by changing the acidity, fertility, or tilth of the soil, then rotating crops (a good policy) is difficult. Raised beds are also quite expensive.

Use common sense in making beds. Match the width of the bed to your arm length and strength of your back. You should be able to reach the middle of the bed easily from both sides. You should never have to walk on the soil in these beds, which eliminates soil compaction. This means beds can be anywhere from 3 to 5 feet wide. Make beds a comfortable length to walk around regularly. Most gardeners like beds no longer than 10 feet, although others build them longer. Some gardeners make much smaller beds, filling them with what amounts to a soilless mix rather than soil. These mixes are loose, hold moisture, and contain no weed seed but, in my opinion, are better in containers than in raised beds, partially because making or buying mixes is extremely expensive. However, if you have limited time and energy, the trade-off in expense may be worth it.

If you make a number of beds, be sure to make paths wide enough for a wheelbarrow to navigate through them. Cover the pathway with shredded bark, which is typically free at compost sites or can be purchased inexpensively from utility companies, especially after storms.

Most people build the sides of raised beds with rot-resistant wood. Use self-screwing stainless steel screws, not nails, for fastening the wood. However, if rocks are plentiful, these can replace wood and be attractive, although weeds do get into the spaces between cracks.

Although you can make permanent beds at any time of year, the best time is in the fall. It's easiest to make beds when the soil is on the dry side, and it's more comfortable making beds when it's cool but not wet. In most areas, there are usually cool, dry spells in the fall when you can work soil easily. Permanent beds should have lots of organic matter mixed in with the soil. If you add this in the fall, it will break down by spring and enrich the bed. And, of course, in the spring permanent beds dry out more quickly than level gardens, even in wet, cold years, giving you a jump on the season.

Straw Bale Gardening

Growing plants in bales of straw is a fun way to introduce kids to gardening or to grow plants in offbeat places where there is little or no soil. It's also handy for people with limited space and limits on the number and types of plants they want to grow. Straw bales are made up of hollow stalks of grain, which may or may not have been grown organically. Contact some local farmers to see whether you can find an organic source. Or buy available straw and take your chances. Straw bales are expensive, heavy, and break down within two to three years. Getting them to your house requires a trailer or a good sense of humor as straw sticks to just about everything, including your clothes and the interior of your car, which you may want to protect by wrapping bales with plastic. Straw is usually clean but may contain the seed heads of thistles.

Choose a spot for your garden with as much sun as possible. Laying down landscape fabric over the "garden" area is optional. Set the bales on their sides in as long or short a row or rows as you choose. The hollow portions of stalks should be up. The strings, usually synthetic, run along the sides of the bale and keep the straw from breaking apart—at least, in theory. You may want to run a couple of strands of wire tightly around the bales to keep them from collapsing.

You can drive posts into the ends of the rows and run wire between them to support some vining plants. The posts will also support a canopy to protect plants during early-spring and late-season cold spells.

About two weeks or so before planting, fertilize and moisten the tops of the bales. Keep doing this every few days. This initiates decomposition of the straw, just as in a compost pile. By adding fertilizer and potting soil to the top of bales, you create a mini-garden in the decomposing organic material. Although straw bales do hold moisture well, consistent watering is critical. Moist straw bales sprout mushrooms like crazy, but this is not a problem as long as you do not eat the abundant fungi.

Straw bale gardening has one advantage over building a typical raised bed: the tops of the bales are well off the ground, which may stop rabbits from damaging plants. However, they aren't high enough to stop deer.

Once the bales break apart, they must be replaced. The straw is an excellent material to add to compost piles, but remove and toss the strings into the garbage. I have given you the principles of this growing method; for more detail, see the book *Straw Bale Gardens* by Joel Karsten.

Straw bales, fine for temporary gardens, should be wired or tied together to prevent them from breaking apart.

Vining plants, such as peas, grow well on wire stretched between deeply planted metal or wooden stakes.

Vertical Gardening

Vertical gardening can be done on its own or in combination with the other styles of gardening. Instead of growing plants on a flat plane, you train them to run up vertical space. This method of gardening works beautifully with vining plants. You prevent many diseases by providing a vertical support for good air circulation and light. It is easy to mulch and fertilize plants growing vertically. Vegetables grown vertically can also be quite beautiful. For instance, the bright red blooms of the scarlet runner bean make for an attractive vining plant. Vegetables and fruits are easier to pick when grown on supports. They are less hidden than on bush plants and seem to dangle in front of your eyes. Picking goes smoothly and fast. However, unless you can improvise vertical support with tree branches (pea stakes) or already have a vertical space set up (fence or wall), creating supports can be expensive. Setting up supports can take a fair amount of time, no matter how easy it looks in books.

Supports must be anchored deeply in the soil and built solidly so they do not blow over in the wind.

Prepare supports before planting the vegetables. You don't want to disturb the roots after they have begun to grow. Plants grown vertically require more attention than others. They have to be guided in the first stages of growth, sometimes even attached to the support with string or a piece of cloth. This is not difficult, but it is meticulous and time-consuming. Whenever attaching any part of a plant to a support, use a figure-eight knot. This stops constriction of the stem as it matures. If you are weaving the ends of vines into netting or wire, be careful not to break off the tender tips. If you bend them too far, they snap off. Melons grown vertically may require some special support. Provide homemade slings made from fabric just as fruit starts to form, or it may break off. Try not to disturb the vines when you do this.

Climbing plants require frequent watering, a real problem in dry or sandy areas, and wind dries them out quickly. Mulch the soil heavily to keep it moist.

Soil

While many conditions contribute to healthy plants, the beginning point is always the quality of your soil. You want to provide vegetables with good topsoil to a depth of 12 inches or more.

So what is good soil? In most cold-climate areas it is a deep-black color, which retains heat from the sun. It is firm enough to hold your plants in place, yet loose enough for easy penetration of water and air to their root systems. You can stick your hand right into really good soils. Good soil drains freely while having the ability to retain moisture during drought and heat waves. Good soil locks in essential nutrients as well and makes them available to plants over a long period of time. Good soil is alive, filled with billions of soil microorganisms. These microscopic creatures benefit the plant by providing nutrients and helping plants take them in. Good soil attracts worms, which tunnel through the ground, keeping it loose and also filling it with nitrogen through their droppings (castings) and the decay of their nitrogen-rich bodies at death. Good soil for most of the plants in this guide should be mildly acidic with a pH ranging from 6 to 7 (more about pH later).

Good soil is composed of both inorganic and organic materials. Inorganic materials are those that do not come from plants or animals: clay, silt, and sand. Clay, usually a light to grayish tan, is made up of minuscule particles. Clay soil is slimy when wet, turns rock hard when dry, and tends to crack apart. It drains poorly, compacts easily, and stays wet for long periods of time. It heats up slowly in spring but cools down slowly in fall. It sticks to your spade and is hard to work. However, nutrients cling to clay. So some clay in your soil is beneficial because it locks in nutrients. Silt is made up of larger particles than clay. When wet, it feels somewhat slippery. Sandy soil is made of large particles and fills gritty when you rub it between your fingers. If you try to form a ball in your hand, it just falls apart. You can feel the sand on your fingertips. It is soft and easy to work. Sandy soil will not retain water or nutrients. It warms up quickly in spring but cools off fast in fall. Having silt and sand in the soil helps keep it loose.

The organic material found in good soils is the result of the decomposition (rotting) of anything once alive. Everything alive eventually dies. When it does, it decomposes. Actually, it is being eaten by billions of different creatures, many of them microscopic. These creatures fall into different categories: some are plants (fungi), others are animals (insects), and some have characteristics of both plants and animals. Organic material is especially attractive to worms. When worms die, their nitrogen-rich bodies decompose to give plants even more valuable food. The wide variety of unseen creatures digest organic material into a light-brown, fluffy material called humus. Humus benefits soil by keeping it loose and airy, holding moisture during drought, containing essential nutrients, and providing a home for helpful soil microorganisms (many of which help plants take in food).

When inorganic and organic materials are mixed together in just the right proportion, the soil is called loam. About 5 to 10 percent of the soil should be organic matter. The rest is best if a combination of clay, silt, and sand in nearly equal parts. If the combination is correct, the soil is said to have good texture. Naturally, no soil will meet these standards exactly, but when soil gets close to these proportions, you will know it. Loam is usually very dark, almost black. Loam with this coloration absorbs sunlight in spring and warms up quickly, and also retains heat in the fall. Loam usually has a loose feel to it. Superb loam is very loose. There is plenty of space between soil particles to hold air and water. You can almost dig into it with your bare hand. Soil matching this description is said to have good structure. It does not get compacted easily, which means that water drains freely through it. Water gets to the roots but does not pool up around them, shutting off air. It drains away, carrying with it toxic salts. The looseness of the soil induces rapid root growth. Often, the root system is much larger than the aboveground portion of the plant. When dry, loam crumbles in your hand. When wet, it is mildly sticky but doesn't form a solid, sticky ball; it will still crumble through

your fingers. Loam has all of the good characteristics of the individual components without the negative ones. For example, the small amount of clay retains nutrients in the soil but doesn't make the soil hard or compacted when dry, and the organic matter maintains soil at just the right pH.

While good soil is important, so is loosening the subsoil, which has few of the qualities of the soil above it. The looser it is, the better. But loosening it can be difficult. If you use a tiller, you end up mixing the topsoil with the subsoil. You don't want to do that unless your topsoil is at least 18 inches deep. The most commonly advocated technique for loosening subsoil is double digging. This technique requires you to dig up the topsoil along the edge of the garden (trench one), place it off to the side or in a wheelbarrow, then loosen the subsoil with a garden fork before filling it in with topsoil taken from an adjacent trench (trench two). In essence, you are digging in and filling in one trench after another throughout the entire garden. If you want a more detailed explanation, read *How to Grow More Vegetables* by John Jeavons. Double digging is a great idea if you have enough topsoil to begin with, at least 8 to 12 inches.

This technique is incredibly difficult in clay or compacted soils. I would rather build a raised bed combining existing topsoil with imported soil. Jeavons also likes raised beds, so we are on the same page in that regard. There is also a tool called a broadfork that some gardeners use to loosen compacted soils without resorting to tilling.

Buying Soil

Many home gardeners do not have enough topsoil to create the best of gardens. If your garden is really small, you can buy soil in bags. For large gardens, the simplest and quickest solution is to buy it in bulk, by the truckload, to fill in raised beds or spread over a level garden. Whether bagged or bulk, all topsoil is not created equal. You want to buy topsoil that is essentially loam, as described earlier, and it should be organic. Read the label carefully to see what it is made of. Buy one bag, and check it out before buying more.

Bulk topsoil, which is expensive, is sold by the cubic yard and can be picked up if you have a trailer or delivered if you don't. Most large nurseries sell soil, often referred to as black dirt. Look at the soil, and ask all the appropriate questions: Where does the soil come from (get a specific location), has it ever been treated with synthetic chemicals or herbicides, and is it mineral based (feel it to see whether it is nice and loose). It should not contain any chemicals and should be as close to loam as possible. Some topsoils are mixed with manures. Ask whether this is the case. There is nothing wrong with some manure being mixed in as long as it has been aged properly. Another option is to find a local grower or landscape designer who makes their own garden or potting soil. Most use loam in their mix. Ask them where they buy their soil. You can ruin a garden by buying the wrong soil, so this is a big decision. Even after asking the right questions, you won't know whether you have gotten honest answers until you begin to grow plants.

Mix the purchased topsoil into whatever amount you have been able to loosen on your own. Note that your soil will degrade unless you add soil amendments each year.

Soil Amendments or Conditioners

Anything added to the soil to change its structure is called a soil amendment. The purpose of these is to get the soil nice and loose so that water will drain freely through it and air can get to the roots of plants. Amendments help retain moisture during dry periods and nutrients throughout the entire growing season. They also reduce soil crusting so seedlings can emerge more easily. Since they break down in time, they need to be added regularly. Following is a description of good soil amendments.

Bark: This amendment must be aged until it is dark brown to black and very crumbly.

Coco peat (coir): Derived from coconut husks. Since it is a renewable resource, it may soon become increasingly available as a replacement for sphagnum peat moss. It has a pH of 6 and absorbs roughly nine times its weight in water. Whether it will be used widely depends on whether it proves to be disease, insect, and weed free—and available.

Compost: The gardener's ace in the hole. I describe how to make it and its benefits following this section.

Leaf mold: A term used to describe decomposed leaves. Mold usually has a negative connotation, but rotted leaves are a blessing to the organic gardener. Leaf mold is one of the best soil conditioners available to the home gardener. Never throw leaves away. It is common to see many bags of leaves in the fall being sent to local compost sites. If you have the stamina and interest, pick these up. Let people in your neighborhood know that you will take their bagged leaves. If you have a large garden and begin to give away some of your produce to people who have supplied you with leaves, the number of bags will increase yearly. Many communities have a "compost" site open to residents. Often these are simply piles of leaves and grass, which, unfortunately, are often mixed with debris that shouldn't be there. Bring the leaves home. You will need a utility trailer to pick up large amounts. Shredded leaves take up a lot less space and decompose more quickly than whole leaves. You don't need a shredder. Just run a rotary lawn mower over the leaves until they are broken into small pieces. The easiest way to do this is to spread dry leaves out as thinly as possible on a driveway

and run over them again and again. Then place them in a pile and keep them moist until the first freeze. No time or energy to shred? Place a thick layer of leaves over the garden in fall. Shred them the following spring to use as a mulch. Leaf mold in most cases is a good replacement for sphagnum peat moss, which is not technically a renewable resource.

Manure: When fully rotted, manure is an excellent soil amendment. It has a good smell, the earthy smell of humus. Contrary to popular belief, it is not high in nutrients. It's light and easy to work with. Don't use fresh manure in spring since it smells, heats up, and can damage plants with excessive nitrogen. Adding fresh manure to the garden in fall is fine since it will break down over the winter months. Manures may contain weed seeds, but so does your soil to the tune of 25 pounds or more of seed per ton of soil. Free manure is available in many areas where horses are boarded, but hauling it may require a trailer. You will need lots of it over the years. It is much better as a soil amendment than a mulch. Note that it does have the potential to be contaminated with pathogens and herbicides, so the longer you can compost it before putting it in the garden, the better. Some organic gardeners are opposed to the use of anything derived from animals, although nature (Earth) makes no such distinction.

Peat moss (sphagnum peat moss): Partially decomposed moss harvested from bogs. Peat is sterile and completely free of chemicals, insects, soluble salts, and weed seeds. It has a pH of 4 and can change soil acidity to some degree depending upon the size of soil particles, from a pH of 7 to 5 in sand, and to 6.8 in clay. But peat is expensive. Peat is sold by volume (cubic foot), not weight, and is available in bales or bags. Most bales sold retail are 3.8 cubic feet. Larger bales are sold wholesale. Peat holds roughly twenty times its weight in water. Getting peat moist the first time can be difficult. Peat absorbs warm or hot water and sheds cold water—still, an even sprinkling of cold water will eventually get it moist. The ecological controversy about the use of peat is heating up, since whether it is truly a renewable resource is debatable. Peat producers insist that peat is being replaced by nature at a rate equal to or greater than that harvested. They claim that of the 280 million acres of peat, a relatively small amount is harvested each year. Those on the other side of the fence would like to see gardeners create their own organic material, available as waste in the local area or from around the home.

Perlite: An inorganic soil amendment made from expanded volcanic rock, often sold in 4-cubic-feet bags. It acts as a spacer between soil particles and is a common ingredient in potting soil mixes. While light and easy to use, it is expensive. It takes a long time to break down, however, and is well worth considering for loosening compacted soil. It is also sterile and weed free. It is most commonly used in growing plants in containers.

Sawdust: Added to soil, sawdust makes it much looser but requires the addition of nitrogen to be valuable.

Vermiculite: Made by heating silica, which forces it to expand. Like perlite, it is an inorganic compound used to lighten the soil and is sterile, weed free, and expensive. It is packaged in a wide range of sizes. Horticultural vermiculite has been tested in Canada and the United States and does not contain significant amounts of asbestos. Look for products with Organic Materials Review Institute (OMRI) approval noted on the bag. Sun Gro has that approval since it tests for asbestos regularly and lists levels as "None Detected." Types of vermiculite sold for other purposes may contain greater amounts of asbestos. Stick to vermiculite specifically labeled for horticultural use. Still, it is wise to moisten vermiculite and wear a mask when using it since it is so "dusty." Vermiculite is more often used in small amounts in furrows when planting seed than as an overall soil amendment. It is also good for a seed-starting mix. Add all soil amendments to the soil in fall, if possible.

Compost

Compost is a unique soil amendment in that you make it by combining every organic material available to you in a pile. The meaning of compost varies according to different publications. *In this guide, compost refers to fully decomposed animal and plant material, not to partially rotted materials.* Fully digested compost is called humus and produces humic acid to improve soil structure and encourage microbial activity that in turn helps provide nutrients to plants. In nature, the earth is carpeted with a rich mat of dead leaves, grass, weeds, and animal remains that decompose over a period of time. Anything that was once alive, whether plant or animal, is referred to as organic matter once it dies. After death, organic matter is immediately eaten by billions of small living creatures and microorganisms, many so tiny that they can be seen only with the aid of a microscope. These microorganisms serve as nature's digestive system by chewing up raw, organic materials, reducing them in bulk as they break down into the material called humus. In nature this material is produced at a rate of 1 inch per century. The process known as composting is a human activity that mimics but speeds up the natural decomposition process. Fully decomposed compost or humus is not a fertilizer but is an excellent soil amendment that makes nutrients available to plants in ways that are only partially understood. Adding as wide a variety of organic materials to the pile as possible supports the diverse needs of various microorganisms. For example,

If compost piles may annoy your neighbors, make them as unobtrusive as possible.

bacteria thrive on plants and grass, while fungi prefer leaves. For this reason, each compost pile is unique but still breaks down into humus, which always enriches the soil.

Here's how microorganisms create humus. Aerobic bacteria thrive in the presence of oxygen. They break down organic material rapidly. They give off no odor. Anaerobic bacteria, which multiply rapidly without oxygen, have essentially the same role as their aerobic counterparts with the additional one of breaking down cellulose. However, they work slowly, at about one-tenth the rate of aerobic bacteria, and cause odors. Both aerobic and anaerobic bacteria produce enzymes to break down complex carbohydrates into simpler forms, which they use as food. Enzymes act as catalysts to biochemical reactions. These enzymes fall into three broad categories: cellulase enzymes, hemicellulase enzymes, and protease enzymes. Cellulase enzymes attack cellulose, breaking down wood and plant fibers as well as paper. Hemicellulase enzymes break down hemicellulose (less strong material than cellulose) and to a lesser degree lignin (another part of the cell wall in plants). The protease enzymes affect the cells of grass and leaves, allowing water

Composting produces humus, a soil amendment nicknamed "black gold" by organic gardeners.

to penetrate into their interior. *The enzymes often remain in the soil and continue to decompose tough organic materials long after the bacteria producing them have died.*

The population of fungi in garden soil is less than that of bacteria, but it is also important in breaking down cellulose and lignin after the faster-acting bacteria have started the reduction process. The best-known microfungi (technically bacteria that have similarities to fungi) are actinomycetes, which secrete digestive enzymes to help decompose lignin, cellulose, protein, and starch. They can work many feet below the soil surface to make food available to deeply rooted plants. The mycorrhizae family of organisms (fungi) live on the roots of some plants and are essential to their growth. The mold inserts its threads (hyphae) directly into the plant's feeder rootlets, conveying food to the plant while making nutrients more available to it at the same time.

Some materials break down easily. Some, such as egg shells and orange rinds, because of their composition, seem to take forever to decompose. But anything that once lived will break down in time. Thickness also makes a difference. A log takes longer to decompose than a weed—a lot longer. The reason for this is that little of the surface of a log is exposed to microorganisms. If the log were chipped up into minuscule pieces, it would decompose more quickly. The other reason is that the log contains more carbon than the weed (more about this later).

Entire books have been written about composting, implying that it has to be difficult, time-consuming, and scientifically done. Nothing could be further from the truth as long as you are not in a hurry. The goal is always the same—humus, a rich, dark, earthy-smelling substance that results from the breakdown of any organic material.

Here's a simple way to compost at home. Choose a level spot in full sun for a compost pile. Generally the best place is near your garden or directly in it. You need to be able to reach it with a hose. It should be a large enough to accommodate a 4-by-4-feet pile of organic matter. If it is in a protected area and not an eyesore to neighbors, all the better. Stack any debris on this spot including grass clippings, kitchen peelings and leftovers, leaves, twigs, weeds from the garden—anything that was once living. Build up organic material into a pile 4 to 5 feet high and roughly 4 to 5 feet wide in whatever time it takes to gather this amount of material. Let the pile sit for as long as it takes to decompose. This could take more than a year. It could take less. It depends on what you put in the pile and how active the soil microorganisms are. Their activity is determined by the weather, both temperature and amount of rainfall, and what you put into the pile. This lazy way of composting works well for many home gardeners who don't have enough organic material to build a large compost pile all at once. They add materials as available. This method may be referred to as cold composting.

The more serious you are about composting, the more time and effort it will take. You will be making what some refer to as hot compost, which has a good chance of killing weed seeds and disease-causing pathogens. It also rewards you with compost (humus) at a faster rate. Here are the main steps in so-called scientific composting. For quick composting, the following things are needed: organic material (grass, leaves, sawdust, weeds, kitchen scraps), water, air, nitrogen, warmth, and soil (for its microorganisms). Here's what you do. Scuff up the top few inches of a 4-by-4-feet area with a spade or rototiller. Do this to a depth of 8 to 12 inches if possible to help the pile drain more freely. If you want several compost piles, scratch up an area 4 feet by 12 feet. With a garden rake push some of the loosened topsoil off to the side of what will become your compost pile. You will be using the soil to speed up the composting process. Compost piles can be either open or enclosed. Enclosed does not mean fully enclosed, since air needs to get into the pile. The sides of enclosed piles should be made of wire with solid supports at three corners. Leave the front open. Now place a foot or so of organic debris on top of the soil. For best results, cover the organic material with an inch or so of manure or sprinkle an organic fertilizer high in nitrogen over the mound. This contains enough nitrogen to help feed the soil microorganisms. This step is optional. If you have the right carbon to nitrogen ratio, described later in this section, it is also unnecessary. Now sprinkle an inch or so of soil over the manure. It adds microorganisms to the mix, helps the pile sink down a little to take up less space, and helps retain moisture. This step is also optional, since organic material will decompose without it. However, it helps speed up the composting process. Water the whole pile with a hose. Get it moist, not soaking wet. It should feel damp, not soggy. If the pile is too dry, the soil microorganisms will not multiply. If the pile is too wet, it may develop an odor (more about that later). Continue with the next layer, following the same steps: organic matter (1 foot), manure or fertilizer (optional), soil (optional), and water. Build the pile up like a club sandwich until it is 4 to 5 feet high.

Now the microorganisms start to go to work. Billions of them begin to feed on the organic matter using the nitrogen in the manure as a kind of booster to really get going. They start to digest the pile, and in the process, the pile gets hotter and hotter, ideally reaching 170°F, more realistically about 135°F. The higher the temperature, the greater the chance of killing weed seeds and a number of plant pathogens (disease-causing organisms). The rapid increase of heat in the pile indicates that there is enough nitrogen to help microorganisms multiply. If a pile is not heating and no manure or organic fertilizer high in nitrogen has been added, mix these into the pile. The pile should start to heat up.

After the pile has had a chance to cook for a week or longer, turn it over, making sure to get all of the material on the outside deep into the center of the pile. The easiest tool to use is a pitchfork. This turning process will get air, moisture, and undigested organic matter into the center of the pile. The digestion process starts all over again. And the temperature in the pile should rise. The more often you turn the pile, the more quickly the material will decompose. Some gardeners say that for every turn you cut the time of decomposition in half. I find that to be an exaggeration. In any event, let the pile heat up inside for several days before turning it. If it takes more than a few days, so be it. Get that pile steaming before turning it. Turning a pile frequently prevents anaerobic bacteria, which multiply without oxygen, from taking over the pile. They are the reason some compost piles smell. It's your choice how often to turn the pile. If you want to turn if every week, every few weeks, or never, the material will still decompose. If you are in a hurry for compost, however, you must turn it more frequently. That is one of the secrets to quick composting. Throughout this process the pile keeps shrinking until it is a fraction of its original size.

Try to keep the compost pile moist at all times. Moist means damp, not soggy. In dry areas, indent the top of the pile to collect as much water as possible. If it doesn't rain, water the pile. Do not worry about chemicals in city water. While they do kill pathogens, they have little overall effect on a pile. If you are in an area with frequent rain, you may want to cover the moist pile with a tarp. If a pile gets too wet, the air-loving microorganisms die, and the ones that don't need oxygen take over. These hardy microorganisms will still do the job, but there's a price. The pile will stink inside, as mentioned earlier. You usually don't smell anything until you turn the pile over. The smell goes away as the anaerobic microorganisms die, and the air-loving micro-

organisms (aerobic) take over, multiplying into the billions within days.

Many companies sell inoculants for compost piles. There is nothing wrong with these, but if you add garden soil and a little manure or organic fertilizer to the pile, they will do just as good a job as an inoculant. Some people use milk, molasses, or sugar to speed up composting. Even without soil and fertilizer, the organic material will break down in time. Although some sources tell you to add lime to the pile to speed up decomposition, it's not really necessary. It makes the pile more alkaline. Organic material breaking down into humus is just about neutral. And that's ideal for all but a few plants in this guide.

Sources often tell you not to put diseased plant material into a compost pile. The problem is that the home gardener may not know whether a weed or plant is diseased. I toss all weeds and plants into the compost pile. Some of these may be diseased. In fact, I'm sure that some of them have been. Perhaps, I have just been lucky. If a single plant wilts and collapses while other plants around it flourish, I would dig it up with the surrounding soil. The usual suggestion is to burn or toss this plant into the garbage. And that is certainly the safest advice. However, burning may be illegal in your area. Tossing organic matter into the garbage is a shame. A compromise is to place plants like this in a clear plastic bag on a hard surface in full sun for several weeks. Then toss the plants into a separate pile devoted to "iffy" plants. This is a bit of a gamble, since some plants may be infected with a disease that can last in the soil for years. However, the sun treatment and isolation in a separate pile allowed to decompose over years may kill off all pathogens.

Sources often tell you not to put weeds in a compost pile. Much of my compost comes from weeds, many of which have mined the soil for nutrients. By all means, toss weeds into the pile. They contain lots of minerals and some nitrogen. Why waste these? However, when I see a weed, such as burdock, with a developed seed head, I snip these heads off into a paper bag, dry them, and then burn them. Do this in a portable grill if burning is prohibited in your area. *There is one weed that I never add to a compost pile: Canada thistle.* Despite caution, some weed seeds will end up in the pile, but I want as much compost as possible and can deal with a few extra weeds to get it. You will also be told not to put dog droppings and cat litter into a pile. Here I agree. The reason is that both might contain organisms harmful to you but not to plants. Dog droppings may contain roundworms (helminths), while cat feces can infect humans with the disease toxoplasmosis. Pregnant women should never handle cat litter.

A key aspect of *quick* composting is the carbon to nitrogen ratio in the pile. Everything once living contains carbon. Organic materials contain carbon and nitrogen but in varying amounts. Generally speaking, it helps to add materials high in nitrogen to the pile. Composting speeds up when the carbon to nitrogen ratio is about thirty parts carbon to one part nitrogen (twenty-five to one is even better). Since some of the materials you will be adding to the pile are extremely high in carbon, adding nitrogen helps in achieving the right ratio or getting closer to it. The carbon to nitrogen ratios found in commonly composted materials are provided in the accompanying table. By mixing these in the right proportion, you will speed up the composting process.

Organic matter containing lots of carbon is often called brown material. Organic matter with a high nitrogen content is often labeled green. So mix brown and green materials to get the right balance for quick composting. For instance, mix leaves and grass clippings. You can always add organic fertilizers high in nitrogen to get the right balance. The more sawdust or wood products in the pile (very high in carbon), the more nitrogen (manure or fertilizer) you will have to add to get the composting process going if you do not have enough green material to overcome the imbalance. That's because of the somewhat finicky carbon to nitrogen ratio just described.

Big things don't decompose quickly. If you can shred everything before putting it in a pile, more surface area is exposed to the microorganisms, which will feed more rapidly on the material, converting it more quickly into humus. That's why a big stick takes such a long time to decompose either in the woods or in a compost pile. That's why shredded leaves will decompose so much faster than whole ones. Some books say that this is a myth. They are wrong. A shredded stick definitely decomposes faster than a big stick. Shredding of hard materials is difficult without a mulcher shredder, but dry leaves are easy to break up on your driveway with a rotary mower. When doing this, wear a mask to avoid inhaling dust, and eye protection, as things sometimes shoot out from the mower in the oddest directions. The other advantage of shredding all materials is that they then take up less space. You can get more debris into each 4-by-4-feet pile. The more material, the more humus. And lots of material in a small space seems to compost better.

There is nothing wrong with having twigs, corn stalks, and so on in a pile, since they help air circulation. But they will not decompose quickly. If your whole pile is made up of twigs and corn stalks, you will have a long wait for humus unless you shred or chip them first.

Many sources tell you not to put meat or fat into a compost pile because it will not decompose quickly. Meat is very high in nitrogen and will decompose. The real fear is that the meat will attract animals. Naturally, exposed meat does attract animals, especially raccoons and dogs. So if you want to put grease or meat scraps into a compost pile, bury them in the center. This extra nitrogen is valuable. Why waste it? What else are you going to do with grease? *Having said this, if there are rats in the vicinity, I would not put meat into a pile.*

Many sources tell you not to add grass clippings treated with herbicides to compost piles. This is a highly controversial issue. Herbicides break down at different rates, some very slowly, others more quickly. Whether herbicide residue remains in compost after thorough decomposition is hotly debated. The high nitrogen content in grass clippings makes them extremely valuable. If you are an organic gardener, you are probably not spraying your lawn with herbicides. So your grass clippings are safe in the compost pile or as a mulch directly in the garden. If you are collecting grass clippings from an unknown source, ask about herbicide use if you are concerned, although information is hard to come by in this situation. To be on the safe side, consider composting them for a year before using them, and even longer if the grass was treated with herbicides such as clopyralid. See the warning later in this section.

Do not add wood ashes to compost piles. They are alkaline and do not help the composting process. Instead, keep them dry in a large metal pail to spread *lightly* over

Carbon to nitrogen ratios found in commonly composted materials

MATERIAL	CARBON/NITROGEN RATIO
alfalfa	13/1
cornstalks	61/1
fruit wastes	35/1
grass clippings	19/1
grease	15/1
green sweet clover	16/1
humus	10/1
leaves	80/1
manure (rotted)	40/1
paper*	170/1
pine needles	80/1
sawdust	500/1
straw	80/1
table scraps	15/1
weeds	20/1
wood	700/1

* Shred paper or cardboard. Avoid either if coated, glossy, or colored.

the vegetable garden in early spring. Do not dump a lot of ashes in any one place, since they will raise the pH of the soil in that area. They are valuable, however, since they contain a high amount of calcium, a small amount of phosphorus, and quite a bit of potassium. Keep them out of beds used to grow acid-loving plants, such as blueberries and potatoes.

All of this makes composting sound more difficult than it really is. Your garden needs organic material, and it will repay you dozens of times over for your effort.

Compost is ready when it turns to humus. This can take as little as a month or two if you work hard at it, or as long as a year or two if you are more casual. The telltale signs of humus are these: it's dark brown, slightly moist, crumbly in texture, and, as hard as it is for some people to believe, has a pleasant, somewhat woodsy smell. You can rub compost through a screen to reduce it to smaller particles, or you can remove larger pieces of debris and toss them into the next compost pile. The larger pieces will decompose in time and will aerate the new pile for you.

While there is nothing magical about making compost, there is something a bit mystical about its effect on growing plants. It may take us many years to know all the reasons why it is so desirable. Knowing why would be wonderful; knowing that it works is good enough for now. Here's what we know it does. It helps smaller soil particles bind together (flocculate). These larger soil "clusters" retain water well and have more space between them. Roots don't have to work hard to grow through them. The more roots a plant has, the better it grows. The roots also can take in nutrients from the air in the soil—critical for healthy growth. Soil that has a lot of humus in it won't crust over. Crust can stop seeds from emerging. You can go to a lot of trouble planting a garden, only to see some seeds never come up. Good soil, rich in humus, retains water so that even during dry spells or droughts your garden stays moist. The humus also prevents erosion during downpours in wet seasons. At the same time water drains freely through humus-rich soil if there is a downpour. The soil never becomes waterlogged. The two statements seem contradictory but are not. Although humus is not particularly fertile, it does contain some of the nutrients essential to plant growth. It's similar to a time capsule, slowly releasing important nutrients as they are needed. Tiny organisms living in the soil thrive on humus. Many of these are very beneficial, actually helping plants to take in nutrients. Some of these are believed to protect plants from disease and attacks by invaders. Just as these microorganisms like humus, so do worms. Worms in your garden mean lots of good things. Worms burrow through the soil and make it nice and loose so that roots can penetrate it

easily. They are constantly eating, and their droppings (castings) fertilize the soil, as do their bodies when they die. The work of the earthworm helps soil retain water and prevents erosion. Humus-rich soil is easy to work and easy to weed, cutting down on one of the more monotonous chores in the garden. Any soil that is rich in humus has a dark color—the color of rich, good earth. This soil absorbs heat from the sun. Your garden warms up faster in the spring and stays warmer in the fall because of this. This way you get an extended season for greater vegetable production. Finally, most plants thrive in soil that is neither too acidic, nor too alkaline. Humus has a way of stabilizing soil so that it stays almost neutral (has a balanced pH).

The problem with composting is that it seems like there is never enough of it. That is why it is often referred to as "black gold" by organic gardeners. Use it wisely. Place it where it will do the most good, as in hills for vining crops, in planting holes, and along furrows. Get it close to seeds and roots.

Throughout the whole year have a small bucket under your sink for kitchen scraps. If you don't, the garbage disposal or garbage become attractive alternatives, and this would be a waste of valuable organic materials. Remove stickers from fruit rinds. Consider putting orange rinds in a blender to break them up into small pieces. Once the bucket is full, dump it into the compost pile. If you add water to the bucket before dumping it, material is less likely to cling to the side of the bucket. Carry a rag with you to wipe it off right at the compost pile before bringing it inside and rinsing it in the sink.

During the winter consider placing a plastic garbage can with a lid in the garage. As the kitchen bucket fills up, dump it into the garbage can. This saves tromping out to the compost pile in winter and trying to bury scraps in a rock-hard compost pile. It also stops animals from eating the kitchen scraps laid out like a smorgasbord on frozen ground. The material settles down and takes up much less space than you might think. As soon as it warms up in spring, dump the scraps into the compost pile. You may have to use a dolly to move the trash can to the pile, since it gets heavy. Material stored in this manner gets smelly, so bury the composting scraps in the pile. The smell dissipates quickly once oxygen-loving bacteria get to work.

Warning: Compost is for sale in many locations. The term *compost* is so vague that you really don't know what you are getting. Unless a bag states clearly that it is OMRI approved, be wary. Black Gold® is an example of one material that is approved. Bags may be labeled "organic" or "natural," but that can be quite misleading. Often you do not know what bagged compost is made of. It may contain bark or sawdust, possibly not aged long enough; biosolids (processed human wastes); chemical contaminants, of which there are thousands; endocrine disruptors; heavy metals; manure that has not been aged properly (gives off an ammonia smell); and solvents. Then there is the catchall of nonspecified inert ingredients. If this seems overly alarmist to you, open a bag. The material should be dark brown to black, light and fluffy (lift the bag), and have a nice smell. In short, it should really be as close to humus as possible. Once you have made your own humus (fully digested compost), you will know exactly what I mean.

Distributors of bulk compost are available in most cities. Composting leaves, grass, and other organic materials is a great idea, but there is a catch. Most compost sites do not test for herbicides, most of which decompose within a year. But not all do. Clopyralid (most commonly sold as Confront®, Curtail®, Lontrel®, Millenium Ultra™, Reclaim®, Stinger®, and Transline®) is an effective broadleaf herbicide that does not break down quickly and even in minute amounts can affect the growth of plants mainly in the bean (Fabaceae), nightshade (Solanaceae), and sunflower (Asteraceae) families. It is particularly damaging to peas, sunflowers, and tomatoes, although it affects other popular crops, including lettuce, peppers, and potatoes. Picloram is another herbicide that is slow to decompose but not as commonly found in bulk compost. Bulk compost may also contain weed seed and bits of shredded plastic. The latter needs to be removed by hand. Bulk compost often varies by the location where it is made. A trip to a few sites may be worth the time and cost of gas. Many gardeners buy bulk compost to cut overall costs. But if you insist on guaranteed organic compost, *the solution, as difficult as it is to accept, is to make your own compost and add soil amendments already mentioned instead, especially leaf mold, since it is so readily available, inexpensive, and effective.* I readily admit that it is hard to ever make enough compost to fulfill all your needs, especially if you have a large garden.

Vermicompost

Compost created with the help of worms is called vermicompost. The work of worms can be done indoors or outdoors. You can capture or buy worms (red wigglers). Here is a synopsis of the process. Get a large plastic bin, and punch holes in it so that water can seep out and air can get in. Lay about a 2- to 3-inch layer of dried grass clippings in the bottom of the bin, and cover it with the same depth of dry horse manure. Then add a cupful of worms before covering them with scraps from the kitchen (no meat or dairy). Scraps smell, so cover these in turn with sphagnum peat moss. It does not have to be a deep layer but enough to cover them well. Moisten the mixture without getting it

really wet. It just has to be barely moist, and kitchen scraps contain quite a bit of water. Place the bin in a warm but shaded area. Water should be able to drain freely from the bottom of the bin, since water will drown the worms. Add kitchen scraps regularly. The worms will work the material into a rich humus-like consistency. The compost is not high in major plant nutrients but has the wonderful benefits of compost. It is also a quick way to break down material. Once the material is crumbly and black, use it, but remove the worms and start the process over again.

If you are seriously interested in vermicomposting, read more about it online, and consider buying a book on this subject alone. Although I'm quite content with regular compost and the work done by worms drawn into the garden with good soil amendments and regular mulching, I think vermicomposting is a great way to make an excellent soil amendment.

pH (Potential Hydrogen)

The term *pH* (potential hydrogen), mentioned several times in this chapter, refers to the relative amounts of either positively charged (hydrogen, technically hydronium) or negatively charged (hydroxide) ions there are in the soil. In simple language, it is a gauge of how acidic or alkaline the soil is. The pH scale runs from 0 (totally acidic) to 14 (totally alkaline). Neutral soil has a pH of 7. Most of the plants in this guide thrive in a slightly acidic soil with a pH of 6 to 6.5. The right pH determines the availability of nutrients to plants. If the pH is too high or too low, many essential plant foods will be locked into the soil and not be absorbed by the roots. (Note: Soil pH values are logarithmic, not arithmetic. A soil with a pH of 5 is ten times as acidic as a soil with a pH of 6. It is one hundred times as acidic as a soil with a pH of 7.)

The pH of soils varies throughout the country. For example, soils in the East are more acidic than those in the West. Home gardeners are successful in all areas despite the difference in soil pH. The pH of city water is often alkaline, but the regular addition of organic matter to the soil usually overcomes this. Generally, hot, dry areas tend to be alkaline. Cool, wet areas tend to be acidic. However, the underlying subsoil in many areas may either be alkaline or acidic depending on its composition. So there are many exceptions to the above rule. Realistically, home gardeners don't have to pay a great deal of attention to the pH of their soil if they follow much of the advice in this guide, including adding lots of organic matter to the soil. Organic matter, breaking down into humus, tends to be neutral. There are a few exceptions. For instance, blueberries really need acidic soil to do well. So you have to make the soil more acidic than would be necessary for most other plants. Acidic soil also protects potatoes from scab. So there is value in lowering the pH for specific crops. Green moss growing on the soil surface is an indicator of acidic soil.

Every time you add something to the soil, there is the potential that it will change the soil pH. Compost, made from decayed organic matter, is usually neutral. Gypsum is often added to soil to increase its calcium content, to break clay down into a more fluffy substance, and to neutralize toxic salts. Some gardeners call gypsum "lime," which it is not. It does not affect soil pH. Cottonseed meal, oak leaves, sphagnum peat moss, pine needles, and sawdust are often recommended to make soil slightly more acidic. The only one proven to do this is sphagnum peat moss. Sulfur, in powder form, is one of the best products to make soil more acidic if a lower pH is needed. It is slow acting, generally applied in fall for results the following spring. Vinegar is often used to make soil in containers more acidic if tap water tends to be alkaline. Add 1 teaspoon to 1 tablespoon per gallon of water. Things that make soil alkaline include animal manures, lime, and wood ash. Add lots of manure to your soil, but go easy on lime and wood ash unless advised otherwise by a soil test. Calcitic limestone (calcium carbonate) and dolomitic limestone (magnesium carbonate) are two forms of lime. Both are slow acting and should be spread over the soil surface (not tilled in) in fall. Wood ash should be kept dry until added *lightly* to the soil in spring.

Soil Testing

Most garden guides strongly recommend a soil test before starting a new garden. Some gardeners, and certainly almost all academicians, insist that it is the single most important step in organic gardening. I consider its value questionable for most home gardeners but worth the cost for mini-farmers. Telling a gardener not to have a soil test is heresy in the gardening world and will be criticized roundly by many. I have never had a soil test in sixty years of gardening in many locations, so my advice is based solely on that experience alone.

Most tests include soil samples from different spots in your garden. The true pH may be different in each spot. Furthermore, the results may be less than reliable. Tests vary according to temperature and soil moisture. And they can be affected by the person taking the soil sample. True soil tests for commercial growers are detailed and expensive. They have great value but are not feasible for home gardeners. Although I have never used one, some gardeners check the soil pH with a handheld meter. The reliability of meters is open to question, but they give you a rough guide. They tell you nothing, however, about the essential nutrients in your soil, which a good soil test does do. Start gardening, and see whether you have any problems. Stunted plants, yellowing leaves, unusual foliage color—these are the real soil test. No problems? Terrific. You have just saved yourself money, time, and trouble. If you follow the tips in this book, the odds are that you will not need a soil test and will have mildly acidic to neutral soil, which is ideal for most of the plants covered in this growing guide. My opinion: if it ain't broke, don't fix it.

But if you have a problem, seek advice. Watch your plants. If they don't measure up to your expectations, now is the time to do something about it. Try to get advice during the growing season. The plants often give professionals or experienced gardeners the clues they need to help you out. The problem may not have anything to do with your soil pH or nutrient level. On the other hand, it could. As with everything, there are exceptions. If you want to grow blueberries, a soil test may be worth the cost. Blueberries can last for decades, and pH is critical to getting them off to a good start and keeping them healthy. Still, in many instances you can get by without a test (see the blueberry section in Part II).

If you decide that you want a test, then contact the nearest university, cooperative, or agricultural extension office. They will tell you what to do and how much it will cost. Mini-farmers may want to get soil tested by Timberleaf, 39648 Old Spring Road, Murrieta, CA 92563; 951-677-7510. I suggest them because they specialize in tests for professional organic growers.

Soil tests are important if you suspect that the soil may contain heavy metals, especially lead, that can cause serious health problems, especially in young children. This heavy metal was and is still used by industry, was in paints until 1978, was in commercial pesticides from 1910 until 1950, and was in leaded gasoline until 1996. If your house was built on a possible industrial site or near one, on an area that was once an orchard, or in a location on the edge of a highway, paying extra for a soil test to check for lead and other heavy metals will give you peace of mind. The level of contamination will determine what you should do. Soil may have to be replaced if levels are high, or raised beds with a geotextile barrier underneath the beds might be suggested if levels are lower. Plants will absorb lead, but it is the soil getting on plants or being eaten accidentally by children that raises the risk of adverse health effects dramatically. With mild levels of lead, keeping the soil above a pH of 6.5, making sure there is enough phosphorus in the soil, and adding lots of organic matter may help reduce the uptake of lead by a crop. Wash leafy and root crops well to remove any soil particles. Also, if you suspect that lead was used in your indoor plumbing, it is worthwhile replacing it if a water test indicates its presence in high enough amounts. Lead solder used to "sweat" copper pipes was not banned until 1986, although some companies stopped using it well before then. Levels of lead do build up in body tissue over time. You also can be tested, and there are ways of eliminating lead from your body.

Arsenic can also be of concern because of health effects. Lumber and timbers treated with chromated copper arsenate (CCA) contain high amounts of arsenic. Do not burn these, but remove or have them removed to specialized waste sites. Newer treated timbers are not as toxic as the older ones. Arsenic may also be found in soil of old orchards once treated with a pesticide called lead arsenate.

Adding Fertilizers to the Soil

Plants vary greatly in their need for major and minor nutrients. Some are heavy feeders, others can withstand benign neglect. The exact requirements of individual plants are provided in detail in Part II. Still, most home gardeners add nutrients to the soil during the preparation of the garden. Some are best added in fall, others in spring. Fertilizers are covered in detail in chapter 4. That section includes information on cover crops that become "green manure" when turned into the soil. Green manures increase microbial activity, add essential nutrients, and improve soil structure. The section also covers other products that improve soil structure, such as gypsum, which applied regularly loosens clay.

CHAPTER 2

PLANTING SEED IN THE GARDEN

When you plant seed in a garden, the process is called direct seeding or planting in situ. It is the most common way to grow vegetables. One of the main goals of this growing guide is to provide you with lists of specific varieties of berries, herbs, and vegetables suited to cold-climate gardening. All of these varieties were available in stores or through mail-order sources at the time of publication. The varieties you choose will depend on what you are after. Qualities that many gardeners look for are quick maturation, superior taste, heavy production, use (fresh, canned, dried, pickled, powdered), color, size (both of fruit and plant), disease resistance, seed saving, and ease of growing. All of these characteristics are covered in the plant descriptions in Part II of this guide.

In the United States the most popular vegetables used in the kitchen are broccoli, cabbage, carrots, celery, corn, lettuce, onions, potatoes, and tomatoes. The top ten vegetables grown in the home garden in one published list in descending order are tomatoes, peppers, green beans, cucumbers, onions, lettuce, squash, carrots, radishes, and corn. In another list they are tomatoes, peppers, cucumbers, onions, green beans, lettuce, carrots, corn, radishes, and cabbage. Ironically, potatoes, the most popular vegetable for cooking in the United States, are on neither list despite the fact that they are easy to grow. And although more corn is grown in the United States than any other crop, it is grown by less than half of home gardeners. These lists reflect the general public's taste but are not included as a way of suggesting what any individual should grow. Grow what you like and constantly experiment.

Buying Seed

Seed is widely available from local outlets and by ordering from the numerous companies listed at the end of this chapter. If you want a specific variety, you may have to order it. The simplest way to find a seed source it to use the Internet. Type in the following: seed source for "name of variety" followed by the type of vegetable. Example: seed source of 'Blue Lake' bean. A single or more than one source should pop up on the screen. You will find that many companies offer seeds both online and through catalogs. There may be a charge for a printed catalog. Some are truly beautiful, and others offer detailed information about the seeds they offer, from growing to cooking instructions. They make great winter reading. Get them as early as possible, and order seeds well in advance before they are sold out. You should always have information on how many seeds are contained in whatever packet you buy. Following are terms commonly used in catalogs.

AAS (All-America Selections): When these letters follow a plant name, they indicate that a plant was selected as superior by testing in a wide range of gardens. For example, 'Sun Drops Hybrid' (AAS-1990) describes a squash chosen as an All-America Selection in 1990. You will find a number of these varieties throughout this growing guide, often going back decades. If listed, they are still available.

Baby: This term does not refer to the size of the plant but to the size of the mature fruit produced by the plant.

Bush: Realizing that many home gardeners have limited space, breeders have worked for years to develop varieties that grow well in a limited area. For example, cucumbers tend to be space hogs with their long vines. But 'Picklebush' doesn't need a lot of space to produce a copious amount of fruit for pickling. By choosing the right plants, you can use far less space than you might think necessary for specific crops. This space-saving and desirable trait is emphasized in catalogs and in this guide when appropriate.

Certified seed: This is a type of seed produced under strict standards. This includes inspections *by a third party* to make sure the seed is what the company says it is. It should be disease free.

Cultivar (cultivated variety): This is the name of any plant cultivated by humans. They may be hybrids or mutations. Cultivars have predictable traits. Their seeds often do not produce plants similar to the mother plant. They are regularly bred by seed producers. Most catalogs simply give the names of cultivars and tell whether the plants are hybrids or open pollinated. In this guide I list all varieties in the same format with single quotation marks around the name, as in 'Discovery Hybrid' cabbage.

Days to maturity: The number of days listed in catalogs and online normally refers to the number of days it takes a seed to mature from the time of planting. However, it may refer to the number of days a transplant takes to mature. This is especially true for plants normally started indoors, such as eggplants, peppers, and tomatoes. Ask if you are not sure. *These numbers are at best approximate and vary by season and region.* They are most useful when comparing plants within a specific plant group (genus), such as one pumpkin to another.

Disease resistance: Certain varieties of vegetables have been bred to resist diseases or to tolerate them better than other varieties. This does not mean these plants cannot be killed off by disease. Disease resistance or tolerance is noted behind particular varieties with letters. For instance, tomatoes are often infected with verticillium wilt (V), fusarium wilt (F), nematodes (N), and tobacco mosaic virus (T). If you see the entry 'Champion II Hybrid' VFNT listed in a catalog, it means that this tomato variety is resistant to verticillium wilt, fusarium wilt, nematodes, and tobacco mosaic virus. These letters are gardening shorthand. Other examples are alternaria or early blight (A), cucumber mosaic virus (CMV), powdery mildew (PM), downy mildew (DM), and common bean mosaic (M). When resistance is particularly important, it is noted in the varietal charts of a few plants in this guide.

Dwarf: This term refers to the size of the plant, not to the size of the vegetable or fruit.

Exclusive: This term means that a seed is available only through a specific company, often one that has supported the breeding program that resulted in its production. These are offered to entice customers to try the seed, test it in the marketplace, and, obviously, to increase profits.

F1 Hybrid: See "Hybrid."

GMO (Genetically Modified Organism): These seeds have been genetically altered, or "engineered," particularly to withstand specific herbicides and to contain substances toxic to insects. *Seeds of this type are not considered organic because the genes of a completely different organism are implanted in the seed, which may be referred to as "transgenic" seed.* Seed referred to as "cisgenic" has a closer relationship between the organisms, but genes are still being altered. There is a great deal of controversy about the safety of these seeds to humans and the environment in the *long* run. Presently tens of thousands of products on grocery store shelves contain ingredients made from plants grown from genetically modified seed. Beets (sugar), corn, peanuts, rape (for canola oil), and soy are the most likely crops to have been grown from this type of seed in cold climates. Research continues to develop additional GMO seed for other plants.

Heirloom: Heirloom seed comes from open-pollinated plants that have shown a remarkable ability to reproduce the qualities of the parent plant over decades. Most of the time they do, but occasionally there are a few "black sheep" that must be pulled up and discarded. Technically, a plant must have originated before 1951 to be called an heirloom, since that was the beginning of widespread modern hybridization. Many people think this is overly liberal, however, and believe that a plant should have originated much earlier to be called a "true" heirloom. The debate is a waste of time. The thing that really counts is that these plants have been kept around for superior characteristics, including taste, earlier or greater yield, resistance to drought, ability to store well, great color, and so on. Since they are open pollinated, they can cross with other plants in the same species. However, they do have a reputation for being more difficult to grow than hybrids, especially regarding resistance to disease and insects.

I do not like the term *heirloom,* because some fine open-pollinated varieties have been introduced after 1951. However, these older plants deserve to be preserved, and if the term will help in that regard, I'm for its use in the sale of seed. Still, remember that heirlooms may have been developed in specific areas of the country and not do as well in other areas. And while their taste may be great, if they are killed off by disease or insects, this becomes a moot point. So, experiment with heirlooms to see how they do in *your* garden.

Hybrid: Hybrids are produced by crossing two genetically different open-pollinated cultivars (plants that have been bred with each other over years to create a stable inbred strain or line—plants essentially identical to each other) in the hope of creating plants with superior qualities, such as disease resistance, better taste, greater yield, and so on. Some are suited for your area, some are not. The seed from a hybrid will not duplicate the parent plant. Hybrids generally cost more than other seed. The term "F1" stands for "first filial" seed (the result of a cross). Hybrids are considered organic in that they occur from controlled but totally natural breeding programs. While the seed of a hybrid usually produces plants dissimilar in some way from the mother plant, a few produce offspring amazingly similar to the mother plant. *This is the exception, rather than the rule.* Ironically, in some cases hybrids bred for resistance to one disease may become more susceptible to another. Hybrids have a way of coming and going. Ones that become popular may be around for decades, others for just a few years. By law when hybrid seed is sold, the word *hybrid* should follow the plant name, for example, 'Packman Hybrid' broccoli.

Open pollinated (nonhybrid): Open-pollinated plants produce seeds that will come true. *Coming true* means that the seeds will produce plants essentially identical to the mother plant. You can save seed from these varieties to plant the following year. You must be careful to avoid having these varieties cross-pollinate with other plants in the same species. This cannot be fully controlled since pollination takes place by wind and insects from gardens that may be as much as a mile away. But it is still worth a try and generally successful.

Organic seed: The plant that produces organic seed must be grown according to National Organic Standards. However, some seed varieties are not available as organic seed. If organic seed is not available for a specific variety and

you want to grow it, make sure that it has not been treated with any chemicals and has not been genetically modified. According to purists, your plants will not have been grown organically if the seeds were not produced by plants grown organically even if you grow the resulting seeds using purely organic methods yourself. Note that many organic gardeners respectfully disagree or feign ignorance. If you are selling produce as organic, you can do neither.

Pelleted or coated seed: Commercial growers often use coated or pelleted seed since every seed is considered an investment. Companies coat the seed with a thin layer of dust, clay, or vermiculite so that even the most minute seed can be planted one seed at a time. Coated seed is obviously expensive, but for controlled gardening it is excellent. Coated seed is especially helpful for people with limited vision or problems using their fingers. You can more easily feel and work with the larger individual seeds. If the seed has been treated with a synthetic fertilizer or pesticide, it is not considered organic. The convenience for a disabled person may be worth a little "organic" denial. However, there are pelleting materials that are organic, so ask when ordering this type of seed.

Primed seeds: These seeds have been treated in ways to make the seed germinate faster. Primed seeds are mostly used in commercial growing. Some methods are organic, others are not. Priming methods used at home are explained later, in the section "Get the Seed Ready" under "Planting Seed."

Provenance: What part of the world a plant comes from is important to know. In this guide I indicate what may be the plant's place of origin. But an even more defined area may be listed in catalogs. Some varieties have been developed with a genetic makeup specifically designed for optimal growth in different parts of the country. This information helps you decide which are the best seeds to buy for your area. Catalogs sometimes tell you, but often do not. Local agricultural extension offices can be helpful, and so can local farmers. Ask growers at local farmers markets about what varieties have grown best for them. Most are generous and will share this information with you. There's an old Mexican saying that "God does not hear those who do not ask." That applies to earthly mentors as well.

Seed tapes: These are typically strips of biodegradable paper embedded with seeds spaced according to the needs of specific plants. You roll them out in a furrow (drill) and cover them with the specified amount of soil. As is pelleted seed, seed tapes are helpful for people with limited vision or problems using their fingers. Again, they are relatively expensive compared to the average seed packets.

Species: A category of plants that occur in nature and

produce seed that will grow into plants similar to the original plant. They are a subdivision of a genus (large plant group). The abbreviation for species is sp. (spp. in the plural).

Treated seed: Some types of vegetables are prone to specific diseases, which can be spread from the surface or inside the seed itself. In some cases, seed grown in certain parts of the country is often infected. By buying treated seed, you can avoid serious problems from the start. Seed can be treated with bleach (sodium hypochlorite) at low doses, with a number of biological agents, such as *Streptomyces lydicus* (Actinovate®), fungicides, insecticides, or with a hot water bath. Organic gardeners do not accept the use of synthetic fungicides and insecticides as a part of their gardening technique. A hot water bath or naturally occurring bacteria are considered natural and acceptable. If this is a concern, always ask about seed treatment when ordering seed. Seed treated with a fungicide is usually pink or light purple—a sign that the treatment was unlikely to be organic. Note that there is ongoing research regarding plant extracts and oils for potential use as seed treatments.

Variety: A variety is a wild plant in any given species that will produce plants identical to itself. When plants have been bred, they should be called cultivated varieties (cultivars). For simplicity, I refer to all plants as varieties whether they are naturally occurring or cultivated. This practice is not technically correct but from a growing standpoint makes no difference. However, plants listed under different varietal headings, as in the onion chapter, are different. For example, the plants listed under *Allium cepa* var. *cepa* are different from those listed under *Allium cepa* var. *aggregatum*. I point out the differences for you so that this becomes less confusing than it seems here.

Viability: Many sources tell you not to store seed for more than the present season. This may be good advice for a perfectionist, but for the rest of us, it is too fussy. As seed ages, the germination rate typically goes down. So what if a few seeds don't sprout? Enough do, and enough is good enough for most of us. However, there are some seeds that do not last. The average length of seed viability is included in each plant description in Part II.

Do store your seeds in a cool, dry, dark place. If you collect seed, place it once it is thoroughly dry in a paper envelope. The first seeds to mature are often the best. Seeds are alive. They absorb oxygen and give off carbon dioxide. Think of them as living and breathing, even while in storage. If you are concerned about high humidity, add a desiccant to the seeds. Calcium chloride absorbs moisture. Dried powdered milk wrapped in tissue also works. I don't store my seeds in desiccants, and they seem to last just fine. Note that seeds are often sold late in the season by mail-order sources at greatly reduced prices. Many of these seeds need to be planted the following spring, so clearly most seed will last more than a year. One other point: when buying seeds, ask how many seeds are in a packet to comparison shop accurately.

Planting Seed

A seed is simply an embryonic plant, waiting for the right conditions to emerge. Your goal is to provide these conditions. The right conditions are warmth, light (if necessary), air, and moisture. Seeds have their own food supplies for initial growth but rely on nature or the home gardener from then on. The first leaves to emerge from the soil are seed leaves, known as cotyledons. Plants that produce one leaf, such as corn, are called monocots. If seeds produce two leaves, they are dicots. Leaves produced after the seed leaves are known as true leaves. Plants that grow from seed to produce seed in the first year are annuals. If they produce seed in the second year, they are biennials. Perennials are plants that will last for years or even decades.

Direct Seeding

Seeds need to be planted at just the right time. Planting dates are related to your growing season and the needs of the vegetables you are planting. Your growing season is defined as the time between the expected last frost in spring and the expected first frost in fall. Since frosts don't follow predetermined timetables, when to start seeds can be hard to determine. Sometimes, the simplest solution is to start small batches of a vegetable three weeks in a row (see "When to Plant," below, for additional tips).

Get the Soil Ready

Once soil is properly prepared, it is ready for direct seeding. If the soil is powdery dry, water it a day or two ahead of time. If it is wet, let it dry out before working it. Spade or till the soil several times if not already done. Remove any debris, such as rocks, clods of earth, weeds, or twigs. Rake the surface of the soil back and forth with a garden rake until the soil is finely pulverized. Some gardeners work fertilizer into the soil at this time. Others place it directly in furrows and hills or broadcast it over raised beds. Either method is fine.

Get the Seed Ready

Most seed is ready for planting without any form of pretreatment. Certain types of seed germinate poorly. These seeds typically have thick or hard outer seed coats that do not allow moisture in, which delays germination. Growers have developed a number of techniques over the years to overcome a seed's resistance to sprouting. For example, soaking the seed of carrots, mints, New Zealand spinach, onions, and parsley for up to twenty-four hours softens the hard outer seed coat and may remove natural chemicals that retard germination. Note that soaking also works for other seeds, such as beans, beets, carrots, corn, cucumbers, muskmelon, squash, peas, and turnips. None of these need a soaking treatment, but the treatment may get them off to a faster start. Whenever you do this, remove any swelling seed from the water and plant immediately! If seeds don't swell, change the water and continue to soak.

You can also presprout seeds by placing them under a damp paper towel in an aluminum pie tin in the refrigerator, or by placing seeds on a damp paper towel covered with plastic and kept at room temperature. Again, once the seeds begin to sprout, they must be planted immediately. Note that old seed can be tested for viability by trying to presprout some of the seeds using these methods in advance of planting.

Prechilling may also hasten germination. Placing seed in a freezer for a specific time helps break the dormancy of some seed, as does placing seed in moist sand, sphagnum peat moss, or vermiculite in an open jar or plastic bag in the crisper of your refrigerator for six weeks or longer. This is called stratification and is commonly recommended for asparagus, mints, New Zealand spinach, onions, parsnips, and parsley. Occasionally, you have to stratify seeds, bring them to room temperature, and stratify them again. During this chilling period never allow the seeds to dry out or get overly wet. Prechilling is only effective if some treated seeds are exposed to light when planting. Press these chilled seeds into the soil or barely cover when planting.

Yet another trick is to nick or penetrate the seed coat with a needle, file, or piece of sandpaper. If you are really careful, you can toss the seeds into a blender and turn it on for a few seconds to nick seeds, which allows water to be absorbed by the seed. Breaking the seed coat in this way is called scarification. Placing seeds briefly in boiling water may break down the seed coat. Commercial growers may use chemicals or acids to increase germination, but this is not recommended for the home gardener.

Good seed companies will tell you whether seed needs special treatment or not to encourage sprouting. When any of these treatments are advised, they are generally printed on the seed packet. Some of these treatments are suggested in this guide for certain plants. Note that seed may be covered with a dusting of fungicide to prevent rotting after it is planted. As already mentioned, this is not considered organic. Seed companies generally note this in their listing of available seed.

Finally, some books suggest dusting specific seeds, especially beans and peas, with an inoculant. I have never found this necessary. Inoculants are an added expense worth trying only after a crop failure. Fortunately, most seed can be direct seeded without any of these pretreatments. Even the seeds mentioned in this section will grow without pretreatment, which is only meant to speed up the germination process—nothing more.

MAKE ROWS OR HILLS

Seeds are typically planted in rows or hills. If you are planting seeds in rows, use a string as a guide. Tie the string to sticks, and pull it taut. The string should be no more than 1 inch above the ground. Then run the pointed portion of a hoe alongside the string to make a furrow (drill). For deeper furrows, repeat this step as many times as necessary. The goal is to get the furrow equally deep along its entire length. After a number of years you can do this without the help of string. For shallow furrows, lay a rake or broom handle on loose soil. Step on it. The depression is an even drill—simple and effective.

If planting extremely fine seed, sift soil, compost, or sphagnum peat moss into the bottom of the furrow. Or rub soil mixed with any of these between your palms until it is pulverized. While doing this, remove any clumps, tiny rocks, or debris. This is time-consuming, but this one step will increase germination and make it more uniform. It is particularly effective in keeping small seed moist until germination.

Some vegetables do well when planted in double rows. The perfect example is garden peas (ones that need to be shelled). When grown close together, they tend to support each other as they grow upward. Double rows are a simple way of getting more yield in less space.

Seed packages will tell you that certain vegetables can be planted in rows or hills. A hill is not necessarily a mound of soil, although it can be. It is just a grouping of seeds in one spot. Seeds are planted in hills in exactly the same way as you would plant them in rows except that you have a small grouping of seeds to be thinned out later to three or four strong plants.

Plants that are grown in hills include corn, cucumbers, melons, pumpkins, and squash. The seeds of all these plants are large. Just lay out the number of seeds you would like in a hill, spacing them appropriately. Then push them one by one to the right depth in the soil. This is a quick and easy way to plant them.

PLANT SEED

Use only the amount of seed necessary to get a little more than what you are after. By planting more than you need, you won't worry about minor loss to insects, marauders, disease, bad weather, or bad luck. The longer you save seed, the worse its germination rate may be. If you are concerned about older seed, plant it more thickly than fresh seed.

Plant large seed one seed at a time. Press the seed into the soil. If you don't want to bend over or get on your knees, just drop them in place, and push down into the soil with the end of a rake. Small seeds can be tricky to plant. Seed planted too thickly causes crowding. This, in turn, causes poor growth. You will be forced to thin ruthlessly to get good growth, and thinning is time-consuming. There are several good methods to prevent overcrowding. One is to mix a small amount of seed with a handful of sand or sphagnum peat moss before sprinkling the material evenly along a row. Or as many experienced gardeners do, just rub the seeds lightly between your thumb and forefinger as you move your hand along the row, as if sprinkling salt on food. You can control them very well in this way. A few gardeners prefer to cut the corner off the seed packet, then gently tap the packet at an angle to control the number of seeds spilling from the packet. Others crease a piece of white paper, pour seeds into the valley, then tilt and tap the paper gently to control the number of seeds spilling from the crease. Another method is to scatter tiny seeds on the surface of the soil and then sift soil on top of them. Certain small seeds are extremely expensive and are best planted one at a time. Tap these out of the seed packet onto a pie tin or shallow bowl. Moisten the end of a toothpick or pencil. Touch individual seeds with the moist end, and place them exactly where you want them.

You have seen the old paintings with a farmer carrying a bag around his shoulder as he sweeps seed from his hand across newly plowed ground. That's broadcasting, one of the oldest and easiest ways to plant seed. Broadcasting works well for crops that can cluster, either to be left that way or transplanted as seedlings. Any leafy vegetable fits this description. So do green manure crops. Broadcast by working your hand back and forth over the wide area to be planted. This can be a block of soil or a broad row. The seeds are exposed at this stage, resting on top of the soil. Seeds can be worked into the soil with a metal garden rake. Just run it back and forth over the surface.

Save extra seed. Place it in envelopes in a dry, cool, dark place. Seed life varies by type of plant but runs from one to seven years.

SPACING

The correct space between seeds is indicated on seed packages. Suggested spacing is not always reliable. Some seed may germinate quickly and uniformly, other seed may not.

Unless you are planting large, expensive seed, consider planting more closely than recommended with the idea of thinning later in the season. However, tiny seed can be hard to plant without extreme overcrowding. Methods for planting this seed were suggested earlier. If you have vision or hand dexterity problems, consider buying pelleted seed coated with a layer of vermiculite or other substances or seed tapes. These are expensive, but pelleted seed is often used by commercial growers, who consider every seed an investment.

Some people use the quick-growing and inexpensive radish as a row marker and spacer. You just mix some radish seed with other seed. The radishes sprout quickly and show you exactly where the other seeds are planted. As the radishes mature, you just pull them out for eating as microgreens or mini-radishes. This leaves space for the main crop. Frankly, this spacing method is a gimmick in most instances but worth trying with minuscule and slow-germinating seed, such as carrots. There are some who are strongly opposed to this "trick," insisting that radishes can carry diseases fatal to other vegetables in the same family (see "Crop Rotation" in chapter 6).

DEPTH

Plant seed according to the depth indicated on the package. Some seed should be barely covered or just pressed into the soil. Lettuce, for example, germinates best if exposed to light. This is true for some other seed as well. Generally, seed is planted at a depth three times the diameter of the seed. However, skilled gardeners vary planting depth according to soil and weather conditions. Plant more deeply in sand and silt soils, which dry out quickly, less deeply in clay. Plant more deeply in hot dry areas or seasons, less deeply in cool, moist areas or seasons. *Seeds need moisture to germinate well.*

COVERING

As mentioned, some seeds grow best if pressed into the soil, since they need light to germinate. Most are planted deeper than this and need to be covered. When planting larger seeds in deeper furrows, hoe or rake the soil into the furrow. Or without lifting your feet, shuffle along the furrow pushing the soil into it with the sides of your feet in a scuffling motion. Firm the soil by sidestepping along the row. Always cover large seeds within minutes of planting. Pick up any seed that accidentally drops on the ground. If exposed, it will attract birds. If a bird finds one exposed seed, it is intelligent enough to dig up an entire row of recently planted seed. Chipmunks will definitely find peanuts. Cover the area with netting, or trap the rodents.

In raised-bed gardens, firm soil with the back of a hoe

or garden rake. Or place a board over the furrow and walk on it—just on the board, not on the soil off to the side.

Getting small seeds, such as carrots, to germinate seems to be a problem for many gardeners. The number one question I have been asked over the years is "what is the secret of getting carrots to grow?" For small seeds, make a shallow furrow, and sprinkle the seeds along it in the way that feels most comfortable to you. I like rubbing seeds between my thumb and forefinger as I move my hand along the row, as described earlier. Then, I grab a handful of peat in one hand and a handful of soil in the other. I rub these materials together between the palms of my hand. If there are debris and small pebbles in the soil, I toss them in a bucket. The remaining mixture is soft and loose, as if pushed through a sieve. Sprinkle this over the seed, and press it firmly in place with your hands to eliminate any air pockets and to get seeds in direct contact with soil particles. I have to repeat this process a number of times as I move along the row, but it is really quick and simple. Of course, I am doing all of this on my knees. If you prefer bending over, you can prepare the peat and soil mix beforehand and carry a bucket of "sieved" soil with you. Firm the soil in place by placing a board over the row and walking on it.

Mulching

Consider covering the soil surface with a very thin layer of mulch, such as pulverized leaves or straw, sphagnum peat moss, or sifted compost. This layer should barely cover the soil. Keep it moist at all times. This prevents soil from crusting (becoming hard on the surface), which may stop seed from popping through the soil as it germinates. As soon as the seeds begin to sprout, gently push the mulch off to one side unless the plants are growing right through it. Check daily, since mulch can damage young seedlings, just as it can inhibit weed growth. Boards, burlap, moist cardboard or paper, and clear plastic are also used by skilled gardeners for the same purpose. However, their use requires attention. Once seeds begin to sprout through the soil, all of these must be removed immediately to prevent killing the seedlings. Lifting up these coverings twice a day to check on germination may be necessary.

Watering

After planting seed, water immediately. Saturate the soil with a gentle mist. Moisten the soil to a depth of 6 to 8 inches. Keep soil evenly moist at all times during the germination period. If seedlings begin to sprout and then dry out, they usually die. You may have to water every day, or even twice a day, in hot, dry weather. Water is critical to quick and uniform germination.

Plant lettuce seedlings close together to conserve moisture, stop weed growth, and improve overall yield.

Label the Row

Always label the row or hill. Labels are important since it is easy to forget what you have planted. Labeling helps you identify young seedlings. It also helps you remember what varieties do best in your soil and climate. Experienced gardeners commonly keep a journal of where and when they planted seed. The simplest and easiest labeling method is to use permanent marker on both sides of inexpensive white plastic knives. You can buy these in large boxes at numerous discount stores at a reasonable price. Just push them into the soil where needed. They are easy to spot at any time in the season. Ink fades but is still legible even after a full season of frequent rain or watering. Wipe them off, and use them again the following season.

Spacing

Every plant is in competition with every other plant for available light, water, and nutrients. So spacing of individual crops is important. Just as weeds choke out garden plants if not pulled, vegetables can do the same.

Although many gardening books include charts showing the amount of space recommended between plants, this is only a general guide, as is the information on seed packets.

Cool-weather seeds and transplants should go into the garden as early as possible in the growing season.

If your plants are doing well, then you have got them spaced properly. If they are stunted, diseased, or produce poorly, then something is wrong—and that something could be poor spacing.

Home gardeners can give each vegetable more attention than can commercial growers. For that reason, try to get more plants in less space than a commercial grower would. A general guide is to have the leaves of mature plants barely touching each other. Recommendations on spacing for individual plants are included in this guide, including exceptions to the general advice.

The goal is to produce as high a yield from as little space as possible. Vertical and container gardening have already

been described. Here are additional techniques that work as well today as they have for thousands of years in other cultures. Some of them are repeated in the section on "Yield" in chapter 7.

Interplanting (Intercropping)

Interplanting means using one space for more than one crop at the same time. The goal is to plant many plants together in a logical pattern. For instance, radishes are often planted in a row of carrots. The radishes germinate quickly and mark the row. The carrots pop through the soil much later, when the radishes are already starting to leaf out. As the radishes mature, you pull them, leaving spaces between the young carrot plants. This spacing is a natural thinning that promotes good root growth in the carrots. Lettuce, spinach, and Swiss chard grow well with broccoli or cauliflower. So do beets. The larger plants shade the leafy vegetables, which thrive in the cool and moist soil under their companion plants. By mixing quick- and slow-maturing crops, you double the production from the same space.

Succession Planting

Succession planting, often called "multiple cropping," is just commonsense gardening. Plant a crop immediately in any space left by the harvest of an earlier crop. Some vegetables, such as lettuce, peas, and radishes, mature quickly. By planting a second crop in the space left by the earlier crop, you double or even triple the number of harvests in a single season. The other advantage of this method is that you can plant small plantings frequently so that a crop doesn't come in all at once. Better a little lettuce every week than lots of lettuce all at once. Interplanting and succession planting are in effect spinoffs of each other. They both are sometimes referred to as "catch cropping," although that term may mean one or the other to specific growers.

Growing Methods

The traditional row is a good way to grow vegetables, but expand your thinking to take advantage of all available space. Consider planting in blocks or in a tight three-two-three configuration. The latter is used by many for lettuce. Plant three plants across, then two a bit back and between the original three, and then three again. This way you are not wasting any space. The plants form a living mulch, need little weeding, and produce prolifically.

When to Plant

Every plant has a temperature that suits it well. Some plants like it cool, others like it hot. By giving the seeds just the right

Spring and fall frost dates by zone

ZONE	AVERAGE LAST FROST DATE	AVERAGE FIRST FROST DATE
2	May	August
3	May	September
4	May	September
5	April	October
6	April	October

soil temperature, you will be off to a good start. In short, plant cool-weather crops in cool weather, warm-weather crops in warm weather.

If you get a late start, plant cool-weather crops but keep them cool with frequent watering and a good mulch. It is possible to beat the odds, and experienced gardeners do it all the time. Still, they get better production from cool-weather plants in cool weather. The reverse is not true. Warm-weather plants need warm weather. Planting corn in a cold, damp soil will end up in dead, damp seeds.

One of the secrets of successful backyard gardening is to vary your planting dates. This helps you hit just the right moment for each vegetable. Judging the perfect planting time can be difficult, even for experienced gardeners. If you plant several plantings of a vegetable, you increase your odds of getting the seed in at just the right time. Do not forget about mid- to late-summer planting for vegetables that like to mature in cool fall weather. A Chinese cabbage such as 'Tatsoi' often bolts when planted in spring but does well if maturing late in the season. Recommendations for late-season planting are given for plants in this guide when appropriate.

When to Plant Seed Outdoors

When to plant vegetables in cold climates can be hard to determine. Your growing season is determined by your last expected frost in spring and earliest expected frost in fall. These published dates rarely match the actual growing season in any given year. They are useful only as rough guides *because they are averages.* Many vegetables can be planted more than once, so knowing both average spring and fall frost dates is helpful. The most common way to determine spring and fall frost dates is the use of a zone map. In recent years, however, these maps have been less useful, since the weather seems to be "softening"—in most years, that is. I have provided the average frost dates by zone. I have also provided state-by-state data, which I prefer, since altitude makes a real difference in spring and fall temperatures. The best source for first and last frost dates for cities (major cities primarily) is the web site victoryseeds.com/frost-zones (thanks to Victory Seeds®).

Equally important is knowing the typical temperatures to expect throughout the growing season. In some cold-climate areas there really is no spring. You jump from freezing to hot temperatures in a brief period. In other cold-climate areas the temperature stays cool even in midsummer, as in high altitudes or in specific locations.

Cool- and Warm-Season Vegetables

As mentioned, plants have different temperature requirements. One of the main secrets of successful gardening is to

Spring and fall frost dates by state

STATE	AREA	LAST SPRING FROST	FIRST FALL FROST
Alaska	Interior	June 15	Aug. 15
	Coast	May 30	Sept. 30
Colorado	West	May 30	Sept. 15
	Northeast	May 10	Sept. 30
	Southeast	April 30	Oct. 10
Connecticut	Entire state	April 30	Oct. 10
Delaware	Entire state	April 15	Oct. 20
Idaho	Entire state	May 30	Sept. 25
Illinois	North	April 30	Oct. 10
	South	April 10	Oct. 20
Indiana	North	April 30	Oct. 10
	South	April 20	Oct. 20
Iowa	North	May 1	Oct. 1
	South	April 30	Oct. 10
Kansas	North	April 30	Oct. 10
	South	April 10	Oct. 20
Maine	North	May 30	Sept. 20
	South	May 10	Oct. 10
Maryland	Entire state	April 20	Oct. 20
Massachusetts	Entire state	April 25	Oct. 25
Michigan	U. P.	May 30	Sept. 20
	North	May 20	Sept. 25
	South	May 10	Oct. 10
Minnesota	North	May 30	Sept. 10
	South	May 10	Sept. 30
Missouri	Entire state	April 20	Oct. 20
Montana	Entire state	May 20	Sept. 20
Nebraska	East	April 30	Oct. 10
	West	May 10	Sept. 30
New Hampshire	Entire state	May 20	Sept. 20
New Jersey	Entire state	April 20	Oct. 20
New York	North	May 20	Sept. 30
	West	May 10	Oct. 5
	East	May 1	Oct. 10
North Dakota	Entire state	May 20	Sept. 20
Ohio	North	May 10	Sept. 20
	South	April 20	Sept. 30
Pennsylvania	East	May 10	Sept. 20
	West	April 20	Oct. 20
Rhode Island	Entire state	April 20	Oct. 20
South Dakota	Entire state	May 10	Sept. 30
Utah	North	May 30	Sept. 30
	South	April 30	Oct. 20
Vermont	Entire state	May 20	Sept. 30
Wisconsin	North	May 20	Sept. 20
	South	May 1	Oct. 15
Wyoming	High areas	June 20	Aug. 20
	Lower areas	May 30	Sept. 30

get your seed or transplants in the garden at just the right time. This increases the yield, prevents stress and disease, and stretches out an already abbreviated season. In cold climates this can be a bit of a guessing game. Skilled gardeners take risks knowing that they may lose some plants either at one end of the season or the other. The hardiness ratings in the accompanying lists of plants are related to original planting times. Some plants fall into more than one hardiness rating.

Very hardy vegetables like cool to cold temperatures, even below freezing. Plant them four to six weeks before the frost-free date. Crocus and daffodils may just be starting to bloom. Plant many of these again in mid-July for a fall harvest. The earlier you get these crops in, the better. Do not plant them if the soil is wet. Gamble with these vegetables.

Get them in as early as possible. If your hands aren't numb, you're not in the garden early enough.

Hardy vegetables like it cool and can stand some light frosts but not hard freezes. Plant them two to four weeks before the frost-free date. Hard frosts rarely occur after oak trees leaf out. Plant hardy vegetables when oak leaves are the size of a squirrel's ear. Plant many of these once again in the summer for a fall crop.

Tender vegetables do not tolerate frost. Plant them after any danger of frost is past.

Very tender vegetables like it hot—the hotter, the better. Soil and air temperatures should be above 70°F, preferably warmer. In cold climates experienced gardeners use special techniques to create artificially warm environments for these plants as a way of getting them into the garden early.

Vegetables grouped by hardiness ratings

VERY HARDY VEGETABLES		HARDY VEGETABLES		
arugula	kale	bean (scarlet runner)	dill	parsley*
asparagus*	kohlrabi	beet	elderberry*	parsnip
beet	leek*	blackberry*	endive	peppercress
Belgian endive	lettuce	blueberry*	escarole	potato (whole)*
broad bean	lovage (plant)*	borage*	fennel (leaf)	radish
broccoli*	mustard	broad bean	Florence fennel	rape
Brussels sprouts*	onion (seed and sets*)	broccoli raab	gooseberry*	raspberry*
cabbage*	ostrich fern*	burdock	horseradish*	rutabaga
carrot	parsley*	caraway*	Jerusalem artichoke	salad burnet
cauliflower*	parsnip	carrot	(sunchoke)*	salsify
celtuce	pea	cauliflower*	lamb's quarters	scorzonera
chicory	potato (whole)*	celeriac*	lavender*	shallot*
Chinese broccoli	radicchio	celery*	leaf celery*	sorrel
Chinese cabbage*	radish	celtuce	lettuce (some types)	strawberry*
chives*	rhubarb*	chervil	lovage (seed)	sunchoke*
collards	rutabaga	Chinese broccoli	malva	sunflower
comfrey*	salad burnet*	Chinese cabbage	miner's lettuce	Swiss chard
corn salad	salsify	Chinese mustard	marigold*	tarragon*
cress	scorzonera	chrysanthemum	mint*	thyme*
dandelion	shallot*	comfrey*	mustard	upland cress
dill	spinach	cress	mustard spinach	watercress*
endive	strawberry*	currant*	nasturtium	
escarole	tarragon*	dandelion	onion (transplant)*	
garlic**	turnip	daylily*	orach	
horseradish*	Tyfon Holland greens			
Italian dandelion	violet*			

* In cool climates plant these as transplants, bare root or potted plants, tubers, or crowns to get a jump on the season.
** Plant garlic in the fall.

When planting transplants, rather than seed, either grow the plants from seed indoors or buy plants at local nursery centers. Whenever possible, buy plants locally. Mail-order companies do a good job shipping bare-root woody plants but not such a good job with seed-sown plants, such as artichokes or tomatoes. The reasons may be poor packing, jostling about during shipping, unforeseen delays during shipping, and fluctuating temperatures. Many times seed-grown plants arrive in horrible condition. A refund helps little compared to the time lost in getting the plants into the ground.

When to Plant by Phases of the Moon

There are gardeners who believe that planting different vegetables during specific phases of the moon helps their growth. Studies on this are limited, but anecdotal reports abound. The book *Supernature* by the late Lyall Watson has some fascinating insight as to why this *may* be true. Whether you believe in this or not, it's a fun read. I don't have time to worry about phases of the moon, but the book almost got me planting potatoes using this principle—almost.

When to Plant Seed Indoors for Spring Transplants

Many plants do not have enough time to mature if planted directly in the garden, so these are started indoors. Starting seed is covered in chapter 3, and when to start seed indoors is mentioned in the "Transplanting" section for each vegetable in Part II.

TENDER VEGETABLES		VERY TENDER VEGETABLES
amaranth	mibuna	amaranth
artichoke*	minutina	basil*
asparagus bean (yardlong bean)	mitsuba	bean (lima)
asparagus pea	mizuna	citron (under watermelon)
bean (shell and snap)	New Zealand spinach	corn (some types)
Cape gooseberry (ground cherry)*	okra	cornichon (under cucumber)
cardoon*	oregano*	cowpea
catnip	peanut	cucumber
chamomile*	perilla	eggplant*
chickpea	potato (cut pieces in cool soil)*	garden huckleberry*
cilantro	pumpkin	gherkin (under cucumber)
corn	purslane	gourds
cowpea	sage*	ground cherry*
ground cherry*	savory*	muskmelon
fennel (leaf)	soybean	okra
lemon balm*	squash	peanut
lemongrass*	thyme*	pepper*
lemon verbena*	tomatillo*	pumpkin (close to tender)
Malabar spinach	tomato*	rosemary*
marjoram (sweet)*	yardlong bean	sage*
		squash
		stevia*
		sunflower
		sweet potato (close to tender)*
		tomatillo*
		tomato*
		watermelon*

Mail-Order Sources

There may be more than seven hundred mail-order sources for seeds and plants in the United States and Canada. Following is a list of some of these. A few of these names are actually offshoots of one company, but most are a single company. The list includes the name of the company, the web address, the telephone number, and the number of open pollinated (OP) or hybrid seeds or plants offered by the company. Note that some companies sell only heirlooms, which are considered open pollinated in this listing. It is smart to search for and read reviews of seed companies online before making a purchase. Many of these companies offer tools and supplies as well.

Only a few Canadian companies have been listed. Some sell only to Canadian residents. For a more complete list of Canadian companies, go to www.seeds.ca/explorer, and enter the common name of the plant group (genus) you are interested in. Numerous companies are listed on this site for Canadian residents.

Not all companies can afford to send out catalogs, but many still do. Catalogs are often a wealth of information. A few companies can take orders only online or by mail.

Every variety in this growing guide was available at the time of writing from at least one of these sources. The simplest way to find a source for a specific plant is to go online and enter "seed source for variety x." Sources for seed and plants can also be found using the web site www.plantinfo.umn.edu. Search either by the varietal name or by the group (genus), such as squash. No site or book can always be up-to-date, since companies frequently change their varietal listings. That is one of the main reasons I have included a number of varieties in each plant description. A number of these varieties have been available for decades, others for a much shorter time. Whenever buying seed, ask how many seeds are in a packet. Most contain far more seed than you will actually need, but not always.

Adaptive Seeds
adaptiveseeds.com
541-367-1105 (400 OP)

Alberta Nurseries (Canada only)
gardenersweb.ca
403-224-3544 (200 OP and hybrids)

Annie's Heirloom Seeds
anniesheirloomseeds.com
800-313-9140 (450 OP)

Artistic Gardens (Le Jardin du Gourmet)
artisticgardens.com
802-748-1446 (360 OP and hybrids)

Baker Creek Heirloom Seeds
rareseeds.com
417-924-8917 (1,500 OP)

Botanical Interests
botanicalinterests.com
877-821-4340 (600 OP and hybrids)

Bountiful Gardens
bountifulgardens.org
707-459-6410 (300 OP)

Burpee®
burpee.com
800-888-1447 (2,500 OP and hybrids)

Cherry Gal
cherrygal.com
888-752-0022 (1,000 OP)

DeGrandchamp Farms
degrandchamps.com
269-637-3915 (blueberries)

Denali Seed Co.
bestcoolseeds.com
907-344-0347 (100 OP and hybrids)

Dixondale Farms
dixondalefarms.com
877-367-1015 (12 varieties of onions)

Dominion Seed House (Canada only)
dominion-seed-house.com
905-873-3037 (100+ OP and hybrids)

D. V. Burrell Seed Growers Co.
burrellseeds.us
719-254-3318 (300 OP and hybrids)

Earl May Seed and Nursery
earlmay.com
800-831-4193 (150 mostly OP)

Ed Hume Seeds
humeseeds.com
253-435-4414 (300 OP and hybrids)

Eternal Seed (Canada only)
eternalseed.ca
604-487-1304 (375 almost all OP)

Farmer Seed & Nursery
farmerseed.com
507-334-1623 (500 OP and hybrids)

Fedco Seeds
fedcoseeds.com
207-426-9900 (1,000 OP and hybrids)

Filaree Farm
filareefarm.com
509-422-6940 (garlic)

Gardens Alive
gardensalive.com
513-354-1482 (250 OP and hybrids)

Goodwin Creek Gardens
goodwincreekgardens.com
800-846-7359 (herbs)

Grand Teton Organics
grandtetonorganics.com
208-313-7303 (100 potatoes)

Gourmet Seed
gourmetseed.com
831-637-2411 (600 mostly OP)

Gurney's
gurneys.com
513-354-1492 (395 OP and hybrids)

Harris® Seeds
harrisseeds.com
800-544-7938 (950 OP and hybrids)

Hartmann's Plant Company
hartmannsplantcompany.com
269-253-4281 (75 berries)

Heirloom Seeds
heirloomseeds.com
724-663-5356 (1,400 OP)

Henry Field's
henryfields.com
513-354-1495 (395 OP and hybrids)

Heritage Harvest Seed (Canada only)
heritageharvestseed.com
204-745-6489 (700 OP)

High Mowing Organic Seeds
highmowingseeds.com
802-472-6174 (630 OP and hybrids)

Hole's Greenhouse & Garden Ltd.
(Canada only)
holesonline.com
780-419-6800 (2,500 OP and hybrids)

Hometown Seeds
hometownseeds.com
888-433-3106 (400 OP and hybrids)

Indiana Berry & Plant Company
indianaberry.com
800-295-2226 (100 berries)

Irish Eyes Garden Seeds
irisheyesgardenseeds.com
509-933-7154 (280 OP; 70 potatoes)

Italian Seed & Tool
italianseedandtool.com
831-637-2411 (400 mostly OP Italian
seeds)

Johnny's Selected Seeds
johnnyseeds.com
877-564-6697 (1,800 mostly hybrids)

Jordan Seeds, Inc.
jordanseeds.com
651-738-3422 (1,000 OP and hybrids)

J. W. Jung
jungseed.com
800-247-5864 (1,500 OP and hybrids)

Kitazawa Seed Company
kitazawaseed.com
510-599-1188 (500 OP and hybrids)

Lake Valley Seed
lakevalleyseed.com
303-449-4882 (800 OP and hybrids)

Lindenberg Seeds Ltd. (Canada only)
lindenbergseeds.ca
204-727-0575 (400 OP and hybrids)

Lockhart Seeds Inc.
no web site
209-466-4401 (350 OP and hybrids)

Meyer Seed Company
meyerseedco.com
410-342-4224 (350 OP and hybrids)

Nichols Garden Nursery
nicholsgardennursery.com
800-422-3985 (900+ mostly OP)

Nourse Farms
noursefarms.com
413-665-2658 (100 mainly berries)

Ontario Seed Company (Canada only)
oscseeds.com
519-886-0557 (600 OP and hybrids)

The Organic Horseradish Company
organichorseradish.com
order online (horseradish roots)

Otis S. Twilley
twilleyseed.com
800-622-7333 (1,500 OP and hybrids)

Park Seed Company
parkseed.com
800-845-3369 (570 OP and hybrids)

Peaceful Valley Farm Supply
groworganic.com
888-784-1722 (500 mostly OP)

Pepper Gal
peppergal.com
954-537-5540 (200 peppers)

Pepper Joe
pepperjoe.com
843-742-5116 (many OP and hybrid
peppers)

Pinetree Garden
superseeds.com
207-926-3400 (400+ OP and hybrids)

Potato Garden
potatogarden.com
877-313-7783 (60 potatoes)

Prairie Garden Seeds (Canada)
prseeds.ca
306-682-1475 (500 OP)

Raintree Nursery
raintreenursery.com
800-391-8892 (50 mostly berries)

Redwood Seed Company
ecoseeds.com
650-325-7333 (115 OP; many peppers)

Renee's Garden Seeds
reneesgarden.com
888-880-7228 (235 OP and hybrids)

R. H. Shumway
rhshumway.com
800-342-9461 (1,200 mostly OP)

Richters Herbs (Canada only)
richters.com
905-640-6677 (800 OP and hybrids)

Rohrer Seeds
rohrerseeds.com
717-299-2571 (1,000 OP and hybrids)

St. Clare Heirloom Seeds
stclareseeds.com
e-mail or mail (500 OP)

Salt Spring Seeds (Canada and U.S.)
saltspringseeds.com
250-537-5269 (600 OP)

Sand Hill Preservation Center
sandhillpreservation.com
563-246-2299 (2,000 OP; many sweet
potatoes)

Sand Mountain Herbs
sandmountainherbs.com
256-659-2726 (400 OP herbs)

Sandy Mush Herb Farm
sandymushherbs.com
828-683-2014 (1,400 plants)

Seeds from Italy
growitalian.com
785-748-0959 (550 mostly OP)

Seeds of Change
seedsofchange.com
888-762-7333 (300 OP and hybrids)

Seed Saver's Exchange
seedsavers.org
563-382-5990 (600 OP)

Seeds Trust High Altitude Gardens
seedstrust.com
720-335-3436 (300 almost all OP)

Southern Exposure Seed Exchange
southernexposure.com
540-894-9480 (800 almost all OP)

Sow True Seed
sowtrueseed.com
828-254-0708 (500 OP)

StarkBro's
starkbros.com
800-325-4180 (125 mainly berries)

Stokes Seeds
stokeseeds.com
800-396-9238 (1,000 mostly hybrids)

Sustainable Seed Company
sustainableseedco.com
877-620-7333 (1,800 mostly OP)

T & T Seeds Ltd. (Canada only)
ttseeds.com
204-895-9962 (250 OP and hybrids)

Territorial Seed Company (also
Abundant Life Seeds)
territorialseed.com
800-626-0866 (2,000 OP and hybrids)

Terroir-Underwood Gardens
underwoodgardens.com
888-878-5247 (600 OP)

Tomato Growers Supply Company
tomatogrowers.com
888-478-7333 (550 OP and hybrids, mostly tomatoes)

Totally Tomatoes
totallytomato.com
800-345-5977 (100 OP and hybrids, mostly tomatoes)

Vermont Bean
vermontbean.com
800-349-1071 (900 OP and hybrids)

Vesey's (Canada and U.S.)
veseys.com
800-363-7333 (550 OP and hybrids)

Victory Seed Company
victoryseeds.com
503-829-3126 (600 OP)

Walker Brothers, Inc.
walkerseed.com
856-358-2548 (asparagus seed and plants)

Well-Sweep Herb Farm
wellsweep.com
908-852-5390 (1,935 plants)

West Coast Seeds (Canada)
westcoastseeds.com
604-952-8820 (700 OP and hybrids)

Wild Garden Seed
wildgardenseed.com
541-929-4068 (220 OP)

Willhite Seed Inc.
willhiteseed.com
817-599-8656 (400+ OP and hybrids)

William Dam Seeds (Canada only)
damseeds.ca
905-628-6641 (450 OP and hybrids)

Wood Prairie Farm
woodprairie.com
800-829-9765 (25 potatoes)

STARTING VEGETABLES FROM
SEED INDOORS (TRANSPLANTING)

CHAPTER 3

hen I first worked as a grower, the job of growing plants from seed belonged to only one man in the company. The seed he worked with was very expensive, often thousands of dollars per ounce. I was handed tiny seedlings to transplant and care for. I respect the ability of any person capable of growing a wide variety of plants from seed, but I also believe that anyone can do it with patience, practice, and a deep-rooted fascination with the process. Learn how to grow vegetables from seed indoors. It may not be magical, but it is somewhat mystical.

Starting Seeds Indoors

These comments about starting seed indoors are meant to encourage the practice but also serve as a guide to realistic expectations.

The Advantages of Starting Vegetables from Seed

Many varieties of vegetables are not available in local stores. Most nurseries stock only the most popular varieties. These may be good, but they are not necessarily the best. If you want other varieties, you have to grow them from seed. Vegetable plants are often available for a limited time, and you may want them before they are on the market. Growing vegetables from seed allows you to get an early start. You may also want some for a late-season planting, when they are not available.

Seeds are generally less expensive than plants, so you can save a lot of money by growing your own. You can plant only the number of seeds you really need, and save the rest of the seed for subsequent seasons, often getting several years of planting from one seed packet.

By growing your own plants, you control how large they are at the time of transplanting—neither too old, nor too young. You also avoid the chance that plants will suffer from being root-bound, which occurs when plants have been grown too long in an individual pot. Seedlings are extremely vulnerable to insects and animal pests. You can protect young plants indoors better than outdoors. If you can get vegetables off to a good start, you often have a better chance of dealing with hazards in the garden. Finally, you

Starting plants in pots before transplanting conserves space and results in more than enough transplants.

can avoid introducing disease into your garden by using safe seed, certified seed from a reputable company, instead of transplants that may harbor disease and insects. Purchased transplants may also have been grown with the use of synthetic chemicals for fertilization and disease control. Your plants will definitely be organic.

Problems with Growing Your Own Vegetables from Seed Indoors

Since light conditions in most homes are poor for growing plants from seed, you may have to set up a growing area, which takes space and some effort to construct. You must buy or prepare the sterile starting mix that seeds require, and this can be expensive or time-consuming. Young plants require lots of attention. If you are going on vacation in late winter or early spring during their growing season, your plants will suffer unless you have an adept house sitter. Some plants really resent being transplanted or don't do better than those seeded directly in the garden.

The Goal

The goal of starting your own plants from seed indoors is to produce healthy stock for your outdoor garden. Healthy plants are short and stocky, with five to seven true leaves, a deep green color, and a thick stem. The root system should

be healthy, but it should not fill the pot and be root-bound. Fruiting vegetables such as eggplant, peppers, and tomatoes are best planted in the garden before they have started to flower. Small plants usually produce better and more fruit than larger plants, which is contrary to what most people think. There are some exceptions, and these are pointed out in the plant descriptions in Part II of this guide.

Step-by-Step Guide to Planting Seeds Indoors

If you follow the tips in this section, you will be highly successful growing vegetables from seed indoors. While this process appears complicated, it becomes much easier once you have done it a few times.

When to Start Seeds

Buy seeds well in advance so you have them in hand. Seeds need to be planted at just the right time. You don't want them to be too big or too little when you put them in the garden. Planting dates are related to your growing season and the needs of the vegetables you are planting. Your growing season is defined as the time between the expected last frost in spring and the expected first frost in fall. Since frosts don't follow predetermined timetables, when to start seeds can be difficult to determine. Sometimes, the simplest solution is to start several small batches of a vegetable three weeks in a row. One batch should be just the right size for planting outdoors.

Choose the Right Container

Seeds can be started in a wide variety of containers. Commercial containers are usually plastic pots, cell packs, or plastic trays. Clay pots used to be popular, but they are now expensive. Vary the size of pots according to the number and size of the plant or plants desired. Pots are fairly inexpensive and can be used time and time again. They must be sterilized after the first use to prevent damping-off.

There are many inexpensive alternatives, however, including the bottom of milk cartons or jugs, plastic containers for strawberries, Styrofoam cups (easy to write the name of what you are growing on the side), plastic cups, the inside of toilet rolls or paper towels, and cans (soup or coffee). It doesn't have to be fancy to work. Some gardeners wrap newspaper, several sheets thick, around the base of pots to make bands. They fold or tape the base of the bands to keep them from popping open. They then pull them off the pot. Once these are filled with starting mix, they are quite strong. However, moisture will break them down, so they must be set firmly against each other in a flat or similar container. The point: be creative to cut costs if money is a concern.

For specific plants that especially resent transplanting, use a 32-ounce plastic container, as for yogurt. Keep the lid, cut out the bottom, and set the container on the lid. Fill it with a sterile starting mix. Plant two to three seeds in it. I recommend this type of pot in the plant descriptions in Part II of this guide when appropriate.

Peat pots are often recommended, but they are OK for some plants, not so good for others. I recommend them in this guide for specific vegetables. The "advertised" advantage of peat pots is that they can be planted directly in the garden. In theory, this means you never have to disturb the roots of the plant during transplanting. Peat pots are also sterile. But they are expensive, and you use them once, and they are gone. Peat pots have some serious drawbacks, which are covered in detail in the section on planting potted plants in the garden, later in this chapter. Compressed peat or coir expandable pellets are also available for seed starting.

For a larger number of plants, use seed trays or flats. Once plants are large enough, prick them out and plant them in larger containers. The starting mix in these can also be cut into blocks, each block planted with a seed or two. You can then scoop out entire blocks and plant them directly in the garden. Commercial growers often use flats and blocks.

Sterilize All Containers

Any container that has been used before should be sterilized. Wash out the container before soaking it in a bleach solution (one part bleach to nine parts water) for no less than thirty minutes and preferably overnight. Bleach is quite toxic, so wear gloves. Some gardeners are now substituting hydrogen peroxide, vinegar, or rubbing alcohol for bleach. Some people believe all of this is unnecessary and just wash out pots with soap and water before rinsing thoroughly or running them through the dishwasher. The idea is to remove any pathogens from the pots. This is especially important with clay pots. You will lose the lovely green patina on the outside of the pots that so many gardeners adore. Keep the patina on the outside of the pot by sterilizing only the inside, and hope that this will be sterile enough for your seedlings.

Get a Sterile Starting Mix

Seeds need something for their roots to grow in freely. That means support in a light starting mix that should retain moisture. The mix does not have to contain fertilizer, since seeds contain enough nutrients to sprout without it. It is critical that starting mixes be sterile to prevent damping-off, the result of a deadly group of diseases that attack young seedlings. Good starting mixes can be made from fully digested compost (humus), perlite, builder's sand or sharp sand (not sea sand), milled sphagnum moss, sphagnum peat moss, and vermiculite.

Compost works well much of the time but may contain soluble salts that could inhibit seed growth. Perlite is a naturally occurring rock that is heated until it pops. It is light and sterile. Sand should be coarse rather than fine. Milled sphagnum moss (pulverized and sifted) is an excellent seed starting medium, but be careful working with it. It has been associated with sporotrichosis, a severe fungal infection. So wear gloves and a long-sleeved shirt. Do not confuse sphagnum moss with sphagnum peat moss. The latter is fully decomposed and safe. It is sterile and holds moisture well once thoroughly moistened with hot water. Vermiculite is exploded mica and completely sterile. Fine grades are best for starting seeds. Look for horticultural vermiculite. Peat and finely ground perlite are often mixed together. Peat holds moisture, while perlite provides space for roots to grow in.

Garden soil is not a good starting mix unless it is completely sterile (technically, pasteurized), which means it must be heated from 140°F up to 180°F for no fewer than thirty minutes. The process can be smelly. Temperatures higher than 180°F up to 212°F (true sterilization) kill off both pathogens and beneficial microbes. High temperatures may result in phytotoxins (related to soluble salts and manganese). Garden soil by itself tends to compact. Although I have used it, the alternatives are much better.

Sterile starting mixes are available in most garden centers and nurseries. Since it is almost as expensive to make your own mix, buying these makes sense.

Fill the Container

Fill containers close to the top with the starting mix. Close means about ⅛ inch for smaller containers, up to a ½ inch for large ones. This allows for good air circulation at the top of the mix, which helps prevent damping-off. Firm the mix with your hands. Get it nice and level, firm but not compacted.

Dampen the Starting Mix

Mist the starting mix until it is thoroughly damp. Inexpensive, plastic misters are critical to growing seeds indoors. A number of products come in misters that you can repurpose (window cleaner, for example). Water the mix until it is thoroughly moist. If you water too heavily, water will gather in the bottom of your container. Tilt the container to remove excess water. Or punch tiny holes in the bottom of the container where excess water will drain out. If soil gets soggy, let it dry out. It should be damp, not wet. You can also set a container with holes in the bottom in a tray of water or buy special water-absorbing mats. The mix will absorb the water through the drainage holes, or if the pot is made of a permeable material, through the pot itself. This is called bottom watering and works through capillary action.

Naturally, if you have holes in the bottom of your containers, make sure to place them on something waterproof. Even when you water carefully, excess water builds up at the bottom of the container and drains out slowly.

Mist just as the surface begins to dry out. If it hardens or forms a crust, the seeds may have a hard time breaking through to the surface. Never scratch or cultivate crust to break it up—always use moisture to soften it.

Label the Container

Mark the container with a label so that you know what plants are growing in that container. Identifying seedlings without labels can be tough, even for experienced gardeners. Good labels are white plastic knives sold in large boxes at inexpensive prices at discount stores. Use a permanent marker to write the name of the plant on the knife. Or, if possible, write the name on the container itself.

Plant the Seeds in the Starting Mix

Plant the seeds according to the instructions on the seed packet. Some seeds are extremely tiny, others are quite large. Sprinkle tiny seeds on the surface of the mix, and press them lightly with the palm of your hand. Larger seeds should go into the soil to a depth roughly three to four times their diameter. Covering seeds is sometimes easiest if you sift some starting mix over the seeds. Do this with a screen, sieve, or flour sifter.

For every plant that you want, plant two or three seeds. You will thin out all but the best one later. Germination is not uniform for some crops. Perhaps only one seed will germinate, and occasionally none, depending on the type and age of seed. Consider starting a few seeds of a specific plant a week or two apart.

Place the Container in a Tent out of Direct Sun

Now put your container or containers in a plastic tent, which you can make from dry cleaning bags or any other clear plastic material. Put some sticks in the mix at the corners of the container to keep the plastic several inches above the mix. Or use wire hangers or plastic straws, whatever works. This tent will retain moisture in the soil, and it will

also ensure high humidity. The key to successful germination of most seeds is moist soil and high humidity at just the right temperature. Some seeds may react badly to overly humid conditions, so cutting slits in the plastic may be helpful in such situations.

Keep the tent out of direct sunlight. The plastic can trap heat and damage the germinating seeds! Although some plants, such as dill, lettuce, and parsley, need light to germinate, that does not mean direct sunlight. Seed packages will give this information.

Control Temperature

The seed of each vegetable germinates best at a specific temperature. This is given on seed packages. However, almost all will sprout at temperatures ranging from 70°F to 75°F.

Heat-loving seeds will sprout best if they have bottom heat. Warming plants from the bottom has several advantages: it causes quick germination, encourages rapid root growth, speeds growth, and helps plants ward off disease caused by excessive or improper watering.

You can provide this in a number of ways, including something as simple as a heating pad, although heating mats are safer. Heat transfers well through metal. I sometimes use shallow metal pans to start finicky heat-loving seeds. These do not have drain holes, so watering must be done extremely carefully. Incandescent bulbs also give off heat, but bottom heat is preferred. Some gardeners place plants on the top of a refrigerator or dryer for bottom heat.

Check Seeds Daily, and Remove the Tent at the Right Time

Check the seeds daily to see whether they are sprouting. Keep the soil damp. You may have to mist it from time to time, even though much of the moisture will be retained in the tent. If your soil dries out, you could lose your plants.

When the seedlings begin to sprout, remove the tent or at least open it up for a good part of the day. The idea is to control humidity, which can cause diseases at this stage.

Provide Good Light

Some plants germinate best in light. Barely cover or press these into the surface of the starting mix. All plants need a good source of light to grow well once they have begun to sprout. Light is essential to help chlorophyll trap energy and aid the process of photosynthesis in which water and carbon dioxide are converted into sugars (a combination of carbon, hydrogen, and oxygen) to feed the plant. In poor light plants grow tall and gangly (leggy). Leggy plants do not make good stock for gardening.

Natural light is often hard to provide indoors. Although light may be good by windows, the area may be too cool for most vegetables. Turn pots and trays one-quarter turn each day if you use natural light. This will keep plants from bending over in one direction and will promote more uniform growth. Also, move the plants away from the windows at night if outside temperatures are cold.

Artificial light works fine for growing plants indoors. Plants need sixteen to eighteen hours per day but should be given a period of darkness each night. Light should be 2 to 3 inches or so from the top of plants early on, and up to 4 to 5 inches as they get taller. Two lights often work better than one.

You do not need expensive grow lights. Simply combine warm and cool fluorescent lights. Both are sold in building supply stores. Warm and cool refers to Kelvin temperature (warm is roughly 3,000 K; cool, roughly 4,000 K). These temperatures are related to light color, not to warmth. Note that light on the ends of fluorescent tubes can be weak, so shift the plants around.

You can use incandescent lights, but fluorescent tubes are longer and easier to use. Incandescent lights usually provide less light and more intense heat, and the latter can be too intense for some plants.

You can buy or create your own growing shelves with lights attached. You should be able to change the position of the shelves easily. Some people just use boards, books, or bricks to move shelves up or down as needed. Or they have lights that can be lifted or lowered easily.

All shelves should have waterproof trays below pots.

Keep Seedlings Watered

Always use a mister when watering young seedlings. The gentle mist gives them plenty of water without knocking them over. Use lukewarm water to keep the soil temperature even. The best time to water seedlings is just as they are exposed to artificial or natural light each day.

The mix can now dry out a little bit more than when your plants were in the tent. But don't let them wilt or dry out for too long. They are very vulnerable at this stage. The mix should be moist, then dry out a bit, then get moistened again. The mix should not be wet.

Some gardeners prefer setting seedling containers directly in water or on moisture-absorbing fiber mats. The soil soaks up water like a sponge. This method is a fine alternative to misting. It is highly recommended for specific vegetables, such as tomatoes. Water is just as important as light for photosynthesis.

Watch the Temperature

Keep plants roughly 10°F warmer in the day than at night. Avoid drafts and cold night air.

Avoid Damping-Off

Watch for a condition called damping-off. The base of the stems of young seedlings begins to rot, causing them to topple over and die. This problem, caused by a number of different pathogens, is common in any mix that is not completely sterile. In fact, it is so common that you should never start seeds in anything but a sterile container and a sterile mix. The disease is not as common outdoors because the pathogens may be killed by ultraviolet light and some soil microorganisms. However, seed and root rot, related problems, do occur outdoors in compacted, saturated soils.

If you notice damping-off, *remove diseased plants immediately.* Stop watering the plants. Let the soil dry out for at least one night. Increase air circulation to reduce humidity. Increase light and heat. Hopefully, this will stop the disease from spreading. The inorganic remedy has long been Captan. An approved, but expensive, organic alternative is the fungicide Actinovate®. Some organic growers claim that dried horsetail *(Equisetum arvense)* boiled for thirty minutes and then strained produces a solution that, once cooled, can be misted on plants to prevent damping-off. Others say that chamomile tea has a similar effect, as does powdered cinnamon. I have tried none of these and relied solely for years on water reduction with good air circulation.

Thin If Necessary

Give plants space to grow. Most don't compete well with each other. For most vegetables you want to end up with only one plant per small pot or cell in a tray. Members of the onion family are notable exceptions. You want even spacing in larger containers, such as a flat. If plants are crowding each other out, thin them by snipping off the excess plants with a cuticle scissors, or pull out gently with a tweezers. Or prick out and pot up.

Don't Pinch Back (Usually)

If you are a flower gardener, you may be tempted to pinch back your vegetable plants to encourage bushy growth. Growing tips are essential for most vegetables, with some exceptions. The plant descriptions in Part II will tell you whether this is a good idea. For example, when basil has several sets of true leaves, pinching back is highly recommended.

Fertilize

Once the seedlings have formed two sets of true leaves, feed them once a week with a mild fertilizer solution. Organic gardeners make up their own formulas. Common ingredients are fish emulsion and seaweed, both heavily diluted. Fish emulsion does smell. Cat owners would be wise to use an alternative. Fertilizer can be applied through foliar feeding, misting the soil, or mixing with water underneath the plants if bottom watering.

Transplanting Young Seedlings (Pricking Out)

As soon as a seedling has a second pair of true leaves, you can safely move it from one container to another, a process known as pricking out. This can be tricky for tiny, tiny seedlings. Some plants, such as asparagus and plants in the onion family, shoot up little spikes rather than a pair of leaves. Prick these out at a few inches tall.

You may not have to prick out plants at all if you are already growing them in a large enough container. Choose any pot that fits the following criteria: it must be sterile, large enough to accommodate the root system of the plant you are growing, and have drainage holes in the bottom so that soil does not get waterlogged.

Fill Pots with Appropriate Growing Mediums

Good growing mediums provide support for the seedlings' root systems, nutrients, and a consistent supply of moisture. *Fully* composted organic material (humus) is an excellent growing medium. It is not particularly fertile, but it is fine as a starting point for young plants. If compost is not fully decomposed, however, it can cause serious problems due to the release of ammonia and high levels of soluble salts.

Potting soil is sold in many stores. The best potting soils consist of a mixture of black earth for nutrients, sphagnum peat moss for water retention, and perlite for good aeration. Many companies sell potting soil that varies from excellent to next to worthless. Sometimes it is really hard to know what is in the bag without carefully reading the ingredients on the bag. Compare the weight of bags. The really heavy ones are mostly soil with little peat or perlite.

Soilless mixes are also fine, especially for anyone interested in growing their vegetables in containers. They are light and easy to work with, provide good aeration and drainage, but retain moisture. They tend to be disease- and weed-free. Most have small amounts of nutrients. Of course, you can make your own potting mix, and many gardeners do using a variety of ingredients including coir, perlite, sand, soil, sphagnum peat moss, and vermiculite. They may also add alfalfa meal, blood meal, bonemeal, Epsom salt, fish emulsion,

greensand, limestone, rock phosphate, and soybean meal. If possible, make potting soils well in advance, and keep warm and moist for several weeks to allow for the release of ammonia and breakdown of organic acids.

Fill Containers with the Medium, and Transplant Seedlings

Fill up the container with growing medium. Firm it lightly. It should be neither loose nor compacted. Poke a hole in the middle of the pot. For pricking out, use any pointed object, even a sharp pencil or a tongue depressor notched into a V shape at the tip. Sometimes you get a bunch of seedlings all in a cluster. You develop a gentle touch to get these apart. Or just leave them together to be thinned later. You may have to shake them lightly to get the roots to come apart. Hold these tiny plants gently by a leaf, not by the stem, which you can damage easily with too much pressure. It takes a few tries to learn how to handle fragile plants. Use just enough pressure on the leaf to hold it, no more. One of the advantages of growing your own is that you don't have to be perfect. If a few don't make it, that's part of learning. Holding the plant by a leaf, gently lower the roots into the hole. Plant the plant no lower than the bottom seed leaves. Firm the medium around the fragile stem. Add a little more medium, and compact it around the plant. Leave at least a ¼- to ½-inch space from the top of the pot to the medium. This leaves room for watering. Now water the plant with a mild transplant solution (diluted fertilizer). Repeat this until you have all the seedlings in individual containers. Put the containers close together to make watering and fertilizing plants easier.

Smokers take note: Wash your hands carefully before touching seedlings, since tobacco may carry tobacco mosaic virus disease. This is particularly important when working with marigold, pepper, and tomato plants, but other vegetables can be infected as well.

Exception to the rule: Leeks and onions do not have to be planted in individual containers. You can grow many of these slender plants (up to twenty-five) in one 4-inch pot. If the leeks or onions begin to get leggy (more than 7 inches high), you can snip them back to 3 to 5 inches. They will regenerate growth. Leeks and onions like cool weather and can be planted in the garden as soon as the soil can be worked.

Planting Seedlings and Potted Plants Outdoors

Seedlings are ready to be planted outdoors after they are growing well in their individual pots and when the weather outside is appropriate for transplanting.

Harden Off the Plants

Young plants are very vulnerable when being moved outdoors. Plants that you have started from seed indoors have been coddled in a hothouse environment. You have got to toughen them up by hardening them off. *Hardening off* is a gardening expression for getting plants acclimated to wind, temperature, and light conditions outdoors. Hardening off typically takes seven to ten days.

Set the plants outside each day somewhere in the shade. Don't put them in direct sunlight. If it is still on the chilly side, protect them from cold. Start off with a few hours, and extend the time outdoors each day. Bring the plants in if there is any danger of frost. Each day expose the plants to a little more light. Do this for about a week. Extreme heat, cold, or heavy winds can do a lot of damage to seedlings, but you still have to harden them off before putting them in the garden. Exposing some plants to colder temperatures can be important. The process is known as vernalization and is suggested when appropriate in the plant descriptions in Part II. It is critical for artichokes.

If you have a cold frame, then set seedlings in the frame, and watch them closely for about a week before planting them in the garden. (For information on cold frames, see "Extending the Growing Season" in chapter 4.)

When the plants can take a full day of direct light, they are ready to be planted, assuming conditions outside are right. This is usually after all danger of frost. There are cold- and warmth-loving plants. Plant seedlings out at the right time. The right time is covered in detail in the plant descriptions in Part II. Even cold-loving plants may need to be protected from unexpected frost or cold spells until they have taken root and are growing well.

If you buy plants from a garden center, hardening off is rarely necessary. They are often sold from racks that have been outside for days.

Planting at the Right Time

Getting plants into the garden at just the right time can be hard to achieve. When to plant is discussed in detail in chapter 2. Read this before planting homegrown or purchased seedlings. The ideal planting time is in the evening on a cloudy day right before a shower. That's asking a lot. Settle for planting in the evening or on a cloudy day. The main enemies of transplants are heat, lack of enough water, or an unexpected frost or freeze. If it is hot or sunny, plants tend to wilt. As long as you keep the plants watered, they will usually survive. Still, why stress them?

Planting Potted Plants

Feel the soil in the pot. If it is dry, water around the base of the plant until the soil is thoroughly moist. Water should drain from the bottom of the pot or plastic container. Let the soil dry out until it is barely moist but not wet or soggy. By letting the plants sit for as long as necessary, you will give the soil a chance to reach the right moisture level. You may have to let the plants drain overnight.

Try to have the space in the garden where you intend to plant seedlings ready before you take them out of their pots or trays. Dig the holes for the seedlings before knocking plants out of pots. Make the hole twice as large as the root ball of the plant. If in doubt, set the pot into the hole to help you decide how deep and wide to dig it. If you are planting seedlings from plastic trays or six-packs (cells), guess how large to make the holes.

In each of the holes sprinkle some compost or well-rotted manure. If you don't have either of these, then a little sphagnum peat moss mixed in with the soil will work well. These materials keep the roots moist by retaining water and promote rapid root growth.

Clay and plastic pots will not break down. Naturally, you take seedlings out of these containers before planting. Very few plants are now being sold in clay pots. To remove plants from plastic pots, place your index finger and middle finger alongside the base of the stem. Tip the pot upside down, supporting the plant with those two fingers. With your free hand, give the pot a whack on the bottom to see whether the seedling will jar loose. If nothing happens, give the pot another whack. Or tap the edge of the pot against a hard surface. Whenever you do this, be sure to support the plant. If you don't, the plant will shoot out of the pot and be damaged when it hits the ground. Occasionally, larger potted plants do not come out easily. If the plant does not jar loose, then slide a knife around the edge of the pot between the soil and the pot itself. Now give the pot another whack on the bottom while holding it upside down. The plant will probably slide out now. If not, check to see whether roots protrude from the bottom drain holes. If they do, just rub them off with your thumb. This minor surgery will not hurt the plant. If the plant still refuses to pop out of the pot with a solid whack, cut off the bottom of the pot. Slit the side of the pot from the bottom up stopping a ½ inch from the top of the plastic pot. Then place the pot in the planting hole, cut off the top ½ inch of plastic, firm soil around the pot, and then pull the pot out of the soil.

To remove larger plants planted in plastic 32-ounce yogurt containers, make a hole in the soil large enough to hold the container. Set the container off to the side of the hole. Slide the plastic lid out from under the container. Cover the bottom where the lid was with your hand, and place the container in the hole. Push soil lightly around the container, and then lift it up and away from the plant. Firm the soil around the plant.

If you are growing your own seedlings in peat pots or buy plants in peat pots, dampen them by setting them in a tray of water. Place the pots into the soil. Make sure that the top of the pot is barely covered with soil. No part of the pot should be exposed. This will stop the pot from acting as a wick—moving moisture from the soil to the air and drying the plant out. Other biodegradable materials, including homemade paper pots, should be treated in the same way. The main goal of growing plants in peat pots is to prevent root disturbance during planting. In theory, roots should grow right through the pots into the soil with the pots degrading over the growing season.

I, along with many gardeners, believe that peat pots in some instances retard growth and break down slowly. If you notice this, the next time you use these pots, remove the upper ½ inch of the already *moistened* pot and tear off its bottom. Then carefully remove the rest of the peat pot just as you place the plant into the soil. This eliminates the potential advantage of peat pots, which is to reduce even minimal root disturbance at the time of planting. Although I do recommend 4-inch peat pots in this guide for specific plants, especially for cucumbers, muskmelons, watermelons, and winter squash, I give an alternative planting method for these in the plant descriptions for gardeners who have had a poor experience with peat pots. Clearly, I am ambivalent about the use of peat pots, knowing that many gardeners and professionals use them without the problems I have experienced. These could be related to the brand of the pot, soil and weather conditions, and so on. Come to your own conclusion by experimenting.

To remove plants from flat-bottomed six-packs, gently squeeze all sides of the pack. This usually loosens the plants enough so that when the pack is tipped on its side, the plants slide out easily in a clump of soil. If plants are in individual cells, squeeze lightly or twist the cell pack before tipping the container on its side. Plants will slide out easily with a gentle tug after this treatment.

Occasionally, two or more plants will be growing in one pot or one cell. Conservative gardeners snip off extra plants with a scissors so that there is only one plant per pot or cell. More daring gardeners want to get the most

plants possible. So they must separate "conjoined" plants. Separating tightly knit plants can be intimidating the first time you try it. Once you have the plants out of the pot or six-pack, tease them apart *gently,* trying to get some soil with each plant. Pull them apart at the base where they are joined together at the soil line. At times you will have to shake the plants apart, loosing most of the soil around the roots in the process. It's always better to keep soil around the roots, but it's often impossible, especially with tiny seedlings growing in tight masses. As long as you plant and water the seedlings *immediately,* they will be OK. Plants do not grow well when crowded or "clump planted," so you are really doing them a favor. If the roots of plants are exposed during transplanting, wilt often results. Plants flop over, may lose lower leaves over a period of days, and look as if they are dying. Keep these plants consistently moist. Generally, they pop back up and look fine after a day of two. If the lower leaves turn yellow, snip or pinch them off. As long as the upper or central leaves are green and growing, the plant is fine. Mulching around the base of the plant will stop the flopping plants from getting covered with soil or sticking to the soil surface. Mulch also helps keep the plants firmly anchored during watering.

When planting seedlings, plant them no deeper than their lower leaves. There are exceptions, and these are noted in descriptions of individual plants in Part II. Hold tender seedlings gently by one leaf as you lower them into the ground. Do not hold them by the stem unless the stems are sturdy and rigid. If you crush or break the stem, the plant may die. Also, protect the growing tip of the plant. This is especially important with broccoli, Brussels sprouts, cabbage, cauliflower, and kohlrabi. If you break off the tip, the plant will not produce properly. If cutworms are a problem in your area, now is the time to slide on a cutworm collar.

Whenever planting seedlings, firm the soil around the roots and base of the plant just under the lower leaves. Press soil firmly around the entire plant with your fingers to eliminate air pockets. The soil should not be loose. Firm soil helps the seedling take in nutrients immediately on planting. If the soil is not firm enough, the plant may topple over when you water it. Pour a cup or two of transplant solution around the base of each seedling. Transplant solution is nothing more than heavily diluted water-soluble fertilizer.

In spring, you may have to protect plants from frost or cold nights. See "Extending the Growing Season" in chapter 4 for suggestions on how to do this.

If the plants will require support, for example, cucumbers, muskmelon, and pole beans, stake them now. Later staking increases the likelihood of root damage.

It is easy to forget what you have planted if you have a large or complicated garden with a wide variety of plants. Most gardeners mark each plant or row of plants with a small marker as a reminder. This may seem unnecessary, but we all forget at times what a plant is—even gardeners with years of experience. Furthermore, some plants look alike, and they can get confused in the early stages of growth. It is also helpful to know the variety of any vegetable and the planting date. By keeping records, you will come up with personal favorites, ones that you can count on year after year. So keeping a journal is a great idea.

Perennials are plants that produce year after year. Locate these in a spot where you will never have to disturb or move them. Perennials include asparagus, blackberries, blueberries, chives, comfrey, horseradish, lovage, mint, onions (certain kinds), raspberries, rhubarb, sorrel, strawberries, sunchokes, and a few others. Most of these plants prefer full sun. Plants generally planted on their own, like rhubarb, are best put in the corner of the garden where they are out of the way. I prefer planting spreading plants in blocks, essentially in contained beds. Some of these can be invasive and can take up much more space than you had originally planned. Chives don't get that large, but they will self-seed freely if you don't remove the flowers. Mint is an aggressive plant that prefers moist soil in a semishaded area. By planting it in a huge plastic pot, you can keep it contained. Cut out the bottom of the pot, and sink it into the ground. Note that sunchokes are highly invasive and best planted where they can go wild.

Buying Potted Plants

If you are going to buy plants at a nursery, try to get the very best for the best price. Most nurseries charge different prices for the same plants. Shop around. Many nurseries do not tell you what variety of plant you are buying. Broccoli is broccoli—that's it. It's a confusing way to sell plants but common. Sometimes, nurseries don't get cool-season plants in early enough in the season to be planted at the right time. This is a good reason to grow your own.

Ask whether the plants have been organically grown. In some nurseries they may not know whether seed has been treated, whether chemical fertilizers have been used, or whether soil has been treated with a pesticide such as a neonicotinoid, commonly imidacloprid. Neonicotinoids are systemic, meaning the pesticide remains in plant tissue. If plants flower, the pollen is believed to kill honeybees and

other insects. Neonics may persist in the soil, causing additional problems. The good news for gardeners is that the sale of truly organically grown plants is increasing each year. Check into farmers markets, where you will often find organic plants for sale.

Choose stocky plants with thick stems and thick, healthy foliage. Big is not necessarily better. Tall plants tend to get leggy, an expression meaning weak and spindly. They do not grow as well as short, compact plants. Avoid plants with pale or faded leaves. Plants should be turgid, not wilted. The soil should be moist and firmly against the rim of the pot. If there is space between the soil and the edge of the pot, this indicates inconsistent watering. Check plants carefully for insects. Hold the plant up to look under leaves. Avoid buying sick plants, even at heavily discounted prices. They can bring disease into the garden, wiping out other valuable plants.

Many plants are sold in trays with six compartments, each one meant to hold one plant. It is very common to find these trays with many more plants than intended. Pick out a tray with extra plants. These can be separated from each other and planted individually, as mentioned earlier.

Buying Plants from Mail-Order Sources

Buying seed from mail-order houses is one thing, buying plants grown from seed is another. Plants must be shipped in appropriate containers, shipped quickly, and, of course, be at the right stage of growth. As soon as you get a package, open it. Follow the directions inside exactly. The roots of mail-order plants generally must be kept moist. Get them into the garden as soon as possible. Some plants can be kept in the refrigerator for delayed planting, as long as they are not affected by ethylene gas, given off by apples, avocados, bananas (ripe), blueberries, green onions, grapes, peaches, pears, potatoes, and tomatoes, to name a few. At least, put ethylene fruits and vegetables in the vegetable bin if you have to store plants in the refrigerator temporarily.

If plants arrive in a damaged condition, call the supplier immediately. Note that some plants look awful but will grow well. Still, let the company know they "look" dead. If once planted, they spring to life, fine. But, if not, you have already set yourself up for a refund or possible replacement.

Buying and Planting Crowns and Woody Plants

Mail-order houses sell a number of plants in a dormant stage, usually referred to as bare root or crowns. These include asparagus, rhubarb, strawberries, and most woody plants, such as raspberries. Plant these in spring, and follow directions carefully. Following are steps most frequently recommended. Get plants out of their packaging immediately. Keep plants out of sun and keep cool. Keep moist if indicated. Plant at the correct depth, firm in place with your fingers, and water well. Keep moist until growing vigorously.

Always order these plants well in advance since some varieties may get sold out. Try to match shipping and planting dates. This is not always possible because weather is so unpredictable, but try anyway. Catalogs offer a far greater selection of bare-root crowns and woody plants than local nurseries. Having said that, always check local suppliers to see whether they are offering bare-root plants of the variety or varieties you want. Local nurseries often offer bare-root plants for a brief period in spring. If you have a problem, it is far easier to deal with them than mail-order houses.

Dig up or buy bare-root raspberries, and get them into the soil as soon as possible.

Plant asparagus crowns with only the roots underground. Firm and water immediately.

CHAPTER 4

CARING FOR VEGETABLES, BERRIES, AND HERBS

Watering

Knowing how and when to water plants is critical. There is no set formula for proper watering, such as "giving plants 1 inch of water per week." Watering depends on the weather, the type of plant being grown, the stage of a plant's growth, the depth, type, and condition of the soil, and other factors covered later in this section and throughout the guide. Water carries nutrients to plants and acts as a nutrient itself since it contains hydrogen needed in the process of photosynthesis. Only with proper watering will plants flourish. Healthy plants are more productive and less prone to damage by insects and disease. They are often more tender and flavorful and possibly more nutritious. Locate your garden close to a water source if possible, so you minimize the time and effort spent watering.

Sometimes, rainfall is sufficient, and there is little need to water, but rainfall amounts cannot be predicted accurately. The goal is to use water wisely as it is a finite and valuable resource. The following suggestions will help you water correctly and efficiently.

Proper soil preparation is essential to effective water-ing. Soil should drain freely but retain moisture during dry periods. The importance of soil preparation has been explained elsewhere in this guide but cannot be understated. The better your soil, the easier it will be to satisfy your plants' moisture needs. Begin by adding lots of organic matter to the soil, such as coir, compost, leaf mold, sphagnum peat moss, or a combination of these. Organic matter retains moisture during dry spells and cuts down on the need for water. Mix in a little organic matter with soil in drills or planting holes. Also, add organic matter to the surface of the soil as a mulch. Mulch keeps the soil moist and deters the growth of weeds, which steal water from the plants you are growing. Always water and loosen the soil before applying mulch.

Weather in cold climates varies dramatically from one year to the next. It also varies from day to day and month to month. Soil tends to retain water during cool to cold spells while losing it rapidly when temperatures soar. Wind also dries out plants quickly as does low humidity. Plants are taking in and giving off water constantly and at different rates at different times of the day. The process is called transpiration and is similar to perspiration in human beings.

Watering needs depend upon mini- or microclimates in your own yard. Are your plants on a slope, by a concrete wall, under an eave, near a tree, exposed to wind, in shade, and so on? Some areas retain moisture well, while others seem to need constant watering. Raised bed and vertical gardens require more watering than level areas. But the value of these types of gardening far outweighs the disadvantage of having to water more frequently.

Seeds need moist soil around them at all times to germinate and grow well. If they are allowed to dry out, they may not germinate. If they start to germinate and then are allowed to dry out, they will often shrivel and die. And if the soil above seeds is allowed to crust or harden, the young plants will not be able to pop through. This can kill them. If you keep soil moist around seeds, you prevent all of these problems. Seeds and seedlings may need to be watered twice a day in dry and windy weather.

If the soil in a container of·transplants is dry, water it before transplanting. Do this far enough ahead of time so that the soil is moist, not soggy, at the time of transplanting. Once transplants have been planted in the garden, water them immediately. Keep their roots moist until

Most plants react well to deep watering, which causes water to pool on the surface of the soil for a brief time.

they are growing vigorously. These first few days are critical to the young plant. If you allow a young transplant to dry out, it may die. Transplants often wilt after transplanting if not enough soil was kept around the roots. Wilting is a sign of acute water loss and stresses plants badly. As long as you keep the soil around them moist, they will spring back within a day or two, take root, and begin to grow. Moisture is the key to getting them off to a good start.

As plants get more mature, they often need less frequent watering. The specific water needs also vary by plant. For example, it is hard to overwater raspberries and mint, while other plants, such as thick-stemmed herbs, will do well with less frequent watering. Suggestions for watering are given for plants in Part II.

When you water more mature plants, soak the base of the plant. Let the water soak in, then water again. Deep watering is important for all but shallow-rooted plants. The soil should be thoroughly moist to a depth of 6 to 8 inches. A good sign that you have watered enough is when water begins to pool up on the surface of the soil. If you water just enough to moisten the soil surface, you are hurting the plants. Roots of deeper-rooted plants will stay shallow, and if the soil dries out, the plant can be damaged. Slow, patient watering is one of the secrets to good vegetable gardening. And how often? Depending upon the weather, this could be once a day, once a week, or more or less. During drought conditions you may have to water twice a day.

Wilting is a sign of water stress. Wilting can result in damage to foliage, loss of blossoms, change in fruit taste and texture, less resistance to disease and insects, and even death. Plants that wilt and are watered usually survive, but often some damage has already occurred. Some plants wilt in the middle of the day as a way of preventing water loss, but if they are wilting in the morning or evening, then water immediately.

Wilting can sometimes be a sign of something other than water stress. If the soil is moist and a plant is wilting, suspect disease or insect infestation. Something other than water stress is especially likely if just one plant in a row or area is wilting while surrounding plants look fine. Often when you dig up a plant in this condition, you will find some sort of root rot or an assortment of root maggots underneath the soil. Dig up the plant and surrounding soil. This will often stop the problem from spreading. Destroy the infected or infested plant and surrounding soil by burning it or tossing it into the garbage. Or place it in a compost pile set aside strictly for sick plants, not in your regular compost pile.

You can prevent wilting by checking the soil daily to see how dry it is. Dig down 6 inches or so with a small trowel or with your hand. Or push your finger into the soil if it is loose enough. Don't judge soil by the top 1 or 2 inches. As long as the soil 6 inches down is moist, your plants will probably not wilt. If the soil is dry, give the plants a thorough watering. And don't be fooled by light rain. Unless it rains long and hard, do not assume the soil has received enough moisture. While it may look wet, dig into it to check. This will give you an accurate idea of how moist the soil is and to what depth. It is not unusual to have to water after a light rain—despite what your neighbors may think as you haul out hoses over a moist driveway.

As with lawns, it is best to water before fertilizing plants and then to water again afterwards. This is especially true when using fertilizers with a high amount of nitrogen on the surface of the soil. The initial watering helps reduce the chance of damage to plant tissue, often referred to as burn. The chance of this damage is low with organic fertilizers but still possible. The second watering helps draw nutrients into the root zone, where they will be most beneficial.

The soil should also be moist around plants before foliar feeding. After using this method of feeding, do not water the foliage for at least twenty-four hours to allow the plant to absorb the nutrients from the diluted fertilizer applied to the leaves.

In general, most publications tell you to water the base of a plant and avoid watering foliage. The reason given is that wet foliage is often more susceptible to disease. Ironically, watering foliage can be useful at times in reducing disease, such as powdery mildew. Spraying off foliage is also recommended for plants covered in dust, as along a rural road. When you get foliage wet also makes a difference, at least, in theory. Many gardeners water in early morning so that water has time to evaporate off foliage during the day. It is usually cooler and less windy in the morning, so there is less water loss. Others prefer late afternoon, insisting that water loss is minor and that foliage has enough time to dry out before night. My practice is simple. I water whenever I can if the soil is drying out and possibly stressing plants. Nature waters at all times of day.

Which brings up the subject of getting water on leaves in intense light. Supposedly, droplets on leaves cause them to act as magnifying glasses and cause damage. I have deliberately watered plants in full sun to see whether this is true and have never noticed this effect. The only drawback of midday watering is water loss, not damage to plants—in my opinion.

While the emphasis in this section has been on watering enough, avoid watering too much. In overly wet soils roots may rot out. A good part of watering is common sense,

which seems to increase dramatically with experience. Plants will let you know if they are getting enough water.

Ways to Water

WATERING WITH A HOSE

Many gardeners water their plants by hand with a hose, preferably one that doesn't kink. Buy a good all-rubber hose with metal fastenings or fittings. Hand watering has a number of advantages: you are aware of what's going on in the garden each day. You can see problems right away, including early signs of disease or insect infestations. You can water selectively, concentrating water where it is needed. You can use nozzles or watering wands, which sprinkle plants with just the right amount of moisture (seeds lightly, seedlings gently, larger plants more deeply). Watering around the base of a plant is usually the best way to water. Water carefully so that soil doesn't splash up on plants. This is more of a problem early in the season before you have mulched around plants. Splashing soil does spread disease. This is an intimate way of gardening, and you may like it. It may also be the only practical way to water depending upon the layout of your yard.

Its disadvantages are clear: it takes up a lot of time, much more time than many people have. And, of course, you can only hand water when you are at home. If you are in a hurry, you may not saturate the soil the way it should be. You may just sprinkle the surface, and this can damage plants. Pulling a hose around can be a chore. If you are not careful, you may pull the hose over plants and damage them in the process. To prevent this, set up hose guards, usually metal stakes or purchased "hose guides." Rebar cut into short lengths works well for guides, but soften the top with duct tape, since it can be rough and sharp. *Do not use a hose if you have a well unless you have enough hoses running to cause your pump to run continuously. With only one hose running, the pump goes on and off constantly and is likely to burn out.*

Most cities require backflow preventers on outdoor faucets, especially ones used to fertilize gardens. Backflow preventers are annoying at worst, critical at best. If you are only running water through your hose and never using hose-end attachments for any other purpose, such as fertilizing or applying pesticides, backflow preventers seem like regulatory overkill. But if you are using hoses for any other purpose than watering, they are essential to stop contaminated water from getting into your household.

Note that drinking from hoses is not recommended. Rubber hoses are usually safer than others if you run out all the water that was in the hose before drinking. If a hose has been sitting in the sun, let the water run until it is cold.

Never drink from a hose that has been used with hose-end attachments for fertilizer or pesticides—never!

Using a Watering Can

A watering can is the old-fashioned way of watering plants, but it works well. You can control flow with a rose, a perforated end cap. I prefer carrying a couple of gallon milk jugs into the garden and watering individual plants that may seem to need it. But this method is impractical for covering wide areas.

Flood Irrigation

Flood irrigation is nothing more than setting a hose with a breaker or bubbler attached on a board or concrete slab and letting it run in the garden. This works fine on level ground and is nearly worthless on sloped areas. It saturates the soil wonderfully, and little of the water is wasted if the area flooded is completely planted in vegetables. Flood irrigation works best for plants such as corn, raspberries, and strawberries. And, of course, you can be doing something else while the hose is flooding the garden.

Sprinklers

Many gardeners prefer to use sprinklers. Sprinklers vary from oscillating types that cover a large portion of ground to small attachments that send out a circular or rectangular, more defined pattern of spray. You can match sprinklers to the size and shape of any garden area by purchasing the right attachment. Sprinklers do get both foliage and soil wet. Wet foliage is reputed to be a cause of disease, but water stress is far more serious.

Quite a bit of water is lost to evaporation when you use sprinklers. In many parts of the country water is so expensive and hard to come by that the use of these doesn't make sense. In other parts of the country the loss is relatively insignificant because water is plentiful or the weather is cooler and more humid. You will lose less water to evaporation if you sprinkle early in the morning, when there is usually less wind and cooler temperatures, or in late evening, giving plants enough time to dry out before dark. A tip: Set sprinklers on raised platforms to cover more area or to stop the spray from hitting nearby vegetation.

Soaker Hoses

Soaker hoses seep water through a porous material. Gardeners run these up and down rows. The hoses weep water along their entire length, watering both plants and soil that may not contain plants. They do keep water near the roots. They are somewhat hard to lay out properly. They are fairly expensive and break down within a few years, but less rap-

idly if covered with mulch. Occasionally, they get kinked or clogged. They may water somewhat unevenly, more closer to the water source, less toward the end.

Soaker hoses are especially attractive to commercial growers, who lay lines out under black or clear plastic, which traps moisture in place, thus reducing water loss due to evaporation from heat and wind. The combination of these hoses and plastic can be duplicated by home gardeners. This method is especially effective for some crops, including cucumbers, eggplants, muskmelons, peppers, pumpkins, squash, strawberries, sweet potatoes, and tomatoes. The plastic holds the water for many days, and this is an ideal way to water these thirsty, mostly warm-weather vegetables. Note the earlier warning about watering if you have a well.

Drip Irrigation

The use of drip irrigation is effective and efficient. Drip irrigation can be set up so that emitters water only plants, not bare soil. Systems can have automatic timers and shutoff valves so water is used just when or as needed. Once set up, the systems reduce unneeded watering and weeding. Many gardeners swear by this method of watering.

Handy home gardeners set up their own systems, while others prefer to have professional help. Some are set up to be permanent, others to be assembled and taken apart for winter storage. Systems can be simple and inexpensive or more complicated and expensive. Most take quite a bit of time to set up, and some must be purged at the end of the season. Emitters do break and may have to be replaced, but that is relatively minor. If you have a well, again be sure that enough water is being used at one time to keep the pump running constantly.

Those gardeners who don't swear by this system, swear at it. The choice to use drip irrigation depends on the type of garden you have, the layout of your property, and even your personality. While most home gardeners view watering as a chore, especially during a period of drought, I'm generally most happy when I'm at the end of a hose.

Placing Milk Jugs near Plants

One of the simplest and most effective ways to water specific plants over a period of time is to fill up a gallon milk jug with water, carry it to the garden, poke pinholes in the bottom, and set the jug beside the plant you want to water, either on or in the ground. Refill as necessary. This works especially well for vine crops, including muskmelon and watermelon. Use a number of these if necessary for individual or numerous plants. This is a useful method for those going on vacation. Test to see how fast water is released to judge how many holes need to be punched into the plastic.

Also, plastic milk jugs filled with water can be left near the garden and used to water just a few plants as needed in dry spells. This is especially helpful if you have to wind and unwind hoses for limited watering.

Rain Barrels

Large rain barrels are useful for collecting water off roofs. They can be set up to deliver water on demand. Cover them to stop mosquitoes from laying eggs in the water.

Water at the Right Time of Day

Many gardening guides tell you to water in the morning. It's a good idea, but many people are unable to do it. Watering late in the day can increase the risk of disease. Still, if your plants need water, it is better to water at night, than not all. If it is your only chance to water, do it. The risk of late-evening watering is real but exaggerated. Compared to the stress on plants by underwatering, it is nothing.

Watering Plants in Containers

Anything that holds soil in which plants can grow is considered a container in this guide. Containers can be resting on the soil, supported by little feet on patios or decks, hanging from hooks, attached to walls as with window boxes, or simply bags of soil cut open and planted with transplants. The type of container, the soil in it, and the placement of the container all affect watering.

Most container gardening is done in pots. These are generally either clay or plastic, although other materials are available. The material that a pot or container is made out of affects the water loss from a plant. Clay pots lose lots of water. It evaporates through the clay itself. Many gardeners soak clay pots overnight before adding a potting mix to them. Overall the regular loss of moisture from clay pots is excellent for plants, as it allows for good air exchange with the root ball. However, this loss demands more frequent watering, which some people view as a chore. For this reason, many people use plastic pots, which lose far less water, are lighter, and are less expensive.

All pots should have drain holes in the bottom so that water can run out freely. Supporting any pot with feet that keep it elevated for easy drainage is highly recommended. Some people double pot, which means placing a plastic pot inside a more decorative pot with coir, peat moss, sand, or sphagnum moss pressed between the two. This helps pots retain moisture and is desirable to many for aesthetic reasons. But many decorative pots do not have drain holes. Place the inner pot on a frog (little pointed metal support) or pea gravel. Tip the pot regularly to drain out excess water so the plant does not develop root rot.

Potting soil or soilless mixes both work well for container gardening. Potting soils should contain soil, perlite, and peat in roughly equal parts. Good soil for containers holds in water and nutrients, is heavy enough to hold the pot in place during gusts of wind, and loose enough to drain freely but containing enough organic matter to hold moisture during dry spells.

Where you place pots also makes a difference to watering. Preferably, put them in a spot close to a water source in the correct light for the plant being grown. Bear in mind that once pots are watered they weigh a lot, so when growing plants in hanging baskets, provide a solid support to prevent them from falling down.

The key to success in growing plants in containers is consistent watering. Frequency of watering depends on the soil, temperature, wind, relative humidity, placement of the plant, and so on. There is no set rule for watering, but in hot, dry periods you may have to water more than once a day. Whenever watering pots, fill the pot to the brim by soaking the soil, not the foliage, with water. If plants are potted correctly, there should be a space between the soil and the upper edge of the pot. Let the soil absorb the water, and then fill the pot again until water drains out the bottom drain holes. This deep watering should be repeated as necessary whenever the soil begins to dry out. Check the soil daily by pushing your finger deep into the soil. Never judge soil moisture by sight with one exception: if the soil is pulling away from the edge of the pot, push it back to fill in the gap, and water immediately. This is a sign that the potted plant is not being watered frequently enough.

You do not want to overwater either. Watering soil that doesn't need it can lead to root rot, foul smelling roots at the base of the pot caused by water pooling in that area. Both under- and overwatering may result in plants wilting. Feel the soil. Too dry? The plants are wilting because of lack of water and the resulting stress. Too wet? Plants may be rotting out at their base. If pots are small enough, lift them after watering. This gives you an idea of the ideal weight. Lift them regularly throughout the season. If they suddenly seem light, they may not have enough water deep in the pot.

If growing plants indoors, place a shallow plastic dish or something more attractive under the plant to catch water that comes out the drain holes. These dishes are sold in most nurseries. Pots should not rest in water. After each watering toss excess water that lies in the plastic dish to prevent root rot. Supporting the pot on attractive rocks or pebbles will also help keep the pot from absorbing too much water resting in the dish. Overwatering is the number one cause of death in growing plants indoors.

Mulch

Mulch is a garden term used to describe any material placed on the surface of the soil to serve varied purposes. Mulches can either be organic (living or made from once-living material) or inorganic (synthetic or stone). Even the so-called inorganic mulches are accepted by many organic gardeners but not by all. In my opinion the best mulch is easy to get, free, effective, easy to apply, and free of weed seeds, disease, and chemicals. If it looks nice, that's an added bonus.

The Advantages of Mulch

Mulch does many good things in the home garden. It cuts off light from germinating weed seeds, so they may not sprout. Weeds compete with vegetables for nutrients and water. They may also act as hosts for insects that spread disease. By stopping weeds from growing, mulch reduces the time and effort needed to weed the garden. Mulch keeps soil temperature from fluctuating wildly. This reduces stress on plants. Mulch retains moisture in the soil. Soil that is consistently moist encourages fast and steady growth. Vegetables and berries produced rapidly have a better size, texture, and taste. Mulch is one of the best ways for the home gardener to ensure quality vegetables.

Mulch encourages earthworms to work the top several inches of the soil. The value of earthworms is enormous. They enrich the soil with their castings (excrement) and dead bodies, they aerate the soil with their tunnels, they spread organic matter throughout the soil as food for microorganisms, and they create better soil structure by creating a slime that binds particles together. In short, they are invaluable in preparing the perfect bed for vegetables and berries. Mulch breaks down and adds organic matter to the soil. This becomes humus as it decomposes with the help of billions of soil microorganisms that help make nutrients available to plants. The humus then makes your garden more productive. It also helps keep soil loose (improves the soil structure), which encourages wider and more rapid root growth. Mulch holds nutrients in the soil. This means that less of your fertilizer runs off in the water (leaches out of the soil). This helps your plants and saves you money. Mulch itself breaks down and adds nutrients to the soil. Naturally, some mulches have more nutrients than others, but all help in the long run.

Mulch keeps soil from splashing on a plant's foliage during watering or heavy rains and reduces disease. It also keeps young plants off the ground, where they can get stuck in the soil. And when plants start to produce fruit, mulch can keep it off the ground, where it may rot.

Mulch reduces soil compaction from hard rains. Roots grow poorly in compacted soil because air cannot reach them. You can walk on mulch without compacting the soil underneath it as much as you would if the soil were bare. This is true even after a rain or watering, although you would be smarter not to walk in the garden at all while the soil is wet. Mulch also prevents soil erosion, either from wind or rain, especially on sloped ground.

While mulch has all of these beneficial qualities, there are some caveats. Mulch needs to be applied at the right time for each plant. It should be at the right depth and not pushed up against the stems of growing plants. In cool, wet seasons it may contribute to an increase in the number of slugs, tiny shell-less snails. So it must be used wisely. Overall, its advantages far outweigh its shortcomings. When to use it for a specific plant is covered in the plant descriptions in Part II.

Organic Mulches

The five most commonly used organic mulches in cold-climate home gardens are grass clippings, cover crops, leaves, pine needles, and straw. Some people also "chop and drop" weeds. This means the weed is cut off at its base and left on the soil. Unfortunately, some weeds take root even when cut

Grass is one of the finest garden mulches and can be used fresh if applied thinly and not against plant stems.

Finely pulverized or rotted leaves keep the soil moist, cool, weed-free, and attractive to worms.

Compostable bags used to collect leaves in the fall make excellent mulch for plants, such as these shallots.

back. This method is most commonly used when weeds have gotten out of hand, created a lot of foliage, and are beginning to go to flower. Do not let them create seeds! I would use the other mulches if at all possible and put weeds into the compost pile.

Grass clippings are the universal mulch, available at no cost whatsoever. Just use a bagging lawn mower to collect them. Lawn services may give them to you free of charge, but compost these for a year before using them since they may contain pesticides and possibly be contaminated by cat or dog feces. Do not worry about using your own grass clippings fresh unless you have pets, despite constantly being told in publications that they must be dried first. I have been using fresh grass clippings for decades. Grass clippings do tend to get hot if applied too thickly. It is better to use 1 to 2 inches and reapply at regular intervals. Do not place the clippings against the stems of growing plants, just on the soil around them. Worms just love the moist soil under clippings.

Cover crops can be cut down and placed on the soil between rows or plants. These are an excellent resource for gardeners who do not have enough grass clippings or leaves. Cover crops are listed in the table of green manures in the section on "Fertilizing" later in this chapter.

Leaves match grass clippings as a universal mulch. They are one of the best soil conditioners and readily available to the home gardener. Never throw them away. Neighbors will often bag leaves for easy pickup in fall. Use shredded leaves instead of whole ones since they allow both air and water to get to the soil more easily. You don't need a shredder to do this. Just run a rotary lawn mower over the leaves, time and again, until they are broken into small pieces. The easiest way to do this is on a driveway. Spread the leaves out as thinly as possible. If they are moist, let them dry out. Then run over them again and again. Pile them up if you have space, or shovel them back into the bags they came in for use the following year. Shred as many leaves as you can. This does take time and energy, but your garden will appreciate it. Soil microorganisms and worms feed on this mulch, so you often have to replace it several times in a growing season. Typically, apply the mulch 2 to 3 inches at a time.

And don't throw away the compostable bags. Cut them along one side, remove the bottom, and spread them out on the soil. They are an ideal mulch for plants, such as shallots, that are often planted fairly far apart. Cut holes through the paper, and plant bulbs and transplants through the openings. The bags break down slowly over the growing season. In my opinion, these bags are much better than sections of

Straw is becoming expensive, but it is a valuable mulch for most plants, including the burdock shown here.

Many communities offer free wood chips, and they make a good mulch under the vines of spreading plants, such as pumpkins and winter squash.

Geotextiles absorb heat from the sun to spur growth of warmth-loving plants, from melons to sweet potatoes.

newspaper or shredded paper, which can also be used as a mulch. All paper products are usually covered with grass clippings or shredded leaves for aesthetic reasons and to hold them in place.

Pine needles work well as a mulch and are common in the far north. You need a good 3 to 5 inches of needles for an effective mulch. They are light and easy to work with. They decay slowly but allow moisture through easily and rarely get compacted. Needles are usually clean and weed-free, but they can be a potential fire hazard. Rake them off the soil at the end of the season, and compost them. They take a long time to break down. Do not work them into the soil. Pine needles were once thought to help acidify soil, but that turns out to be untrue.

Straw is the stems of grain crops. It is an excellent mulch but increasingly expensive. It is readily available, easy to use, and extremely effective. It is the easiest mulch to take on and off during cool spells when you want to protect plants at night and expose them in the day. It may contain weed seeds, pose a fire hazard, and act as a home for rodents. Moist straw is much easier to work with than dry. Sprinkle it with a hose; then it won't stick to your clothes or blow around in the wind. You can also pulverize it with a rotary lawn mower as you would leaves. In this form it attracts worms readily if kept consistently moist. But it does break down a lot faster than if kept whole.

Other mulches include bark, which varies in size from large chunks to fine shreds (good only for covering soil around vining plants); buckwheat hulls; cardboard; cocoa bean hulls (expensive and possibly toxic to dogs); corn cobs (ground up); cottonseed hulls (rarely available in cold climates); hay (rotted or rotting; good source of nitrogen but often contains seeds); leaf bags (the kind people use to bag leaves in fall, as already mentioned); marsh grass from freshwater areas; newspaper in sections (avoid colored pages); paper (such as grocery bags, but not photocopy or wax paper); pomace (leftover material from squeezing juice from apples and grapes); salt marsh hay; sawdust (OK for blueberries); seaweed (wash, dry, and shred with a lawn mower before using); weeds (dry them out first); and wood chips (only around vining crops).

As garden crops mature with their leaves nearly touching, they shade weeds and create a "living mulch." Soil stays damp longer as well under a leafy canopy.

Inorganic Mulches

Inorganic mulches are synthetic products or naturally occurring stone. Stone is rarely used in home vegetable gardens, other than for walls or pathways. The most common inorganic mulches are plastic (black or clear) and geotextiles (landscape fabric).

Black plastic is a synthetic, petroleum-based product and not considered organic by some growers. The main purpose of plastic is to generate heat for warmth-loving plants. The plastic is often placed over the ground or elevated soil and anchored in place either in spring or fall. Holes are then slit into the plastic to make an opening for planting transplants. The thickness of plastic is important. Most gardeners use plastic that is at least 4 mils ($^{4}/_{1000}$ of an inch) thick or thicker. It is easier to work with and stronger than thinner sheets of plastic, which admittedly warm soil better than thicker ones.

Clear plastic may generate as much as 8°F more heat than black plastic. Use it carefully since it can overheat the soil in extreme summer temperatures. Also, clear plastic does not inhibit weed growth as well as black. You can, however, kill sprouting weeds by covering clear plastic with shredded leaves or grass clippings later in the season after the plastic has served its purpose of warming the soil.

Advocates for the use of plastic say that it is effective in maintaining soil moisture with the use of soaker hoses, reduces the use of pesticides, protects vegetables from touching the soil and rotting, and controls weeds well. Detractors don't like that it is petroleum based, doesn't let water and air through for the benefit of the soil below, doesn't break down and provide nutrients to the soil, and has to be disposed of when it begins to crack or break apart. It is nonrecyclable, although if rolled up and kept dry, it can last for a few years. Note that there are biodegradable plastic mulches, but the breakdown is not uniform and is believed to release a large amount of carbon dioxide into the air.

There is a great deal of research taking place on plastics, mainly considering color as a deterrent to pests. The main colors being tested are blue, red, silver, and white. There is even an infrared-transmitting (IRT) plastic that has been developed to suppress weeds but allow infrared light through to warm the soil beneath.

Unlike plastic, landscape fabrics (geotextiles) let air and water through to the soil beneath while keeping weeds from coming up. They can be either woven or unwoven. Unwoven is plastic with holes punched in it. Woven is better but more expensive. Landscape fabrics have some of the same drawbacks as plastic. They are petroleum products. When exposed to light, they degrade over time. Weeds grow up into the landscape fabric, creating problems when you want to remove it.

I do not like inorganic mulches. I might use black plastic for one season to get a good crop of a warmth-loving plant, such as muskmelons or sweet potatoes. Then I would move the plastic to another area the following season and rework the soil that was originally covered by it.

No matter what kind of mulch you use, always remove all weeds and aerate the soil before applying it. Stir the soil up lightly as you put it in place. If you have to walk on soil to apply mulch, you will compact it. Loosen the soil with a pronged hoe (cultivator), and walk backwards, applying the mulch and stirring up any compacted area in the process. When gardening in raised beds, you can often apply mulch without walking on the soil at all. Once the mulch is in place, water the garden well.

Mulching Pathways

The soil in any area used as a pathway becomes compacted quickly. At some point in the future you may change your garden and use the pathways as a growing area. The easiest and least expensive way to protect the soil in the pathway is to lay down paper (leaf bags or sections of noncolored newspaper) and cover it with a deep layer of organic mulch. Some gardeners use straw, but bales are expensive unless you live in a rural area. Instead, use grass clippings or leaves. Cover these with a thick layer of wood chips, which are easy to lay down, attractive, and durable. In many areas there are piles of wood chips at composting sites available for free. Tree and utility companies will also deliver wood chips but generally charge a fee. The purpose of this mulch is not only to prevent soil compaction but also to stop weeds from sprouting. They should be removed before converting a pathway back to a garden area. They temporarily make nitrogen less available to plants as they decompose, although in the long run the nitrogen is returned to the soil. The mulch under the wood chips will probably have decomposed and can be worked into the soil without causing problems.

Mulching for Winter

Mulch can be used to protect plants in the winter and to store plants in the soil. But it can also be used to improve soil during the cold winter months. Till or stir up the soil in late fall after garden cleanup. Then cover the entire garden with a thick bed of leaves, readily available at this time of year. They do not have to be pulverized. Moisten them with a hose until the first freeze so that they won't blow away. This thick mat of leaves draws in worms, which work like underground tillers. You won't believe the number of worms at the soil line as the weather warms up the following spring. Dry and pulverize the leaves used as a winter mulch in spring for a summer mulch, unless you want to leave some in place. For example, you may want to plant squash along the edge of a bed and let vines roam over the covered area. Or you may want to leave the winter mulch in place for part of the growing season to keep worms at work to improve the underlying soil structure and fertility.

Fertilizing

Think of fertilizing as helping soil provide plants with a healthy diet—not too much, not too little of the sixteen chemicals needed by them to grow well. Nature replaces some of these, including carbon, hydrogen, and oxygen, but you must help out by providing additional chemicals as needed if you want to be a successful gardener. Nitrogen, phosphorus, and potassium are primary nutrients (macronutrients). Slightly less important elements, often labeled secondary nutrients, are calcium, magnesium, and sulfur. Finally, plants need tiny amounts of seven other micronutrients, or trace elements. These are boron, chlorine, copper, iron, manganese, molybdenum, and zinc. Micronutrients may be brought to the soil surface by roots penetrating deep into the earth and by worms. But the organic gardener must provide adequate amounts of the other nutrients. You do this by applying organic fertilizers, growing green manure or cover crops, and making proper use of compost and mulch.

Organic gardeners use organic fertilizers rather than synthetic fertilizers. Organic fertilizers are safe if handled properly. They can be used when starting seeds, whereas synthetic chemicals can kill germinating seedlings. They provide plants with essential nutrients while increasing the number of soil microorganisms. Organic fertilizers are slow to release nutrients, including micronutrients, but long acting. They do not contain potentially harmful soluble salts found in synthetic fertilizers. These salts are dissolved in water in the soil. In high enough concentrations they can harm a wide variety of plants, although specific plants are more prone to injury than others. They may also harm beneficial soil organisms. By using organic fertilizers, you reduce this concern.

Organic fertilizers do not leach through the soil as fast as synthetic ones and are less likely to get into surface or underground water. Still, they are capable of leaching and should be used carefully. The goal of the organic gardener is to build up fertile soil over a period of years to promote good plant growth without harming the environment.

The reason that people have relied on synthetic fertilizers is that they are easy to find, relatively inexpensive, and act quickly. Synthetic chemicals are sometimes referred to as petrochemicals because they are produced using large amounts of petroleum and natural gas. This is yet another reason that organic gardeners are opposed to their use, since the goal is not only to improve the soil but to protect the environment.

Essential Elements for Growing Healthy Plants

Boron (B): Needed in minute quantities. Important to cell division, flower formation, and pollination. Helps vegetables absorb and use nutrients, especially calcium. Ample amount exists in most soil. Augment when needed by adding borax (11 percent boron), fish emulsion, granite dust, or manure to the soil. Boron is especially important for beets, cauliflower, and celery. (.005 percent of plant tissue)

Calcium (Ca): Needed in moderate amounts. Important to cell structure and good root growth. Gets plants off to good early growth. Helps feed soil microorganisms and increases the activity of nitrogen-fixing bacteria. Unnatural curling of leaves, blossom drop, and yellowing of leaf edges can be caused by calcium deficiency. Ample amount exists in most soil. Found in gypsum (calcium sulfate), which is sometimes added to soil to get rid of salt deposits and "loosen" clay soils. Augment by adding bonemeal; hardwood ash (contains more calcium than softwood ash); or pulverized clam shells (50 percent calcium but alkaline), oyster shells (45 percent calcium but alkaline), or egg shells (94 percent calcium carbonate) to the soil. Important to cabbage, carrot, celery, escarole, lettuce, parsnip, pepper, tomato, and watermelon. (.6 percent of plant tissue)

Carbon (C): Needed in large amounts. Ample supply in air. (44 percent of plant tissue)

Chlorine (Cl): Needed in minute quantities. Important in transfer of water and minerals into cells and in photosynthesis. Leaves turning brown on their tips or turning yellow and falling off are possible signs of chlorine deficiency. Ample supply exists in soil and city water. (.015 percent of plant tissue)

Copper (Cu): Needed in minute quantities. Important in stem development and color. Essential in enzyme formation, root growth, and respiration, which is the process by which cells produce energy using chemicals. (Respiration is often confused with transpiration, the evaporation of water from plants.) Ample amount exists in most soil. (.001 percent of plant tissue)

Hydrogen (H): Needed in large amounts. Ample supply exists in water. (6 percent of plant tissue)

Iron (Fe): Needed in minute quantities. Important in chlorophyll formation and for proper plant respiration. Stunted growth and yellowing leaves with green veins are signs of possible deficiency. Ample amount exists in most soil. Augment by adding bonemeal, compost, or seaweed to the soil. (.02 percent of plant tissue)

Magnesium (Mg): Needed in small amounts. Important in chlorophyll formation and respiration. Essential for healthy foliage and disease resistance. Found in soil, but augmented by adding bonemeal or dolomitic limestone to the soil and by the use of Epsom salt, fish emulsion, liquid seaweed, or Sul-Po-Mag as fertilizers. (0.3 percent of plant tissue)

Manganese (Mn): Needed in minute quantities. Important in chlorophyll formation and the production of food through photosynthesis. An enzyme regulator. Helps plants, especially corn and onions, use nitrogen. Watch for whitish patches on older leaves between the leaf veins, which indicate a manganese deficiency. Ample amount in most soil. (0.5 percent of plant tissue)

Molybdenum (Mo): Needed in minute quantities. Helps plants use nitrogen for vigorous growth. Essential for enzyme formation, root growth, and respiration. Pale-green to yellow leaves may indicate a possible deficiency. Ample amount exists in most soil. Augment by tilling vetch into the soil. (.0001 percent of plant tissue)

Nitrogen (N): Needed in large amounts by most (not all) vegetables. Critical to healthy growth, lush foliage, and flower and fruit formation. Important in cell growth and plant respiration. Essential food for soil microorganisms. Too much nitrogen may cause an abundance of foliage at the expense of proper fruit formation. Too little can lead to limited foliage with poor color. Look for yellowing leaves and stunted plants. Must be added to the soil regularly. Note that the nitrogen in organic matter must be broken down by microbes into ammonium and nitrate to be useful to plants. Both are technically inorganic forms of nitrogen. Ammonium lasts longer in the soil than nitrates. The latter may be lost to leaching, water runoff, and conversion to gas released into the air. Microbes are most active in warm, moist, rather than cool, dry, soil. Add nitrogen to the soil in spring using blood meal, feather meal, or fish emulsion. Hold nitrogen in the soil in fall with a cover crop. Especially important to beans and corn. (2 percent of plant tissue)

Oxygen (O): Needed in large amounts. Ample supply exists in both air and water. Note that plants release oxygen into the air during the day as a by-product of photosynthesis. They retain the amount of oxygen needed but release far more than they use. (45 percent of plant tissue)

Phosphorus (P): Needed in large amounts. Essential to rapid growth. Important to proper formation of stems, flowers, fruit, and seed, as it is a component of all cell membranes. Augment yearly with the use of organic fertilizers, such as bonemeal, fish meal, and manure, or the use of rock phosphate. Also found in compost and crop debris. Watch foliage, especially for reddening of lower leaves and stems and bleached or pale upper leaves, which indicate a phosphorus deficiency. (0.5 percent of plant tissue)

Potassium (K): Often referred to as potash. Needed in large amounts. Important to root growth and formation of blossoms for greater yield. Helps create sturdy stems and promotes disease and drought resistance. Critical in forming sugars and starches through photosynthesis. Stunted plants and malformed or discolored leaves may indicate a deficiency. Must be added to the soil regularly in the form of organic fertilizers, such as kelp, green sand (3 to 5 percent), or wood ash. (1 percent of plant tissue)

Sulfur (S): Needed in small amounts. Keeps soil at the right pH (slightly acidic). Important in formation of plant proteins needed for good health and root growth. Ample amount is supplied in rain. Can be augmented if necessary with the use of calcium sulfate (gypsum) and magnesium sulfate, commonly sold as Epsom salt. Gypsum is 13 percent sulfur, while Epsom salt is 10 percent. Pure sulfur is used to acidify the soil, which may be necessary for growing blueberries. (0.4 percent of plant tissue)

Zinc (Zn): Needed in minute quantities. Important in stem and flower bud formation. Essential to enzyme formation, root growth, and respiration. Ample amount exists in most soil. Augmented by adding rock phosphate to the soil or tilling in vetch. Very important to beans and corn. (.01 percent of plant tissue)

Organic Fertilizers

Gardeners have been growing plants without synthetic fertilizers for thousands of years. Organic gardeners insist on continuing to do this because they believe that man-made fertilizers harm the soil through salt buildup that inhibits the intake of water by plants. Chemically, there is no difference between nitrogen ions produced by the decomposition of organic matter and those produced by inorganic fertilizers. The difference is that nutrients are released slowly in decomposition of organic matter, and rapidly from man-made chemicals. Using organic fertilizers reduces, but does not eliminate, the chance of nutrients leaching into groundwater, which can have adverse effects on the environment.

The most commonly used organic fertilizers in the home garden are blood meal for nitrogen, bonemeal for phosphorus, and fish emulsion and kelp products for potassium. Wood ash is also commonly available as a source of potassium. Keep it dry until you are ready to use it. Use it sparingly since it can raise the soil pH.

Manures are also popular to provide essential nutrients as well as organic matter to the soil. If there are farms in your area, ask whether you can pick up manure from them. You will need an appropriate vehicle with a hitch and a trailer to pick up larger amounts. For many, this is impractical. Animal manures sold by the bag are an expensive alternative. While manures do not contain a high amount of nutrients, adding them to your garden regularly ends up producing remarkable results. Avoid the use of fresh manures directly in the garden since they may contain the pathogens *Escherichia coli* (*E. coli*), *Listeria monocytogenes,* and *Salmonella* species, which can come from sick animals. Fresh manures also may contain antibiotics, pesticides, and weed seeds. Either apply fresh manures to the soil in fall to decompose over the winter, or compost them for use after they are well rotted. Fully rotted manures are an excellent addition to the garden and have been used for centuries without problems. Note that when gathering or working with manure, you should use gloves and a face mask. Make sure that you have had a tetanus shot in the past ten years to avoid being infected by the bacterium *Clostridium tetani,* which causes tetanus, a serious and sometimes fatal disease (sometimes referred to as lockjaw).

Many companies sell products made from organic materials either in solid or liquid form. On packages of dried organic material, compare the actual amounts of nitrogen, phosphorus, and potassium to get good value for your money. The values of N-P-K (nitrogen-phosphorus-potassium) are listed as a percentage of the weight of the product. If you have a 100-pound bag of organic fertilizer with a 10 percent value of nitrogen (N), then you have 10 pounds of nitrogen in that product. For example, Sustane® (4-6-4), a product made from turkey litter, contains 4 pounds of nitrogen, 6 of phosphorus, and 4 of potassium. These percentages do not match those for turkey litter in the table of organic fertilizers, which shows that there is no exact agreement on the analysis of any of these organic substances.

Organic fertilizer is usually sold in much smaller bags

N-P-K values of organic fertilizers (percentage by weight)

ORGANIC FERTILIZERS	NITROGEN (N)	PHOSPHORUS (P)	POTASSIUM (K)
Alfalfa hay	2.5	0.5	2.0
Alfalfa meal (rabbit pellets)	2.0–5.0	1.0	1.0–2.0
Animal tankage (ground animal tissue)	8.0	10.0	0.5–1.5
Apple pomace	0.7	1.5	0.8
Banana peels	0.0	3.0	42.0
Bat guano	9.0	3.0	1.0
Beef manure	1.2	2.0	2.1
Blood meal (dried blood) (acidic)	15.0	2.0	1.0
Bonemeal (raw) (alkaline)	3.0	22.0	0.0
Bonemeal (steamed) (alkaline)	0.0–1.0	12.0	0.0
Brewer's grains	0.9	0.5	0.1
Castor pomace	5.5	1.5	1.3
Cattle manure (alkaline)	3.0	1.8	2.0
Chicken manure (highly variable)	4.0	4.0	1.5
Cocoa shells	1.0	1.5	2.7
Coffee grounds	2.0	0.4	0.7
Colloidal phosphate	0.0	25.0	0.0
Compost	3.5	1.0	2.5
Corn gluten meal	10.0	0.0	0.0
Cornstalks	0.8	0.4	0.7
Cottonseed meal (acidic)	7.0	3.0	2.0
Cow manure	0.6–2.0	0.2–3.2	0.3–3.0
Crab meal (lots of calcium)	2.0	3.0	0.0
Duck manure	1.1	1.4	0.5
Eggshells (high in calcium)	1.2	0.4	0.1
Feather meal (acidic)	12.0	0.0	0.0
Fish emulsion (fluid from processing fish)	5.0	2.0	2.0
Fish meal (dried ground-up fish)	9.5	4.5–7.0	0.0
Goat manure	1.5	1.0	1.8
Granite dust	0.0	0.3	2.0
Granite meal	0.0	0.3	2.0
Grape pomace	1.5	1.5	0.8
Grass clippings (variable)	1.5	0.5	1.0
Grass hay	1.2	0.4	1.8
Greensand (glauconite)	0.0	0.0	3.0

with lower levels of major nutrients than synthetic fertilizers. That's part of the reason why buying synthetic fertilizers is so tempting. However, organic fertilizers often contain micronutrients, absent from synthetic ones. Organic gardeners have the patience necessary to build up their soil fertility over a period of years. This patience pays off with an increase in beneficial soil microorganisms and earthworms.

Alfalfa meal: A fast-acting fertilizer with a good amount of nitrogen. Do not use it directly in a planting hole since it may burn roots, but spread it around lightly and work it into the soil around plants. Alfalfa meal is ground-up alfalfa and may be sold that way or as rabbit pellets, which you can dissolve in a large bucket of water. It does contain micronutrients and a plant hormone (triacontanol), which many gardeners believe triggers accelerated growth in plants. When buying pellets, make sure that alfalfa is the first ingredient listed.

Blood meal: A fast-release source of nitrogen. It can burn seedlings. Do not place it directly in furrows when planting seed. Instead, dig it into soil before planting in spring. Use

ORGANIC FERTILIZERS	NITROGEN (N)	PHOSPHORUS (P)	POTASSIUM (K)
Guano (bat)	14.0	2.0–4.0	0–2.0
Guano (pigeon)	4.2	3.0	1.4
Guano (seabird)	8–16	8.0–12.0	2.0–3.0
Hoof and horn meal	12.5	1.8	0.0
Hops	0.5	2.0	0.5
Horse manure (alkaline)	0.7	0.3	0.5
Leather dust	5.5	0.0	0.0
Leaves	1.5	0.4	0.2–0.4
Linseed meal	5.5	2.0	1.5
Mushroom compost (alkaline)	0.7	0.3	1.5
Olive pomace	1.2	0.8	0.5
Peanut hulls	1.5	0.1	0.8
Pig manure	0.6	0.4	0.1
Pine needles	0.5	0.1	0.0
Potassium sulfate	0.0	0.0	50.0
Poultry manure	2.0	1.9	1.9
Rabbit manure	2.4–3.5	1.4	0.1
Rock phosphate	0.0	20.0–30.0	0.0
Salt hay grass (Spartina patens)	1.1	0.3	0.8
Sawdust (acidic)	0.2	0.1	0.2
Seafood wastes	8.0	5.0	1.0
Seaweed or kelp (liquid and meal)	0.3–2.0	0.2–1.3	1.0–5.0+
Sheep manure (alkaline)	1.5–2.0	1.0–1.5	1.8–3.0
Soybean meal (acidic)	7.0	1.5	2.5
Sphagnum peat moss (acidic)	0.6–1.4	0.05	0.08
Sul–Po–Mag (langbeinite)	0.0	0.0	22.0
Tobacco stems	4.0	0.5	7.0
Tomato sludge	1.0	0.5	0.6
Turkey litter	5.0	2.0	4.0
Urine (human)	10.0	1.0	3.0
Vermicompost (variable)	1.0	0.5	0.0
Wheat straw	0.5	0.2	0.8
Wood ash (potash) (alkaline)	0.0	1.0–2.0	3.0–10.0
Worm castings	0.5–3.0	0.5–1.0	0.3–2.0

it throughout the growing season. Consider mixing it with water and using around leafy plants.

Bonemeal: Slow acting but an excellent source of phosphorus. It is typically steam sterilized. Despite rumors, it has not been a source of bovine spongiform encephalopathy (BSE, referred to as mad cow disease). It does contain micronutrients and calcium.

Corn gluten meal: Contains a high level of nitrogen. If you use it, be careful. It kills seeds just as they germinate. Use it around actively growing plants only, if at all.

Cottonseed meal: Since cotton may come from GMO plants treated with pesticides, cottonseed meal is somewhat controversial. It acidifies soil and releases nitrogen into it quite slowly.

Crab meal: Contains chitin, said to increase microbial activity and reduce harmful nematodes when tilled into the soil in spring.

Feather meal: Breaks down slowly and should be added to the soil in early spring. Otherwise, its valuable nitrogen content may be lost.

Fish emulsion: May contain many micronutrients, possibly some growth hormones, and helpful enzymes. It does smell and is fast acting but contains a good amount of nitrogen. Pour it around the base of plants already growing well, or use it for foliar feeding after it has been heavily diluted.

Guano (bat or bird droppings): High in nitrogen and fast acting. Mix droppings into the soil, but do not place them directly in furrows alongside seeds. Some organic gardeners insist that harvesting guano is not ecologically friendly.

Kelp and other seaweed products: Contain negligible amounts of major nutrients but numerous micronutrients. They are believed to be extremely helpful in increasing populations of soil microorganisms. They are often used in drip irrigation systems rather than fish emulsion, which may clog the emitters. On plants producing fruit from flowers, use kelp only after flowers form. Otherwise, it may cause premature flowering, according to some gardeners. If collecting seaweed, let rain wash off salts before use in the garden, or compost it for several months. Salt on seaweed may repel worms.

Manures: Excellent fertilizers. Note that contamination from fresh manures has been linked to the outbreak of deadly illness here and abroad, usually from the runoff of feces-contaminated water from farms into nearby crops. Manure poses a very low threat if fully composted for at least four to six months or spread over the garden in fall to decompose over the winter. Do wear gloves when working with it. A mask is a good idea as well. If loading it into a trailer or back of a pickup, a pitchfork is the easiest tool to use. Pick up manure that drops to the ground with a large flat shovel.

Milorganite®: *Not considered organic* and not legally labeled as deer repellent, but it does repel deer. It is a sewer/sludge fertilizer that is principally banned for organic use because it is supposed to contain too many heavy metals.

Pomace: The pulpy residue left over from squeezing juice from fruits.

Potash: The term for ashes soaked in water, this was at one time a source of potassium.

Seafood waste: Contains chitin, believed to be effective against nematodes. It may contain small amounts of arsenic.

Soybean meal: A slow-acting fertilizer that is good for gardens and lawns. It acidifies soil.

Urine: Not only high in nitrogen, but its smell sometimes deters deer from entering an area. Gardeners can also pour it into compost piles to increase the rate of decomposition of organic material.

Vermicompost: May be low in essential nutrients, but this is misleading. It has properties making it a great food for plants.

Wood ash: High in potassium and quick acting. Keep it dry until ready to be used. Spread just a couple of pounds per 100 square feet every two to three years. It does raise the soil pH. Never use it around blueberries.

Note that the availability of nutrients in any of these products is affected by the type of soil, moisture levels, temperature, pH, and the overall amount of organic material in the soil.

Nature provides quite a bit of ammonia (NH_3) and nitrates (NO_3) through lightning in thunderstorms. These are also generated ("fixed") by microorganisms in the soil.

Using Organic Fertilizers

Plants grow well when nutrients are available at different depths. If you have lots of organic material, work it into the entire garden, trying to keep it within 6 inches of the soil surface. You need more nutrients in sandy soils than in loam or clay. Water washes through sand, carrying nutrients away. Keep adding organic matter to sandy soil to help it hold more nutrients in place. If you grow lots of plants in a small space (intensive gardening), you will need more fertilizer per square foot. One of the secrets of organic gardening is to add organic fertilizers regularly. Regular application builds up essential nutrients over a period of years and sustains the soil, which should be viewed as a living organism, not an inanimate substance.

What constitutes the right amount of nutrients depends on what you are growing, so proper fertilizing is plant specific and covered in detail in plant descriptions in Part II. For example, some plants need lots of nitrogen, while others may do poorly if given too much. Still, you have to start somewhere. If available, cover the entire surface of the garden with well-aged manure in fall. With every rain or watering during the growing season, nutrients are carried into the soil, where the roots can absorb them easily. This is referred to as a topdressing and only practical in areas where manures are readily available in bulk.

At time of planting, add a little fertilizer to the bottom of a furrow or hole. Mix it in with the soil. This will stimulate rapid root growth and plant vigor. Referred to as base-dressing, this method of fertilizing is a more concentrated use of fertilizer than topdressing. The method is often more practical for the home gardener who must buy smaller amounts of fertilizer at local nurseries.

Pouring a solution of diluted fertilizer around the base of a seedling when it is newly planted stimulates quick growth. The diluted fertilizer is referred to as a starter or transplant solution.

During the growing season, sprinkle fertilizer off to the sides of rows of plants or encircle individual plants. Water immediately for best results. This method is referred to as side-dressing. The amount of fertilizer needed is often quite small. If plants are growing well, it may not even be necessary. Again, this is plant specific and covered in Part II.

Foliar feeding is a method of fertilizing plants by applying fertilizer directly to the leaves, branches, and stems of growing plants. The food is absorbed by the plant and used almost immediately. It promotes vegetative growth, the formation of flower buds and flowers, and the development of fruit. *It augments, but cannot take the place of, adding nutrients to the soil directly.* Some organic gardeners do it regularly; others don't do it at all. Foliar feeding may help prevent certain diseases, such as powdery mildew on cucumbers and melons. It is believed to increase solids in vegetables, which enhances their flavor. It may increase the number of blossoms on flowering plants and thereby increase overall yield. It can provide trace elements directly to the plant, depending on the spray used.

Common organic substances used in foliar feeding include blood meal, fish emulsion, and liquid seaweed. There are numerous organic products on the market for foliar feeding and "home-grown" recipes. Foliar feeding proponents are constantly developing their own formulas, many of which include teas made from herbs or barks. Some of these recipes may contain substances that are not safe.

Spray plants either very early in the morning or in late afternoon. Cover both the upper and lower surfaces of the leaves. Spray the entire stem and branches. Cover the entire plant with a fine mist—almost like dew. Lightly spray the soil as well. Don't spray or sprinkle foliage with water for twenty-four hours, until the plant has a chance to absorb the fertilizer. Respray if it rains within twenty-four hours. Foliar feeding is effective throughout the entire growing season but should match the needs of individual plants. There are a number of products on the market said to enhance the absorption of nutrients, often called wetting or delivery agents. Try these if your first attempts at foliar feeding fall short of your expectations.

Always water the soil before and after fertilizing to avoid any chance of plant burn, the withdrawal of water from plant tissue. Burn is most common with synthetic or fresh organic fertilizers, neither of which you should be using. Still, proper watering gets nutrients to the roots quickly and helps with their absorption. Water dissipates quickly in hot weather, so fertilize in spring and fall when it is cool if possible. Otherwise, fertilize lightly and water frequently.

Earthworms

One of your main allies is worms. Draw them into the garden with a thick layer of organic mulch kept consistently moist. This is both their food and "clothing," as it protects them from the sun. Worms breathe through their skin. If it gets dried out, they die. More than three thousand species of worms exist worldwide. They vary in size from 1 inch to 9 feet in parts of Australia. Healthy organic-rich soil may contain as many as fifty thousand night crawlers (*Lumbricus terrestris*) per acre. When adding other types of worms to this total, some estimates reach into the millions per acre. Three different types of earthworms feed and thrive in different parts of the soil: those that thrive near or on the soil surface (epigeic), those that live and move laterally through the upper part of the soil (endogeic), and those that dive deep into the soil and create permanent burrows (anecic). The latter include night crawlers, which come to the soil surface to find food, which they pull deep into the soil.

All of these types work their way through the soil to eat available organic matter. In this process they improve the soil in a number of ways. The first is by leaving behind as much as 18 tons of nutrient-rich castings (excrement) per acre per year under optimal conditions. These nutrients act as free fertilizer for your plants. Worms secrete a sticky substance in their castings that binds soil particles together to form larger clumps

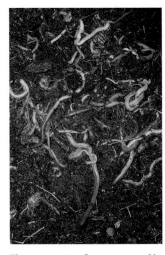

The many species of worms attracted by moist organic matter help loosen and fertilize soil.

(aggregates). This means there is more space between the particles. This space and the tunnels (channels) created by the worms as they move through the soil result in looser soil that doesn't compact as easily as the original soil. Less compacting makes it easier for roots to penetrate the soil and stops soil from crusting as easily on the soil surface. The result is that seeds can pop through the soil more easily. An added advantage of the larger soil particles and numerous channels is that air and water can move more easily in the soil and can be stored in the openings (pores) between the particles.

In effect, worms act as underground tillers, loosening the soil, bringing organic matter into the earth, eating some of it, and leaving part of it behind to feed the billions of soil microorganisms that depend on it for life. These microorganisms break the organic matter down into humus. Worms move deeper into the soil as winter approaches, because they can freeze to death. As worms die, their bodies may supply as much as 40 pounds of nitrogen per acre. If you till or spade the garden in fall, cover the garden with grass clippings or leaves to renew the food supply for worms, which breed readily in spring when the soil is moist and beginning to warm up again. Note that some organic gardeners are opposed to tilling because they are concerned it breaks down the tunnels (burrows) of worms. This may be true, but worms will return in great numbers if organic matter is added to the soil regularly and an organic mulch is laid down on the soil surface each year.

Manure, Compost, and Plant Teas

For decades, gardeners have been brewing manure and compost teas and then pouring a cup or so of this solution around transplants or young seedlings to stimulate initial growth. They make these teas by soaking well-rotted manure or fully digested compost in nonchlorinated water (if possible, such as from a dehumidifier or rain barrel) for several days or longer, the components typically enclosed in cloth bags to keep solids from mixing into the solution. Another method is to drop aged manure or compost broken down into humus into a large container and let it soak for a few days or longer while the solids sink to the bottom of the barrel.

Other gardeners do something similar with a combination of the foliage of comfrey and stinging nettle plants. They press the plants into a container, add water, and stir over time until the mixture turns black. Then the mixture is diluted with more water (one part plant material to fifteen parts water) and used as a "tea." These plants, referred to as dynamic accumulators, are believed by some to draw up valuable nutrients from deep in the soil. Other plants that fall into this group but are rarely made into teas include dandelion, lamb's quarters, parsley, plantain, salad burnet, watercress, and yarrow (*Achillea millefolium*). The latter is a lovely perennial that comes in a vast array of colors. The goal of all these controversial teas is to inoculate the soil or the plant itself with billions of beneficial microorganisms and to fertilize the plant.

Having used compost and manure teas myself and seeing what I thought were excellent results, I was surprised to learn that I was potentially exposing myself and others to infection by *Escherichia coli*, *Listeria monocytogenes,* and *Salmonella* species (as pointed out earlier). However, I never added any "artificial" ingredients to the manure or compost in the tea-making process. Some gardeners have been adding various ingredients, such as molasses, that apparently increase the risk of creating a pathogenic soup. I also used only fully decomposed compost and well-rotted manure, both of which rarely contain pathogens (many disagree with this statement), and stirred the mixture occasionally for aeration. (Aeration can be improved greatly with bubblers, similar to those found in fish tanks or sold to keep minnows alive.) Also, using these teas on the soil only early in a plant's growth, well before harvest, reduces any chance of contamination greatly. I also did not use the

It is a controversial belief that plants like comfrey draw nutrients from the subsoil as dynamic accumulators.

The leaves of nettle are often mixed with comfrey to form a "tea" poured around plants to stimulate growth.

teas as foliar sprays, which is highly recommended by some and considered very dangerous by others.

Academicians do not agree on the value of any of these teas. Some think they work well. Others insist that they do not promote growth, do not help plants ward off diseases, and pose significant health risks when used on edible crops. How to make compost teas or whether to make them at all is so controversial that I suggest reading every article and book on this subject you can find so you can make up your own mind. Or skip them altogether, and concentrate on adding soil amendments to the soil and using mulch on top of it to help earthworms and all manner of soil organisms to flourish. This is what I am now doing, having taken all points of view into consideration.

Green Manure (Cover Crops, Catch Crops, Compost Crops)

Plants used to suppress weed growth while improving the structure of the soil are called cover crops. They may also be referred to as catch crops if they are quick maturing and used to cover bare space between plantings of main crops. When cover crops are tilled or spaded into the soil, they become green manures. These green manures add organic matter to the soil, which helps retain moisture during dry spells, feeds soil microorganisms that may help prevent root disease, loosens the soil, holds nitrogen in the soil, and protects soil from erosion by water and wind. Cover crops have extensive root systems. One winter rye plant may penetrate the soil to a depth of 4 to 5 feet, while producing hundreds of miles of roots. These roots bring micronutrients to the soil surface from the subsoil. And they break up compacted soil, improving its overall structure. The loosened soil becomes aerated and will drain more freely. This change in soil structure is one of the most important values of green manure crops. The soil becomes much easier to dig or till.

Nitrogen-fixing cover crops are especially valuable. They have little nodules on their roots. These contain rhizobia, bacteria that take in nitrogen from the air and convert it for use by the plant, which in turn supplies them with ample amounts of carbohydrates as food. Add nitrogen to the soil by plowing these crops under. Nitrogen fixation will not occur in acidic soil with a pH below 5.5 or in soils lacking calcium, magnesium, or molybdenum. It will also not occur if soil is already rich in nitrogen or if the soil is too dry. And, finally, it will not occur if the temperature at planting time is inappropriate. Plants that are not fixing nitrogen properly often have yellowing leaves or are growing poorly. If curious, dig up a plant, and look for nodules on the roots. Cut one open. If it is white or gray on the inside, the plant is not

Peas, peanuts, and other legumes enrich the soil with nitrogen, reducing the demand for expensive fertilizers.

fixing nitrogen. It should be pink to pinkish red when fixation is occurring.

Typically, the home gardener digs or tills the more persistent cover crops into the soil in midgrowth, usually when the plants are still somewhat tender and before they have flowered. They decompose most quickly at this stage. Some plants can be invasive if they go to seed. Cut these back before they flower. The seed of others provides additional nitrogen to the soil and can be spaded or tilled into the soil after the plants die back. Since some of these plants can get tall, it is easier to cut them down and compost the stems than to work the entire plant into the soil. You can also mow over the stubble before digging the root system under.

When you till or spade the soil, try not to bury the crop. Just work it into the soil surface to a depth no deeper than 6 inches. Till roughly, or turn it at an angle with a spade. Let the crops decompose for at least a month or longer before planting.

As mentioned, once a cover crop is dug or tilled into the soil, it becomes a green manure. The organic matter, much of it in the form of roots, begins to decompose slowly, providing nutrients as if it were a slow-release time capsule. It encourages the growth of microorganisms, which help plants absorb these nutrients. It also attracts earthworms, which continue to improve the soil structure as they tunnel through it and add additional nutrients to the soil in the form of castings and the decay of their bodies.

Alfalfa and clover are great green manure crops for farmers with the kind of equipment needed to turn them into the soil, but they are not recommended for the home gardener. The long, thick roots are great in the field, a nightmare in the home garden. Cover crops are sometimes broadcast over existing crops a few weeks before harvest, so that the cover crop is already growing before the area is left bare. There are as many systems for green manuring or cover cropping as there are garden layouts, and many ways to add organic matter with these plants.

The term *flower* in the table of green manures means flowers or seed heads. Winter rye and buckwheat are allelopathic and will stop small seeds from germinating if not allowed to break down for a few weeks before planting. Buckwheat is neither a wheat nor a grass but related to

rhubarb. Its seeds look like, but are not, a grain. For lots of green material (biomass), grow hairy vetch, rape, rye, and sorghum-sudangrass. Cut plants down when they reach 3 feet, and either use them as a garden mulch or add them to the compost pile. Plants grown late in the season pick up available nitrogen from the soil rather than having it leach out over the winter. Oats are easily found in feed stores and ideal for this use.

There are a few nitrogen-fixing plants not commonly mentioned as green manures that add beauty to the landscape and nitrogen to the soil. The foliage of these plants can be added to compost for additional nitrogen. The roots fix nitrogen in the soil. *Baptisia australis* (blue wild indigo) is a perennial that I have added to my vegetable garden both for its gorgeous bloom spikes and nitrogen-fixing benefits. *Apios americana* (groundnut) has gorgeous flowers and edible roots. I have not grown this vine, but it is well suited to the edges of woods and will increase nitrogen in the soil. *Phaseolus coccineus* (scarlet runner bean) is another vine with spectacular scarlet flowers. This plant I have grown and would do so again for its edible flowers alone.

GREEN MANURE (COVER CROP)	FIXES NITROGEN	WHEN TO PLANT	WHEN TO DIG OR TILL IN
Annual ryegrass (*Lolium multiflorum*)	No	Throughout the season	Before it flowers or after it dies back
Barley (*Hordeum* species)	No	Throughout the season	Before it flowers or in spring
Bean (*Phaseolus* species)	Yes	When fully warm	When it dies back
Broad bean (*Vicia faba*)	Yes	Very early spring	When it dies back
Buckwheat (*Fagopyrum esculentum*)	No	When fully warm	Before it flowers
Chickpea (*Cicer arietinum*)	Yes	After danger of frost	When it dies back
Cowpea (*Vigna unguiculata*)	Yes	When fully warm	When it dies back
Hairy vetch (winter vetch) (*Vicia villosa*)	Yes	Spring or fall	Before it flowers
Kale (*Brassica oleracea*)	No	Spring into summer	Whenever
Lentil (*Lens culinaris*)	Yes	Very early spring	When it dies back
Lupine (*Lupinus angustifolius*)	Yes	Spring	Within 3 months
Mustard (*Sinapsis alba*)	No	Throughout growing season	Before it flowers
Oat (*Avena sativa*)	No	Spring or late summer	Before it flowers or in spring
Pea (*Pisum sativum* species)	Yes	Very early spring	When it flowers or dies back
Peanut (*Arachnis hypogea*)	Yes	When fully warm	When it dies back
Radish (*Brassica* 'Tillage Radish®' daikon radish)	No	After July 15	Remove fall flowers; till in spring
Rape (*Brassica napus*)	No	Summer	Before it flowers
Sorghum-sudangrass (*Sorghum bicolor* var. *sudanense*)	No	When fully warm	After cutting back multiple times
Soybean (*Glycine max*)	Yes	When fully warm	When it dies back
Sunflower (*Helianthus* species)	No	When fully warm	When stems are still tender
Winter rye (*Secale cereale*)	No	Late summer into fall	Very early following spring
Winter wheat (*Triticum* species)	No	Late summer into fall	Early following spring

Accepted Inorganic Fertilizers

Some inorganic products are accepted for use in organic gardens.

Azomite®: A mined mineral noted for containing trace minerals.

Borax (sodium tetraborate decahydrate): A good source of boron. Use 1 tablespoon 20 Mule Team Borax per 100 feet of row. Boron deficiency is rare but sometimes affects broccoli and cauliflower. It is toxic at high levels and sometimes used to kill weeds. I cannot advocate its use as a weed killer.

Chilean nitrate (16-0-0): The same as sodium nitrate. It is readily usable by plants but leaches through soil quickly. Its use is controversial, and some organic growers will not use it.

Epsom salt (magnesium sulfate): Consist of 10 percent magnesium and 13 percent sulfur. Both elements are needed in small quantities by growing plants. Some gardeners mix 1 tablespoon per gallon of water and spray pepper and tomato foliage when the plants begin to bloom.

Granite dust (0-0.3-2): A good slow-release source of potassium.

Greensand (green sand) (0-0-3): Also known as glauconite, used to provide the soil with potassium (K) and trace elements. Apply greensand in the fall. It is powdered iron potassium phyllosilicate and is slow acting, but lasts for years, helps break down clay, and contains valuable trace elements. Both granite dust and greensand work best when combined with lots of organic matter in the soil.

Gypsum (calcium sulfate): Accepted for organic use if it has been mined. It is an excellent source of calcium but also acts as a superb soil conditioner. It is commonly used to break up clay soils to improve drainage by getting its tiny particles to cling together (aggregate) and to leach salts from the soil. It consists of approximately 29 percent calcium and 23 percent sulfur. It has no effect on the soil pH.

Langbeinite (Sul-Po-Mag): Sulfate of potassium and magnesium mixed with potassium sulfate. It contains 11 percent magnesium, 22 percent potassium, and 22 percent sulfur.

Lime, calcitic (up to 90 percent calcium carbonate): A form of lime (40 percent calcium and 0.2 percent magnesium) that should be applied to the soil surface in fall and not added at the same time as fertilizers. Add fertilizers in spring. Lime breaks up clay. It does increase the soil pH and should not be overused. Typically, it is sprinkled lightly on the soil surface in fall every few years. Choose a product with as small a particle size as possible, since it will be faster acting.

Limestone, dolomitic (calcium magnesium carbonate): Also known as dolomite lime, it is used to add calcium to the soil. Dolomitic limestone (60 percent calcium carbonate and 40 percent magnesium carbonate) has high levels of both calcium (21 to 46 percent) and magnesium (11 to 38 percent), the actual amount varying according to the source of information on this product. When reading the packaging on lime, look for two things: the CCE (calcium carbonate equivalent) and the mesh number. The higher both numbers are the better. The CCE indicates overall "availability" of nutrients; the mesh number is related to the size of particles that can pass through a "mesh." Smaller particles are preferred in gardening; they pass through the mesh more readily, increasing the mesh number.

Marl (calcified seaweed): Mined lake or sea sediments noted for high concentrations of calcium (up to 50 percent), magnesium carbonate (up to 10 percent), and trace elements. The product is often used to take the place of lime in other countries. It is still not commonly found in the United States. Calcified seaweed is believed to encourage the growth of soil bacteria, break up heavy clay soils, and cause soil particles to come together (aggregate). It is applied in fall and will raise the soil pH.

Rock phosphate: Hard rock phosphate is a source of phosphorus and trace elements. Its value is related to particle size. Although rock phosphate is considered to be organic, it is released extremely slowly into the soil. Hard rock phosphate is 20 percent phosphorus and 48 percent calcium. Soft rock phosphate is sometimes called colloidal phosphate. It is 16 to 20 percent phosphorus, 10 to 15 percent calcium, and does contain trace elements. It is a better choice than hard rock phosphate since it is released a bit more quickly into the soil. Some organic gardeners are opposed to the use of rock phosphates since they are not a truly renewable resource.

Sulfate of potash (potassium sulfate): Extremely high in potassium (0-0-50). It is approved for organic use only if produced in a specific manner. It must be made from langbeinite or nonsynthetic materials.

Sulfur (S): 100 percent sulfur is used to make soil more acidic and has been used for years as an organic pesticide. It may also make calcium more available to plants, and like gypsum, it helps improve soil structure.

Support

Some plants will topple over and grow poorly without support. Others will grow well on the ground but take up a lot of space. Supporting plants can reduce disease by providing better air circulation and spread production of fruit, such as pole beans, over a longer period of time. During harvesting what needs to be picked is easier to see, and you don't have to bend over. Furthermore, vegetables are usually much cleaner than when grown on the ground. Weeding around the base of vining plants growing on supports is also easier than pulling out weeds sprouting through foliage of plants

A Japanese tomato ring serves two purposes: the inside is a compost pile, and the outside is a support for plants.

A nearly invisible green stake supports okra and is aesthetically appealing.

Crisscrossed poles: Anchor two poles into the ground at an angle, so they look like an inverted V. Do this again about 10 to 12 feet away. Place a horizontal pole between these vertical supports. Tie the horizontal pole to both sets of inverted poles. Add additional poles as necessary, or drop wire or synthetic twine down from the horizontal pole at appropriate intervals. Anchor these into the ground. Place plants at the base of each piece of wire or twine.

Fences: Wire fences make excellent supports for a wide variety of vining plants. Many of these need chicken wire or string as initial support to guide them to the fence. If plants have tendrils, interweave early growth into the wire. If creating a fence in the garden, pull wire taut between solid supports. Plant on both sides whenever possible to increase your yield.

Japanese tomato rings: The Japanese tomato ring is an interesting variation of the tomato cage. You make a larger ring and plant tomatoes, usually three or four plants, around the outside of the ring. You can also plant any number of vining plants at the base of the ring, not just tomatoes. As the season progresses, you dump all your garden refuse in the center of the ring, where it turns to compost. So the ring serves two purposes. The theory is that the compost gives off nutrients and keeps the roots of the plants moist. You end up with good fruits and compost for the garden. This method has the added advantage of taking up relatively little space. You do have to tie the stems of nonvining plants to the wires of the cage. As the plants grow, you may have to tie up additional growth throughout the season.

The ring should be 4 to 6 feet across. To make one you need 13 to 15 feet of wire, wire cutters, and something to attach the wire together. For keeping the wire in place long-term, hog rings work the best and can be found in feed stores. There's a little tool you buy that pushes hog rings together. Just ask how to use it. It will save you lots of time. You can also use short pieces of wire or twine to attach the sides of the wire, but this is a bit of a pain. Cable ties are easier to use and inexpensive when purchased in bulk. They are easy to cut off at the end of the season if you prefer to store the wire rather than leave it in place.

You will probably notice that one side of the ring gets more shade than the others. The plants on the shaded side will not grow as tall and well as the other plants. Keep

on the ground. Certain plants, such as cucumbers, supposedly produce straighter fruit on supports.

The disadvantages of supports are their potential cost, the time and effort it takes to set them up, and wind damage during storms, either to the supports or to the vegetables themselves. While all plants are susceptible to damage by deer, it is much easier for these animals to nibble off foliage on supports. Finally, plants grown on supports may require more watering than plants grown on the ground.

All supports should be put in place before or at the time of planting, not at a later date. This eliminates the potential for root damage and also ensures that you will have the supports in place before the plants get too large to work with. When tying plants to supports, use a figure-eight knot. Jute twine or soft fabric is less likely to damage stems but can be replaced with synthetic material. Avoid tight tying, which may crimp the stem. Also, if you have to weave the tips of growing stems through a support, do it gently. The tips are often fragile and break off easily.

Here are some of the many methods used by home gardeners for growing plants vertically.

A-frames: This support looks like an inverted V with sides spread out at the bottom and coming together at the top. The way they are put together can be complicated or as simple as leaning two pieces of remesh against each other (42½ by 72 inches.) Remesh is sold in big-box stores. I have been told that some gardeners place the wire in old box springs against each other.

notes for the following season, and avoid planting warmth-loving plants on the one "bad" side. Consider planting peas there.

Pea stakes: Sharpen the end of short branches and push them into the ground so that the tops angle inward. If you live near a woods, these are easy to come by and cost nothing. Although often mentioned in books and articles, they are a nuisance to work with and, I would add, unnecessary if garden peas, the ones that need to be shelled, are planted close together in double rows. The peas end up being self-supporting in this way.

Peony rings: Place peony rings upright or upside down to contain or support vegetables. A secondary use is to wrap these with cloth and use them as cloches to protect plants in early spring.

Staking: The majority of home gardeners use stakes in one way or another. Stakes are usually at least 8 feet long—6 feet aboveground, 2 feet below. You can tie a tomato or other plant directly to a stake driven in the ground with a heavy stake driver. Use soft ties in a figure-eight knot. Place plants at the bottom of each stake, generally about 12 to 18 inches apart. Some gardeners drive stakes into the ground about 6 feet apart and string a strand of 9-gauge wire between them. They then tie strings to the wire and pull them taut by attaching them to a stake in the ground, similar to the crisscrossed pole method. The strings are then used as vertical support for the plants. This method should not be used in windy locations since plants will flop around and possibly be damaged. An alternate method (basket weaving) is to run string between the stakes horizontally, essentially capturing the growth in bands of undulating string held tautly between the poles.

The advantages of staking are that you can prune plants to the exact number of main stems you want. Fruits are easy to see and pick. Staking takes up less space than some of the other methods. Weeding is easy. Fruit stays off the ground. The disadvantage is that whatever staking method you use, you have to buy supports, put them up, and tie plants to them. Some gardeners argue that staked plants use more water.

Stakes should be strong and rot resistant. The easiest way to get stakes in the ground is with a stake driver, but if you do not have one, use a hose to start a hole for you and to moisten the underlying soil. The pressure of the water opens the ground. The moisture makes inserting the stake easier. Pound the stake down into the hole and softened earth. Always get your supports in before planting.

Tepee or tripod: Tie three or more poles together at the top to form a triangle or a circle at the base. Anchor the poles by pushing them into the soil at an angle. Weave synthetic twine around the structures at 1-foot intervals for additional support. Plant one plant at the base of each pole. Plant shade-tolerant vegetables, such as lettuce or spinach, underneath the structure.

Tomato cages: Wire cages and rings help support plants with abundant fruit and large, heavy stems or vines. Cages are wire enclosures, generally made out of galvanized welded wire. Cages are usually at least 5 feet tall with openings large

Tie plants to supports using a loose figure-eight knot made with twine or strips of cloth.

Bamboo circled with twine is an ideal support for the upward-growing vines of acorn squash.

Acorn squash, despite its weight, grows on strong vertical supports without help.

The tomato cage is one of the simplest and most popular methods of supporting plants.

Pole beans and other vining plants produce well when grown vertically on solid metal or wood supports.

Peas cling readily to chicken wire, while their tendrils attach to twine strung above.

enough to get your hands through—at least 6 inches. Cages can vary in size from 12 to 30 inches across. You need 3 feet of wire per 1 foot of diameter. It is a good idea to anchor the cage with some sort of stake or stakes pounded firmly into the ground. You place the cage directly over the plant. The cage acts as a good support for the plant and keeps all fruit off the ground. It takes up little space. You can surround the lower 24 inches of the cage with tar paper or plastic early in the season. This traps heat and protects young plants from wind, but the heat trap should be removed once summer heat hits. Plants grow up inside the cage without any staking, tying, or pruning if desired. Still, some gardeners stake plants inside the cage for additional support. Tomato cages can be used for many vegetables other than tomatoes.

Trellises: As vines start to grow, weave them in and out of the trellis openings. Individual plants may produce several growing tips. Guide these in several directions to fill up all available space. A tuteur is a four-sided trellis in the form of a pyramid. Trellises can be made from thin pieces of wood or synthetic netting tacked onto supports.

Wire or string supports: Stretch wires or synthetic string between solid supports. One wire is usually 10 to 12 inches off the ground, the other anywhere from 36 to 72 inches. Plants can be tied to the wires directly as they mature, or string can be stretched between the wires at set intervals (basket weaving) and used to support individual plants, or string can be pulled in a zigzag fashion up and down between the wires. Use tough string between the poles but softer and rougher string to guide plants upward and outward along the

wire trellis. A variation of this is to use chicken wire along the base to get plants started in the right direction.

Weeding

Weeds are just plants that are out of place. Grass is nice as a lawn, but it is a weed in the garden. However, the presence of weeds in a potential garden site is a good sign. Where weeds can grow, so can vegetables. But weeds are thieves. They steal light, nutrients, and moisture from your garden plants while stopping air movement, which can help reduce disease. Weeds also harbor plant pests and carry disease. Before planting a garden, get rid of all weeds in the garden area and surrounding area if possible. Never let weeds go to seed. Respect the old saying, "One year seeding, seven years weeding." Without any question weeding is the least popular chore in the home vegetable garden. Sometimes, especially after an illness, weeds get out of hand. Mow and till them into the soil to let them decompose.

It is easy to confuse young desirable plants with weeds, which often mimic specific seedlings. When planting a vegetable for the first time, sprout a few in a pot so that you know what the seedling will look like. Note that weeds often grow faster than desirable plants! Most of the following information applies primarily to level and raised-bed gardens. It is of far less value to gardeners growing plants in compost, lasagna, mulched (no-till), or straw-bale gardens. All of these are promoted as being essentially weed-free, which is almost true.

When starting or renewing a garden overrun with weeds, mow and till the area to bring it (and you) back from despair.

Making Weeding Less of a Chore

There are three types of weeds: annual weeds, which grow and produce seed in the first year; biennials, which flower and produce seed in the second year; and perennial weeds, which continue to grow over a period of years, often producing copious amounts of seed once fully mature. Your soil is filled with millions of seeds. Some of these seeds live for a few years, but others can live for decades. Most seeds are in the top 6 inches of soil but only germinate in the top 1 to 2 inches, where there is enough light and moisture. Every time you disturb the soil, you bring weed seeds to the surface.

To reduce the amount of weeding, your goal is to reduce the amount of seed in the soil over a period of years. This is called reducing the seed bank. Think of each seed as a penny in a piggy bank. Each time you remove a penny, there are fewer left to spend. You will never get rid of all seeds, but there are ways to nearly empty the bank. Seeds are blown in by the wind, carried by

animals, and brought in with transplants. So the idea of a weed-free garden is a pipe dream.

Many farmers and small-scale professional gardeners reduce the seed bank by using two methods, referred to as the false-bed and the stale-bed techniques, which although often used as synonyms, are a little different. In the false-bed technique, till the soil, and remove weeds that have been disturbed. Moisten the soil, and let weed seeds emerge. Till again but never deeper than 2 inches. Rake out weeds, and plant.

The stale-bed technique is slightly different in that the soil is tilled, a crop is planted, and the weeds destroyed after they emerge. By doing this year after year, you reduce the number of seeds in the upper surface of the soil. The technique works well but creates a dilemma for the home gardener. In some springs the weather goes from frigid to warm in a week or two. Many seeds are best planted as soon as possible. There is simply not enough time to till, wait for weeds to grow, till lightly again, and then plant. Also, it is a poor idea to till soil when it is wet. This is especially true of soils with a high clay content. When clay is tilled while wet, it will often compact and form nearly rocklike clumps. So, instead of doing this in spring, try it in fall. Till the soil deeply after removing debris from the garden. Hopefully, the weather will still be warm enough for weed seeds to germinate. Let them grow for a couple of weeks, and till lightly again to remove them. Then cover the whole garden with a thick mat of leaves, unless you have planted a cover crop.

If you do not have a rototiller, you can spade the soil deeply, removing all weeds in the process. Then moisten the soil, let weeds germinate, and spade lightly again, removing the young weeds with a garden rake. Good hand tools to

Pull up lamb's quarters, an edible weed, when young, as it will grow up to 8 feet tall when it self-seeds profusely.

Purslane is edible, spreads to form a mat, and self-seeds like lamb's quarters.

Burdock can be a tenacious weed. It is best dug up in early growth—as many times as necessary to kill it.

Cut back Canada thistle in the bud stage as often as necessary to deplete the food source stored in its roots.

have for weeding whether you till or spade the garden, are a garden spade, garden rake, hoe (whichever type you prefer), four-pronged hoe, small hoe-fork combination (mattock), and a dandelion digger or similar tool to dig up long-rooted plants. Keep your hoe sharp. This will cut down on the weeding time. If you work without gloves, keep the handle smooth to prevent blisters. Sand off rough edges, and apply linseed oil if it's dry. A good hoe makes weeding far less of a chore.

There are two perennial weeds that are difficult to remove. One is burdock *(Arctium lappa)*, difficult but possible to dig up with its ultralong, thick taproot. You may have to use a posthole digger off to one side and then slide the root out into the hole created by the digger. You may have to dig up burdock several times, since it has a way of resprouting from any missed portion of root. But this is possible. See the information on burdock in the section "Unique Plants" in Part II.

The other difficult weed to kill is Canada thistle *(Circium arvense)* with its prickly leaves and long, white, thin roots that break off easily. If allowed to go to seed, it may produce as many as five thousand seeds once fully mature. Its seeds can last in the soil for years. Some say two decades. This plant has been nicknamed the "Lettuce from Hell Thistle." It shoots up as a thin, prickly point, matures into a plant with a prickly stem supporting numerous prickly leaves, forms buds that open up to a pretty purple flower, and matures into a seed head with white, downy fibers with tiny seeds at their base. The down floats in the wind and spreads widely. The usual advice in dealing with Canada thistle is to dig it up. Unfortunately, Canada thistle is a whole different story from burdock. It is the cancer of the weed world. No matter how wide and deep you dig, you somehow leave behind a tiny bit of root that invariably comes up again. This is especially true in clay soil with rocks buried here and there. It often comes back as a group of plants, rather than a single plant.

The only organic way to kill this thistle is to deplete its food reserves. Never pull up the weed by its base. This just signals the plant to shoot up plants around it in all directions. *Instead, cut the plant off at its base once it is tall enough to form flower buds.* Do not let it go to seed. Burn the flower heads, since they may continue to mature even once cut off the plant. If the thistle comes back to life, let it grow again to the bud stage, and whack it off at its base a second time. This is a war of attrition. Each time the plant grows, it is using up the energy reserves stored in its roots—in theory. Be patient. Eventually, the plant gives up. I have also had success covering Canada thistle with paper leaf bags under a thick layer of organic mulch spread out well beyond the site of the original plant. However, it may take two to three years to kill the plant with this method. Canada thistle does not compete well with thick growth, so you can also try planting a quick-growing cover crop to compete with it. Again, you may have to do this several years in a row. Frankly, this is only practical in larger gardens. All of the other methods outlined in most books and articles haven't worked for me. This includes using vinegar (acetic acid) and other products, which kill the foliage but not the roots. The roots are the problem. Some sources say to pour salt into the hollow stem. Not all, but some stems of this plant are solid, so this is not as simple as it sounds. Inorganic products containing clopyralid will kill this thistle but at a price. This product kills off soil microorganisms and is long lasting. Its presence in the soil is toxic to a wide range of vegetables. Some gardeners get so frustrated that they insert Roundup® into the stem with a hypodermic needle. That's definitely straying from the straight and narrow organic path. It also may not work. If sprayed on the plant, it just kills off the foliage. The roots will live and shoot up a second or new batch of plants.

While burdock and Canada thistle are on the most-wanted list, any deep-rooted or spreading weeds and grasses are tough to kill, such as quack grass and crabgrass. Be sure to dig out the entire root system, or little bits of root will grow into another plant. If a plant of this type reemerges, dig it out as soon as you see it, again trying to track down and remove every bit of root. Just regular lawn grass can be a problem, so pull it out before its underground roots (stolons and rhizomes) begin to spread. If your garden is surrounded by lawn, consider blocking it with a barrier made of cement, plastic, or rock. Grass is tenacious, and its underground roots are capable of creeping under barriers.

The key to weeding in spring is to start early, even if it's for just a short time each day. This way weeding will not turn into a nightmare. It will just be a mild headache. Whack weeds off at their base with a sharp hoe. Most weeds die if their stems are cut. Some grow back from the roots. Dig these up with a spade or dandelion digger, making sure to get the entire root. Hand weeding is preferred by some and easy if the soil is moist. Slide your hand down to the base of larger weeds and pull up gently. If they resist, moisten the soil, or use a dandelion digger to remove them. If a weed is close to a desired seedling, hold the desired plant in place as you pull up on the weed next to it. Or snip the weed off with a pair of scissors. As vegetables mature, weeds hide under the leaves. Lift up the leaves, and pull out weeds close to the plant. Occasionally, weeds grow right in the center of some plants. Moisten the plant, slide your thumb and forefinger down to the base of the weed, and then pull it up, starting off gently and increasing pressure as the weed begins to

give way. Toss all weeds into a wheelbarrow or a bucket as you work. Compost all debris, since it will break down into valuable humus—never throw away or burn weeds. It would be a waste of valuable nutrients.

In level gardens you can mow weeds down if the soil is not rocky. Till or spade the garden. Then smooth out the soil with a garden rake. At the same time remove and compost all the uprooted weeds. New weeds will grow from the disturbed soil, but if you keep after them from the start, weeding is relatively easy.

Begin planting as soon as you can. Dense plantings often compete well with weeds. If you are not going to use some of your garden, plant it with a cover crop. These compete well with weeds and help your garden in numerous ways. Good cover crops are buckwheat in summer and rye in fall.

One of the simplest ways to reduce weeding time is to use mulch. Mulch inhibits the germination of weed seeds and deprives them of the light they need to grow. It's never perfect, but it's good. The section in this chapter on mulch is essential reading. But always weed a garden thoroughly before setting down a mulch. Organic mulch does not stop weeds completely. Occasionally, you will have to work your way through the garden, pulling weeds by hand. Weeds are often found at the base of plants, where they do the most damage. Pull these weeds as carefully as possible by hand so as not to damage the root system of the plant you are growing. Mulch keeps the ground very moist, which makes weeding easy. If the ground gets dry or hard, water the garden, and let it sit for a few hours. Come back and weed later when the weeds will slide easily from the soil. *Don't cultivate a garden once covered with mulch.* This will only bring weed seeds to the surface, where they will germinate and cause problems.

Some gardeners kill weeds with flamers, mechanical propane gas torches. Flamers will kill some seeds near the surface of the soil if you water the area first. To kill weeds that have already sprouted, shoot the flame over each weed for less than a second. The high heat causes the plant's cells to burst. You are not trying to burn up weeds but just to damage them so that they will die. Do this early or late in the season before applying mulch or after removing it. Never use this method near dry mulch or during dry periods. While this method sounds simple enough, the cost of the equipment and propane makes it impractical for many home gardeners.

Corn gluten is often mentioned as an "organic" pre-emergent herbicide. I do not use it, but I have included it as an "organic" fertilizer in the fertilizer section of this chapter. Some will consider this inappropriate since the product is principally made from GMO (genetically modified) corn. However, as far as I can determine, it is not toxic to humans, beneficial insects, or soil organisms—just to germinating seeds. It is expensive and must be applied at exactly the right time, just as weed seeds begin to germinate, to be effective. Its value as an herbicide is "iffy" in any event. Also, it will kill all seeds, not just weed seeds. However, its value as a high-nitrogen fertilizer is not disputed. It is certainly a step up in many ways from a synthetic fertilizer.

Thinning

Once plants are growing in the garden, thinning them out is just another form of weeding. Not all plants need to be thinned, but many do. Each plant has a different need for space, but most grow best with a little elbow room. This reduces competition for water and nutrients, provides better air circulation, and increases yields. However, experiment with this. There are times when you can crowd plants much closer together than recommended in books or on seed packages. This can only be learned through *personal* experience, although tips are given in the plant descriptions.

When growing plants from seed indoors, end up with only one plant per small pot or cell in a tray (members of the onion family are exceptions). You want even spacing in larger containers, such as a flat. If plants are crowding each other out, thin them by snipping off the excess plants with a cuticle scissors, or pull out gently with a tweezers.

When you buy plants at a nursery, there may be several plants per pot or tray. For example, basil is often sold as a cluster of plants. Tease these apart and plant them as single plants. Give them space to mature. If you plant them as a group, growth will be stunted. When planted separately, each plant will get large and bushy.

Water the garden lightly the night before you plan to thin—it's easier to pull up plants from moist earth. When thinning, you don't want to disturb the root system of the plants you intend to use later. Using one hand, push down on the soil around the plants you want to keep. Pull out the others. Pinch them between your thumb and forefinger or with a pair of tweezers, and pull up. Firm the soil gently around the remaining plants. Just push the soil lightly back in place to anchor the roots. Water the thinned plants immediately to help them overcome any shock from root disturbance. If thinning this way proves too difficult, cut plants with a pair of cuticle scissors. Toss prunings into a bucket and then into the compost pile. More ruthless and impatient gardeners pull a garden rake through the row to be thinned. This takes a little experience and lots of confidence.

Thinning does not have to be done all at once. You can thin crops over a period of weeks. A number of gardeners do this with root crops. When thinning root crops, pull out the larger ones first. Pull them out just as they reach edible size. Lettuce, spinach, greens, beets—all can be tiny and still good to eat as microgreens. The smaller remaining plants will now take over and develop healthy roots.

Pruning

Pruning is cutting off a portion of a plant. There are a number of reasons to prune plants. Some of the few woody plants in this guide need some pruning to keep fruit production at its best. Pruning techniques for these are covered in the plant descriptions in Part II. Many plants tend to bolt, which means a plant starts to send up a flower shoot. Sometimes, by cutting off this shoot, you can keep the mother plant producing edible leaves for a longer period of time. Cutting back plants to a point just above the growing tip

When plants, such as parsnip, grow too close together, they must be thinned.

With proper space between plants, the roots will produce large leaves that provide food to enlarging roots.

Few gardeners know that when a cabbage head is removed, smaller heads will develop if allowed to.

To stop garlic chives and flowering vegetables from self-seeding, cut off the flower heads as they emerge.

Many vegetables, including leaf celery, can be cut back to produce new growth as "cut and come again" plants.

Several plants, such as these raspberries, have dead cane or stems that should be cut out in winter or very early spring.

Remove whole or portions of dead stems from plants such as sage.

Cut the stems back to any emerging new growth.

may result in a second or even third crop. This is common with a number of greens. These are referred to as "cut and come again" crops. Pruning may be necessary if a part of a plant is diseased or covered with insects. Snipping off the infected tissue may save the rest of the plant. If a plant is producing lots of small fruits, some gardeners snip off a few to end up with fewer, larger ones. They may also cut off the top of the stem late in the season to direct all energy to ripening fruit below.

To prune properly, have a pair of scissors for soft-stemmed plants; pruning shears for harder-stemmed plants, also called hand shears or secateurs; gloves for thorny plants; protective glasses for thorny plants; and loppers for thicker woody stems. Tools should be sharp and disinfected between cuts, at least on plants that produce canes. A bleach solution of nine parts water to one part bleach has traditionally been recommended, but many organic gardeners are switching to rubbing alcohol (isopropyl or ethyl alcohol) or hydrogen peroxide, which are less toxic. Toss prunings into a bucket, and add to the compost pile. If you are pruning raspberries

If young plants develop flower or fruit early in the season, as on this tomatillo, snip them off to direct energy to new growth.

Cover plants with leaves or straw, and keep them in the garden under snow to be harvested late in the season.

Late in the season, snip off the tips of tomato stems to encourage remaining fruit to ripen more quickly.

or plants with thorns, consider burning the cuttings to prevent sticking yourself by accident when working with the compost. Leaving any pruned plant part on the ground can attract insects and increase the chance of disease. When to prune is covered in the plant descriptions in Part II.

Winter Protection

This cold-climate growing guide is aimed at gardeners living in areas that can get as cold as −20°F or colder. Winter cold is most relevant when growing perennial plants. The hardiness of these is included in the plant descriptions in Part II so that you can choose varieties best suited to your area. The foliage of some perennial plants dies off, but the plants spring back to life the following season without any winter protection at all. Other perennials, however, including a number of herbs, are best protected by placing an 8- to 12-inch covering of loose straw over them as soon as the ground freezes. Do not cover these plants too early, since rodents may then use them as a winter home. Adding an additional layer of pine boughs after Christmas adds to this protection. All protection must be removed as soon as the weather warms up in spring to prevent the plants from rotting out. Overall, the best winter protection is a deep layer of snow.

Winter protection allows for some plants to be harvested all winter long. Winter protection is also useful to seed savers trying to get biennials to survive and flower in the second year of growth. However, even with protection some biennials rarely survive in the garden. These are usually dug up and placed in moist sand or sphagnum peat moss in a large container kept in an area where the roots stay cold but do not freeze. Suggestions for when to do this are covered in the plant descriptions.

Extending the Growing Season

There's a saying about cold climates, "If frost doesn't get you at one end, it will at the other." To extend the growing season, plants need to be protected from the cold. Spring and fall strategies are usually different, but a few are the same. I explain them here in abbreviated form since there are entire books written on this subject. One assumption is made: you do not have a greenhouse or complicated structures such as tall, protective plant tunnels, the kind used by professionals to market produce well into the winter months. Still, without all the protective paraphernalia, the home gardener can extend the season in areas that are "nine months of winter and three months of poor sledding."

Cold frames, easily converted into hotbeds, are relatively simple to construct. A cold frame is a box with a clear plastic or glass lid. It acts like a miniature greenhouse. Using a cold frame can extend your growing season by several weeks in spring and, sometimes, quite a bit longer in fall. Its use is versatile: hardening off plants, starting plants from seed, and even growing a few cold-tolerant vegetables in fall.

The basic cold frame is 10 to 12 inches above the soil line on the south or southeast side and 6 inches higher on the north with the sides slanted down from one side to the other. The overall size can vary, but you should be able to reach every spot within the cold frame easily. Using plywood for all sides works fine. Screw all sides together, and anchor them 2 inches or more into the soil. Bank soil up around the sides to make it less wobbly and provide a bit of insulation. Lay hardware cloth (really wire) with its fine mesh on the soil inside the cold frame to keep rodents out. Some gardeners place a couple of inches of Styrofoam on top of this, but that is optional. Now place 4 inches of rich soil over the hardware cloth or Styrofoam. You can use whatever is available as a cover, which should angle down at 45 degrees to catch the sun's rays. An old window works fine if you can hinge it to the frame. Clear plastic is lighter and easier to work with. Devise your own method for rolling it up and down. If the cover is solid, make a notched stick to hold it up at different levels. You will want to be able to reduce heat and humidity on hot days. A solid cover stands up much better to snow and hard rain. Cover cold frames at night with a blanket to keep heat loss to a minimum. The blanket works well during snowfalls. You can just lift it up and shake off the snow.

An even simpler cold frame is just a deep hole in the ground with a clear lid. It works just fine, but most people prefer an aboveground area to work. Mark it well so no one steps into it. The plastic lean-to is a variation on the cold frame. It can be as simple as tacking clear plastic on the side of a garage and staking it to the ground. The advantage of the lean-to is that you can walk right in, put it up and take it down in minutes, and store it easily by rolling it up for the next season. It is messy and awkward to deal with, but it does work.

As soon as the ground freezes, protect tender plants with a cover of straw.

A hotbed is a cold frame with heating cables under it. Or it can be a cold frame with no more than one light-bulb providing heat. When using heating cables, place them under 1 inch of soil, cover with a screen, and then add another 5 inches of soil. Set the temperature at 70°F. Anything electric should be plugged into a GFI (ground fault interrupter) outlet. The old-style hotbed was a cold frame built over a couple of feet of fresh manure covered with 6 inches of soil. The decomposing manure gave off heat. Unfortunately, most of us do not have immediate access to that amount of manure.

If you have ever thrown ashes from your fireplace on snow, you have probably noticed that area melting quickly in spring. Black plastic mulch warms up soil and encourages warm-weather plants to put on a fantastic display of growth. If you are going to use this technique, prepare a bed in fall, and cover it with plastic at that time. This works well for cucumbers, eggplants, muskmelons, peppers, squash, tomatoes, and watermelons.

Cover individual plants in spring to extend the season. HotKaps® are little domes placed over new transplants to keep heat in overnight in cold weather. Any device used in this way is referred to as a cloche and can be as simple as an ice cream bucket or milk jug with the bottom cut out. Save the lid or cap to put on at night. Some gardeners enclose plants under baskets or buckets. The use of a cloche takes some attention. The plants need to be warm, but they should not be overheated in bright sunshine during the day without some form of ventilation. At night they must stay fully enclosed if temperatures are expected to drop below freezing. Plant enclosures also protect young plants against wind, some marauders, and some insects.

Wall O' Water plant protectors allow plants to be put into the ground earlier.

day for good air circulation if necessary. Close them at night to retain heat, as you would with a cloche. Check city regulations if constructing large tunnels. They are effective but may be eyesores to your neighbors.

Light and heavy row covers also work well to provide protection during spring and fall. While they are primarily used to protect plants from insects, they will keep the temperature from fluctuating as much as it would around completely exposed plants. Temperatures are also somewhat higher under fabric covers but not nearly as much as under plastic tunnels. Fabric covers should be supported, whether heavy or not, to prevent damage to plant foliage and stems.

Stack black plastic bags filled with leaves or straw around plants during cold spells. Use a heat trap to shelter plants and encourage quick growth. Bales of straw with a south-facing opening trap heat and encourage growth in warmth-loving plants. Cover the entire trap at night during cold snaps with a 6-mil piece of plastic or a cloth tarp. Black roofing paper wrapped around wire also acts as a good heat trap. The black paper absorbs heat. At night you place a piece of roofing paper over the cylinder until day and nighttime temperatures pose no threat to the young plant. Place a board over the paper to prevent it blowing off. It's easy to put together, take apart, and store. Surrounding cages with plastic also works well. Some gardeners double cage using chicken wire, a layer of cardboard around it, then thick plastic. These could really be called cold greenhouses that take advantage of the sun's warming influence. Cover all openings with cloth at night.

Using sprinklers to drench plants during an unexpected cold spell may also prevent overnight damage. It is unrealistic to expect anyone to leave the sprinklers on all night, but getting plants thoroughly soaked is sometimes good enough to stop them from dying off completely. This is most commonly done in fall, when plants are mature.

Plants can also be covered with sheets in fall for temporary protection. Always get the sheets on during the warmest part of the day. The goal is to hold the heat in, not keep the cold out. Use cloth, not plastic, for this purpose. Plastic does not insulate as well and may cause condensation to form on leaves just below it. This freezes and damages leaves. For even more warmth, fill milk jugs with warm water and place them under the cloth covering.

In cold climates gardeners must expect the unexpected, such as a really late cold snap in spring. If corn, for example, is already sprouting, bury it before the cold hits. Do not remove the soil, and hope that the corn keeps growing and sprouts through the protective layer of soil. Constantly think outside the box.

Surrounding plants with Wall O' Water plant protectors in spring may add three weeks to the growing season. These are plastic walls filled with water to absorb energy from the sun in the day and to give off heat at night. A little chlorine in the water helps prevent it from getting cloudy. Gallon plastic milk jugs or plastic soda bottles filled with water and placed around plants are an inexpensive substitute. Keep the lids for these bottles so that you can pop them on at night to prevent heat loss. Flop a blanket over the space left between these at night to conserve more heat.

Plastic tunnels work well to extend the growing season in both spring and fall. Use clear plastic over supports to form a tunnel. You can buy supports or make your own from flexible ½-inch PVC pipes, used in plumbing. Tunnels of varying sizes are also offered for sale but are expensive. Tunnels work especially well for cucumbers, muskmelons, okra, squash, and watermelons. Open the ends during the

Bringing Pots Indoors

Lack of light and low humidity are the main problems of bringing plants indoors during winter months. But this may be your only choice if you want to keep more tender plants alive. Bring these in toward the end of the season. Do not expect wonders. The main goal is to keep them alive, even if they simply limp along. Some plants, such as lemon verbena, will drop their leaves, but do not assume that they are dead. Give them as much sun as possible, go easy on the watering, and only harvest parts of a plant if it is growing vigorously. Ideally, place plants under grow lights for twelve to fourteen hours a day. Placing them on a water-filled tray will help with humidity, but the pots should be resting on pebbles so that the lower portion of soil in the pot is not soggy. Sometimes, it's simpler to take cuttings and start new plants from scratch so that they do not take up as much space.

Winter Mulch

A few gardeners use a thick winter mulch as a way of elongating the harvesting season or protecting plants during winter cold. When to use winter mulch is covered in plant descriptions in Part II. It is especially good for carrots, garlic, horseradish, leeks, parsnips, radishes (winter), salsify, scorzonera, and turnips. The most commonly used winter mulch is straw placed over plants to a depth of 10 to 12 inches. Straw, even when covered with snow, seems to compact less than whole leaves. When using leaves as a winter mulch, never break them down. Try to use whole oak leaves if possible. They fall late in the season and don't pack down as easily as other leaves. Don't forget to mark the plants with tall stakes. Paint the tops orange.

All winter mulches should be removed as soon as the weather warms up in spring. Sometimes, you have to do this over a period of days since the lower portion of mulch may still be frozen. This is more of a problem with leaves than straw.

You extend the season by gambling on early and late plantings. Sometimes, you lose, other times you win. The cost of the loss of some seed is worth the gamble.

CHAPTER 5

PROPAGATION

How to propagate specific vegetables is covered in detail in the plant descriptions in Part II. I would like to emphasize that if allowed to mature, many plants self-seed prolifically. Little seedlings pop up where the mother plant was grown the season before. Each year it's fun to see what emerges from what appears to be bare soil.

Following are the most popular methods used by home gardeners to create new plants from existing vegetables, herbs, and berries. I have listed them alphabetically, not by preference of one over the other.

Bulbs, bulbils, and bulblets: Onions and their relatives are the most common vegetables to form bulbs, bulbils, and bulblets. If you grow onions from seed, they form small bulbs. These are brought indoors at the end of the season, either to be eaten if large enough or to be planted the following spring. Egyptian onions form little bulbs called bulblets on the tips of their stems, which topple over so that the bulblets can take root to form new plants.

Cloves and bulbils: Break garlic bulbs into separate cloves. Plant each of these late in the year to get bulbs the following season. Bulbils form in the flowers of some gar-lics. See the chapter on garlic for more information on planting and growing these.

Softwood cuttings: These cuttings are taken from the soft tips of stems. Cut off the top 4 to 6 inches. The cutting should have several nodes, places where leaves join the stem. Cut ¼ inch below the lowest node of the cutting with a razor blade or sharp knife. Do not use pruners, which tend to compress the plant tissue at the cut. Take cuttings in late morning. Remove the lower leaves around the bottom node. Place the base of the cutting in water, and change it every day. Cuttings will often form roots faster in an opaque rather than a clear container. Cuttings for woody plants can also be grown in sterile mix kept evenly moist. Once the cuttings form roots, plant them in the garden when the weather matches the needs of the plant. One of the most common vegetables propagated in this manner is sweet potatoes.

Hardwood cuttings: Cuttings can also be taken from more mature stem tissue. Known as hardwood cuttings, they are done to propagate plants such as blueberries, currants, gooseberries, lavender, and so on. Cut out a 6- to 8-inch piece of the stem during the dormant season from one-year-old wood. Again, make a cut under a node. Plant

Scatter garlic bulbils like seed in a shallow furrow or over a block of soil in the fall for microgreens the following season.

Cut stems from sprouting sweet potatoes, and place them in water to create little "bare-root" plantlets. The cuttings shown here have more and longer roots than necessary, but this later-stage photo is easier to understand.

immediately, or place the cutting in moist peat moss in the refrigerator until spring. You have several planting options. The first is to plant the cuttings in sterile starting mix kept consistently moist until roots form. The second is to dip the base of the cuttings in honey and plant immediately in sterile starting mix. The third is to soak the base of the stem in willow water overnight before planting in a sterile starting mix. To make willow water, cut off new growth from the branches of willows, strip off the leaves, cut the stems into small pieces, allow them to soak in water for several days, and pour the water through a sieve, preserving only the water. Then soak the base of the cuttings in the willow water overnight before planting in a sterile starting mix. Willow water contains indolebutyric acid (IBA), found in many rooting hormones, and salicylic acid, which helps keep the water sterile. (A similar compound, acetylsalicylic acid, is found in aspirin, which some people use in plant propagation.) Getting cuttings to root may take time or not succeed at all. Experiment.

Bud cuttings: For this kind of cutting, only a bud is removed off hardwood. This is done to propagate blackberries, although tip layering, described later, is much easier for the home gardener. Again, always cut just below a node, since roots form more quickly from this portion of stem. Hardwood and bud cuttings can be challenging to grow, but I describe them here for those interested.

Division: Division is the process of dividing a large plant into smaller pieces, which are then planted to create new plants. This is one of the oldest and simplest ways of propagation. Normally divide plants just as new growth emerges in spring. Dig around the mother plant, and lift it from the ground, or slice off a portion with a spade. If you lift it from the ground, divide it with a spade or a knife into pieces each containing buds connected to a healthy portion of root. Plant immediately at the same depth in well-prepared soil. Water deeply, and keep the plant well watered until it is growing vigorously.

Grafting: In this process part of one plant (scion) is inserted into the rootstock of a different plant. The rootstock imparts some favorable characteristic to the grafted portion of the plant. Grafting is most commonly done to increase the disease resistance of heirloom varieties. These plants are expensive, and whether the extra expense is worth it is up for debate. The stems of the upper portion (scion) should

This mature rhubarb plant can be cut into pieces for new plants.

Use a sharp knife or spade to cut rhubarb plants apart, and plant them immediately as a bare-root plant. For ease of illustration, this photo was taken later in the season than you would normally divide a plant.

Snip the stem connecting a small strawberry to its "mother," and plant it immediately.

never be planted under the soil surface. Any growth emerging from the rootstock should be removed immediately.

Mound layering: Also called stooling or stool bedding, mound layering is used primarily in producing blueberries and gooseberries in the home garden. In early spring before new growth starts, cut back a mother plant nearly to the ground, leaving about 3 inches of stem tissue. Then cover the plant with soil (amended with sphagnum peat moss for blueberries). Shoots will develop from the mother plant, and as they grow, they will form roots. Once roots form, cut off the shoots, and plant as you would a bare-root plant. The process generally takes about a year, so new plants can be planted the following spring.

Rhizomes, runners, and stolons: Many plants form stems that grow horizontally on or just below the surface of the soil. When aboveground, they are referred to as runners or stolons; when below, as rhizomes. Strawberries are a good example of plants that form numerous runners. Mint may form runners and rhizomes. Cut these off and plant. Keep moist until growing well.

Seed: Some plants produce seed prolifically, others hardly at all. Most sources say to save seed from open-pollinated (heirloom) varieties only, not from hybrids. That is certainly the safest way to get new plants that match the mother plant, but it is surprising how many hybrids produce seeds that develop into fairly close replicas of the mother plant. Seed is produced when pollen from the male flower (stamen with anthers) of one plant (or the same plant) is carried by wind, insects, or you (with a painter's brush or cotton swab) into a female flower (pistil with stigma) of the same or different plant. Pollination results in a fertilized egg (zygote) in the ovary of the female flower. Note that some plants pollinate themselves. Not all plants produce flowers in the first year, and seed saving is more difficult if plants produce flowers only in the second year. Many of these have a tendency to die off in cold-climate areas. A few, such as parsnips, seem to survive well and produce seed.

Plants in the same family may cross-pollinate. Different varieties in the same species will cross-pollinate. So growing only one open-pollinated variety makes sense for seed

Snip off parsnip seed heads into a paper bag, let dry, and remove all debris except for seed.

line the bottom of the bag. Remove the debris. Then run the seeds through a sieve to remove tiny particles of unwanted material. Place the seeds in an envelope. Write the name of the variety on the envelope and the date. Seal the envelope, and keep it in a dark, cool, dry place. If seeds get moist or are exposed to light, they may begin to germinate. If they get too hot, they may die. The ideal temperature is 50°F, but seed will live in higher temperatures than that. Find as cool a spot as possible. Some seed is best saved in a refrigerator, but the average home gardener doesn't have the space for this.

Seed savers generally treat tomato seeds differently, using the "wet method." Let tomatoes develop on the vine until completely mature and a bit beyond. Admittedly, they may get a bit mushy. Pick the earliest-maturing fruit for seed-saving purposes. Scoop out the interior of the thoroughly cleaned fruit. Mash the pulp in a bowl, adding a few tablespoons of water (optional). Stirring the mixture each day, let the pulp ferment covered or uncovered at 70°F for at least three days to kill germs. At this point spoon off the surface. Most viable seeds sink. Add water, and carefully pour out any debris. Keep doing this, making sure not to lose the seeds in the rinsing process. Tap or push the seeds into a sieve, and wash them thoroughly in cold water. Then lay them out in a single layer on a hard plate (they stick to paper) or cookie sheet to dry. They dry best if they are not touching. That means pushing the seeds around until they are separated from each other. Move the seeds around as often as you can. Let them dry until they slide around easily when pushed lightly. This can take a week or longer. Be patient. Place them in a paper envelope. Keep them dry, cool, and dark until planting time.

Biennials occasionally do produce flowers and seeds in the first year, generally under some form of stress. However, if they don't, the following, somewhat burdensome procedure may work. In late fall as temperatures dip, dig up the plant. Remove any ragged leaves, and keep the stem or head along with the roots. Shake off any soil from the roots. Then, place plants in moist sphagnum peat moss, sand, or sawdust in a large container in a cool, but not freezing, place. The roots of cabbage, for example, should be tucked into the material with the heads sticking up. Carrots can be placed lying flat in layers separated by the moist medium. Use common sense. If during storage they begin to rot or deteriorate, remove rotted leaves or tissue if possible. A minimum of six plants should be stored in this way to preserve genetic diversity. The following year, plant the overwintered biennial as you would a transplant. Keep well watered, and hope the stem and roots are still alive and capable of producing new growth. Note that a number of biennials can be "stored" right in the garden with a thick layer of mulch.

savers. And that variety should not be close to the flowers of another plant in the same family. Note too that your plants may be pollinated by others as much as a quarter of a mile to a mile away. So if you are surrounded by lots of families growing vegetables, it's possible for unwanted cross-pollination to occur. But don't worry about it. Give it a try.

Let seeds mature on any given plant for as long as possible. Flower heads usually turn brown at this stage. Seeds are carried in a wide variety of structures, from pods to umbrella-like clusters. It takes a little experience to know when to cut off the structures carrying seed. If you do it too early, the seeds have not developed enough to be viable. If you wait too long, then seeds may fall off the plant and make harvesting difficult. Fruits that open up to release seed are called dehiscent; fruit that stays intact, as on a sunflower, is referred to as indehiscent. Knowing what type of plant you are dealing with helps in deciding how vigilant you must be in collecting the seed at just the right time.

When you believe the seeds are fully mature, cut off the plant part carrying the seed into a paper bag. Let the seeds dry in an open bag indoors for two to three weeks. Then squeeze the seed heads in your hand. The seeds pop out and

Seeds are living organisms. The viability of seed varies with each plant but is no less than one year. Plant the seed the following year if possible. Germination rates go down as seed ages. If you get hooked on seed saving, then buy a book that deals with this subject, since the information here is an oversimplification of a fascinating aspect of gardening. A recent book is *The Seed Garden,* edited by Lee Buttala and Shanyn Siegel. Clearly, the process of seed saving can be incredibly easy to extremely difficult, depending on the plant.

Suckers: If you have ever grown raspberries, you have seen little plants form off to the side of the mother plant. These are known as suckers or offshoots. Dig these up in spring, and plant as you would a bare-root plant. Try to keep as much soil around the roots as possible, and sever the plant from the mother plant just as little green buds barely begin to sprout on the stem or earlier.

Tip layering: The canes of blackberries cascade toward the ground. Where the tips of the canes touch the ground, the stems often take root. Let this take place naturally. Once little plantlets are growing from the tips, sever them from the mother plant and get into the ground immediately. Treat as a bare-root plant—consistent watering is the key to success. To propagate blueberries, in the fall, bend a branch down to the ground. Make a narrow cut into the branch about 6 inches from the end. Stick a toothpick into the wound to keep it open. Pin the wounded area down. Cover it with moist soil mixed with peat. Keep the stem moist until the first freeze and throughout the following season. The wounded stem often takes root within one to two years. At that point, sever it from the mother plant, and plant as a bare-root plant.

Tissue culture (micropropagation): This is one of the most fascinating ways to create plants, and it is done in sterile conditions with the goal of creating plants that are completely disease-free. The tissue of a plant is broken down, and its cells are placed into a sterile growing medium. While some home gardeners have grown plants in this manner, it is best left in the hands of professionals.

Dig up suckers that sprout off the sides of raspberry plants, and get them into the ground quickly. Ideally, do this before the plant leafs out, as shown in this photo.

Blueberries and potatoes are examples of plants that have been grown using tissue culture.

Tuber: A tuber is a portion of swollen stem tissue. Unlike an onion, it consists of solid flesh rather than overlapping layers. However, the tuber can be divided into pieces. Each piece that contains an eye, a little indentation in the skin, can grow into a new plant. This is a common way to plant potatoes. If a tuber is small and has only one or a few eyes, it is best to plant it whole. Even potatoes with numerous eyes can be planted whole.

CHAPTER 6

SOLVING GROWING PROBLEMS

Organic gardeners may face many problems in the garden—insects, disease, and marauders. Plants may suffer physiological disorders. There is no Garden of Eden, but any gardener can take steps to keep problems to a minimum. Like a medical student, you may conclude that your garden has a host of problems more severe than they really are. It's important to have the right frame of mind. You can't control everything, and by accepting that all gardens suffer some loss, your gardening experience will be far more enjoyable. Organic gardening aims to deal with problems as simply and naturally as possible.

Tips to Reduce the Use of Pesticides

In the hands of professionals who have been trained in their use and need them for survival of crops to make a living, pesticides may seem justified, but the average home gardener can learn to deal without them. Pesticides affect the soil, may kill more than seventy million birds a year, kill beneficial insects and butterflies, and along with fertilizers use tens of millions of barrels of oil in their production each year. I refuse to use chemicals in the home garden. I like the peaceful feeling of knowing that my family is eating chemical-free produce. I believe that chemicals destroy a delicate natural balance in the environment. Here are ways to avoid pesticides.

Get into the garden, and begin to observe what is happening. Got slugs? Slide them off leaves at night with the help of a flashlight, or put up with the holes they chew in leaves. Got Japanese beetles? Take a shallow dish, and place it under the beetle while you try to pinch it with your fingers. If you don't get it, it will drop into the dish, where you can kill it. Got egg masses on leaves? Squish them with your finger or with a cotton swab if squeamish. Furthermore, many insects infest plants, cause a great deal of damage, and eventually kill the plant, but you have still been able to harvest more than enough of what you are growing. I have squash bugs destroying the stems of my zucchini plants every year. After eating and giving away more squash then any family could hope for, I finally take my hat off to the bugs and go on with life. This may seem like a cavalier way to deal with disease and insects, but gardens don't have to be perfect to be good. *Like my insistence on the importance of creating great soil, this attitude regarding disease and insect problems in the garden is one of the most important points in this guide.* Accept the loss of some plants as part of the price for fresh, chemical-free produce. Plant a few more plants than you really need.

Select varieties of transplants and seeds according to their ability to resist disease and insects. This is emphasized in seed catalogs. Breeders have spent a lot of time, energy, and money to create these varieties. Take advantage of this. Make sure seed is certified disease-free. Buy seed of varieties suited to your climate. This growing guide will help you do that.

Use physical barriers to stop insects from attacking your plants. Row covers come in different weights. All allow sun and rain to reach plants underneath them. Lightweight (floating) covers can actually rest on some vegetables, but they are most commonly supported by hoops to eliminate any damage to foliage. Hoops can be made of 9-gauge wire or flexible ½-inch PVC pipe used by plumbers. Supports can be both under and over the fabric to keep it from blowing away. Fabric is fragile and should be handled with care. Note that row covers do more than protect plants from insects. They also reduce temperature fluctuations and loss of moisture from plants and soil. To be effective, they must be anchored to the soil on both the ends and sides with whatever heavy materials are available. U-shaped pins are sold through catalogs for this purpose. The covers, consisting of a synthetic fabric, can be wrapped around wire cages enclosing plants, such as tomatoes. For protection against frost use the heavier grades. Another commonly used physical barrier is a mat to prevent cutworms from encircling stems.

Whenever practical or possible, start your plants from transplants if they lend themselves to being transplanted. These young plants are more resistant to problems than seedlings emerging from seed in the garden. Of course, only specific plants are typically transplanted. This is covered in the plant descriptions in Part II.

Grow healthy plants. Plants actually have chemicals in them to help ward off disease and protect themselves from insects. The healthier a plant is, the less susceptible it is to disease and insect problems. That does not mean that healthy plants will not be affected. They will. But stressed plants are an open invitation to increased damage by disease and insects.

Protect beneficial insects by not using pesticides. This way they can actually do what nature intended them to do—to kill insects either by eating them (predators) or laying eggs in their larvae (parasites). True, some eat both good and bad insects, but let nature take its course. In case you are interested in delving deeper into this subject, I have provided a list of common beneficial insects. There is also a belief by some that certain plants provide a good refuge for beneficial insects. Those most commonly recommended are listed here.

Don't buy predator or parasitic insects. Predator insects sometimes eat each other en route to your house. In the wild, predator or parasitic insects will attack only certain prey. Therefore, their use is immediately limited to specific insects. If prey is in short supply, the predators move on. Your money literally flies or crawls away. Most home gardens do not have enough insects to maintain a large colony of predator or parasitic insects. Some of the predators you introduce, such as praying mantises, will eat beneficial as well as harmful insects. In short, bees may be the dessert after a batch of cabbage butterflies.

Beneficial Insects

ant lion (doodle bug)	ground beetle	praying mantis (eats both good and bad insects)
aphid lion (lacewing)	honeybee	
assassin bug	hover flies (also known as syrphid fly)	spiders (not spider mites)
bumblebee	lacewings (green)	syrphid flies (also known as hover fly)
centipedes	lady beetle (also known as ladybird beetle or ladybug)	tachinid flies
damsel bug		wasps (parasitic)
devil's coach horse	minute pirate bug	yellow jackets (they have nests in the ground; do not disturb these)
dragonflies (can kill thousands of flying insects)	mites (some good, some bad)	
	nematodes (mostly good, some bad)	

Plants That Provide Refuge for Beneficial Insects

anthemis	leaf fennel	rudbeckia	tanacetum	vetch
basil	marigold	sage	tansy	yarrow
cosmos	monarda	spearmint	thyme	zinnia
dill	morning glory	sunflower	tritonia	

Protect your allies no matter how much they make you flinch or squirm. By encouraging them, you can keep many insects in check and improve the quality of your soil and crop. Allies include bats (build bat houses), birds (build birdhouses and provide a birdbath), bees (may visit a single flower more than eight hundred times to collect pollen), frogs, lizards, salamanders, snakes (garter snakes eat worms and rodents), and toads (may eat fifteen thousand insects in one season). Lure toads into the garden with a shallow dish filled with water and set into the ground with its rim at soil level. This dish must be in the shade. Change the water daily since mosquitoes need water to breed and can carry encephalitis and West Nile virus. Change the water in your birdbath routinely for the same reason. And draw worms into the garden with a thick layer of mulch.

Keep your garden and tools clean. Pick up all debris. Quickly remove foliage infected with disease or infested with insects to prevent their spread. Dig up badly diseased plants, and burn them. Many communities allow fire pits even when open burning is illegal. Or buy a grill, and burn debris in it. Carry a container filled with a mild bleach solution (one part bleach to nine parts water), rubbing alcohol, or vinegar when pruning. Dip the pruners in this solution

Planting marigolds throughout the garden may deter pests, according to advocates of "companion planting."

after each cut. This is most important for woody plants, such as currants or raspberries, if they show signs of disease. At the end of the season remove and compost all dead plants. These can serve as a winter refuge for insects or harbor disease-causing pathogens.

Plant lots of different plants in the garden. Mix it up with vegetables, herbs, berries, and flowering plants. This diversity does remarkable things. Grow plants that you may not even intend to use if they produce flowers that will attract pollinators or act as deterrents to harmful insects. I don't use borage, but I grow it. It produces copious amounts of foliage and huge clusters of lovely flowers that attract bees. Who knows whether marigolds really repel insects. I don't, but they are beautiful. When a variety of plants are combined, insects seem to be less of a problem. This may have given birth to the concept of companion planting, which is almost completely unproven and mostly anecdotal but remarkably popular. Books on companion planting claim that certain plants grow well together, while others don't. I have tested this claim for years, seen contradictory advice in articles and books, and have come to the conclusion that people choose to believe what they want to believe. I just garden.

Trap cropping is sometimes listed as a companion planting strategy. The idea is to sacrifice one crop for another. The

Reduce the chance of asparagus beetle damage in spring by removing dead asparagus stems in fall.

trap crop is planted on the perimeter of the garden. Since insects are drawn to specific plants, the idea is to get them to attack the one you don't care about to save the one you do. Figuring out which plant to use as a trap for a specific insect is not as easy as it might sound. However, there have been studies that prove that it does work in principle. Once the trap crop is covered in insects, the plant and insects are destroyed. This method is better suited to commercial situations than the home garden, but it is an interesting concept in need of much further study.

A final strategy is to plant the same plant in different parts of the garden or in different places in your yard. Insects may get one crop and miss the other altogether. This way both you and the insects win. Many of these suggestions and those in following sections are part of what has been labeled Integrated Pest Management (IPM). I prefer calling it intelligent pest management, which has evolved over decades since the introduction of synthetic pesticides.

Using Organic Chemicals

Losses are minimal in most organic gardens but, admittedly, could be prevented by organic pesticides. The word *organic* has come to mean safe, and, yet this is not really true. Some of the organic controls offered years ago are off the market, just as many synthetic chemicals have come and gone. Organic products still kill bees and beneficial insects. Read the labels. They can also harm you. Diatomaceous earth may be effective for solving certain problems, but it is made up of sharp particles that can cause lung damage if inhaled. My question is, how much time, effort, and money do you want to spend worrying about problems that cause only a small percentage of damage in the home garden? One estimate is that disease and insects cause only about 15 percent of damage done to vegetables in the home garden. Far more destructive are environmental factors including lack of water, heavy wind, and fluctuating temperature; improper use of chemicals including pesticides and fertilizers; poor light; mechanical damage; salt used on ice during winter; and so on. Not to mention marauders (more about these later).

Chemicals cost money. Some are more expensive than the crop you are trying to save. However, the urge to control and protect a crop started from seed or transplants in your own garden is extremely strong. I have used a few chemicals occasionally during the past sixty years but have come to the conclusion that for the average home garden they are not necessary with one exception: asparagus, a perennial crop. If you have asparagus beetles, treat plants with an organic spray if absolutely necessary.

What I have against pesticides is more than just an emotional reaction. Pesticides may have to be used often to be effective, most kill insects indiscriminately, many kill bees, some kill amphibians, some kill fish, some are phytotoxic (disfigure or kill foliage), some are dangerous to pets, some are dangerous to people, some build up heavy metal in the soil, some don't work unless combined with other substances, some are only effective at specific temperatures and humidity, some are being used so often that insects are building up resistance, and so on. *I repeat, the term* organic *does not mean safe.*

Many organic gardeners disagree, contending that you can prevent loss with a limited use of chemicals to destroy unwanted insect pests and to stop disease. They claim that poisons properly used at the right time do not pose any health problems if gardeners follow the directions on the label and use the poisons only when absolutely necessary. However, many have the potential to kill beneficial insects. Follow label instructions to cut down on "collateral damage." For those who want to use pesticides, there are dozens of products on the market used as bactericides (poisons that kill bacteria), fungicides (poisons that kill fungi), herbicides (poisons that kill plants), insecticides (poisons that kill insects), molluscicides (poisons that kill slugs and snails), and rodenticides (poisons to kill mice and rats). If you want specific recommendations on controlling disease or killing insects, search this site: https://attra.ncat.org/attra-pub/biorationals/index.php. Here you will find a list of diseases and insects, chemical controls, and products containing these. To verify that a product is organic, cross-check with lists from the Organic Materials Review Institute (OMRI). They publish a directory of products for organic use. Here's a sampling.

Actinovate®: A fungicide that deals with a wide range of diseases.

AzaGuard®: An insecticide that kills a wide range of insects. Both Actinovate® and AzaGuard® are as expensive as they are effective.

Bacillus thuringiensis (Bt): A naturally occurring bacteria that can be commercially cultured to be sprayed on leaves, flowers, and fruits to kill a wide variety of larvae. There are various types of *Bt,* and the product may kill the larvae of butterflies. It does not harm humans.

Bicarbonates: Baking soda (sodium bicarbonate) is a fungicide when mixed with oil. However, if used frequently, the salt buildup can be toxic to plants. Ammonium bicarbonate and potassium bicarbonate are more commonly recommended because they contain plant nutrients. However, their effect on different plants varies, making them complicated to use.

Bordeaux mixture: A combination of lime and copper

sulfate used to kill blights and mildews. While it is based on natural products, its use has restrictions applied to it. It can damage foliage if applied during cold wet weather.

Copper: Used in a number of products to kill bacteria and fungi. However, it is a heavy metal and can build up in the soil.

Derris: Derris consists of the powdered roots of tropical plants in the *Derris* genus. It is a source of rotenone and used as an insecticide.

Diatomaceous earth (DE): This powder consists of the ground-up, dried skeletons of microscopic sea creatures (diatoms). It is dusted on plants and soil to control a wide range of insects. Unfortunately, it kills spiders and beneficial insects as well. Always wear goggles and a mask when using it. It works best in dry weather.

Horticultural oils: There are many types of oils on the market that are considered organic. However, they should not be used when temperatures are higher than 90°F or lower than 40°F. They also should not be used when humidity is above 65 percent.

Insecticidal soap: Fatty acids toxic to soft-bodied insects. Use on a small infested area, and wait forty-eight hours to see whether plant tissue is affected. If it is, don't use the soap.

Kaolin clay (Surround® WP): A naturally occurring clay made into a powder, mixed with water, and sprayed on plants to protect them from insects. It is more commonly used by mini-farmers than home gardeners.

Lime sulfur: This smelly liquid is used to kill bacteria, fungi, and insects, primarily on the canes of dormant plants. Never apply it at temperatures over 80°F. It is considered organic with restrictions.

Milky spore disease (*Paenibacillus popilliae*, formerly *Bacillus popilliae*): A naturally occurring bacteria that kills the grubs of Japanese beetles. It is considered to be less effective in cold climates than in milder ones. Anyway, Japanese beetles can fly into your garden from a mile or more away. I include it only because it is mentioned so frequently in publications as a control for this pest.

Neem (azadirachtin): The crushed seeds of the neem tree produce an oil that has proven toxic to a wide range of insects. The product kills some insects slowly or makes them less likely to feed on sprayed foliage. It may also be effective at killing powdery mildew spores.

Permethrin: *Do not confuse this with pyrethrum or pyrethrin.* This is a synthetic insecticide, one of the pyrethroids, which also include bifenthrin and d-phenothrin (sumithrin). The product kills fish, and many believe it kills bees as well. This product is toxic to cats. It is commonly available, but do not use it.

Pyrethrins: Pyrethrins are the insecticidal components of pyrethrum often mixed with rotenone and piperonyl butoxide, the latter known as a synergist, an agent that helps the insecticides become more potent. Pyrethrins do not kill spider mites but do kill fish. Piperonyl butoxide should not be considered organic.

Pyrethroids: Pyrethroids are synthetic compounds made to act like pyrethrins. They are very toxic to beneficial insects and long lasting. Their use is widespread, but they have no place in the organic garden.

Pyrethrum: This is an insecticide made from the dried and pulverized flowers of *Tanacetum cinerariifolium (Chrysanthemum cinerariaefolium)* and *Tanacetum coccineum (Chrysanthemum coccineum)*.

Rotenone: This dust or wettable powder comes from the roots of *Derris elliptica* and is both a contact and stomach poison. Some organic gardeners will use it, others won't, depending on which branch of the organic gardening fraternity they belong to. Rotenone, already potent, is often mixed with pyrethrin to make it even more effective against many insects. Rotenone is toxic to bees, fish, and beneficial insects, including ladybugs. Depending on its formulation it may be more toxic than Sevin® (carbaryl), which is the most commonly used *synthetic* insecticide in the United States. Carbaryl is considered to be carcinogenic, and its use has been banned in many European countries.

Ryania: This dust is made from the stems of a South American shrub (*Ryania speciosa*). It is both a contact and stomach poison used in foliar sprays to kill a wide number of insects.

Sabadilla: This dust is the pulverized seeds of a South American lily (*Schoenocaulon officinale*) and acts as a contact and stomach poison for a number of insects. It does kill bees. Wear a mask if using this.

Spinosad (pronounced spine-OH-sad): A bacteria (*Saccharopolyspora spinosa*) that must be ingested by insects to be fatal. It needs regular reapplication to be effective. It is deadly to bees.

Sulfur: Used for thousands of years as a fungicide and is especially effective on rust, which should be a rare problem in cold climates.

If put on the spot, I would use only *Bt*, insecticidal soap, pyrethrum, and spinosad in my garden. The overuse of *Bt* may lead to resistance in targeted insects but is presently still effective. The other products do kill beneficial insects, but they are relatively safe to use if directions on the label are followed to the letter. These products are available in many nurseries and online. Still, I do not use them.

Note that organic gardeners have come up with hundreds of recipes for sprays to deal with disease and kill insects.

Commonly included in these potions are detergent (this can damage foliage), garlic, geranium leaves, horsetail *(Equisetum arvense)*, milk (for powdery mildew), mint, molasses (fifty parts water to one part molasses), onions (green), pepper, self-rising flour (1 cup flour, 1¼ teaspoon baking powder, ¼ teaspoon salt), shallots, soap (not detergent), stinging nettle, thyme (lemon scented), tomato (blended leaves), and wood ash. Since I don't use any of these, I have no idea whether they work. I often think the effort, time, and money spent on making and testing these is better used in looking after the garden itself.

Insects

I have spent years studying the life cycles of insects. I have portfolios outlining what to do with which insect, photos of what they look like, and so on. Yes, I have had trouble with a dozen or so insects, sometimes quite a bit, but I have learned that with patience I can deal with them.

While I do not use pesticides in the garden, I realize that knowing something about common insects will be helpful. Many of these can be controlled by simple or-

Many plants, such as garden huckleberry, can be ravaged by insects and still produce a reasonable crop.

ganic methods, such as handpicking adults, crushing egg masses, spraying plants off with water, using row covers and physical barriers to stop damage, avoiding heavily promoted pheromone traps, and so on. The number of possible insects that could be included in this section is extensive, so this is just a selection of those you are most likely to encounter. Included is a short description and possible control that does not require a pesticide. A note on pheromone traps: They do work, but you don't need to draw insects into the garden. If a neighbor is not a gardener, ask them if you can put a trap in their yard. Or just skip them altogether.

When checking plants for insects, it helps to have a magnifying glass or a photographer's magnifying glass (loupe). This way you can check colors, shapes, and sizes of insects more easily. Some insects are large and easily identified, but others are difficult to identify, and a few are essentially invisible. When crushing insects, you may want to wear gloves. Some discolor your skin, and some can be quite smelly. Neither result is more than a nuisance if you prefer to capture them barehanded.

Aphids (many species in the Aphididae family): Aphids (also known as blackflies, green flies, plant lice) are ¹⁄₁₀-inch, black, brown, green, pink, red, tan, white, or yellow soft-bodied, pear-shaped insects that often cluster along tips of stems or undersides of leaves. As they pierce tissue to suck out juices, they inject a toxin. Kill nearby ants, cut off and destroy heavily infested plant parts, spray off with a hose, rinse with nondetergent soapy water (1 tablespoon per gallon).

Asparagus beetles (*Crioceris* species): The common asparagus beetle *(Crioceris asparagi)* is ¼ inch long with a blue-black head, reddish body, and wings with pale patches edged red. Its larvae are grayish green with black heads. Both the larva and adult of this species feed on the young plants. The twelve-spotted asparagus beetle *(Crioceris duodecimpunctata)* is slightly larger with a reddish-orange body, black head, and six black dots on each wing. Its larvae are yellow orange with black heads. Adults of this species attack new growth and cause substantial damage. Both beetles cause the ends of emerging asparagus to curl into a shepherd's crook. Handpick if possible; clean out all asparagus ferns in the fall. Use an organic insecticide—my one exception, since this is a perennial plant. Or wait them out over a two- to three-year period. This sometimes works.

Cabbage looper (*Trichoplusia ni*): Cabbage loopers are the larvae of a brownish-gray night-flying moth with about a 1½-inch wingspan. The moth lays round, white eggs on plants in spring, which develop into light-green caterpillars with thin white to light-yellow lines on each side. They move in a looping motion, from which they get their name.

Cabbage loopers eat holes in leaves, leaving them looking ragged. Cover plants with row covers to stop the moth from laying eggs on the plants; handpick larvae.

Cabbage root maggot (*Delia brassicas* and *Delia radicum*): The cabbage root fly (*Delia brassicas*) looks like a ¼-inch housefly. Its eggs develop into ¼-inch, white, soft, legless maggots (*Delia radicum*) that eat into roots of brassicas. Plants usually wilt even when well watered. Use row covers to keep flies away. Or place 6-inch-square pieces of carpet pad around the base of each plant *when planting.*

Carrot rust fly (*Psila rosae*): A ¼-inch black fly with yellowish hairs, head, and legs. Its eggs develop into ½-inch-long, white to yellowish maggots that nibble on roots and introduce bacteria to the wound. Plants often wilt and rot. Avoid damaging foliage, which may emit an odor that attracts the fly. Cover emerging plants with a row cover.

Colorado potato beetle (*Leptinotarsa decemlineata*): The adult beetle, often referred to as the potato bug, resembles a ⅜-inch ladybug with an orange head but a body with black and yellow stripes on its hard, outer wing covers. The adult lays yellowish-orange eggs in clusters on the undersides of leaves. These develop in stages into pinkish-orange humpbacked larvae with two rows of black spots on each side. These pupate in the soil. The adults and larvae skeletonize foliage and stems as they feed voraciously. Place row covers over young plants. Use a thick mulch (up to 12 inches deep). Handpick adults daily. Destroy egg masses.

Corn earworm (also known as tomato fruitworm) (*Helicoverpa zea* or *Heliothis zea*): This 1½-inch, yellowish-tan to grayish-brown, night-flying moth (noctuid) lays yellowish eggs on the undersides of leaves. These develop into larvae that may be green white, pinkish, or brown and will mature to a length of roughly 1¾ inches. The insect has light stripes on its side and back. Early maturing larvae eat leaves; ones that mature later attack fruits. When the larvae feed on the silk and tender kernels of corn at the tip of the ear, they are known as corn earworms. When they invade the fruit of tomatoes, they are called tomato fruitworms, but they are the same insect. Cut out worms from corn before eating. Handpick insects off tomatoes.

Corn rootworm (*Diabrotica* species): The ¼-inch adults of northern corn rootworm (*Diabrotica barberi*) are cream colored when young, maturing to a tannish green, while the ⁵⁄₁₆-inch adults of western corn rootworm (*Diabrotica virgifera* var. *virgifera*) are yellowish green with black stripes. The adults lay eggs in the soil late in the season. These hatch the following spring. The slender, white larvae with brown heads are up to ½ inch long. They develop in stages before pupating, then emerge as adults, sometimes in one season, occasionally in two. The adults feed on pollen, silk, and leaves. Damage to silk often interferes with pollination so that ears contain few developed kernels. Adults are most active in the morning and late afternoon. The larvae feed on roots, causing minor to serious damage, the latter resulting in distorted or weak stalks susceptible to disease and death. Nothing is effective against these rootworms.

Cutworm (species in the Noctuidae family): Cutworms are the larvae of night-flying moths. There are many species of cutworms, which may be black, brown, or gray and spotted or striped but generally have smooth, soft bodies. Most are about 1 inch or a little longer, and they will curl up into a C when poked. They feed at night, typically on plant tissue at the soil surface, but this can vary. Cutworms curl around the base of many vegetables, killing them by eating a ring around the stem until the plant topples over. Protect the base of seedlings with cutworm collars, any material wrapped or placed around the stem when planting. These should be at least 2 inches above the soil and 1 inch below and roughly ½ inch away from the stem itself. Collars can be as simple as a ring of newspaper or cardboard, the bottom of a plastic bottle (bottom removed and slit upwards), two split straws facing each other around the stem, the cardboard center of toilet paper, and so on. Another measure is to place a toothpick or wooden match on each side of the lower portion of stem. This may prevent the cutworm from being able to encircle the area. Also definitely effective is to check the base of plants at night with a flashlight, handpick the cutworms, and squish them on the spot. Look for slugs at the same time.

Earwig (*Forficula auricularia*): Earwigs, "pincher bugs," are elongated, ¾-inch, reddish to blackish-brown insects with little pincers on their rear ends. Generally, they do little damage and do eat some harmful insects. If they go after your plants, that's another matter. They are night feeders, hiding in the day. They sometimes feed on seedlings and young foliage. Put 12-inch pieces of hose or rolled-up newspaper (bound with twine or rubber bands) in the garden at night. In the day dump the earwigs from their hiding place into hot water.

European corn borer (*Ostrinia nubilalis*): This roughly 1-inch, yellowish-brown, night-flying moth lays cream-colored eggs on the undersides of leaves. These develop into 1-inch, light-pink to gray larvae with brown heads and spots on their sides. These larvae (borers) eat into the stalk of the plant and cause damage by interfering with the movement of fluids from the roots to the stem and leaves. Stagger plantings. Get stalks out of the garden as soon as corn is picked.

Flea beetle (species in the Chrysomelidae family): Flea beetles, often no larger than 1/16 inch, are typically black, brown, gray, green, or yellowish. These ultratiny, round, shiny insects have an awesome jumping ability and an equal appetite. Look for them with a magnifying glass. They and their larvae leave seedlings looking like they have been shot with a miniature shotgun. Protect plants with row covers. Run a greased board above the plants. They jump up and get stuck—at least in theory (I have only read about this).

Grasshopper (species in the Locustidae and Tettigoniidae families): Grasshoppers are elongated insects that vary in color but have long hind legs and hard body coverings. A few grasshoppers do little damage, but when concentrated, especially during drought, they destroy entire patches of vegetables by eating foliage. Till gardens thoroughly in the fall to expose clusters of rice-like eggs to birds. Catch by hand (use net if necessary), and do this early in the day, when they are sluggish.

Grubs (white grubs): The C-shaped white grub is the larva stage of 1,500 species of beetles. The larvae usually have brown to blackish heads and soft, mushy, fleshy bodies. Grubs may damage the roots of many edible crops. Till the soil well in spring and fall. This brings grubs to the surface, where birds can feast on them. Destroy any you see, although they make excellent fish bait.

Harlequin bug (*Acrocinus longimanus* or *Murgantia histrionica*): This shiny, black and red bug, found mostly in the South, reaches about ¼ inch and has a large triangle on its back. Adults are shield shaped, while nymphs are more rounded. It sucks juices from foliage, which turns a blotchy white and transmits disease in the process. Handpick.

Imported cabbage worm (*Pieris rapae*): This is a white, day-flying butterfly with black spots on its wings. It lays clusters of tiny, green eggs. Look for these in the crotches of leaves next to the stem. These hatch into cabbage worms, light green with a yellow stripe, which have the most incredible appetites. When you see shredded leaves dangling from your once-healthy plants, you have been blitzed by these bad guys. Cover cole crops with a gauzelike netting or row cover. Capture and kill using butterfly nets, but they are so common and plentiful that this can be time-consuming and borders on pointless. Crush eggs with your finger or a cotton swab. Handpick worms.

Japanese beetle (*Popillia japonica*): Japanese beetles are shiny, ¼- to ½-inch insects, usually coppery brown with green heads and white tufts of hair on their bellies. They feed voraciously, leaving behind skeletonized leaves. Adults lay eggs in the soil. These develop into grayish-white grubs with brown heads and emerge as adults the following season. The grubs feed on roots; the adults, on leaves. Never use traps laced with sex hormones (pheromones). Handpick daily, preferably in early morning, when beetles are lethargic. Squish or drop into soapy or vinegary water. Beetles often drop as you try to handpick them. Have a container just below to catch them as they fall. Milky spore, used against these beetles, is not effective in cold climates.

Leafhopper (species in the Cicadellidae family): There are a number of species of leafhoppers affecting a variety of crops. Depending on their stage of maturity, they can move sideways, fly, or hop (from which they get their names). Adult leafhoppers are ⅛-inch, wedge-shaped insects with slender iridescent green wings held like a roof above the body. They lay eggs on the undersides of leaves. These develop into paler-green nymphs that mature in stages to adults. Nymphs and adults suck juice from foliage and inject a toxin at the same time, which causes leaves to discolor, turning whitish to yellow to brown as if scorched. Leaves may also appear distorted, curl in from the edges, or wilt. Infested plants are often stunted and lack vigor. The insects also transmit diseases (viruses and mycoplasma). Protect plants with row covers. Remove infested leaves early on. Get rid of perennial weeds in the area, such as thistles and dandelions.

Leafminer (*Liriomyza trifoli, Phytomyza miniscula,* and many others): Small, black and yellow flies insert eggs inside leaf tissue. These develop into thin, pale-green to yellowish, ⅛- to ¼-inch maggots. They eat channels ("mines") into the foliage, causing blistering, blotching, and discoloration of leaf surfaces. Leaves may shrivel, turn whitish, and drop off. Larvae fall to the ground and pupate. There are dozens of different leafminers that do similar damage. Protect plants with row covers. Remove and destroy the blotchy leaves as soon as possible.

Maggots: See cabbage root maggot, carrot rust fly, onion maggot, and seed corn maggot.

Mexican bean beetle (*Epilachna varivestis*): Mexican bean beetles look like a ¼-inch, copper-colored ladybug with eight black spots on each wing cover. They lay yellow-orange eggs on the undersides of leaves. These become ⅓-inch, yellow-orange larvae. Both adults and larvae chew holes in leaves, stems, and pods. They eat most of the leaf but not the veins, so leaves end up with a lacy appearance. Handpick and destroy adults and eggs.

Onion maggot (*Delia antique*): Onion root maggot flies are grayish brown with humped backs. The ⅓-inch flies are most active in cool, moist weather and often emerge as dandelions begin to bloom. The fly lays white, elongated, ¹⁄₂₅-inch eggs at the base of the plant. These hatch into ⅓-inch, cream larvae that penetrate bulbs and feed on roots, stem, and the bulb itself. Foliage discolors and wilts; bulbs often rot. The insects survive winters as pupae that look like brownish grains of wheat. Start onions as sets, not seed or plants, since thinning often attracts the fly. Plant in several locations, not all in one spot.

Seed corn maggot *(Delia platura)*: The adult is a ⅕-inch gray fly, similar to, but more frail-looking, than a housefly. It lays eggs that turn into ¼-inch maggots that destroy corn seeds, especially in cool, wet soil. Plant seed in warm soil so that it sprouts quickly. Add manure to soil in fall, not spring.

Slugs and snails (a number of species in varied families): Slugs are snails without a shell. These moist mollusks (not insects) work at night, leaving behind a slimy trail that sparkles silver in the morning sun. They are most common in moist areas. They skeletonize leaves with rasping tongues covered with thousands of miniscule teeth. Go outside with a flashlight at night, and hunt them down. Grab them with tweezers if you don't like handling them. Toss them into a can filled with salt water or vinegar. Or in the evening, lay warped boards or black plastic on the ground. Slugs will slide and hide under them as daylight approaches. Lift these in the morning, and remove and destroy slugs. Toads eat slugs. Attract them into the garden with shallow bowls of water. The edge must be level with the soil surface. Iron phosphate pellets scattered throughout the garden will kill slugs and are much safer than poisoned baits. They should not come in contact with stems or foliage.

Southern rootworm: See spotted cucumber beetle.

Spider mites (varying species in the Tetranychidae family): Spider mites with their eight legs are not insects but are related to spiders and ticks. They are most common in hot, dry weather. It's difficult to see them since they are less than the size of a pinhead. Slip white paper under a leaf, and tap it hard. Mites pop off and show up as tiny red specks. A fine webbing on the underside of leaves is a good sign of an infestation. Spider mites suck sap from foliage and inject a toxin at the same time. Plants are often stunted and have discolored foliage, which may drop off. Dust plants with lime sulfur as a last resort. Water late in the day to increase humidity (an exception to the general rule). Spray off foliage with a jet of water.

Spotted cucumber beetle *(Diabrotica undecimpunctata)*: The ¼-inch, spotted cucumber beetle is yellowish orange with six black spots on each side of its back. Their whitish larvae, known as southern rootworms, develop from orange eggs and are about ½ inch long with brown heads. They feed on roots, while the adults chew on leaves and stems. The adults transmit bacterial wilt and mosaic virus, which may cause plants to wilt and die. Cover with row covers. Handpick adults, and drop into soapy water.

Spotted wing drosophila *(Drosophila suzukii)*: At one time blueberries rarely had problems with insects. Unfortunately, in recent years the spotted wing drosophila has become a serious pest to blueberries and brambles in cold climates. These tiny, yellowish-brown flies with clear wings deposit eggs that turn into damaging larvae up to ⅛ inch as they mature. The adults can be killed in traps. The University of Minnesota recommends drilling several ⅜-inch holes in a 32-ounce cup, baiting the trap with 1 inch of apple cider vinegar, and placing yellow sticky cards inside. Get these traps in place immediately once the insects appear. This is usually just as a crop begins to turn color. Use pyrethrum or spinosad as a last resort.

Squash bug *(Anasa tristis)*: The shield-shaped squash bug looks like, but is not, a stinkbug. It's a flat-backed insect, grayish black, and about ⅝ inch long. It lays clusters of 1⁄16-inch eggs on the undersides of leaves. These tiny eggs, shaped like miniature footballs, change color as they mature and may appear brown, red, or yellowish. Adults and their young, grayish-green, ½-inch nymphs pierce and suck juice from leaves, causing them to wilt and dry. Protect plants with row covers. Handpick and destroy adults and egg clusters. Lay boards on the ground to attract the insects. Lift up early in the morning to spot and kill the adults. Remove mulch, and don't mulch the following year, since mulch can be a hiding place for these insects.

Squash vine borer *(Melittia cucurbitae)*: The adult squash borer, sometimes mistaken for a colorful wasp, is actually a 1½-inch, daytime-flying moth with orange and black markings. It lays greenish-brown to reddish eggs on stems and leaf stalks at the base of the plant. In about a week eggs hatch into whitish-green larvae with brown heads. They grow to about 1 inch long when mature. The larvae bore into a stem, usually as plants begin to flower. As they drill into the stem, they leave behind a sawdust-like, greenish-yellow to orange excrement called frass near a small hole at the base of the plant. After feeding, they burrow into the soil to pupate, forming a protective cover to get them through the winter. The boring damages stems, and plants suddenly wilt and may die. Anchor floating row covers over young plants. Remove these once plants begin to flower. Place yellow buckets filled with water around plants in June and July. Moths may be attracted to these and drown. Once they are into a plant, surgery is required. Make an incision by the hole at the base of the plant, and cut up the stem until you find the larvae. Stab them with any thin, pointed object. Cover the cut stem with a mound of soil. If the plant has begun to spread out, bury the vine at every fifth node to make it take root. Start a second planting. This one will usually be free of infestation, but it may be too late for a good crop.

Stink bug (brown marmorated stink bug *[Halymorpha halys]*, brown stink bug *[Eucchistis servus]*, southern green stink bug *[Nezara viridula]*): Stink bugs are all shield shaped but vary in color and size, although most adults are roughly ⅝ inch. The brown marmorated stink bug (creamy brown), brown stink bug (dark brown), and southern green stink bug (green with white specks) all lay clusters of elliptical to barrel-shaped eggs on the undersides of leaves. The eggs develop in stages into nymphs. The insects overwinter as adults in available shelter. The nymphs and adults pierce plants and suck out juices. Foliage may curl up and be malformed. Fruit may be spotted, pimpled, or warted. Protect plants with floating row covers. With a gloved hand, knock the insects into soapy water or crush eggs. Place a can under the insect, since it may drop when disturbed. Remove organic mulch if stink bugs are present. They use it as a hiding place.

Striped cucumber beetle (Acalymma vittatum): The ¼-inch, striped cucumber beetle is yellow with three black stripes running down its back. Their orange eggs develop into white larvae that feed on roots, while adults chew on leaves and stems. They transmit bacterial wilt (Erwinia aracheuphilia) and viruses that may cause plants to wilt and die. Protect plants with row covers. Handpick.

Tomato fruitworm: See corn earworm.

Tomato hornworm (Protoparce quinquemaculata or Manduca quinquemaculata): The grayish hawk moth with an orange-spotted body and a wingspan of up to 5 inches can be mistaken for a hummingbird in flight. It lays round, greenish-yellow to pale-green eggs on the undersides of leaves. These develop into fat, pale-green, white-striped larvae up to 4 inches long. The caterpillar (larva) gets its name from a harmless red to brown thorn, or "horn," that sticks up from its hind end. It is often attacked by parasitic wasps. It does damage by feeding on leaves, stems, and fruit. The larvae pupate over winter. Pick them by hand at night or early in the morning, and destroy in a bleach solution. Till soil in fall to expose pupae. Note that if you find a hornworm covered with white eggs that look like little white cocoons, you should leave it alone. The eggs will develop into parasitic wasps, allies in your garden. Move if off the plant to a different place along with some tomato foliage. It will not live long.

White cabbage butterfly: See imported cabbage worm.

Whitefly (Trialeurodes vaporariorum and others): Whiteflies are ¹⁄₁₀-inch or smaller, winged insects that swirl up in a cloud when disturbed. They lay eggs on the undersides of leaves. These develop into flat, oval to oblong "scales," usually whitish green to yellow. In turn these mature into legless, greenish-yellow nymphs. The insects suck juices from plants and often infect plants with viral diseases. Damage usually consists of leaves turning yellow, curling up, and dying. The insects secrete a sticky "honeydew," which may turn into a black mold. Paint molded areas with bleach (1½ percent sodium hypochlorite), and hose off with water within thirty minutes. Snip off infested leaves early. Cut thin strips of plastic from yellow antifreeze bottles. Cover these with petroleum jelly. Hang these near infested plants. Whiteflies will be attracted to the color and will get stuck. Clean regularly.

Wireworm (Alaus or Conoderus species): Wireworms are slender, almost hard-shelled creatures (⅓ to 1½ inches), usually dark brown, orange, or yellow and cylindrical. They have jointed bodies and appear shiny. They won't curl up if you touch them. They lay eggs in soil. These develop into larvae. Adults and larvae attack the roots and tubers (occasionally seeds and stems) of many plants. They are most common when a wild or sodded area is first converted into a vegetable garden. Put potato slices on a shish kebab skewer, and stick it into the soil, or place one large slice of potato cut end down about 1 inch deep. Dig up after two days, and destroy the worms. Till soil in spring and fall to expose eggs and adults to birds. Kill any you see.

Disease

In 1986 I bought the book *Vegetable Diseases and Their Control* by Arden F. Sherf and Alan A. MacNab. It's 728 pages and may be a great book, but I don't use it. It sits on my shelf as a reminder that much of what we worry about never comes true. Professionals with years of experience look at diseased plants and say they would have to take a sample back to the laboratory to determine the problem—a bacteria, fungus, mycoplasma (virus-bacteria combination), or a virus? What home gardener has that kind of luxury? And how much loss really can be contributed to disease each year? Always some, but not much. The same cannot be said for commercial crops grown in large fields, but this growing guide is primarily for the home gardener.

While I have provided a list of insects that may be a problem for your garden, not only because they damage plants but also because they carry disease, I am not going to do the same for diseases. You can examine an insect and identify what it is, but as I said above, you can't determine what disease is affecting your plant merely by looking at blotches, discoloration, stunting, wilting, and so on. Once plants are infected, it may be too late anyway. Disease prevention is expensive and introduces chemicals into the garden that affect the natural order, whereas you can do something to get rid of insects *without chemicals*.

There are natural ways to prevent disease in the garden. These have been practiced for centuries, and they work well for the home gardener. Plant disease-resistant varieties, and choose varieties suited to cold climates. Buy certified

Corn smut, an ugly fungal growth, is a delicacy in some countries, where it is harvested young, well before it turns black.

seed or plants. Plant the same seed in more than one location. Protect young plants with row covers to prevent insects from spreading disease. Stake or cage plants to keep mature fruit off the ground. Use mulch to stop soil from splashing up on foliage during wet weather or watering. Disinfect tools. Kill weeds in and around the garden. Don't wound the stems or roots of plants. Never smoke in the garden, and wash your hands before working with plants if you are a smoker. Avoid working in the garden when it is wet. Cut off diseased foliage as soon as you see it, and dig up and destroy wilted plants if they do not respond to watering. Till or spade organic matter into the garden each fall. Clean up all dead plants from the garden in fall.

Crop Rotation

One thing mentioned on almost every seed package is crop rotation. The concept behind crop rotation is simple. Different families of plants are susceptible to completely different diseases. Don't plant vegetables within the same family in the same spot each year. Commercial growers practice this routinely. The home gardener is at a disadvantage since

space may be limited. But you can plant a tomato in one corner of the garden one year, then in another the next. In larger gardens you can build a number of beds. Change the crops grown in each one each year. This is especially important when you have already had a disease problem with a specific crop. Plant a different group of plants in that area the following year. Think of each family as if it were one plant. Do not plant the same plant in the same location year after year.

Some gardeners disagree with this strategy since it leads to planting members of the same family in proximity in one bed one year and close together in a different bed the following year. They view this as putting all of your eggs in one basket. Instead, they place plants willy-nilly throughout the garden and change the planting area each year, which is in essence a form of disorganized rotation. Experiment. For those who want to follow traditional advice, I have provided a list of families.

Solarization

While less commonly recommended than crop rotation, solarization is another technique available to organic gardeners to fight disease in the home garden. It also helps break down organic matter in the soil to release nitrogen, which becomes readily available to plants. The idea is to heat soil to as high a temperature as possible to kill many disease-causing organisms (fungal and bacterial pathogens), insects, nematodes, and weed seeds. This is done using the energy from the sun. It is easy to do, but it requires the area being solarized to be taken out of production for weeks.

First, pull up and remove all weeds, till the soil lightly, and rake smooth, making sure that it is ready for planting after the heat treatment. Dig a 6- to 8-inch trench around the area being solarized. Saturate the soil to a depth of 12 inches. Then cover the area with clear plastic, tucking the plastic tightly into place, and fill in the trench so the plastic remains in direct contact with the soil. Anchor the edges of the plastic so that air cannot get in. Solarization is most effective when plastic hugs the soil.

Solarize in the hottest part of the summer for four to eight weeks. In full sun the temperatures under the plastic may get up to 140°F on the soil surface but increasingly less hot deeper down. The hotter the temperature, the better. In cool or cloudy weather the process may take longer. Also, weed seeds may sprout if the temperature is too cool or if air is allowed to get under the plastic. Thin plastic 1 mil thick (1/1000 of an inch) heats soil better than thicker plastics, but it is easily damaged. Most gardeners go with thicker, 4-mil plastic, the type used by painters

Plant Families

Adoxaceae (muskroot family), formerly Caprifoliaceae (honeysuckle family)
- elderberry

Aizoaceae (carpetweed family)
- New Zealand spinach

Alliaceae or Amaryllidaceae (onion or amaryllis family), formerly Liliaceae (lily family)
- chives
- garlic
- leeks
- onion
- ramps
- scallion
- shallot

Amaranthaceae (amaranth or goosefoot family), formerly Chenopodiaceae (goosefoot family)
- amaranth (grain)
- amaranth (vegetable)
- beet (beetroot)
- lamb's quarters
- orach (mountain spinach)
- spinach
- Swiss chard

Apiaceae (parsley family), formerly Umbelliferae
- caraway
- carrot
- celeriac
- celery
- chervil
- cilantro (coriander)
- dill
- fennel, bulb
- fennel, leaf or sweet
- Florence fennel
- Hamburg parsley (turnip-rooted parsley)
- lovage
- mitsuba
- parsley
- parsnip

Apocynaceae (dogbane family), formerly Asclepiadaceae (milkweed family)
- milkweed

Asparagaceae (asparagus family), formerly Liliaceae (lily family)
- asparagus

Asteraceae (sunflower family), formerly Compositae
- artichoke, globe
- Belgian endive
- burdock
- cardoon
- celtuce (stem lettuce)
- chamomile
- chrysanthemum
- dandelion
- endive
- escarole
- Italian dandelion
- lettuce
- marigold
- radicchio
- salsify
- scorzonera
- stevia
- sunchoke (Jerusalem artichoke)
- sunflower
- tarragon

Basellaceae (Malabar spinach family)
- Malabar spinach

Boraginaceae (borage family)
- borage
- comfrey, Russian

Brassicaceae (cabbage or mustard family), formerly Cruciferae
- arugula (rocket)
- broccoli
- broccoli raab (rapini)
- Brussels sprouts
- cabbage
- cauliflower
- Chinese broccoli (gai-lan) (Chinese kale)
- Chinese cabbage
- Chinese mustard
- collards
- garden cress
- horseradish
- Japanese horseradish (wasabi)
- kale (borecole)
- kohlrabi
- mibuna
- mizuna
- mustard
- mustard spinach (komatsuna)
- radish
- rape
- rutabaga
- turnip
- Tyfon Holland Greens
- upland cress
- watercress

Convolvulaceae (morning glory family)
- sweet potato

Cucurbitaceae (cucumber, gourd, or squash family)
- bitter melon (bitter gourd)
- cucumber (gherkin)
- gourds
- muskmelon
- pumpkin
- squash (summer and winter)
- watermelon

Ericaceae (heath family)
- blueberry

Fabaceae (pea or pulse family), formerly Leguminosae
- asparagus bean (yardlong bean)
- asparagus pea
- bean
- broad bean (fava bean)
- chickpea (garbanzo bean)
- cowpea (southern pea)
- ground nut (Indian potato)
- peas
- peanut
- soybean
- yardlong bean

Grossulariaceae (currant family)
- currant
- gooseberry

Lamiaceae (mint family), formerly Labiatae
- basil
- catnip
- lavender
- lemon balm
- marjoram, sweet
- mint
- oregano
- perilla
- rosemary
- sage
- savory
- thyme

Malvaceae (mallow family)
- malva
- okra

Onocleaceae (wood fern family), formerly under Dryopteridaceae
- ostrich fern

Plantaginaceae (plantain family)
- minutina
- plantain

Poaceae (grass family), formerly Gramineae
- cat grass
- corn
- lemongrass
- wheatgrass

Polygonaceae (buckwheat or knotweed family)
- rhubarb
- sorrel (spinach dock)

Portulacaceae (purslane family)
- miner's lettuce (claytonia)
- purslane

Rosaceae (rose family)
- blackberry
- raspberry
- salad burnet
- strawberry

Solanaceae (nightshade family)
- eggplant
- garden huckleberry
- ground cherry
- peppers
- potato (Irish or white)
- tomatillo
- tomato
- wonderberry (garden huckleberry)

Tetragoniaceae (New Zealand spinach family)
- New Zealand spinach

Tropaeolaceae (nasturtium family)
- nasturtium

Urticaceae (nettle family)
- nettle

Valerianaceae (valerian family)
- corn salad (mâche)

Verbenaceae (verbena family)
- lemon verbena

Violaceae (violet family)
- violet

Xanthorrhoeaceae (grass tree family)
- daylily

when painting a house. This reduces the chance of having to cover the first sheet of plastic with a second as the first deteriorates or gets torn.

Once the area has been solarized, lift up the plastic, and plant a crop. Do not disturb more than the top 2 inches of soil, or you will bring weed seeds to the surface.

Do not expect this heat treatment to kill deep-rooted perennial weeds. The temperature achieved by solarization is not high enough to kill some pathogens, including some viruses. While it does kill some beneficial microorganisms, their population explodes once the plastic is removed. Worms are not affected since they can tunnel down to cooler areas.

To solarize soil for containers, place it in black bags or large buckets no deeper than a foot, and wrap with a layer of clear plastic held firmly in place in a bright, sunny location. The bags or pots should be raised off any hard surface to allow air circulation to raise temperatures both on top and underneath the containers. Under ideal conditions the temperature may reach 160°F; however, it only needs to get to 140°F for roughly an hour to be effective. For even hotter temperatures, some gardeners place a second layer over the first, using spacers such as cans or water bottles to keep the two separated. The sunlight heats the upper layer, the air in between, and then the lower layer of plastic. This method results in a dramatic increase in temperature, soaring well above 160°F.

If you have only a small amount of soil to "sterilize," pour boiling water over it. Baking soil in an oven is sometimes suggested as well, but the mess and smell turn most people off. Unless the temperature of the soil reaches 180°F for an extended period of time, the process should be called soil pasteurization. Pasteurization rather than true sterilization preserves at least some beneficial soil microorganisms.

Marauders

A foolproof cure for garden marauders would be worth a million dollars. Here are some suggestions for dealing with the most common.

Birds: When planting large seeds, do not let any lie on top of the soil. If crows see these, they are smart enough to peck into the soil for hidden treasure. During the growing season, scare off birds with waving or flashy materials. This doesn't always work, so protect individual fruiting plants with netting. Grouse will eat blueberry flower buds in the far north. Protect each plant with a wire enclosure.

Cats: Cats don't do much damage in the garden, but they will use loose soil as litter. Keep them indoors unless you want them to hunt down rabbit nests. Unfortunately,

Stop deer from eating tips off Belgian endive and similar plants by constructing a good fence.

outdoor cats are estimated to kill between two and four billion birds each year in the United States alone. Since birds are one of your main allies in the garden, it makes sense not to let cats run loose.

Chipmunks: Chipmunks are generally a minor nuisance in the vegetable garden, but they do like to nibble on strawberries. If this is a severe problem, you can kill chipmunks with rat traps placed near their runs.

Deer: Deer will eat just about anything if they are hungry enough. The amount of damage they can do in one night of feeding is remarkable. To keep deer out of the garden, two types of fencing are recommended. The first is a 10-feet-high fence. This is allowed in rural areas but does not usually meet code in suburban areas. A 4- to 6-feet fence becomes effective if you stretch a second fence out and downward at a 45-degree angle from the main fence. Or stretch wire or strong fishing line between metal posts just a few feet outside the main fence. Deer do not like double fencing. Just laying a fence on the ground sometimes stops deer in their tracks.

Alternatives to fencing include expensive repellents or simple ones such as human hair or urine, soap hung off

Keep birds from devouring gooseberries and similar crops by covering the plants with netting early on.

the ground, sprays made with eggs mixed with water, and Milorganite® applied around, but not in, the garden—it is not considered an organic product.

Dogs: Like cats, the main problem in the garden is dogs' droppings, which are a health hazard.

Gophers (pocket and thirteen-lined ground squirrels): If the burrowing and damage by these rodents becomes a headache, use specialized traps to kill them. Avoid poisoned baits.

Groundhogs (also known as woodchucks): These animals are voracious feeders of anything green. The typical recommendation for keeping them out of the garden is a fence anchored at least 12 inches into the soil. The problem with this is that they can climb over and dig under fences. They form two holes for each tunnel. Shove wire into one, and place a live trap baited with vegetable scraps at the entrance to the other. Once trapped, move them to an area more than 10 miles away, or destroy them if allowed by local laws.

Mice: Mice will nibble on a few vegetables, such as tomatoes, during the growing season, but they are more of a health hazard than a garden marauder. Trap mice in the fall inside the garage, garden shed, or home. Bait the traps with ordinary American cheese or peanut butter. Snapping traps that kill mice instantly are far more humane than sticky traps or poison.

Moles: Moles kill many destructive insects. Trap them in active tunnels only if they are doing a lot of damage.

Rabbits: Rabbits are the scourge of home gardeners. They nibble on just about anything green during the growing season and forage on the stems of woody plants, such as blueberries, in the winter. High raised beds often deter rabbit damage but are expensive to build. Where allowed, people shoot rabbits. There are all sorts of repellents on the market. They are expensive and must be reapplied regularly.

A better solution is to build a fence and then encircle it with rabbit wire with holes so small that even baby rabbits cannot get through it. This double fencing is also expensive and takes effort and time to install, but it does work and is permanent. A compromise is to encircle prized plants with rabbit wire, leaving the rest of the garden more vulnerable. Many plants can sustain considerable damage and still spring back to life, providing a decent, if delayed, harvest.

Raccoons: These animals are perhaps the smartest of all marauders. They invade the garden at night and are especially fond of fresh corn, eating it just a few days before it matures. Electric wires running around the top of a fence are the best way to shock sense into these thieves, but this type of wiring is often prohibited in city and suburban areas. Live traps baited with fish or vegetable scraps work well and allow you to move the animals to distant locations or to destroy them according to local laws.

Skunks: Skunks often do more damage to lawns than vegetable gardens. Still, if they are a serious nuisance, live-trap them like raccoons. To avoid being sprayed when catching them, hold a long towel in front of you as you approach the trap, then drop it over the trap once close enough. This tip is courtesy of Havahart® traps.

Squirrels: When you plant peanuts, cover the areas with netting. Otherwise, you may find little peanut plants sprouting in the oddest places around your garden and yard. In general, squirrels are not a major problem for most vegetable gardeners, but there are exceptions. In these cases, livetrap the squirrels using peanuts or peanut butter as bait. Move or destroy the animals according to local laws.

Physiological Problems

It is sometimes difficult to tell the cause of a problem. Physiological problems often appear to be diseases or the result of insect infestations. Most physiological problems can be avoided by preparing the soil properly, keeping it properly fertilized and watered, and planting seeds and transplants when they should be. Following are a few problems not caused by disease or insects. There is one exception, shepherd's crook, which looks like it is physiological but is not.

Blossom end rot: Occasionally the end of the fruit farthest from the stem (the blossom end) may rot. This problem is caused by a lack of calcium in the soil or by the inability of the plant to absorb calcium. It is most commonly a problem with eggplant, peppers, and tomatoes. Keep the pH of the soil near neutral, and water plants consistently. Add calcium-rich gypsum or lime to the soil in case that nutrient is missing. Add these in the fall for the following year's crop.

Bolting: Plants that begin to go to seed too early are said to be bolting. This is one of the most common problems in the garden. Bolting is usually the result of too low or too high temperatures related to the plant's actual needs. Planting seed and transplants at the correct time in the growing season reduces bolting dramatically. Sometimes, removing the developing flower stalks prolongs the harvest. Some plants are bolt resistant, so read catalogs carefully.

Buttoning: The premature formation of cauliflower heads is not common in the home garden. Buttoning may occur, however, if seedlings are damaged by frost or improper handling, as in breaking off the growing tip, or if seedlings are allowed to get root-bound in a pot. Buttoning may also occur if plants are crowded, underfed (lack nitrogen), or too dry in the early stages of growth, and, possibly, if too many leaves are damaged by careless gardening. Transplant shock has also been blamed for buttoning.

Catfacing: This term describes fruit deformity, typically on tomatoes. It is probably caused by cool (50°F) nighttime temperatures while fruits are forming. The problem affects single fruits, so discard them, or cut good flesh off the fruit.

Color changes in foliage: Some color changes may be natural or a sign of nutrient deficiency. Keep your soil properly fertilized and at a near neutral pH. For example, if plants develop purplish coloration in their leaves, the soil may be deficient in phosphorus, which helps the plants move sugars properly throughout the plant rather than accumulate in the leaves.

Cracking fruit: Cracking of fruit, for example, tomatoes, is a mystery. The most common cause cited is inconsistent watering and fluctuations in weather conditions. Water

Cutting off the flowers of plants such as broccoli before they bloom stimulates additional edible growth.

Burdock and other root crops will form crooked roots if they bump into stones as they grow into the ground.

well during hot, dry weather. Cracking may also be related to the variety grown.

Flowers dropping off (blossom drop): On many vining plants the first flowers are male and simply drop off. This is not a problem. On other plants blossoms may drop off because of inconsistent water or fluctuations in temperature. This is usually a temporary problem.

Forked roots: Occasionally, root crops have forked roots. Two things are believed to cause this: rocks in the soil, and transplanting of plants that resent this. Some gardeners believe that the use of manure may also be responsible. In most instances, however, debris in the soil is the culprit.

Leaf curling: This problem is generally caused from overly wet conditions, as after a period of frequent, heavy rains. Other possible causes are overpruning, uneven watering, and spells of extremely high temperatures. Unfortunately, it may also be a sign of disease or lack of nutrients, commonly calcium. If the plant forms fruit, don't worry about it.

Leaf distortion: While this problem can have many causes, one that often goes by undetected is damage from herbicides such as 2,4-D (2,4-Dichlorophenoxyacetic acid) and dicamba, both used to kill broadleaf weeds in lawns. If these are applied to lawns as a fine mist, they can be carried by wind (drift). On still days, herbicides can evaporate and be circulated in the air (volatilization). Plants affected by drift or volatilization include beans, corn, cucumbers, muskmelons, pumpkins, soybeans, squash, and tomatoes. While you may not be using these products, neighbors might. More than a thousand products contain these substances. The only option is to talk with your neighbor in a friendly manner and ask to see the label of the product they are using. Supplying your neighbor with produce regularly doesn't hurt if you ask them to be more careful in following label directions. Companies that specialize in lawn care can also be responsible for damage to your plants. Unfortunately, they spray somewhat indiscriminately. Cut off damaged foliage, and water plants deeply if you suspect herbicide damage. Do this as quickly as possible.

Poor flavor or texture: Weather and inconsistent watering can affect the flavor and texture of vegetables. For example, hot weather often causes radishes to become overly hot and woody.

Poor or no fruiting: Poor fruit set is generally caused by lack of pollination in cold, rainy, or cloudy weather. If you experience this kind of weather while plants are blooming, hand pollinate. In artichokes it is caused by not letting young plants be exposed to cool temperatures for long enough in early growth, a process known as vernalization.

Cabbages and radishes will split if improperly watered or left to mature too long.

If plants are producing lots of foliage but no fruit, the soil probably contains too much nitrogen. In some cases the season is not long enough for some plants to produce in cold climates. Choose varieties that have shorter growing seasons.

Rotting of stems or foliage: Keep mulch away from stems. If water pools in foliage, it may cause rot. This is generally related to prolonged rains accompanied by cool temperatures. There is not much you can do about it except give plants more space for better air circulation.

Shepherd's crook: When asparagus forms spears in the form of a shepherd's crook or spears with overly dense foliage, this is not a physiological problem but the result of an asparagus beetle infestation.

Splitting roots (radish) or heads (cabbage): Heavy rain after drought, too much fertilizer, insect damage, and delayed harvest—all have been blamed for splitting. Too much watering once cabbage heads form seems the most likely cause early in the season; letting heads mature too long is more likely late in the season. Harvest plants on time. Although there are varieties that resist splitting, they won't last forever if not harvested in a timely manner.

Rot in root interiors: This may be caused by a boron deficiency in the soil. Sometimes, fruits, such as strawberries, are hollow and not rotted. Cut down on your use of nitrogen.

Sunscald: Large, white blisters are caused by overexposure to the sun. Heavy pruning or loss of foliage from disease may allow too much light to hit developing fruit. Remove fruit, and compost. In the case of woody plants, stems may be damaged by reflected light during the winter. Woody tissue swells during warm periods, only to burst open when temperatures drop. Blueberry bushes covered with snow or protected by black plastic bags filled with leaves rarely suffer from sunscald.

Variation in yields: It is normal for plants to have varying yields. However, to increase yields on some plants, you may have to hand pollinate flowers, especially if weather is cold and rainy.

Wilting: When plants droop over, they usually are short on water. Feel the soil. It's probably dry. Soak the soil thoroughly, getting water deep down to the roots. If the plant does not respond, it is probably infected with a fatal disease. Wait a day or two. If the plant doesn't look better, dig it up, and dispose of it. Normal advice is to burn or toss it into the garbage.

CHAPTER 7

HARVESTING AND CULINARY USES

Harvesting

Expand your horizons by harvesting vegetables at various stages of growth and by eating parts of the plant you may never have tried before. For example, many leafy plants can be cut back during the early stage of growth and are now being sold as microgreens. Rather than buying these, grow your own. When and how to harvest individual plants is covered in each plant description in Part II. The critical thing to remember is that timing is everything when it comes to flavor and nutrient levels. Eating vegetables as quickly as possible after harvesting is extremely important for taste and nutrition. *Vegetables deteriorate rapidly once harvested.* The higher the temperature, the faster the deterioration. There are exceptions. Certain plants do not do well chilled. A few examples are basil, okra, and tomatoes. If a plant resents chilling, this is pointed out in its description.

Here are a few general tips concerning harvesting that are not repeated in the plant descriptions. When harvesting, avoid damaging the plant. Use scissors or a knife to snip or cut off fruit if necessary. Tugging on plants often dislodges roots and slows down or stops continued growth. Avoid har-

vesting in wet periods if possible. As you harvest, you may carry disease from one plant to another. This is possible at any time, but moisture helps pathogens increase in numbers.

Many plants have the best taste and possibly a higher nutrient level early and late in the day. In general, pick vegetables that mature aboveground late in the day, and those that mature below the ground early in the day. Compare taste and texture for yourself to see whether you agree. Herbs are often best harvested just as they dry in the morning. This is the point when their essential oils are at their peak. Some vegetables taste better after a frost or hard freeze; pick them at that time to let starches turn into sugars. Some vegetables will be ruined by cold, however, and must be picked before they are damaged. (This information is given in plant descriptions in Part II.)

Carry a container of cold water into the garden with you when harvesting crops that tend to wilt quickly. This is especially helpful with greens. If you are sensitive to prickly plants, wear gloves.

Organic vegetables often look worse than store-bought produce. A little clip here and there may be necessary to remove an affected plant part, but don't discard vegetables

This corn is not yet ready to pick: the silk has not begun to turn brown.

The tops of these onions have died back, showing that they are more than ready to be harvested.

simply because they are somewhat marred. If they are clearly diseased, overly bruised, or rotting, toss them into the compost pile. The idea of throwing diseased plant tissue into compost piles really bothers some gardeners and is controversial. I can only say that I have been doing it for more than half a century and have as healthy a garden as those who criticize this "habit."

Yield

Gardeners are often surprised by how much can be grown in a relatively small area. In larger gardens the amounts can be far more than one family needs, and you might give away much of what you produce. This leads some people into mini-farming for profit. Yield is affected by a number of factors.

Vegetable Choice and Varietal Choice

Different vegetables produce a lot in a little space. Beets, carrots, and lettuce are good examples. Others roam, taking up large amounts of space. Examples of space hogs are pumpkins and winter squash. Their production is also limited, considering the space they are taking up.

Numerous varieties are described in this guide. Some take up little space and produce prolifically. For example, 'Picklebush', a type of cucumber, doesn't ramble as much as other varieties and produces an incredible number of fruits. The experience of local gardeners and farmers can supplement the varietal information in this guide. Ask at farmers' markets. The people selling produce are growing it locally so will know which plants are most productive and best suited to your area.

Garden Types

Increase yield by using vertical gardens, where you grow appropriate crops on supports. Pole beans generally produce more beans over a longer period of time than bush beans. Peas can be grown on both sides of a wire fence, doubling the overall yield.

Raised beds tend to warm up faster in spring and are easily covered during cold snaps. They can extend your growing season by several weeks in any given spring. See "Extending the Growing Season" in chapter 4 for additional tips to increase yearly yield.

Weather

You have no control over the weather, but experienced gardeners pick up on cues that suggest changes from one year

Enjoying the bounty of fall on a dry, sunny day offers a special sense of accomplishment.

to the next. I have planted corn in April only once during sixty years of gardening, but the weather was so warm for so long and predicted to continue that I gambled and had corn well over my head by July 4. It was a gamble based on observation. Most years are more unpredictable. First and last frost dates are *averages,* and thus they are merely guides. Still, planting time does affect yield. When to plant is one of the main topics in Part II. Get seeds and plants into the garden when they should be planted, and your yield will change dramatically. But follow your instincts. Definitely gamble by planting a small number of seeds earlier and later than typically recommended.

Spacing

This is one of the more controversial subjects in gardening. What might make sense to someone growing crops for a living may have little to do with spacing in the home garden. Seed packages give suggested spacing. In reality, a number of gardeners ignore this and plant closer together than may be recommended. The spacing that works best for you in getting the most of any given vegetable is what counts. Try planting in double rows or in small or large blocks. Plant leafy plants in a three-two-three pattern, often called triangular or hexagonal planting. This ends up filling in empty space typically seen in straight rows. Experiment.

Proper Growing

Higher yields depend on how you grow plants. Providing them with the right conditions makes a huge difference in production. Following the recommendations in this guide, from soil preparation to proper care throughout a plant's life cycle, is critical to high yields. Any kind of stress can lower yield. You want plants to grow evenly throughout the season. The most common cause of "stop and start" growing is uneven watering.

Successive Planting

Experienced gardeners learn that planting some vegetables in small amounts every two to three weeks produces more than planting a larger crop all at once. Or they will plant one type of vegetable early and a different vegetable in the same area immediately after harvesting the first crop. This way the garden is always in use. Many people know about successive planting but don't do it as often as they could—including me. We live busy lives and sometimes don't have the time or energy to do this. But it does increase yields. Note that in a few cases successive planting makes less sense than one larger one. For example, if you freeze beans, you might want one large crop that you can process all at once rather than smaller crops spread out over time.

Plant quick-maturing plants, such as lettuce, between slower-maturing plants, such as carrots, in order to use space wisely.

Interplanting and Companion Planting

Some vegetables sprint to maturity, while others linger. By planting different crops together, called interplanting or catch cropping, you take advantage of all available space. For example, you can plant lettuce between broccoli or cabbage. As the latter grow, harvest the lettuce, and then remove the plants once the other crops begin to spread out. This is difficult to do for commercial farmers but relatively easy in the home garden.

Some people believe that you increase yields by planting specific plants next to each other, called companion planting. They even go further by stating that some plants react badly to others. Experienced gardeners agree or disagree adamantly about this idea. There is no question that in areas such as rain forests there are symbiotic relationships between plants, but can the same be true for annuals? I have tried companion planting and come to one conclusion: the greater the diversity of plants in the garden, the better. And that has nothing really to do with companion planting. It's simply throwing together vegetables, herbs, flowers, berries, and so on in a different manner each year. It is the opposite of monoculture, which is the norm today in agriculture. Diversity increases yield by decreasing problems with disease and insects.

Multiple Cropping

Many plants will produce more than once. Many greens can be cut back and will regrow. These are referred to as "cut and come again" crops. As long as you do not damage the growing point of the plant, you can get multiple harvests. Always water after cutting plants back. Also, some plants such as broccoli and cabbage can have their main heads removed but still produce smaller heads in the weeks to come. This too results in more than one crop.

Pollinators

A number of plants are self-fertile, but many require insects for proper pollination. Attract as many pollinators as you can by growing a wide variety of flowering plants in or near the garden. Consider letting vegetables go to seed even though they may no longer be of use in the kitchen. For example, once lettuce bolts (goes to flower), it is next to inedible, but the flowers it forms are attractive to a wide variety of insects that act as pollinators for many flowering vegetables in the garden. The better the rate of pollination, the higher the yield. It certainly beats having to hand pollinate the flowers of plants such as pumpkins and squash. Adding pollinators to the garden is sometimes recommended in discussion of companion planting.

Reducing Damage to Plants

Your yield will go up dramatically if you can keep animals out of the garden. See the section on "Marauders" in chapter 6.

Some gardeners believe that you increase the yield of desirable crops by luring insects away from them with trap crops, other plants that act like a "dessert" instead of a main course. The dessert crop may be planted around the edge of the garden or next to the crop you want to save. This is considered by some to be part of companion planting. Once again, gardeners disagree about its effectiveness. One of the problems is that the dessert crop may be no more desirable than the crop you want to save. I must admit that I have seen insects drawn to specific plants in any given year while leaving other plants alone, so I believe this strategy could work if you are willing to sacrifice one crop for another. However, like so many aspects of companion planting, the specific information on how to put this into practice is missing. Universities are studying this, but more for use by commercial growers than home gardeners. Also, the trap crops are often sprayed with pesticides to decimate the undesirable insects, and I am fundamentally opposed to the use of poisons.

Special techniques, such as presprouting (chitting) potatoes, result in earlier and sometimes larger yields.

Seed Pretreatment and Presprouting

Pretreatment of seeds is covered in detail in chapter 2. Increase potato yields by getting them to produce sprouts before planting. Potatoes are produced off to the sides of the stem. Although some gardeners allow only a few eyes to sprout, potatoes will produce fine without all the fuss. Presprouting, or chitting, is considered obsolete by some, but the late Robert Lobitz, who produced an amazing assortment of quality potatoes, believed that presprouting was essential to his success.

Storing

Most vegetables provide more nutrients when eaten fresh, although a few vitamins and phytochemicals are increased when plants are cooked or dried. Storing aims to keep the flavor and nutrient level as high as possible for extended use past the usual harvesting time. Information about how to store vegetables is provided in the plant descriptions in Part II.

Following are brief descriptions of storing methods. When storing root crops, remove the foliage for longer storage life. They are often sold in grocery stores with foliage, but it draws moisture out of the crops. Good examples are radishes and carrots.

Leaving Vegetables in the Garden

Some vegetables can be left in the ground and covered with mulch for extended use into the fall and even until the following spring. Others can be buried in the garden or covered with a mound of soil, which is in turn covered with a thick layer of straw. The mound usually looks like an inverted V. This is known by some as "clamping." Note that a number of vegetables actually taste better after a hard frost.

Storing in Moist Medium

A number of vegetables can be dug up and placed in moist sand, sawdust, sphagnum peat moss, or similar moisture-retentive material. The key to success is keeping them cool and moist but not wet. If they freeze, they will rot.

Storing in Cool Spaces

One of the simplest ways of storing a number of vegetables is to place them in a cool, dry spot on a flat sheet of cardboard or in a cardboard box with part of its sides cut out. Place the vegetables on a shelf or right on the floor. This works well for garlic, onions, potatoes, shallots, and winter squash, which can be stored in this way for months. You can also hang garlic, onions, and shallots in mesh bags, and use over the coming months. If any bulbs begin to sprout, use those first.

Relatively few people have root cellars, but these are excellent places to store vegetables that need high humidity and cool, but not freezing, temperatures.

Most vegetables will last for at least a short period of time in the refrigerator. Note that ethylene gas emitted by apples may cause problems with some vegetables.

Curing

This is the process of letting starch convert to sugar over a period of weeks or even months and is especially important for squash. A butternut squash sweetens with age and is often sold in stores before it has reached peak flavor.

Preservation Methods

Freezing is the easiest and most efficient way to preserve the color, flavor, and nutrients of most fresh vegetables for long periods of time. However, texture is affected. Many vegetables need to be blanched before freezing. Blanching kills off microorganisms and inactivates enzymes that could cause deterioration. Vegetables are typically placed in relatively small amounts in a wire basket and immersed in boiling water. The amount of time varies by vegetable and is specified in plant descriptions. Immediately after blanching, the vegetables should be plunged into ice-cold water or flash frozen in as thin a layer as possible on a cookie sheet in the

Vegetables such as garlic, onions, and shallots store well in orange mesh bags or can be placed on cardboard in a cool, dry place with other vegetables such as potatoes, pumpkins, and squash.

freezer. After cooling, place immediately in a freezer bag with as much air removed as possible to prevent oxidation. Mark the bags with content and date.

Watery vegetables such as asparagus, cucumbers, greens, and radishes do not freeze well. Note that beets should be cooked completely before freezing, or they will become rubbery if simply blanched.

A number of herbs and berries can be flash frozen without blanching. Herbs may be dried and pulverized before blending with oil. Freeze this combination immediately to prevent botulism (caused by *Clostridium botulinum* bacteria). Blueberries, raspberries, and strawberries flash freeze quickly if there is space between each berry. They do not need to be washed. You can do the same with tomatoes, or purée them for tomato sauce to conserve space. An extra freezer is a necessity for storing large amounts of vegetables.

A few vegetables and many herbs dry well. Sun drying is generally not recommended in cold climates because temperature and humidity are not conducive to proper drying. The foliage of herbs can be air dried either by placing it on screens or hanging stems tied in small bunches upside down in a warm, dry, airy place but not in direct sun, which

There are many ways to preserve berries, herbs, and vegetables, including canning, drying, freezing, pickling, and making jams and jellies.

Many of the fruits in this guide can be preserved by making them into syrups, jams, and jellies. Syrups may be used fresh or added to fruit being frozen. Syrups usually contain sugar, may be mixed with water, and can be flavored with herbs.

Buying Organic Produce for Storage

You may want to buy large quantities of organic produce for storage. Be aware of the different labeling requirements. According to the National Cooperative Grocers Association and the U.S. Department of Agriculture, labels fall into four categories: 100 percent organic (100 percent organic ingredients), organic (no less than 95 percent organic ingredients), made with organic foods (between 70 to 95 percent organic ingredients), and no organic claim on the label (less than 70 percent organic ingredients or none at all). Simply washing nonorganic produce may remove as little as 25 percent of pesticide residue, some of which is absorbed by plant tissue itself. The terms *free-range, hormone-free, natural,* and *all natural* do not mean organic, although products labeled with these terms must be what they are labeled.

produces UV rays that can affect flavor and nutrition. Air drying must be done quickly. If whole leaves or sprigs begin to mildew, discard them. Chopping herbs in a blender and then drying them reduces the chance of mildew. Herbs are often stored with rice or dried milk in little bags to act as desiccants. Drying in an oven or microwave also works. A dehydrator is safer and easier to use. Follow closely the directions provided with a dehydrator for best results.

The key to drying is to get the water content very low. Dried vegetables and herbs should be brittle. In some cases the flavor is preserved well, in others flavor is either more or less intense. Drying increases the nutrients in tomatoes but reduces it in most vegetables and herbs. Whole leaves store better than shredded ones. Moisture, heat, and sunlight can cause dried products to deteriorate badly. Note that storing dried materials in a refrigerator reduces the chance of spoilage.

Canning is one of the most popular ways of preserving vegetables, but it must be done precisely to be safe. Problems with bacteria, mold, and yeast can be serious. Particularly deadly is botulism *(Clostridium botulinum)*. Get the "USDA Complete Guide to Home Canning" or a similar book.

Pickling, or brining, consists of cleaning and then preserving vegetables in a solution of salted vinegar. Many more vegetables can be pickled than beets and cucumbers. Tastes of pickled produce vary by region because each area has unique bacteria and yeast that are needed for fermentation.

Culinary Uses

Growing vegetables well is great, but knowing what parts of the plant are edible and how you can use them is essential to getting the most out of your garden. Most fresh vegetables have a different taste from ones frozen or sold in stores. The emphasis in this guide is *fresh,* so each vegetable section includes tips on proper harvesting and cooking. The taste of produce varies by soil, variety, and weather. One of the nice things about cooking vegetables is that recipes do not have to be complicated—many of the suggestions here are simple and quick. The capacity to taste depends on the ability to smell and varies by individual DNA. Body chemistry also plays a part in why some people love or hate specific plants, such as arugula and cilantro—both detested by Julia Child. Genes are especially important in the detection of bitter compounds found in vegetables such as Brussels sprouts and kale.

Culinary Terms

aioli: Dip or sauce made from a garlic paste combined with egg yolk, lemon juice, mustard, and olive oil. Some refer to it as garlic-flavored mayonnaise, combined with spices to taste.

bake: To cook in an oven at desired temperature. A form of dry cooking. Vegetables cooked in this way should have enough space between them for good air circulation.

barbecue: See **grill.**

béarnaise: Sauce typically made using shallot or onion along with egg, lemon juice, mustard, tarragon, and white wine vinegar.

béchamel: Sauce typically made with broth, butter, cream, flour, nutmeg, and salt.

Bercy: White sauce often served on fish. Ingredients usually include fish stock, parsley, shallots, and white wine.

blanch: To cook briefly in boiling water before plunging into ice water to stop the cooking process. Critical in freezing most vegetables since it cleans them while stopping the work of enzymes that could affect the flavor, color, and vitamin content of the food being frozen. Blanching may also refer to excluding light from the base of certain vegetables, such as asparagus and celery, to keep them white and tender.

boil: To cook by placing in boiling water. Vegetables will cook more evenly if of the same size or thickness. Nutrients are lost in this process, and the water is often saved for use in sauces, soup, or stock.

bouquet garni: Herbs tied up and wrapped in cheesecloth to be added to soups, stocks, and stews, then removed before serving. Herbs most commonly used are basil, bay leaf, chervil, lovage, parsley, salad burnet, rosemary, savory, tarragon, and thyme.

braise: To sear before cooking in liquid under a cover, or to sauté lightly, then cook in liquid.

butter, herbal or seasoned: Butter typically flavored with edible flowers, garlic, herbs (chives and dill most common), or lemon.

butter steam: To cook by stir-frying with butter instead of oil. Once partially cooked, small amounts of water or broth can be added to the pan to continue the cooking process briefly. Best results are achieved by cooking in several batches rather than one large one.

can: To treat with heat and preserve. Canning can be problematic, so a *current* canning guide is recommended. Many vegetables are not acidic enough to prevent botulism. The amount of cooking necessary to prevent botulism destroys nutrients. That is why freezing is such a good option.

caramelize: To cook a vegetable with sugar to give it a "caramel" coating. If a vegetable naturally contains sugar, such as onions, the addition of sugar is unnecessary.

chiffonade: To cut leafy vegetables into thin strips.

chop: To cut into small pieces that vary in size.

coulis: Sauce made from puréed vegetables and fruits. It can be strained to remove seeds or fibrous material.

cream: To combine sugar with butter in baking; to beat into a creamy texture.

crudités: Raw vegetables, generally served on a platter with a dipping sauce.

cube: To cut into square pieces.

deep-fry: To immerse completely in hot oil.

dehydrate: To remove moisture to keep a product from spoiling. Dehydrators are recommended over open-air or oven drying, although the latter are possible with some plants.

dice: To cut into small pieces.

dry: To remove moisture using the sun, an oven, or a dehydrator. Food should not be dried in sunlight at a high humidity. Oven dry at 150°F for four to twelve hours, then cure for seven to fourteen days in a hot, dry, airy place. Or follow directions for specific foods when using a dehydrator.

dust: To cover lightly with superfine sugar to make candied flowers.

fines herbes (pronounced "feen-erb"): Seasoning typically consisting of finely chopped chervil, chives, parsley, and tarragon; used fresh or dried.

freeze: To place in a freezer until frozen solid. Flash freezing is doing this as quickly as possible. Vegetables with space between them freeze faster. Note that frost-free freezers go through freezing and thawing cycles and will not keep vegetables for as long as many gardeners believe. Still, freezing is one of the safest and easiest forms of preserving most vegetables.

French: To cut beans into long pieces for quicker cooking.

fry: To cook as quickly as possible in hot oil to preserve nutrients.

garnish: To add a vegetable or flower to a dish for color.

grate: To rub against an abrasive surface, reducing vegetables into small pieces or fragments or even into a powder.

grill: To cook with dry heat from above or below. Barbecuing is a form of grilling. Thin bamboo or metal skewers are often used to hold sliced or cubed vegetables in place. Bamboo should be soaked in water for twenty to thirty minutes before grilling. Most vegetables are coated with oil or butter before being placed on an oiled grill.

herbes de Provence: Seasoning that almost always includes dried basil, fennel seed, marjoram, oregano, rosemary, savory, and thyme. Optional are bay, Italian parsley, lavender, and tarragon.

hollandaise: Sauce typically made with butter, egg, Dijon mustard, and lemon juice or white wine vinegar.

juice: To blend vegetables in a blender or juicer to reduce to a liquid. Some vegetables will not release all of their nutrients unless juiced to a high degree. Wheatgrass is a good example.

julienne: To cut into thin strips like matches.

The stems of asparagus are at their best when the bud scales at the tips are still tightly compressed.

Freshly picked coriander seeds can be used whole or be ground into a fine powder for seasoning.

mandolin (mandoline): Instrument used to cut vegetables into thin slices.

marinate: To flavor or tenderize food by soaking it in a solution, called marinade, usually of oil or vinegar mixed with spices or herbs. Commonly done with fish, meat, and vegetables for varying lengths of time before cooking.

mayonnaise: Sauce made from beaten egg yolks, oil, and vinegar or lemon juice.

mesclun: Mix of various greens. There are no specific plants required for this mix. Seeds sold as mesclun mixes may not result in a mix, since the plants mature at different times.

microgreens: Plants harvested when only a few inches tall. Microgreens are used for texture, taste, and visual appeal. These young plants often are delicate and have outstanding flavor.

microwave: To cook in a microwave until desired doneness; often recommended for vegetables to preserve nutrients. This method of cooking also preserves color and texture better than other methods.

mince: To cut into fine or small pieces.

Mornay: Sauce similar to béchamel but with red pepper instead of nutmeg, and grated Gruyère, Parmesan, or Swiss cheese.

oil: Used for cooking and sometimes to store plant parts. *The latter is not safe except for a day or two, since oil is not acidic.* Bacteria, especially *Clostridium botulinum*, can grow in oil, resulting in botulism unless the oil preserving the plant part is kept frozen until use. Use vinegar instead.

panfry: See **sauté**.

pan-sear: See **sear**.

parboil: To cook part way by boiling.

pare: To cut off the outer skin; to cut into thin slices.

paste: Crushed or mashed vegetables or herbs, used fresh, or frozen for later use. Pesto is one of the most common.

peel: To remove outer skin, usually with a vegetable peeler or with a knife.

pickle: To preserve in vinegar or brine. Almost anything can be pickled and be safe to eat because of the vinegar's acidity.

poach: To simmer lightly in a sweetened liquid. This is done mainly with fruits, rarely with vegetables.

powder: To dry thoroughly before grinding or pulverizing into a dustlike material.

purée: To cook and make into a creamy consistency by blending. May be done before freezing some vegetables for the purpose of taking up less space. Purée can be frozen in ice cube trays, then removed and placed in a freezer bag.

rémoulade: Dressing or sauce with a mayonnaise base (egg yolks, oil, vinegar) similar to tartar sauce. May be flavored with anchovies, capers, mustard, pickles, and a variety of herbs or spices (most commonly curry).

ribbon: When referring to vegetables, to ribbon means to cut into wide but thin slices or strips. Can be done with a potato peeler or a spiral vegetable slicer. Slices can be straight or made into curls and served raw or cooked.

roast: To bake uncovered in an oven.

sauce: Any liquid used to moisten or flavor food.

sauté: To cook in a small amount of oil or fat at a high temperature while flipping continuously to get even heat on all sides of the cut vegetables.

score: To cut into base of vegetable to help it cook faster.

sear: To char or scorch the surface with high heat. Cut vegetables into small pieces, heat olive oil to medium-high temperature in a pan, and sear both sides for two minutes or until blackened.

shred: To cut, slice, or tear into pieces. Similar to grating, but the pieces are usually longer, thicker, or wider.

simmer: To cook in water just below the boiling point. The water may be bubbling ever so lightly.

slice: To cut across or diagonally into pieces. The size of the pieces varies by use.

sofrito: Sauce popular in the Caribbean and Latin America. Highly variable but often consists of small bits of onions, peppers, and tomatoes cooked with garlic, spices, and herbs.

sprout: To get seeds moist enough to germinate, forming small stems and seed leaves. Color will depend on seeds and exposure to light. Flavor varies considerably from one seed to the next. Make sure seeds are untreated and sterile. For specific seeds and more information, check sproutpeople.org.

The flower stems of garlic are often clipped off and discarded, but they are considered a delicacy by many.

Plant 'Magentaspreen', a pretty version of lamb's-quarters, in a bold block to be eaten as microgreens.

The leaves and flowers of nasturtiums are edible, and the pods can be pickled as a caper substitute.

If radishes bolt, save a few plants for their edible flowers and plump pods.

Squash flowers stuffed or fried in batter as tempura are popular in many cultures.

Few gardeners know that the buds of some vegetables, such as sunflowers, are edible.

steam: To place above boiling water to cook in rising steam, which is at same temperature as boiling water, or to wrap a vegetable in foil or paper to cook in its own moisture. Preserves nutrients better than boiling.

stew: To simmer or boil slowly.

stir-fry: To cook rapidly in an oiled and highly heated pan, such as a wok. Vegetables sliced into small pieces are cooked over high heat while being stirred continuously until to the desired doneness. May be combined with braising for fibrous vegetables, such as broccoli stems. Sauce made from cornstarch, soy sauce, and water is often used as seasoning. Peanut oil is most highly recommended for cooking in high heat. Vegetable oils are also fine. Olive oil is generally used at lower temperatures. Cooking quickly in as little oil as possible preserves nutrients. *Do not crowd vegetables.* Make more than one batch if necessary.

stock: Liquid from boiling bones, meat, or vegetables for use as soup or flavoring in dishes.

sweat: To cook in butter or oil at a low temperature while stirring frequently until vegetables become soft and tender.

tartar sauce: Mayonnaise flavored with chopped pickles. May be flavored with anchovy paste, capers, lemon juice, onions, parsley, tarragon, or other ingredients to taste.

tempura: Vegetables dipped in batter and fried.

vinaigrette: Dressing made with Dijon mustard, oil, and vinegar (optional lemon, pepper, shallot or red onion).

vinegar, flavored: Vinegar to which plants and herbs are added to change its color and taste. This is safe since vinegar is acidic.

wilt: To cook greens gently until they are no longer crispy.

zest: Typically grated lime, lemon, or orange peel—just the surface of the peel.

Nutrition

The nutrients produced by plants include carbohydrates, minerals, protein, and vitamins. One major advantage of growing your own vegetables is that they contain the most nutrients when picked fully mature and just before eating. There are a few exceptions, such as some winter squash, which are best eaten after appropriate storage times. Sprouts, germinating seeds, although not covered in detail in this guide, are also extremely nutritious. The emphasis on eating *fresh* vegetables cannot be overemphasized. When these are grown without the use of either organic or synthetic pesticides, they are also considerably safer. Whether organically grown produce is more nutritious than plants grown with synthetic fertilizers, assuming that both are eaten quickly after harvesting, is hotly disputed. The debate should be encouraged because the more research done on this subject, the better. Everyone agrees that foods grown organically without the use of either organic or synthetic pesticides are more environmentally friendly.

Many parts of plants may be edible, including roots, stems, leaves, flowers, and seeds. Some parts may be more nutrient rich than others, but taken as a group they provide a wide range of minerals and vitamins essential to a healthy diet.

Plants also provide dietary fiber (roughage), which is critical in digestion and the elimination of potentially toxic wastes from the body. The recommended daily allowance of fiber is roughly 20 to 35 grams per day.

Diets high in nutrition derived from plants are believed to help prevent the development of many illnesses. These include diseases causing thousands of deaths each year, such as cancer, diabetes, and heart disease. These diseases are also linked to genes, lack of exercise, too much red meat, not enough whole grains, and overuse of alcohol, but almost all medical professionals agree that a primarily plant-based diet is good for your health. The more varied the diet, the bet-

ter. By eating a wide range of vegetables and berries, you increase the chance of getting just the right balance of nutrients. However, plants do not produce all nutrients necessary for good health, such as small amounts of fat and appropriate doses of calcium, iodized salt, iron, vitamin B12 (cobalamin), and vitamin D3. Anyone on a strictly plant-based diet (vegan) should consult with a nutritionist or medical professional for additional advice. Vitamin B12 and vitamin D3 are often deficient even in people who are not vegans, especially as they age. *This book is a growing guide and should not be relied on for medical advice.*

In recent years there has been an increasing interest in chemicals produced by plants. These phytochemicals are believed to protect plants against disease and insects. They are also believed by some to do the same for humans. The exact number of phytochemicals is still unknown but may be as high as ten thousand or significantly higher. Only a few have been studied. Much of the evidence as to their value is anecdotal or preliminary. More than likely they work together. It may take years of research to know exactly how. By eating a variety of plants you may increase your HDL (high-density lipoprotein), known as good cholesterol, while lowering your LDL (low-density lipoprotein),

Beet greens, along with numerous vegetable greens, are often more nutritious than roots or stems.

known as bad cholesterol, which helps prevent heart disease and reduces the risk of stroke; may reduce your blood pressure; may reduce your chance of getting cancer or diabetes; may reduce your chance of macular degeneration as you age; may boost your immune system; may reduce inflammation throughout your body; and so on. An interesting theory is that plants not sprayed with either organic or synthetic pesticides are forced to produce greater amounts of phytochemicals to survive. They are therefore more healthful to us.

Different plants contain different phytochemicals. Carrots alone are believed to have at least a hundred. The most well known are listed in the accompanying table. Many of the phytochemicals in this list are antioxidants, which are believed to pick up free radicals (unstable molecules) that may cause cell damage in the body leading to cancer and heart disease.

Nutrients are available in different amounts depending on whether they are eaten raw or cooked. In general, nutrients are lost in cooking but not always. Steaming or, at least cooking vegetables quickly, is often the best way to preserve nutrients if vegetables are not eaten raw. Phytochemicals also vary in their availability. Some may be lost in cooking. However, lycopene in tomatoes becomes more readily absorbed if tomatoes are cooked or made into paste. The addition of oil also increases availability of phytochemicals

The high amount of protein in broad beans has given rise to their nickname "vegetable meat."

Phytochemicals in plants and their health benefits

PHYTOCHEMICAL	PLANTS CONTAINING PHYTOCHEMICAL	HEALTH BENEFIT
Allyl sulfides	Garlic and onions	May boost the immune system
Anthocyanins	Blackberries, blueberries, raspberries, and vegetables with a dark-red to purple coloration	May reduce inflammations and the risk of tumors
Carotenoids (antioxidant)	Carrots, muskmelon, pumpkin, squash, sweet potatoes, and a number of leafy vegetables	Believed to promote eye health
Ellagic acid (antioxidant)	Blackberries, raspberries, and strawberries	Believed to fight cancer
Flavonoids (antioxidant)	Chickpeas and soybeans	May reduce risk of cancer and possibly help prevent heart disease
Isoflavones (plant estrogens) (antioxidant)	Soybeans	May help prevent cancer, heart disease, and possibly osteoporosis
Isothiocyanates	Broccoli, Brussels sprouts, cabbage, cauliflower, Chinese cabbage, collards, horseradish, kale, kohlrabi, mustard greens, onions, radish, rutabaga, turnip greens, and watercress	Believed to help prevent cancer
Lutein (carotenoid)	Primarily in kale and spinach but other greens as well	Believed to prevent cancer
Lycopene (antioxidant)	Tomatoes and watermelon	May help prevent cancer
Resveratrol	Peanuts	May help prevent heart disease
Sulforaphane (antioxidant)	Arugula and broccoli	May help prevent cancer
Zeaxanthin (carotenoid)	Primarily in kale and spinach but in other greens as well	May help prevent cancer

Eating raw garlic is believed to provide healthful benefits for the heart.

Sunflower seeds removed from the flower heads and toasted are high in minerals, protein, and vitamins.

in some vegetables, including tomatoes. Blackberries and raspberries appear to provide more phytochemicals if freeze dried. We simply do not yet fully understand the best way to preserve phytochemicals in all plants.

It should be noted that many supplements are on the market containing these chemicals. These are not controlled by the FDA, may contain varying amounts of the chemical, and may actually be harmful, since accurate dosing is next to impossible to determine. *Almost all medical advice is to get phytochemicals naturally by eating a wide variety of vegetables and berries.* Part of that advice comes from the fear of potential interactions of phytochemicals with prescription drugs. Consult a medical professional before taking supplements. Also, note that synthetic vitamins may be metabolized differently from those occurring naturally in plants.

While vegetables, berries, and herbs generally promote health, that is not always the case. Health concerns of specific plants are described in Part II. For example, the oxalic acid in beet greens and spinach may be a problem for someone with kidney disease, since kidney stones are calcium oxalate. This acid is actually toxic in rhubarb leaves if eaten

in large amounts. As you study the potential health benefits of specific vegetables, you soon learn that eating too much of any one vegetable is rarely advised. A diet including a wide variety of vegetables seems to be the most effective and healthful. Bear in mind that juicing tends to concentrate the intake of specific chemicals contained in vegetables. It's also the only way to make vitamins available from some plants, such as wheatgrass. Vary the vegetables juiced on a regular basis to avoid potential problems. In effect, everything natural has the potential to be toxic depending on the quantity eaten. The old adage of "everything in moderation" applies.

Finally, the sooner people begin to eat vegetables, the better. In our society it is difficult to get children to eat them. By combining vegetables, especially greens, with what children see as more "edible" food, you can often incorporate them in their diet. Also, children will eat snacks, such as sliced carrots and celery, if they are hungry enough and do not have less healthful foods available. One way to reverse the severe obesity problem in this country is to introduce children to healthful foods at a young age. Many parents have already begun to do this with some remarkable results.

CHAPTER 8

TOOLS, MATERIALS, AND GARDENING AIDS

Following are some suggestions for tools and materials you may need for an organic garden. Whether you will need them depends on your gardening style and the size of your garden. The list does not include some of the more sophisticated tools commonly used in mini-farming. Whatever you need, buy the best you can afford. In the long run you will save money. Since tools can be expensive, check online for used tools if money is tight. Used tools can be perfectly good. I have used some of the same tools for decades. Stock up in the fall if you have room.

Keep metal sharp and clean. Disinfect tools and supports regularly to stop the spread of disease. Paint a portion of each tool red, or encircle the top with reflective tape. Red is fine, white is better. If you lose a tool in the garden, go out at night and shine a flashlight into the garden. The tape will pinpoint its location.

As for keeping fuel in power tools, there is a debate. Some say to run the tools until all fuel is consumed at the end of the season. Others fill up the tool with fuel mixed with a stabilizer. I side with the second group. But I run the power tool long enough for some of the stabilizer to work its way through the engine just before storage.

The most important tool of all is your body. Protect it with a tetanus shot every ten years, use appropriate clothing including gloves if necessary, and apply sunscreen. Use tools correctly to avoid sprains and strains. Lift only what is reasonable for your strength and back.

Some communities are allowing residents to raise chickens and other poultry. If you are raising chickens, you could contract histoplasmosis, a disease caused by inhalation of the spores of the fungus *Histoplasma capsulatum*. Symptoms are vaguely flu-like and often not present at all. If you feel sick and see a doctor, mention that you are raising birds. Most cases resolve on their own, but more severe ones require medication. The disease is somewhat similar to tuberculosis. If you have a lung disorder or any illness causing a weakened immune system, raising chickens may be ill advised. Check with your doctor. Note that other diseases exist that are transmitted from birds to humans.

When buying starter mixes, growing mediums, fertilizers, pesticides, and so on, you may want to check that they are approved for organic gardening. There are two main organizations that deal with the somewhat complicated issue about what is considered organic and what is not. They are the Organic Materials Review Institute (OMRI) and the National Organic Program (NOP), part of the U.S. Department of Agriculture. OMRI produces written materials. NOP gives out information in an online handbook at http://www.ams.usda.gov/rules-regulations/organic/handbook. These two organizations are primarily aimed at commercial growers. Also, if you are interested in mini-farming, go online to http://misadocuments.info/PHH_Long_02.22.15.pdf. This is a realistic look at what it takes to sell safe produce once harvested. I have dealt with this issue throughout this guide, so that you do not have to try to find out what is or is not organic. Still, the definition of "organic" is somewhat a moving target and not everyone agrees. While this issue is certainly important to the home gardener, it is far more critical for someone wanting to get organic certification to sell produce.

National Organic Program
1400 Independence Avenue Southwest
Room 2642-South, Stop 0268
Washington, D.C. 20250-0268
202-720-3252

Organic Materials Review Institute (OMRI)
2649 Willamette Street
Eugene, OR 97405
541-343-7600

Tools and Garden Products

Backflow preventer: This device can be added to any water spigot to prevent polluted water from getting into your home. It is critical if hoses have attachments for fertilizing or applying pesticides.

Boards: Most raised beds are built with cedar (brown or green treated) or pine boards. Cedar is lovely, long lasting, and the most expensive material. My experience is that the boards should be at least 2 inches (actually ends up being 1½ inches) thick. Thinner boards tend to warp and bow. The length and height of the boards depends on how far you can reach into the bed without stepping into it. Typical board heights range from 6 to 12 inches, and lengths from 8 to 10 feet. Three 10-foot boards can make a 5-by-10-feet raised bed. Cut one board in half, and use it for the ends. Dig into the soil and make sure that all four sides are level. Note that many companies sell kits for raised beds. Some are easy to put together and take apart if you want to move them. They are unlikely to match the quality of do-it-yourself beds.

Boots (rubber): Tall rubber boots that go almost up to your knee provide little support but lots of protection from slime and grime.

Broadfork or deep spader: This tool loosens subsoil and is used by some to avoid the need for tilling.

Buckets or pails: A bucket or large pail is useful to throw weeds into or to carry tools around the garden. Laundry detergent is sold in rectangular containers that are excellent for this use. Drywall installers dispose of buckets regularly. Ask them to save a few for you. Or buy them at a store.

Cable ties: While commonly used to keep cables in place, they are excellent for tying wire together. They can even be used to support plants against supports, but leave space for stems to grow. They are inexpensive when purchased in bulk.

Capillary mat: This water-absorbing material is placed under pots. The water is absorbed into the starting mix by capillary action. This is bottom watering. It is an alternative to misting plants, which requires constant vigilance so that seedlings do not dry out or get overly wet, which results in damping-off, a collection of diseases that cause seedlings to topple over. Bottom watering also requires care in that you don't want starting mix to get waterlogged.

Catalogs: These give you valuable information: names of varieties, days to maturity (more or less), whether seeds are organic, whether they are open pollinated (heirlooms) or hybrids, their resistance to disease, growing tips, preferred planting dates, and whether or not they are All-America Selections (AAS) winners. This guide supplies much of the same information but narrows choices even further since some plants do better in cold climates than others.

Chain saw: This tool is expensive, but essential, if removing trees from a potential garden area.

Coir: Shredded coconut husks are used as a soil amendment. It is considered a renewable resource and touted by many organic gardeners as the future replacement for sphagnum peat moss.

Compost pile enclosure: Use four wooden or four steel T posts dug or driven deep into the ground as end supports for wire running around them. Leave one side open. Another simple encloser is a Japanese tomato ring, a circle of wire with a 4-foot diameter set in the garden. Attach the ends of the wire together. These rings can be unfastened and moved from one place to another easily. Pallets are often suggested as good enclosures. While you can often find them for free if you ask around, they are heavy and hard to move—I have used them but never again. My advice is to keep your piles simple and as inexpensive as possible. *Compost piles do not have to be enclosed and can be made right in larger gardens, either as single or multiple piles.*

Conduit (electrical): This material makes good supports and is excellent for hose guides. You can have it cut at big-box stores to the size you want.

Crowbar: A long-handled crowbar with a flattened base can act as a lever to move stones trapped in the soil.

Cultivator (pronged hoe): This tool has a long handle and four tines to pull through the earth. It works beautifully.

Dandelion digger: There are both short- and long-handled dandelion diggers. The short is especially helpful digging out long-rooted weeds. The more open the V at the end of the blade, the better. It can also be used to harvest asparagus, although the base of the stalks are extremely tough. Use a sharp knife instead.

Dibble or multidibble: A fancy garden term for something that will make a hole in soil for planting seeds or transplants. My dibble is my forefinger or hand.

Disinfectant: Cleaning and disinfecting tools and supports will cut down on disease. Commonly recommended products contain chlorine or rubbing alcohol. Some gardeners simply scrape off tools and wash them in soap and water. You can buy products for this use that have been OMRI approved, such as Oxidate®.

Drip irrigation (soaker hoses): These can be hoses or actual systems set up for watering. Water loss from these is minimal. Some gardeners swear by them; others, at them. If you have a well, use some other system since these do not draw enough water to keep the pump running continuously, which is necessary to stop it from burning out. Systems may include timers and shutoff valves for specific lines. The water source should have an antisiphon valve (similar, but not exactly the same as, a backflow preventer). Systems may also require some sort of filter. Note that most gardeners are better off with professional advice when installing any form of drip irrigation, even if that means just talking to someone before installing a system on your own.

Earplugs: These help protect your ears from damage when using power equipment.

Edger: This tool is used to cut deeply between lawns and gardens. The kind with a rounded (crescent) blade works best.

Eyeglasses: When mulching leaves on a driveway, wear something to protect your eyes. Safety glasses that have sides on them are even better.

Fence post drivers: Heavy, hollow metal tubes with handles on the side—the heavier, the better. Slide them over posts tilted at an angle, lift up, and pound posts down. They are much more efficient than trying to drive posts into the ground with a sledgehammer.

Fence posts: Metal posts are fine, but timbers are more attractive. T posts (also called U posts or Y posts) are steel with a bumpy edge and wedge at their base. Anchor wood or metal posts firmly in the ground so that they cannot budge once wire is attached to them. Synthetic netting can also be pulled taut between them to support the vertical growth of many plants.

Fencing: Gardens need protection from marauders. Some communities have tight regulations on the height of fences. There are relatively lightweight synthetic fences on the market for those who don't like to work with wire. You can generally get away with using these, since they are high but barely noticeable. When you first put them up, tie little pieces of cloth to them so that deer know that something in their life has changed.

Fertilizers: If possible, buy these ahead of the spring planting season. The variety of organic fertilizers presently on the market is staggering. Study catalogs, online sites, and the shelves of local nurseries to compare prices.

File or grindstone: Have something on hand to sharpen tools, or check with local hardware stores to see what the cost is for sharpening individual tools. Sharp tools make gardening much easier. Files come in various grades; a mill bastard file is one that is neither too coarse, nor too fine to sharpen tools. Attachments for power drills also are available.

Freezer: If you can afford it and have the space, buy an extra freezer. Your garden often produces far more than you can use at any one time. Freezing is one of the easiest and best ways to preserve nutrients in vegetables.

Garden fork: This is a tool with solid prongs, not a pitchfork. It is very strong and used to dig up soil and root crops.

Garden, hard, iron, or steel rake: This long-handled tool has a solid, well-built head with deep, thick prongs. You will use it over and over again to prepare soil for planting. Heads vary in size; the wider ones are the most practical. Use the front to dig into soil, the back to smooth soil out.

Gloves: Some gardeners love gloves, others despise them. While they are not necessary, they do prevent blisters when working with tools, do prevent some minor wounds when working with soil, and definitely help when picking berries from brambles. *All gardeners should wear gloves when working with manure and compost.* Leather gloves are much longer lasting than ones made of other materials.

Gloves (rubber): Absolutely essential if you are working with any toxic liquids. Hopefully, you will not have to.

Hat: Broad-brimmed hats are best for sun protection.

Heating pad or mat: For starting seeds indoors, it is helpful to have bottom heat.

Hedge trimmers: This tool is excellent for cutting down multistemmed plants at the end of the season.

Hoe: Catalogs are filled with all sorts of hoes. A simple flat-bladed hoe works just fine. Simply turn it an angle to make furrows. Sharpen edges of all cutting tools regularly.

Hoe-fork combination (mattock): This is a tool with

a short handle. On one end are sharp spikes, on the other end a small, flat hoe. It is one of the easiest and most useful tools to use in the garden. It does require you to work on your knees.

Hog rings and pliers: These are sharp metal rings crimped together with a tool (pliers) that are ideal for attaching wire fences and remesh together quickly. Once attached, they are sturdy and will last for years. Use them to make permanent wire rings, including regular and Japanese tomato rings. They can be hard to find except in rural areas.

Hoops: You can purchase or make your own hoops to hold up row covers. PVC pipe works well and will bend easily if no more than 1/2 inch thick. Hoops should be high enough so that the covers do not touch the plants.

Hoses: Do not try to save money on hoses. Buy hoses guaranteed not to kink. Rubber hoses with metal fittings are recommended. Never drink from a hose if you have used attachments to apply fertilizers or pesticides. Drinking from hoses is not recommended at all. Gardeners that do should run water long enough to flush out any water that was sitting in the hose before turning it on. Soaker hoses weep water into the soil. Lay these out along the base of plants. *If you have a well, make sure you are using enough water to keep the pump running constantly to avoid burning it out, since it goes on and off with varying water demands.* The simplest way to avoid this problem is to water with a number of hoses running all at the same time.

Insect repellent: Repellent protects you from mosquitoes and ticks. Deer ticks carry Lyme disease.

Journal: I have always wished I started keeping notes much earlier in my life. Journals can be invaluable as the years go by, not only to you but also to family members and friends. Keep track of what, when, and where you plant. Keep notes on the season as well.

Kneeling pad: This cushions whatever surface you are working on. Lots of work is easiest done while kneeling down rather than bending over, which ends up hurting your back. Buy a simple, flat pad that you lay below your knees and can move easily from one place to the next. Ones that encircle your knees are cumbersome, uncomfortable, and unnecessary.

Knife: A good knife makes harvesting plants a breeze.

Labels: The least expensive labels are white plastic knives sold in large boxes at major discount stores. They are light and easy to mark with a permanent marker. The white color stands out in the garden. They last several years but eventually break down.

Landscape fabric: This fabric can be used in place of plastic to control weeds, hold moisture in the soil, and especially to increase soil temperature.

Lawn mower: A small mower can not only collect grass but also shred leaves in fall for compost or mulch.

Leaf bags (compostable): Each fall, you can gather filled leaf bags and use the leaves for mulch, and the bags for a similar purpose.

Leaf rake: While not used often in the garden itself, it is essential for gathering leaves in the fall.

Lights: To start seedlings indoors, you need good light, as much as sixteen to eighteen hours a day. You do not need expensive grow lights.

Mask: Wear a mask when shredding leaves in the fall to be used as a mulch the following spring. Wearing a mask when working with manure, especially bird droppings, or compost is also highly recommended.

Metal snips: Use this tool to cut hardware cloth and rabbit wire—much easier than using wire cutters.

Mister: A simple hand mister makes watering seeds indoors easy. It gives you good control, so that you do not overwater.

Moisture meter (gauge): This tool is for those gardeners who don't want to get their fingers dirty.

Netting (nylon): Netting is a good substitute for wire when growing plants vertically. It is extremely strong.

Nozzle: This attachment is critical for hand watering with a hose to control the force of the spray from a gentle mist to a near geyser.

Peat moss (sphagnum peat moss): This is one of the most readily available soil amendments sold in bags and bales. Bales are harder to move around but much more economical. Sphagnum peat moss is slightly acidic. Some organic gardeners will not use it, believing that it is not a sustainable resource. The industry claims that bogs are creating it as fast as it is being used. If coir were more readily available, perhaps less peat moss would be used.

Perlite: This is one of the best soil conditioners for making potting soil, but it is ultra-expensive in small quantities. Look online for a local distributor selling it in larger quantities. Some farm stores carry it.

Permanent marker: Use a permanent marker to write on plastic labels, but do not expect the writing to be permanent. When naming plants, write the variety on both sides of the label.

Pickaxe: This tool is essential in making a garden in areas where the soil contains lots of stones. Some can be very large and hard to budge.

Pitchfork: This tool is by far the easiest to use to lift and turn organic matter, especially debris or cuttings of green manure or mounds of animal manure.

Plastic: This material can be used as a soil cover to stop weeds and increase moisture, but especially to increase soil temperature for warm-weather crops. It comes in many colors and thicknesses, the latter measured in mils (1/1000 of an inch).

Posthole digger: In addition to digging holes, this tool can help you dig up root crops that dive deep into the soil. It is also helpful in digging up burdock, both a weed and a vegetable.

Pots: It is nice to have a variety of pots, from utilitarian to decorative. Pots can be made from a wide variety of materials, vary in size and weight, and can be cheap or ultra-expensive.

Potting soil: Either make your own or buy some. The larger bags are harder to handle but less expensive. The best potting soils are made with a good deal of sphagnum peat moss and perlite. Miracle-Gro® potting mix is sold just about everywhere. There is a tiny amount of synthetic fertilizer in the regular mix. If tempted to buy the purely organic mix, make your own instead.

Potting table: A table makes potting much easier since materials can be laid out at the right height for easy potting. It is nice to have but not essential.

Pruners (secateurs): This tool is used for cutting hard stem tissue. Get the kind with blades that cross each other. Pay the extra money for a good pair, since they can last for years. Sharpen or get them sharpened regularly for clean cuts.

Rain gauge: A gauge collects rain and gives you an accurate idea of how much fell. An open bucket or upright wheelbarrow is effective enough for me.

Ramp: A ramp or large boards are necessary to get large equipment into a trailer.

Rose (rosette): A cap with small holes placed on the spout of a watering can breaks up the water and is sometimes referred to as a "water breaker." These vary in shape from round to wide and flared.

Rototiller: A power tool with rotating blades (tines) that cut into the soil to loosen it up. Many gardeners cannot live without it; others say it destroys the earth. Neither side will ever convince the other. There are both front and rear tillers. The types with tines in front are less expensive but harder to handle. The rear types are expensive, easier to use, and more versatile.

Row covers: These come in various weights. Light fabric, a floating row cover, is used to protect plants from insects. It does let in light and water while maintaining an even humidity and temperature underneath. It should always float above and not touch the foliage of plants underneath it. This is especially true for vining plants, such as cucumbers. Foliage entangled in covers is easily damaged. Use hoops both below and over row covers to keep them

in place. Note that some gardeners use plants to support row covers. For example, they plant broad beans early in the season, and then a warmth-loving plant, such as cucumber, later. The broad beans hold up the cover as the cucumbers begin to grow and spread out. The broad beans are then pulled up once the cucumbers start to flower, and the row covers are removed. The broad beans add nitrogen to the soil and are composted, rather than allowed to produce a crop. I have never tried this, but the idea is intriguing.

Scissors: You should have a pair dedicated just to the garden. It will be used time and again.

Scythe: This tool is useful when cutting down weeds in an open area or cutting cover crops for use as a mulch or for an addition to compost.

Seed: Buy it well in advance if local stores do not carry the varieties you want. Keep it in a dark, cool place until ready to be used. Never allow it to get wet before planting.

Seed-saving box: Have a box or place to store seed. Buy a box of envelopes, place seed or seed packages in the envelopes, and then place the envelopes in the box. No fuss, no muss, no waste.

Seed starter mix: This refers to any material used to start seeds indoors. Make sure that it is sterile.

Shed: Either have a shed or some place to store tools, as in the garage on hooks or in a large plastic garbage can with the handles down.

Sheets (old): Use these to cover plants in a late-season cold snap. Use them to move whole leaves around. Pull all four ends together, lift up, and carry the bundle like Santa Claus, or pull them along the ground to where you want them. If leaves are shredded, use a wheelbarrow. They become heavy once broken down.

Shelving: When starting seeds indoors, shelving of some sort is a must. It does not have to be fancy but must be able to be raised up and down easily. Some gardeners simply use books or bricks to raise or lower shelves.

Shovel (spade): A shovel, often called a spade, is used for digging. It should have a long, solid handle and a rounded head that comes to a point, like the spade in a deck of playing cards. When spading soil, step down on the edge with the full weight of your body to get the spade into the soil as far as possible. It is surprising how fast you can dig up a garden with this tool. I prefer the kinds with synthetic, rather than wood, handles, but I have used both for years.

Sifter: Fasten four boards together into a square or rectangle that will fit on the sides of your wheelbarrow. Attach rabbit wire on the bottom. Lay this on the wheelbarrow, shovel soil onto the wire, and move about with a gloved hand. Rocks and debris will remain, and sifted soil will drop down.

Soil: For filling raised beds or adding soil to the garden in large amounts, buy soil by the truck load. Look at the soil before you buy it. Make sure it is loose. Dig into it with your hand. Squeeze it. See whether it falls apart or forms a tight ball. Soil should be loose and crumbly. Ask where it comes from. Then ask to see where it is being "mined." The last thing you need is soil that contains pesticides or salts left over from years of fertilization, such as soil from conventional farms. *Soil is the life blood of the organic garden.* Choosing the right soil is critical, since it will be the basis for your garden for years to come.

Spade (shovel): Spades have a flat bottom and vary in size. They are not meant to dig into the soil but to create flat areas, such as the bottom of trenches in the garden, or to scoop up material from the ground or a hard surface. I have always called these shovels.

Timbers are heavy and hard to work with but especially helpful when building high raised beds.

Sprayer: If you plan on foliar feeding, get a sprayer. Use a fine mist on both the top and bottom of leaves.

Sprinklers: These come in many models, from the oscillating kind, which covers a broad area, to little metal sprinklers with holes in them. The latter are made to cover circular, rectangular, and square areas.

Stake driver: A heavy, hollow metal tube with side handles. Place it over a stake, lift it up, and drive it down sharply. The stake will be driven into the soil. This is effective on metal stakes but works well on wood ones as well. The wood does sometimes get beaten up.

Stakes: Anything upright with a sharp point that can be driven into the ground is a stake. Use stakes of various sizes and heights to support individual plants, fences, and trellises; to lay out a garden; to mark rows; and so on. Materials include bamboo, electrical conduit, rebar, and wood, among others. If money is limited, collect broken hockey sticks, use sturdy saplings from a nearby woods (with permission), or anything that is sturdy. For some crops, brush is enough (pea stakes).

Straw: Do not confuse straw (stalks of grains) with hay. Straw makes an excellent summer and winter mulch. It is sold in bales, generally wrapped tightly in synthetic twine. The bales are heavy and scratchy. Wear gloves, and pull the separate twines together on one side of the bale to lift them into or out of your vehicle or trailer.

String: I define string in this guide as an organic material used to tie plants to supports or to make straight furrows. It does decompose over a long period of time. You may want to replace it with twine.

Sunscreen: You should use sunscreen for obvious reasons.

Supports: This term is used generically to cover any kind of support used for vertical gardening, from stakes to Japanese tomato rings.

Synthetic mulches: Plastics and geotextiles are sold in many nurseries to be used as mulches. Most commonly used are black or clear plastic.

Tape: There are many different types of tape useful in gardening. Many gardeners would be wise to use a circle of reflective tape, preferably white, around the top of each tool. If you lose a tool, shine a flashlight into the garden at night. The tool will light up like a star.

Thermometer (outdoor and soil): Get two types of thermometers, one to check air temperature, the other with a probe to check soil temperature. There are even compost thermometers for ardent gardeners.

Timbers: Although expensive, timbers are effective to create low or high raised beds. See the section "Constructing Raised Beds," below.

Tire pump: If you have a wheelbarrow with inflatable tires, then have a tire pump on hand. Squishy tires make heavy loads heavier.

Trailer: A trailer is a luxury worth its weight in gold over a period of years. It is ideal for picking up manures and compostable materials, such as leaves and wood chips, and also useful for hauling materials needed for all aspects of gardening. It does require a trailer hitch on your vehicle. The price of a trailer and hitch is high, but for the serious gardener they are well worth the investment.

Traps: Dealing with marauders effectively often requires the use of traps. Some kill animals; others trap them alive.

Trellis: Trellises are wooden or metal vertical supports. Make your own, or buy them in just about any shape and size imaginable.

Trowel: This tool is commonly used to dig up plants for transplanting, making holes, and so on.

Twine: Although twine can be made from natural materials, in this guide the term arbitrarily refers to a synthetic material that is used to tie plants to supports. It is generally green or tan, and it does not decompose. Some organic gardeners prefer jute, not only because it is soft but also because it is a natural plant fiber. It does break down and fray.

Vermiculite: This substance, mica heated to expand, is used in potting mixes.

Wall O' Water: This brand is one of the most popular types of cloches on the market. The home gardener can make many types of cloches without buying these, but this product does work remarkably well to keep plants warm in cold springs.

Watering can: A watering can is helpful for anyone doing a lot of container gardening. It provides excellent control over the amount of water being used per container.

Watering wand: This attachment is a type of nozzle that juts out to make it easier to reach plants far away from you. It should have a shutoff valve right on the wand. This tool makes it easy to water the base of plants instead of the whole plant.

Wheelbarrow: Get the largest wheelbarrow you can handle. If you have trouble pushing it up a slope, pull it up instead.

Wire: Wire fences and rolls of single-stranded wire come in various gauges (thickness of the wire) and heights. The lower the gauge, the stronger and more expensive the wire. Check your zoning laws before purchasing wire fencing. They often will not allow fences higher than 6 feet. Remesh is a thick wire often sold in 42½-inch-by-72-inch sections in big-box stores. It is made to reinforce concrete but is excellent as a support for vining plants. The wire can

be supported in an upright position. Some gardeners simply lean two pieces against each other at a low angle and let vines ramble over them. This skips the need for building supports but does take up more space. Welded wire with various size openings and various strengths is good for fencing, supports, and Japanese tomato rings.

Wire cutters: This is an indispensable tool when working with wire.

Zip or cable ties: These plastic strips allow you to attach remesh and wire together quickly and easily. They are not as quick as hog rings and pliers but are easy to detach at the end of the growing season. They are also readily available in hardware and big-box stores and inexpensive. Do not use them to attach plants to supports unless there is foam placed between them and the stem of the plant.

Constructing Raised Beds

The sides of enclosed raised beds can be made of many different products. Ideally, if using wood, it should be free of toxins. Pressure-treated boards and timbers once contained chromated copper arsenate (CCA). They are now pressure treated with different chemicals: alkaline copper quaternary (ACQ), copper azole (CA), and micronized copper quatemary (MCQ). These treated boards may last for up to twenty years in moist conditions. However, most organic gardeners are wary of these new pressure-treated woods because they fear harmful chemicals may leach into the soil. Boards made from recycled plastic are also on the market. The ones from high-density polyethylene (HDPE) are extremely heavy and expensive but are claimed not to leach any toxins into the soil. If you prefer non–pressure-treated wood, you have a choice of pine or cedar, which comes in a variety of grades. The better grades resist rot longer. Pine will last four to five years; cedar, perhaps twice as long. But cedar is extremely expensive per linear foot. Some people retard pine from rotting by attaching black plastic to the board wherever it will come in contact with the soil. (Note: Although commonly used for raised beds, railroad ties are not recommended. They are treated with creosote, which is a substance not recommended for landscape use.)

Boards should be at least 2 inches thick, since enclosed soil tends to bulge out. In longer and higher beds, secure the center of the bed with an additional board either at or below soil level. It acts as a stabilizer. Many gardeners building high raised beds run square posts deep into the soil at each end of the bed and secure boards to them with lag bolts (lag screws) over washers.

When making high raised beds with timbers, level the soil surface, and lay down the timbers. The key is to anchor

Lock high raised beds into supports with lag bolts to stop them from bowing and coming apart.

the timbers in place with special galvanized spikes that penetrate both the timber and the one below, to nail these into both sides of a joint, and to place timbers back into the soil as "dead men." Also, by placing each row of timbers a tiny bit back from the previous row, you reduce the chance of soil pushing the timbers out. Look online, or talk to someone who has built a timber wall for an explanation of this process. You are probably capable of doing this yourself and will save a lot of money if you do.

When fastening lower beds together, do not use nails. Use expensive 3-inch trimhead self-screwing stainless steel deck screws or less expensive ordinary stainless steel screws. The deck screws are the easiest to use since they are thin and very sharp, but you may have to call around to find them. Some people will not know what you are talking about. Small lumber yards often do. You will need a power drill with a specific bit to screw these in. Predrilling holes is helpful with regular stainless steel screws and not necessary with the self-screwing type.

Most raised beds are squares or rectangles. To avoid a lopsided bed, do the following: in clockwise fashion label each corner A, B, C, and D. Run a line (twine or rope) from A to C and from B to D. If both are the same length, your bed is square.

PART II

Vegetables, Berries, and Herbs

Vegetables, Berries, and Herbs

This part of the book is devoted to specific plants. Each plant description follows the same format, but the information under each heading is specific to that plant and can make a big difference in your success growing it.

Each plant listing begins with the common name of the plant described in that section. Underneath the common name are the genus and the species, and under that the family name. For example, Sweet Potato, *Ipomoea batatas,* Morning Glory Family (Convolvulaceae): sweet potato is the common name; the overall group, or genus, is *Ipomoea*; the species is *batatas.* In some sections there is not one specific species but many. The family name is important if you want to try crop rotation (see chapter 6).

The brief introduction to the plant explains whether the plant prefers cold or warm weather, why you might want to grow it, and where the plant may have originated. This is followed by a short description of how the plant grows. The goal is to give you a more intimate feeling about the plant and tell you how much effort and time are required to grow it. Since some of the plants are not ideally suited to cold climates, this section may serve as a warning that success could be difficult, but it is possible to grow all of the plants in this growing guide if you follow the steps outlined in the individual descriptions.

The nutrient charts in the plant descriptions list the quantities of nutrients present in the plant in significant amounts and what percentage of the daily recommended values (% DV) those quantities represent. The amounts are *approximate* and in most instances come from the USDA National Nutrient Database and NutritionData.com. Plants contain many more nutrients than those listed but in relatively small amounts. The purpose of these charts is to make nutrient comparison between plants quick and easy. Note that folate may be referred to as vitamin B9 and occurs naturally in plants. It is sometimes referred to as folic acid, which it is not. Folic acid is a synthetic product. Niacin is the same as vitamin B3; pantothenic acid, the same as vitamin B5; riboflavin, the same as vitamin B2; and thiamin (originally spelled thiamine), the same as vitamin B1.

The varieties listed at the end of the chapter are suggested for growing in cold climates. The varietal lists indicate whether the plant is a hybrid, open pollinated (OP), or an heirloom. Heirlooms are all open pollinated. Anyone planning on saving seed needs to know this since only open-pollinated plants will produce seed that duplicates the parent plant. Also listed are the days to maturity, either from seed or from date of transplant. The colder your climate, the more important it is to choose varieties that mature quickly.

Some plant names are followed by five asterisks (*****). These are not necessarily the best plants in any given group but rather the ones recommended as a good place to start for comparison. If possible, always grow more than one plant in the varietal list. Each year keep plants you like, and try others. Over a period of time you will find your personal favorites. How plants thrive varies from one garden to another; even the taste may vary. Your list will be garden specific.

All of these plants were available at the time this guide was written, but varieties do come and go. For information on the sources for plants, see "Mail-Order Sources" in chapter 2.

Three sections cover plants in a different format: "Greens," "Herbs," and "Unique Plants." Some of these plants are difficult to grow in cold climates; others are simply not well known or not as popular. The plants listed as greens are important for their high nutritional value. The herb section, which includes a few flowers, is clearly aimed at cooks looking to add special flavors to their dishes. Cooking vegetables does not have to be complicated, and herbs add a delicious touch to even the simplest dish. Unique plants require special growing techniques or are unfamiliar to most gardeners. Some may be quite difficult to grow in cold areas with short seasons.

Read through the glossary at the end of the book to learn gardening terms; understanding the language of gardening can be challenging at first. The glossary also includes information that will be helpful as you continue to read about organic gardening.

Wait until asparagus is at least the width of a pencil before harvesting.

ASPARAGUS

Asparagus officinalis, **also known as** *Asparagus officinalis* var. *altilis*
**Asparagus Family (Asparagaceae), formerly Amaryllis (Amaryllidaceae),
Lily (Liliaceae), or Onion (Alliaceae) Families**

Asparagus is a very hardy, cold-season perennial. It requires extreme patience to get it established, but once growing vigorously it produces for decades. Many gardeners await its arrival in early spring with anticipation. It is without question one of the most interesting and rewarding vegetables to grow. Asparagus probably originated in the eastern Mediterranean but may also have come from northern Africa or western Asia.

How Asparagus Grows

Asparagus starts as a small, black seed (950 to 1,200 seeds per ounce), which sprouts and produces a thin, frail, upright asparagus spear (stem). This tiny spear sends off little side branches that give the plant a fernlike appearance. Food produced by the foliage helps the young plant create an increasingly extensive root system that shoots out laterally like tentacles of an octopus. The roots look like thin, fleshy fingers attached to a crown, the thick lower portion of stem known as a rhizome. The underground crown enlarges throughout the growing season. On its top it produces new buds (nodes) that look like little white bumps. Asparagus spears emerge from these nodes each season to create ever larger mounds of green foliage, which turn yellowish brown and finally dry up in the fall. The plant goes into a dormant period during the winter. Each year the crown gets bigger and creates more and larger asparagus spears. Each plant will be either male or female. Mature female plants blossom with tiny, yellowish-green, bell-shaped flowers, which mature into soft, deep-red berries with two or more hard, black seeds inside to begin the life cycle anew. The seeds are mildly poisonous and if eaten, can cause vomiting and pain.

Where to Plant Asparagus
Site and Light

Asparagus thrives in full sun. The more sun you can provide, the better. A south-facing slope in cold climate areas is ideal. But don't worry. Asparagus is adaptable and will do well in a wide variety of locations even if they aren't

Nutrition Facts
Serving size: 100 grams (3.5 ounces)

	AMOUNT PER RAW SERVING	% DV	AMOUNT PER COOKED SERVING	% DV
Calories	20	1%	18	1%
Carbohydrate	4 g	1%	2 g	1%
Copper	0.2 mg	9%	0.1 mg	5%
Dietary fiber	2 g	8%	2 g	6%
Folate	50 mcg	13%	140 mcg	35%
Manganese	0.2 mg	8%	0.1 mg	7%
Protein	2 g	4%	3 g	6%
Riboflavin	0.1 mg	8%	0.1 mg	6%
Thiamin	0.2 mg	11%	0.1 mg	4%
Vitamin A	755 IU	15%	1,005 IU	20%
Vitamin C	5.6 mg	9%	21 mg	40%
Vitamin E	1.5 mg	7%	1.2 mg	6%
Vitamin K	40 mg	50%	80 mcg	100%

"perfect." Since asparagus will be growing in the same spot for years, choose your planting site carefully. You never want to transplant asparagus. Avoid planting asparagus in a low-lying frost pocket or wet area. Roots will rot out in overly wet soil. You can plant asparagus in rows on one side of the garden or right down the middle, or in its own special bed separate from other vegetables. Planting on the side of the garden is most commonly done. The plants are out of the way, but weeds do tend to go unnoticed, and asparagus competes poorly with them. Planting in the middle of the garden draws your attention to any weeds that do sprout. There is no one right answer.

Soil and Moisture

Asparagus flourishes in rich soil that retains moisture but is loose and drains freely. The ideal pH is from 6 to 7 or even a bit higher. Soil preparation should be done during the fall before a spring planting if possible. Preparing the bed can be arduous work. The planting area should be deep and wide—at least 16 inches deep and several feet wide. The average home garden does not have good soil to this depth. If you do, loosen it thoroughly with a spade or rototiller, removing all rocks and debris. If you don't, you can either replace the subsoil with loam or build a raised bed. In both cases you may have to purchase loam from a nursery. Proper bed preparation is worth it for perennial plants that can produce well for 20 years or longer.

Once the soil is loosened or replaced, dig a trench 16 inches deep and 1 foot wide for the full length of the proposed asparagus bed. The fastest way to do this is by digging down as deeply as possible with a pointed spade and setting the soil off to the side of the trench. Fill the bottom 4 to 8 inches with a mixture of compost, rotted leaves (leaf mold), and rotted manure if available. If not, just place loose soil amended with sphagnum peat moss back into the trench. Add organic fertilizer to the soil including bonemeal, blood meal, and rock phosphate. Other organic fertilizers are fine as long as the mix contains enough phosphorus, potassium, and nitrogen. A little lime or wood ash can also be added, especially if using peat as a soil amendment. Mix all of this together, and level the trench, marking the ends so that you know where to plant the following year.

If all of this seems overwhelming, you can dig individual holes for each crown. Each hole should be deep and wide. If the soil is poor, replace and amend it as if making a trench. The one danger with this method is that water tends to pool in heavy soils, such as clay. Asparagus does not like wet feet and may die out. If your overall planting area is loose and sandy, this is less of a concern.

Planting
Seed

It takes three years to grow asparagus from seed. Still, there are many advantages. Seeds are inexpensive, and almost all the seeds germinate. You can try a number of unusual varieties that may be hard to find locally or as crowns. Rarely is fusarium root rot brought in with seeds, whereas this can be a problem with crowns purchased locally or through mail order.

Asparagus likes 75°F soil for peak germination, but ignore this and get the seeds into the ground as soon as the soil can be worked when temperatures are as low as 50°F. This will allow the seeds to absorb moisture, and they will sprout as soon as the soil temperature suits them. Plant them ½ to 1 inch deep about 2 to 3 inches apart. Seed germination generally occurs within 21 days.

Plant the seeds in rows. When the seeds sprout, you will see thin, fernlike plants popping through the soil. The most important requirement for starting asparagus from seed outdoors is to keep the plants moist at all times. The following spring the seedlings can be transplanted to a permanent location.

You can also start seed indoors at least 12 weeks before outdoor planting. Soak the hard seeds in tepid water for up to 2 days as long as you change the water several times per day. Fill containers with sterile starting mix, place seeds about ½ inch deep, and moisten with a mister. The seeds germinate best in warm soil (77°–86°F). Place the pots on a heating pad. If not available, plants will still grow at 70°F. Provide light as seeds pop up, and water when soil just begins to dry out.

Transplants

Most gardeners start asparagus beds from crowns purchased in local garden stores or from mail-order houses. Crowns are sold according to age or size. Plants older than 1 year are hard to find, and most guides tell you to buy 1-year-old crowns. They claim that they grow better than older plants, which suffer transplant shock. A high-quality asparagus crown will have a healthy root system. The roots will be firm but pliable. Each crown should have several growing buds, little protrusions, on the top of the plant. These will grow into asparagus spears. The more of these, the better. Larger crowns usually have longer and larger roots and more buds on each. When buying crowns, ask about their age and size.

Check the roots carefully. If roots have mushy ends, snip the damaged portion off with scissors. If the entire root is mushy, return the plant. If there is a little white mold, soak the plants for 30 seconds in a solution of 1 part bleach and 9 parts water. Then rinse. If any other color mold is present, return the crowns.

Then check the buds. Make sure that they have not been knocked off or damaged. Damage to these buds is common. Sometimes, they are completely absent, making the crown next to worthless.

Look at each crown closely to see whether several crowns are intertwined. If they are, gently pull them apart under running water. You may get as many as three or four small crowns from some of these clumps.

If you buy plants locally, buy them as soon as they are available—the less time in the package or in open bins, the better. Open the package immediately, even in the store. Check them out. Do not have overly high expectations. Roots are often quite small with limited root systems. As long as each crown has a few firm bumps on top and firm roots, they will grow. If necessary, you can store them *briefly* at home in your refrigerator. Keep them cool and dry. Wet or frozen crowns will rot.

When you are ready to plant, soak the crowns in a bucket of water for at least 30 minutes. You can carry the crowns in the bucket while you plant so that they stay moist until they are buried in the ground.

Your bed or planting holes should already be prepared. Dig a deep trench the full length of the planting bed where it was prepared in fall. Then make a ridge in the center of the trench by drawing up soil toward the middle. The ridge acts as support for crowns. If possible the top of the ridge should be 6 to 8 inches below the surrounding soil. If planting in individual holes, make a mound in the center of the hole with its top 6 to 8 inches below the surrounding soil. The deeper you plant asparagus, the later it will emerge in the spring. In cold climates deeper planting can be an advantage since air temperature will be warmer when the spears pop through the soil.

Set the crowns on top of the ridge or mound. Spread the roots out in all directions as if setting a wig on the soil. Plant the buds up. Fill in the trench or planting hole just enough to cover all the roots and the crown to the base of the buds. Firm the soil around each crown, being careful not to break off the buds. Water the newly planted crowns thoroughly. After the water has drained down through the soil, cover the crowns with 2 inches of soil mixed with some fully decomposed organic matter. Water again. When the soil settles, the very tips of the buds will be almost at the soil surface. Over the coming days or weeks gradually fill in the trench as the spears grow, always leaving a few inches of stem and maturing foliage exposed to light. By planting on a ridge or mound, you decrease the chance of root rot.

Spacing

Asparagus plants grow over time to several feet tall and a little less wide. A typical plant can send out roots for up to 6 feet in all directions. Spacing helps with air circulation, which prevents disease. However, some gardeners plant them closer together than commonly recommended to stop the heavy foliage from toppling over. Planting in all directions varies from 18 to 24 inches or more depending upon the philosophy of an individual gardener. Do not interplant asparagus with other vegetables. It needs all the water and nutrients it can get.

When to Plant

Get seed and plants into the soil as early in spring as possible for a long growing season. This helps plants create an extensive root system and lots of foliage to form food for the underground crown. The soil has to be 50°F for seed to germinate. Plant crowns up to 4 weeks after the frost-free date at the latest.

Support

Asparagus plants can get gangly. Some gardeners stake the four corners of the bed and run nylon string or wire along the outside edges between the supports. This keeps the ferns from weeping over and taking up even more space. This is why planting asparagus in a separate bed outside the main garden appeals to many.

How to Care for Asparagus
Water

Asparagus is the camel of the plant world. Frequent, deep waterings will stimulate lush growth, lots of food storage in the crown, and beautiful spears the following year. Water is especially important as spears begin to form foliage. The more foliage, the better. It's almost impossible to overwater plants in full growth in well-drained soil. Even so, once mature, asparagus is drought tolerant, and too much water can be a problem in more compact soil.

Mulch

Keep the beds mulched at all times to cut down on weeds and to increase soil moisture, essential for good foliage growth. Apply mulch as soon as the spears emerge from the ground in spring. Good mulch includes straw (7 inches thick), grass clippings (3 inches thick), shredded leaves (3 inches thick), or any other organic material available locally. Apply mulch up to, but not over, the crowns. Add mulch as needed throughout the growing season.

Fertilizing

Although you have prepared the bed with major nutrients, asparagus is a heavy feeder and needs to form lush, ferny foliage to produce food for the crown. Side-dress the crowns throughout the growing season with manure and compost if available. Feed regularly with organic fertilizers high in nitrogen, such as blood meal, cottonseed meal, or guano. Some growers use corn gluten meal, which is high in nitrogen and kills weed seeds just as they begin to sprout. It does not kill weeds once they have emerged from the ground.

At the end of the season, remove all mulch, weeds, and dried foliage. Cultivate the soil around the crowns with a pronged hoe. Never dig deep. Just scratch the soil. Then cover the asparagus bed, but not the crowns themselves, with a 2- to 3-inch mat of well-rotted manure. If no manure is available, use compost. Not enough compost? Then settle for loose soil supplemented with organic fertilizers including blood meal, bonemeal, fish emulsion, and rock phosphate. Fish emulsion and bonemeal add calcium to the soil. Fish emulsion is a rich source of micronutrients as well. Note that this covering should be loose and not at all compacted.

Weeding

Asparagus has an extensive root system that goes both deep and wide. The plants compete poorly with weeds, especially perennial weeds that steal valuable nutrients and water from the crowns. *Kill all perennial weeds before planting the bed.* Hand pull any weeds that sprout through the mulch. Salt was once used by growers to kill weeds, but I do not advise its use by the home gardener, since once it reaches a certain level, it becomes toxic—way too much of a gamble.

Thinning

If there are female plants in the garden, they may self-seed. The tiny, emerging plants can be pulled out or transplanted. In cold climates they often die off if not given special attention. So, thinning is rarely a problem.

Pruning

At the end of the season, clean up your asparagus bed by cutting back all the dead stems to ground level with hedge trimmers or hand pruners. Don't do this while the plants are still green; wait until they are completely dry. Pruning gets rid of winter habitat for insects and reduces the chance of disease the following season. Compost the debris. If you have had asparagus beetles or problems with disease, burn the foliage.

Winter Protection

Many cold-climate gardeners mulch asparagus beds in the winter, most commonly in the first year. A 6- to 8-inch layer of straw is the easiest winter mulch to use, but pine boughs do a good job in the far north. Both trap snow and protect the plants beautifully.

Special Considerations

Blanching asparagus by hilling up soil around the spears is possible. The spears turn white and are tender, but the loss of vitamins makes this practice seem archaic, at least to me.

For most people, urine smells after eating asparagus since the plant contains asparagusic acid, which is converted into a smelly, sulfurous compound after consumption. It is not at all harmful, just noticeable and annoying.

Problems

Insects

While a number of insects will infest these plants, asparagus beetles are the major problem. Both the adults and larvae of the common asparagus beetle (wings with yellowish patches) can cause considerable damage to spears. The adults of the twelve-spotted asparagus beetle (red with six black dots on each wing) also damage spears, causing them to come up from the soil bent to one side, looking like a shepherd's crook. Handpicking and destroying both types of adult beetles is the usual advice. Asparagus aphids also cause shoots to come up and form bushy foliage. Treat as for shepherd's crook, or simply wait them out. It may take several years for their population to decline.

Salt is sometimes recommended to control weeds and asparagus beetles. Its buildup can be toxic and requires extreme monitoring. Don't use it. Do remove and burn all brown foliage at the end of the season.

For serious infestations causing major damage, consider resorting to the organic pesticide pyrethrin. This is one of only two instances noted in this guide where use of a pesticide makes sense since this is a *perennial* crop that can be severely weakened over a period of years. Repeated applications will be necessary since asparagus grows rapidly.

Disease

Asparagus planted in low, wet areas is prone to disease. Avoid planting in such a location. Keep your bed free of weeds that harbor insects.

Asparagus can be affected by various types of fusarium. Infection generally shows up as yellowing foliage in early to midseason, well before foliage should deteriorate. If a plant starts to turn yellow in midseason, dig it up and get rid of it. Usually, the crown will be rotting underneath the soil surface. Note that many varieties are tolerant of fusarium rot. Remember that all asparagus turns from yellow to brown at the end of the season. This is not a sign of disease but rather a natural part of the plant's life cycle.

Rust *(Puccinia asparagi)* gives a reddish hue to stems and branches and causes them to wither. If rust develops, dust the plants with sulfur. Rust is usually brought in on infected plants and occasionally on strawberries. When buying asparagus seed or crowns, consider disease resistance. No variety will be completely disease-free, but start off on the right foot.

Marauders

It's rare for asparagus to be affected by marauders, with the possible exception of soil-dwelling rodents. Trap these if they become a nuisance.

Physiological

Asparagus is a really tough plant, but fluctuating spring temperatures can cause problems. Once growing, spears subjected to a late freeze in spring are best cut off immediately to encourage new growth from buds below. This is a relatively rare problem.

Propagation

Female plants will form little round fruits toward the end of the season. Let these mature. Then squeeze them between your fingers to pop out the tiny, hard, black seeds inside. Wash and dry these. Place in an envelop, and store in cool, dark place. Or plant them in a cold frame for moist chilling (stratification) over the winter. They will sprout early in spring. Seed will last for about 3 years and up to 5 in ideal conditions.

When you dig up a large plant, you may discover that it has formed more than one crown. If you can pull these apart, you will essentially be dividing the plant. But do not divide a solid single crown as you would for rhubarb. How to divide is a concern only when you are trying to relocate mature plants to a new area. This is challenging and not recommended.

Harvesting

When to harvest and for how long depends specifically on the age of the plant. When starting plants from seed, wait at least 2 to 3 years to harvest any asparagus. If planting 1-year-old crowns, harvest lightly the following year, if at all. Remove spears larger in circumference than a pencil for no more than 1 to 2 weeks. Let all of the other spears grow to produce as much ferny foliage as possible. In the third year harvest larger spears for a few weeks. In the fourth year harvest for about 4 weeks. From then on, harvest until spears are smaller than a pencil. Every year you want some spears to form lots of foliage to supply the crown with enough food to survive and thrive. If you are impatient and harvest too heavily too early, you may cause permanent damage to your crop.

To simplify, don't pick any asparagus until the spears are pencil-size. Always let at least five and preferably more spears go to fern on every plant each season.

Harvest spears when about 6 to 10 inches tall. The head of the spear should be compact with bud scales not starting to bush out into a fern. The lower part of a stem is usually whitish and woody; the upper part, green and tender.

The easiest way to pick asparagus is to bend it to one side from the top of the spear until it breaks. The entire piece that snaps off will be tender and delicious, not at all stringy or tough like some of the spears you buy in a store. Then remove the lower portion of stalk just below the soil surface. Note that once asparagus has been harvested, it begins to deteriorate by becoming increasingly stringy. That is why fresh asparagus is so much better than store-bought. Pick just before eating.

Alternatively, cut the spears off at the base or just under the soil surface with a sharp knife. The reason that commercial growers cut asparagus with much of the lower (whitish) stalk intact is to preserve moisture. This method of cutting can damage the crowns, and no home gardener needs to do it. Still, some do, often using an ultrasharp knife to sever the stem without pushing into the crown. The base of the spear can be tough to sever.

Storing

Asparagus deteriorates extremely rapidly. Bunches sold in stores often have wrinkled or frayed tips, a sign that the spears are not fresh. Both flavor and nutrition are lost as spears age when exposed to heat and light.

Asparagus stores poorly. To store, place the lower portion of unwashed stems in a glass of water in the refrigerator. Cover with plastic wrap. Or wrap the base of the spears in a moist paper towel. Use within 2 days or sooner if possible.

To freeze, wash, leave whole, or slice into pieces. Blanch 2 to 4 minutes depending on the thickness of stems. Cool in ice water for 3 minutes. Drain, lay on a tray, and freeze for 30 minutes. Pack in airtight bags, and freeze. Much of the texture and flavor is lost in this process. Note that asparagus can be pickled.

Culinary Uses

Do not eat asparagus flowers or berries.

Asparagus is edible raw or cooked. Raw asparagus is considered mildly toxic, but some gardeners snack on tips right in the garden as they would fresh strawberries. Pieces or thin strips can be added raw to salads along with bits of orange and Parmesan cheese, or can be blanched lightly, cooled quickly, and then added. Asparagus can be cooked in a wide variety of ways: boiling, grilling, microwaving, roasting, sautéing, steaming, or stir-frying.

To prepare, gently bend each spear if harvested from its base. The more tender portion will break off from the tougher lower portion. Set the tougher pieces aside to make soup. Some cooks peel stems; most don't. Asparagus is most attractive served whole, but it can be chopped or sliced if preferred.

Don't overcook asparagus. To boil, place spears in a flat pan of boiling water, and cook until tender but still firm. To grill, brush with oil, and roast, turning often to "char" all sides. To sauté, place in hot oil, and turn until done. To microwave, place in a little water, and cook just until tender. To roast, follow the same steps as for grilling. To steam, place bunches of upright stems in a pan filled with a couple of inches of water. Cover if possible. Bring the water to boil, and let the upper tips cook in the steam. To stir-fry, cut diagonally into 1-inch pieces. Cook in oil at high heat for 1 minute, add ½ cup broth, turn down the heat, and steam until tender.

Pieces of cooked asparagus are delicious added to any number of recipes but especially to omelets and pasta dishes. Asparagus makes a great side dish and can be covered in butter and spiced to taste or topped with cheese. While the asparagus tips are the delicacy, you can use the tougher bottom pieces in cream of asparagus soup. Cook, drain, purée, strain, and add to cream. Straining removes the stringy fiber in the lower portion of the spears.

Note that purple varieties turn green when cooked.

Varieties

Numerous varieties are offered in catalogs. The following are the best for cold climates. The all-male (androecious) varieties are popular because the spears are thick and succulent. However, the term *all male* should be changed to *mostly male*. The common belief is that thick spears taste better than thin ones: this is simply not true. They are just bigger, not necessarily better. For this reason, the older, open-pollinated (heirloom) varieties still have a faithful following. They produce both male and female plants and appeal to seed savers.

Note that many of these seed-grown varieties have "Washington" in their name. Seeds from these will produce perfectly good asparagus but cannot be considered specific varieties since seed has gotten mixed up over the years.

Resistance or at least tolerance to rust, fusarium wilt, and crown rot is certainly worth considering when choosing plants. Resistance indicates a higher level of protection than tolerance, but no asparagus plant is completely resistant to disease.

VARIETY	MOSTLY MALE	DISEASE TOLERANCE
'Jersey Giant Hybrid'	Yes	Good disease tolerance
'Jersey Knight Hybrid'	Yes	Good disease tolerance
'Jersey Supreme Hybrid'	Yes	Good disease tolerance
'Millennium Hybrid'	Yes	Some disease tolerance
'Purple Passion' (heirloom)	No	NA
'Sweet Purple' (OP)	No	NA
'Walker Deluxe Hybrid'	Yes	Good disease tolerance

Even just brushing past basil plants as you walk through the garden creates a wonderful scent.

BASIL

Ocimum basilicum species
Mint Family (Lamiaceae, formerly Labiatae)

Basil is a tender, warm-season perennial grown as an annual in cold climates. Even in warmer climates, it is short-lived. The delightful fragrance and rich taste of basil make it worth growing. The foliage of different varieties varies in color from light green to deep purple. Every time you water the garden the plant gives off a pervasive, sweet scent. The delicate flowers of some varieties are eye-catching. Basil is easy to grow, and you can start it each year from seed without a lot of fuss. It also takes up little space for all the pleasure it gives. You need only a pinch of leaves to give omelets, salads, soups, and stews a distinctive flavor. And it is, of course, the main ingredient in fresh pesto sauce. Basil is believed to be native to Asia, Iran, and the Middle East. Varieties may have also originated in India to be imported to Europe centuries ago.

How Basil Grows

Basil germinates from tiny, almost round to oval, dark-brown to black seed (about 13,000 to 18,000 seeds per ounce). The plants grow rapidly once they take root in the garden. The stems are four-sided with leaves varying in color, shape, size, and texture by variety. They all exude an exquisite and unique aroma when brushed. The scent comes from essential oils, which vary from one variety to the next. Plants form whorled flower heads (calyxes) made up of tiny flowers, which also vary in color by variety. Some are so lovely that the plants are considered prized ornamentals by some home gardeners. The shape of the flower heads does vary by variety. The flowers will form seed (nutlets) if flower heads are allowed to mature. Seed is easily collected for next year's crop.

Where to Plant Basil
Site and Light

Basil thrives in a warm, sheltered, sunny location. Plants will tolerate light shade if summers are extremely hot, but full sun is the preferred location. Basil is extremely susceptible to frost either in spring or fall, so avoid planting it in low-lying frost pockets. Ideally, plant basil somewhere close to the kitchen. If you have to run a marathon each time you

Nutrition Facts

Serving size: 100 grams (3.5 ounces)

	AMOUNT PER RAW SERVING	% DV
Calcium	175 mg	18%
Calories	23	1%
Carbohydrates	3 g	1%
Copper	0.4 mg	19%
Dietary fiber	2 g	6%
Folate	68 mcg	17%
Iron	3.2 mg	18%
Magnesium	64 mg	16%
Manganese	1.1 mg	57%
Potassium	295 mg	8%
Protein	3 g	6%
Vitamin A	5,275 IU	105%
Vitamin B6	0.2 mg	8%
Vitamin C	18 mg	30%
Vitamin K	415 mcg	520%

need it, you may not use it as often. Consider growing it in a perennial border for its lush and colorful foliage.

Soil and Moisture

Basil thrives in loose, rich garden soil that drains freely. If you have compacted soil, build a raised bed. Since basil needs consistent moisture, add organic matter to the soil. Basil thrives in a slightly acidic soil with a pH of 5.5 to 6.5, so adding sphagnum peat moss to the soil is highly recommended.

Container

'Cuban', 'Green Bouquet', 'Minimum', 'Piccolo', and 'Spicy Globe' are varieties that grow well in 12-inch pots filled with a potting mix made of sphagnum peat moss, perlite, and garden soil. Enrich the mixture with organic fertilizer. Keep the containers only steps away from the kitchen in a sunny spot. Other varieties also grow well but demand larger containers.

Planting

Seed

Seeding basil directly in the garden is possible, but starting plants indoors or purchasing transplants from a local nursery is recommended. The soil must be at least 60°F before you plant seed outdoors. Plant seed about ⅛ to ¼ inch deep depending on the texture of your soil. Keep the soil consistently moist to aid germination. Seed that is moist and warm generally germinates within a week. Seed placed in cool soil rots. Germinating seed allowed to dry out will die.

When growing purple-leaved varieties, pull up and eat any seedlings with green markings on the leaves.

Transplants

Start seed indoors in a sterile starting mix about 4 to 6 weeks before planting outdoors. Press into the soil surface, leaving seeds exposed to light. Keep the mix moist and warm: at least 70°F or higher during the day, and 50° to 65°F at night. Once growing, plants need good light, up to 16 hours per day, to become stocky. Bottom watering is effective, but don't let soil get soggy. Potting up is highly recommended when plants have two sets of true leaves. Feed with highly diluted organic fertilizer to spur growth. Pinch off growing tips if plants begin to get gangly.

Spacing

Spacing between individual plants is critical for basil to produce lush, full foliage. Plants should be at least 8 inches apart, preferably more. If planted too closely together, none of the plants will do well. One plant growing on its own will produce far more leaves than a bunch of plants planted closely together. Good air circulation around the plants also reduces the chance of disease.

Basil bought from a nursery often has a number of plants per pot. Tap the root ball out of the pot, and gently tease the roots apart. Keeping soil around the roots is difficult, but avoid damaging the roots themselves as best you can. Each plant should have a solid stem attached to a cluster of roots. Get these into the soil immediately, and give plenty of room to mature. Firm the soil around the roots, and water the plants well. Plants often wilt initially but will spring back to life if the weather is warm and if you keep the soil moist. A mild transplant solution is recommended at this time, as is a *thin* layer of mulch around the plants, which often topple over and get stuck in the soil.

When to Plant

Basil is a tender plant and extremely frost sensitive. You gain nothing by trying to plant seeds or transplants too early. Successive plantings are one way to ensure healthy plants throughout a longer growing season. However, you will be harvesting leaves from young rather than mature plants with later plantings. Wait until temperatures are in the 65° to 70°F range for best results.

Support

Basil can get large. Plants are remarkably sturdy, but support doesn't hurt, especially when growing the plant in containers. Get supports in place early. Tie plants to the support with loose figure-eight knots made of fabric or soft material.

How to Care for Basil

Water

Keep young plants moist until growing vigorously. At that stage let the soil dry out between deep waterings around the base of the plant. Don't let it wilt; if it does, it may lose some of its essential oils.

Mulch

Basil needs lots of moisture and warm soil. When the soil is very warm, apply a 1- to 3-inch layer of mulch around the plant. This helps preserve moisture. Grass clippings are easy to use, readily available, and effective. Some people dry these before use in the garden. I never have, but I do not apply them thickly. Shredded leaves and straw also work well and are more attractive.

Fertilizing

Leafy plants need enough fertilizer to maintain uniform and consistent growth. If your soil is rich enough to begin with, you may not need additional fertilizer in the growing season. If leaves begin to turn pale, side-dress with an organic fertilizer high in nitrogen, such as blood meal. Fish emulsion is another good fertilizer to use throughout the growing season.

Weeding

Keep the area weed-free throughout the entire growing season. Avoid cultivating around the plant to avoid damaging the shallow roots. Pull weeds near the stem by hand.

Thinning

If you have planted basil as described earlier, no thinning is necessary.

Pruning or Pinching Back

You grow basil primarily for its scented leaves. The more leaves a plant produces, the better. The simplest way to get lots of leaves is to pinch back the growing tips on all stems and branches regularly. Pinching back really means pinching or snipping off the last inch or so of growth just above a pair of leaves. Whenever basil begins to form a flower, pinch it out between your thumb and forefinger. The plant will then send off side shoots like little branches. These in turn mature and produce leaves. The tips of the side shoots can in turn be pinched back to encourage even more growth. If a plant gets really bushy with multiple flower heads, shear them off with a scissors. Alternatively, you can begin cutting back plants when young to three sets of leaves. New branches will form and can be cut back in the same manner.

The plant gets increasingly bushy. Experiment with both methods to settle on the one you prefer.

Special Considerations

Basil is reputed to keep flies and mosquitoes away on decks and patios. This has not been my experience, but I have not grown types with a camphor or turpentine scent. The various scents of listed varieties comes from essential oils: eugenol (clove scent), linalool (lavender or floral), and methyl chavicol or estragole (fruity anise).

Extending the Season

Basil is extremely frost sensitive. Consider growing a plant in a pot to bring indoors at the end of the season. Place it in a sunny window sill. Don't expect too much.

Problems

Insects

Aphids can be a problem. Spray them off with a jet of water, or remove any infested leaves. Handpick grasshoppers and Japanese beetles. Slugs occasionally damage leaves, so using a flashlight, pick them off at night.

Disease

Basil was once considered relatively disease-free. In recent years basil downy mildew has been spreading, possibly from contaminated seed. It shows up as purplish-gray spores on the undersides of yellowing leaves. Some varieties appear to be more resistant than others. Ask when purchasing seed. Fusarium can also be a problem. If a plant suddenly wilts and does not respond to watering, dig it up and burn it. The disease is fatal, and you want to get rid of the plant as quickly as possible. 'Nufar Hybrid' is resistant to fusarium wilt but not downy mildew. Buy your seed from a trusted source. Finally, prevent leaf drop and spotting with proper spacing for good air circulation and the use of mulch to stop soil from splashing up on the leaves.

Propagation

Basil is insect pollinated. To save seed, let some shoots go to flower. Once the plant forms seeds, it will deteriorate. Its mission is complete. Let flowers dry. Late on a sunny, hot day, clip the seed heads off. Strip the dried, circular disks surrounding the stem into a bag with one swipe of your hand. Break these apart when fully dry to separate out the seeds. Let dry further. Seal in an envelope. Seed lasts about 3 to 5 years and even longer if kept frozen in an airtight plastic freezer bag. Varieties will cross, so grow only one variety at a time, or remove all flowers from all but one variety.

For cuttings, cut a 4-inch piece of stem with several pairs of leaves from the tip of a nonflowering stem. Cut just below a leaf node. Strip off all but the top set of leaves. Place the stem in water in an opaque container or cup. Change the water daily to keep it clean and oxygenated. Once roots form, plant in sterile starting mix in a pot until growing vigorously. Then plant outdoors. This is a good way to get true purple plants from ones beginning to have green spots on the foliage. Take cuttings with only purple foliage to start new plants.

Harvesting

There are varying opinions about how and when to harvest basil. Letting the plant mature until it has at least several sets of leaves is important. Some people let the plant mature much longer, but it is up to you.

You can either harvest small amounts of leaves from the top of individual plants or cut the stem off just above a set of leaves below. New growth will emerge from the leaf axils, places where leaves join the stem, just below the cut.

Enjoy the scent and beauty of the plant indoors by cutting off a stem and placing it in room temperature water. Combined with Italian parsley, it makes a lovely edible arrangement. Change the water daily. Adding a little sugar and lemon juice to the water may help the stems last longer.

Any part of the plant pinched off during the season can be used in cooking. This includes the whorls at the tips of the plants as they begin to form flowers. Don't toss these away as many people do. They are delicious.

Storing

The simplest way to store basil for a few days is to strip off only the lower leaves of several stems, place the stems in a container filled with water, and cover with a plastic bag. Keep in a cool place out of direct sun. If you place leafy stems in the refrigerator, they often turn color, although some people do wrap stems in moist paper and store in a plastic bag for a few days.

Basil leaves can be either dried or frozen. Cut the stems off the plant, hang them upside down in a dry place, strip off the leaves when they are completely dry, or place leaves on a screen in an airy spot outdoors but not in direct sunlight. Leaves may turn dark brown to black. They are dry when they become brittle. Possibly the best way to dry leaves is in an oven at low heat, roughly 150°F with the door open a crack. Store dried leaves whole, not crumbled up, in an opaque, airtight jar in a dark place.

To freeze, strip off leaves from stems, then flash freeze in a single layer on a cookie sheet covered with wax or parchment paper. Remove from tray when frozen, and place in plastic freezer bags. Leaves may turn black. When needed, do not thaw. Break off pieces of frozen basil, and toss into cooked dishes as late as possible in the cooking process. Or make into pesto (see below).

Culinary Uses

Basil, often referred to as the "Queen of Herbs," offers a wide variety of scents, colors, and flavors. It is commonly used in fish, poultry, and rice dishes. It is added to tomato sauces and put fresh on top of pizzas. The leaves and seeds of some varieties are used in desserts and sweet drinks. Whenever using fresh basil for a salad or dish, cut it at the last possible moment. It tends to turn color if cut or torn apart too soon. Cooking often intensifies the flavor.

One of the simplest uses for basil is to place leaves alongside freshly sliced tomatoes and splash with olive oil. Or mix with diced tomatoes and cubed mozzarella cheese. Butter flavored with basil is a delight. Chop up the basil in a processor. Add garlic and spices to taste. Mix into butter, and chill before serving.

The varieties with small leaves are excellent for bruschetta. Eat the leaf, stem and all, for this dish. A number of varieties have deep-red to purple leaves. Add some of these to vinegar for a rich red or opal coloration. Pack them into a glass jar. Pour white vinegar over the leaves. Seal the jar. Place it in a dark spot at room temperature. Let the vinegar absorb the flavor and color of the leaves for at least 2 weeks. Store in a dark closet to retain color. The leaves left in the vinegar are lovely.

Here's a recipe for pesto from Oregon State's extension service:

> ¼ cup pine nuts (or sunflower seeds, walnuts, or a combination)
> 3 cloves garlic
> 2 cups fresh basil leaves (or 1 cup basil and 1 cup parsley leaves)
> ¼ cup grated Parmesan cheese
> ¼ teaspoon salt
> ½ cup olive oil

Finely chop nuts and garlic in a food processor. (A blender can also be used, but it is more time consuming). Add basil, and chop really fine. Add Parmesan cheese and salt. Mix well. When everything is blended, add oil, and mix all ingredients together.

Some cooks season with pepper as well. Place paste in an

ice cube tray, and freeze. Add cubes to dishes without thawing. The classic variety used to make pesto is 'Genovese', although many other varieties serve that purpose well.

The flowers are edible and should be picked just as they open. Add them to salads, or sprinkle into soups or over pasta dishes. Do not use seeds for sprouts, since they turn slimy.

Varieties

There are more than thirty different species of basil. The most common is sweet basil *(Ocimum basilicum)* available in an incredible number of varieties with various aromas, leaf colors, sizes, and tastes. Other popular subspecies and crosses include *Ocimum basilicum* var. *citriodorum* (lemon basil), *Ocimum basilicum* var. *crispum* (lettuce leaf basil), *Ocimum basilicum* 'Minimum' (dwarf green basil), and *Ocimum basilicum* var. *purpurascens* (purple-leafed basil).

Many basils are used as ornamentals. *Ocimum basilicum* var. *canum, sanctum,* or *tenuiflorum* (holy basil) is one noted for the beauty of its pinkish-purple blossoms, although many edible varieties have distinctive blooms as well. *Ocimum selloi* is unusual in that it has the look and taste of peppers. *Ocimum kilimandscharicum* (camphor basil) grows up to 36 inches and is reported to repel insects (mostly anecdotal evidence). It is not included in the varietal table.

Many of the purple-leaved varieties are noted for reverting to plants with green markings on the foliage. This includes both 'Dark Opal' and 'Purple Ruffles'. For uniform color, 'Red Rubin' may be the best choice. Purples do not grow as fast or vigorously as green types. The charming 'Well-Sweep Purple Miniature' is grown only from cuttings, which are available from Well-Sweep Herb Farm. Note that 'Cuban' basil is fairly cold tolerant, while 'Green Pepper' basil can withstand a mild frost. Finally, confusion regarding the names of different varieties and what species they come from has been a problem for years. The names in this chart are presently being used in catalogs. Worry less about a plant's background and more about how the plants perform for you.

VARIETIES	DAYS	FOLIAGE/STEM/FLOWERS	TASTE	HEIGHT (INCHES)
'Amethyst Improved'	60–70	Blackish purple/purple/purple	Anise licorice	16–20
'Anise'	75	Dark green serrated/red purple/light pink	Anise licorice	24
'Cinnamon'	70–80	Veined narrow green/purplish/lavender pink	Cinnamon	12–24+
'Cuban'	75	Medium green/green/white (rarely flowers)	Spicy sweet basil	18
'Dark Opal' (AAS-1962) (var. *purpurascens*)	70–80	Maroon green/reddish/lilac purple pink	Flowery to bitter	18
'Dwarf Green Bush'	75	Light to medium green/green/white	Sweet with lemon	8–10
'Genoa Green' (see 'Genovese')				
'Genoa Green Improved' (see 'Genovese')				
'Genovese' (heirloom)*****	70–80	Pointed, shiny green, curled under/green/white	Sweet peppery	18–26
'Genovese Verde Migliorato' (see 'Genovese')				
'Green Bouquet'	60–80	Tiny/green/white	Sweet basil	12
'Green Pepper' (*O. selloi*)	75	Glossy green leathery/green/maroon pink	Green bell pepper	24–36
'Green Ruffles'	60–90	Large, green, quilted/green/white	Subtle sweet basil	24
'Holy Basil Nicobar' (Thai basil)	90	Light green/purple/purple	Clove	18–24
'Holy Basil Samui' (Thai basil)	90	Light green purple/purple/purple	Clove	18–24
'Horapha' (see 'Thai Sweet Basil')				
'Italian Cameo'*****	60–70	Pointed, indented, lime green/green/white	Sweet basil	8–12
'Italian Genovese' (see 'Genovese')				
'Italian Large Leaf' (see 'Large Leaved Italian')				
'Langkuri' (Thai sweet)	80	Shiny bright green/purplish green/deep red purple	Mild licorice basil	12–24
'Large Leaved Italian' (heirloom)	60–90	Large, crumpled, green/green/white	Sweet basil	24–30
'Lemon' (var. *citriodorum*)	80	Light to medium green/green/white	Citrus lemon	18
'Lettuce Leaf' (var. *crispum*)	85	Frilly, large, thick green/green/white	Subtle anise minty	16–24
'Licorice' (see 'Anise')				
'Lime' (var. *citriodorum*)	60	Bright green/green/white	Citrus lime	16–20
'Magical Michael' (AAS-2002)	80	Olive green/purplish/purple white	Sweet basil	16

VARIETIES	DAYS	FOLIAGE/STEM/FLOWERS	TASTE	HEIGHT (INCHES)
'Mammoth'	80	Huge, shiny yellowish green/green/white	Subtle sweet basil	18
var. *minimum*	70–90	Tiny, medium green/green/white	Clove	6–12
'Mrs. Burn's Lemon' (var. *citriodorum*)*****	75–90	Bright green/green/white pink	Strong citrus lemon	18–30+
'Napoletano'*****	60–70	Huge, light green, puckered/green/white	Anise mint	18–22
'New Guinea'	60–70	Arrow-like, green-tinted purple/purple/violet purple	Anise	18
'Nufar Hybrid'*****	85–90	Wrinkled, medium, green oval/green/white	Sweet basil	18–24+
'Opal' (see 'Dark Opal')				
'Osmin Purple'	70	Dark purple/purplish/lavender purple	Sweet fruity	12–24
'Penang' (var. *citriodorum*)	80	Light to medium green/green/purplish	Citrus lemon	18–24
'Piccolo' (heirloom)	70–80	Tiny, medium green/green/white	Mild sweet basil	12–20
'Profuma di Genova'	75–90	Large, light green/green/whitish	Sweet basil	12–18
'Purple Passion' (see 'Red Rubin')				
'Purple Ruffles' (AAS-1987) (var. *purpurascens*)	85	Purple/purple/purple pink	Cinnamon licorice	18–24
'Queenette' (Thai sweet)	75–85	Narrow green/purple/purplish	Clove mint	18
'Red Rubin'*****	75–80	Deep warm red/purplish/deep pink lavender	Strong sweet basil	12–18
'Rubin' (see 'Red Rubin')				
'Siam Queen' (AAS-1997)	70–80	Dark green/purple red/pink purple	Licorice basil	18–24
'Spicy Globe' (var. *minimum*)	60–80	Tiny, green/green/white	Sweet basil	12
'Sweet Basil'*****	85	Glossy medium green/green/white	Sweet basil	18
'Sweet Dani Hybrid' (AAS-1998)*****	75–90	Large olive green/green/white	Citrus lemon	18–26
'Sweet Green' (see 'Sweet Basil')				
'Sweet Thai' (see 'Thai')				
'Thai' or 'Thai Sweet'	65–90	Bright green/purple/purple	Anise clove	18–24
'Thai Magic'	65	Shiny, long, green/green/magenta	Sweet anise	18–24
'Thai Red Stem'	70–80	Deep green/purple/purple	Anise clove	18–24
'Thai Siam Queen' (see 'Siam Queen')				
'Verde Fino' (see 'Piccolo')				
'Well-Sweep Purple Miniature' (var. *minimum*)	30	Tiny purple/purple/pink	Subtle sweet basil	10
'Windowbox'	70–80	Pointed, narrow, green/green/white	Subtle sweet basil	6–8

BEANS

Phaseolus **species**
Legume or Pea Family (Fabaceae, formerly Leguminosae)

Most beans are tender, warm-season annuals, with the exception of the scarlet runner bean, which can be planted in cool soil. Beans are easy and inexpensive to grow. They are good for eating, great for your health, and wonderful for the garden with a root system that is highly beneficial to the structure of your soil. There are hundreds of bean varieties suited to many uses. A few of these varieties are called "peas" in the South, but they are actually beans. Bean plants are prolific and take up little space. Beans originated in Africa, Asia, Latin America, the Mediterranean, and South America.

How Beans Grow

Bean seed varies in shape, color, and size (anywhere from 30 to 150 seeds per ounce). It tends to be large and easy to work with. The seed leaves are easily noticeable as they emerge, and the true leaves are even larger. Beans form thick, but somewhat brittle, stems and a great deal of foliage. The short, stubby bush beans grow to a specific height (determinate), while pole beans are vining plants that continue growing in size (indeterminate). All varieties of beans produce lovely butterfly flowers in shades of pink, scarlet, and white depending on the variety. These flowers may be self-fertilizing or be pollinated by insects. Once pollinated, young beans begin to form. These pods can be eaten when they are young and green (French, snap, or string beans), or the seeds in the pods can be eaten when immature (lima or butter beans), or the seeds in the pods can be allowed to dry out (dry beans). A few varieties produce beans that are good in all three stages of growth.

Where to Plant Beans
Site and Light

Plant beans in full sun, a requirement of any vegetable that flowers and produces a fruit—in this case, pods. Place pole beans on the north side of the garden, since they grow tall and can shade other plants. The use of black fabric or plastic to warm up the soil and keep it warm throughout the season is highly recommended for lima beans. Ironically, runner beans do not like it hot and will not produce beans

Nutrition Facts

Serving size: 100 grams (3.5 ounces)

	SNAP BEAN		LIMA BEAN		DRY BEAN	
	AMOUNT PER COOKED SERVING	% DV	AMOUNT PER COOKED SERVING	% DV	AMOUNT PER COOKED SERVING	% DV
Calories	35	2%	115	6%	145	7%
Carbohydrates	8 g	3%	21 g	7%	26 g	9%
Copper	0.1 mg	3%	0.2 mg	12%	0.2 mg	11%
Dietary fiber	3 g	14%	7 g	28%	9 g	36%
Folate	33 mg	8%	83 mcg	21%	170 mcg	43%
Iron	0.7 mg	4%	2.4 mg	13%	2.1 mg	12%
Magnesium	18 mg	5%	43 mg	11%	60 mg	14%
Manganese	0.3 mg	14%	0.5 mg	26%	0.5 mg	23%
Phosphorus	30 mg	3%	110 mg	11%	145 mg	15%
Potassium	145 mg	4%	510 mg	15%	435 mg	12%
Protein	2 g	4%	8 g	16%	9 g	18%
Selenium	0.0 mcg	0%	4.5 mcg	6%	6.2 mcg	9%
Thiamin	0.1 mg	5%	0.2 mg	11%	0.2 mg	13%
Vitamin A	700 IU	14%	0.0 IU	0%	0.0 IU	0%
Vitamin B6	0.1 mg	3%	0.2 mg	8%	0.2 mg	11%
Vitamin C	10 mg	16%	0.0 mg	0%	1.5 mg	2%
Vitamin K	16 mcg	20%	2 mcg	2%	0.5 mcg	0.5%

in temperatures over 85°F. Place them where they will be cool during the summer.

Soil and Moisture

Beans prefer loose soil that drains freely. Add lots of organic matter to the soil. It provides some nutrients to the plants and helps retain moisture in the soil. Beans prefer mildly acidic soil in the 6.0 to 6.8 pH range but will tolerate fluctuation. Note that most soils loaded with organic matter fall into this range. If your garden has compacted or rocky soil, build a raised bed. The bed will get warm early in the season, and the soil will never get soggy.

Container

You can grow a few bean plants in a large container, at least 3-gallon size. Combine equal parts sphagnum peat moss, perlite, and rich soil to fill the pot. Plant six seeds, trying varieties such as 'Big Kahuna' or 'Mascotte'. Any of the smaller bush snap beans will do well.

Planting

Seed

Do not soak seed in water. The use of an inoculant is often recommended but is unnecessary in most instances. If you do use it, follow the directions on the package. Dust the seed, or place the inoculum in the soil. The bacteria are alive, and there is an expiration date on the package. Plant seeds about 1 to 1½ inches deep. Slightly deeper planting is fine in sandy soil. Seeds of all varieties generally germinate in fewer than 14 days. Although it is commonly recommended to plant the eye down, it is really not necessary. At best, they will germinate a bit faster.

Transplants

Few people go to the trouble of starting snap beans indoors. However, dry, lima, and runner beans need more time to mature and produce a good crop. If you live in the far north, consider starting these indoors in small individual pots 2 to 4 weeks before the frost-free date, setting them outside under cloches as close to the frost-free date as possible. Scarlet runner beans are a bit more hardy than dry and limas but still do not tolerate frost.

Spacing

Spacing depends on the type of bean. Bush beans are usually planted several inches apart and then thinned once growing. The same is true for lima and dry beans. Some gardeners prefer double to single rows. Many home gardeners place rows closer together than the typical recommendation of 24 inches. This helps plants stay upright, as they support each other and act as a living mulch to conserve moisture and reduce weeds, but it also increases the chance of disease.

If you have limited space, plant bush snap or lima beans in between hills of vining plants. The beans are quick growing and can mature while vines are forming. Wide row planting also works well. Creating a block of plants rather than a row increases the number of beans per square foot. However, leaning over to pick the beans without stepping into the bed can be hard for some gardeners.

Plant pole beans in hills 2 to 3 feet apart, with four or five seeds per pole. After the beans have sprouted, thin to three plants or fewer per pole. Other supports are fine. The term *pole* refers to the vertical growth pattern. Give scarlet runner beans support as well, and space them far enough apart for good air circulation around the vines. For the climbing types, this means spacing of 6 to 8 inches at the base of the support.

When to Plant

Plant all bean seeds in the garden well after any chance of frost. Beans need warm weather and warm soil to thrive. At the minimum, soil temperature should be 60°F or preferably higher, especially for dry beans. Lima beans are even more tender than bush beans. They will germinate at 60°F but prefer soils in the 80° to 85°F range, as do dry beans. All bean seeds will rot in cold, wet soil. They are fragile, so it doesn't pay to hurry the season. Still, some home gardeners do with an extra small planting and occasionally win the gamble.

If you are growing bush snap beans, try to plant several different crops throughout the season. As one crop peters out, the next is just coming into production. When the second set of true leaves emerges on your first planting, plant your second crop.

Many people stop planting snap beans too soon. Although beans cannot tolerate frost, the later harvests are often the most delicious of the season. Late plantings are often damaged less by insects. Plant bush snap bean varieties up to 2 months before your first expected fall frost.

Plant pole, lima, and dry beans only once. Do this as soon as the weather warms up. For the later-maturing varieties, getting seed into the ground on time is critical. Otherwise, frost will hit before your beans mature. If you start any of these beans indoors, transplant them outside several weeks after the frost-free date, or plant them earlier using any method to keep them warmer than if fully exposed.

Support

Pole beans grow to match the height of whatever support you give them. They prefer going up to going out. For example, a 10-foot-high pole would be more appealing to a pole bean than a 20-foot-long, 7-foot-high fence, although the later is much more practical. Get your supports in before you plant the seeds. Pole beans need support to grow properly. If they don't have support, they don't do much of anything. Popular pole structures include tepees made from cedar stakes or bamboo poles, high chicken-wire fences supported by posts, tall poles for individual groupings of plants, trellises, and ordinary fences protecting the garden from marauders. Supports with rough surfaces seem to work best. For example, cedar is better than bamboo. Make sure any support is sturdy and wind resistant. The weight of the vines increases with the length of the season and makes any weak structure wobbly and easy to knock over in a storm. So set it at least 12 inches into the soil. Nylon string stretched between supports works well for many vegetables but not so well for pole beans. The plants can be damaged as they flop around in the wind. Plastic netting is better.

When you are growing pole beans, you sometimes have to help nature out by wrapping the plants around the support to get them started in the right direction. Once they get going, they take off on their own. Tie them in place only if necessary.

Since these structures are relatively high, keep in mind that they will shade nearby areas. You may use this to your advantage by planting cool-loving vegetables at the base of the beans or in the shaded area. Native Americans used to grow pole beans on corn. Traditionally, they got corn off to a good start and then planted pole beans at the base of the growing corn 3 weeks later. The vines would curl up the corn stalks. They added squash in between the plants. This makes sense for dried corn, dried beans, and winter squash. Otherwise, you will be tromping on vines and breaking bean stalks in the process of harvesting earlier-maturing beans and corn. If you want to give the "Three Sisters Method" a try, use 'Genuine Cornfield' bean to stick with tradition.

How to Care for Beans
Water

Bean seeds, especially lima, have a tough time breaking through hard or crusty soil. If you keep your soil moist, your rate of germination will be higher. Once plants are growing well, water whenever the soil dries out. Keep the soil consistently moist but not soggy. Moisture is especially important when the beans burst into bloom. Watering at this time causes the blossoms to open fully, exposing them to pollinating bees. When string beans or lima bean pods are forming, the plants need lots of water. Let your water run on the soil at the base of the plants like an irrigation project. Do this in the evening, since daytime heat dissipates moisture from the young beans. Avoid spraying the foliage, since this can increase the chance of disease. Spraying the foliage of lima beans can knock off the pods. Water immediately after picking to encourage the formation of new blossoms and additional harvests. If you grow runner beans on a sunny wall under an eave, water regularly since the area underneath is often dry.

Mulch

Beans like uniform moisture. Once they are 6 inches high, surround the plants with mulch such as shredded leaves or grass clippings. Do not place the mulch against the stems.

Fertilizer

A well-prepared soil rich in organic matter and rotted manure usually contains enough fertilizer for beans. Beans create their own nitrogen with the help of rhizobia bacteria in the soil. Beans do need phosphorus and potassium. Provide these by adding appropriate organic fertilizers to the soil being prepared in the previous fall.

Weeding

The roots close to the plant are quite vulnerable. Hand weed around the base of the plants for the entire growth cycle. Mulch stops most weed growth. If not using a mulch, shave off the soil surface with a sharp hoe outside the leaf canopy. Avoid spreading diseases by working in the bean patch only when it is dry.

Thinning

Let your plants guide you. If they seem to be overcrowded, thin them. Different varieties grow differently, and you simply adapt to their growth pattern.

Pruning

There are many methods of growing pole beans. Not all of us are willing to build giant supports for them. If you have a structure of limited height, pinch off the growing tip of the bean vine between your thumb and forefinger just as the vine reaches the top of its support. This may cause the bean to branch. Pinch off the tip of shell or dry bean plants when pods start to form to speed up seed development as the end of the growing season nears. Pinch off the tip of runner bean vines once they have begun flowering and have reached the top of the support. This may encourage the formation of beans.

Special Considerations

Bush beans are easy to grow, but don't expect all your seeds to germinate. Some gardeners use a booster powder inoculant available in some nurseries to increase germination and yield. In my opinion the cost doesn't justify the benefit.

Bush beans sometimes get knocked over by heavy winds. Push mulch aside. Hold the plant upright and mound soil around its base. This extra soil will prop up the plant so that it can continue to produce beans. In temperatures more than 90°F plants may stop producing beans. Flowers may also drop off. This problem takes care of itself as temperatures drop. After your lima beans bloom, the tiny pods will set. Do not disturb plants during this vulnerable period, since the pods may drop to the ground. This is not a problem with snap beans.

Beans fix nitrogen in the soil, a tremendous benefit to any garden. Never dig up their roots. Cut off the plant at soil level, and let the roots decompose in the soil. This is giving your soil a nitrogen shot in the arm. Compost the severed upper portion of the bean plant.

Extending the Season

Beans produce many beans, sometimes more than you can eat at any one time. If this happens, continue to pick the beans anyway. Don't let them mature on the plant, or the bean plant will die. By picking all the beans, you will encourage the plant to live and produce more beans for weeks of delicious eating. If you continually and religiously pick all the beans off a plant, you can have beans right up until the first frost.

Problems

Insects

Bean leaf beetles (yellowish with six spots) chew holes in the leaves of bean plants. Prevent some beetle damage by tilling or spading soil several times in spring to kill the bean leaf larvae. You can avoid a lot of bean leaf beetle damage by planting early-maturing bean varieties. Don't worry about the loss of a few leaves or plants. Mexican bean beetles (look like sixteen-spotted ladybugs) feed on beans both as adults and larvae (orangish yellow). Pick these off. Spider mites cause bean leaves to turn yellow and wither. These are most common in hot, dry weather. Normally, damage is so limited that it's not worth worrying about. Just spray off the foliage with water. Other beetles also attack bean plants. If you experience problems early in the season, deter beetles with row covers. These have an added advantage of keeping plants warm.

Disease

Beans are susceptible to a wide variety of diseases. A few are anthracnose (red to black sunken spots on different portions of the plant), bacterial blight (brown patches on the leaves), mosaics (crinkly mottled leaves and stunted growth), and rust (yellowing leaves drop off). Buy disease-resistant varieties. Good seed catalogs list disease resistance for each variety. Bean plants should be planted in a new spot each year if possible. This may prevent some root diseases. Rotation is part of good hygiene. Remember that peas and beans are in the same family, so don't plant beans in a spot occupied by peas the year before.

Reduce the incidence of anthracnose and bacterial blight by not working in the bean patch when the leaves are wet. Leaves tend to be wet from morning dew or, naturally, after a rain. Kill aphids to cut down on mosaic. Occasionally, a plant or two will die. Do not try to save it. Uproot and toss it into the center of an active compost pile. Burning or tossing any diseased plant material into the garbage is commonly recommended if you are worried about spreading disease through compost. If pole beans are diseased one season, do not use the same poles the following year without sterilizing them. Wipe them down with bleach or another disinfectant.

Marauders

Rabbits love to nibble off the tops of sprouting bean plants. So do deer. The only solution is a good fence.

Physiological

Under stress, usually when it is hot, dry, and windy, blossoms may drop off. Without blossoms no beans will form. Once the weather changes, the plant should start blooming and forming beans again.

Propagation

Beans are self-pollinating. The seed of open-pollinated varieties is worth saving. Let pods mature on the plant until the seeds inside are dry. Remove the seeds from the pod. If you see mildew on the beans or if disease has been a problem in the growing season, don't use them. Start with fresh seed. If insects have been a problem, place the seed in a container in the freezer for a couple of days. Remove and let the container warm up before opening; otherwise, moisture may condense on the cold seeds. Place good, dry seed in an envelope and keep them in a cool, dark place. Seed often stores for up to 3 to 4 years.

Avid lovers of scarlet runner beans dig up the crown in fall, place it in moist sand, and keep it cool until planting the following spring. This is similar to preserving dahlias. If successful, it gives you a giant head start the following season.

Harvesting

Pick snap beans when they are only partially developed. Length varies by variety, but all snap beans should be picked thin—not at all the size of beans in most markets or grocery stores. They are too big if the seeds inside are bulging through the skin. The new varieties really do snap if you break them in two. Try beans at different stages of maturity to see which size appeals to you most. Beans are usually ready to pick within 3 weeks of first blossoming, so check the plants daily. Never let beans mature on the plant, since this is a signal to the plant to stop producing. When you are picking beans, there will still be blossoms on the plant. These will continue to mature and produce additional beans.

Don't tug at beans to pick them. You can damage the plant if you are too rough. Hold the stem just above the bean as you pinch or snip it from the plant.

Some gardeners do pull up entire plants, pick off the beans, and toss the plant into the compost. If you have planted a number of plants, succession crops, and are just eating fresh beans, this actually makes a lot of sense if you want to plant the area with a different crop. Hang the plant upside down to pick off the dangling snap beans in a "snap."

Whenever you pick beans during the day, don't leave them in the sun. Keep them in the shade or in a container filled with ice. Beans that stay cool, stay crisp and tasty. Wilted beans lose flavor rapidly. A wilted bean is one that will bend almost in two without snapping.

According to some experts, you should pick beans at night for best flavor and texture. Unfortunately, mosquitoes find that we improve in flavor at the same time. I do my picking in the day, thanks.

Check your lima beans frequently as they approach maturity. Like peas, they have to be picked at just the right moment to be right—not too big, not too small. It can be hard to tell when they are ripe. Feel the pods. The end of the pod should feel somewhat spongy. If necessary, open one to check the seed size. Lima beans are best when no larger than a pea. The beans should be green and tender. If the pods turn yellow, the seeds inside will be large. Keep checking pods to make sure that you don't let them get overripe. Overly mature beans lose most of their flavor. Store your limas in the pod. Shell them just before eating.

Dry beans should not be harvested until the vine is dead. The leaves drop off, and the beans rattle in the papery pod if you shake the vine. The pods should be brittle but not cracking open. Yank up the vine by its roots. Dry out the vines by hanging them upside down in a dry area. When the beans are dry (carefully bite a bean to see if it's rock hard), put the vines in a burlap or cloth bag (old pillow case) and beat them to separate the beans. Don't do this on a hard surface like concrete, or you will smash the beans to bits. You can also whack the vines against the side of a clean garbage can or place them on a board and walk on them gently. Separate the beans from the dried pods and stem (chaff) by throwing them up in the air over a tarp or blanket on a windy day. Sort out the good beans, and dry them for 3 weeks in a warm, well-ventilated spot on a screen or bed sheet. The screen provides better air circulation.

Storing

Green beans will keep well if stored in ice water for a few hours. If you intend to keep them longer, do not wash them, as this leads to decay. Put them completely dry in a plastic bag in the refrigerator crisper. Use them as soon as possible, certainly within 3 days. Some people disagree and keep moist beans in an open container. Try both methods to see which works best for you.

To freeze snap beans, snip or pinch off ends. Leave whole, cut into pieces, or French (slice lengthwise down the middle). Blanch for 2 to 3 minutes, cool immediately in ice water for 2 minutes, drain, spread on a tray to freeze for 30 minutes, place in a plastic bag, and freeze.

To dry snap beans, wash, snap or cut off ends, cut diagonally into 1-inch pieces, blanch for up to 4 minutes depending on thickness, steam for an additional 4 minutes, and dry in a dehydrator. The beans may last up to 4 months.

To pickle, use your favorite recipe. Consider adding garlic or other spices to the vinegar.

To freeze lima beans, shell, blanch 2 to 4 minutes depending on size, cool, drain, dry, and pack. To freeze runner beans, clean, cut into thin slices, blanch for 2 minutes, cool, drain, dry, and pack.

To store dry beans, dry completely; as protection against a wormy surprise, freeze for 3 days, or bake the beans in an oven at 180°F for 15 minutes; cool; dry again; then place in closed containers. Keep as close to 32°F as possible. They may last up to 1 year stored in this way, but check regularly for any signs of mold. No room in the refrigerator? Keep them cool and dry. Some people use little packets of dried milk in each jar to absorb moisture. Check the beans occasionally. If they are moist at all, mold will develop. Keep colorful beans out of sun to preserve color.

Culinary Uses

Pick snap beans of all types when young and thin. The flat-podded Romano varieties have a distinct taste. All snap beans should be firm and make a snapping noise when bent in two. The little seeds inside should be barely noticeable. Purple varieties will turn green when cooked.

Snap beans are edible raw, but do not eat other types this way, since they contain small amounts of cyanide. Cut off the tops and tails of raw beans. Slice them into strips (French) to be served in salads or placed on platters for dips. For salads, they are also delicious cooked lightly, cooled, and then added to the dish.

To cook fresh snap beans, pinch or cut off the ends. Leave them whole, break or cut into pieces, or French. Blanch, microwave, steam, or stir-fry them until tender. Cook briefly, no more than 2 to 3 minutes. A simple dish is to steam snap beans, smother them with butter, and season with garlic.

Beans are also excellent as a dip. Cook briefly, purée, and cool.

Lima beans are eaten for their seeds. Pods can be hard to open. Cut off one end, and then press on the stem. Pop the pod open. Limas vary in the number and size of seeds inside. Cook them until tender. The French flageolet has its own unique taste. Sauté immature beans in butter, and season with fresh herbs. Once the beans are fully mature, dry them to make cassoulet or bean stew, traditionally served with roasted lamb.

Lima beans can be allowed to mature to the dry stage. At this point, they may be referred to as butter beans, although this term is sometimes used as a synonym for lima beans at any stage.

Dry beans are exceptionally high in protein. Rinse the beans in cold water. Soak them overnight in cold water (3 cups water to 1 cup beans). Soaking minimizes problems with gas created by fermentation in the large intestine and helps beans retain their natural shape. Discard the water. Drain. Cook in 2 cups water to 1 cup beans. Adding salt to the water may make the beans tougher. Heat the beans to just below the boiling point, simmer with the cover slightly open until tender. This can take up to an hour or longer. You can also boil beans for 30 minutes, although boiling may break down the beans. Don't overcook. Mix with other ingredients if desired.

Scarlet runner bean flowers are gorgeous and edible. Pick them as they open and eat them by themselves, or add them to salads. Since these plants do not produce many beans in cold climates, they are grown primarily for the beauty and taste of the flowers. You will get a few beans but not nearly as many as on an average bush of snap beans. Think about letting the pods go to seed, not only to try them as a dried bean but to save seed for the following year.

Varieties

Bush beans are easy to grow and produce well. Pods come in a wide variety of colors. Some gardeners choose yellow wax beans simply because they are easy to see for picking. Pole beans grown on vertical supports are an excellent use of space. Some gardeners detect a difference in taste from the bush beans and find it preferable. Pole beans produce more abundantly than bush beans but do come in later. You do not have to bend over to pick them. Most cold-climate gardeners grow at least one type of bush bean since they mature rapidly and are easy to grow in successive plantings. Add to this one vining variety for an ideal combination.

Snap beans actually do snap when they are bent in two. They are green, purple, or yellow. Snap beans go by a number of names: garden, green, French or French filet (haricots verts), Roma or Romano also know as Italian, string, and wax. French filet beans are very long and thin, referred to occasionally as "shoestring beans." The Italian green pod, Roma, or Romano beans are wide and flat. Snap beans were once quite stringy, giving rise to the name "string bean." Most newer varieties are far less stringy. The name of wax beans may be derived from their light-yellow to golden wax-like color.

Lima beans are grown for their ¾-moon-shaped seeds, not their pods. You shell them like peas, usually two to five per pod. Lima beans are called "butter beans" in the South. Butter beans generally refer to lighter-colored beans that have a creamy texture when cooked. 'Henderson's Bush' is a good example. Regular limas are larger with a more mealy texture, such as 'Fordhook's 242'. Other names for lima beans are civet, seewee, shell, and sieva beans. *Baby lima* refers to the size of the bean, not the size of the plant. (*Bush* and *pole* do refer to plant size.) Lima beans are more difficult to grow in cold climates. They like lots of heat and do poorly in cool, wet summers. Pole limas may be out of reach to the cold-climate gardener because of the length of time they take to mature.

Dry or shell beans also take a long time to mature. They are tough to grow to the fully dry stage in cold climates, but some gardeners find the challenge rewarding. The days listed to maturity in many catalogs and in the list below may be off by as much as a month depending on the season. Try a bush variety first to increase your odds of success. There are usually five to ten beans per pod. Many can be eaten as snap, lima, or dried beans. For this reason Borlotto, French flageolet, and horticultural beans are sometimes listed as lima beans in catalogs. 'Great Northern' are excellent puréed for cream soups; kidney types, good in chilies; black

The brilliant blooms of the scarlet runner bean are ornamental and edible.

or turtle beans, delightful in tacos and tostadas; and pintos, good for refried beans. While dry beans taste great and are highly nutritious, many gardeners do not grow them considering the limited yield for the time and effort involved.

Runner beans are perennials grown as annuals in cold climates. The seed leaves (cotyledons) are produced underground. In warmer climates the roots can get as big as an arm. The vines produce lovely bicolor, pink, red, or white flowers, which may attract hummingbirds. Red-flowered varieties with their delicate bean flavor are the most popular. On some varieties beans can be as long as 16 inches. Runner beans require pollination, and if they develop, they have a fuzzy coat that sticks to cloth. They have a nutty taste, but pods are neither tender nor sweet. They get tough and fibrous if too mature. Let them mature completely for dry seeds. You will often get primarily flowers—the bean is worth growing for those alone. Birds sometimes damage these. Try wintering over the large roots as you would a dahlia. Runner beans are sometimes called case knife, multiflora, and painted lady beans.

VARIETY	DAYS	HEIGHT (INCHES)	POD COLOR/LENGTH (INCHES)
Snap beans (bush and pole)			
Phaseolus vulgaris			
'Beurre de Rocquencourt' (see 'Rocquencourt')			
'Black Valentine' (heirloom)*****	70	18	Green to 6 (black seed)
'Big Kahuna' (OP)	60	24	Green to 11
'Blue Lake' (heirloom)	70	72	Dark green to 6
'Blue Lake Bush 274' (heirloom)	60	18	Green to 6
'Bountiful' (heirloom)	45	18	Green to 7
'Burpee's Stringless' (heirloom)	50	20	Green to 6
'Cherokee Wax' (heirloom) (AAS-1948)	50	18	Golden yellow to 5
'Contender' (heirloom)*****	55	18	Green to 6
'Derby' (OP) (AAS-1990) (beans on top)*****	60	18	Green to 7
'Dragon Langerie' (heirloom)*****	60	24	Cream streaked purple to 8
'Dragon's Tongue' (see 'Dragon Langerie')			
'Early Riser' (heirloom)*****	55	72	Green to 8 (romano)
'Empress' (heirloom)*****	55	18	Green to 6
'E-Z Pick' (heirloom)*****	55	18	Green to 6
'Fin de Bagnol' (heirloom)	60	18	Green to 7 (filet)
'Fortex' (heirloom)*****	60	84	Dark green to 11 (filet)
'Genuine Cornfield' (heirloom)	85	72	Green to 7
'Gold of Bacau' (heirloom)	65	72	Golden to 8 (romano)
'Goldcrop' (OP) (AAS-1974)*****	55	18	Golden yellow to 6
'Goldkist' (OP)	60	18	Golden yellow to 6
'Golden Wax' (heirloom)	50	18	Golden yellow to 5
'Golden Wax Improved' (heirloom)	50	18	Golden yellow to 5
'Greencrop' (OP) (AAS-1957)*****	50	18	Green to 8 (flat)
'Improved Commodore' (heirloom) (AAS-1945)	65	18	Dark green to 8
'Jade' (heirloom)*****	60	20	Very dark green to 6
'Kentucky Blue Pole' (OP) (AAS-1991)*****	65	72	Green to 7+
'Kentucky Wonder Bush' (see 'Improved Commodore')			
'Kentucky Wonder Pole' (see 'Old Homestead')			
'Mascotte' (OP) (AAS-2014)	50	18	Green to 6
'Masai' (OP)	55	14	Green to 4 (filet)
'Mon Petit Chéri' (OP)*****	60	24	Green to 7
'Maxibel' (heirloom)	60	24	Green to 7 (filet)
'Neckargold' (heirloom)	75	72	Golden yellow to 7 (filet)
'Old Dutch Half Runner' (heirloom)	60	36	Light green to 5
'Old Homestead' (heirloom)	65	60	Medium silver green to 8
'Pencil Pod Black Wax' (heirloom)	60	18	Golden yellow to 6 (black seeds)
'Pencil Pod Golden Wax' (heirloom)	60	18	Golden yellow to 6
'Provider' (heirloom)*****	50	18	Medium green to 6+
'Purple Queen' (heirloom)	50	18	Purple to 7
'Purple Teepee' (heirloom) (beans on top)*****	50	18	Purple to 6
'Rocquencourt' (heirloom)	55	22	Yellow gold to 5
'Roc d'Or' (heirloom)*****	55	20	Gold to 6 (filet)
'Roma II' (heirloom)	60	18	Green to 5 (romano)
'Romanette' (heirloom)	55	22	Green to 6 (romano)
'Romano' (heirloom)	65	18	Green to 6 (romano)
'Romano Gold' (heirloom)*****	55	18	Light yellow to 5 (romano)
'Romano Pole' (heirloom)	70	72	Green to 6 (romano)

VARIETY	DAYS	HEIGHT (INCHES)	POD COLOR/LENGTH (INCHES)
'Royalty Purple Pod' (heirloom)*****	55	18+	Purple to 5 (green when cooked)
'Shoestring Bean' (see 'Fin de Bagnol')			
'Slenderette' (heirloom)	55	20	Green to 6
'Slenderwax' (heirloom)	60	16	Bright yellow to 6
'Straight 'N' Narrow' (OP)	55	18	Dark green to 5 (filet)
'Strike' (heirloom)*****	55	18	Green to 5
'Tavera' (heirloom)*****	55	18	Green to 5 (filet)
'Tema' (OP)	55	18	Dark green to 5
'Tenderette' (heirloom)	60	20	Green to 6
'Tendergreen' (heirloom)	55	24+	Green to 6
'Tendergreen Improved' (heirloom)	55	20	Medium green to 6
'Top Crop' ('Topcrop') (heirloom) (AAS-1950)*****	50	18	Medium green to 6
'Topnotch' (see 'Golden Wax')			
'Triomphe de Farcy' (heirloom)*****	60	20	Green striped purple to 6 (filet)
'Trionfo Violetto' (heirloom)	75	72	Purple to 6

VARIETY	DAYS	HEIGHT (INCHES)	BEAN COLOR
Lima beans			
Phaseolus lunatus or *limensis*			
'Burpee Improved Bush Lima' (heirloom)	80	20	Whitish green
'Bush Fordhook® 242' (heirloom) (AAS-1945)*****	75	18	Pale green
'Cangreen' (see 'Thorogreen')			
'Christmas Large Speckled' (heirloom)	90	84	Cream marked red
'Dixie Speckled Butterpea' (heirloom)	75	24	Almost white
'Dwarf Sieva' (see 'Henderson Bush')			
'Henderson Bush' (heirloom)	70	24	Small creamy
'Jackson Wonder' (heirloom)*****	75	24	Purple speckled
'King of the Garden' (heirloom)	90	96	Light green
'Large Speckled' (see 'Christmas Large Speckled')			
'Thorogreen' (heirloom)*****	75	20	Pale green

VARIETY	DAYS	HEIGHT (INCHES)	COLOR AT DRY BEAN STAGE
Dry bean			
Phaseolus vulgaris			
'Black Turtle' (heirloom)	95	12	Small jet-black oblong
'Borlotto Lingua di Fuoco' (see 'Tongue of Fire')			
'Borlotto Solista' (heirloom)	95	72	Rose-red cream oblong
'Dark Red Kidney' (heirloom)	95	16	Mahogany-red kidney
'Dwarf Horticultural-Taylor Strain' (heirloom)	65	18	Pale pink blotched red oblong
'Flageolet Vert' (heirloom)	80	24	Light-green kidney
'French Horticultural' (heirloom)	70	20	Cream-yellow with red oblong
'Great Northern' (heirloom)	90	24	White navy-like oblong
'Jacob's Cattle' (heirloom)	100	24	White speckled red kidney
'Navy Bean' (heirloom)	90	20	White oblong
'Pinto Bean' (heirloom)	95	20+	Tan speckled brown oblong
'Light Red Kidney' (heirloom)***** (Chili-refried-baked)	85	16	Brownish-red kidney
'Soldier' (heirloom)	100	18	White with red-brown eye oblong
'Tongue of Fire' (heirloom–bush)	70	24	Light white pink streaked red oblong
'Tongue of Fire' (heirloom–climbing)	95	72	Light white pink streaked red oblong

VARIETY	DAYS	HEIGHT (INCHES)	COLOR AT DRY BEAN STAGE
'Trout' (see 'Jacob's Cattle')			
'True Red Cranberry' (heirloom)	95	72	Dark-red rounded
'Vermont Cranberry' (heirloom)*****	85	24	Tan maroon speckled brown oblong

VARIETY	DAYS	HEIGHT (INCHES)	POD/FLOWER COLORS
Runner beans (scarlet)			
Phaseolus coccineus			
'Painted Lady Improved' (heirloom)	80	72+	Green/scarlet cream
'Scarlet Emperor' (heirloom)	80	72+	Green/bright orange red
'Scarlet Runner' (generic)*****	80	72+	Green/rich red

It's easy to find and pick wax beans, since they stand out so clearly from the foliage.

Most beets are best when harvested quite small.

BEET (BEET ROOT)

Beta vulgaris ssp. *vulgaris*
Amaranth or Goosefoot Family (Amaranthaceae, formerly Chenopodiaceae)

Beets are biennials grown as annuals. They are a hardy, cool- to cold-season crop. Beets are easy to grow, tough, relatively pest-free, and produce quickly. Most people grow beets just for the roots, but others have learned that the beet greens (leaves) are delicious both raw and cooked. Think of beets as a dual crop, roots and greens. The deep-green leaves, often veined or fringed red, are especially decorative, making them a good choice for border, container, and patio gardens. They are also extremely nutritious. Beets probably originated in European or west Asian coastal areas.

How Beets Grow

The seed (a fruit) is tan, fairly large (about 1,500 to 2,000 seeds per ounce), and rough. Its surface is irregular. Each little pod contains a number of seeds. As these germinate, they form seed leaves and then delicate true leaves. The latter become increasingly larger and send nutrients to the developing root system. The base of the plant begins to bulge. The root continues to swell until harvested, often coming out from the soil surface. If the beet could survive cold winters, it would send up stems with bumpy, little, greenish-tan to pink flowers that would form seed once mature.

Where to Plant Beets
Site and Light

Beets can tolerate a wide range of light conditions, although they prefer a sunny area. The sweetest beets are grown in full sun in cool weather, although they will grow in partial shade.

Soil and Moisture

Although beets tolerate a wide variety of soils, they thrive in moist, fertile soil that drains freely. If you have rocky or clay soil, consider building a raised bed. This will give you an ideal garden for any root crop, beets included.

Add lots of organic matter to the soil at planting time. The soil should have a pH of 6.5 to 7.5, which is neutral to slightly alkaline. Horse manure is excellent since it is slightly alkaline and holds moisture in the soil. Adding a

Nutrition Facts

Serving size: 100 grams (3.5 ounces)

	BEETS		BEET GREENS COOKED	
	AMOUNT PER SERVING	% DV	AMOUNT PER SERVING	% DV
Calcium	16 mg	2%	114 mg	11%
Calories	44	2%	27	1%
Carbohydrate	10 g	3%	5 g	2%
Copper	0.1 mg	4%	0.3 mg	13%
Dietary fiber	2 g	8%	3 g	12%
Folate	80 mcg	20%	14 mcg	3%
Iron	0.8 mg	4%	1.9 mg	11%
Magnesium	23 mg	6%	69 mg	17%
Manganese	0.3 mg	16%	0.5 mg	26%
Potassium	305 mg	9%	910 mg	26%
Protein	2 g	3%	3 g	5%
Riboflavin	minimal		0.3 mg	17%
Thiamin	minimal		0.1 mg	8%
Vitamin A	minimal		7,650 IU	155%
Vitamin B6	minimal		0.1 mg	7%
Vitamin C	3.6 mg	6%	25 mg	42%
Vitamin K	minimal		485 mcg	605%

little lime for magnesium or wood ash for potassium in the preceding fall helps. Lime also creates a more alkaline soil. Don't go overboard—just a little of each. A small amount of bonemeal is a good source of phosphorus, which promotes healthy root growth. Beets also need boron to avoid physiological problems, covered later. Soil amended with compost or kelp products usually provides enough. Beets are quite salt tolerant.

Note that experts disagree about the effect of manure on root crops. Apparently, it makes them "hairy." I have grown many excellent root crops amended with well-aged horse manure and have never encountered the problem.

Containers

Beets grow well in containers. Plant several seeds per pot, at least 10 to 12 inches wide. Mixing peat, perlite, and some garden soil makes a good potting soil.

Planting
Seed

The spiny, little seeds are really pods, which usually contain three to six embryos. So when you plant a seed, you may get three or four plants in one spot. Beet seeds are notorious for being unpredictable. Try soaking the seed in cold water for several hours up to a full day before planting, or wash them in cold water to remove chemicals that inhibit germination. Plant them immediately after soaking. Even more unpredictable are the golden varieties. 'Touchstone Gold Hybrid' purports to be a more reliable germinator.

Since germination may be erratic, plant them ½ inch deep and 1 to 2 inches apart. If they all sprout, you can thin them later. Keep the soil around the seeds moist at all times. This will help germination and make it easy for the seedling to pop through the soil surface.

To prevent crusting of the soil surface, add a thin layer, ½ inch or less, of grass clippings or shredded leaves over the planting row. This will also retain moisture in the soil. As soon as the plants start to pop through the soil, move the mulch just off to the side unless the seedlings are growing right through it vigorously.

Transplants

If you love beets so much that you want to get a a month's jump on the season, plant seeds indoors 3 to 4 weeks ahead of the time you would like to get them in the garden. Plant several seeds in each container or cell pack. For a week before you plant the beets in the garden, set the young transplants outside on a porch or walkway so they get used to being outdoors. If there is a chance of a hard frost, bring the plants in at night.

Spacing

Spacing depends on your intended use. For leaves, plant close together; for beet roots, farther apart. See "Thinning."

When to Plant

Begin planting as soon as the ground can be worked in early spring, even as early as 2 to 4 weeks before the last expected frost. Beet seed can germinate in soil with a temperature of 40°F, although optimum germination occurs at higher temperatures. Germination generally begins within 10 days. Plant again 2 weeks later. Beets grow poorly in high heat and drought. Still, it's worth planting some seeds 6 to 10 weeks before the first expected fall frost. It's a gamble, but at the very least you will get good greens.

How to Care for Beets
Water

Beets need an even supply of moisture to grow evenly and rapidly. They are sweet and tender when they do. If stressed from lack of water, beets can be discolored, tough, and woody. They may also bolt. When the soil starts to dry out, water, but avoid overwatering.

Mulch

Beets like it moist and cool. Mulch takes care of both needs. Good mulches are grass clippings and shredded leaves. Start with a light mulch early and build it up to 3 or 4 inches as the season progresses. The mulch should be off to the side of the plants and not touching the stems or developing roots.

Fertilizing

If soil is properly prepared and amended with organic matter and fertilizer, beets may not need additional fertilizing throughout the growing season. Let growth be your guide. Side-dress if necessary to encourage good foliage growth. Fertilize lightly. Place compost along the row, or a little diluted fish emulsion or liquid seaweed.

Weeding

Weeding can be difficult. Pulling up weeds between or close to newly emerging beets may pull the young seedlings from the soil. Snipping the weeds off with scissors works well. Once beets are larger, weeding becomes a lot easier, especially if you use mulch around the plants. To avoid damaging the roots, do not cultivate close to the plants.

Thinning

Beets grow quite well close together, but they do need a little elbow room. As soon as they pop through the soil, thin them to one plant per 1 inch of row. You can do this by hand or by running a steel rake lightly across the row. The rake technique works, but first-time gardeners are really reluctant to do it. Don't push the rake deep into the soil; just let it run across the surface. It will thin the row to a manageable number of seedlings. Still, for beets I prefer hand thinning since they often pop up in little clumps of plants. Place your fingers on the soil around the beet you want to save while pulling or snipping out the others. Thinning is easiest if the soil is slightly damp, neither dry nor soggy. If the soil is dusty, water it in the morning, and thin in the evening. Wash and eat the tiny seedlings.

Don't thin them at this stage if you want to grow beets for greens. Tight planting encourages lots of leaf growth at the expense of the roots.

When the young plants are 4 to 6 inches tall, thin them again. The actual space between each plant should match the potential size of the beet and may also depend on your gardening style. The thinnings make a delicious meal even though the roots are not yet fully formed.

These plants can also be transplanted if you thin carefully. Try to keep as much soil around the roots as possible when moving plants. Water them immediately to help the roots heal. Note that this process is a hassle and not always successful. It's much easier to start a new batch of beets in a successive planting.

Most gardeners begin eating beets when they are quite small, less than 2 inches. This leaves room for the remaining beets to mature. So early harvesting is really a form of thinning.

Pruning

Snip off insect-damaged or yellowing leaves. Otherwise, leave the foliage alone other than to harvest greens as needed.

Winter Protection

This is not commonly done in cold areas. See "Propagation."

Special Considerations

There is one beet (*Beta vulgaris* var. *cicla)* known for ornamental use. It has large green leaves with scarlet tones in its midribs. Boil the base of the stem, and then submerge it in cold water before placing it in an arrangement. It is not included in the varietal list.

Although beet greens are highly nutritious, they do contain oxalic acid. Cooking does reduce the amount but also reduces the nutrient value of the greens. Eat all greens containing oxalic acid in moderate amounts. Skip only if your doctor tells you to.

Extending the Season

In spring you can start plants indoors. Or plant seeds under a cloche even if there is danger of a freeze. Watch the plants carefully during the day to make sure that they don't overheat. You may have to remove protection if it gets too warm or sunny, only to replace the cloche in the evening when the temperature drops. Since you can plant beets in the garden so early in spring, these methods seem overkill to me.

Plant beets late in the season for a fall harvest. Beets cannot take temperatures lower than 25°F, so the first hard frost can signal trouble. If you leave beets in the ground, they must be protected. If you expect a freeze, then cover the beets with 12 to 18 inches of straw or whole leaves. After a freeze you can move the mulch aside to harvest the beets. Do not leave beets unprotected in the garden to rot during the winter. This only encourages problems with disease and insects the following season.

Problems

Insects

Aphids, flea beetles, leafhoppers, and leafminers are potential problems. Frankly, one of the joys of gardening is growing more than you need so that you don't have to worry about losing a few plants to pests, and so you don't have to worry about buying and using poisons unless absolutely necessary. If some leaves are damaged, snip them off. If badly damaged, plant another crop.

Disease

Beets are susceptible to leaf damage from mildews and leaf spot disease *(Cercospora)*. 'Pacemaker III' and 'Red Ace Hybrid' are quite resistant to this disease. The simplest way to handle beets with damaged leaves is to remove the leaves and toss them into the center of an active compost pile. Save and eat the beet roots.

Marauders

Beet greens are sweet. The tops often get nibbled off, especially early in the season, by deer and rabbits. The only effective way to keep them out of the garden is with a high fence. Be patient. The greens often regrow.

Physiological

If you notice corky black areas on your beets, they need some boron. Dilute 1/18 teaspoon of borax in a gallon of water. Treat the soil around beets *lightly* with this solution. Note that boron is also present in cantaloupe leaves, compost, and kelp.

Propagation

Beets are wind pollinated; the pollen is fine, light, and plentiful. It is difficult to get enough plants, at least a half dozen, through the winter for proper seed production. Try by covering them with 12 inches of straw. Do not expect success. Digging up and storing roots in cool, but not freezing, damp peat moss or sand may get the roots through the winter to be planted the following spring. The flowers contain both male and female organs. You may have to support the flower stalks. The seed is technically a fruit. Note that beets do cross-pollinate with each other and with Swiss chard. Grow only one open-pollinated variety for best results. Beet seeds will last up to 3 to 5 years if kept cool, dry, and dark.

Harvesting

Most early-variety beets are the best eating when no more than 2 inches in diameter. At this stage they are juicy and tender—not at all like many you will find in markets or stores. Older beets of the early-maturing varieties tend to get tough and woody. The later-maturing varieties can often be good when bigger. Experiment with each variety to find your preferred stage of maturity.

Beet greens have more vitamins than the root. Start picking them young at 4 to 6 inches tall. Harvest the largest leaves first, and let the smaller ones continue to grow.

When digging or pulling up the root, cut or twist off the foliage about 1 to 2 inches above the beet so it will not draw out moisture from the beet. Keep the nicest leaves, and compost the rest. If you cut lower, the beet will bleed. Don't cut the tap root. That will bleed too. Note that some varieties of golden and white beets don't bleed.

Do the same when you plan to store beets. Leave a short portion of the stem on. The later-maturing varieties of beets are usually best for storage and should be allowed to mature. They will be larger than the early-maturing varieties and still taste quite good.

Storing

For temporary storage, cut off all but 1 to 2 inches of stem from each beet. Do not cut off roots. Place unwashed in a plastic bag in the refrigerator. Beets will last for up to 7 days this way and sometimes much longer, even up to 1 to 3 months if the humidity is high enough.

For longer storage, dig up beets on a dry day. Take only the best of the lot for storage. Eat the rest. Let the beets dry out for a couple of hours. Much of the loose soil will drop off, but don't wash or brush the beets. Snip off the foliage to within 1 inch of the top of the root. If you cut into the beet by accident or damage it in any way, don't store but eat it.

Beets can be stored in moist, not wet, sphagnum peat moss, sawdust, or sand in a plastic garbage can in an unheated but insulated garage where temperatures range from 35° to 40°F. Place the root with an inch of stem upright in the packing material. Beets should not touch one another or the side of the container. Cover each beet completely. Place the beets in layers until the container is full. The moisture will keep the beets from drying out. Beets will last for several months stored this way.

The key is to store beets at high humidity as close to freezing as possible without letting them freeze. This prevents water loss. And of course, you should not put any damaged beets into the containers, where they will rot and infect the other beets. Beets may last up to 3 months or longer stored in this way.

If you don't have a root cellar or an insulated garage, freeze the beets. To freeze beet roots, wear plastic gloves, trim tops back to ½ inch, and wash. Boil until tender (usually 25 to 50 minutes). Slip off skins while submerged in cool water. Cut in two, place the flat end down, and cut with a french fry cutter or egg slicer. Place in ice water, then in freezer bags. Or freeze baby beets whole. *Beets are not blanched, but fully cooked, before freezing.*

To dry, cut off tops to within 1 inch of beet, wash, and steam until barely tender. Peel, cut into ⅛-inch strips, and dry. These beets may last up to 4 months.

Baby beets are excellent for canning whole. 'Detroit Little Ball' and 'Little Chicago' are good choices for this. 'Bull's Blood' and many other beets are good substitutions for true baby beets if dug or pulled at 1½ inches. Cylindrical beets look like long carrots and can be up to 8 inches long. They provide uniform slices for pickling. They are under the section "Beets, Cylindra type" in the varietal table.

Beet greens do not store for a long time. Keep them cool while picking. As with other leafy vegetables, they may collect a little coating of soil. Rinse them under cold running water, and shake off excess moisture. Roll leaves in a paper towel so that each leaf is sandwiched between paper. Place the rolled-up leaves in a plastic bag in the crisper of the refrigerator. Use the leaves as soon as possible since they become tougher with age—within 2 days if possible. Certainly, no longer than 7.

To freeze beet greens, pick young, or remove stems from older leaves, wash, pat, and pack dry. Label and freeze. Blanching leaves for 1½ minutes before freezing is recommended by some.

Culinary Uses

Beet roots can be eaten raw. Slice thinly, or grate roots into salads. Excellent sweet hybrid varieties for this use are 'Kestrel', 'Merlin', 'Red Ace', 'Red Cloud', and 'Solo'. Use fresh greens in salads when they are 4 to 6 inches long. 'Bull's Blood' and 'Golden Detroit' are popular for this use.

Cook beet roots by baking, boiling, grilling, microwaving, roasting, or steaming. Match sizes for uniform cooking, and keep 1 inch of stem on each beet. This reduces the chance of bleeding. Still, when working with red beets, wear gloves to avoid stains. White and golden beets do not bleed. Once cooked, remove skins under running water. Beets are done when you can press a fork into them easily.

Simmer whole beets in salted or sugared water for up to 45 minutes, pour cold water over them, slip skins off, and serve whole, sliced, or cut into cubes. Melt butter over them. Add a little orange juice, lemon, mint, vinegar, or a favorite herb to the butter for added flavor. Cooked beets can also be chilled and sliced into salads.

Beets may also be baked at 350° to 400°F or roasted whole. Brush with olive oil, place on or wrap with foil, and cook. The beets will shed their skins when fully cooked. 'Crapaudine' is a French heirloom often roasted before the crinkly skin is removed and then seasoned to taste. Other excellent heirlooms for roasting are 'Detroit Dark Red' and 'Detroit Supreme'. Good hybrids for this purpose are 'Eagle', 'Kestrel', and 'Merlin'.

Borscht, a beet soup, can be made in numerous ways and is one of the more popular culinary uses.

Sauté mature greens in oil until wilted. Then steam them until tender, or boil them in bouillon dissolved in water for 5 to 6 minutes or until tender. Before serving, drench them in butter, or splash them with vinegar. If greens have thick stems, remove and chop these into small pieces. Cook them longer than the leaves. Cooked greens are sometimes referred to as *verdure cotte*. The varieties marked with five stars under the "Greens" heading in the variety table are among the best for this use.

Varieties

Beets may be called blood turnip, garden beet, red beet, or table beet. They are all the same. Sugar beets are grown commercially for sugar production and are not included here, nor are mangel beets, most commonly used to feed livestock. Beets may also be tilled under for green manure.

The varietal list includes a wide selection of beets in varied colors, shapes, and sizes. There are both early (quick-maturing) and late (slow-maturing) varieties. The later-maturing varieties, such as 'Lutz Green Leaf', can get large and are better for storage. Some varieties are grown just for their greens, either when tiny (microgreens) or fully matured. Although included in the following list are a few miniature or baby beets, you can duplicate them quite easily by picking other varieties of beets when they are very young.

While most beets produce a number of plants from each pod (multigerm seeds), monogerm varieties produce only one. Monogerm varieties listed below are 'Alvro Mono', 'Moneta', 'Pacemaker III', and 'Solo'. The size of the beets is the approximate stage at which they would be eaten.

VARIETIES	DAYS	EXTERIOR/INTERIOR/SHAPE	GREENS
Beet, globe type			
'Albino' (heirloom)	55	Greenish white/white/top-like to 3 in	Light green
'Alvro Mono' (OP) (monogerm)	55	Red/red/mildly elongated globe to 3 in	Green with red stems
'Betterave Rouge de Bassano' (see 'Chioggia')			
'Blankoma' (heirloom)	55	White/white/round tapered to 3 in	Light green
'Boro Hybrid'	50+	Red/dark red/round to 4 in	Green with red stems
'Bull's Blood' (heirloom)*****	60	Red/striped/flattened globe to 3 in	Deep burgundy***** (microgreens)
'Burpee's Golden' (heirloom)*****	55	Orange/yellow gold/round to 2 in	Light green
'Burpee's Red Ball' (OP)	60	Red/red/round to 3 in	Green with red stems
'Candystripe' (see 'Chioggia')			
'Chioggia' (heirloom)	55	Red/red white circles/round to 2 in	Light green
'Detroit' (heirloom)*****	60	Deep red/red/globe oval to 3 in	Glossy dark green with red stems
'Detroit Dark Red' (see 'Detroit')			
'Detroit Little Ball' (OP)*****	55	Red/red/round baby to 1½ in	Green with red stems
'Detroit Supreme' (OP)*****	65	Red/red/round oval to 3 in	Glossy dark green with red stems*****
'Eagle Hybrid'	55	Purplish red/red/round to 4 in	Green with red stems
'Early Wonder Tall Top' (heirloom)	55	Purplish red/red/flat globe to 3 in	Green with red stems*****
'Egyptian' (heirloom)	50	Red/varied red/flattened heart to 4 in	Green with red stems
'Golden Beet' (see 'Burpee's Golden')			
'Golden Detroit' (heirloom)	55	Orange/buttery yellow/round to 3 in	Light green (microgreens)
'Harrier Hybrid'	50	Red/red/round to 5 in	Green with red stems
'Kestrel Hybrid'*****	55	Red/red/round to 1½ in	Green with red stems
'Kleine Bol' (see 'Detroit Little Ball')			
'Little Ball' (see 'Detroit Little Ball')			
'Little Chicago Hybrid'	55	Red/red/round baby to 1½ in	Green with red stems
'Lutz Green Leaf' (heirloom)*****	80	Purplish/deep red/top shaped to 7 lb	Green with red stems*****
'Merlin Hybrid'*****	55	Red/red/round to 3 in	Green with red stems*****
'Mona Lisa' (OP) (monogerm)	55	Red/red/round (eat as baby beet)	Green with red stems
'Moneta Hybrid' (monogerm)	60	Red/red/round to 3 in	Green with red stems
'Pacemaker III Hybrid' (monogerm)	55	Red/red/round to 3 in	Green with red stems
'Perfected Detroit' (OP)	60	Red/red/round to 3 in	Green with red stems
'Pronto' (OP)	60	Red/red/round mildly tapered to 3 in	Green with red stems
'Red Ace Hybrid'*****	55	Red/red/round to 3 in	Green with red stems*****
'Red Cloud Hybrid'	60	Red/red/round mildly tapered to 3 in	Green with red stems
'Ruby Queen' (heirloom) (AAS-1957)	55	Red/red/round to 3 in	Green with red stems
'Solo Hybrid' (monogerm)*****	50	Red/red/globe to 3 in	Dark green with red stems*****
'Shiraz Tall Top' (heirloom)	55	Red/red/round to 3 in	Green with red stems*****
'Touchstone Gold Hybrid'*****	60	Orange/gold/round top shape to 3 in	Light green *****
'White Detroit' (heirloom)	55	White tan/white/top shaped to 3 in	Light green
'Winter Keeper' (see 'Lutz Green Leaf')			

VARIETIES	DAYS	EXTERIOR/INTERIOR/SHAPE	GREENS
Beet, Cylindra type			
'Butter Slicer' (see 'Cylindra')			
'Cheltenham Green Top' (heirloom)	55	Purplish red/red/tapered to 9 in	Light green with red stems
'Crapaudine' (heirloom)*****	70	Rough black/dark red/carrot-like to 8 in	Purplish with red stems
'Cylindra' (OP)	60	Dark red/red/carrot-like to 8 in	Green with red stems*****
'Formanova' (see 'Cylindra')			
'Forono' (OP)	60	Dark red/red/carrot-like to 8 in	Green with red stems
'Lady Toad' (see 'Crapaudine')			
'Rodina Hybrid'	60	Purplish red/red/carrot-like to 6 in	Green with red stems

Although many people prefer small beet greens, the larger leaves when properly prepared are delicious and nutritious as verdure cotte.

Blueberries ripen over time and must be protected from birds with netting.

BLUEBERRY

***Vaccinium* species**
Heath Family (Ericaceae)

Blueberries produce a plentiful crop of edible berries that can be enjoyed either by you or by wildlife. Bushes are neat. The fall foliage, usually reddish yellow to fiery red, is especially attractive. Stems may also take on a yellow to reddish hue in fall and winter to brighten winter days. Blueberries will live for decades if cared for properly. Blueberries are exacting in their cultural needs and take roughly 9 years to peak, but do start producing nice crops of berries in 3 to 4 years. The following information is geared to cold climates. Do not follow instructions from other books, often aimed at growing plants in warmer areas. *These plants are only worth growing if you have enough time and energy to take care of them properly.* Blueberries originated mainly in North America, but some species may have originated in Africa, Asia, and Europe as well.

duce numerous stems covered with deep-green, often glossy, somewhat leathery leaves vaguely reminiscent of holly. Each plant produces flower and leaf buds in the fall. The flower buds are larger and more rounded than the pointed leaf buds. Both buds are produced only on new growth. The flower buds burst into small, fragrant, white blossoms, a little like lily-of-the-valley flowers, in spring. Each variety requires a different variety close by for cross-pollination necessary to produce an abundance of berries. Bees or other insects are critical to proper pollination. Bees have a hard time pollinating blueberry flowers if the temperature falls below 55°F, if winds are higher than 15 miles per hour, or if it is raining. Pollinated flowers form berries during the summer. The berries turn from green to red and then to blue. These blue berries ripen over a period of days and sometimes weeks depending on the season and variety.

How Blueberries Grow

Blueberry bushes have a fibrous, shallow root system. They lack the delicate root hairs of many other plants and rely on a fungus to draw in nutrients for them. Each plant will pro-

Where to Plant Blueberries
Site and Light

Plant blueberries in full sun. Blueberries will grow in partial shade, but they produce many more berries in bright

light. Select a protected site or one that you can protect with a windbreak such as a fence, hedge, or wall. Heavy winds damage blueberry plants, so block them from prevailing winds.

Soil and Moisture

Ninety percent of success with blueberries depends on soil preparation. Getting a blueberry bed prepared can take from 1 to 2 years. Blueberries have two basic requirements: the right soil pH and loose soil with lots of organic matter in it. Soil must drain freely but retain moisture during dry periods.

Prepare the bed in fall by spading or tilling. Sandy soil is ideal. Build raised beds if your soil is compacted or rocky. Raised beds do have the disadvantage of exposing blueberry plants to winterkill by raising them higher than ground level so that they are less likely to be covered by snow. Blueberries demand a pH of 4.5 to 5.5. If the pH is higher than this, the plants may not survive or will do extremely poorly. Add sphagnum peat moss to your soil. It will lower the soil pH, help the soil stay loose, but retain moisture during dry spells. At least one-third of the soil should be peat; one-third, other organic matter such as rotted leaves; and the last third, garden soil. Peat lowers pH from 7 to 5 in sandy soil, only to 6.8 in clay. Peat also helps plant roots take in nutrients, particularly iron. Do not add lime to the soil. Although it contains nutrients, it increases the soil pH. Wood ash also increases soil pH and is best avoided. To lower the pH, add sulfur to the soil. Most products sold as sulfur are 88 percent to 100 percent sulfur and take about 3 to 4 months to lower soil pH, so fall is a good time to get soil ready for spring planting.

It's smart to test the pH in the planting area for blueberries. Test kits and pH meters are available, but more reliable are soil-testing laboratories. Extension offices can tell you where these are. Have a soil test done if you want to be exact. Whenever you order this test, tell the lab that you want to grow blueberries organically. The lab will return the test with exact instructions on how to prepare the soil. Most tests will indicate that you have to lower the soil pH. If you add sulfur to the soil in the fall, repeat the soil test again in the spring. If you add sulfur in the spring, test again in late fall. It's an added expense but cheaper than losing all of your blueberry plants. Older blueberry plants are expensive but worth it, and they will last for years if properly taken care of.

Some people don't want to go through the trouble and expense of soil testing and have had success just by using peat in the planting hole and sulfur as an acidifying agent. It's a gamble. Nonorganic growers use ammonium sulfate, not aluminum sulfate.

Nutrition Facts

Serving size: 100 grams (3.5 ounces)

	AMOUNT PER RAW SERVING	% DV
Calories	57	3%
Carbohydrates	14 g	5%
Dietary fiber	2.5 g	10%
Manganese	0.3 mg	17%
Protein	1 g	1%
Vitamin C	10 mg	16%
Vitamin K	20 mcg	25%

Container

It is possible to grow 'Top Hat' in a 5-gallon container filled with an acidic potting mix loaded with organic matter. The soil should drain freely through holes in the bottom of the container. Keep the soil moist at all times. Place plants in full sun. Repot after several years, and trim off some of the roots at that time.

Planting
Seed

Blueberries are rarely grown from seed. See "Propagation."

If protected from birds and cold, blueberry buds burst into gorgeous white bells in spring.

Bare Root

Bare-root plants are sold at many stages of growth. The tiniest plants, called microcuttings, are extremely small and the least expensive. If possible, buy older and larger bare-root plants. Remove plants from their shipping package immediately on arrival. Soak them in room-temperature water overnight before planting. Then plant them immediately with the soil line 3 to 4 inches above the top roots. Place a small amount of bonemeal in the base of the planting hole, and cover it with several inches of soil. If you are already growing some blueberries, grab a handful of soil from around the crown of a standing plant, and toss it in the hole as well. According to some growers, this soil is likely to contain the fungus that helps blueberries take in nutrients. Spread the roots out over a cone of well-prepared soil, and fill the hole with the same planting mix. Firm soil around the roots to remove air pockets, and water immediately. Pour ½ cup of a starter solution around the base of each plant. Fish emulsion works well.

Potted and Containerized Plants

Just like bare-root plants, potted and containerized blueberries are sold at many stages of growth. Plugs are 1- to 3-inch rooted plantlets. Mini-liners are 4 to 6 inches tall and sold in 2-inch pots. One-year-old plants are 10 to 14 inches tall and normally potted up in 4-inch pots. Two-year-old plants are a bit larger, more expensive, and planted in larger pots. Two-year-old plants are the best to buy since they mature more quickly and suffer less transplant shock. Plant potted plants as soon as you can in spring after all danger of frost has passed.

If the soil in the pot is dry, soak and let it drain overnight before planting. Carefully remove the plant from the container so as not to break the root ball. Plant at the same depth as in the container after preparing the hole in a similar manner as that for a bare-root plant. Fill the hole with well-prepared soil, firm with your fingers, and water immediately. Use ½ cup of starter solution around the base of the plant.

Spacing

Plant blueberries 24 to 36 inches apart or more in all directions. If you are gambling with larger and less winter-hardy varieties, space them 4 feet apart. This gives each plant plenty of room to expand and cuts down competition for nutrients and water. Space allows for good air circulation to prevent disease. It also lets lots of sun hit the berries during the entire season. The more sun, the better. When planting different varieties, plant them alternately in a row. This increases pollen exchange between the different varieties.

Cross-pollination increases the number and size of berries on the different varieties. It may also cause fruit to come in earlier and possibly to have better flavor. Not all pollinated blossoms set fruit.

When to Plant Blueberries

Get the plants into the soil as soon as it warms up in spring after any chance of a severe frost. Early planting gives them a good chance to take root during the summer. This will help them survive their first winter.

How to Care for Blueberries
Water

Keep the soil evenly moist, but not soggy, from spring until the soil freezes in fall. Consistent watering is critical throughout the shrub's entire life. In the early part of the season it stimulates flowering and good berry growth. In the second half of the season it helps the stems form lots of leaf and flower buds. Always saturate the soil deeply with each watering. Hand water, soaking the base evenly and deeply around all sides of the plant. When the top 2 inches of soil dry out, water. During hot, dry periods, mist foliage in the morning with a fine spray to ward off spider mites, wash off dust, and cool plants down. Do not spray water on berries if possible. This may cause cracking of the fruit. In some areas water is very alkaline, and heavy waterings can cause a change in pH. You can overcome this by applying acidic fertilizers to the soil each year.

Mulch

Place a 4- to 6-inch layer of mulch around the base of each plant. The mulch shelters the roots, keeping them moist and at an even temperature while it cuts back on weeding. Rotted oak leaves, pine needles, or composted sawdust from pine trees are most commonly recommended. These are all mildly acidic but do not reduce the pH as much as sphagnum peat moss added to the soil at the time of planting. Add additional mulch as necessary throughout the growing season. When using wood products, remember to add more nitrogen to the soil than you normally would since soil microorganisms need it to break down the mulch. The nitrogen will be depleted temporarily but released later.

Fertilizing

Getting blueberries off to a good start means fertilizing them regularly with sulfur to keep the soil acidic. Organic fertilizers high in nitrogen are also recommended for good growth. Blood meal and soybean meal are effective.

In the first year, six weeks after initial planting, fertilize each blueberry bush with blood meal. Spread it around the base of the plant, and water well to carry nutrients to the root zone. Six weeks later do the same.

Every year thereafter, spread organic fertilizer around the base of the plant as soon as the snow melts. Add sulfur regularly to the soil as well to keep the pH low. At bloom time sprinkle blood meal around the base of each plant. Six weeks later do the same. Do not fertilize plants later in the year than this. You might stimulate late growth, which is vulnerable to winterkill.

If plants produce lots of foliage and little bloom, cut back on the use of nitrogen. If the soil pH is too high, the leaves of blueberry plants will turn yellow. This is the result of inadequate uptake of iron from the soil. Professional *nonorganic* growers use ammonium sulfate (not aluminum sulfate) to keep soil acidic and well fed.

Weeding

To encourage heavy growth, keep the area around each bush free of weeds and grass. If weeds sprout, pull them out by hand. Don't cultivate around the bushes, since the roots are shallow and easily damaged. Use a mulch to reduce the need for weeding. The few weeds that do pop up are easy to pull out from moist mulch.

Pruning

Picking off flower blossoms for the first two years may encourage better root development. This takes a lot of time and patience but may result in a bushier plant with greater fruit production in future years.

As new growth emerges in spring, cut off any wood that died from exposure during the winter. Cut stems back to the first healthy bud. Slant the cut about ¼ inch above the bud. Keep as much of each stem as possible to conserve flower buds. If a stem is dead all the way to the ground, cut it off flush with the soil surface. If plants produce horizontal stems close to the ground, snip these off.

After the third year of growth, remove any twiggy or weak lateral growth while the bushes are still dormant. Leave the larger new laterals alone. Remember that plants form leaf and flower buds on new growth only. So keep pruning to a minimum.

When the plant is 5 or 6 years old, cut out one or two of the older canes each year. Do this in late winter. These older canes do not produce as well as the younger ones. Too many canes sap the plant of its strength. Vigorous bushes contain four to six old canes, and two to four new ones for a total of six to ten stems per bush. Healthy plants will produce new canes from the base of the plant each year. In effect, the plant is constantly regenerating as it should. Your job is to keep the older stems from interfering with the plant's overall health.

Whenever you prune blueberries, carry a small bottle filled with 1 part bleach and 9 parts water. Dip the pruning shears in the solution after working with each plant. This helps prevent the spread of disease. Some home gardeners are replacing bleach with rubbing alcohol.

Keep the bed clean. Toss all trimmings into the compost pile.

Winter Protection

Blueberries are only marginally hardy in extreme cold and can die back to the ground if not protected. If they are partially protected by snow, they will often die back to the snow line. The flower buds are even more sensitive. These are formed in the fall. If these buds are damaged by cold, they will not produce flowers even though the plants seem to be doing fine. The best protection for blueberries, both plants and flower buds, is snow. If the plants are completely covered with snow, the buds will survive the brutal cold and chilling winds of midwinter. Placing snow fences in strategic locations to force drifts over the plants is one way of protecting blueberries. You can also shovel snow over the plants. This is not practical in commercial production, but it is easily done to a few plants in a home garden.

Some gardeners fill plastic bags with leaves and set them around their blueberry plants. Do this after a few hard freezes. Whenever it snows, you can shovel snow onto these bags. If it doesn't snow at all, these leaf-filled bags provide minimal protection. Straw does not provide blueberries with enough protection during cold winters. Whole leaves are better, but snow is best. Several synthetic products have been tested and work well for winter protection. Netting should have ¼- to ½-inch mesh. All are very good at trapping snow, but they are less effective in dry, snow-free winters. Some commercial growers use plastic to protect plants during the winter, but using it takes skill, so use another method to protect your bushes. Remove any winter protection as soon as the snow melts and before buds begin to swell on the bushes.

Extending the Season

You can plant varieties that mature at different dates for a prolonged harvest. This is more practical for commercial growers.

Problems

Insects

At one time blueberries rarely had problems with insects. Unfortunately, in recent years the spotted wing drosophila (*Drosophila suzukii*) has become a serious pest to blueberries and brambles in cold climates.

Disease

Blueberries are susceptible to fungal diseases that cause cankers to form on the stems. These diseases are directly related to winter damage. Winter damage includes sunscald (see below), which results in open wounds that become easily infected. If some branches do die, remove them immediately in spring. Always cut stems off if they have any open sores. The removal and destruction of infected cane often stop the spread of fungal disease before it becomes a major problem. Avoid other serious infections by buying plants certified to be disease-free.

Blueberries will develop root rot if the soil does not drain freely. Add enough peat to help acidify the soil, but don't add so much organic matter that the soil remains soggy over a long period of time.

Marauders

In most instances birds are great allies in the home garden since many species eat thousands of insects during the growing season. Yet, they have an insatiable appetite for ripening blueberries. Birds can be frustrating to deal with, since it can take up to 3 weeks for blueberries to ripen even after initially turning blue. There are many folk remedies for this problem, such as hanging pie tins from the bushes, but the only effective way to protect berries is to cover them with nylon bird netting. Cover entire patches by stretching netting over supports that keep the material off the plants themselves. The netting should be anchored around the base of plants so that birds cannot get in from the bottom. Remove this netting immediately after all berries have been picked.

Birds, especially grouse, are a problem in northern areas during the winter. They eat the flower buds. Protect plants as you would in the summer with netting or fencing. Rabbits eat plants at any time of year. Completely surround growing areas with chicken wire to prevent rabbit damage.

Physiological

Sunscald is damage caused to exposed canes by reflected light during the winter. The tissue swells during warm periods, only to burst open when temperatures drop. Blueberry bushes covered with snow or protected by black plastic bags filled with leaves rarely suffer from sunscald.

Propagation

It is possible to grow blueberries from cuttings, mound layering, seed, soil layering, suckers, and tissue culture.

Harvesting

Fruit on different varieties ripens at different times. Fruit from a cross-pollinated plant will ripen faster than fruit from a self-pollinated bush. Blueberries turn blue before they are completely ripe. If you pick them too soon, they may be bitter. They are usually sweet when every hint of red has disappeared from the berry. Look at the place where the stem joins the berry. If it is pinkish, the fruit may not yet be ripe. Ripe berries also come off more easily from the bush when you touch them gently. The only way to know exactly when to pick them is by taste.

Storing

Some people insist that if you refrigerate blueberries, they lose some of their sweet flavor. So compare berries at room temperature with a few that have been chilled to see whether you agree. Keeping them chilled is the only practical way of storing them for short periods of time—about a week. Lay them on a plate in a single layer, not crammed on top of each other.

To freeze, remove any debris or stems, but don't wash the berries. They freeze better if dry. Flash freeze in single layer on metal tray before placing them into freezer bags. Don't freeze berries in large clumps unless you plan to make jelly from them at a later date. Small bags of berries are much easier to use when you need just a few. They do not have to be thawed to be used.

To dry, wash, remove stems, and dry in a dehydrator. They may last up to 6 months if fully dry.

Culinary Uses

Blueberries are great fresh in any number of ways. They are wonderful as jams and jellies and in pies. To make a simple blueberry syrup, cook 2 cups berries with ⅓ cup sugar and the juice of a lemon.

Varieties

Following are some of the most popular blueberries for fruit and ornamental purposes. They are commonly hybrids of *Vaccinium angustifolium* (lowbush blueberry) and *Vaccinium corymbosum* (highbush blueberry). The approximate date of first fruiting is listed under season and varies from early to late season. The time span from early to late is about 1 month or a bit longer. Cross-pollination is critical for large berries and abundant berry production. It may also help berries come in sooner and sweeter. For example, when 'Northsky' is cross-pollinated, its berry weight goes from .4 ounce to .8 ounce, and its fruit set rises from 14 percent to 87 percent. Plant 'Northblue' with 'Northcountry' for good fruit production. 'Top Hat' is self-pollinating and primarily an ornamental plant.

VARIETY	SIZE/COLOR	SEASON	YIELD (LB)	HEIGHT/ WIDTH (FEET)	HARDINESS
var. *angustifolium*	Small/light blue to dark blue	Very early	Variable	½/1½	-35°F
'Bluecrop'	Large, bright blue	Mid	3–6	6/6	-15°F
'Bluetta'	Medium/slightly dark blue	Early	5–6	5/5	-20°F
'Bluegold'	Medium large/sky blue	Early to mid	7	4½/5	-20°F
'Blueray' ('Blue Ray')	Very large/bright blue	Mid	3–6	6/6	-15°F
'Chippewa'	Medium/light blue	Mid	4–7	4/4	-25°F
'Northblue'*****	Very large/dark blue	Early to mid	3–9	2/3	-30°F
'Northcountry'	Small, sky blue	Early to mid	2	2/3	-30°F
'Northland'	Very small/dark blue	Early to mid	4–7	4/5	-25°F
'Northsky'	Small/sky blue	Early to mid	1–3	1½/3	-30°F
'Patriot'	Very large/light blue	Early to mid	9–12	6/5	-20°F
'Pink Popcorn'™	Medium/cream pink	Early to mid	5	4/5	-25°F
'Polaris'	Medium/light blue	Early mid	3–7	4/4	-25°F
'Reka'	Fairly large/light blue	Early mid	8	5/5	-20°F
'St. Cloud'	Medium large/deep blue	Early	2–7	4/4	-30°F
'Superior'*****	Very large/light to medium blue	Late	5–6	4/4	-35°F
'Top Hat'	Small/light blue	Late	1–2	1½/1½	-20°F

BROAD BEAN (FAVA BEAN)

Vicia faba species
Legume or Pea Family (Fabaceae, formerly Leguminosae)

Broad bean is a hardy, cool-season annual. It goes by many different names, including bell bean, English bean, fava bean, field bean, horse bean, pigeon bean, tick bean, and Windsor bean. In cold climates it makes an excellent substitute for finicky lima beans. It is easy to grow as long as you plant it early. Its flowers are lovely, and as a bonus, it adds nitrogen to the soil. It is so high in protein that it is sometimes called "vegetable meat." Broad beans probably originated in the Middle East.

How Broad Beans Grow

Seed varies in color but is usually very large and somewhat wrinkled (about 15 to 20 seeds per ounce). The leaves often look like a cross between a bean and a pea. Stems get thick but are brittle. Most varieties produce white flowers with a black blotch in the center, but there are some delightful exceptions. The flowers drop off as fuzzy lima bean–like pods begin to form from the bottom up. The flat (broad) pods vary considerably in length (2 to 12 inches) depending on the variety and produce varied numbers, colors, and sizes of beans (seeds). The pods and seeds are edible as is the cluster of leaves on the tips of stems.

Where to Plant Broad Beans
Site and Light

Broad beans thrive in bright light. Plant them in full sun. At the same time they like it cool. Summer heat can be a problem, as foliage may burn, and pollination may suffer in higher temperatures. The solution is to get seeds into the ground early in the season. Since the stems of the plants are brittle, choose a location protected from prevailing winds.

Soil and Moisture

Broad beans like loose, well-drained, and rich soil. Add lots of organic matter to the soil to retain moisture and keep soil temperatures even. Well-rotted manure is the ideal soil amendment. Additional fertilizer is not necessary. A pH of 6 to 6.8 is recommended.

Container

It is certainly possible to grow the smaller varieties in large pots, but it is rarely done. However, 'The Sutton' is a good choice if you decide to give it a try. It is available from several British companies.

Planting

Seed

Direct seeding is the most common method for growing broad beans. Plant seeds from 1 inch to 2 inches deep depending on the texture of your soil. Germination is erratic, occurring as early as 10 days and as late as 21.

Transplants

It is possible to start broad beans indoors, but it is not recommended, as they do not transplant well. Young plants can stand some light frost, but indoor seeding is more bother than the average gardener will want to go to.

Spacing

Spacing depends on your style of gardening. If planting in rows, place seed about 3 to 6 inches apart. Another method is to plant seeds 12 inches apart in all directions with the hope that plants will support each other as they mature.

When to Plant

Get the seed into the ground as soon as the soil can be worked in spring, which is usually 2 to 4 weeks before the last expected frost. Ideally, you want plants to bloom in cool weather. Seed will begin to germinate at temperatures just above 40°F, although the optimum temperature is higher. Succession planting is highly recommended to spread out the harvest time. Blossoms may drop in temperatures above 90°F; at the very least, pod set may be poor.

Support

Many varieties get tall and can be easily damaged by winds. The plant stems are brittle and will break if mishandled or blown over. Pound stakes into the ground about 4 feet apart. Then run string back and forth through the growing plants at various heights to hold them in place. Some gardeners dispense with this by planting them closer together than normally recommended. This is a gamble that usually pays off.

How to Care for Broad Beans

Water

Broad beans grow best with consistent moisture. It is especially important to water plants well while they are flowering and forming pods. Do not let the soil dry out at that time. Few or deformed pods may result from water stress. Drip irrigation works well, or hand water the base of plants as necessary in the morning.

Nutrition Facts

Serving size: 100 grams (3.5 ounces)

	AMOUNT PER COOKED SERVING	% DV
Calories	110	5%
Carbohydrates	20 g	7%
Copper	0.3 mg	13%
Dietary fiber	5 g	22%
Folate	105 mcg	25%
Iron	1.5 mg	8%
Magnesium	43 mg	11%
Manganese	0.4 mg	21%
Phosphorus	125 mg	12%
Potassium	268 mg	8%
Protein	8 g	15%
Zinc	1 mg	7%

Mulch

Mulch with an organic mulch once the seedlings emerge. The mulch keeps the soil moist and cool, just the way broad beans like it. Do not touch the base of the stems with the mulch but spread it out thickly in the area between the plants. Mulch also stops soil from splattering up on the leaves if you water by hand.

Fertilizing

Fertilizing is unnecessary and may promote lush foliage at the expense of fruit. As a legume, the broad bean gets nutrients from nitrogen-fixing bacteria on its roots. Broad beans make a good green manure when plowed under.

Weeding

Get rid of all weeds by hand pulling them around the base of the plant. Weeds compete with the plants for moisture, and broad beans need consistent moisture to develop well.

Thinning

Plants should have enough space to grow freely but be close enough to support each other. The space between plants will vary with variety. Follow your instincts.

Pruning

As the flowers begin to wilt and pods start to form, pinch out the top cluster of leaves on the tip of the stem. This directs

Broad beans are an ideal source of protein for vegetarians.

all of the plant's energy into pod formation. These little clusters are edible and should not be thrown away. Some refer to them as a spinach substitute, but they have their own distinct flavor.

Winter Protection

Broad beans often are planted in fall in moderate climates, but this is not the case in colder areas.

Special Considerations

Most people have no allergic-like reaction to working with or eating broad beans. However, roughly 10 percent of black people, about 1 percent of people of Mediterranean descent, and a small number of people from different backgrounds are "allergic" to them because of an inherited G6PD deficiency, which predisposes them to hemolysis, the spontaneous destruction of red blood cells. This response to broad beans is known as favism and can be serious. When eating broad beans for the first time, eat just a small amount. When growing broad beans, sensitive individuals can react to the pollen as if they had eaten the beans.

Anyone taking MAOI (monoamine oxidase inhibitors) for depression should talk to a doctor before consuming broad beans.

Broad beans make an excellent cover crop to add nutrients and organic matter to the soil.

Extending the Season

Although you can plant broad beans under plastic tunnels to get a jump on the season, few people do. Get the seeds into the ground as soon as possible with the hope that the broad beans will begin to mature in relatively cool weather.

Problems

Insects

Not many insects affect this crop in the home garden. Watch for aphids. Break off and destroy heavily infested parts, and wash off the rest with a hose. Slugs are a potential problem in wet weather.

Disease

Leaf spots and gray mold (botrytis) show up occasionally. Give more space for better air circulation the next time you plant them.

Physiological

Flower drop may occur in higher temperatures. Uneven watering may also be to blame.

Propagation

Broad beans are self-pollinating. Home gardeners should grow only one variety because different varieties will cross-pollinate if they bloom at the same time and if there is sufficient insect activity. Let the beans dry on the plant. Remove them when fully dry. Place them in an envelope. Keep in a cool, dark, dry place. They often stay viable for 3 or more years.

Harvesting

There are three potential times to harvest broad beans. At any time do not tug the beans off the plant; use a scissors or pruning shears to snip them off. Stems are easily damaged. When picking beans, always start from the bottom up. The lower beans mature first. The first harvest can take place when the pods are young and tender. You can eat the pod at this stage. However, broad beans are more commonly picked at the "lima bean" stage. The pods will get plump as the beans swell inside. Check inside one pod. If the scar on the bean is greenish white, begin picking. Once the scar turns black, the beans are past their prime. Broad beans do not mature all at once. Check them every few days. If beans get overly mature, just let them continue to develop. Wait until the pods turn black. The beans inside should be dry. Hang them in a warm, dry place, then shell. Toss plants into a compost pile after picking.

Storing

To store in a refrigerator, place unwashed whole pods or shelled beans in a plastic bag in the crisper, where they may last for up to 10 days. Try to eat them within 4 days if possible.

If you can't eat all of the beans at the "lima bean" stage, do not store them in their pods. Freeze them instead. Remove freshly picked beans from the shell, rinse, blanch in boiling water for 1½ to 3 minutes, plunge immediately into ice-cold water for 2 minutes, lay on a tray and freeze for 30 minutes, place in locking freezer bags, and freeze for up to 6 months.

Culinary Uses

When you pinch back the plants during the growing season, keep the tops, and stir-fry them in butter. Or add them to quiches or omelets as you would spinach. The tips are best just as beans begin to appear. Note that these tips are edible raw as well.

The beans themselves can be eaten at an early stage as you would snap beans. Both pods and tiny beans can be eaten a little later like snap peas. At a later stage, the seeds make an excellent substitute for lima beans. They can also be eaten once fully mature and dry. Place dry beans in an oven at 135°F to destroy insect eggs.

Young beans, when they are still tender, are delicious raw or cooked. As the pods mature, they become tough and stringy. However, the developing beans inside are excellent. Remove the pod, and cook the beans until tender, for about 3 to 5 minutes. The cooking time does vary by variety. Do not overcook the beans, or they will become mushy. Then pop the beans out of their covering. This is like skinning each bean with your fingers. Once skinned, they are delicious cooked with garlic, or they can be puréed and made into a soup.

Soak dry beans overnight. Then cook them until tender. They are excellent seasoned with garlic, lemon, and olive oil. Purée them for a spread. Or grind them into a high-protein flour and use to make bread. You can also pop the beans like popcorn (well, sort of). The variety 'Coffee Bean' can be dried and ground into a coffee substitute.

Varieties

Choose varieties by size, date of maturation, and seed production. All have lovely flowers, but those of 'Crimson Flowered' stand out for rich color. These are all heirloom varieties, many of which are in danger of perishing. If you intend to save seed, grow one variety at a time to prevent cross-pollination. Some are available only through British or Canadian seed sources.

VARIETIES	DAYS	HEIGHT (INCHES)	POD LENGTH (INCHES)	SEEDS PER POD
'5B's Choice'	80	40	8	Up to 6 large, lime green
'Aprovecho Select'	75	40	7	Up to 6 very large, tan
'Aquadulce'*****	75	24	7–10	Up to 8 large, greenish
'Aquadulce Claudia'	90	38	9	Up to 8 light green
'Aztec Yellow'	65	36	3	Up to 3 large, yellow
'Black Fava'	75	24	2	Up to 3 small, black
'Broad Improved Long Pod'	85	36–40	4–7	Up to 6 large, pale green
'Broad Windsor'*****	75	36–48	5–8	Up to 5 very large, white green
'Broad Windsor Long Pod'	75	24	8	Up to 7 greenish white
'Bunyard's Exhibition'	80	48	12	Up to 7 white
'Claudia' (see 'Aquadulce Claudia')				
'Coffee Bean'	75	24	2–3	Up to 4 tan mottled black
'Con Amore'	70	30	3	Up to 5 medium, pale green
'Copper Fava'	85	30	3	Up to 3 medium, copper
'Crimson Flowered'	75	36	3–4	Up to 4 light green
'Exhibition Long Pod'	80	42	9	Up to 7 greenish white
'Express'*****	80	36	5–6	Up to 6 light green
'Green Windsor'	70	36	5–6	Up to 8 bright green
'Imperial Green Longpod'	85	36	14	Up to 9 large, green
'Jubilee Hysor'	75	42	6	Up to 8 large, light green
'Martoc' ('Martock')	90	22	3	Up to 4 small, tan (for dry beans)
'Masterpiece Green Long Pod'*****	80	36	8	Up to 8 green
'Polar'	65	24	4	Up to 5 medium, white
'Primo' (see 'Express')				
'Purple Fava'	80	48	5	Up to 4 royal purple
'Red Epicure'	75	36	5	Up to 5 large, chestnut red
'Scabiola Verde' (see 'Aquadulce')				
'Statissa'	90	30	5	Up to 4 medium, light green
'Sweet Lorane'	80	48	4	Up to 5 small, light beige (for dry beans)
'Swiss'	75	28	5	Up to 5 large, blond
'The Sutton'	65	16	3	Up to 6 white blond
'Threefold White'	75	36	8	Up to 8 small, white
'Witkiem Manita'*****	65	40	5	Up to 6 white
'Windsor' (see 'Broad Windsor')				

Pick broccoli when the tiny flower buds are still tight.

BROCCOLI

Brassica oleracea var. **italica,** or Italica Group
Cabbage or Mustard Family (Brassicaceae, formerly Cruciferae)

Broccoli is a very hardy, cold-season annual. Broccoli is a fun and relatively easy plant to grow. Each plant will reward you with many delicious meals. However, broccoli is just as much a favorite with insects and animals. So you may have to devise plant protection methods if you want to be successful. Broccoli probably originated in the eastern Mediterranean, possibly coming from Turkey into Italy.

How Broccoli Grows

Broccoli seed is small (about 6,000 to 8,000 seeds per ounce), round, and usually dark brown to purplish. The plant grows rapidly from a tiny but sturdy seedling into a large, leafy plant. As it matures, an immature flower begins to form at the growing tip. This enlarges into a head similar to the one you buy in the store. It is made up of numerous flower buds. If you do not cut off this head, the buds will turn into bright, yellow flowers. These may or may not form elongated pods filled with seeds in the first year.

Where to Plant Broccoli
Site and Light

Although broccoli is a cool- to cold-weather plant, it likes a bright, sunny location.

Soil and Moisture

Broccoli grows rapidly and requires lots of moisture and a rich, fertile soil that drains freely. As with most plants, it thrives in loam amended with lots of organic matter, which releases nutrients slowly, loosens the soil, and yet retains moisture during dry spells. If your soil is compacted, build a raised bed. If compost or manure is in short supply, just toss a few cupfuls into the hole when planting. Enrich the soil with a variety of organic fertilizers. Adding a little lime or wood ash in fall is fine and may help prevent clubroot. Gypsum is also valuable for its calcium. The ideal pH is from 6.5 to 7.2, which means the soil can be slightly alkaline.

Nutrition Facts

Serving size: 100 grams (3.5 ounces)

	AMOUNT PER RAW SERVING	% DV	AMOUNT PER COOKED SERVING	% DV
Calories	35	2%	35	2%
Calcium	47 mg	5%	40 mg	4%
Carbohydrates	7 g	2%	7 g	2%
Dietary fiber	3 g	12%	3 g	12%
Folate	63 mcg	16%	108 mcg	27%
Iron	0.7 mg	4%	0.7	4%
Manganese	0.2 mg	10%	0.2 mg	10%
Phosphorus	65 mg	7%	65 mg	7%
Potassium	315 mg	9%	295 mg	8%
Protein	3 g	6%	3 g	6%
Riboflavin	0.1 mg	7%	0.1 mg	7%
Vitamin A	625 IU	12%	1,550 IU	30%
Vitamin C	90 mg	150%	65 mg	110%
Vitamin B6	0.2 mg	10%	0.2 mg	10%
Vitamin E	0.8 mg	4%	1.5 mg	7%
Vitamin K	100 mcg	125%	140 mcg	175%

Container

It is possible to grow broccoli in a container, but few people do. Grow only one plant per large container. 'Munchkin' and 'Small Miracle Hybrid' form small heads but are probably your best choices.

Planting

Seed

You can gamble with direct seeding for a fall crop. Timing is difficult since plants can react badly to high heat or to early fall frosts. However, broccoli matures well in the fall, so the gamble is well worth it. Plant seed about ½ inch deep. Keep consistently moist.

Transplants

Broccoli is easy to grow from seed, which you can order from mail-order companies. One big advantage of growing broccoli from seed is that you select the variety or varieties to grow. Experiment each year. Most plants sold in garden centers are simply labeled "broccoli." You have no idea what variety they are, how long they will take to mature, and whether they are disease resistant. If you buy plants, choose packs with short (roughly 4 inches), stocky plants with good color. One pack may have more plants than another. Choose the one with the most plants, and tease them apart for planting.

Start your own broccoli seed indoors 4 to 6 weeks before the time you plan to set your transplants in the garden, which is roughly 3 to 4 weeks before the last expected frost. Plant seed at different times to ensure having them at the right size, since weather is so unpredictable. Save the remaining seed for the next season. Plant in sterile starting mix about ¼ to ½ inch deep. Keep moist and warm at 70°F, with a drop of 10 degrees at night. Seeds should sprout within 10 days. Harden off before planting outdoors.

Be careful when working with young broccoli seedlings. Don't bend or break the tip of the plant. Strip off any lower leaves if they have turned yellow. When you do this, don't tear them off—pinch them between your thumb and forefinger. Plant as deep as the lower leaf. Firm the soil around the base of the plant with your fingers. Pour a transplant solution around the seedling. Keep consistently moist. Note that root disturbance does retard growth slightly. Keep as much soil around the root system as possible.

Spacing

There is no specific spacing required, but plants are usually planted no closer than 12 inches apart and often up to 18 to 24 inches. It is easier to harvest side shoots with more space between plants, and wider spacing may help reduce disease. Broccoli planted at 18- to 24-inch intervals will produce larger heads than broccoli planted close together. But the total production from patches planted in different styles will be about the same.

Some gardeners harvest only the central bud. They then tear out the plant and replace it with a different crop. Most gardeners find the side buds provide a wonderful extended crop.

When to Plant

Set seedlings outdoors as soon as you can work the soil, generally 3 to 4 weeks before the last expected frost. If frost threatens, protect the seedlings with a cloche, HotKap®, or thick layer of mulch. Plants can take cold after they have several pairs of true leaves, but don't gamble with frost or severe cold.

Get the plants in very early since buds form best in cooler weather. During the growing season the ideal temperature is 60°F to 65°F, but heads will still form up to 80°F.

Direct seed for a fall harvest 10 to 12 weeks before the first expected fall frost. The seed package will tell the number of days to maturity. Count backwards from the first expected frost date to figure out when to plant the seeds for the fall crop. Give yourself an extra two weeks leeway since daylight diminishes late in the season. Older broccoli plants can tolerate frosts and temperatures as low as 25°F in the fall. A hard freeze will kill them. Fall-harvested broccoli is ideal for freezing.

How to Care for Broccoli

Water

Make sure transplants or seeds planted directly in the garden are kept consistently moist until growing well. Once they are growing vigorously, you can water less. Still, don't let them get stressed from lack of water. When the head begins to form, water deeply and frequently. Water the base of the plant, not the leaves, to reduce the chance of disease.

Mulch

Broccoli responds beautifully to a thick layer of organic mulch. The mulch keeps the soil weed-free, moist, and cool. Get the mulch on early in the season, but don't touch the stems with it.

Fertilizing

Use a transplant solution high in phosphorus when you plant seedlings. Either give plants a heavy feeding after 3 weeks and again 2 weeks later or small feedings weekly. Using a variety of organic fertilizers to provide varied nutrients makes sense. Good fertilizers include blood meal, bonemeal, fish emulsion, and rotted manures. Properly prepared soil will contain enough boron and calcium, which are important for good growth. Foliar sprays are excellent for micronutrients. Broccoli is a heavy feeder.

Weeding

To avoid damaging the root system, do not cultivate deeply around the base of the plants. Hand pull all weeds in the root zone. If you're using mulch, you won't have to disturb the soil at all. If any weeds pop up through the mulch, remove them immediately.

Thinning

When direct seeding, sprinkle seed in the furrow. When seedlings have true leaves, prick them out, and space as you would transplants.

Pruning

Harvest all buds as they mature, even if you don't need them at the moment. Or at least freeze them. Once the plant starts to flower, it deteriorates.

Special Considerations

Broccoli may bolt in hot weather. If you are a seed saver, let the plant flower, and hope that pods will form and have enough time left in the season to form viable seed. Otherwise, pull up the plant, compost, and plant a new crop.

Broccoli may taste differently to different people because of their genetic makeup. Some people find it extremely bitter, but most don't.

Extending the Season

The best way to extend the season is to get plants in early with protection and then plant a second set of plants to mature in the fall. Broccoli is not as frost resistant as cabbage but produces nicely in cool weather. It will tolerate light frost if growing vigorously. Some varieties can even withstand temperatures down to 20°F. Some good fall varieties are listed in the varietal table.

Problems

Insects

Transplants and seeds grow quickly and beautifully in the garden, but seedlings are very prone to insect damage when immature. There are numerous insects that feed on broccoli. Aphids, cabbage worms, cutworms, flea beetles, and root maggots are the most common. Cutworms attack the stems of young plants, which collapse. Root maggots work below the soil and typically kill older plants, which suddenly wilt for no apparent reason. Two types of cabbage worms make a smorgasbord of leaves. The loss of a plant or two does not warrant the expense of typical controls. Till green manure or leaf mold into the soil in fall to reduce the chance of root maggot damage. Covering young plants with row covers reduces the more common insect problems.

Disease

A number of diseases may affect broccoli. Disease is usually less of a problem than insect infestations in the home garden. However, fusarium yellows can be serious if it gets into the soil from infected nursery plants or seed. Clubroot is fairly common, causing plants to wilt and die. When you pull up the plant, the roots resemble an enlarged club, giving the disease its name. To reduce the incidence of this disease, add limestone to the soil in fall. Limestone causes a change in the soil pH, so use it sparingly. Black rot and downy mildew occur occasionally.

Prevent most disease by buying certified seed of disease-resistant varieties, providing enough space for air circulation, and planting cole crops, which include broccoli, in a different place each year. Since you cannot know the background of transplants purchased from a local nursery, consider growing your own plants each year.

Marauders

Rabbits can wipe out a dozen young broccoli plants in one evening. They often go down a row, eating out the crucial growing tips from each plant. Woodchucks do the same. Animals much prefer young plants to older ones and look at broccoli as a spring delicacy. Year in and year out marauders do more damage to broccoli than insects and disease. This is just as true in the middle of a suburban area as out on the farm.

The best defense is a good fence. Consider a really good one right from the start. Mini-fences, cages around plants, will protect plants against rabbits. They do nothing to stop woodchucks and deer, which when hungry enough will eat just about anything. The second best defense against marauders is an aware and aggressive dog. However, dogs may not be roaming at night, when rabbits often do their dirty work.

Physiological

There are several physiological disorders causing poor growth (hollow stems and discolored heads), poor head formation (buttoning), bolting, or few heads at all (blindness). With adequate soil preparation and consistent watering, all are uncommon in the home garden. Hollow stems and brownish heads are commonly caused by a lack of boron in the soil, which is rare if you are adding organic matter to the soil. Buttoning may result from poor drainage, a lack of nitrogen, overly cold weather as transplants are being planted, and inconsistent watering. Bolting is generally caused by overly hot weather. Damage to the growing tip, caused by either you or marauders, may result in no heading.

Propagation

Broccoli is hermaphroditic, having both male and female organs. However, it must be insect pollinated. Isolate it from any other flowering plants in the same family. Let plants go to seed. Let pods dry on the plant until just before they begin to split. Snip off pods, break open, separate seed from debris, and store in a dark, dry, cool place for up to 3 to 5 years. The best seed is produced when at least a dozen plants are allowed to flower together. While I think it's smart to grow more than one variety each year, this would defeat the purpose of seed savers since varieties can cross-pollinate.

Harvesting

As broccoli plants grow wider and taller, they begin to form a large, green central flower head at the top of the plant. This is made up of hundreds of little florets or flower buds tightly pressed together. Rub your fingers over these. Let the bud continue to grow until the bumps just begin to loosen up. This is a sign that the plant is about to go to flower. Harvest the head when it looks like the broccoli you buy at the grocery store. Heads that start to flower are past their prime, although the flowers are decorative and edible.

Cut off the head with a knife an inch or two down the stalk. Do not cut farther down the stem, because you want the plant to produce an additional crop of smaller buds. These form at the end of shoots springing out of leaf axils, the place where leaves join the stem, below the central head after it has been harvested. Cut these off in the same way as the original, larger head.

You may get many 1- to 2-inch side shoots from each plant, smaller and smaller as the season progresses. You will keep getting broccoli as long as you leave as much stem tissue and leaves intact as possible. If you originally cut farther down the stalk (12 inches below the head), you will have fewer but bigger side shoots. The choice is yours.

Never let any heads bloom. If you let the plant go to flower, it will stop producing. Its job is done as soon as flowers go to seed. As long as you keep cutting all the smaller heads off, you encourage the plant to send out more and more side shoots. When these become sporadic or so small they are barely worth harvesting, pull up and compost the plant.

Storing

To store in the refrigerator, place heads unwashed in a perforated plastic bag for up to 7 days, but they are best eaten within 3.

To freeze, wash and soak in salt water to remove worms, remove any leaves, break off florets, pare and cut stems into 1 inch pieces, blanch for 3 to 4 minutes, plunge into ice water for 3 to 4 minutes, place immediately in airtight freezer bags, and freeze.

Culinary Uses

Broccoli is edible raw or cooked. Use broccoli immediately if possible. If you can't, place it in the refrigerator. Do not wash broccoli until you are ready to use it. Fresh broccoli is a delicacy, not only for you but also for little green worms, which hide in the heads. Soak fresh broccoli in salt water for 10 to 15 minutes but not longer. The little worms react to this bath by floating to the surface of the water, where you can skim them off. You can do the same in warm water with a dash of white vinegar. These worms are a good indication that your heads have truly been grown in a pesticide-free environment.

Add raw broccoli to salads, or serve on a vegetable platter with dip. If broccoli flowers, add blossoms to salads. They are edible and ornamental. Young leaves are also edible, but as they get old, they turn bitter.

Snap or cut off florets that make up a broccoli head. These are the tight, bright-green little clumps. Peel and split the stems before cutting them into thin slices, either rounds or on the diagonal. Both the florets and stems can be boiled, butter steamed, microwaved, roasted, sautéed, or steamed. Cook only until tender to preserve color, flavor, and nutrition.

Cook, purée, and mix with a variety of ingredients for a delicious cream of broccoli soup. Look up the recipe for *bagna cauda,* a mix of olive oil or butter, garlic, anchovies, and chili flakes, dusted with parsley leaves. Steam briefly, then sauté in olive oil, and cover with parmesan cheese. Cook until tender, and smother in cheese or hollandaise sauce. Flavor cooked broccoli with dill, lemon, or rosemary for a change of flavors.

Varieties

It is confusing, but what is sold in supermarkets is not really broccoli, but calabrese. It forms a large head in one season and smaller side heads after the main head is cut off. True broccoli, sometimes called sprouting broccoli, doesn't form a large central head, but numerous smaller ones. It is better suited to milder climates. To add to the confusion, the variety 'Italian Green Sprouting' is calabrese.

Many varieties do well in the home garden. Try two each year. Pick the one you like best, and grow it again the following year with yet another variety. Keep doing this each year. This is a fun and simple way to find out which variety does best in your specific location. Purple cauliflower is really a broccoli, but I have included it in the cauliflower section since it is most commonly sold that way. It has a head that looks like cauliflower but is really made up of tiny flower buds. 'Piracicaba' (pronounced peer-uh-see-CAH-buh) is like a broccoli crossed with broccoli raab. It has lots of small loose heads and numerous side shoots. Romanesco broccoli is really a cauliflower, and a number of varieties are listed in the cauliflower section, although one is listed below, as it is commonly sold as if it were a broccoli. A cross between broccoli and cauliflower is called broccoflower or floccoli and is listed in the section on cauliflower.

All of the varieties listed in the table will produce a nice central head and a number of decent-sized side shoots. Head size is highly variable, and the chart gives an educated guess at best. Good fall varieties include 'Arcadia Hybrid', 'Atlantic', 'Eureka', 'Green Belt Hybrid', 'Gypsy Hybrid', 'Marathon Hybrid', 'Premium Crop Hybrid', and 'Waltham 29'. 'Emperor' takes a while to mature but is still a good spring variety since it tolerates heat well.

VARIETY	DAYS	HEAD COLOR	HEAD SIZE (INCHES)
'Amadeus Hybrid'	60	Blue green	4
'Arcadia Hybrid'*****	65–85	Purplish green	6
'Atlantic' (heirloom)	70	Blue green	6
'Batavia Hybrid'	65	Deep green	8
'Belstar Hybrid'	65–75	Blue green	6
'Blue Wind Hybrid'	50	Blue green	4
'Bonanza Hybrid'	55	Deep green	8
'Captain Hybrid'	60	Blue green	6
'Coronado Crown Hybrid'	60	Green	6
'Early Dividend Hybrid'	45	Blue green	6
'Emperor Hybrid'	70	Blue green	8
'Eureka' (an improved 'Green Valiant')	60–90	Deep green	8
'Express Broccoli Hybrid'	75	Blue green	6
'Flash Hybrid'	50	Blue green	6
'Green Belt Hybrid'	90	Medium green	5
'Green Comet Hybrid' (AAS-1969)	55–65	Deep green	5
'Green Goliath' (OP)*****	60–75	Blue green	8
'Green Magic Hybrid'	60	Blue green	6
'Gypsy Hybrid'	60	Medium green	6
'Italian Green Sprouting' (heirloom)	60	Blue green	5
'Marathon Hybrid'	70	Blue green	5
'Munchkin' (OP)	60	Medium green	6
'Nutribud' (OP)	65–70	Medium green	6
'Packman Hybrid'*****	60	Deep green	8
'Piracicaba' (heirloom)	56	Green	Many small heads
'Premium Crop Hybrid' (AAS-1975)*****	55–75	Green (one head)	8
'Romanesco' (heirloom) (really cauliflower)	75–90	Apple green	Spiral cone
'Small Miracle Hybrid'	55	Dark green	5
'Southern Comet Hybrid'	80	Medium green	7
'Thompson' (OP)	70	Green	4
'Waltham 29' (heirloom)*****	60–90	Blue green	6
'Windsor Hybrid'	60–90	Blue green	6

BRUSSELS SPROUTS

***Brassica oleracea* var. *gemmifera,* or Gemmifera Group**
Cabbage or Mustard Family (Brassicaceae, formerly Cruciferae)

Brussels sprouts are very hardy, cold-season biennials grown as annuals. Brussels sprouts, bred from kale, are much more popular in continental Europe than in the United States, probably because they are rarely harvested and cooked properly here. Each plant produces fifty to a hundred sprouts, or miniature "cabbages," about the size of a walnut. They usually taste best after being sweetened by a fall frost. This is an easy vegetable to grow, but it does require a long season to mature. Although the exact origin is unknown, they may have originated either in the Mediterranean (possibly in Italy) or along the Atlantic coast of Europe. They get their name from their popularity in Belgium in the sixteenth century.

How Brussels Sprouts Grow

Brussels sprouts seeds are round, hard, and usually brown to black (about 6,000 to 8,000 seeds per ounce). They grow into young plants that look very much like cabbage or broccoli seedlings. The seedling matures into an odd-looking plant: a tall stem with a bushy rosette of large, floppy leaves on top. The stem becomes thick and hard. Where the leaves meet the stem, tiny little "cabbages," or "buttons," form. These are really small buds referred to as sprouts, which mature from the bottom up over a period of months. If the plant were to survive a winter, it would produce numerous flower stems with bright-yellow flowers, which mature into pods filled with seed.

Where to Plant Brussels Sprouts
Site and Light

Brussels sprouts like a bright, sunny spot in the garden. Full sun is best, but they will tolerate light shade. Shelter from wind reduces the chance of plants toppling over.

Soil and Moisture

Brussels sprouts grow best in loose, fertile soil that drains freely. If your soil is compacted, build a raised bed. Add lots of organic matter, which helps loosen the soil but retains moisture during dry periods. Mix in various organic fertilizers. Blood meal is high in nitrogen; bonemeal, in

Nutrition Facts

Serving size: 100 grams (3.5 ounces)

	AMOUNT PER COOKED SERVING	% DV
Calories	36	2%
Carbohydrates	7 g	2%
Dietary fiber	3 g	10%
Folate	60 mcg	15%
Iron	1.2 mg	7%
Manganese	0.2 mg	11%
Phosphorus	56 mg	6%
Potassium	320 mg	9%
Protein	2.5 g	5%
Vitamin A	775 IU	15%
Vitamin B6	0.2 mg	9%
Vitamin C	62 mg	105%
Vitamin K	140 mcg	175%

phosphorus; and wood ash, in potassium. The latter tends to make soil more alkaline, which helps prevent clubroot. A little lime is also fine for the same reason. If possible, prepare your bed in fall, mixing in the organic matter and fertilizers at that time. A pH of 6 to 6.8 is good, but if clubroot becomes a problem, make it more alkaline (with wood ash and lime).

Container

Few people grow Brussels sprouts in containers, although it is certainly possible. For ornamental purposes, choose one of the red varieties. For sprouts, choose a short plant, and stake it from the start.

Planting

Seed

It is possible to direct seed in the garden. Seed will germinate at temperatures as low as 45°F. Seeds grown in this manner are vulnerable to rabbits and insects. It is often easier to start plants indoors, where they can be grown in more favorable conditions.

Transplants

Starting plants from seed indoors has several advantages. You can select exactly the right variety for your area and experiment with different varieties each year to find the one that you like best or that does the best in your climate.

Grow a few more plants than you will eventually need, and save the remaining seed for the next season.

Start seed indoors 3 to 6 weeks before the time you plan to set your transplants in the garden, which is roughly 4 to 6 weeks before the last expected frost. Plant in sterile starting mix about ¼ to ½ inch deep. Keep moist and warm at 65° to 70°F with a drop of 10 degrees at night. Seed generally sprouts within 10 days. Consider a staggered planting by starting seed 2 weeks apart in three cell packs. Before planting outdoors, harden off the young seedlings.

Many nurseries offer seedlings in the spring. Usually, you can find Brussels sprouts but not always. Trays are frequently labeled "Brussels sprouts" with no indication of variety. If you buy plants, choose packs with short, stocky plants with good color. One pack may have more plants than another. Choose the one with the most plants, and tease them apart for planting.

Be careful when working with young Brussels sprouts seedlings. Don't bend or break the tip of the plant. Strip off any lower leaves if they have turned yellow. When you do this, don't tear them off—pinch them between your thumb and forefinger. Plant as deep as the lower leaf. Firm the soil around the base of the plant with your fingers. Pour a transplant solution around the seedling. Keep consistently moist. Note that root disturbance does retard growth slightly, but plants usually recover fine.

Spacing

Spacing depends somewhat on the variety, but Brussels sprouts tend to be large plants taking up more space than you might think. Space transplants 18 to 24 inches apart in rows about 30 inches apart. This gives enough space for air circulation and prevents plants from competing for available water and nutrients.

When to Plant

Get Brussels sprouts transplants into the garden roughly 4 to 6 weeks before the last expected frost. If a hard frost threatens, cover the young plants with a cloche.

Support

By planting Brussels sprouts in a protected location, you can eliminate the need for support. If this is not possible, stake plants early in the season, tying the stem to a support with a figure-eight knot. Use a soft piece of cloth that will expand as the stem enlarges. While support is commonly recommended, I have never found that Brussels sprouts needed it. They have thick, strong stems, but once producing heavily, who knows what will happen in strong winds?

How to Care for Brussels Sprouts

Water

Water plants frequently until they are growing vigorously. Consistent moisture throughout the growing season is important, especially during hot, dry spells in the summer. When you water, water deeply around the base of the plant.

Mulch

Mulch keeps the ground moist and cool, just the way Brussels sprouts like it. It also prevents most weed growth. Get mulch in early, and replenish it as the season progresses.

Fertilizing

Brussels sprouts are heavy feeders. Prepare your bed appropriately. Pour a transplant solution around seedlings when you first get them into the garden. Then side-dress 3 weeks later and again 2 weeks after that. Or feed lightly but regularly throughout the season until plants begin to form small sprouts. Stop feeding at that time. Use a variety of organic fertilizers for best results. Do not go overboard in the use of nitrogen, which may result in more foliage than sprouts and may make the plant more susceptible to disease.

Weeding

Brussels sprouts have a dense but shallow root system. Avoid cultivating close to the base of the plant. The use of mulch makes cultivation there unnecessary and prevents potential damage. Pull by hand any weeds appearing around the base of the plant.

Thinning

You do not need to thin unless you are planting seed directly in the garden. This is not common since plants take a long time to mature, even from transplants.

Pruning

Remove all dead or yellowing leaves during the active growing season. Removing leaves below harvested buds is optional. If you want to get a few sprouts to mature early in the season, just snip off the growing tip of the plant. Wait until there are many small sprouts already growing in the axils along the stem. When you cut off the top of the plant, you divert energy to the sprouts, which mature more rapidly. Don't do this on all plants, just on one or two for an early meal of sprouts. Do exactly the same thing to get sprouts to mature before a cold snap. Sometimes, the plants just keep getting bigger and bigger in the fall, using energy for growth and not for the sprouts. Cutting off the top of the plant often results in more usable sprouts before a freeze.

Special Considerations

Plants can get tall. A few may require staking or hilling up of soil at their base. The stems of taller varieties make decent walking sticks. The stem and foliage of 'Rubine Red' are lovely in arrangements. Note that the plant itself is not a great choice for sprouts and is included in the varietal chart primarily for its beauty. If you are on a blood thinner such as warfarin (Coumadin), talk to your doctor. Brussels sprouts are high in vitamin K.

Extending the Season

Measures to extend the season are not necessary. Plants often survive frost, which helps the sprouts develop an even better flavor. Some will survive down to 15°F. It is possible to pick off sprouts from plants covered in snow.

Problems

Insects

Brussels sprouts are potentially susceptible to a number of insects, including aphids, cabbage worms, cutworms, flea beetles, grasshoppers, and root maggots. The root maggot problem may be reduced by tilling alfalfa meal, leaf mold, or green manure into the soil in fall. Floating row covers are helpful in stopping damage to seedlings.

Disease

Although Brussels sprouts are susceptible to a number of diseases, clubroot is the most common problem. It causes plants to wilt and die. When you pull up the plant, the roots resemble an enlarged club, giving the disease its name. You can discourage clubroot by adding wood ash or limestone to your soil in the fall before the spring planting season. Use light applications since both increase the soil pH. Another potential threat is fusarium yellows. Growing your own seedlings using seed certified to be disease-free decreases your chance of infection. Note that some varieties, such as 'Jade Cross Hybrid', have resistance to this disease.

Marauders

Rabbits often are a problem early in the season when transplants are still young. Once plants get larger, damage is limited. Woodchucks on the other hand are a problem throughout the entire season. The solution as always is a good fence or live trap.

Physiological

As with cabbages, it is possible for sprouts to split if not grown with consistent moisture. Heat and lack of moisture may also be responsible for overly bitter sprouts. If the top of the plant turns brown or black and begins to dry up, it is suffering from "tip burn," a condition caused by lack of calcium uptake into the plant. Inconsistent watering is the most common cause, although fertilization after sprouts form may also be a factor. As do other cole crops, Brussels sprouts may bolt in hot weather.

Propagation

Brussels sprouts are hermaphroditic, having both male and female organs, but they must be insect pollinated. They must be isolated from all members of their family. You need a group of plants for adequate pollination. If plants do flower in the first season, let seedpods mature on the plant. Once dry, remove the pods and seed immediately. Seed will store for about 4 to 5 years if kept dark, cool, and dry.

Harvesting

When to begin harvesting is a matter of personal choice. The best-tasting sprouts are compact and only about 1 inch or less in diameter. Always pick the larger, lower sprouts first. You will be picking from the bottom up. Press down and twist firmly to snap them off. Or just cut them off with a knife. If frost threatens, don't worry; the plants will not be harmed. Brussels sprouts often taste better after a hard frost, which concentrates sugar in the little heads. These can be picked even when covered with snow. Still, you do not want them to freeze.

Storing

Brussels sprouts will store for about a week in the refrigerator. Do not store them with apples, which give off ethylene gas and may cause them to become bitter. Place them unwashed in a plastic bag. Try to use within 3 days if possible.

To freeze, cut an X in the base, or cut in half, blanch 2 to 5 minutes depending on size, chill in ice water, drain, package in airtight freezer bags, and freeze.

Culinary Uses

Brussels sprouts can be eaten raw but rarely are, although some gardeners chop or shred them into salads. More often they are baked, butter steamed, fried, grilled, microwaved, pan-seared, roasted, sautéed, or steamed. Avoid overcooking sprouts, since this often leads to an "off" odor of sulfur, a bitter taste, and mushy texture. Avoid boiling, which leads to loss of nutrients. Steam lightly instead. To speed up cooking, cut a deep X in the base. Breaking the sprouts apart into individual leaves results in fast cooking, which results in a much better taste. Lightly cover with oil before broiling or roasting.

To roast, cut in half, toss in olive oil, sprinkle with salt and pepper, cook on a baking sheet at 425°F, turn as desired, and cook no longer than until tender. Sauté in garlic butter or with onions. Or use garlic butter or hollandaise as a sauce. For superfast cooking, cut sprouts in two, remove the core (looks like small wedge), slice into thin strips, cook in hot oil for 1 minute, and season to taste. The British, who say this is their least favorite vegetable, might even like this last dish. Lemon goes especially well with Brussels sprouts.

Note that leaves, the large ones on the plant, are edible. Usually, the upper ones are best, look like collards, and have a taste reminiscent of cabbage. These too should be sliced into thin strips before rapid cooking, commonly done in oil seasoned with garlic.

Varieties

The hybrids of Brussels sprouts are more reliable than the open-pollinated varieties. Reds have been included in this list; they are ornamental and far more temperamental than the greens. Still, some insist the flavor is better, and they do mature late in the season, when frosts can enhance taste. 'Diablo Hybrid' also matures late, so it would make a good taste test comparison.

VARIETIES	DAYS	COLOR	HEIGHT (INCHES)
'Bubbles Hybrid'	80–90	Dark green	36
'Catskill' (heirloom)	85–100	Dark green	20–24
'Churchill Hybrid'	90–100	Medium green	24–36
'Diablo Hybrid'*****	110–120	Medium green	26–30
'Dimitri Hybrid'	85–110	Medium green	24–28
'Early Marvel Hybrid'	85	Medium green	36
'Evesham Special' (heirloom)	80–115	Medium green	24
'Falstaff' (heirloom)	90–120	Purplish red	36
'Franklin Hybrid'	80	Green blue	24–36
'Gustus Hybrid'	100	Medium green	24–36
'Igor Hybrid'	90–110+	Medium green	36
'Jade Cross Hybrid' (AAS-1959)	80–90	Medium bluish green	30
'Jade Cross E Hybrid'*****	85–90	Deep green	30–32
'Mezzo Nano' (heirloom)	110	Deep green	36
'Nautic Hybrid'	105	Blue green	30
'Nelson Hybrid'	90	Medium green	24–36
'Octia' (OP)	80	Medium green	36
'Roodnerf' (heirloom)	100	Medium green	24–36
'Royal Marvel Hybrid'	85	Medium to dark green	30–36
'Rubine Red' (heirloom)	100–105	Purplish red	36

Brussels sprouts look like miniature cabbages growing just above each leaf. They taste best after an early frost.

The home gardener can produce lovely heads of cabbage without pesticides despite this vegetable's affinity for insects.

CABBAGE

***Brassica oleracea* species**
Cabbage or Mustard Family (Brassicaceae, formerly Cruciferae)

Cabbage is a very hardy, cool- to cold-season biennial grown as an annual. It is easy to grow and popular with its varied colors, shapes, and textures. By choosing early-, mid-, and late-season varieties, the home gardener can enjoy cabbage over a period of months. Cabbage is an insect magnet. Grow enough and there will be plenty for you and the bugs. Cabbage may have originated in southern or western Europe, possibly along the English Channel or northern Mediterranean area.

How Cabbage Grows

Cabbage seed is small (about 6,000 to 8,000 seeds per ounce), round, and brown to blackish. Seedlings are easy to spot as they sprout from what will become a dense but shallow root system. Depending on the variety, curly, smooth, or wrinkled leaves develop on a short, fleshy central stem and are wide and thick as they mature. Leaves mature first on the outside and then on the inside. As the season progresses, the new outer leaves begin to envelop the interior leaves. As they curl in, they form a tight ball (head) around the central bud. If plants were to survive winters, they would flower the following year. The four-petaled, yellow flowers will produce seed in elongated pods. Occasionally, plants will bolt in the first year.

Where to Plant Cabbage
Site and Light

Cabbage thrives in full sun but likes it cool. In areas with cool summers this is not a problem. If your summers tend to be hot, cabbages will do fine in partial shade. What cabbages really like is extended light. In Alaska cabbages can weigh 60 to 70 pounds thanks to the extremely long days. Cabbage makes an interesting addition to a flower bed.

Soil and Moisture

Cabbage thrives in cool, moist soil enriched with lots of organic matter and fertilizer. Soil should be loose, drain freely, and have a pH of 6 to 7.5. Slightly alkaline soil may cut down on the incidence of clubroot disease, so adding a little lime or hardwood ash to the soil in fall from time to time may be helpful. If soil is compacted, build a raised bed, but realize that soil in these tends to be warmer and dryer. Since cabbage likes it moist and cool, overcome this handicap with mulch and consistent watering.

Container

You can grow cabbages in containers. Choose early maturing varieties with smaller heads. Plant one plant per large container. Clay pots tend to get hot, so either double pot or use a plastic container.

Planting

Seed

Planting seed directly in the garden is possible. Most people plant seed in a small area with the idea of transplanting seedlings later on. Transplanting often results in shock, which delays heading by 10 to 15 days. Plant seed at a depth of ¼ to ½ inch depending on your soil type. Seed should germinate within 10 days at a soil temperature of 45°F. Transplant seedlings when they form several sets of true leaves. Direct seeding is most commonly done for late maturing varieties, which means most direct seeding is done at a soil temperature of around 65°F.

Transplants

Cabbage is easy to grow from seed, which you can order from mail-order companies or buy at local stores. One big advantage of growing cabbage from seed is that you select the variety or varieties to grow. You know whether it's disease resistant or heat tolerant and whether it's an early-, mid-, or late-season variety. Experiment each year.

Most nurseries sell plants in plastic trays with a minimum of six plants. Plants sold by garden centers may simply be labeled "cabbage." You may have no idea what variety it is, other than a green or red cabbage. Choose packs with short, stocky plants with good color. One pack may have more plants than another. Choose the one with the most plants, and tease them apart for planting.

Start your own cabbage seed indoors 4 to 6 weeks before the time you plan to set your transplants in the garden, which is roughly 4 to 6 weeks before the last expected frost. Grow a few more plants than you will eventually need, and save the remaining seed for the next season. Plant in sterile starting mix about ¼ to ½ inch deep. Keep moist and warm at 70°F with a drop of 10 degrees at night. Seeds should sprout within 10 days. The main problem with growing cabbage indoors is that young plants become spindly without proper light. Use grow lights. Keep them on 16 hours a day. Plants should have a good root system, four to six leaves,

Nutrition Facts
Serving size: 100 grams (3.5 ounces)

	AMOUNT PER RAW SERVING	% DV	AMOUNT PER COOKED SERVING	% DV
Calcium	40 mg	4%	48 mg	5%
Calories	25	1%	23	1%
Carbohydrates	6 g	2%	6 g	2%
Dietary fiber	3 g	10%	2 g	8%
Folate	45 mcg	11%	30 mcg	8%
Potassium	170 mg	5%	195 mg	6%
Protein	1 g	3%	1 g	3%
Vitamin B6	0.1 mg	6%	0.1 mg	6%
Vitamin C	37 mg	60%	38 mg	62%
Vitamin K	75 mcg	95%	110 mcg	135%

and be no larger than 4 inches tall when transplanted. Begin hardening off early to get stocky and cold-resistant plants, as many as 14 to 21 days in advance of planting in the garden.

When planting seedlings, be careful not to break off the growing point or tip of the plant. If you do, the plant may not form a head but a bunch of smaller heads instead. Strip off any lower leaves if they have turned yellow. When you do this, don't tear them off—pinch them between your thumb and forefinger. Plant as deep as the lower leaf. Firm the soil around the base of the plant with your fingers. Pour a transplant solution around the seedling. Keep consistently moist. Note that root disturbance does retard growth slightly.

When cabbage plants are still in the seedling stage, they can be damaged by frost. If you set them out especially early, protect them. You can use mulch, HotKaps®, or any shield to capture heat from the soil around the plants. Once the plants take root and are growing, they resist frost well. Note that extreme cold on a young plant can cause it to go to seed later on in the season, just as hot weather and long days make spinach bolt.

Spacing

Cabbage planted at 18-inch intervals will produce larger heads than if planted closer together. Closer planting makes sense for early plantings. Give cabbages maturing late more space for good air circulation during summer heat and humidity. The most common way of planting cabbage in a home garden is in the three-two-three style. This cuts down on wasted space.

When to Plant

The earlier you get early- and midseason varieties into the garden, the better. Plant transplants 2 to 4 weeks or longer before the frost-free date, just as soon as you can work the soil. If there is an unexpected frost, use a cloche to protect the young plants. Plant midseason (for a second time) and late-season varieties later in the season, about 10 weeks before the first expected fall frost. The late-season varieties can mature after light frosts, and some varieties will take hard freezes.

Support

A few gardeners place wire cages around plants not so much for support but to keep marauders at bay.

How to Care for Cabbage

Water

Keep the soil consistently moist, especially early in the plant's growth. In really hot weather give the plants thorough soakings, not light sprinklings, two or even three times a week. Moisture encourages quick and uniform growth for the best-tasting heads. Once heads get closer to maturity, cut back on watering. Watering also helps plants take in small amounts of boron and calcium, both essential for healthy growth.

Mulch

From the time they are planted until they mature, cabbage plants need a cool, moist root run. Place a 2-inch layer of mulch around the base of transplants immediately. Do not touch the stems. Add mulch to a greater depth once plants are growing vigorously. This helps retain moisture in the soil, and cabbage plants need lots of it to form dense heads. Use an organic mulch such as shredded leaves or grass clippings.

Fertilizing

Treat young plants to a cup of transplant solution as you place them in the garden. This will encourage quick root growth and get the cabbage off to a good start. During the season you have options: feed heavily with organic fertilizer after 3 weeks and again 2 weeks later, or give plants light feedings once a week until the head forms. Good natural fertilizers include blood meal, compost, fish emulsion, lake weed, or rotted manure. Go easy on nitrogen with later-maturing varieties.

Weeding

Remove all weeds before setting transplants into the garden. Watch for weeds sprouting through mulch. Hand pull them carefully from around the base of the plant. Clipping weeds in this area with scissors is obsessive but effective. Don't cultivate deeply around cabbage plants, because they have a shallow (if extensive) root system. Any weeds that do sprout through mulch should be easy to pull.

Thinning

Close planting makes for smaller cabbages. Thin plants only if you have planted seed in the garden. Plant these as transplants if you want to.

Pruning

Do not prune. When you cut off the head, leave the plant in place if you want to develop a second round of little heads, more like elongated bunches of leaves.

Special Considerations

Early transplants exposed to prolonged cold temperatures may bolt, but this is rare.

When you harvest cabbage heads, cut just underneath the head. Leave the bottom leaves sticking out from the stem. Make a ½-inch wound in the shape of a cross or X through the stump. This may stimulate the formation of additional little cabbage heads. Even if you don't do this, cabbages often create mini-cabbages on their own. Remove all but one as they emerge. If none sprout, dig up and compost the stump.

If you are on a blood thinner such as warfarin (Coumadin), talk to your doctor. Cabbage is high in vitamin K but not nearly as high as a number of other greens.

Extending the Season

Get plants into the ground as early as possible. Protect transplants from freezing in spring by protecting them with cloches or plastic tunnels. Many late-maturing varieties can withstand frosts, and some will tolerate temperatures as low as 20°F. So the season is already long. Storing, rather than protecting them late in the season, makes sense.

Problems

Insects

Numerous insects feed on cabbage. Aphids, cabbage worms, cutworms, flea beetles, and root maggots are the most common. Cutworms attack the stems of young plants, which collapse. Root maggots work below the soil and typically kill older plants, which suddenly wilt for no apparent reason. Two types of cabbage worms make a smorgasbord of leaves. In most instances the loss of a plant or two does not warrant the expense of typical controls. Till green manure or leaf mold into the soil in fall to reduce the chance of root maggot damage. Covering young plants with row covers reduces the more common insect problems.

Disease

In the home garden insects are generally more of a problem than disease. Still, cabbage can be infected with a number of diseases, such as blackleg, black rot, black speck, cabbage yellows (fusarium), powdery mildew, and clubroot. Discourage clubroot disease by adding limestone to the soil in the fall before planting. Clubroot causes plants to wilt and die. When you pull up the plant, the roots resemble an enlarged club, giving the disease its name. Lime does change the soil pH, so use it sparingly. Prevent cabbage yellows (yellowing and browning of lower leaves) by buying varieties resistant to this disease. Resistant does not mean immune. Practice crop rotation to take care of most other diseases.

Marauders

Rabbits and woodchucks can do a lot of damage in a short time, especially to younger plants. Fencing keeps out rabbits, but woodchucks may have to be livetrapped and dealt with as you feel appropriate.

Physiological

Mature cabbage heads occasionally split, which means that they crack open. Some varieties resist splitting, while others split more often. Cabbage with smaller heads split less often than those with larger ones. Heavy rain after drought, too much fertilizer, insect damage, and delayed harvest—all have been blamed for this. Too much watering once heads form seems the most logical cause early in the season; letting heads mature too long is more logical later in the year.

Cabbages may, but often don't, bolt in high temperatures. Seed savers like it when cabbages send up flower stalks prematurely, but those who are growing cabbage for food see bolting in a different light. There is little to do about soaring temperatures except to choose bolt-resistant varieties and to get cabbages planted at the right time.

Occasionally, cabbages don't form heads. This may be caused by you or a marauder breaking off the growing tip. That tip is the beginning of a head. Occasionally, growing tips are eaten off by insects, like cutworms. There are a few other potential problems, but proper soil preparation, fertilizing, and consistent watering virtually eliminate them.

Propagation

Cabbage is hermaphroditic but must be insect pollinated. It is difficult to get enough plants, at least a half dozen, through the winter for proper seed production. Try by covering them with 12 inches of straw. Do not expect success. A better idea is to dig up several plants. Strip off the larger outer leaves, and brush or shake off soil from the roots. Place them in a large container, pushing moist sphagnum peat moss or sand around the base of each plant. Store these in a cool spot. Do not let the plants freeze. Plant the roots in spring. If cabbages form flowers, let the pods mature and dry on the plant. Pick just as they become brittle, before they crack, shatter, and scatter seeds in all directions. Seed will last up to 4 to 5 years.

Harvesting

Cabbage can be harvested for its leaves before it's completely mature, and when fully mature, it can be stored if kept cool and humid.

Harvest early types for fresh use as soon as suitable size leaves begin to form. Begin with the outside leaves. Leave as many plants to form heads as you think you will need at a later date. Begin your harvest before all heads mature completely. Pick small heads whenever you need them. Unless you need a half dozen heads all at once, there is no point in waiting longer. Let the midseason varieties mature in the garden until they form firm heads. The later varieties can withstand cold and actually taste better after a frost. The later varieties get larger heads than the earlier ones but are not suited for areas with extremely short growing seasons. The flavor of savoy cabbage also improves with a little cold, and it can be kept in the ground until there is a threat of a hard frost. To harvest early- and midseason cabbage, use a sharp knife to slice the stem, or twist the head off with a forceful motion of your hand. Leave five or six outer leaves.

Storing

Green and red cabbage can be stored for relatively long periods of time. Savoy cabbage is more perishable and should be used as soon as possible. Storing reduces nutrients. To harvest late-season cabbage, cut heads off for immediate use, and pull up plants with roots attached for storage. Cabbage can be kept for a few weeks by hanging it upside down from its roots in a cool place. Cabbage will store for a longer period of time in a cold frame or root cellar. If placing in a cold frame, do not remove the roots, and cover well with straw. Cabbage will last up to 4 months at just above 32°F in humid conditions. If you don't have a root cellar, dig a trench. Line it with straw, lay the plants roots and all on the straw, and cover with 6 inches of soil (the soil removed from the trench) and another layer of straw. This insulates the uprooted plants from cold and snow but is clearly a hassle.

To store in the refrigerator, do not cut the cabbage into pieces. Keep heads close to freezing at high humidity for up to 3 to 4 weeks. To freeze, wash, cut into quarters or eighths if large, blanch in boiling water for 3 minutes, plunge into ice water, drain, and place in freezer bags with as much air removed as possible. Freeze immediately. Cut the blanching time to 1½ minutes if freezing shredded leaves. To pickle, make sauerkraut.

Culinary Uses

All cabbages are excellent raw. Use leaves early in the season. They are nutritious and delicious at this stage. All types of cabbage are suited for making coleslaw, shredding into green salads, or juicing. Remove leaves, and cut out the core.

Both young and mature leaves can be lightly boiled, microwaved, or steamed; drenched in butter; and seasoned to taste to make a delicious dish. Do not overcook cabbage. It will smell, as hydrogen sulfide gas is released, and both taste and nutrient value are affected. Consider slicing leaves into thin strips before sautéing for as little as 2 minutes or a bit longer. Or stir-fry leaves in soy sauce spiced with ginger.

Cabbage and beets are essential ingredients in borscht, a classic beet soup. German red cabbage makes a sweet and tart combination when mixed with apples and onions cooked in vinegar and sugar with a variety of spices added. Note: use vinegar when cooking red cabbage to maintain its rich color. The later varieties with their larger heads are ideal for sauerkraut.

Note that frost improves the flavor of late-maturing cabbage including savoys. Savoys may look almost like kale. Leaves can be pickled or used as a wrapping for stuffed dishes.

Varieties

The days listed in the table are from transplants. There are early (matures in 50 to 60 days), midseason (70 to 85), and late (more than 85) varieties of cabbage. If you want to eat cabbage fresh, then the early- and midseason varieties make sense. If you want to store cabbage, then you want your plants maturing late in the season. For this reason, it's smart to grow an assortment of varieties so that you will have heads forming at different times of the year.

Here are various terms used to describe cabbages: drumhead (round and flattened), Dutch (white cabbage), oxheart (oval or conical), green or white cabbage (green outer leaves and whitish inner), pickling (usually refers to red cabbage or any cabbage used to make sauerkraut), red cabbage (round head with red leaves), salad savoy (refers to edible ornamental kale and not savoy cabbage), savoy (compact with frilly or curly leaves with a blistered or bubbly texture), and winter cabbage (overwinters in mild areas). Note that green is occasionally called yellow cabbage.

The varieties listed below represent a range in color, days to maturity from transplants, resistance to cabbage yellows (represented by the letter "F" under resistance), and the approximate weight of the heads at maturity. A few varieties resist bolting in torrid summer heat. Others resist splitting, cracking apart as they mature. These traits are listed under comments.

VARIETIES	DAYS	RESISTANCE	WEIGHT (POUNDS)	COMMENTS
Green cabbage				
Brassica oleracea ssp. *capitata* or Capitata Group				
'All Seasons' (heirloom)	85–95	F	10–12	Resists bolting somewhat
'Amager' (see 'Danish Ballhead')				
'Blue Vantage Hybrid'	70–75	F	3+	
'Bravo Hybrid'	85		3–4	
'Brunswick' (heirloom)	70–85		4–5+	
'Charmant Hybrid'	65–70		3–4	
'Cheers Hybrid'	75	F	5	Resists bolting somewhat
'Copenhagen Market' (heirloom)*****	65–70		3–4	Resists splitting
'Cuor di Bue Grosso' (heirloom)	65–75		3–4	Conical
'Danish Ballhead' (heirloom)	100–110		5–7	Resists splitting and bolting
'Drumhead' (see 'Premium Late Flat Dutch')				
'Dynamo Hybrid' (AAS-1997)*****	65–70	F	2½	
'Earliana' (heirloom)	60		2	
'Early Jersey Wakefield' (heirloom)*****	65–75	F	2–3	Conical
'Early Round Dutch' (heirloom)	70–75		4–5	
'Emerald Cross Hybrid' (AAS-1963)	65–75		1–2	Resists bolting somewhat
'Glory of Enkhuizen' (heirloom)	75–80		8–10	
'Golden Acre' (heirloom)*****	65–70	F	3–4	
'Gonzales Hybrid'	65		1–2	
'Grenadier Hybrid'	55–65		2½	
'Premium Late Flat Dutch' (heirloom)	105–115		10–15	
'Stein's Late Flat Dutch' (heirloom)	65–70		Variable	
'Stonehead Hybrid' (AAS-1969)*****	65–70	F	3–4	
Red cabbage				
Brassica oleracea ssp. *capitata* or Capitata Group				
'Mammoth Red Rock' (heirloom)	90–110		4–7	
'Red Acre' (heirloom)*****	70–75	F	2–4	Resists splitting
'Red Danish' (see 'Mammoth Red Rock')				
'Red Dynasty CMS Hybrid'	75–80		3–5	
'Red Express' (heirloom)*****	62		2–3	
'Ruby Ball Hybrid' (AAS-1972)*****	70–80	F	3–4	Resists splitting
'Ruby Perfection Hybrid'*****	80		3–4	Resists splitting
'Salad Delight' (heirloom)	50		3	
'Super Red 80 Hybrid'	75		3–5	Resists splitting
Savoy cabbage				
Brassica oleracea var. *sabauda*				
'Chieftain' (heirloom) (AAS-1938)*****	90		4–6	
'Deadon Hybrid'	105	F	3–6	Red exterior, green inside
'Des Vertus' (heirloom)	95		4–6	
'Large Drumhead Savoy' (see 'Des Vertus')				
'Perfection Drumhead' (heirloom)	85–90		3–4	
'Savoy Ace Hybrid' (AAS-1977)*****	75–85		3–4	
'Savoy Express Hybrid' (AAS-2000)	65–75		1–2	
'Savoy King Hybrid' (AAS-1965)*****	85–90	F	4	
'Savoy Perfection' (heirloom)	90		6–8	
'Savoy Queen Hybrid'	90	F	5	

Carrots, best harvested young, are offered in an amazing array of sizes and colors.

CARROT

Daucus carota* var. (or ssp.) *sativus
Carrot or Parsley Family (Apiaceae, formerly Umbelliferae)

Carrots are hardy to very hardy, cool- to cold-season biennials grown as annuals. They take up very little space, produce a nice nutritious crop over a long period of time, and are much sweeter than store-bought produce. They do germinate erratically and can be difficult to weed, but the effort is well worth the effort and time. Carrots originally came from Afghanistan.

How Carrots Grow

Carrots grow from small (about 19,000 to 22,000 seeds per ounce), tan, indented, rounded spear-like seeds. The germinating seeds create a thin, ferny spike. As the plant matures, foliage expands and sends food to developing roots below the soil. These roots swell and continue to grow until late in the season. If the carrots survive the winter, they may form flower stalks tipped with a ball composed of dozens of delicate, white flowers in the second season. These produce seed to complete the life cycle.

Where to Plant Carrots

Site and Light

Plant carrots in full sun. They grow poorly in deep shade but do tolerate partial shade.

Soil and Moisture

Provide carrots with a bed made up of very deep, loose, fertile soil. If you have compacted soil, build a raised bed. Sandy soil is ideal. However, carrots grow well in other soils as well. Work compost, leaf mold (rotted leaves), well-rotted manure, or sphagnum peat moss into the soil. The use of manure is said to cause root crops to be hairy or forked. Well-rotted manure has served home gardeners well for centuries—use it, if available.

Forking will definitely be caused by roots bumping into hard objects in the soil. Remove all debris when loosening the planting bed. This means even the tiniest rocks, stones, or roots. Break up the soil as you are working it with a garden rake. Debris often hides in clumps. The soil should not only be loose but fine. Run it through a sieve or screen wherever seed will be planted. Or simply rub it between your hands to remove bits of clay and small rocks. The soil pH should be in the range of 6.5 to 7.

Container

Carrots grow well in larger containers, at least 12-inch or larger pots. Three excellent choices are 'Little Finger', 'Parmex', and 'Thumbelina Hybrid'. The other baby types listed in the varietal chart are equally good but a little harder to find.

Planting

Seed

In theory, carrot seed should sprout within 10 to 14 days. In reality, carrot seed is notorious for germinating erratically, sometimes fast, sometimes slow, sometimes at different times, and rarely not at all. Gardeners use many tricks to speed up germination, such as soaking seed overnight before planting, presprouting seed by rolling it in a moist towel, or putting it in a sprouting jar. Presprouting requires your attention. Check on the seed every day. If using a sprouting jar, rinse the seed with fresh water daily, just as you would alfalfa or other sprouts. As soon as the seed begins to germinate, plant it immediately. I don't use any of these methods.

Carrot seed is somewhat difficult to plant. If you have poor eyesight, you can buy coated or pelleted seed. This kind of seed is used by commercial growers who view every seed as extremely valuable. You can also buy bands that you lay down. Both pelleted seed and bands are expensive. I don't use these either.

To plant, cut a ¼- to ½-inch-deep furrow into the soil with a pointed hoe, or lay the handle of a tool down and step on it to create a shallow furrow.

There are several ways of planting this fine seed. One is to cut off a corner of the seed package and tap it lightly as you sprinkle seed into the furrow. If you have trouble with this method, sprinkle some seed into the palm of your hand. Then with your other hand pinch the seeds between your thumb and forefinger as if pinching salt. Salt the soil with a sprinkling of seeds as you move along the furrow. Plant less deep in heavier soil, a little deeper in sand. Plant less deep in cool weather, deeper in hot. This works well if you are patient and don't let too many seeds drop at a time. This reduces thinning later in the season. Once the seed has been scattered along the row, grab a handful of soil, mix it with a little sphagnum peat moss, and rub it between your hands into a small pile. As you do this, remove small pebbles, tiny bits of debris, and any soil that clumps together. You end up with a fine mix as if it has gone through a sieve. Now barely

Nutrition Facts
Serving size: 100 grams (3.5 ounces)

	AMOUNT PER RAW SERVING	% DV	AMOUNT PER COOKED SERVING	% DV
Calories	40	2%	35	2%
Carbohydrates	10 g	3%	8 g	3%
Dietary fiber	3 g	11%	3 g	12%
Manganese	0.1 mg	7%	0.2 mg	8%
Potassium	320 mg	9%	235 mg	7%
Protein	1.0 g	2%	1.0 g	2%
Vitamin A	16,700 IU	335%	17,035 IU	340%
Vitamin B6	0.2 mg	8%	0.1 mg	7%
Vitamin C	6 mg	10%	3.6 mg	6%
Vitamin K	13 mcg	16%	14 mcg	17%

cover the seed with this mix, and press down so that seed is in firm contact with the soil. You may have to rub several handfuls of soil with peat to get enough material to cover all of the seed. Water immediately with a fine spray. The peat moss retains moisture and prevents crusting, which may stop fine seeds from sprouting. More people have asked me about the secret to getting carrot seeds to sprout than any other topic. This method has worked for me, not only with carrots but with numerous other small-seed crops for years. See "Water" for the second key to success.

Note that some gardeners plant carrots in blocks rather than rows, but if you do, make sure you can reach each plant without stepping on the soil.

Transplants

It is possible to start seed indoors roughly 4 weeks before transplanting, but there is little advantage in doing this. Besides, carrots resent transplanting. Just get seed into the garden early.

Spacing

Carrots need space to mature properly. The more space, the more rapid the growth (see "Thinning").

When to Plant

Get carrot seeds into the ground as soon as you can work the soil in spring. Plants actually germinate best at 65° to 80°F, but get them in early anyway. This is roughly 2 to 4 weeks before the last frost. Seed will germinate at temperatures as low as 40°F to as high as 95°F. The soil should be mildly moist but crumbly, not sticky and wet. Plant a second and even a third crop at 2-week intervals. Your fall crop should be in by midsummer. This fall crop is often neglected and one of the best. The roots are harvested small after temperatures drop. At this point starches have been converted to sugar, and carrots are especially sweet.

How to Care for Carrots

Water

Once you have planted seeds, it is critical to keep the soil moist until seedlings emerge. To keep soil evenly moist, consider covering the planting area with an ultrathin layer of cardboard, cloth, or mulch. The soil and covering must be kept moist at all times, and the cardboard or cloth needs to be removed immediately once seedlings break through the soil. They will often grow through an ultrathin layer of mulch. You can also do nothing except keep the planting area moist at all times with regular sprinkling with a fine mist. That means checking the soil every day, sometimes twice a day, and watering if necessary. *Uniform moisture is the second secret to success in getting carrots off to a good start.* If you have sandy soil or are planting in a raised bed, remember that these dry out quickly in warm or windy weather.

Carrots tend to be sweeter if grown rapidly. One of the secrets to fast growth is consistent watering, especially when the plants are young. Deep watering during hot, dry weather is particularly important as plants mature. Always water after thinning to help plants overcome root disturbance. Carrots can become tough if not watered properly.

Mulch

Mulch is one of the best ways to deal with the problem of weeds. It won't stop them all, but it stops a lot of them. Pulverized leaves or grass clippings work well. They also keep the soil moist and cool. Place mulch close to, but not touching, the stems. It does not have to be thick, 1 to 2 inches are fine, but replenish it as it disappears throughout the growing season.

Fertilizing

Lush foliage helps create larger roots. Let it be your guide. If foliage is weak, apply organic fertilizers to the side of the plant during the growing season. Feed lightly until the plant responds.

Weeding

Keep carrot patches weed-free right from the start. Mulch works well around carrots to keep them moist and almost weed-free, but some weeds will still grow. Don't let the weeds get big. When you pull large weeds, young carrots are torn up at the same time.

The less weeding you have to do with carrots, the better. You practically need a tweezers to take out weeds from emerging carrot plants. Be as delicate as you can when removing weeds.

Weeding can sometimes hurt the root system of these delicate plants. The solution is to water the row after any weeding. This helps the carrots overcome the shock of root disturbance. Weeding is also easier if the soil is moist, not wet. One solution is to water in the morning and weed in the evening.

Thinning

When too many carrot plants grow side by side, they can develop lots of tops and no roots. Excess carrot plants are essentially weeds. Carrot seeds are so small that it's difficult to plant them without needing to thin them later on. There are several different approaches to this problem.

One method is to thin the plants when they are just poking through the soil and are about 1 inch tall. Run a steel garden rake at right angles over the row—very gently. Don't pull down hard, or you will pull all of the young plants up. The best time to do this is after a light rain. No rain? Water in the morning, thin in the evening. Water after using any method of thinning. This can be repeated again later on if the first thinning was not quite good enough. This method takes a little practice, and many first-time gardeners are reluctant to do it, but it does work.

Other people prefer to thin the rows by hand, pulling up plants to provide 1 to 2 inches of space between each carrot as they mature. This is meticulous work and time-consuming. If there are any weeds in the row, it can be difficult. Consider snipping off emerging foliage with a scissors.

Another approach is to do nothing at all. Just let the plants begin to mature. When some of the carrots get big enough and begin to bulge on top, you can pull them, leaving the smaller ones to mature on their own. This works well as long as you don't sow the seeds too thickly in the first place.

I like thinning by hand and then pulling up small carrots to let larger ones mature—a combination of two thinning techniques that works extremely well.

Special Considerations

Pick carrots before their shoulders begin to turn green. Green shoulders are not the end of the world—cut them off before cooking. If your carrots have forked roots, rework the bed the following spring to remove overlooked debris. Roots splitting may be caused by erratic watering, such as heavy watering after a drought. Water consistently.

Extending the Season

Have a number of plants maturing late in the season. Leave the plants in the soil until the first hard frost. Cover them in stages with loose straw or whole leaves to harvest late into the season and, sometimes, in winter.

Problems

Insects

Carrots can be attractive to a range of insects including carrot rust fly, leafhoppers, leafminers, and root maggots. If you have problems with any of these, use row covers the following year.

Disease

A disease known as aster yellows is carried by leafhoppers. It shows up as dying, yellow foliage. By controlling leafhoppers, you stop the spread of the disease. If other diseases, including root rot, occur, dig up and destroy plants. Once a problem exists, plant carrots in a different location later in the same year or in the following year.

Marauders

Rabbits sometimes eat just foliage early in the season. While this affects growth, carrots often form new foliage and edible roots. If possible, prevent damage in the first place with a fence.

Physiological

Occasionally, carrots have forked roots or split. Two things are believed to cause this: rocks in the soil and transplanting, which is not advised. Some people believe that the use of manure may also be responsible.

Propagation

Carrots are insect pollinated and self-fertile, having both male and female organs. You might be able to get plants to produce seed if you can get them through the winter with a thick layer of mulch. Replanting stored roots in spring also works, but it is difficult to store roots that long. If you intend to collect seed, buy open-pollinated (heirloom) varieties. Let the plant form white, umbrella-like flowers, which will mature and turn brown. Collect once dry, and separate from debris. Seed will store for about 3 years if kept cool and dry in an envelope. Note that for good seed, you may need dozens of plants placed close together because female flowers are not always receptive when pollen has been formed on one plant or another. Professionals enclose areas with netting and introduce insects for pollination. If Queen Anne's lace is growing in your area, it can cross with carrots. Get rid of it if you are a serious seed saver!

Harvesting

Begin harvesting carrots as soon as they are large enough to eat. If you pull up carrots as a way of thinning, pull up the larger carrots first, leaving the smaller ones to mature. Small carrots are less fibrous than older ones and considered to be at their sweetest at this stage. The tops of carrot roots bulge and turn orange as they mature. As you walk along a row, you can tell which roots are ready for harvesting. If you use the mound method of raising carrots, pull some of the soil away from the side of the plant to judge the overall maturity of the root. If you are growing carrots in a level row, pull the carrot firmly and steadily at the base of its leaves just above the root. If the soil is loose, the carrot will pop out. This sounds much easier than it sometimes is. Carrots can stick solidly in the ground. Try watering them a few hours before pulling, or run a hose over roots to loosen them. In compacted soil, dig up roots with a spading fork. If you are careful, you can slide immature roots back into the ground for further growth. If soil gets this hard, you are dealing with clay—add lots of organic matter to it each year when you prepare the bed.

Cut the tops off the carrots in the garden, not in the kitchen. Toss them on the compost pile, or use them as described under "Culinary Uses." Brush off any loose soil, but do not wash carrots until you are ready to use them. Get carrots into a cool place as soon as possible. They lose vitamins and begin to get limp if in too much heat.

Storing

Carrots are really tough. Store them right in the garden. Some gardeners cut off the tops before covering them with a 1- to 2-foot covering of straw mulch. Straw is highly recommended since it is relatively easy to move once a snow falls. Continue to harvest roots right into the winter. Note that snow is the best mulch there is for winter protection. Carrots often get sweeter once chilled. They will rot if they freeze. Technically, they are safe only to 20°F, when protected, but, again, they often make it through colder winters with enough winter protection. Be sure to harvest before they start growing the following spring.

For long-term storage once harvested, dig up carrots on a dry day. Take only the very best of the lot for storage. Eat the rest. Let the carrots dry out for a couple of hours. Much of the loose soil will drop off, but don't wash or brush them off. Snip off the foliage to within 1 inch of the top of the root. If you cut into the carrot by accident or damage it any way, don't store but eat it.

Fill the bottom of a deep box or plastic trash barrel with 4 inches of barely moist sphagnum peat moss or sand. Put down a layer of carrots. Don't let them touch each other or the side of the box. Cover them on all sides with 2 to 4 inches of sphagnum peat moss. Repeat the procedure over and over until the box is full. If you don't have peat, then use whole leaves instead. Store the box in a cool place, such as an unheated but insulated garage where temperatures should range from 35° to 40°F. Do not let the carrots freeze. These are more accessible than carrots left in the garden, but check them regularly for rot. The moisture will keep the carrots from drying out. Carrots will last for several months stored in this way. If you don't have a root cellar or an insulated garage, freeze them as described later.

To store in the refrigerator, wash, trim off greens keeping ½ inch of stem, place in a perforated plastic bag, and eat ones that begin to get hairy right away. If kept near freezing at high humidity, they may last for up to 4 to 6 months. Do not store them near apples, which give off ethylene gas and may cause carrots to be bitter.

To freeze, remove tops, scrub, rinse. Leave small carrots whole. Cut large carrots lengthwise into thin strips, or across into thin slices, or cube. If older carrots have formed a core, remove. Scald 2 to 5 minutes depending on thickness, plunge into ice water, drain, package in airtight freezer bags, and freeze.

To dry, remove tops, wash, scrub or scrape the skin, dice or slice into ¼-inch pieces, blanch up to 3 minutes, steam blanch for 4 minutes, and dry. They may last up to 6 months.

To pickle, cut into small, finger-size pieces, boil for 1 minute, rinse in cold water, add to your favorite brine mixture brought to a boil, remove from stove, let cook until cool, place in jars in refrigerator, and eat within 1 month. Or follow more intricate pickling methods for longer storage.

Culinary Uses

Most people are familiar with dozens of potential uses for carrots, including juicing. Never peel carrots; just scrub them down, or you will lose valuable nutrients in the skin. If you intend to eat them raw, remove the core if there is any. If you intend to cook carrots, leave the core in. It will become tender. Note that some gardeners insist that carrots taste best if chilled, either by cold outdoors or by 7 days of storage in the refrigerator. I like them right out of the garden, no matter what the temperature is.

Both raw and cooked carrots are good for you. There appear to be health advantages to both, so eat them raw and cooked for maximum benefit.

Eat them raw whole or sliced for vegetable platters. Shred, grate, or julienne them for salads. Eat them cooked baked in a honey glaze, boiled, microwaved, pan-seared, puréed, roasted with mint and honey, steamed, or stir-fried—diced, julienned, shredded, sliced, or whole. They are delicious in soups and cakes.

The leaves are edible but strongly flavored either fresh or cooked and generally used in tiny amounts as a flavoring, not as a side dish or main ingredient. Some people juice them to take advantage of their nutrients. Others use them in making vegetable stock. It may sound a bit over the top, but there are even recipes for carrot-top pesto. As with many other root crops, the roots may be roasted as a coffee substitute.

Varieties

If you have deep, loose soil, you can grow some of the longer-rooted varieties. If you have clay or somewhat compacted soil, stick to the stubbier crops. Experiment each year with new varieties to find the ones that do well in your garden. You will never understand how much the taste and texture of different varieties vary until you have grown your own.

The following varieties were chosen to give you a wide range of types; colors including orange, purple, red, white, and yellow; and shapes from tiny round to long and thin. Included are excellent hybrids with good disease resistance and some open-pollinated (heirloom) types noted for superb color and taste. 'Flyaway' is said to be resistant to carrot rust fly. Deep-orange, purple, and red varieties contain higher levels of beta carotene. Note that 'Atomic Red' and 'Red Samurai' have a richer coloration once cooked. For late planting, try 'Napoli' and 'Minicor'. They are wonderful, sweet baby carrots.

Here is useful information on the types of carrots in the varietal list.

Baby or mini: Sometimes referred to as Paris Market or planet-type carrots, they are small carrots that mature quickly and are suited to growing in heavy soil or containers.

Chantenay: These are cylindrical carrots with broad shoulders. They are usually fairly short, growing to about 6 inches in length. They typically have a blunt, rounded tip. Harvest them young, since they have fairly hard cores. These are suited to growing in heavier soils.

Danvers: These are a bit longer than Chantenay and a bit shorter than imperator-type carrots. Their growing tip is conical. Harvest them young for best flavor. Many consider these the best for juicing.

Imperator: These are thin, cylindrical carrots up to 12 inches long with a tapered point. This is the type of carrot commonly sold in grocery stores. They are hard to grow unless you have sandy or deep, loose soil. They store well.

Nantes: These carrots are cylindrical with mildly blunt tips. They look a bit like a cigar and are the easiest carrots for home gardeners to grow. They generally are 6 to 7 inches long with fairly tender cores and a sweet taste.

VARIETY	DAYS	COLOR	SHAPE AND LENGTH (INCHES)
'Apache Hybrid'	65	Deep orange	Imperator to 9
'A#1 Hybrid'	65–70	Deep orange	Imperator type to 10
'Atomic Red' (heirloom)	75	Pink to deep red	Imperator type to 8+
'Babette Hybrid'	70	Deep orange	Nantes baby to 3
'Baltimore Hybrid'	75	Bright orange	Nantes to 6
'Bolero Hybrid'*****	70–75	Deep orange	Nantes to 7
'Chantenay Red Cored' (see 'Red Cored Chantenay')			
'Crème de Lite Hybrid'	70	Creamy yellow	Imperator type to 9
'Danvers' (heirloom-1871)	65–85	Bright orange	Danvers to 8
'Danvers 126' (heirloom-1947)	75	Deep orange	Danvers to 6
'Danvers 126 Half Long' (heirloom-1886)	75	Deep orange	Danvers to 6
'Deep Purple Hybrid'	75	Purple	Imperator to 8+
'Dragon' (heirloom)	75–90	Purple red/orange	Danvers to 8
'Early Coreless' (see 'Scarlet Nantes')			
'Flyaway Hybrid'	75	Bright orange	Nantes to 6
'Hercules Hybrid'	65	Bright orange	Chantenay to 6
'Imperator 58' (heirloom)	65–75	Deep orange	Danvers to 9
'Ingot Hybrid'	70	Dark orange	Nantes to 8
'King Midas Hybrid'	75	Deep orange	Imperator to 9
'Little Finger' (heirloom)	55–60	Gold orange	Nantes type baby to 3
'Minicor' (heirloom)*****	50–55	Deep orange	Baby cylindrical to 3
'Mokum Hybrid'	35–55	Orange	Nantes baby to 6
'Nantes Coreless' or 'Nantes Half Long' (see 'Scarlet Nantes')			
'Napa Hybrid'	55–65	Dark orange	Nantes to 8
'Napoli Hybrid'	50–60	Dark orange	Nantes to 8
'Nectar Hybrid'	70	Orange	Nantes to 8
'Nelson Hybrid'	60	Deep orange	Nantes to 7
'Nutrired' (heirloom)	75–80	Red	Imperator type to 9
'Parabel' or 'Parabell' (see 'Paris Market' as a substitute)			
'Paris Market' (heirloom)	50	Bright orange	Baby round to 2
'Parmex' (OP)	45–50	Bright orange	Baby round to 2
'Purple Haze Hybrid' (AAS-2006)	70	Purple/orange core	Imperator to 12
'Rainbow Hybrid'	60–75	Orange, gold, white	Imperator to 9
'Red Cored Chantenay' (heirloom)*****	65–70	Gold orange	Chantenay to 5
'Red Samurai' (heirloom)	75	Pink (cooks to rose red)	Imperator to 11
'Romeo' ('Round Romeo') (heirloom)	45–50	Orange	Baby round to 2
'Royal Chantenay' (heirloom)	60–70	Bright orange	Chantenay to 5
'Scarlet Keeper' (heirloom)	85	Orange	Danvers to 9
'Scarlet Nantes' (heirloom)*****	65–70	Bright orange	Nantes to 5
'Short 'N' Sweet' (OP)	70	Bright orange	Nantes type baby to 3
'Sugarsnax 54 Hybrid'	70	Bright orange	Imperator 9–12
'Sweetness II Hybrid #192'	65–70	Bright orange	Nantes to 8
'Tendersweet' (heirloom)*****	75	Orange	Imperator to 10
'Thumbelina Hybrid' (AAS-1992)	60–70	Deep orange	Baby round to 2
'Tonda di Parigi' (heirloom)*****	65	Deep orange	Baby round to 1½
'Touchon' (heirloom)*****	65–70	Bright orange	Nantes to 6
'White Satin Hybrid'	70	White	Nantes to 8
'Yaya Hybrid'	60	Orange	Nantes to 6
'Yellowstone Hybrid'	70–75	Yellow	Danvers to 10

Cauliflower has a reputation of being difficult to grow, but don't give up before trying.

CAULIFLOWER

Brassica oleracea var. **botrytis,** or Botrytis Group
Cabbage or Mustard Family (Brassicaceae, formerly Cruciferae)

Cauliflower is a hardy to very hardy, cool- to cold-season, biennial crop grown as an annual. It is grown for its edible stem head (curd). Its name means "cabbage flower." It is not really a flower but developing stem tissue. While a little more finicky than broccoli, don't be intimidated by its "difficult to grow" reputation. A good harvest of cauliflower depends on cool temperatures, ample moisture, and plenty of rich organic matter in the soil. Cauliflower probably originated in the Mediterranean area, possibly in Italy or Turkey.

How Cauliflower Grows

Cauliflower seed is tiny (about 6,000 to 8,500 seeds per ounce), round, and brown to blackish. The seedlings look much like broccoli or cabbage when young. The plants grow large, broad leaves. In the center of the plant, a portion of the stem develops into a head (curd). This is not a flower head as with broccoli. If the plant were allowed to mature completely, it would form a stem and blossom with four-petaled, yellow flowers in its second year of growth.

Where to Plant Cauliflower

Site and Light

Plant cauliflower in full sun. It needs bright light to develop thick foliage.

Soil and Moisture

Cauliflower grows rapidly and requires lots of moisture and a rich, fertile soil that drains freely. As with most plants, it thrives in loam with lots of organic matter. If compost or manure is in short supply, just toss a few cupfuls into the hole when planting. The ideal pH is from 6.5 to 7.5, which means the soil can be slightly alkaline. Adding a little lime to the planting area in fall is fine and may help prevent clubroot.

Container

It is possible to grow cauliflower in a container, but few people do. Grow only one plant per container, the larger, the better. Soil must remain consistently moist but not soggy.

Planting

Seed

Although it is possible to plant seed directly in the garden, it is uncommon in cold climates. Starting plants indoors to be transplanted outdoors makes more sense since plants mature best in cooler weather. You can gamble with direct seeding for a fall crop. Timing is difficult since plants can react badly to high heat.

Transplants

Cauliflower is easy to grow from seed, which you can order from mail-order companies. One big advantage of growing cauliflower from seed is that you select the variety or varieties to grow. Experiment each year. If available at all, most plants sold in garden centers are simply labeled "cauliflower." You have no idea what variety they are, how long they will take to mature, and whether they are disease resistant. If you buy plants, choose packs with short, stocky plants with good color. One pack may have more plants than another. Choose the one with the most plants, and tease them apart for planting.

Start cauliflower 4 to 8 weeks before the time you plan to set your transplants in the garden. Plant in sterile starting mix about ¼ to ½ inch deep. Keep moist and at 65° to 70°F, although seeds will germinate down to 45°F and as high as 95°F. Mist when the surface dries out. Seeds should sprout within 10 days. Month-old plants will do better than older ones. You want plants that are 4 inches tall and stocky for outdoor planting. Young plants often become tall and spindly unless you grow them under fluorescent lights. Keep the lights on for at least 16 hours a day. Harden off before planting outdoors.

When planting seedlings, be careful not to break off the growing point or tip of the plant. The loss of the tip could mean the plant will not form a curd. Strip off any lower leaves if they have turned yellow. When you do this, don't tear them off—pinch them between your thumb and forefinger. Plant as deep as the lower leaf. Firm the soil around the base of the plant with your fingers. Pour a transplant solution around the seedling. Keep consistently moist. Note that root disturbance does retard growth slightly.

Spacing

Transplants should be roughly 18 to 30 inches apart. Since plants can get large, wide spacing is usually wise. It also allows for better air circulation.

When to Plant

Planting cauliflower at the right time is more difficult than planting broccoli and cabbage. When growing your own

Nutrition Facts

Serving size: 100 grams (3.5 ounces)

	AMOUNT PER RAW SERVING	% DV	AMOUNT PER COOKED SERVING	% DV
Calories	25	1%	23	1%
Carbohydrates	5 g	2%	4 g	1%
Dietary fiber	3 g	10%	2 g	9%
Folate	57 mcg	14%	44 mcg	11%
Manganese	0.2 mg	8%	0.1 mg	7%
Potassium	305 mg	9%	140 mg	4%
Protein	2 g	4%	2 g	4%
Vitamin B6	0.2 mg	11%	0.2 mg	9%
Vitamin C	45 mg	75%	45 mg	75%
Vitamin K	16 mcg	20%	14 mcg	17%

plants, start them indoors at different times. This way you can get plants into the garden at different points in the season. You need only a few plants maturing at the same time, so this spreads out the harvest date. Unlike cabbage, which can stay in place for weeks, sometimes months, cauliflower must be picked as soon as the curds mature.

Plant seedlings on the frost-free date. Or gamble, getting the young seedlings into the ground 2 to 4 weeks before then with protection. Once growing vigorously, plants can handle a light frost, but they are less cold resistant than broccoli and cabbage. Having said that, frost in the early stages of growth may on occasion cause the premature formation of a small and unusable curd, a process known as "buttoning." Also, prolonged temperatures less than 50°F may cause the plants to bolt.

Consider another gamble by planting seeds directly in the garden later in the season for a fall harvest. Since it takes a long time for most cauliflower plants to mature from seed, start at about 10 weeks before the first expected fall frost. Vary planting dates as you would for indoor plants to increase the chance of success. The key is to time all plantings so that heads form in cool temperatures, if possible.

How to Care for Cauliflower

Water

Keep soil consistently moist. Don't hesitate to water the plants immediately once the soil starts to dry out. Moisture keeps the soil temperature down and spurs lush growth. One of the essential secrets of getting good cauliflower is to keep the plant growing rapidly at all times. Water is critical to this process, especially as the curd is forming

Mulch

Any organic mulch works wonders on cauliflower by keeping the surrounding soil moist and cool—cauliflower couldn't ask for more. Straw, grass clippings, compost, shredded leaves, and lake weed will work well in the garden. Get the mulch on early in the season, but don't touch the stems with it.

Fertilizing

Either give plants a heavy feeding after 3 weeks and again 2 weeks later or small feedings weekly. Fertilizers such as fish emulsion, fish meal, or seaweed provide plants with valuable micronutrients. Cauliflower needs nitrogen but just enough to keep foliage lush.

Weeding

To avoid damaging the shallow root system, do not cultivate deeply around the base of the plants. Hand pull all weeds in the root zone. If you are using mulch, you won't have to disturb the soil at all. If any weeds pop up through the mulch, remove them immediately.

Thinning

Thinning is not necessary unless you are starting seed outdoors in a block for later transplanting.

Pruning

Clip off any yellowing foliage around the base of the stem.

Special Considerations

Blanching describes the process of pulling leaves over and around a maturing head (curd) to keep it white. It comes from the French word *blanche,* meaning "white." If you don't blanch the heads, they may become coarse and discolored. Plants that form green, orange, or purple heads do not require blanching. Orange varieties need sun to retain their color. Self-blanching (self-wrapping) varieties have leaves that naturally bend over the curds. In theory, these do not need to be blanched. In reality, they sometimes need a little help. When the small white heads or curds get to be about 2 inches in diameter, pull the outer leaves in, and tie them with a piece of string so that the head is in a leafy cocoon. As long as light can't get to the head, it will turn a bright white. Tie the leaves loosely toward the top to give the head plenty of room to expand. Do this on a dry day to avoid trapping moisture inside the head. This could cause rot, which is possible in hot, wet weather. Blanching takes anywhere from 5 to 12 days, rarely less or longer. The warmer it is, the faster the curds mature. Untie the leaves regularly, and peek inside to see if the heads are big and mature. If

they are not, tie the leaves up again. Blanching is not tough, yet it seems to scare even veteran gardeners.

A few people are allergic to cauliflower but not many. Doctors may advise anyone with gout or kidney stones to avoid eating cauliflower.

If you are interested in botany, study Fibonacci numbers. Growth patterns following this sequence allow more sun to get to growing plant parts. The sequence of swirling petals or similar plant parts is always the sum of the previous numbers: 0, 1, 1, 2, 3, 5, 8, 13, 21, and so on. The curd of cauliflower is a good example of this principle.

Extending the Season

The best way to extend the season is to get plants in early with protection and then plant a second set of plants to mature in the fall, when they may again need protection from frost. Cauliflower is not as frost resistant as cabbage but heads up nicely in cool weather and will survive a temperature down to 20°F if growing vigorously.

Problems
Insects

Numerous insects feed on cauliflower. Aphids, cabbage worms, cutworms, flea beetles, and root maggots are the most common. Cutworms attack the stems of young plants, which collapse. Root maggots work below the soil and typically kill older plants, which suddenly wilt for no apparent reason. Two types of cabbage worms make a smorgasbord of leaves. In most instances the loss of a plant or two does not warrant the expense of typical controls. Till green manure or leaf mold into the soil in fall to reduce the chance of root maggot damage. Covering young plants with row covers reduces the more common insect problems. Once plants are more mature, they can survive attack more easily.

Disease

A number of diseases may affect cauliflower. Disease is usually less of a problem than insect infestations in the home garden. However, fusarium yellows can be serious if it gets into the soil from infected nursery plants or seed. Clubroot is fairly common, causing plants to wilt and die. When you pull up the plant, the roots resemble an enlarged club, giving the disease its name. To reduce the incidence of this disease, add limestone to the soil in fall. Limestone causes a change in your soil pH, so use it sparingly.

Prevent most disease by buying certified seed of disease-resistant varieties, providing enough space for air circulation, and planting cole crops, which include broccoli and cabbage, in a different place each year. Since you cannot know the background of transplants purchased from a local nursery, consider growing your own plants each year.

Marauders

Rabbits and woodchucks seem to have an emotional attachment to young plants, especially those in the mustard family. While they might choose broccoli over cauliflower, they seem to have enough time for an extended banquet. The problem is that they are fond of nibbling off the growing tips—no tips, no curds.

The best defense is a good fence. Consider a good one right from the start. Mini-fences, cages around plants, will protect plants against rabbits. They do nothing to stop woodchucks and deer, which when hungry enough will eat just about anything. The second best defense against marauders is an aware and aggressive dog. However, dogs may not be roaming at night when rabbits often do their dirty work.

Physiological

Buttoning, the premature formation of cauliflower heads, may occur if plants are left growing too long indoors; if seedlings are damaged by frost or kept under 50°F for a prolonged period; if transplants are allowed to get root-bound in a pot; if plants are kept crowded, underfed (too little nitrogen), or too dry in the early stages of growth; and, possibly, if too many leaves are damaged by careless gardening. Transplant shock has also been blamed for buttoning. This list makes it sound almost impossible to get it right. Prepare soil well, grow or buy transplants at the right stage of growth, and transplant carefully.

No head at all is generally caused by breaking off the growing tip of transplants. Discolored and deformed heads indicate possible nutrient deficiencies. This is extremely rare in a garden with lots of organic matter and fertilizer added to the soil regularly. Very small heads may be caused by a lack of boron in the soil. Plants need very little boron, which is supplied in organic matter and kelp. On occasion, a dilute solution of borax may need to be applied to the soil in fall before spring planting. Use 1 ounce to 1 gallon of water per 500 square feet. More is not better, since boron can be toxic if the level in the soil is too high.

"Whiptail" describes the formation of narrow leaves without normal growth of the head. Anything that interferes with consistent growth may result in this condition. It may also be a sign that the soil is too acidic. If the soil pH is within the recommended range, this condition is rare because necessary nutrients (molybdenum) can be taken in by the plant. Lack of nutrients, improper watering, and bad luck with weather conditions are the major causes of physiological problems.

If the temperature gets warmer than 77°F, plants may bolt. Higher temperatures than this are common as cauliflower matures in cold climates. My cauliflower has not bolted at higher temperatures, but that doesn't discredit this general warning, which comes from commercial growers.

Propagation

Cauliflower is hermaphroditic, having both male and female organs. It is not self-fertile but must be insect pollinated. Isolate it from any other flowering plants in the same family. This plant is a biennial, but high heat may cause it to bolt, forming flower stems showered in four-petaled, yellow flowers in the first year. Let plants go to seed. Let pods dry on the plant until just before they begin to split. Snip off pods, break open, separate seed from debris, and store in dark, dry, cool place for up to 3 to 5 years. The best seed is produced when at least a dozen plants are allowed to flower together.

Harvesting

Cauliflower matures more rapidly in warm weather than in cold. Once heads have begun to form, check on them daily in warm weather, every other day in cool, to see how they are doing. On most varieties, mature heads are large and compact with tight buds. Don't let them get overripe, when heads have a "ricey" look and texture. White varieties may turn tan or brownish but are still edible. It is preferable to cut heads a little early than a little late. Cut them in the morning if possible, when they are most firm. Bend back the leaves, and cut off the head with a sharp knife. Or cut the head with a few leaves intact—just enough to cover the head loosely. Now you have a prize well worth the effort. If a head gets frozen at the end of the season, cut it off and use immediately.

Storing

When harvesting in fall, store cauliflower plants with roots and leaves attached by hanging them upside down in a cool (34°F) place for about a month. Spray them occasionally with water to keep them fresh. Do not let them freeze— why not blanch and freeze them instead?

For short-term storage, strip off damaged outside leaves. Do not break up the curd into small florets, since these deteriorate rapidly. Do not wash curds until you are ready to use them. Curds will last longer in the refrigerator if you wrap them loosely in a perforated plastic bag with the stem down. In theory, this should stop moisture from collecting on the top of the head. Cauliflower does not last long, from 7 to 10 days at best.

To freeze, wash, break into small pieces (florets), soak in salt water if worms have been a problem, place in strainer, dip into boiling water for 3 to 4 minutes, remove and plunge into ice water until chilled, drain, place in freezer bags, label, and freeze. Adding 1 tablespoon of lemon juice or a little citric acid to water may help discoloration during blanching. When pickling, use your favorite recipe. Typically, white wine vinegar is recommended for pickling.

Culinary Uses

Cauliflower is delicious and most nutritious eaten raw on vegetable platters and in salads. It is equally delicious, but less nutritious, cooked. You can cook the curd whole or broken into florets. Cook by baking, boiling, frying, microwaving, sautéing, steaming, or stir-frying. Never overcook it, or it will produce an "off" odor. Use stainless-steel cookware to avoid discoloration as chemicals in the plant may react with aluminum or iron. Boiling is best if you intend to mash it as you would potatoes. In fact, the taste of the two blended is a favorite of many cooks. Some cooks mash either one or both with garlic and oil or butter and dust with Parmesan cheese. Cooked cauliflower is delicious covered in béchamel, cheese, or hollandaise sauce.

The stems are good if cut into thin strips and cooked like the curd. The leaves, referred to as cauliflower greens, are edible, but barely, in my opinion. Considering their importance to the formation of the flower head, leave them alone. There are a lot better greens to be had in the home garden. However, as an experiment, roast a leaf or two, and dust with salt to see whether you disagree.

Purple cauliflower, really a broccoli, turns green when cooked and tastes like broccoli. 'Graffiti' sometimes retains a purplish tinge. Orange cauliflower 'Sunset Hybrid' and 'Cheddar Hybrid' claim to retain their color. There are conflicting reports about this.

Varieties

In the following chart, CMS stands for cytoplasmic male sterility, a breeding term of little importance to the home gardener. More important is to grow cauliflowers that mature at different times so that you can spread out the growing season. The head sizes listed are dependent on how plants are grown and weather conditions. Just getting a firm, flavorful curd should satisfy any home gardener. Small curds are as tasty as large ones. Some gardeners actually prefer cutting off curds before fully mature.

Cauliflower (White)

Many of the following cauliflowers will have leaves that fold up to protect developing heads from the sun, so that the curds will stay white. Once curds begin to develop, if leaves are not fully covering the curds, tie the leaves together. This is important to preserve the color and texture of the curds.

VARIETIES	DAYS	HEAD SIZE (INCHES)
'All the Year Round' (heirloom)	70–100	6
'Amazing' (OP)	75	8–10
'Apex Hybrid'	70	7–8
'Bishop Hybrid'	65	7
'Candid Charm Hybrid'*****	65–70	8
'Cloud Hybrid'	65–75	5–7
'Denali Hybrid'	75	7
'Early Snowball' (heirloom)	60–75	6–7
'First White Hybrid'	50	10–12
'Fremont Hybrid'*****	65	7
'Freedom CMS Hybrid'	65–70	7
'Giant of Naples' (heirloom)	80	10–12
'Igloo' (heirloom)	70	7
'Imperial 10–6' (OP)	60	7
'Le Cerf' (heirloom)	70	7
'Minuteman Hybrid'	50–60	6–8

VARIETIES	DAYS	HEAD SIZE (INCHES)
'Self Blanche or Self Blanching' (heirloom)*****	70	7–8
'Skywalker Hybrid'	80	6–8
'Snowball' (see 'Early Snowball')		
'Snowball Y Improved' (heirloom)	70–80	6
'Snow Crown Hybrid' (AAS-1975)*****	50–60	6–8
'White Cloud Hybrid'	75	6
'White Sails Hybrid'*****	70	7–8

Cauliflower (Orange)

The orange varieties get their color from beta-carotene, as do carrots, so are especially healthful. They may retain their color when cooked, but there are contradictory reports regarding this trait. Do not tie leaves over these curds.

VARIETIES	DAYS	HEAD SIZE (INCHES)
'Cheddar Hybrid'*****	70	4–7
'Orange Burst Hybrid'	80–90	4–6
'Sunset Hybrid'	70	Variable

Cauliflower (Purple)

Purple cauliflowers are actually broccolis. They contain anthocyanin, believed to be an important nutrient. Do not tie leaves over these curds.

VARIETIES	DAYS	HEAD SIZE (INCHES)
'Graffiti Hybrid'*****	80–90	6–8
'Purple of Sicily' (heirloom)	90	6–8
'Rosalind' (heirloom)	65	6
'Violet Queen Hybrid'*****	70–80	6–7

Cauliflower, Broccoflower™ (Light Green)

Light-green broccoflower™ is a cauliflower-broccoli cross that looks like cauliflower but tastes more like broccoli. It does not need to be blanched by tying leaves over its head.

VARIETIES	DAYS	HEAD SIZE (INCHES)
'Green Harmony Hybrid'	55–60	8–10
'Panther Hybrid'	75	10–12
'Verdi Hybrid'	90	7–8
'Vitaverde CMS Hybrid'	75	8

Cauliflower, Romanesco (Light Green)

Romanesco, often sold as broccoli, is a cauliflower with spiky pinnacles spiraling around a pyramidal curd. Some gardeners say they are more difficult to grow. I have not grown these and cannot comment on these reports.

VARIETIES	DAYS	HEAD SIZE (INCHES)
'Orbit Hybrid'	75	Pyramid
'Romanesco' (heirloom)	75	Pyramid
'Veronica Hybrid'*****	80	Pyramid

Start harvesting homegrown celery young, and expect it to have a stronger flavor than if it were store-bought.

CELERIES

Apium graveolens species
Carrot or Parsley Family (Apiaceae, formerly Umbelliferae)

There are three types of celery covered in this section: stalk celery, bulb celery (celeriac), and leaf celery. They are half-hardy, cool-season biennials grown as annuals. The names describe which part of the plant is eaten. Celeries have a reputation of being difficult to grow. There are three reasons for this: sometimes seeds are difficult to get to germinate (not always), you have to start the seeds 8 to 12 weeks before outside planting, and both stalk and bulb celeries need a long growing season to mature. Patience, then, is the real key to success with this plant. These plants probably originated in the Mediterranean region.

How Celeries Grow

The tan seed of celeries looks like an indented tooth or spearhead (about 50,000 to 75,000 seeds per ounce). These grow into plants with a dense, fibrous root system. All celeries form leaves, but they vary in size and use. *Stalk* celery forms long, thick, indented leaf stems. The plant is grown just for these. *Bulb* celery also forms leaves, which send nutrients down to the base of the plant, which swells into a large bulb. The leaves are discarded, and the bulb is eaten. *Leaf* celery forms a dense grouping of thin leaves, which are eaten like stalk celery. If these plants are able to mature, they produce umbrella-like clusters of small, white to creamy-yellow flowers. These will produce seed.

Where to Plant Celeries
Site and Light

Celeries prefer full sun but will grow in light shade.

Soil and Moisture

The wild ancestors of celeries grew well in almost boggy, acidic soil. Modern varieties do well in deep, fertile, well-drained soil with a pH of 6 to 7. If soil is compacted, build a raised bed. Mix in as much organic matter as possible, including well-aged manure if available. Mix in organic fertilizers high in phosphorus and potassium in the fall before planting. Mix a nitrogen-rich fertilizer into the soil in early spring. The organic matter and organic fertilizers generally provide enough boron and calcium to eliminate the chance of physiological problems later in the season.

Container

Leaf celery is the easiest of the celeries to grow in a large container filled with potting soil or soilless mix. Keep the soil consistently moist.

Planting

Seed

Celeries are started indoors and planted into the garden as transplants.

Transplants

Start seed indoors 8 to 12 weeks before the frost-free date in your area. Plant seeds in individual pots or plastic trays with a half dozen individual cells. Celeries are noted for erratic germination, which generally occurs within 21 days. Try overcoming this by soaking the seeds overnight in tepid water before planting them in a sterile starting mix. Press them into the soil surface or barely cover so that they "sense" light. Or wrap the seeds in a moist paper towel until they start to sprout. You can also use a sprouting jar and "grow" them as you would sprouts with one exception: as soon as the seeds start to sprout, plant them immediately. Just barely cover the "sprouts." Keep at 65°F to 70°F during the day and 10 degrees lower at night. Keep moist under a tent to increase humidity. The key is to keep the soil moist but not wet. Bottom watering is highly recommended.

Once sprouting, keep seedlings at 60°F during the day and 5 degrees lower at night if possible. Reduce humidity gradually by removing the tent for a longer period of time each day. Use grow lights to keep seedlings from getting tall and spindly.

Try to time your planting so that you can transplant seedlings when they are 4 to 5 inches tall. You may have to start several batches of plants to do this since outdoor temperatures are so unpredictable. Seeds are inexpensive, and starting a dozen or so each week for several weeks is worth a try. Before planting outdoors, harden off for 7 to 10 days. Bring plants indoors if temperatures threaten to drop below 45°F. Some gardeners do not harden off but reduce water to next to nothing for about a week as a way of getting transplants ready to be planted outdoors. Experiment with these techniques, especially with leaf celery.

It can be hard to find celery seedlings in garden centers, so call ahead in fall to see whether they will be available or could be grown for you. Seedlings from a nursery are usually sold in packets of six with individual planting

Nutrition Facts
Serving size: 100 grams (3.5 ounces)

	AMOUNT PER RAW SERVING	% DV	AMOUNT PER COOKED SERVING	% DV
Stalk celery				
Calories	16	1%	18	1%
Carbohydrates	3 g	1%	4 g	1%
Dietary fiber	2 g	6%	2 g	6%
Folate	36 mcg	9%	22 mcg	5%
Potassium	260 mg	7%	285 mg	8%
Protein	0.7 g	1%	0.8 g	1%
Vitamin A	450 IU	9%	520 IU	10%
Vitamin C	3 mg	5%	6 mg	10%
Vitamin K	29 mcg	37%	38 mcg	45%
Bulb celery (celeriac)				
Calories	42	2%	27	1%
Carbohydrates	9 g	3%	6 g	2%
Dietary fiber	2 g	7%	1 g	5%
Manganese	0.2 mg	8%	0.1 mg	5%
Phosphorus	115 mg	12%	66 mg	7%
Protein	1.5 g	3%	1 g	2%
Vitamin B6	0.2	8%	0.1 mg	5%
Vitamin C	8 mg	13%	3.5 mg	6%
Vitamin K	41 mcg	50%	32 mcg	40%

pockets or cells for each plant. The plants are generally 4 to 6 inches tall and ideal for planting in a home garden. Seedlings bought at a nursery are often dry. If this is the case, water the plants immediately. Let them drain for an hour or so. Then gently squeeze the bottom of each pocket of the plastic tray, and tap the container against your hand. Plants will usually slide out. Break or cut the plastic to get the plants out of these packets if you have to. It's better to discard the plastic packet than to damage the root system of the young plants. To keep soil around the roots, squeeze the root ball of moist soil gently. Place the root ball of each plant in a planting hole. Firm the soil around the base of the plant with your fingers. Pour a transplant solution around the seedling. Keep consistently moist.

Spacing

Place individual stalk celery plants 12 to 18 inches apart, closer if you intend to pick regularly before plants have a chance to mature. Plant bulb celery (celeriac) 10 to 12 inches apart. If you buy bulb celery seedlings from a nursery, what looks like one plant may be two or more. If this is the case, gently pull the seedlings apart with each thin stem supporting a small root system. If you do not separate the plants, they will form two interconnected bulbs next to impossible to use. Leaf celery can be planted about a foot apart.

When to Plant

Plant after apple blossoms fall, usually 2 to 4 weeks before the frost-free date. If temperatures will drop below 45°F or stay below 50°F for 10 days or so in a row, then protect the plants with cloches or row covers. Celeries are frost tolerant, but a hard frost or cold snap can kill seedlings or cause plants to bolt (flower prematurely) later on. To play it safe, plant after the frost-free date.

How to Care for Celeries

Water

The single most important secret to succulent celeries is water. It is best to water these plants along the ground. Let the hose run at the base of the plants as if you were creating a miniature flood zone around them. This soaking is essential to healthy growth. Try to avoid getting moisture on the growing leaves, but don't be paranoid about it. Overhead spraying occasionally deters insects. If you don't water consistently, stalk celery in particular tends to be hollow or stringy. Erratic watering reduces the uptake of essential micronutrients in the soil, and this can cause physiological problems, described later.

Mulch

Place a 1- to 2-inch layer of organic mulch around the base of the plant, but do not touch the stems. Good organic mulches are shredded leaves and grass clippings. They don't have to be deep to be effective but will need to be replaced as the season progresses.

Fertilizing

Celeries are heavy feeders. Either fertilize heavily after 3 weeks and then again 2 weeks later, or supply plants with small amounts of organic fertilizer weekly. By adding lots of organic material including manure to the soil at planting time, you can cut down on fertilization dramatically—to even nothing at all. Fish emulsion and seaweed products are good organic fertilizers containing essential trace elements.

Weeding

If the plants are surrounded by mulch, weeding usually takes a few minutes at most. Pull the weeds up by hand. Do this as soon as weeds start to spring up. Do not cultivate close to celery plants. You may damage their shallow roots. Mulch essentially eliminates or dramatically reduces the need for cultivation.

Thinning

Most home gardeners grow no more than a half dozen or so plants. Place plants where you want them to mature from the start. When this is done, no thinning is required.

Pruning

No pruning is necessary except to remove any yellowing leaves. Snip them off at their base. Some gardeners pull off a *few* lower shoots of bulb celery, hoping to get larger, cleaner bulbs.

Special Considerations

While it is best to get plants into the ground early in the season, prolonged exposure to temperatures under 50°F may cause plants to bolt. This is relatively rare. 'Golden Self Blanching' is bolt resistant.

Some people blanch stalk celery to turn it white. While this may make the stems less bitter and more tender, it destroys a number of vitamins at the same time. They blanch stems by excluding light from the stalks long enough to stop the formation of chlorophyll, which keeps plants green. By starting stalk celery seedlings in trenches, you can fill in the trench during the last few weeks of growth to blanch the lower portion of the stems. Note that some varieties are sold as self-blanching.

An easier method of blanching, which avoids the need to dig trenches, is to exclude light from the bottom of the plant by wrapping it with a thick layer of newspaper or pliable cardboard secured in place with twine. Do this when the plant is dry. Once the stems are covered with paper, mound up soil around the base of the plant. Do this for 2 to 3 weeks before harvesting. This method makes more sense to me since no dirt gets in between the stems.

Some people also blanch bulb celery. This should only be done 2 to 3 weeks before harvesting. Mound soil up over the bulb. The bulbs are said to become more tender. I don't blanch celeries, because a little extra tenderness is not worth the loss of nutrients to me, and there is a chance that stalks or bulbs will rot if they get wet during this process.

Leaf celery is lovely added to flower arrangements. Its deep-green, curly foliage is long lasting.

Extending the Season

Celeries can often withstand hard frosts in the fall without dying back. Some are even usable after a snowfall. Of course, this is pushing it, but it shows that even in cold climates you can extend the season into early or mid-November. Plants turn mushy if they freeze. They can be protected with a 12-inch layer of straw covered in soil or pulled up and placed in a cold frame with a similar protective blanket.

Problems

Insects

Plants may suffer occasional attacks by insects, but these are relatively rare in the home garden. Most common are aphids and leafhoppers. Spray off aphids with a forceful stream of water, and cover young plants with row covers if leafhoppers or other insects become a problem.

Disease

The most common disease is fusarium yellows, commonly spread by leafhoppers. Other problems are blights (early and late), rot, powdery mildew, and a virus spread by aphids. If a plant is severely damaged, dig it up, and settle for a little less. Prevent disease by making sure the soil has plenty of micronutrients; by watering regularly but not too much, preferably in the morning; by reducing insect infestations with the use of row covers, if necessary; and by buying disease-resistant varieties.

Marauders

Any animal that is hungry enough will eat just about anything. However, celeries are not high on any specific animal's hit list, especially if there are other preferred crops close by.

Physiological

Celeries must have enough boron, calcium, and magnesium. Lack of boron may cause stems of stalk celery to crack or have brown streaks inside. This can also be caused by too much nitrogen. Not enough calcium is believed to cause black heart, a condition where leaf tips turn watery and portions of the plant turn black. Leaves that turn yellow but have green veins indicate a lack of magnesium. By adding lots of organic matter to the soil and fertilizing with a variety of organic fertilizers, you reduce the incidence of these problems. Kelp products are effective in this regard.

Propagation

Celeries are insect pollinated. Unless a plant bolts prematurely in the first season, you are unlikely to see flowers (umbels)—no flowers, no seed. You can cut leaf and stalk celeries to a healthy-sized stub in fall, winter protect them, and hope that they produce flowers in the following season, but don't count on the plants surviving.

Harvesting

As soon as stalk celery is producing edible-sized stems, start cutting them off from the outside as needed. Do not pull the stalks off. Make a clean cut at the base of the stem. Leave the central core (bud) and most of the stems alone. This way you enjoy celery all season long. At the end of the season, pull up the entire plant, cut off the roots, and enjoy.

Harvest bulb celery whenever the bulbs are large enough to eat. Cut the root just below the bulb. Trim off the leaves, and use immediately. Bulb celery often tastes better after a frost, but no home gardener is likely to harvest bulbs all at once.

Leaf celery does not have large stalks but typically rounded and thin ones. Most cooks prefer them young, but they are good even when mature. As the name implies, leaf celery is grown mainly for its leaves. It is a "cut and come again" plant. Cut stems off at the base starting from the outside. Do not cut all the stems off a single plant. Plants regenerate new stems.

Storing

Keep celeries in the garden for as long as possible. Since they are remarkably cold hardy, this can be late into fall. Do not let them freeze.

To store stalk celery, cut off foliage to within 1 inch of stems, let soil dry, rub it off, do not wash, place in a perforated plastic bag in the crisper of your refrigerator. For longer storage, place roots upright in moist, not wet, sphagnum peat moss, sawdust, or sand in a plastic garbage can in an unheated but insulated garage where temperatures range from 35° to 40°F. The stems should not be touching one another or the side of the container. Cover each plant completely. Place them in layers until the container is full. The moisture will keep the roots from drying out. The stalks may last for several months stored in this way.

To freeze stalk celery stems, wash, remove strings, cut into pieces or strips appropriate for their final use, and freeze immediately. Use these within 2 months. Or blanch pieces for 2 to 3 minutes, plunge into ice water for same amount of time, drain, and freeze immediately in airtight freezer bags. Frozen stems are mushy and only useful in cooked dishes, such as casseroles, sauces, soups, stews, stir-fries, stock, and stuffing. Note that celery can be sautéed before freezing. It can also be puréed with seasonings, placed in ice cube trays, popped out, then kept in freezer bags until ready to be added directly without thawing to cooked dishes.

To freeze stalk celery leaves, roll them into a long "log" roll, and freeze in a freezer bag. Open the bag, and slice off only what you need, returning the remainder of the roll to the freezer.

To dry stalks, wash, cut crosswise into ¼-inch slices, blanch 1 to 2 minutes, cool in ice water for the same time, dry in a dehydrator, or for hours in an open oven preheated to 140°F. Store in a glass jar. More highly recommended is to dry the *leaves* of stalk and leaf celeries. They can be dried at any time during the season for later use in soups and stews. The leaf varieties are naturals for this. Lay leaves out on a screen and air-dry, or hang leaves upside down in a dry, airy spot. Or dry in a dehydrator. Dry until crispy. Do not break the leaves apart until ready to be used. Keep in an airtight jar.

To store bulb celery, cut off foliage to within 1 inch of the bulb, let soil dry, rub it off, remove rootlets, do not wash, and place in a perforated plastic bag in the crisper of your refrigerator. For longer storage, follow the same steps described for stalk celery.

Culinary Uses

Stalk celery is excellent raw or cooked. Compared to store-bought celery, plants grown in the home garden are usually a much deeper green with a stronger, even intense, flavor. The leaves of stalk celery and leaf celery contain more nutrition than the stalks. Use raw stalk celery on vegetable platters, filled with peanut butter for the kids, or chopped into egg, green, potato, or tuna salads. If stalks are a bit stringy on the outer surface, strip off the strings with a knife from the top down. Note that stalk and leaf celeries will wilt if exposed to heat. If this happens, put their bases into cold water in the refrigerator. They usually snap right back.

Stalk celery stems are delicious in casseroles, soups, stews, and stir-fries. Bake, boil, broil, or steam half stalks for an outstanding side dish. Use the nutritious leaves as a flavoring in hot dishes, soups, stocks, and stuffings.

Leaf varieties have a different taste, in some cases more like parsley. They make colorful garnishes. However, they are usually cooked and used as you would the leaves of stalk celery and have all of its nutritional benefits as well.

Both types of celery can be juiced. Although you can juice using a blender, a juicer is more highly recommended. With a blender you have to add water to get juice and must strain out the pulp, removing healthful nutrients in the process.

Bulb celery is delicious raw or cooked. It has a firm, dense texture, often described as "nutty," and a mild flavor with hints of both celery and parsley. Cut off top and bottom (often indented with soil, forcing you to remove more than you might like), peel off outer skin (some people blanch the bulb to make this easier), cut out any pits as you would with a potato, cut in two. Plunge into 4 cups water with 3 tablespoons lemon juice or vinegar. Soak for at least 15 minutes. This stops the white flesh from turning brown. Soak in a favorite marinade if desired.

For fresh use, cube, dice, grate, juice, julienne, shred, or slice. Add to greens for salad, or eat it by itself. It has a wonderful crisp texture. Drench in vinaigrette.

To cook, cut into desired shape and size. Boil, braise, butter steam, fry, roast, or sauté lightly. Do not overcook. Steam, purée, and mash into potatoes to give them a unique flavor. Add pieces to soups or stews, or make cream of celeriac soup. Good complements to bulb celery are butter, dill weed, green onion, mint, parsley, and tarragon. Salt and pepper to taste. Bulb celery can be pickled like beets. Most people do not eat the leaves, but they are edible. They can be dried and added to soups as a flavoring.

To freeze, peel, dip into lemon water, cut into desired shape and size, blanch for 1 to 3 minutes depending on the size of the pieces, plunge into ice water for the same amount of time, place in freezer bags, and eat within 1 month.

Should any of these celeries have a chance to flower, the petals are edible and make colorful additions to salads.

Varieties

Disease resistance does vary by variety. Generally, hybrids show more disease resistance than open-pollinated (heirloom) varieties. Actual resistance tends to be a gray area. The term should probably be *tolerant* rather than *resistant,* which implies that a variety is fully immune. Furthermore, information on resistance varies by source.

Stalk Celery *(Apium graveolens* var. *dulce)*

This is the type of celery most people are familiar with. It has thick, succulent stalks and is one of the main vegetables sold in grocery stores. 'Giant Red Celery' and 'Redventure' have deep-red tones in the stalks. Some gardeners plant celery in trenches to blanch the bottom portion of stem to make it more tender. "Self-blanching" in the name implies that the plants do this naturally. The base of the stems are simply golden, not truly fully blanched.

VARIETIES	DAYS TO MATURITY FROM TRANSPLANTS
'Conquistador' (heirloom)*****	80
'Giant Pascal' (heirloom)	130
'Giant Red Celery' (heirloom)	100
'Golden Pascal' (heirloom)	90–115
'Golden Self-Blanching' (heirloom)*****	90–115
'Paris Golden Self-Blanching' (see 'Golden Self-Blanching')	
'Redventure' ('Red Venture') (heirloom)	95–100
'Tall Utah' (heirloom)	125
'Tall Utah 52-70 R' (heirloom)	100–120
'Tango Hybrid'*****	80–90
'Tendercrisp' (heirloom)	90–110
'Utah' (heirloom)	90–125
'Victoria Hybrid'	100

Bulb Celery (Celeriac) *(Apium graveolens* var. *rapaceum)*

Celeriac is one of those vegetables that few people have grown. It's sometimes known as celery knob, celery root, knob celery, or turnip-rooted celery. Indeed, it is very similar to celery. It can be eaten raw or cooked. Its leaves are edible but rarely used unless dried. Some gardeners dig it up in fall, cut leaves back, and pot up to bring indoors. They then eat emerging leaves as they would leaf celery.

VARIETIES	DAYS
'Alabaster' (see 'White Alabaster')	
'Brilliant' (OP)*****	100–110
'Diamant' (OP)	100–110
'Large (Giant) Smooth Prague' (heirloom)*****	110
'Mars' (OP)	95–105
'Monarch' (OP)*****	100–120
'President' (OP)	105–110
'Prinz' (OP)	95–105
'White Alabaster' (OP)	90–120

Celeriac takes up quite a bit of space but is especially memorable in cream of celeriac soup.

Leaf Celery *(Apium graveolens* var. *secalinum)*

Leaf celery may be called celery leaf, Chinese celery, Chinese golden, cutting celery, da Taglio, French celery, German celery, soup celery, parcel (Par-Cel), or even smallage (the wild plant from which it is derived). It looks like parsley with its thin stalks and curly leaves. The stems of 'Red Stem' are partially red; the stems of 'White Queen' are thin and are an example of Chinese celery. Most plants range from 12 to 24 inches tall. Days to maturity is misleading in that most gardeners begin to pick leaf celery at an early stage, but the stems are nice when picked much later. *This is a great celery and too often overlooked by the home gardener. Note that the leaves can be dried.*

VARIETIES	DAYS TO MATURITY FROM TRANSPLANT
'Afina' (OP)	60–90
'Amsterdam Fine Seasoning' (heirloom)	75
'Amsterdam Seasoning' (see 'Amsterdam Fine Seasoning')	
'Dinant' (OP)	60
'Golden Leaf' (OP)	75
'Parcel' (see 'Zwolsche Krul')	
'Red Stem' (OP)	85
'Safir' (OP)	75
'Soup Celery' (heirloom)	
'Zwolsche Krul' (heirloom)*****	60–70
'White Queen' (OP)	60–80

Leaf celery grows prolifically and can be cut back for another crop.

Picked at just the right moment, corn is one of the most popular vegetables in the country.

CORN

Zea mays **species**
Grass Family (Poaceae, formerly Gramineae)

Corn is a tender to very tender, warm-season annual. Fresh corn may well be the most prized vegetable, actually a cereal or grain, in the United States. The home gardener will be surprised by the sweetness of freshly cooked corn. Corn is easy to grow but takes up a lot of space in the garden. It is equally prized by raccoons and deer, which do far more damage in general than insects or disease. Corn is called maize in most countries. Corn originated in Mexico.

How Corn Grows

Corn grows from a large (about 100 to 190 seeds per ounce), sometimes wrinkled seed into a growing point, which breaks through the soil surface. As the plant grows, increasingly larger leaves unfurl from its stem. As the plant approaches maturity, it produces a male flower (tassel) on its top and a female flower (ear shoot) below. Up to a thousand strands of fine silk protrude from the end of each ear shoot. The tassel above releases up to several million grains of pollen (male sex cells) in midmorning, which drift in the wind and

land on the exposed silk of any plant. The silk (style) is covered with sticky hairs to help trap the pollen. Each delicate strand of silk must be individually pollinated. A fertilized silk creates a pollen tube, which runs down to an ovule at its base and fertilizes it. The fertilized ovule develops into a kernel of corn. If silk is damaged or not pollinated, no kernel will develop at its base. Each kernel matures over a period of time and eventually dries into a seed.

Where to Plant Corn
Site and Light

Corn needs lots of open space in full sun. Many gardeners plant it on the north side of the home garden to avoid shading other sun-loving plants. The more light and warmth, the better.

Soil and Moisture

The soil in your corn bed should be loose to the depth of a foot. Work manure, compost, sphagnum peat moss, or any available organic matter into the soil. This helps soil retain

Nutrition Facts

Serving size: 100 grams (3.5 ounces)

	AMOUNT PER COOKED SERVING	% DV
Calories	365	18%
Carbohydrates	75 g	25%
Copper	0.3 mg	15%
Dietary fiber	7 g	30%
Iron	2.7 mg	15%
Magnesium	125 mg	30%
Manganese	0.5 mg	25%
Niacin	3.6 mg	18%
Phosphorus	210 mg	20%
Potassium	285 mg	8%
Protein	9.5 g	20%
Riboflavin	0.2 mg	12%
Selenium	15.5 mcg	20%
Thiamin	0.4 mg	25%
Vitamin B6	0.6 mg	30%
Zinc	2.2 mg	15%

moisture and attracts worms, which enrich the soil with their castings (excrement). The soil should drain freely. If necessary, build a deep raised bed over rocky or compacted soil. Add lots of organic fertilizer to the soil in fall. Corn is a heavy feeder and likes its soil rich. Add nitrogen to the soil in spring before planting. With lots of organic matter, the soil should have a pH of 6 to 6.8, which is ideal for corn.

Planting
Seed

Most gardeners plant seed directly in the garden, either in rows or hills. Corn is wind pollinated, so plant in a block of four short rows, rather than in one long row. If corn is planted too thinly, the silk will not get fertilized, and the ears will not form properly.

Dig a furrow 3 inches deep. Place the seed in the furrow, and cover with 1 inch of soil. Once the seeds are germinating, push the remaining soil over them. Shallow planting is important for sh2 varieties, so don't plant quite as deep.

Luther Burbank, the great plant propagator, used to get a jump on his neighbors by soaking corn seeds in water for a day before planting. He insisted that it speeded up germination. This is highly recommended for finicky sh2 varieties. Soaking the furrow or hill with water after planting seems to work well enough for other types. Seeds usually sprout within 14 days at 58° to 68°F and faster when the soil is warmer.

Transplants

Few people start seed indoors. In my opinion, the advantage is minimal unless you are trying to get sh2 varieties off to a good start or you live in the far north. They can be quite finicky about soil temperature and moisture. Starting means presprouting in this instance. Place seed on the surface of a moist, sterile starting mix. Keep humidity high by covering the mix with a plastic tent. When seeds start to break open, get them into a furrow *immediately.*

Corn can be planted in cell packs roughly 2 to 3 weeks in advance of the frost-free date. They prefer 80°F and will usually germinate within 10 days. This strategy makes sense in the far north and for commercial growers who want to profit from early sales. Plant when only a few inches tall.

Spacing

Plant seeds 4 inches apart, possibly to be thinned later. Rows should be about 2 feet apart. You can also plant corn in hills spaced 18 to 24 inches apart in all directions to form a grid of plants. A hill is a gardening term meaning several seeds in one spot—it does not necessarily mean a mound of earth, although it can. If planting corn in hills, sow five seeds to a hill. Two possible advantages of hills are easier cultivation and greater wind resistance in storms. It is also easier to mound up plants knocked over after a storm with the added space between the hills. Still, most home gardeners plant in blocks of four to six rows.

When to Plant

There's no advantage to planting corn before the soil has warmed up to 60°F. Corn seeds often rot in cool, damp soil. This is particularly important for sh2 and popcorn varieties. Corn planted late has a way of catching up with corn planted early, so successive plantings often mature at the same time. There's an old saying that corn is ready to be planted when the oak leaves are the size of a squirrel's ears.

Disbelievers and gamblers should plant some corn (not sh2) 2 weeks before the last expected spring frost. If it germinates and starts to pop up during a frost, cover the emerging plants with soil. This gamble occasionally pays off. The most you have to lose is some seed, time, and effort.

Plant two or more different varieties with different maturation dates if you want corn coming in at varying times. Also, this planting schedule is used with varieties potentially damaged by cross-pollination, as covered in more detail later. While this sounds good in theory, it doesn't always work. For some reason, different varieties may mature at the same time despite listed days to maturity in catalogs—maybe I'm doing something wrong.

Support

Corn does fall over in strong gusts of wind, but supporting corn takes a lot of effort. The large corn roots near the surface of the soil are shallow, but in reality the plant has many other roots diving deep into the ground. Unfortunately, these do not support the plant as do the ones near the surface. See "Special Considerations."

How to Care for Corn

Water

Keep the soil moist to speed germination. This is particularly important for sh2 types of corn. The smaller seed has a tendency to dry out or die off without enough moisture.

The leaves of corn are shaped to funnel all rain to the stem. The water runs down the stem to the base of the plant, where it does the most good. The larger roots around the base of the plant seem shallow and don't support it in strong gusts of wind; however, corn has an extensive root system that can grow deep into the ground in search of water.

Still, corn needs heavy moisture to grow well. A couple of good rains a week is enough for corn, but during dry periods you will have to soak the ground. The best way is to flood the base of the plants with water by letting the hose run in the middle of the patch. The water will spread out. In larger patches you will have to move the hose a couple of times. Place the end of the hose on a board or it will make a hole in the soil. It is especially important to keep corn well watered when it begins to form cobs.

Soaker hoses interfere with cultivation and also hilling up the base of plants blown over in heavy winds. Overhead sprinkling, while not recommended, usually is only a problem once the corn begins to tassel. Water only the base of the plants at that time.

Note that corn curls or rolls up if stressed by water loss. Water immediately!

Mulch

Place a thick layer of organic mulch around plants when about 1 foot tall. Good mulches are hay, straw, and grass clippings. Pulverized leaves also work well. Replenish the mulch as it "dissolves" into the soil.

Fertilizing

Native Americans used to put a fish about 6 inches under each mound of corn plants. As the fish decomposed, it gave off nitrogen, which fed the growing plants. The point is that corn needs a rich soil high in nitrogen. The growing crop and soil microorganisms use up available nitrogen rapidly. Fertilize at least twice with an organic fertilizer high in

Every kernel of corn is produced as pollen travels down hundreds of individual strands of silk.

Corn tassels produce millions of grains of pollen to fertilize the silk.

nitrogen. Do this once when the plants are a foot tall and once again as they begin to tassel or form silk. Fish emulsion is excellent but so are other high nitrogen fertilizers.

Weeding

Cultivate lightly until you place mulch around the base of plants. Do not disturb the root system. The larger roots around the base of the plant are shallow, although the root system dives deep into the soil. Hand weed around the base of the plant if necessary. Once mulch is in place, it will stop the growth of most weeds. The weeds that do pop up are easy to pull.

Thinning

The typical recommendation is to thin corn plants to 1 foot apart. You can get away with less if you provide plants with lots of care. Compact patches do extremely well in the home garden where space is at a premium. Try at least one planting spaced 6 to 10 inches apart. Thin plants when they are about 5 to 6 inches high.

Pruning

Suckers shoot off from the base of some corn plants. They look like miniature stalks of corn. Do not pull these off. These suckers help the plant develop a strong root system. *This is in direct contradiction to many articles and other books.*

Special Considerations

Patches of corn can be damaged by high winds, especially when plants are tall. If your corn gets blown over (lodges), don't despair. Tilt the plants upright, and mound soil around the roots. If you use enough soil and pack it tight at the base of the plant, the corn will remain upright and produce a good crop. To do this, you have to remove mulch temporarily. Some gardeners actually push up soil around young plants as a preventative measure to wind damage. If your garden is in a wind tunnel, then you may have to pound stakes into the ground and run twine along the inside and outside edges of each two rows of corn. Do this at various heights as the corn grows. Begin when corn reaches a height of 2 feet.

Corn cross-pollinates. This means that one type of corn can fertilize another variety close by. This cross-fertilization (or pollination) can change the texture and taste of the preferred variety. There are two ways of handling this problem. The first is to grow two varieties with widely varying maturation dates so that one variety has been pollinated before the next variety tassels out. The second solution is to isolate each type of corn. The corn has to be far enough away from the other patch to prevent cross-pollination. The minimum

recommended distance is 150 feet. For most home gardeners, this isn't practical.

Pull up the corn stalks as soon as you pick corn. They are much easier to chop up and place in the compost pile at this stage, rather than later when they become stiff and hard.

Extending the Season

Extend the season by getting corn planted as soon as possible in spring and by planting varieties that mature at different times, even into fall. Planting through plastic or geotextile and insulating sprouting seedlings with a light cloth allow you to get a jump on the season. Sprouting seedlings can also be covered with earth if planted early and endangered by a frost, as mentioned earlier.

Problems

Insects

Commercial corn growers have suffered huge crop losses from insects and disease. These losses make home growers nervous. But the diversity of seed used in the home garden is so great that problems are far less common. There are many insects that could harm your crop. These include beetles, corn earworms, corn maggots, cutworms, European corn borers, grasshoppers, and rootworms. Severe infestations of any of these are rare in the home garden. True, you will occasionally find a worm nibbling on a few kernels at the tip of an ear. Cut it out. Most of the ear will be fine.

Disease

As with insects, disease is somewhat uncommon in the home garden. Corn diseases include anthracnose leaf spot, bacterial wilt, common smut, maize dwarf mosaic virus, northern corn leaf blight, rust, southern corn leaf blight, and Stewart's wilt. Catalogs list the disease resistance of specific varieties. Most of these are hybrids. Keep an eye out for smut, which forms a big black ball on infected ears. Remove it as soon as you see it. In Mexico, corn stalks are deliberately wounded to encourage the formation of this fungus, considered an edible delicacy known as *huitlacoche* (pronounced weet-la-KOH-chay). This gives you a good idea of exactly what not to do to avoid smut on your plants. It occurs occasionally on an ear or two in the home garden.

Marauders

Here's the real problem in growing corn at home. Deer will nibble off corn at any stage. Sometimes, young corn will recuperate, but that's not certain. More frustrating is when deer munch on mature corn plants or maturing ears.

Raccoons have an uncanny sense of knowing when to eat corn—exactly a few days before you intend to pick it. It is said that you can plant sweet corn in the middle of acres of field corn, and raccoons will still find it. They think of sweet corn as their personal crop, a kind of summer banquet. Protect the crop from deer and raccoons by building a high fence around the patch. Run a wire around the top, and connect it to a battery. One jolt from an electric fence is all it takes to educate wily raccoons. Fencing does work, but it is expensive.

Other home remedies that people swear by are placing human hair around the corn patch (easily gotten at salons by the bagful—not my bag) after every rain or hanging a bar of Dial soap 6 inches above the ground in various locations. Apparently, mice eat it if you place it directly on the ground. Other simple measures, including growing pumpkins and squash in a corn patch or caressing each ear with your hand to leave human scent, have never worked for me. Some gardeners insist that covering nearly mature ears with lunch bags can protect them from raccoons. I have never tried this. A radio on at night has provided some relief, but it must be protected from rain. More importantly, you have to remember to turn it on and off. And neighbors may not appreciate your choice of music.

It is possible to trap raccoons in a Havahart® trap using fish, chicken, and even some vegetables as bait. Now you have an ethical problem. Do you transport the animal miles away and give someone else a headache? The other option is clear.

Other furry and feathery pests are birds, mice, rats, squirrels, and woodchucks. A loose dog or cat discourages them but is rarely allowed in city and suburban settings. Woodchucks are easily trapped in live traps with vegetables as bait, Again, you face the dilemma of what to do with them. They are feisty and smelly. Fortunately, these latter intruders are not common in most home gardens, but when present, they are frustrating.

Physiological

Smut, technically a fungal disease, looks like a gall with highly irregular swellings. This strange growth, considered disgusting or a gourmet's delight, may be caused by wounding stems during weeding. Pick it when it is young and gives gently to the touch. Think of it as a rare mushroom. When it turns black, it is way past its prime and useless.

Propagation

Corn is cross-pollinating. Pollen from nearby plants is carried by wind to the silk of another plant. It generally falls fairly close to a crop, but in a heavy wind can be blown much farther. Exactly how far is still hotly debated. A limited number of open-pollinated varieties are still available for seed savers. Let sweet corn dry on the stalk, but pick before kernels begin to ferment. Let other types of corn dry on the stalk as long as possible. Shuck ears, and continue drying indoors in an airy, well-ventilated place. Do not save seed from hybrids. Do not save seed if an open-pollinated variety has been grown near another variety. Sweet corn seed will store for about 2 years, while other types store much longer. If you grow 'Country Gentleman', don't expect the kernels to line up in neat, tidy rows. The irregular kernel pattern is normal. Note that seed must be saved from up to a hundred plants to keep seed producing the best crops possible.

Harvesting

As ears mature, the sheaths turn a deep green. If they get too mature, they begin to get pale or whitish. Also, as corn matures, the silk begins to turn brown. The more brown and dry it becomes, the more mature the corn. On some varieties the silk just begins to turn brown when the corn should be picked. Mature ears of corn feel more solid and round than immature ones. The tip of mature ears feels flat and rounded, not pointed.

Test one ear of corn by pulling down on the outer leaves just under the silk. The kernels on the top of the ear are always the last to mature. If they are large, you are picking the corn too late. If they are just beginning to fill in, then the corn may be ripe. You may want to shuck one of the most mature ears to be sure.

The perfect moment to pick standard (su) corn is when the kernels are filled with a milky substance. Push in on a kernel with a fingernail. It should pop and bleed with milk. When the milk turns pasty like toothpaste, the kernels are too mature. Sugars have been converted to starch. Corn at this stage is tough and loses its sweet taste. This test is not reliable with the se, sh2, and se-sh2 varieties. They contain less starch and may exude a clear fluid when punctured.

To pick corn, pull down sharply. This will snap the ear off the main stalk. If a second ear is developing on the same stalk, hold the stalk with your hand to prevent damaging it. Pick corn just before you cook it, although some gardeners insist it is at its best in the morning and should be kept cool until an evening meal. The sugar in standard (su) corn starts turning into starch immediately after picking. This is less of a problem with the higher sugar varieties (se, sh2, and se-sh2).

To get miniature corn for Chinese cooking or pickling, pick the regular varieties early, as the silk starts to emerge.

A good variety for this use is 'Bodacious'. It is not technically a baby corn, and gourmets may insist that true baby corns are better than regular varieties picked at an immature stage. The advantage of growing the regular varieties is that you can harvest some baby corn and some larger ears from the same patch.

Don't pick the ears of popcorn or ornamental corn until the entire plant has dried out in the fall. This is usually after the first frost. Kernels should be hard and glossy. Pull off the husks, and hang the bare cobs in a mesh bag or place on a screen in a dry, warm, well-ventilated area for 3 weeks. Strip the kernels by hand or by rubbing cobs together. If the kernels do not come off easily, dry some more. Try popping a few kernels. If they don't pop well, dry out the ears some more. Drying can take up to 3 months. However, if they get too dry, they may not pop. In this case sprinkle them with water, and let sit for an hour or so.

Storing

It is best to cook corn just after picking it, certainly no longer than an hour off the plant. Standard corn begins to deteriorate as soon as it has been picked. If you have to keep it for more than an hour, pick it early in the morning, wrap unhusked in a damp paper towel, place in the refrigerator, and keep as close to freezing as possible. It may last up to 1 week. Se, sh2, and se-sh2 varieties hold better than the older, open-pollinated and hybrid corn because of the higher sugar content in individual kernels.

To freeze, husk, remove all silk, cut the base of each cob flat, blanch three to four ears at a time for 4½ minutes, plunge into ice water for same time, cut kernels off as cob rests on its flat end, spread kernels out in a single layer on a metal tray, freeze for 30 minutes, place in freezer bags, and freeze. When about to use, let the package thaw before use. Most other vegetables do not require this thawing process.

To dry, steam for 3 to 5 minutes, cool in ice water, cut off kernels, lay in a single layer on a cookie sheet in an oven preheated to 140°F until brittle (takes anywhere from 2 to 4 hours), stir a few times for even drying, cool at room temperature for several days, store in an airtight glass container, and check for mold weekly. Use later by soaking in water for up to 8 hours and then cooking at a slow boil for up to 2 hours. Or dry in a dehydrator.

Culinary Uses

Sprouts just emerging from the ground are edible, but few people grow corn for these. If thinning early in the season,

consider trying them. On another note, baby corn can be eaten husk and all.

Corn can be baked, boiled, grilled, microwaved, roasted, or steamed. For baking, leave the husks on. For boiling, have the water boiling before you pick the corn. Mark Twain insisted that the boiling pot of water should be carried right into the corn patch. Shuck and boil just until tender. Do not overcook corn. Do not put salt in the water since this actually toughens the kernels. Some cooks suggest putting in a tablespoon of sugar instead, claiming it enhances the taste of fresh corn. Leave the husks on if you microwave fresh corn. It generally takes about 10 minutes. Grilled or roasted shucked corn is delicious drenched in honey-sweetened soy sauce. Turn corn to get all sides charred a bit. Corns primarily grown for ornamental purposes are good if picked when immature and grilled this way. Shuck corn for steaming.

The secret to good popcorn is the moisture level in the kernels. Twist off the kernels from the bottom of the cob up. They should come off fairly easily if they are dry enough. Try popping some in a hot air popper. If they are too dry or too wet, they won't pop well. If they pop, store them in a glass jar at room temperature. If they don't pop, place them in a jar in the refrigerator. Add 1 tablespoon of water to ¾ quart of popcorn. Shake the jar regularly for several days. Try again with ½ cup of the moistened corn. Kernels still not popping? Grind them up for cornmeal.

Note that smut is considered a delicacy in some cultures, where it is called maize mushroom or Mexican truffle. Pick it young before it starts to turn black. Parboil it for 10 minutes or so, and then sauté it in butter spiced to taste.

Varieties

For a more prolonged harvest throughout the summer and into the fall, plant some of the early (65–80 days), midseason (81–90 days), and late varieties (91–110 days). As noted before, they may still all mature about the same time.

Both popcorn and the supersweet (sh2) hybrids grow well in home gardens but must be isolated to stop cross-pollination with other varieties. There are two ways to do this: isolate by time (have crops tassel at different times), or isolate by space (have 1,000 feet between different varieties). Obviously, the easiest and most practical for home gardeners is to isolate by time. As mentioned, that may or may not work. How far pollen will travel is controversial: no more than 150 feet typically but up to a mile in a strong wind.

Varieties of popcorn can be decorative and come in a broad range of colors. A few varieties are included in the table below.

Standard-type corn is open pollinated with an average

sugar and starch content. It may appear as su (sugary) in catalogs. It should be eaten immediately after picking, or it begins to deteriorate. The se designation stands for sugar enhanced or sugar extender and may also be listed as EH (Everlasting Heritage) in catalogs. It is very sweet, with more sugar than starch. Some of the varieties, such as 'Kandy Korn Hybrid', have reddish tones in the husks. Cross-pollination is less of a problem with these than with sh2 varieties. When both parents are se types, the plants are called homozygous. If only one parent is se, the plant is heterozygous. Sh2 types have been bred with the shrunken-2 gene, which gets its name from the shrunken appearance of the dried kernels. These should not be grown with other types of corn, since cross-pollination will affect the extremely high sugar content of the kernels. These varieties can be picked and stored for a longer time. Sh2 types may also be called shrunken, extra sweet, supersweet, and ultrasweet. Se-sh2 crosses are referred to as synergistic corn, often listed as sy in catalogs. The se parent gives the cross better tolerance to cold; however, the sh2 parent means the corn must be isolated for good taste. Many of these varieties are listed as Triplesweet™ varieties.

Organic gardeners should ask for untreated (UT) seed. Otherwise, you may get seed that has been coated with a fungicide to prevent rot in cool spring soil. Also, some sources insist that open-pollinated varieties have greater nutritional value than modern hybrids.

Yellow corns are a mutation from white corns, which are more common in other countries. Yellow may be more nutritious than white because of higher concentration of carotenoids (beta-carotene). There is a debate whether se, se-sh2, and sh2 are more or less nutritious than the others. Many of the multicolored corns have a higher percentage of protein than sweet corns.

Sweet Corn (*Zea mays* var. *saccharata*)

VARIETY	DAYS	HEIGHT (INCHES)	TYPE	COLOR/SIZE OF EAR (INCHES)
'Ambrosia Hybrid'*****	75	72	se	Bicolor to 8
'Applause Hybrid'	75	80	se-sh2	Yellow to 8
'Argent Hybrid'*****	85	80	se	White to 8
'Ashworth' (heirloom)	69	60	Standard	Yellow to 7
'Avalon Hybrid'	80	65	se-sh2	White to 8
'Bodacious Hybrid'*****	72	84	se	Yellow to 8
'Butter 'N' Sugar Hybrid'*****	75	80	Standard	Bicolor to 7
'Captivate Hybrid'	90	90	se-sh2	White to 8
'Country Gentleman' (heirloom)*****	90	84	Standard	White to 7
'Delectable Hybrid'	85	90	se	Bicolor to 9
'Earlivee Hybrid'	55	40	Standard	Yellow to 7
'Early Sunglow'	65	48	Standard	Yellow to 6
'Early Xtra Sweet Hybrid' (AAS-1971)*****	70	70	sh2	Yellow to 9
'Golden Bantam' (heirloom)	75	60	Standard	Yellow to 7
'Golden Queen Hybrid'	95	96	Standard	Yellow to 8
'Honey & Cream Hybrid'	80	72	Standard	Bicolor to 7
'Honey 'N' Pearl Hybrid' (AAS-1988)*****	78	72	sh2	Bicolor to 9
'Honey Select Hybrid' (AAS-2001)*****	80	78	se-sh2	Yellow to 8
'How Sweet It Is Hybrid' (AAS-1986) *****	83	80	sh2	White to 8
'Illini Xtra Sweet Hybrid'	80	72	sh2	Yellow to 8
'Incredible Hybrid'	85	96	se	Yellow to 9
'Iochief Hybrid' (AAS-1951)	85	80	Standard	Yellow to 8
'Jubilee Hybrid'	82	96	Standard	Yellow to 9
'Jubilee Supersweet Hybrid'	83	96	sh2	Yellow to 9
'Kandy Korn Hybrid'*****	90	96	se	Yellow to 8
'Miracle Hybrid'	80	94	se	Yellow to 9
'Northern Xtra Sweet Hybrid'*****	68	60	sh2	Yellow to 9
'Pay Dirt Hybrid'	70	65	se-sh2	Bicolor to 8
'Peaches & Cream Hybrid'	80	80	se	Bicolor to 7

VARIETY	DAYS	HEIGHT (INCHES)	TYPE	COLOR/SIZE OF EAR (INCHES)
'Providence Hybrid'	85	84	se-sh2	Bicolor to 8
'Quickie Hybrid'	62	60	se	Bicolor to 7
'Seneca Horizon Hybrid'	65	65	Standard	Yellow to 8
'Serendipity Hybrid'	85	96	se-sh2	Bicolor to 8
'Silver King Hybrid'	85	72	se	White to 8
'Silver Queen Hybrid'*****	95	90	Standard	White to 9
'Spring Treat Hybrid'	70	60	se	Yellow to 7
'Stowell's Evergreen Hybrid' (AAS-1934)*****	95	96	Standard	White to 8
'Sugar Baby Hybrid'	65	72	se	Bicolor to 8
'Sugar 'N' Gold Hybrid'	62	50	Standard	Bicolor to 7
'Sugar Buns Hybrid'	70	76	se	Yellow to 7
'Sweet Temptation Hybrid'*****	72	72	se	Bicolor to 8

Popcorn and Ornamental (*Zea mays* var. *everta* or *praecox*)

Under color, the first color describes the cob, the second the popcorn.

VARIETY	DAYS	HEIGHT (INCHES)	TYPE	COLOR/SIZE OF EAR (INCHES)
'Dynamite' (see 'South American Yellow')				
'Japanese Hulless' (heirloom)	110	60	Standard	Yellow to 4 (white)
'Pretty Pops®' (OP)*****	100	96	Standard	Varied to 3–5 (tinted)
'Robust Yellow Hybrid'	110	86	Standard	Gold yellow to 7 (white)
'South American Yellow' (heirloom)	115	60	Standard	Yellow to 6 (white)
'Strawberry' (heirloom)	105	48	Standard	Mahogany to 2 (white)
'Tom Thumb' (see 'Japanese Hulless')				

Cornmeal, Flour, Ornamental, Roasting

Flour corn is *Zea mays* var. *amylacea*. Field or dent corn is *Zea mays* var. *indentata*. Flint, grinding, or Indian corn is *Zea mays* var. *indurata*.

VARIETY	DAYS	HEIGHT (INCHES)	TYPE	COLOR/SIZE OF EAR (INCHES)
'Black Aztec' (heirloom)	85–100	78	Standard	Blue black to 8
'Bloody Butcher' (heirloom)	100–120	120	Standard	Red black maroon to 10
'Blue Hopi' (see 'Hopi Blue Flour')				
'Calais Flint' (see 'Roy's Calais Flint')				
'Fiesta Hybrid'	100	84	Standard	Multi colored to 8
'Hickory King' (heirloom)	115	96	Standard	White or yellow to 9
'Hooker's Sweet Indian Corn' (heirloom)	80	72	Standard	Variegated red to 6
'Hopi Blue Flour' (heirloom)	110	84	Standard	Blackish purple to 10
'Indian Ornamental' (see 'Rainbow')				
'Mandan Bride' (heirloom)	85–90	72	Standard	Multicolored to 7
'Painted Mountain' (heirloom)	90	60	Standard	Multicolored to 7
'Rainbow' (heirloom)	110	84	Standard	Multicolored to 8
'Roy's Calais Flint' (heirloom)	90–95	72	Standard	Gold yellow to maroon to 10
'Truckers Favorite' (heirloom)	80–100	96	Standard	White to 10

'Straight Eight' is a crisp, award-winning heirloom that lives up to its name.

CUCUMBER (CORNICHON, GHERKIN)

Cucumis sativus
Cucumber or Gourd Family (Cucurbitaceae)

Cucumbers are very tender, warm-season annuals. Cucumbers are one of the easiest vegetables to grow and are adaptable to different growing methods. A few plants will supply the average family with more than enough fruits for pickling and fresh use. Fresh cucumbers picked at the right stage are crispy, juicy, and less bitter than store-bought fruits. Cucumbers are vulnerable to insects and disease but somehow manage to produce decent crops even when troubled by these. Cucumbers probably originated in India.

How Cucumbers Grow

The seeds are thin, typically light tan, and look like the end of a spear (about 1,000 seeds per ounce). The seeds germinate quickly and break through the soil with easy to spot seed leaves (cotyledons). The true leaves, which appear shortly after, are triangular with serrated edges. The plant forms prickly stems that are often brittle. The foliage enlarges and matures into larger leaves sending energy into the plant, which then produces lovely, but small, yellow, bell-shaped flowers. Each plant on many varieties has both male and female flowers produced at alternating nodes (where leaves join the stems). The early flowers are all male, but soon after both male and female flowers appear. Plants with differing ways of reproducing are covered in "Varieties." Insects transfer pollen from the male to the female flowers, which have a bulge (embryo) at their base. Once fertilized, these develop into fruit, which matures to form seed for the next generation of plants.

Where to Plant Cucumbers
Site and Light

Cucumbers grow best in bright, sunny locations that stay as warm as possible and are sheltered from prevailing winds. So plant them in full sun in a protected area.

Soil and Moisture

Moisture and heat—those are the two main secrets for growing cucumbers. Properly prepared soil will provide even moisture throughout the season. If possible, prepare the growing

Nutrition Facts

Serving size: 100 grams (3.5 ounces)

	AMOUNT PER RAW SERVING	% DV
Calories	15	1%
Carbohydrates	4 g	1%
Dietary fiber	0.5 g	2%
Protein	0.7 g	1%
Vitamin C	3 mg	5%
Vitamin K	16 mcg	20%

bed in fall. Raised beds are especially effective since they warm up quickly in spring. You can also make 6-inch or higher mounds or hills several feet wide in the planting area. Add lots of organic matter to the soil. Compost, sphagnum peat moss, and rotted manures are excellent soil amendments. Work the soil until it is loose. Add organic fertilizers to enrich it. You want the soil to be rich, loose (drain freely), and moisture retentive. Once you have made the bed, don't walk on it. Avoid compacting the soil that you have worked so hard to keep aerated. With all of the organic matter added to the soil, it probably will be mildly acidic with a pH close to 6.5 to 7. That's ideal for cucumbers.

Covering the soil with black plastic or permeable landscape fabric is highly recommended in areas with cool summers. If using black plastic, which repels water, consider placing soaker hoses underneath it. Instead of evaporating, water gets trapped underneath it and keeps the soil moist. Permeable landscape fabric heats up soil like black plastic but allows water through. Light also gets through, so you may want to cover it with a thick organic mulch once plants are growing vigorously and air temperatures are high.

Containers

Some varieties of cucumbers grow well in containers. Home gardeners often come up with their own formula for potting soil. The base for most of these is a combination of peat, perlite, and loose garden soil. Add organic fertilizers to the soil before planting. For a slicer, try 'Bush Champion', 'Salad Bush Hybrid', or 'Spacemaker 80'. For a pickler, try 'Picklebush'.

Planting

Seed

Most gardeners plant seed directly in the garden. The soil temperature should be at least 70°F, but warmer is even better. Place six seeds several inches apart on top of the hill. Seeing them on the soil surface makes spacing easy. Just press them down into the loose soil with your finger to about ½ to

1 inch deep depending on your soil type. Then firm the top of the hill with your hand. Water immediately. Seeds usually sprout within 10 days.

A common misconception is that the soil must be mounded, but this is a matter of choice. The advantage of raised hills is that they drain well and dry out quickly in spring like miniature raised beds. Planting on a level surface is fine as long as you have prepared the soil as you would for a hill or raised bed. The spacing of hills (raised or level) depends on the potential size of the plant. Typically, a few feet is fine for bush types; farther apart, for vining varieties.

If using black plastic or black landscape fabric to heat up an area, make small holes or slits. Plant the seeds in the soil through these. This technique is most valuable in northern areas where it can get cool at night.

Transplants

Cucumbers really dislike being transplanted. Root disturbance sets them back. When transplants and seeds are planted in the same hill at the same time, the seeds often do as well or outperform the transplants. If transplants are set in the garden and kept artificially warm in plastic tunnels, they do get a head start. Since cucumbers grow rapidly, this extra work makes sense only to the avid home gardener.

The avid home gardener should start seeds indoors about 3 to 4 weeks before expected outdoor planting time. Don't start them too early, because they grow quickly. Use a 32-ounce plastic container. Keep the lid, cut out the bottom, set the container on the lid. Fill it with a sterile starting mix. Plant two to three seeds in it. Keep the mix moist. Soil should be at least 70°F, preferably 85°F, with a 5 to 10 degree drop of temperature at night. Use a heating mat if necessary. Seeds should germinate within 10 days. Snip out all but the one healthiest plant. If the plant gets taller than 6 inches, pinch off the growing tip. The plant will branch, but this rarely results in better or more fruit. It's best to time planting so that plants are less than 6 inches tall when set out. Alternatively, use a 4-inch peat pot. Plant several seeds in it and thin to one before planting.

Harden the plants off slowly before planting in the garden. Make a hole in the soil large enough to hold the container. Set the container off to the side of the hole. Slide the plastic lid out from under the container. Cover the bottom where the lid was with your hand, and place the container in the hole. Push soil lightly around the container, and then lift it up and away from the plant. Firm the soil around the plant. Water immediately. If the weather is not stable, protect the plant until it warms up. Using a large container and planting carefully to avoid root disturbance are the critical elements of this method. If this is too much effort, use a peat pot, and plant it in the ground so that the top of the pot is barely covered with soil.

Spacing

There is no set rule for spacing cucumbers since they can be grown in so many ways. However, you do not want plants growing from the same spot to be too close together. In short, two or three plants growing from one hill will be more productive than six growing from that same spot. Plants should not compete with each other for water and nutrients.

When to Plant

Cucumbers are tropical plants. They do not tolerate frost, either in spring or fall. So direct seed them only after the soil has warmed up to at least 60°F and preferably higher. Unless you are willing to protect transplants with plastic tunnels or individual cloches, plant them when both the air and soil temperature are warm, certainly no sooner than 2 weeks after the frost-free date and later if possible. Use floating row covers for protection from insects. These should be supported and not touching the plants.

You may have success with a late planting in early July for a fall crop. Taking the gamble with a few seeds is certainly worth the risk.

Support

Most cucumbers tend by nature to be vining plants. You can grow them on a support or on the ground. If using a support, they may need a little help to get them started in the right direction. As soon as the plants begin to vine, tie them to the support with a soft piece of fabric tied in a loose figure-eight knot. Try to keep vines growing on one side of the support if possible. Ideally, the vines should be facing south.

The advantages of growing cucumbers this way are that they take up less space and are exposed to bright light; air circulation is good and cuts down on disease; pollination may be improved; pruning is simple; and maturing fruit is easy to spot and pick. Cucumbers grown this way do require more watering; however, you can easily water just the base of the plant and not water the foliage at all. So vertical growth is both a disadvantage and an advantage when it comes to watering.

Good supports include A-frames (place two pieces of concrete remesh against each other), fences, Japanese tomato rings, tomato cages, trellises, and wigwams, which are three or more poles angled upward and tied together at the top. They should be no taller than 6 feet, so that reaching fruit is comfortable. Cucumbers can be grown in other places than in the garden—on the back of a garage, on the side of a

wall—you name it. These areas tend to be warm, since heat is retained by building materials. Always get your supports in place before planting seeds. They should be sturdy and, if possible, out of prevailing winds.

Again and again, I read how cucumbers grown on supports are straighter than those grown on the ground. Having photographed cucumbers for years, I can say that's not necessarily true. If you have enough space, don't worry about growing cucumbers on the ground. You will have plenty of straight fruits. Having said this, if you want straight cucumbers longer than 9 inches, support is recommended. Also, when you grow cucumbers on the ground, they can be harder to spot. Don't let any get overly ripe, which could stop the plant from producing additional cucumbers.

How to Care for Cucumbers

Water

Once cucumbers are growing well, water them only when the top inch of soil is dry. Pushing your fingers into the soil is the only reliable way to know whether it is dry. Cucumbers watered only when the soil has dried out will develop deeper roots, which help them ward off disease and withstand hot and dry conditions later in the season. If plants are under row covers, water them deeply and do not water again until the soil dries out, which can be many days later.

Whenever you water, saturate the soil around the base of the plant. Avoid spraying the foliage, which may increase the chance of disease. Uneven watering can result in bitter fruit. Cucumber vines tend to wilt in the afternoon, but if they are wilting in the morning or evening, water immediately. The use of soaker hoses is effective with these plants, especially under black plastic. The water goes into the soil, not on the leaves. A number of varieties are extremely water sensitive while flowering and fruiting. So don't skimp on water at these times. While water is critical to lush growth and fruit development, overwatering can result in root rot. Yellowing leaves are a symptom of this problem.

Mulch

If you live in an area where summers are usually cool, plant cucumbers through a black fabric or plastic mulch. In areas where temperatures soar in midsummer, use a thick organic mulch *once the soil and air temperatures are high.* Place 3 to 4 inches of organic mulch around the young plants after they have formed a few true leaves and, again, only once the weather is really warm. Do not touch the base of the plant with the mulch. Mulch keeps the soil moist and stops soil from splashing onto the leaves. If you are allowing these plants to ramble, set the mulch in place as far out as the plant can grow. The vines roam over the mulch. This stops you from having to pull weeds from in between the vines.

Fertilizing

Cucumbers like rich soil. If you have properly prepared the soil and added nutrients to it, you are off to a good start. Supplemental feeding is highly recommended at two times during the growing season, once when the plants begin to vine, and again as they begin to flower. Sprinkle organic fertilizer around the base of the plants at this time. Foliar feeding with an organic fertilizer high in nitrogen also works well. Fish emulsion is popular for this use. Stop foliar feeding once plants begin to bloom. Cucumbers are heavy feeders, so don't be afraid to spoil them. However, if you are getting more leaves than fruit, stop fertilizing.

Weeding

Keep the area around the base of the plant weed-free. Pull up weeds gently as soon as they appear. If they get large, snip them off at the base. In removing weeds, you do not want to disturb the cucumber's shallow root system. By mulching you reduce the chance of doing this. As vines spread out, they sometimes get entangled in weeds. Cut, rather than pull, these weeds out. Clearly, it is far better to use a mulch and prevent weed growth from the start.

Thinning

When you plant seed in a hill, you usually plant more seeds than you need. Save only two or three of the strongest plants. Don't pull out the weaker ones; snip them off with a scissors. By doing this, you avoid disturbing the root system of the remaining plants.

Pruning

If you are growing plants on the ground, pinch off the tips of the vines whenever they are growing longer than you want. The plant will often send off side branches. You get more growth in a more confined area. Pinching may result in more foliage than fruit, but there is generally enough fruit for the average family. If vines outgrow their support, pinch off the growing tip. This just keeps the plant more manageable and sends energy into the fruit below. Roughly 3 to 4 weeks before your first expected frost, pinch off all flowers and immature fruit to cause the remaining fruit to mature more rapidly. If there isn't much fruit on the vine, let it be. Whenever pinching back, do it at a leaf axil, the place where a leaf joins the stem. Snipping off excess growth with a pair of scissors is the same thing as pinching back, which is a general term for the removal of excess growth for a specific reason.

Special Considerations

The darker green the cucumber, the more nutritious it is believed to be. Darker green fruits contain higher amounts of lutein, a carotenoid.

Although rare, cucumbers can revert to plants similar to wild plants in their genetic background. The fruits of these plants are especially bitter. They contain a high amount of cucurbitacin and should not be eaten. Mild, but tolerable, bitterness may be caused by inconsistent watering, extreme temperature fluctuations, or getting a "bad" seed in a packet with genes that lead to a more bitter taste. The latter is uncommon.

Bee activity can be limited or even absent in urban areas. It can also be limited anywhere in cold, rainy, or cloudy weather. If your plants are not forming fruits, hand pollinate the blossoms. Use a camel hair brush to collect pollen from a male flower, and dab the pollen into a female blossom. Or cut a male blossom off the plant, and strip off the petals. Then push it lightly against the stigma in the center of a female flower. Do this in the morning when plants are in full bloom.

Try not to disturb or crack the vines at any time. This may result in reduced production. For example, if the vines are not crawling along the ground in the "right" direction, leave them alone. You do have to move vines a bit at an early stage if you are trying to get them to climb a vertical support, but this can be done carefully without damaging the stems.

Extending the Season

Cucumbers are extremely frost tender. However, they still produce fruit in cool weather. To extend the season, protect young plants in spring with plastic tunnels or cloches. Consider a midsummer planting for a fall harvest. Cover the plant in fall with row covers or sheets if there is a threat of frost.

Problems
Insects

Unfortunately, cucumbers do attract insects. The most common invaders are aphids, cucumber beetles, flea beetles, leafhoppers, leafminers, squash borers, and squash bugs. Protecting plants early in the season by covering them with cheese cloth or floating row covers is effective against a number of these but not easy to do on some vertical supports. Cucumber beetles are common and spread disease, including bacterial wilt. Covers on ground-hugging plants should be supported and removed as soon as the foliage begins to touch the fabric. Definitely remove covers once the vines begin to flower so that pollination can take place freely.

Disease

Cucumbers are also vulnerable to a number of diseases. The most common are angular leaf spot, anthracnose, bacterial leaf and fruit spot, bacterial wilt, cucumber mosaic virus, downy mildew, powdery mildew, and scab. A number of varieties have resistance to some of these diseases. Avoid some disease by keeping insects off the plants. Disease resistance is reported in most catalogs.

Marauders

Rabbits and woodchucks are said to like some varieties more than others. But they are not *that* selective, nor are other common marauders. Deer do prefer squash to cucumbers, but they will nibble off the tops of vines growing on a support and sometimes a bit of foliage on cucumbers planted on level ground.

Physiological

Poorly shaped fruit may be the result of not enough fertilizer, disease and insect problems, or inconsistent watering. As long as all fruits are not misshapen, it really is of little concern.

Propagation

Cucumbers are cross-pollinating. Save seed only from open-pollinated varieties. Grow only one variety at a time to prevent cross-pollination with a different variety. Note that cross-pollination does not affect the taste of cucumbers in the first season. It does, however, affect the genetic makeup of seed. Grow at least five plants of the variety to be saved. Cucumbers do not cross-pollinate with muskmelon, pumpkin, squash, or watermelon.

Let a cucumber mature until big and bloated. Then store inside for another 3 weeks. Cut open, remove seeds, let them ferment in a glass of water for 3 days, wash thoroughly, then place in water, keep only seeds that sink, dry in a single layer on a plate for as long as necessary to become hard, and store in a sealed envelope. Seed may last up to 5 years or longer under favorable conditions.

Harvesting

With some notable exceptions, pick cucumbers for any use when they are young, not the size found in grocery stores. Cucumbers are crisp and delicious, rather than bitter, when they are not overly mature and contain far fewer seeds. The best time to pick is in the morning when they are still turgid. Some gardeners pick picklers before the sun rises, because they insist they are at their best at this time. Others wait until dew dries to avoid spreading disease. Cucumbers are at their peak for a short time.

Use a knife, pruners, or a pair of scissors to sever the fruit from the vine. Hold the fruit while cutting it from the vine. Cut off each pickling cucumber with a tiny portion of stem attached. Traditional sweet pickles are usually 2 to 3 inches long; dill, 5 to 6. Pick the variety 'Lemon Cucumber' when no larger than 2 inches. Pick cornichons and gherkins at ½ to ¾ inch. Pick slicers when they are deep green and before they form seeds, usually about 6 inches long. There are a few varieties that are better picked when larger or more mature, and these are noted in "Varieties."

Avoid damaging the vine, which may cause the plant to stop producing. Don't lift up vines growing on the ground. Don't twist or bend any stems. Don't let cucumbers go to seed on the vine. Each day, pick off all cucumbers of eating size and give away or compost the ones you can't use. A single ripe, bloated fruit turning light green to white (on white-spined varieties) or yellow to orange (on black-spined varieties) may stop the plant from producing more cucumbers. That one mature fruit may give off a hormone causing the vine to die. If going on a vacation, strip off all the fruit and flowers from each vine.

Vines will produce for about 2 months. After this period, the cucumbers tend to get bitter. Some gardeners don't let the pickling varieties produce any larger fruits for slicing. They say this will cut down on the production of additional fruit. I let picklers form one larger fruit at a time for slicing and haven't noticed any change in production of smaller fruits.

'Poona Kheera' is unique in that it can be eaten from when it is light colored to when it is deep tan. When picked with a deeper color, it is sweeter. It's a unique variety from India, not familiar to the average American. 'Lemon Cucumber' is another offbeat cucumber. Pick it just with a touch of yellow. While pretty when bright yellow, it is overly mature.

Storing

Refrigerate both slicing and pickling cucumbers immediately. Cover slicers with plastic, or they will shrivel. Or place them in an unsealed plastic bag. Keep them cool in the crisper of your refrigerator. Keep them away from ethylene gas, emitted by apples. They ripen more quickly and may turn yellow. Eat them within a few days if possible.

For pickles, pick and pickle cucumbers as quickly as

Unlike most cucumbers, 'Poona Kheera' actually tastes better as it matures to a yellowish-brown color.

Few people realize that cucumbers are good cooked. Cut them into slices, roll in flour, and sauté in butter. Peel, seed, and cut into strips before butter steaming them for 2 to 3 minutes. They should be barely cooked, somewhat tender, but still crisp. Drench them with hot butter seasoned with your favorite herb or spice.

Varieties

There are two basic types: slicing cucumbers and pickling cucumbers. Slicing varieties are delicious in salads and can be picked young for pickles. Pickling varieties produce many, short fruits. These usually have thin skin and may appear warty. Their spines are white or black. The white types are a bit more popular. Picklers are juicy and firm. When allowed to get a little large, they make delicious slicers. Both slicing and pickling cucumbers may be sold as bush (dwarf), semibush (intermediate), or vining (long) varieties. This vegetable is relatively easy to grow—much easier than muskmelons and winter squash.

Here are a few terms that are helpful to know.

Andromonoecious: Having two types of flowers on the same plant. Some are male while others are perfect, meaning they contain both male and female organs.

Apple or lemon cucumbers: Rounded to oval, creamy to light-yellow, sweet cucumbers. They can be both slicing and pickling cucumbers, although they are most commonly eaten raw like an apple. Most people prefer them just as they turn yellow, but a few like them more mature when the skin thickens. Two varieties, 'Crystal Apple' and 'Lemon', are listed in the varietal chart.

Armenian cucumbers: Also known as snake cucumber or snake melon, uri melon, metki, mikti, and yard-long cucumber *(Cucumis melo* var. *flexuosus),* these "cucumbers" are actually melons. The fruits are ribbed with a thin, pale-green skin. They are good eaten raw up to a foot long and are often not peeled. They can be pickled when small, up to 6 inches, or cooked like summer squash when larger. They are considered "burpless cucumbers." Armenian cucumbers will not cross with other cucumbers but will with melons. Most catalogs suggest growing them on supports for straight fruit. I have grown mine on the ground and have had beautiful long fruits.

Burpless: A generic term referring to long fruits that have tender skins and mild flesh. In theory, they are easier to digest than thicker-skinned varieties. They may be called Asian (Oriental), Chinese, Dutch, English, European, gourmet, greenhouse, long, or seedless cucumbers.

Gherkins *(Cucumis anguria)*: These are not true cucumbers, but they grow in the same manner so are included

possible. There is an old saying, "from vine to brine in 24 hours." Cucumbers can be pickled whole or sliced and seasoned to be sour, spiced, or sweet. Avoid using alum, which is high in aluminum. Bread-and-butter pickles are sweet pickles seasoned to taste, dill pickles are, obviously, made with dill, kosher pickles (nothing to do with religion) are made with garlic and dill, and sweet-and-sour pickles are made with ingredients that combine the sour taste of vinegar with sugar and spices added to taste.

Do not freeze cucumbers.

Culinary Uses

Both slicing and pickling cucumbers are delicious raw in salads and sandwiches. If prickly, rub off the spines with a cloth. Then wash in cold water. Cut crosswise into thin slices. Or slice into spears for a vegetable platter. Cucumbers have little nutritional value, but fresh or pickled, they make up for it in taste. While the skin of the cucumber may be somewhat bitter, peeling it off removes much of the already limited nutritional value. Temperatures above 100°F make the skin even more bitter. If fruit is a little too mature, cut it in half, and scoop out seeds with a spoon.

here for convenience. They are called *cornichons* in French. Gherkins have smaller leaves and vines than cucumbers. Pick the spiny oval fruits when they are very small, at ½ to ¾ inch, no more than an inch. Pickle immediately. Do not confuse these with Mexican sour gherkin cucumbers, which are in a different plant group (genus), *Melothria scabra*. The latter look like tiny green to white watermelons.

Gynoecious: Producing only or mostly female flowers. From the beginning of the season the flowers will produce fruit as long as they are pollinated by a separate variety. Seed companies include one or more seeds in the packets of gynoecious varieties to act as pollinators. These may be colored to distinguish them from the other seeds. *The key point is that you need a pollinator.*

Hermaphroditic: Having only perfect flowers, ones that have both male and female organs.

Monoecious: Producing both male and female flowers. The first flowers of the season are all male and drop off until female flowers appear later in the season. At that point insects transfer pollen from the male flowers to fertilize the female flowers. Once fertilized, the flowers swell into fruits. Growing two varieties of these results in better pollination. However, seeds from crosses cannot be saved. If you grow just one open-pollinated monoecious variety, you can save the seed. These varieties tend to produce fruits later in the season but over a longer period of time than other types.

Parthenocarpic: Producing fruit without pollination and with no seeds or nearly none. *To produce seedless fruit, they must be isolated and not pollinated by another variety.* They were intended to be grown in greenhouses but can be grown outdoors if there are no other cucumber types in the garden or nearby. Pollinated fruit may be distorted. The dark-green fruits are usually long and thin with tender skin. Middle Eastern (Beit Alpha) and Persian cucumbers fall into this category.

The following chart lists some fine cucumbers arbitrarily divided into five groups. There are three groups of slicers. The first (regular) consists of the typical cucumbers that home gardeners have grown for years either for slicing or pickling when small. The second (Oriental) is cucumbers that stay unusually narrow and may get long before they are picked as slicers but can be picked at an early stage for pickling. The third group (unusual) separates somewhat offbeat varieties that are fun to grow and eaten differently from the other two slicer groups. The groups picklers and gherkins are self-explanatory, but many gardeners do not realize that picklers also make excellent slicers if allowed to mature more than normal.

VARIETIES	DAYS	VINE	TYPE	FRUIT COLOR AND LENGTH (INCHES)
Slicers (regular)				
'Bush Champion' (OP)*****	55	Bush	Monoecious	Bright green to 10
'Dasher II Hybrid'	60	Vining	Predominantly gynoecious	Dark green to 8
'Fanfare Hybrid' (AAS-1994)*****	65	Semibush	Monoecious	Dark green to 8
'Garden Sweet' (OP)	55	Vining	Monoecious	Dark green to 10 (burpless)
'Long Green Improved' (heirloom)*****	65	Vining	Monoecious	Medium to dark green to 10
'Marketmore 76' (OP)*****	65	Vining	Monoecious	Dark green to 9
'Raider 52 Hybrid'	55	Vining	Gynoecious	Dark green to 8
'Salad Bush Hybrid' (AAS-1988)	60	Bush	Monoecious	Dark green to 8
'Slicemaster Hybrid'	55	Vining	Predominantly gynoecious	Very dark green to 9
'Spacemaster 80' (OP)	60	Bush	Monoecious	Dark green to 7 (non-bitter)
'Straight 8' (heirloom) (AAS-1935)*****	65	Vining	Monoecious	Dark green to 8
'Sweet Slice Hybrid'	65	Vining	Monoecious	Dark green to 10 (burpless)
'Sweet Success Hybrid' (AAS-1983)	55	Vining	Gynoecious/parthenocarpic	Medium green to 12 (burpless)
'Tasty Green Hybrid'	65	Vining	Monoecious	Deep green slim to 10 (burpless)
Slicers (Oriental)				
'Diva Hybrid' (AAS-2002)*****	60	Vining	Gynoecious/parthenocarpic	Bright green to 8 (burpless)
'Japanese Climbing' (heirloom)	65	Vining	Monoecious	Light green curved to 8
'Orient Express Hybrid'	65	Semivining	Gynoecious	Mid green curved to 14 (burpless)
'Socrates Hybrid' (Beit Alpha)	55	Vining	Parthenocarpic	Medium green to 7
'Suhyo' ('Suyo') Long' (heirloom)	60	Vining	Monoecious	Medium green curved to 15 (burpless)

VARIETIES	DAYS	VINE	TYPE	FRUIT COLOR AND LENGTH (INCHES)
Slicers (unusual)				
'Albino' (see 'White Wonder')				
'Armenian' (heirloom)*****	70	Semi to vining	Monoecious	Light green ribbed to 20 (burpless)
'Crystal Apple' (heirloom)	65	Semibush	Hermaphroditic	Greenish white apple
'Lemon Cucumber' (heirloom)	65	Vining	Andromonoecious	Green to yellow apple to 3
'Long White' (see 'White Wonder')				
'Poona Kheera' (heirloom)	55	Vining	Monoecious	Light to darker tan large potato-like
'Serpentine' (see 'Armenian')				
'Snake Melon' (see 'Armenian')				
'White Wonder' (heirloom)	60	Bush	Monoecious	White to 7
'Yard Long' (see 'Armenian')				
Picklers				
'Addis' (heirloom)*****	55	Vining	Monoecious	Dark green white spine
'Calypso Hybrid'	50	Vining	Predominantly gynoecious	Dark green white spine
'Carolina Hybrid'	55	Vining	Predominantly gynoecious	Medium green white spine
'County Fair Hybrid'	60	Vining	Predominantly gynoecious	Medium green black spine
'H-19 Little Leaf' (OP)	60	Very bush	Parthenocarpic	Medium green white spine (very small leaves)
'Eureka Hybrid'	55	Vining	Monoecious	Very dark green white spine
'National Pickling' (heirloom)	55	Vining	Monoecious	Dark green black spine
'Northern Pickling' (OP)	55	Bush	Monoecious	Medium green black spine
'Picklebush' (OP)*****	50	Bush	Monoecious	Medium green white spine
'Pioneer Hybrid'	55	Vining	Predominantly gynoecious	Medium green black spine
'Regal Hybrid'	55	Semivining	Predominantly gynoecious	Medium green white spine
Gherkin *(Cucumis anguria)*				
'Burr gherkin' (see 'West Indian Gherkin')				
'West Indian Gherkin' (heirloom)	60	Vining	Monoecious	Prickly green ball to 2

Give eggplant plenty of warmth and sunshine to grow into beautiful, glossy fruit.

EGGPLANT (AUBERGINE)

***Solanum melongena* species**
Nightshade Family (Solanaceae)

Eggplants are very tender, warm-season perennials grown as annuals in cold climates. Most people really enjoy growing eggplants. The leafy plants, colorful blossoms, and unusual fruit are all beautiful. The fruits vary slightly in taste but a great deal in color and shape, making them fanciful additions to the home garden. However, eggplants demand a long period of warm weather to mature properly. Eggplants are sometimes referred to as aubergines. Eggplants may have originated in Asia, possibly in India.

How Eggplant Grows

Eggplant seed is small, flat, tan, and light (about 6,000 to 7,000 seeds per ounce). As the young seedlings mature, they form lush plants with large, downy leaves. The stems become sturdy and somewhat prickly. Once mature, the plants blossom with star-shaped flowers, generally in shades of purple with a bright-yellow center. The plants are self-fertile, but cross-pollination is possible. Once fertilized, the flowers form fruits that vary in size, shape, and color depending on

the variety. These in turn form seed if allowed to mature on the plant.

Where to Plant Eggplant

Site and Light

Plant eggplants in full sun. If possible, choose an area out of prevailing winds. Avoid low-lying frost pockets. These plants want as much warmth and light as possible. A good choice is the south side of a fence. An area like this traps heat, provides both direct and reflected light, and curtails damage from winds.

Soil and Moisture

Eggplants demand loose, rich soil that retains moisture but drains freely. Add lots of organic matter to the soil. If compost, leaf mold, or rotted manure is in short supply, add it directly to the planting hole rather than throughout the entire planting bed. Adding organic fertilizers to the soil before planting is also helpful, since eggplants are heavy feeders. If you have compacted soil, build a raised bed. These

Nutrition Facts

Serving size: 100 grams (3.5 ounces)

	AMOUNT PER COOKED SERVING	% DV
Calories	33	2%
Carbohydrates	8 g	3%
Dietary fiber	3 g	10%
Protein	1 g	2%

tend to warm up quickly in spring compared to level gardens, but they also dry out faster as well. The preferred pH is in the 6 to 6.5 range.

Container

Eggplants grow well in containers. While it is possible to plant several plants in one container, they seem to do best if planted alone. Large 3- to 5-gallon pots are recommended for larger varieties such as 'Black Beauty' or 'Dusky Hybrid'. Smaller pots are fine for smaller plants such as 'Bambino' and 'Pot Black'. Buy or create your own potting mix by combining sphagnum peat moss, perlite, and compost or well-rotted manure. Mix in a blend of organic fertilizers. The idea is to keep the soil light and loose. Ideally, you want to be able to move the container around without harming yourself. All pots should have drainage holes and be kept off hard surfaces with spacers. Concrete is a good base for pots since it warms up a lot during the day and stays warmer at night. When planting transplants in pots, get stakes in place immediately. These will be used to support the plants as they mature.

Planting
Seed

Do not direct seed in the garden. Start plants indoors, or buy transplants from a garden center.

Transplants

Start seeds indoors about 6 to 8 weeks before your last expected spring frost. Seed can be presoaked. Use a 32-ounce plastic container per desired plant. Keep the lid, cut out the bottom, set the container on the lid. Fill it with a sterile starting mix. Plant two to three seeds in it about ¼ inch deep. Keep the mix moist and warm, preferably between 75° and 85°F, although they will germinate at 70°F. Place the container on a heating pad if necessary. Seeds should germinate within 14 days. Once germinating, they grow well at 60° to 65°F indoors. Let them form their first true leaves. Snip out all but the one healthiest plant.

Harden the plants off for 7 to 10 days. Make a hole in the garden large enough to hold the container. Set the container off to the side of the hole. Slide the plastic lid out from under the container. Cover the bottom where the lid was with your hand, and place the container in the hole. Push soil lightly around the container, and then lift it up and away from the plant. Firm the soil around the plant. Water immediately. If the weather is not stable, protect the plant until it warms up with row covers or cloches. Using a large container and planting carefully to avoid root disturbance are the critical elements of this method.

If you don't want to start your own, buy eggplants at a local garden center. They are usually sold when roughly 6 weeks old. Plants should be stocky with deep-green foliage.

Spacing

Spacing depends on the potential size of the variety being grown. Two feet apart in all directions is a good guide for larger plants, less for smaller.

When to Plant

Plant outside when daytime temperatures are above 70°F, nighttime above 60°F, for several days in a row. The soil temperature should be at least 60°F. Increase soil temperatures by covering the planting area with black landscape fabric. If an unexpected cold snap hits, protect individual plants with a cloche. Eggplants grow best in temperatures between 75°F and 86°F but can usually be set outdoors 3 weeks after the frost-free date and a bit earlier with protection.

Support

Plants may topple over either because they are blown about in wind or from the overall weight of the fruit. Some plants will produce up to six fruits at a time. At planting time push supports into the soil close to the stem. Use bamboo or similar stakes. As the plant grows, tie its stem to the stake with a soft piece of cloth in a figure-eight knot. Plants do not have to be particularly tall to topple. So supporting them from the start makes sense.

How to Care for Eggplant
Water

Keep the soil around eggplants consistently moist throughout the season. Water frequently and deeply in dry or hot weather. Eggplants love it hot but not dry.

Mulch

The use of black landscape fabric around eggplants is optional. It does heat up the soil and prevent some weed growth.

If you do not use fabric, wait until the soil is very warm before applying an organic mulch around the plants. If you apply it too soon, you keep the soil too cool. Mulch will keep the soil moist at any time and reduce the amount of weeding.

Fertilizing

Apply organic fertilizers around the base of each eggplant several times throughout the growing season. Pale foliage indicates a lack of nutrients. Fertilize as soon as fruits start to form and then again 4 weeks later. Fish emulsion is highly recommended. So is any fertilizer high in potassium, such as kelp products and wood ash (use sparingly, as it increases soil pH).

Weeding

If using a mulch, hand pull any weeds that sprout. If not using a mulch, avoid deep cultivation around the plant's shallow root system. Weed only in dry weather. If leaves are wet, you risk spreading disease.

Pruning

Pruning is optional. For large plants, pinch off the growing tip when the plant is 12 inches tall. You can also pinch back side shoots. The idea is to create a bushier plant with a limited number of fruits, usually five per plant. Once the desired number of fruits are forming, pick off all additional blossoms. While this may reduce the need for staking, it also limits production. Many gardeners let plants grow naturally. So do I.

However, approximately 4 weeks before the first expected fall frost, pinch off all blossoms and small immature fruit if there are larger fruits developing. This will encourage the plants to put all their growing power into the few remaining fruits before frost hits.

Extending the Season

Eggplants are extremely sensitive to cold both in spring and fall. If you really want to extend the season, consider growing an eggplant or two in containers, which can be brought indoors at the first threat of a fall frost and then placed outside in full sun once the weather warms up. Although it is common in cold climates to have a week or two of nice weather after the first frost, it will not be that warm, and fruit production will be low.

Problems
Insects

Aphids, Colorado potato beetles, cutworms, flea beetles, tomato fruitworms, leafhoppers, spider mites, nematodes, stink-bugs, tomato hornworms, and whiteflies have been known to damage eggplants. The two main culprits are Colorado potato and flea beetles. Row covers will discourage both but are unnecessary unless they have been a problem in the past.

Disease

Leaf spots, phomopsis rot, root knot, tobacco mosaic virus, and verticillium wilt occasionally show up in the home garden. Avoid most problems by planting eggplants in a new location each year, one where plants in the same family were not grown the year before. Many varieties of eggplants are resistant to specific diseases. Consider this when buying seed.

Marauders

While some insects like eggplants, few animals seem to. Having said that, a wily creature, such as a woodchuck, will prove me wrong.

Physiological

Occasionally the end of the fruit farthest from the stem (the blossom end) may rot. This may be caused by uneven watering or a lack of calcium getting into the plant. Keep the soil consistently moist. Add calcium-rich gypsum or lime to the soil in case that nutrient is missing.

Too much nitrogen in fertilizers can result in abundant foliage with limited fruit production. Cool nights and wet weather can also reduce the number of fruits. Blossoms may drop off in these situations. A turnaround in the weather often results in new fruits forming.

Propagation

Eggplants are self-pollinating. Let them mature on the plant. They often become dull, dry, and discolored. Do not let them rot. Cut open, remove pulpy interior with seeds, place in bowl of water, swish around, pour out pulp and any seeds that float, keeping the ones that sink, do this several times, strain, spread out seed one layer thick on a plate, dry out of the sun for several days or longer, place in envelope, and store for up to 4 to 5 years.

Harvesting

When you pick eggplants is a matter of personal preference. Younger eggplants are firmer than older ones but also a lot smaller. Eggplants are ready to be picked as soon as they turn bright and glossy. Small fruited varieties get seedy quickly. Although eggplants are mildly bitter, seeds just increase this trait. So don't let the fruit get overripe.

Don't try to pull eggplants off the plant. They hang down from the plant and appear fragile but aren't. Cut the stem about an inch above the eggplant with one snip of a pruning shears, leaving the calyx on the fruit. Many gardeners wear gloves when doing this since the stems are prickly.

Don't let eggplant ripen completely on the vine. This will shut off production. Keep picking even if you have enough eggplants. It stimulates other fruits to form. This extends the harvest over a much longer period.

As the season ends, begin removing blossoms about 4 weeks before the first expected frost. Fruit won't set if temperatures dip below 60°F. If there is any danger of frost, pick all remaining fruits. They will be damaged by the cold. You can cover plants with a sheet or row cover if you think the cold spell is just temporary—a day or two at most.

Storing

Use eggplants as soon as possible after picking. They store poorly, even in the refrigerator, where cool temperatures increase bitterness. Keep them up to 5 days in a plastic bag in the crisper of your refrigerator.

To freeze, peel, slice, immerse in salt water to stop darkening, scald 4 to 4½ minutes in salt water, chill, drain, place in airtight plastic bags, and freeze. Or salt slices, place in a bowl, let stand for up to 20 minutes, pour off any liquid, batter if desired, sauté lightly until tender, place in airtight bags, and freeze. Or simply cook a favorite dish, such as ratatouille, and freeze. Cooking is preferred over blanching.

To pickle, choose an eggplant that is firm and not overripe, cut into strips, and remove as much moisture from it as possible following your favorite recipe. Make sure that the pieces are stored in an acidic solution, not just oil alone. Usually the strips are cooked in a solution containing boiling vinegar. The process is more like canning than pickling.

Culinary Uses

Do not eat eggplant flowers. Do not eat raw eggplant. As with all members of the nightshade family, it contains chemicals that can be irritating if ingested.

The popularity of white or striped eggplants comes from the flavor of the flesh, which appeals to some more than the greenish-white flesh of darker-skinned varieties. The distinction is quite subtle, and some gardeners dislike it. If you pick fruits young on all varieties, the taste is better and the skin much thinner.

Peeled eggplant tends to brown. Sprinkle it with lemon juice to help retain the original color. Remove excess water in slices of eggplant by soaking them in salt water for 30 minutes, or cover with salt, and let them bleed for an hour or two. Rinse off the salt, and then pat dry before using in such wonderful dishes as moussaka or ratatouille. Or sauté breaded or floured slices in oil, or cook plain slices in a broth.

Grill slices of eggplant with the skin on. Paint the flesh with oil or soy sauce spiced with grated ginger. Flip and paint again. Or peel and slice eggplant, dip in tempura batter, and fry in 375°F oil.

Flavors that go nicely with eggplant are basil, garlic butter, marjoram, oregano, and minced parsley. Popular is a combination of eggplant with melted cheese in hot dishes and sandwiches.

Varieties

The following varieties were chosen to give you a varied selection of colors, shapes, and sizes. The days to maturity represent the time it takes for fruit to develop from transplants, not from seed. These are all good plants, and some have been standard selections for years. There is a subtle difference in taste between varieties. Some ethnic groups prefer 'Kermit' and 'Listada de Gandia' for their bitterness. Although not as disease resistant, try at least one open-pollinated or heirloom variety for taste alone.

VARIETIES	DAYS	COLOR/SHAPE	HEIGHT (INCHES)
'Amethyst Hybrid'	65	Deep purple/small teardrop	20
'Antigua' (heirloom)	75	White streaked lavender/long cylinder	20
'Applegreen' (heirloom)	70	Pale green/small, rounded oval	30
'Bambino Hybrid'	45	Purplish black/miniature round	12
'Barbarella Hybrid'	65	Dark purple/small, round decorative	36
'Black Bell Hybrid'	65	Black purple/round to oval large	28
'Black Beauty' (heirloom)	80	Dark purple/round to oval large	24
'Burpee Hybrid'*****	75	Glossy purple/oval large	24
'Casper' (heirloom)	70	White/elongated short	32
'Classic Hybrid'	75	Purplish black/elongated oval large	36
'Dancer Hybrid'	65	Purplish pink/elongated cylinder	28
'Dusky Hybrid'*****	70	Purple to black/oval to pear medium	30
'Fairy Tale Hybrid' (AAS-2005)*****	65	Purple striped white/small elongated	18
'Ghostbuster Hybrid'*****	80	White/oval large	36
'Green Goddess Hybrid'*****	60	Pale green/elongated	30
'Gretel Hybrid' (AAS-2009)	55	Shiny white/elongated short in clusters	36
'Hansel Hybrid' (AAS-2008)*****	55	Dark purple/short elongated	36
'Ichiban Improved Hybrid'*****	70	Dark purple/elongated long	48
'Kermit Hybrid'	60	Green white/small, round golf ball	48
'Listada de Gandia' (heirloom)	75	Purple striped white/elongated teardrop	16
'Little Fingers' (heirloom)	68	Dark purple/elongated, short in clusters	36
'Machiaw Hybrid'	65	Pale lavender/elongated, long cucumber-like	36
'Millionaire Hybrid'	65	Glossy black/long elongated	30
'Nadia Hybrid'*****	70	Dark purple/large oval	30
'Orient Charm Hybrid'	65	Pinkish white/long slender	36
'Orient Express Hybrid'	60	Black purple/long slender	28
'Ping Tung' (heirloom)*****	70	Violet/long slender	36
'Pot Black' (OP)	60	Purple black/baby oval	24
'Rosa Bianca' (heirloom)	80	Lavender splashed white/round ribbed small	28
'Slim Jim' (OP)	75	Lavender/short elongated	36
'Traviata Hybrid'	70	Dark purple/large oval	28
'Vittoria Hybrid'	65	Dark purple/elongated long	36
'White Lightning Hybrid'	60	White/teardrop medium	30

The crisp bulbs of Florence fennel add a licorice flavor to salads and cooked dishes.

FLORENCE FENNEL

Foeniculum vulgare var. *dulce* or *azoricum*
Carrot or Parsley Family (Apiaceae, formerly Umbelliferae)

Florence fennel is a hardy, cool-season perennial grown as an annual. It is extremely popular in Italy, where it is called *finocchio*. Florence fennel is a bulb fennel, rather than an herb fennel, which means that it is grown primarily for its whitish-green bulbous base rather than for its green ferny foliage. Although not yet grown by many cold-climate gardeners, it is relatively easy to grow and well worth trying. It is considered a delicacy by many. It probably originated in the Mediterranean area.

How Florence Fennel Grows

Florence fennel seed (roughly 6,250 seeds per ounce) looks like an indented spear, dark in the indentation and light tan on the outside edges. As the seedlings mature, they form feathery foliage on enlarged, flattened leaf stalks. The base of the plant looks like and often is referred to as a bulb, but it is really a series of overlapping leaf stems. If plants were to survive, they would produce yellow flowers and fruits (seeds) in the second year of growth. The plant has a noticeable licorice or anise scent.

Where to Plant Florence Fennel
Site and Light

Plant Florence fennel in full sun. Since the plant prefers cool weather, it will tolerate partial shade in hot, dry periods. Too much shade may result in the plant going to seed prematurely.

Soil and Moisture

Although the bulbous base of this plant is above the soil surface, the plant still does best in deep, fertile soil that drains freely. Adding lots of organic matter to the soil is particularly important in keeping even moisture around the plant's roots. If your soil is compacted or rocky, build a raised bed. The ideal pH is 6 to 6.8.

Container

If you have no other choice, then planting in a container is worth a try.

Planting

Seed

Plant seed in finely worked soil at a depth of ¼ inch. Keep the seed evenly moist until germination, which typically occurs within 14 days.

Transplants

It is possible, but not recommended, to start these plants indoors. The advantage is minimal since seeds can be planted directly in the garden early in the season. Furthermore, the growth of Florence fennel is often retarded by any root disturbance. If you want to try, use individual containers filled with a sterile starting mix kept at 65° to 75°F. Start roughly 4 weeks before the frost-free date in your area. Harden off and plant outdoors.

Spacing

Plant seed about 2 to 3 inches apart with the understanding that thinning will be necessary and plants will end up roughly 12 inches apart at maturity.

When to Plant

Florence fennel is best if it matures in cool weather, either in spring or fall. Direct seed as soon as you can work the ground in spring. Night temperatures are typically above 45°F at this stage of the season. Once seedlings are growing well, they can even withstand light frost. Cold temperatures early in the season may cause plants to bolt later on. However, by making successive plantings, you can ensure at least one healthy crop or more. Also, consider an additional planting later in the season to take advantage of cooler fall temperatures.

How to Care for Florence Fennel

Water

Steady moisture is one of the secrets of growing Florence fennel. Plants stressed by drought may go to seed prematurely.

Mulch

A thick layer of mulch helps cut down on the chore of watering by keeping the soil evenly moist for a longer period of time during dry spells. It also reduces the number of weeds that compete with the bulbs for available moisture and nutrients.

Nutrition Facts

Serving size: 100 grams (3.5 ounces)

	AMOUNT PER RAW SERVING	% DV
Calories	31	2%
Carbohydrates	7 g	3%
Dietary fiber	3 g	15%
Folate	27 mcg	7%
Manganese	0.2 mg	9%
Phosphorus	50 mg	7%
Potassium	415 mg	9%
Protein	1.25 g	2%
Vitamin C	12 mg	20%

Fertilizing

Start out with fertile soil, and then fertilize the plants every 2 to 3 weeks with any organic fertilizer high in nitrogen. Fish emulsion and liquid kelp are highly recommended. This extra fertilizing may be unnecessary if the plants are growing vigorously.

Weeding

Keep the area around bulbs weed-free. Pull weeds by hand. This is not difficult if you keep the area well mulched.

Thinning

If you plant seeds close together, begin thinning as soon as seedlings are a few inches tall. Keep thinning until more mature plants are roughly 8 inches apart. The few plants that mature completely will be about 12 inches apart. Wash and use the plants pulled up throughout the season during this thinning process. Add them to salads or stir-fries.

Pruning

The foliage is edible and in some varieties ornamental. Removing foliage inhibits the growth of the bulb, but some gardeners accept the trade-off. Although relatively rare, stems producing flowers may form in the first year. Cut these off immediately to encourage healthy bulb formation.

Special Considerations

Florence fennel can be finicky. Cold early in the season and drought during the main season may cause the plant to bolt. There is even speculation that root ball disturbance or too little light may be partially to blame for bolting. Planting seeds at the right time in full sun and keeping soil consistently moist throughout the growing season reduces the chance of bolting to slim.

There are some articles and books that recommend

blanching the bulbs by hilling up soil around the base when bulbs are the size of a golf ball, or excluding light with cardboard collars. The theory is that this creates more tender bulbs. I have never done this.

Problems

Insects

Occasionally, caterpillars and slugs appear on plants, but they are usually not a major problem.

Physiological

Bolting, which seems to be unpredictable, is the only physiological problem.

Propagation

Propagation is difficult because plants normally flower in the second year of growth. If plants do flower, they will cross-pollinate with caraway, coriander, and dill. Seeds are viable from 3 to 4 years if kept in a cool, dry, dark place.

Harvesting

Harvesting begins with thinning. The seedlings are edible and may be used in salads and stir-fries. Begin eating the bulbs when they are no more than a few inches in diameter. Smaller bulbs are the most tender. Larger ones can become a bit tough and stringy.

Harvesting Florence fennel is easy. Push the soil away from the stem, and cut it just below the bulging area. Cut off the leaves to within ¾ inch of the bulb. Both the leaves and bulbs are edible. Note that harvested plants may sprout secondary shoots. If interested in these, do not pull up the plant by its roots.

Storing

To store either leaves or bulbs for about a week, place them unwashed in a perforated plastic bag in the crisper of your refrigerator. To freeze bulbs, clean carefully, keep only the inner bulb, slice into a suitable size, blanch for 3 minutes in salt water, chill in ice water for same time, drain, pack in plastic freezer bags in water used for blanching, cool water down, and freeze. Dry the fine and feathery leaves in a dehydrator. Crumble and store in an airtight jar until use.

Culinary Uses

Although Florence fennel is grown primarily for its bulbs, both they and the leaves are edible raw or cooked. The raw bulb has the crunchy texture of celery and a strong licorice taste. Bulbs are often grated or sliced into salads. Raw slices can also be dipped into hot butter as an hors d'oeuvre.

Mince leaves, and add small amounts to fresh salads, or sprinkle the fine pieces over egg and fish dishes. Or place fresh leaves under fish on a platter. Or lay leaf stalks like celery on a vegetable platter. Dried leaves make a nice anise-flavored tea.

Cooked Florence fennel has a milder taste than raw. Trim off the base. Cook bulbs whole, or cube, dice, julienne, or slice them. The bulb lends itself to virtually every method of cooking. Here are some of the more popular ways. After parboiling, bake in butter before sprinkling with cheese. Boil ½-inch slices for 8 to 10 minutes. Butter steam or steam slices for 2 to 18 minutes depending on preparation and desired texture. Marinate quartered bulbs for up to an hour before grilling or roasting for 10 to 20 minutes. Sauté in olive oil until tender. Slice and cook rapidly in a stir-fry. Add pieces to soups and stews.

Grating Parmesan or Swiss cheese over cooked Florence fennel is commonly recommended, as is the addition of a little lemon or orange zest.

Varieties

Leaf fennel, including some lovely ornamental varieties, is described in the section "Herbs." The following varieties are grown for their elongated or round bulbs, although the foliage is edible. The height of most of these plants is around 24 to 30 inches.

VARIETIES	DAYS	SHAPE	RESISTS BOLTING
'Colossal' (OP)	65–80	Flat rounded (large)	Yes
'di Firenze' (OP)	65–80	Round	Somewhat
'Fennel Finale' (OP)	65–80	Flat rounded	Yes
'Fino' (see 'Zefa Fino')			
'Florence Fennel' (heirloom)	60–90	Flat rounded	Somewhat
'Orion Hybrid'	65–80	Round	Yes
'Selma Fino' (OP)	65–80	Flat rounded	Yes
'Victorio Hybrid'	65–80	Rounded	Yes
'Zefa Fino' (OP)*****	65–80	Flat rounded	Yes

GARLIC

Garlic is a staple of healthful cooking, and its many varieties offer a wide selection of tastes.

Allium sativum species
Onion or Amaryllis Family (Alliaceae or Amaryllidaceae), formerly Lily Family (Liliaceae)

Garlic is a hardy, cold-season biennial that can be grown as a perennial. Many home gardeners are learning that growing garlic is relatively easy as long as you plant it at the right time. They are also realizing that store-bought garlic represents only one of many possible tastes. Expand your culinary experience by growing several varieties suited to cold-climate conditions. Garlic probably originated in central Asia.

How Garlic Grows

Garlic grows from "seed," really bulbs separated into cloves. Each clove sends up a small green shoot. This is followed by additional leaves that arch outward and down. These leaves can rise 2 or more feet above the soil line depending on the variety. The leaves nourish the underground bulbs, which swell, creating a number of cloves. The overall bulb is protected by a papery covering, as are all of the individual cloves. There are ten major types of garlic, but for the sake of simplicity I am dividing garlic into two categories: hardneck and softneck. The ones that usually do best in cold climates are hardneck varieties. These will produce flower stems (scapes) that curl around in different patterns according to the variety being grown, while the softneck varieties generally do not flower. On top of the flower stems a lovely round bulbil capsule (called by some a flower head or umbel) forms over a period of weeks. It is covered with a sheath (spathe). Tiny bulbils (aerial cloves) form inside around inconspicuous true flowers. These bulbils planted and replanted over a period of years will form garlic bulbs.

Where to Plant Garlic
Site and Light

Garlic grows best in full sun.

Soil and Moisture

Garlic demands loose soil that drains freely but retains moisture during dry spells. When loosening the soil in fall, add organic matter and fertilizer. Garlic is a relatively heavy feeder. If your soil is compacted or rocky, build a raised bed. Garlic will rot out in soggy soils. Mixing blood meal

Nutrition Facts

Serving size: 100 grams (3.5 ounces)

	AMOUNT PER RAW SERVING	% DV
Calcium	180 mg	18%
Calories	150	7%
Carbohydrates	33 g	10%
Copper	0.3 mg	15%
Dietary fiber	2 g	8%
Iron	1.7 mg	9%
Manganese	1.7 mg	85%
Phosphorus	155 mg	15%
Potassium	400 mg	10%
Protein	6 g	13%
Thiamin	0.2 mg	13%
Vitamin B6	1.2 mg	60%
Vitamin C	30 mg	50%

into the soil in spring will add nitrogen and make it slightly acidic. Garlic thrives in soil with a pH of 6 to 7, which is mildly acidic.

Planting

Seed and Bulbils

When garlic forms "flowers," inside are true flowers and tiny bulbils that look like enlarged grains of rice. Professionals remove all the bulbils, allowing only the flowers to form seed. The flowers do not always cooperate, and seed collected in this way often does not germinate. So home growers do not grow garlic from true seed. However, the bulbils can be planted in fall and will produce a tiny bulb the following year. The tiny bulbs are harvested and then planted again and again until large enough to be split into cloves, which are called seed in catalogs.

Seed

The term *seed* refers to cloves in a garlic bulb. Separate the cloves from the bulb just before planting. Larger bulbs usually have larger cloves. The larger the clove, the better the results. Cloves have a pointed top and a blunt bottom. Plant the cloves with the pointed top facing up. The base of the blunt end should be planted 1 to 2 inches below the soil surface. A simple way of gauging the right depth is to poke your index finger into the loose soil up to the second joint. Pop the clove into the hole, and firm the soil around it.

Spacing

Space the cloves about 4 to 6 inches apart. Closer planting results in smaller bulbs if left to mature, but you can harvest some plants early as if they were green onions to increase spacing between remaining bulbs.

When to Plant

Garlic thrives in cool weather. It needs a cold period to produce well. Plant cloves in late fall 1 to 2 weeks after a killing frost when the temperature dips for the first time below freezing. Sometimes, the clove will produce a little green spike late in the season. If it does, don't worry about it. Very early spring planting is also possible, but resulting bulbs are usually smaller.

How to Care for Garlic

Water

Watering garlic takes some attention. Keep the soil moist after fall planting until the first freeze. In spring, water whenever the soil starts to dry out. The plants have shallow roots and will deteriorate if allowed to dry out too much. However, they do not tolerate soggy soil. Water throughout the season to prevent stress during hot and dry periods. As the season progresses into late summer, the plants will begin a natural process of dying back. Yellowing leaves at this time is normal. Stop watering.

Fertilizing

Garlic needs enough nitrogen to form lush foliage. As the cloves begin to sprout green shoots in spring, sprinkle some blood meal or liquid fish emulsion (4 tablespoons per gallon) around the young plants. Do this again several weeks later. Foliage will remain a deep green if fertilized properly and may encourage larger bulb formation.

Weeding

As mentioned, garlic has a shallow root system and does not compete well with weeds for available moisture and nutrients. Hand pull any weeds that pop up through the mulch. The mulch itself will stop many annual weeds from sprouting.

Pruning

During the growing season, flower stems shoot up from hardneck varieties of garlic. The flower stem (scape) will curl at the end as it begins to mature. Just as these curls begin to form a loop with an immature bud at the end, clip them off just above the uppermost leaf. By removing the flower stem, all of the plant's energy goes into creating a larger bulb—at least, in theory.

Winter Protection

After a hard freeze, cover the recently planted seed with 4 to 6 inches of straw as a winter mulch. Putting it on any earlier may attract rodents looking for a winter home. The winter mulch prevents heaving of the bulbs as the temperature fluctuates. It will settle over the winter. Leave it on. It is now a summer mulch, which keeps soil moisture and temperature even while preventing the growth of some weeds. The garlic leaves will push up through it.

Special Considerations

Raw garlic contains a compound (allicin) that may lower blood pressure, the incidence of cancer, and triglycerides for better heart health. It is highly perishable and should be used raw quickly after being crushed. Garlic is also being studied for its effects when crushed and added to bathwater as a way of curing infections. Garlic contains inulin, a polysaccharide, that may be useful for diabetics.

Weather, soil, and curing may affect the taste of garlic, so the same variety can taste somewhat different from year to year.

Extending the Season

Although it is preferable to plant all garlic in the fall, the one softneck variety listed in the varietal section can be planted as soon as the soil can be worked in spring. Harvesting will be later than normal.

Problems

Insects

In general, garlic is not bothered by many insects in the home garden. However, onion maggots and thrips can be a problem. Soapy water helps control thrips, and regular crop rotation helps prevent problems with onion maggots. If you plant garlic in an area recently covered with sod, you could have a problem with wireworms. Make sure to buy garlic from a reputable source, since nematodes can be carried into the garden with seed that is already infested with these microscopic worms.

Disease

Garlic is susceptible to several diseases, including botrytis (gray mold), fusarium, rust (orange spots on leaves), and white rot (root rot). Do not wound cloves while planting, or plants while weeding. Rotate crops regularly. If a plant yellows early in the season, remove it immediately and burn.

Marauders

Animals are not a major problem with garlic, although gophers can be. If you mulch bulbs too early, rodents may be tempted to use it for their winter home.

Physiological

If you wait too long to harvest garlic, bulbs may split. They will not store well this way.

Propagation

Take one or more of your larger bulbs, and break off the cloves after curing them. Eat the smaller ones, plant the larger ones as described earlier. In this way you will have garlic for years to come. You can also plant the bulbils in mature flowers, but don't expect large bulbs for at least 3 years and possibly longer. Most people eat the sprouting bulbils as green garlic.

Harvesting

As previously mentioned, on hardneck varieties stems will curl and begin to form a flower bud during the growing season. When pruning these off, don't throw them away. This curly portion with its swollen head is considered a delicacy by some and is most tender when the bud just begins to form. Although some people yank on it to pull it free from the plant, it is easier to snip it off with scissors above the uppermost leaf. Younger flower stalks (scapes) are more tender than older ones. Some people snip off the bud itself; others find it quite tender and delicious. Do snip off the pointy portion sticking out beyond the bud, as it is very stringy.

I always let several plants complete the flowering cycle. The flower petals are mixed together with tiny, rice-like bulbils. Pull out the flowers, and use them in dishes. Let the bulbils mature, and cure them as you would the underground bulbs. Crush them, and use as you would garlic cloves, or, better yet, plant them in fall alongside larger cloves. The little bulbils send up tender shoots in spring that look a bit like grass and can be eaten as a replacement for "garlic greens," a name given to young garlic bulbs pulled early and eaten like scallions.

In cold climates harvesting mature garlic bulbs occurs in mid- to late summer. Actual dates vary by season and location. If you wait too long to harvest garlic, the bulbs will begin to come apart in the soil. The clue that it is time to harvest comes from the plants. Leaves begin to turn yellow from the bottom of the plant up. Harvest hardneck varieties when half of the leaves are yellow, the other half green. This is usually about 3 weeks after the first leaves begin to yellow. Harvest softneck varieties when leaves turn yellow and topple over. To confirm a bulb's maturity, dig soil away from the side of the bulbs. Then feel them. If bumpy, they are ready for harvest. Dig up the plants at this time with a flat shovel, being careful not to damage the bulbs. Do not pull on the stems, since these may break off from the bulb. Keep the shoots and bulbs together at this stage. Do not wash the bulbs.

Instead, dry them with leaves and roots attached. Do not dry them in the sun, as this can change the flavor. Hang them in a warm, dry place out of direct light for several weeks. Proper ventilation is important. Air circulating around the bulbs helps them dry properly. An open shed is ideal, but an enclosed area with a large fan is OK. Once thoroughly dry, brush off any soil with a swipe of a gloved hand. Leave the papery skin on the bulb. Cut off all roots roughly ¼ inch from the bulb. Trim back the leaves of hardneck varieties to 1 inch above the bulb. Cutting back the leaves on softneck varieties is optional. If you want to braid softneck garlic bulbs, don't cut off the leaves, but do reinforce the braid with string or wire.

Storing

At 60°F and 60 percent humidity, hardneck varieties may last for up to 4 months; softneck, up to 8 months. These conditions are hard to provide in the average home; they are more likely in a partially heated garage. Store them in any dry place if necessary. If bulbs start to sprout, use them as soon as possible.

To make garlic powder, remove skin from cloves, and dehydrate in a dehydrator. Or slice into thin slices, and dry in an oven at 130° to 150°F until hard and light tan (not overcooked to brown). Then grind in a blender, and shake through a sieve. Keep in an airtight jar in a cool place, or freeze.

Although often recommended, never place peeled cloves in oil but instead in vinegar. Oil is not acidic enough to kill bacteria that may cause botulism. Use the cloves as desired. The vinegar now has the delightful scent and flavor of garlic. Some people eat garlic like "pickles."

To freeze, separate cloves from the bulb, peel, lay out on a cookie sheet, place in a freezer until frozen, remove, place in airtight freezer bags, and freeze for a few months. Frozen cloves do deteriorate in taste and texture.

To freeze flower stalks, cut into small pieces, and flash freeze. Or make them into a pesto, which can be frozen in an ice cube tray and popped out into a freezer bag to be stored as cubes.

Culinary Uses

Using garlic raw is the healthiest way to eat it. Garlic contains a compound called allicin, believed to promote heart health. Eat garlic raw to benefit from it, since it is apparently destroyed in cooking or by processing in any way. Garlic leaves and the little curly ends nipped off the top of flower stalks can be used in a number of ways. Snip them into bits for salads. Sauté them, steam them with vegetables, add them to stir-fries or as flavoring to any cooked dish. The little pods can even be pickled. When preparing flower stems, leave the flower bud on, but remove the little pointy portion that sticks out past the bud. Although some cooks claim the buds are stringy, I have found them to be quite tender compared to the stalks themselves, which if allowed to mature too long, remind me of the old-fashioned "string beans" that really were stringy. If "flowers" are allowed to form, pick them just as they open and break apart. They are milder than the bulb and delicious in salads.

Grate raw garlic cloves over salads or any of your favorite dishes where it would complement the taste. To use mature cloves in cooking, cut off the root end, press down on an individual clove with a large knife, peel off the skin, and place the clove in a garlic press to mince it. Use it as a flavoring for escargots, rubbed over meats, or added to baked dishes. Whole cloves are made sweeter as they are cooked. Roast whole bulbs for about an hour at 325°F. Let cool slightly. Pick off individual cloves, and squeeze into your mouth or into your favorite dish or even onto a cracker as a spread. 'Chesnok Red' is a favorite baked in this manner. It has even been mixed with vanilla ice cream and refrozen to make "butter brickle." When sautéing garlic in oil, remember that it will turn bitter if allowed to burn at all.

Varieties

As mentioned, there are two general categories of garlic: hardneck and softneck. Hardnecks are well suited to cold-climate gardening. The softneck types are less so. Within these broad categories there are ten major types of garlic, of which four are represented in the varietal list. These plants are available and have proven themselves in cold climates over a period of years. The average number of cloves of any type varies by the variety and is given in the chart below.

Although the artichoke type 'Inchelium Red' is a softneck garlic, plants may form flower stalks after a severe winter without adequate snow cover. If bulbils form, they tend to be purplish. The bulb itself is white with purplish tones and has up to twenty cloves. The porcelain type will produce flower stems. If bulbils are allowed to form, they typically are white. The large, white bulbs may have up to nine cloves. The purple stripe type also produces flower stems. If bulbils are allowed to form, they are purple. The name of this type comes from the purplish streaks on the bulb, which may have up to twelve cloves. Rocambole (ROCK-uhm-bowl) is sometimes referred to as serpent garlic or top-setting garlic. It is one garlic that can be counted on to form pea-size "bulbils" at the end of its flower stem if left on until the plant matures.

Softnecks are the types most commonly sold in grocery stores. Individual cloves are usually small, *may be diseased*, and are suited to warm climates. However, cloves planted in early spring will produce bulbs, which are small, with even smaller cloves than those planted. Still, they are usable but not nearly as good as the ones listed below. Experiment with replanting, even if small, to see whether the plant adapts to the climate over a period of years and slowly increases in size. Note that hardneck garlic may be available in organic-oriented stores in fall, but you will not know the variety. Look for bulbs with large cloves. This is an inexpensive way to experiment with your first garlic planting.

'Russian Red' is sometimes confused with elephant garlic, which is actually a leek and not truly hardy for over-wintering in cold climates.

VARIETIES	TYPES	CLOVES	TASTE
Hardneck (*Allium sativum* var. *ophioscorodon*)			
'Chesnok Red'	Purple stripe	Up to 10+	Mild, lingering, great in cooking
'Cichisdzhvari' (see 'Georgian Crystal')			
'German Red'	Rocambole	Up to 9	Hot, rich
'Georgian Crystal'	Porcelain	Up to 5 to 6	Mild, mellow, rich, good raw
'Georgian Fire'	Porcelain	Up to 6	Robust, hot, great in salsas
'Music' ('Musik')*****	Porcelain	Up to 7	Medium-hot raw, mildly sweet cooked; lingering
'Russian Giant'	Purple stripe	Up to 7	Mild; delicious roasted or sautéed
Softneck (*Allium sativum* var. *sativum*)			
'Inchelium Red'	Artichoke	Up to 20	Spicy, lingering

GREENS

This diverse group of nutritious plants are placed together in this section because they are less commonly grown or are even considered "weeds." Flavors vary dramatically from one plant to the next. Most are usually appreciated, but others demand an "acquired" taste—they are not for everyone. One example is cilantro, a favorite of some but detested by others (including Julia Child). Taste may be genetic, so vive la différence. I hope this section will introduce you to plants that will be your friends for years to come.

Mesclun is a seed mix containing a variety of greens. Skip packages labeled this way. Grow a selected number of specific greens to make your own mix.

Unless noted otherwise, the plants all do well in similar growing conditions: full sun, fertile soil, good drainage, lots of organic matter in the soil, regular watering, average pH between 6 to 7, no competition with weeds, and regular mulch. Many do well in large containers. The descriptions also mention when the plants are invasive or commonly bothered by insects.

A number of these plants make good "cut and come again" plants, so you can harvest them over a long period of time. Many can be harvested from the microgreen to the mature stage. A *microgreen* is a plant harvested when very young, past the sprout stage, when true leaves emerge. Dozens of other plants in this growing guide are delicious as microgreens, not just plants known as "greens."

Greens are grown close to the ground and often eaten raw. Wash them well to remove any trace of soil and to kill off potential pathogens. You may have to wash them more than once. Spray them with a jet of water, and dry them in a salad spinner. If there is any dirt in the bowl of the spinner, clean it out. Wash the greens again before spinning a second time. Be as gentle as possible in this process, but make sure that they are completely clean.

Amaranth
Amaranthus species
Amaranth or Goosefoot Family
(Amaranthaceae, formerly Chenopodiaceae)

Amaranth is a tender, warm-season annual. Both vegetable and grain amaranths produce colorful edible leaves. The round, shiny seed of both types is incredibly small and varies in color by variety (37,500 seeds per ounce). Vegetable amaranths may be called Asian spinach, callaloo, Chinese spinach, or tampala. It is related to a number of weeds referred to as pigweed. Both vegetable and grain amaranth are easy to grow for greens, but grain amaranth is primarily grown for seed and should be considered a novelty crop in cold climates. Even if seed ripens, it is a chore to collect.

The leaves of vegetable amaranth have a sharp taste faintly reminiscent of chard, mustard, and spinach. Pick only tender, young leaves, which have the best taste and texture; older leaves become pungent and stringy, although some people still prepare them as cooked "greens." There are three methods for harvesting these immature leaves. The first is to pull up the entire plant when young (6 to 8 inches tall). The second is to cut it back repeatedly as a "cut and come again" crop, as you would leaf lettuce. Do this as many times as the plant resprouts. The third method is to let it grow, and pick off the small leaves at the tip of the plant and at the end of side branches. Do this only as long as the leaves remain tender and tasty. If they get bitter, pull up the plant. This is a good reason for planting successive crops. Leaves have a tendency to lose moisture rapidly, so pick them early in the morning or late afternoon. Use as soon as possible.

I like the taste of cooked amaranth better than I do raw. The leaves are excellent added to soups, steamed like greens, added to stir-fries (cook for 1 to 2 minutes), or made into delicious soufflés. Do not overcook amaranth, or it turns "gummy."

Grain amaranths are long-season plants. Note that the name *grain amaranth* is misleading in that the plant does not produce grain but seed. Although the leaves are edible, the plants are grown primarily for their protein-rich seeds. The range of colors of the leaves and flowers is remarkable. Pick leaves when they are small and tender, then let the plant develop for the rest of the season until it forms lovely, decorative plumes.

Let the seed heads stay on the plant as long as possible. In cold climates this is typically 10 days after a killing frost has damaged the foliage. Cut the seed heads off before they start to shatter. Chew several seeds to test them. They should be firm, not doughy. If you wait too long, the seeds will shoot off in all directions. On a dry, sunny day cut the entire seed head off into a paper bag. Let the seed head dry in the bag until it becomes brittle. To remove the seed, reach in with a gloved hand, and crunch the seeds from the stem. Or place the seed heads in a pillow case, and press down on it firmly or walk on it with bare feet. Alternatively, rub the seed heads over a window screen with a bucket underneath to catch the seed. Remove all the debris. Tossing the seeds

The leaves of grain amaranth are edible, and the plant will form gorgeous flower plumes in the fall.

and debris up in the air in a mild breeze over a tarp is a simple way to separate out the seeds. Using a blower on low speed also works. There are no hulls to remove as on cereal grains since "grain" amaranth forms only seeds.

Sometimes, seeds begin to form before a hard frost. Rub a flower head to see whether seeds fall off. If they do, bend the heads over a large bucket or wheelbarrow. Rub and shake the flower head to dislodge the seed. Occasionally, flowers are still brightly colored, so don't use color as a gauge. Also, harvesting in this case may take place over a period of days. If seeds are spilling out, do not cut off the heads as described earlier; collect seed day after day. Wash the seed. Place it in a thin layer on a cookie sheet, and let dry at room temperature. Seeds should not be at all moist and not cling together. Once thoroughly dry, place in an airtight container in a cool, dark place.

Seed can be cooked like rice, ground into powder, popped (toasted), or sprouted. To cook, bring to boil, then simmer in water for 10 to 15 minutes until soft but not mushy. When fully cooked, it will make a sound as air bubbles through the mixture. Cover and let sit for 10 minutes.

Amaranth Nutrition Facts

Serving size: 100 grams (3.5 ounces)

	VEGETABLE		GRAIN	
	AMOUNT PER COOKED SERVING	% DV	AMOUNT PER COOKED SERVING	% DV
Calcium	209 mg	21%	47 mg	5%
Calories	21	1%	102	5%
Carbohydrates	4 g	1%	19 g	6%
Copper	0.2 mg	8%	0.2	8%
Dietary fiber	0.0	0.0%	2 g	8%
Folate	57 mg	14%	22 mg	5%
Iron	2.3 mg	13%	2.1 mg	12%
Magnesium	55 mg	14%	65 mg	16%
Manganese	0.9 mg	43%	0.6 mg	32%
Phosphorus	72 mg	7%	148 mg	15%
Protein	2 g	4%	3.8 g	8%
Vitamin A	2,770 IU	55%	0.0	0.0%
Vitamin B6	0.2 mg	9%	0.1 mg	6%
Vitamin C	41 mg	69%	0.0	0.0%
Zinc	0.9	6%	0.9 mg	6%

The color of grain amaranth plumes depends on the variety, but all produce copious amounts of seed in ideal weather.

Grind in a coffee grinder when dry, or toast first, then grind. Seeds are small, and this works only marginally well. To pop (toast), place 1 tablespoon of seed sprinkled lightly with water in a hot pan without any oil. Each popped or toasted grain is tiny but is delicious mixed with honey (*alegría* candy) or sprinkled on cereal. Toasting adds a nuttiness to the flavor. To sprout, moisten and sprout like alfalfa sprouts, washing out the container each day.

Amaranth seed makes an excellent replacement for poppy seeds. Add seeds or amaranth flour for extra protein to bread, cookies, crackers, pancakes, and tortillas (tostadas). Amaranth flour can be mixed with regular flour or used on its own. Depending on how fine you want the flour, use a coffee grinder (rough flour), a seed mill (finer), or an electric flour mill (very fine).

Although there are numerous varieties of grain amaranth, 'Burgundy' and 'Golden Giant' stand out. Both are white-seeded types, the ones most appreciated by cooks. 'Golden Giant' and 'Burgundy' produce lovely foliage and deep-gold and brilliant-purple plumes, respectively. *They are worth growing just for their beauty alone.* For food, the majority of gardeners grow vegetable amaranth. Again, there are numerous varieties. Start with the species *Amaranthus tricolor,* or 'Green Callaloo'. Note that 'Joseph's Coat' is used primarily for ornamental purposes.

Amaranth species probably originated in China, Greece, Mexico, the United States, and West Africa.

Arugula
Eruca vesicaria ssp. *sativa* and *Diplotaxis* species
Cabbage or Mustard Family (Brassicaceae, formerly Cruciferae)

Arugula (uh-ROO-guh-luh) is a hardy to very hardy, cool- to cold-season annual or biennial grown for its pungent leaves used fresh or cooked. Many gourmets consider this plant a delicacy. Others find it less so. Since taste does vary by variety, maturity, and growing conditions, it is a hard plant to judge without growing it on your own. Fortunately, it is easy to grow and matures quickly, so that taste testing is easy. Arugula is also known as arrugola, garden rocket, Italian cress, Mediterranean rocket, rocket, rocket salad, rocola, roquette, ruchetta, rucola, rughetta, rugola, rugula, and tira.

Arugula seed is very small, round, and tan to brown (roughly 15,000 seeds per ounce). Plants germinate quickly and form light- to dark-green leaves that are frilly, lobed, indented, or serrated, depending on the variety. Plants produce loose foliage or a rosette of leaves before going to seed. The flower stems are deep pink and bear small, cross-shaped, delicate flowers varying in color from white with red veins to yellow, formed in loose clusters. These in turn produce plump, elongated, pointed pods containing numerous seeds.

Arugula tastes best when it matures in cool weather. Plant it in spring and again late in the summer. The first planting can begin as soon as the soil can be worked in spring when soil temperature is at least 40°F. Plants are cold tolerant, so gamble by getting them in early. If a hard frost threatens, cover the planting area with a sheet or row cover. Make successive plantings 2 weeks apart to ensure a steady crop early in the season. Plant again in late summer to take advantage of cool fall temperatures. Some gardeners insist the fall planting results in better-tasting arugula.

There are several ways of harvesting arugula. No matter which method you choose, the leaves are best when immature. Older leaves often turn quite bitter. Leaves may be harvested individually. Snip them off when they are about 3 to 4 inches long. Start from the outside and work in. Leave the immature leaves in the center alone. Do this over a period of several weeks. You can also cut all the leaves back to ground level. New leaves often form to be harvested later as a "cut and come again" crop. Another option is to pull up young plants roots and all. This last method is best if you plan to store the plant for a couple of days. It also results in less bruising of individual leaves, but it only makes sense if you have done successive sowings.

The leaves, flower stems, flowers, and seeds are all edible. They are noted for their pungent, peppery taste. When you work with them, they often leave a smell on your hands. This is often referred to as a "skunky" scent, but it is not nearly that harsh. Do not wash the leaves until ready to use, but wash them well when you do, as soil may cling to them. The leaves are highly perishable. Try to use them as quickly as possible, storing them at most for a few days in the refrigerator.

Leaves are most commonly added to salads, but they can be blended to flavor dishes as you would herbs. Some nutrients are more available in raw arugula, while others may be more available when leaves are cooked lightly. Sauté them quickly in oil for maximum flavor and health benefits. They should be limp but still mildly crisp ("wilted"). Arugula loses some of its bitterness when cooked. When placing it on a pizza, always wait until the pizza is almost done before placing leaves on it. The same can be said for adding the whole or chopped up leaves to any cooked dish, including pastas. Try using arugula as a spinach substitute in a creamed soup, which is delicious hot or cold.

Arugula flowers are delicate and quite pretty. Add them to salads, or sprinkle them into stir-fries at the last minute. Or chop finely, and add to soft cheese.

Arugula Nutrition Facts

Serving size: 100 grams (3.5 ounces)

	AMOUNT PER RAW SERVING	% DV
Calcium	160 mg	16%
Calories	25	1%
Dietary fiber	1.6 g	6%
Folate	97 mcg	24%
Iron	1.5 mg	8%
Magnesium	47 mg	12%
Manganese	0.3 mg	16%
Potassium	370 mg	11%
Protein	2.5 g	5%
Vitamin A	2,373 IU	47%
Vitamin C	15 mg	25%
Vitamin K	109 mcg	136%

Plant short rows of arugula a few weeks apart; these leaves taste best young.

Note that arugula seeds make poor sprouts, because they turn slimy (mucilaginous), but once growing, they make excellent microgreens.

There are numerous varieties of arugula with varied genetic backgrounds based on species. Start with a generic

Broccoli Raab or Rabe Nutrition Facts

Serving size: 100 grams (3.5 ounces)

	AMOUNT PER COOKED SERVING	% DV
Calcium	118 mg	12%
Calories	33	2%
Carbohydrates	3 g	1%
Dietary fiber	3 g	11%
Folate	71 mcg	18%
Iron	1.3 mg	7%
Magnesium	27 mg	7%
Manganese	0.4 mg	19%
Niacin	2 mg	10%
Phosphorus	82 mg	8%
Potassium	345 mg	10%
Protein	3–4 g	8%
Riboflavin	0.1 mg	8%
Thiamin	0.2 mg	11%
Vitamin A	4,535 IU	91%
Vitamin B6	0.2 mg	11%
Vitamin C	37 mg	62%
Vitamin E	2.5 mg	13%
Vitamin K	256 mcg	320%

The young leaves and budding flower tips of broccoli raab are popular with gourmet cooks.

arugula seed packet, and compare it to named varieties, such as 'Olive Leaf Arugula' *(Diplotaxis tenuifolia f. integrifolia)* and 'Runway' *(Eruca sativa).* To mimic wasabi paste (Japanese horseradish), try arugula 'Wasabi' *(Diplotaxis erucoides).*

Arugula probably originated in southern Europe, most likely in the Mediterranean area.

Broccoli Raab or Rabe
Brassica species
Cabbage or Mustard Family (Brassicaceae, formerly Cruciferae)

Broccoli raab is a hardy, cool-season annual or biennial grown as an annual. Although broccoli raab is edible raw, it is most often cooked. There are three types of broccoli raab, depending on their intended use. Some are grown for their bud clusters including leaves and stems just below; others, primarily for their stems; and still others, for their leaves. The latter would be better named "leaf broccolis." Leaves can either be smooth *(liscia)* or curly *(riccia).* Broccoli raab is also known as broccoletti, cima di rapa, friarielli, grelos, Italian mustard or turnip, raab or rabe (pronounced rob), rapa, rapine or rapini, rappone, ruvo kale, salit raab, sprarachetti, spring broccoli, taitcat, and turnip broccoli. The taste is most commonly described as tangy, peppery, or biting, which some translate into bitter. The leaves and buds are very rich in nutrients. Rapini (cima di rapa) is technically not broccoli raab, but it is often sold that way. The flavor is so close that the average person doesn't care. The genetic background of plants sold as broccoli raab is convoluted. Focus on growing the plants and enjoying them as the nutritious greens they are.

Broccoli raab grows from tiny, round, dark-brown to red-black seed (7,500 to 10,500 seeds per ounce) into a plant with many broad, smooth to frilly leaves. Stems shoot up as plants mature. These produce clusters of buds, which open into brilliant-yellow flowers if allowed to. These then form pods, which contain seeds that could be planted for next year's crop. The choice of varieties is staggering. Any source specializing in Italian seeds will describe these well.

When and how you harvest these plants depends on the type you are growing. For budding types, cut off the top 4 inches or so just as buds begin to form and before flowering. Side shoots may appear with additional buds. Cook these until tender, although Italians often cook them much longer. For stem types, harvest when stems are still tender. Although these are delicious when young, they can become woody and bitter with age. Steam them like asparagus. And for leaf types, snip off leaves as desired. Consider blanching the leaves lightly and discarding the water to get rid of any bitter taste. Then sauté them in olive oil with garlic or onion and flakes of red pepper. To disguise the flavor of broccoli raab, many cooks smother these greens in grated cheese or hollandaise sauce.

Grow 'Sessantina' or 'Sorrento' for large bud clusters, 'Rapini' for stems, and 'Spigariello Liscia' for leaves. Because of its small size, 'Quarantina' makes a particularly good container plant and produces small bud clusters. Another factor in choosing varieties is matching them to the season when they grow best. Try 'Sessantina' in spring and 'Early Fall Rapini' (small bud clusters) for a late-season planting.

Broccoli raab may have originated in China or in the Mediterranean area.

Cat Grass (Catgrass)
Avena sativa
Grass family (Poaceae, formerly Gramineae)

No one knows why cats like cat grass. It may taste good or possibly provide nutrients, but it does not offer the high of catnip, described in "Herbs." It often induces vomiting, which brings up hair balls. Many grains can be grown and labeled cat grass, but the most common is oats. Oats are large, long, thin, light-tan seeds slightly indented on one side (about 950 seeds per ounce). They grow rapidly. Plant seeds in a pot right next to each other just under the soil surface. Keep moist, and expect quick germination. The seed forms a thick mat of grass for cats to eat. Place it next to the water or food bowl, and let cats eat it for just a few minutes. Do this every day. Replant as necessary.

Chinese Broccoli
(Broccolini, Brokali)
Brassica oleracea var. *alboglabra*
Cabbage or Mustard Family (Brassicaceae, formerly Cruciferae)

Chinese broccoli is a hardy, cool-season annual that does surprisingly well in warmer weather. The plant is grown for its tender tips and flower buds, which are a bit stronger and more bitter than broccoli. Plants are easy to grow but are not well known to gardeners. The plant is also known as Chinese kale, gai lan (gai lohn or gai lon), kailaan (kai-lan or kalan), and white-flowering broccoli or kale. It is not a broccoli or a kale, although a number of varieties are Chinese broccoli-kale hybrids.

Chinese broccoli grows from small, round, deep-brown seeds (11,500 per ounce) into a plant roughly 8 to 12 inches tall. The plant is not nearly as vigorous as regular broccoli

Cat grass, which seems to mysteriously appeal to cats, is easy to grow in small containers.

and produces blue-green leaves reminiscent of tender collard greens. Small flower buds appear at the tip of the stems as the plant matures. They are like a miniaturized version of broccoli. If the buds are allowed to flower, they are usually white in the shape of a small cross. Developing fruits (siliques) are long and narrow.

If rabbits are a problem, grow Chinese broccoli in a container. The plants are prone to slug and insect damage and benefit from being protected with a row cover.

Harvest when flower buds begin to form. Cut off the top 4 to 6 inches. The stalks, leaves, and buds are all edible. They are best cooked fresh from the garden. Peeling stalks is optional. Cooking methods include quick boiling, braising, sautéing, steaming, and stir-frying. Sauté in olive or sesame oil. Steam, then flavor with oyster or soy sauce. Stir-fry with garlic, ginger, sugar, or a mixture of these in rice wine. The secret is to preserve taste and nutrition by cooking quickly until the vegetable just begins to turn limp. If stems are thick, slice them in two to help them cook quickly. Any part of the plant can be battered and deep-fried for tempura or added to soups or soup-like dishes, including sukiyaki. Add at the last minute for optimal flavor. Both leaves and

Chinese Broccoli (Broccolini, Brokali) Nutrition Facts

Serving size: 100 grams (3.5 ounces)

	AMOUNT PER COOKED SERVING	% DV
Calcium	100 mg	10%
Calories	22	1%
Carbohydrates	4 g	1%
Dietary fiber	3 g	10%
Folate	99 mcg	25%
Manganese	0.3 mg	13%
Potassium	260 mg	7%
Protein	1 g	2%
Riboflavin	0.1 mg	9%
Vitamin A	1,640 IU	33%
Vitamin C	28 mg	47%
Vitamin K	85 mg	106%

Chinese broccoli is grown for its tender young leaves and stems tipped with flower buds.

stems can be a bit stringy if stressed during the season or overly mature.

Numerous varieties of Chinese broccoli are available from catalogs specializing in Asian vegetables, but 'Blue Star' and 'Green Lance' are two of the most popular varieties. Broccolini® *(Brassica oleracea italica × alboglabra)* is a hybrid between broccoli and Chinese broccoli. It has loose florets similar to broccoli and slender stalks similar to Chinese broccoli. It tastes much like broccoli. In Great Britain it is commonly referred to as "tender stem broccoli." Brokali *(Brassica oleracea)* is a cross between Calabrese broccoli and Chinese broccoli. Plants may produce side shoots as well as heads at the tip of the main stem. 'Apollo Hybrid' is a variety usually sold as a type of broccoli, which it is not.

Chinese broccoli may have originated in the Mediterranean area or Southeast Asia, possibly in China.

Chinese Cabbage
Brassica rapa species
Cabbage or Mustard Family
(Brassicaceae, formerly Cruciferae)

Chinese cabbage is a hardy to very hardy, cool- to cold-season biennial grown as an annual in cold climates. Plants take up a relatively small amount of space. Chinese cabbage can be easy or difficult to grow depending on the variety. Chinese cabbage grows rapidly from tiny, round, blackish-purple seed (about 7,000 to 11,000 seeds per ounce) into many different forms.

Chinese cabbages are known by so many different names that it seems difficult to get them straight. The *barrel-head* type refers to upright and compact heads with outer green leaves covering a white to yellowish interior. In the United States this type is most commonly called Napa or Nappa cabbage. It also goes by the names celery cabbage and Wong Bok. These can be challenging to grow in cold climates where summers get hot and days long. Start them as early as possible or late to have them mature in cool weather. I have grown 'Bilko Hybrid', and it was a lovely plant that didn't bolt.

The *cylindrical-head* type grows upright like the barrel type, but its leaves are softer and looser. The center gets blanched by the outer leaves, as with the barrel-head type. It is commonly referred to as Michihili cabbage, that name coming from one popular variety in this group. In cold climates it is most commonly planted to mature in the fall. For a spring planting, try 'Taiwan Express Hybrid'.

Flowering Chinese cabbage, closely related to bok choy, is divided into two groups: *green choy sum* (also known as edible rape and yu choy) and *white choy sum* (also known as bok choy sum). Green choy sum has green stalks and leaves that vary in color and shape by variety. Some varieties are chosen for tasty yellow flower buds as well. They are similar to mustard greens but less bitter. Try 'Spring Express Hybrid', which matures rapidly with smooth, deep-green leaves and green stems. White Choy Sum is grown for its delicious thick white stems, green leaves, and flower buds. Once the plant flowers, the stems become bitter. *Choy sum* refers to the combination of stems, leaves, and buds in Chinese. Unlike some other Chinese cabbages, these varieties are not frost hardy. These plants may be listed in catalogs as flowering pak choy, flowering rape, or flowering white cabbage. Consider 'Long White Stalk'.

Fluffy top describes one unique variety, 'Kaisan Hakusai'. It can be eaten fresh or cooked like other Chinese cabbages. *Loose leaf* (small) is a catchall for plants that are not tall and whose leaves do not form a tight head. These grow quickly and are ready to be harvested in less than a month. They are reasonably heat tolerant. Both the light-green leaves and leaf stalks are tender, typically used in stir-fries. Begin with 'Fong San Improved'. *Loose leaf–head* cabbages are similar but tend to have more densely packed leaves. 'Yukina Savoy' forms a rosette of leathery, crumpled, dark-green leaves with a pale green stalk.

Pak choy or *bok choy* falls into two groups. The first is regularly sized plants; the second, miniature or "baby" types. This plant has thick, succulent leaf stems or stalks (petioles) and dark, spoon-shaped leaves. The stems do vary in color and thickness, but most are white or pale green and crunchy like celery. The smooth or ribbed foliage is reminiscent of dark-green mustard leaves. The plants are upright with stems varying from open to fairly tight. This plant form is often described as an upright rosette. In some ways they look like thick-stemmed Swiss chard. Pak choy is fairly easy to grow and matures fast enough to be a good choice for cold-climate gardeners. It may be listed in catalogs as Chinese celery cabbage or mustard, Chinese chard, Chinese mustard or white cabbage, Japanese white celery mustard, non-heading celery cabbage, mustard cabbage, spoon cabbage or mustard, or white celery mustard. 'Joi Choi Hybrid' lasted all season for me. The baby pak choy varieties are ideal for container planting. They range from 6 to 8 inches and are eaten young, often snipped off as a whole plant and steamed that way. A good choice is 'Mei Qing Choi Hybrid'. Rosette pak choi includes varieties with unique colors, delicate leaves, and an interesting peppery taste. Rosette pak choi may be called flat cabbage, flat black cabbage, or spoon cabbage. 'Tatsoi' is commonly recommended and a nice cabbage, but it tends to bolt quickly if spring turns into summer overnight. Consider planting it later in the season to develop in fall. It's still a gamble. I have both won and lost with this variety.

All types can be used in the kitchen in a variety of ways. Leaves are edible raw, but their taste varies by type and variety. Some are similar to mustard greens. They can be used as wraps to replace bread, or shredded and added to salads, or made into coleslaw. Leaves, stems, buds, and flowers

Chinese Cabbage Nutrition Facts

Serving size: 100 grams (3.5 ounces)

	AMOUNT PER RAW SERVING	% DV	AMOUNT PER COOKED SERVING	% DV
Calcium	105 mg	10%	95 mg	10%
Calories	13	1%	12	1%
Carbohydrates	2 g	1%	2 g	1%
Dietary fiber	1 g	4%	1 g	4%
Folate	65 mcg	15%	40 mcg	10%
Manganese	0.2 mg	8%	0.1 mg	7%
Potassium	250 mg	7%	370 mg	10%
Protein	1.5 g	3%	2 g	3%
Vitamin A	4,470 IU	90%	4,250 IU	85%
Vitamin B6	0.2 mg	10%	0.2 mg	8%
Vitamin K	45 mcg	55%	35 mcg	40%

'Joi Choi' pak choi and 'Bilko' barrel-head hybrids are easy to grow.

Plant 'Tatsoi' to develop in fall, when it forms a deep-green rosette of leaves.

Chinese Mustard (Gai Choi)
Brassica juncea
Cabbage or Mustard Family
(Brassicaceae, formerly Cruciferae)

Chinese mustard is a cool-season annual. It grows from tiny, reddish-brown seeds (10,000 to 15,000 seeds per ounce) and, depending on the variety, forms leaves or semiheading plants with a spicy flavor that increases as the plant matures. Leaves form quickly and may bolt with bright-yellow, four-petaled flowers. The plant is vulnerable to insects and may need to be protected with row covers if planted early in the season when flea beetles and slugs are active. Plant it in spring or fall when the weather will be cool as it matures.

The most popular variety is 'Gai Choi', which has become synonymous with Chinese mustard. The leaves are most commonly braised, pickled, or added to soups in Asian cooking. It can also be mixed with horseradish to mimic wasabi, served in Japanese restaurants as a condiment.

Chinese mustard probably originated in Central Asia, possibly from India.

Chrysanthemum
(Edible Chrysanthemum)
Glebionis coronarium or *coronaria,* also known as *Chrysanthemum spatiosum* or *Xanthophthalmum coronarium,* formerly *Chrysanthemum coronarium* and *Leucanthemum coronarium*
Aster, Daisy, or Sunflower Family
(Asteraceae, formerly Compositae)

Chrysanthemum is a hardy, cool-season annual. It grows from a small, thin, pointed to curved, tannish deep-brown seed (about 14,500 seeds per ounce) into a plant with lacy green leaves and yellow to orangish flowers. It makes a good container or garden plant. It grows best in cool conditions and will even tolerate light frost in fall. So get seeds into the ground in early spring or late summer to mature in fall. Successive plantings are recommended. Barely cover the seed.

The leaves have an acquired taste, which is pungent or even bitter. If you crush the leaves, the taste is similar to their scent. The leaves are best harvested young when only a few inches tall, or pinched off the tips of plants less than 12 inches tall. Many gardeners cut plants back regularly to stop them from flowering and to get a "cut and come again" crop of tender young leaves. The leaves are edible raw or cooked. The young leaves are often separated from the stems and added sparingly to salads, either raw or briefly blanched. If using stems, cook them lightly since overcooking makes them especially bitter. The young leaves can be

are edible on all types. They can be boiled, microwaved, sautéed, steamed, or stir-fried. They are delicious added to soups. The stems, as those of Swiss chard, are considered a delicacy by many. Some cooks trim off the green leaf edges and eat the stems alone, either as a single dish or mixed with other vegetables, as in stir-fries. Many recipes use ginger or soy sauce as a spice with roasted sesame seeds as a final touch, but many leaves are delicious simply covered in melted butter. Do *not* eat Chinese cabbage seeds, reputed to be poisonous.

Plant seed directly in the garden as early in spring as possible. Unlike "regular" cabbage, it thoroughly resents transplanting. Still, it's worth trying. Otherwise, read the section on cabbage for general information on care and dealing with potential problems. Note that Chinese cabbage does not store well fresh. Seed densely enough to eat smaller plants throughout the growing season, and let the remaining plants last well into late fall, even after a hard frost, for most types. Freeze finely shredded leaves, and either pickle or dry some for long-term storage.

Chinese cabbage originated primarily in China, but some species may have come from Korea as well.

Chinese Mustard (Gai Choi) Nutrition Facts

Serving size: 100 grams (3.5 ounces)

	AMOUNT PER RAW SERVING	% DV	AMOUNT PER COOKED SERVING	% DV
Calcium	105	10%	75 mg	7%
Calories	25	1%	15	1%
Carbohydrates	5 g	2%	2 g	1%
Dietary fiber	3 g	13%	2 g	8%
Folate	185 mcg	45%	75 mcg	18%
Iron	1.5 mg	8%	0.7 mg	4%
Magnesium	32 mg	8%	15 mg	4%
Manganese	0.5 mg	24%	0.3 mg	14%
Potassium	355 mg	10%	200 mg	6%
Protein	3 g	5%	2 g	5%
Vitamin B6	0.2 mg	9%	0.1	5%
Vitamin C	70 mg	115%	25 mg	45%
Vitamin E	2 mg	10%	1.2 mg	6%
Vitamin K	500 mcg	625%	300	375%

The young leaves of Chinese mustard are popular with insects as well as cooks, so protect them with row covers.

cooked lightly like spinach, used to flavor bottled vinegar, or chopped and added to soups. They are used as main ingredients of chop suey, shabu-shabu, stir-fries, and sukiyaki, and in tempura.

The flowers look like little, yellow to orange daisies and are edible. They are sometimes added fresh to soups or boiled either fresh or dried for teas—preferably fresh. For other dishes, cut off the flower base, and use the petals only. Blanch lightly, and toss into salads. Fry petals briefly in oil before adding to salads, soups, or stir-fries. Always cook quickly for the best flavor and most nutrition.

Plants are called chop suey or chrysanthemum greens, crown daisy in Great Britain, garland chrysanthemum or daisy, shungiku in Japanese, and tong hao in Chinese. In Greece they are known as mandilida, which is actually a varietal name. Varieties vary some in pungency and leaf color but are similar. Ones on the market include 'Broad Leaf', 'Koni Shungiku Salada', 'Garland Round Leaf', 'Garland Serrated', and 'Tiger Eye'.

Note that the leaves irritate the hands of some people and may cause indigestion in others. *Do not eat flowers of* Tanacetum cinerariifolium (Chrysanthemum cinerariae-folium) *or* Tanacetum coccineum (Chrysanthemum coccineum), *used in making the insecticide pyrethrum.*

The plant probably originated in the Mediterranean or East Asia.

Edible chrysanthemums grow quite large, but the leaves are best eaten when the plant is young.

Chrysanthemum (Edible Chrysanthemum) Nutrition Facts

Serving size: 100 grams (3.5 ounces)

	AMOUNT PER RAW SERVING	% DV	AMOUNT PER COOKED SERVING	% DV
Calcium	115 mg	10%	70 mg	7%
Calories	24	1%	24	1%
Carbohydrates	3 g	1%	4 g	1%
Dietary fiber	3 g	12%	2 g	9%
Folate	180 mcg	45%	50 mcg	12%
Iron	2.3 mg	13%	3.75 mg	20%
Magnesium	30 mg	8%	18 mg	5%
Manganese	0.1 mg	45%	0.35 mg	18%
Potassium	565 mg	15%	565 mg	15%
Protein	3.5 g	7%	2 g	3%
Thiamin	0.1 mg	9%	0.02	1%
Vitamin A	1,870 IU	35%	2,575 IU	50%
Vitamin B6	0.2 mg	9%	0.2 mg	9%
Vitamin C	1.4 mg	2%	24 mg	40%
Vitamin K	350 mcg	440%	145 mcg	180%

Cilantro (Coriander)
Coriandrum sativum
Carrot or Parsley Family
(Apiaceae, formerly Umbelliferae)

Cilantro is a cool-season annual. In the United States *cilantro* is the name given to the leaves of the plant, while the seeds are referred to as coriander. This pungent and highly nutritious plant is a favorite ingredient in various cuisines. It is easy to grow and often lasts well into early fall. It is sometimes listed as Chinese, Indian, or Mexican parsley. The seed is round, hard, small (about 2,500 seeds per ounce), indented, and tan. The plant forms feathery, ferny leaves that look like flat-leaf parsley. Plants will shoot up flower stalks once mature. These form small, umbrella-like clusters of tiny, white to pale cream to pinkish-white flowers. As the plant continues to mature, it forms tight groups of small, round, green balls with miniscule spikes sticking out from one end. These are the fruit of the plant, which dry to a dark brown, and will produce two seeds each. Plants self-seed freely if seed is not harvested and you plant it early enough. Make successive plantings a few weeks apart to ensure a steady supply of leaves. If you want seeds, plant early, and let plants bolt. In cold climates getting seed can be difficult.

All parts of this plant are edible including the root, stems and leaves, flowers, seedpods, and seeds. The different parts of the plant have different tastes. The stems are more pungent than the leaves, the flowers have a delicate flavor, the immature seedpods (fruits) are milder than the stems and leaves, while the powdered dried seeds have a lemony taste. The roots are popular in Thai cuisine. The foliage is used in many cuisines. It is generally used fresh since it dries poorly and loses much of its fresh flavor when cooked. Try it in Asian chutneys, salads, and salsas (sauces); added as sprigs to soups and stews at the last minute; mixed into dishes such as guacamole; or even made into pesto as a basil replacement. Cilantro pesto freezes well, although the leaves by themselves do not.

The delicate flowers may be added to fruit salads, mixed into cream cheese, or sprinkled on desserts for color and flavoring. The immature pods are eaten by some as a side dish or used to flavor drinks. The seeds, either crushed, ground, or whole, are popular in a wide variety of cuisines. Seeds can be ground in a mill like pepper. Crushed seeds may be added to beans, cakes, cookies, ice cream, and stews. Some cooks roast them before grinding to enhance the flavor. Ground coriander is an essential ingredient in curry powders and can be used by itself to flavor meats, especially sausage. Whole seeds are generally soaked for several hours before use in a wide variety of dishes and are sometimes added to breads.

Although there are many named varieties, consider buying the generic seed or 'Calypso Hybrid', which is slow to bolt. Or try 'Delfino' (AAS-2006), which has lacy, dill-like foliage rather than the typical flat-leaf parsley look.

Cilantro may have originated in southwestern Asia, southern Europe, or North Africa.

Mexican cilantro, *(Eryngium foetidum)*, is a short-lived, tender, *warm*-season biennial grown as an annual in cold climates. Note that while in the same family as cilantro, Mexican cilantro is a different plant. I have included information on this plant to differentiate it from the cilantro that truly is suited to cold climates. Popular in varied cuisines, it goes by a wide variety of names, including culantro, fitweed, long coriander, ngo gai, recao, sawleaf or saw-tooth herb, spiny coriander, Tabasco parsley, and thorny coriander. The seed needs a high temperature to germinate (at least 75°F) and may be started indoors 6 to 8 weeks before planting out in warm weather in partial shade. It demands heat and consistent watering. Consider growing it as a house plant. Long, fairly broad, serrated leaves grow out from the base of the plant, forming a rosette.

Mexican cilantro has a similar, but stronger, flavor than cilantro. Its leaves can be dried and still retain their flavor. Leaves should be harvested before the plant bolts and shoots up stems with spiny, thimble-shaped flowers. Cut these off

Cilantro (Coriander) Nutrition Facts

Serving size: 100 grams (3.5 ounces)

	AMOUNT PER RAW SERVING	% DV
Calcium	65 mg	7%
Calories	23	1%
Carbohydrates	4 g	1%
Copper	0.2 mg	10%
Dietary fiber	3 g	11%
Folate	60 mg	15%
Iron	1.8 mg	10%
Manganese	0.4 mg	20%
Niacin	1.1 mg	6%
Potassium	520 mg	15%
Protein	2 g	4%
Riboflavin	0.2 mg	10%
Vitamin A	6,750 IU	135%
Vitamin C	27 mg	45%
Vitamin E	2.5 mg	13%
Vitamin K	310 mg	390%

Many people love the taste of cilantro, but 10 percent of people hate it, which could be a genetic taste preference.

Plant cilantro early in the season to give plants enough time to form seeds, known as coriander.

Mexican cilantro produces more foliage when flower stems (shown here) are removed immediately.

Collards
Nutrition Facts

Serving size: 100 grams (3.5 ounces)

	AMOUNT PER RAW SERVING	% DV	AMOUNT PER COOKED SERVING	% DV
Calcium	145 mg	15%	145 mg	15%
Calories	30	2%	25	1%
Carbohydrates	6 g	2%	5 g	2%
Dietary fiber	4 g	15%	3 g	10%
Folate	165 mcg	40%	95 mcg	25%
Manganese	0.3 mg	15%	0.4 mg	20%
Protein	2 g	5%	2 g	5%
Riboflavin	0.1 mg	8%	0.05 mg	6%
Vitamin A	6,670 IU	135%	8,115 IU	160%
Vitamin B6	0.2 mg	8%	0.1 mg	6%
Vitamin C	35 mg	60%	18 mg	30%
Vitamin E	2.5 mg	10%	0.1 mg	4%
Vitamin K	510 mcg	640%	440 mcg	550%

Collards are popular in the South. Cold-climate gardeners may want to give these greens a try.

at the base as soon as they begin to appear. The leaves and roots are commonly used in sauces, soups, and stews. It can be combined with a wide variety of herbs and vegetables and sautéed or braised. Leaves can be blended in a food processor with olive oil and frozen. Recaíto and sofrito, two popular sauces containing Mexican cilantro, are used in making a number of dishes in Puerto Rico.

The plant probably originated in Central America, Mexico, or South America.

Collards
Brassica oleracea var. *acephala*
or Acephala Group
Cabbage or Mustard Family
(Brassicaceae, formerly Cruciferae)

Collards, sometimes referred to as collard greens, are hardy to very hardy, cool- to cold-season biennials typically grown as annuals. Collards are a cabbage substitute, most popular in the South where cabbage is difficult to grow. Collards are sometimes referred to as non-heading cabbage or tree-cabbage. Collards grow well in cold climates and are becoming increasingly popular. Although collards like it cool, they tolerate hot weather and rarely bolt. Their tolerance for varied temperatures make them an ideal multiseason crop.

Collards grow from a round, hard, purplish-brown seed (about 8,500 to 9,000 seeds per ounce) into plants that resemble young cabbage seedlings. Instead of forming a head, like cabbage, collards create either a lovely rosette or a more open stalk with firm, fleshy leaves. The leaves are the main edible part of the plant. The finger-length leaves may be used in salads. They are sweeter if grown at the end of the season and hit by a frost or kept in the refrigerator for a few days but no longer. Cook collards by boiling, braising, microwaving, steaming, or stir-frying. Cook briefly, or they may emit a sulfurous smell. Remove the ribs from older leaves. Chop or shred the leaves and cook as quickly as possible. Collards are often cooked with bacon for added flavor, or braised with olive oil and garlic. Make *caldo verde,* a Portuguese "green soup," using collards instead of kale. If you boil greens, many of the nutrients end up in the water, which can be reserved for soups. The cooking water is called pot likker in the South and was originally eaten with unleavened corn bread (corn pone). It is now eaten with corn bread.

Eat the flower stems in the bud stage before flowers open. These taste much like broccolini®, a cross between broccoli and Chinese broccoli (kai-lan). This is only possible if plants overwinter or bolt. Collards are hardy, withstanding frosts at the end of the season. Covering them with a 12-inch-thick layer of straw may get them through the winter. If it does, harvest the flower stalks as they appear.

Collards can be frozen. Younger leaves are much better than older. Wash, remove stems from older leaves, cut into strips, place in a sieve, plunge into boiling water for 30 seconds to 1½ minutes depending on the thickness of leaves, lift up, drain, place into ice water for 2 minutes, then into airtight freezer bags, and freeze. Note that greens do lose vitamins when blanched. Some people prefer cooking them in a microwave instead of plunging them into boiling water. Chop moist leaves, and place a in microwave-safe dish. Cook just until tender, and proceed as if they were blanched.

The naming of varieties can be confusing. Catalogs may list almost identical plants under different names, and they may have slight differences. Commonly recommended for cold climates are 'Vates', a compact plant with smooth leaves, and the taller 'Georgia', which has mildly crinkly leaves.

Collards are high in vitamin K. If you are on a blood thinner such as warfarin (Coumadin), talk to your doctor.

Collards likely originated in the eastern Mediterranean or Asia Minor, possibly Turkey, and from western Europe along the Atlantic Coast.

Corn Salad (Mâche)
Valerianella locusta var. *olitaria*
Valerian Family (Valerianaceae)

Corn salad is a hardy to very hardy, cool- to cold-season annual. It has been a favorite in France for years. Eat it either raw or cooked like spinach. Other common names are doucette, feldsalat, fetticus, field lettuce or salad, lamb's lettuce, lamb's tongue, loblollie, mâche, nut lettuce, and rapunzel. Do not confuse it with lamb's quarters (*Chenopodium album*). Its tan seed is small, indented, and irregularly rounded (about 21,000 to 30,000 seeds per ounce). The plant forms a low mound or rosette of rounded to elongated leaves. It is slow growing and relatively short-lived. It has a dense, shallow root system and if allowed to mature, looks a bit like 'Deer Tongue' leaf lettuce. It will form clusters of silvery blue to white flowers if not deadheaded. The plant can become invasive if flowers are allowed to go to seed.

As soon as the leaves are large enough to eat, begin harvesting. You can cut the entire plant off just above the soil line, but many backyard gardeners prefer cutting just the outer leaves when no larger than a few inches as needed, letting the inner ones mature for a later harvest. Use a pair of scissors to snip off the leaves. The plant resents harvesting. However, if you let it get too large or go to flower, the taste becomes poor. The flowers are edible. Consider successive planting in spring and a late planting since corn salad can withstand frost and even light freezes. Said to be hardy to 5°F and even colder if covered with a thick layer of mulch, it is a good late-season substitute for lettuce. It is not so good in the heat of summer and may bolt if temperatures reach 80°F.

The taste of corn salad is mild and often described as "nutty," but the taste changes some from raw to cooked. The texture tends to be more tender or succulent than crisp.

Corn Salad (Mâche) Nutrition Facts

Serving size: 100 grams (3.5 ounces)

	AMOUNT PER RAW SERVING	% DV
Calories	20	1%
Carbohydrates	4 g	1%
Iron	2.2 mg	12%
Manganese	0.4 mg	18%
Potassium	460 mg	13%
Protein	2 g	4%
Vitamin A	7,100 IU	140%
Vitamin B6	0.2 mg	14%
Vitamin C	38 mg	65%

Corn salad, which goes by many names, has become a popular green in upscale restaurants.

Buttery is a good description. Raw, it makes an excellent salad by itself with a little olive oil and lemon or a vinaigrette. Toppings often include cheese or nuts, such as sliced and toasted almonds or walnuts.

Dutch and English varieties have larger and more elongated leaves, while the French form a rosette of smaller leaves. Varieties are further divided into what are called large- and small-seeded varieties. The large-seeded types tend to stand up to heat better and should be planted when the soil temperature is around 65°F, while the small-seeded are more cold resistant and can be planted when the soil temperature reaches 50°F. Both are notorious for poor germination, so try to match the seed type to the soil temperature. Some gardeners insist the small have a better flavor. Some good large-seeded types are 'A Grosse Graine', 'd'Olanda', 'Valgros', and 'Vit'. For small-seeded types, try 'Coquille de Louviers', 'Verte à Coeur Plein', 'Verte de Cambrai', and 'Verte d'Etampes'.

Corn salad probably originated in Europe.

Dandelion
Taraxacum officinale
Aster, Daisy, or Sunflower Family
(Asteraceae, formerly Compositae)

This hardy, cold-season perennial is despised by many and adored by others. It amazes many gardeners that anyone would purposefully grow dandelions, no more than a common weed. In fact, the French consider young dandelions a delicacy. Turn over a new leaf by trying some of the cultivated varieties. The plant grows from an ultratiny, thin, tan, mildly curved seed (35,000 seeds per ounce) into pale, tender, light-green leaves the first year and a rosette of in-

Dandelions grown from seed produce delicate leaves eaten as greens in salads or side dishes.

dented or toothed leaves in the second. Press into soil in early spring so that the seed "senses" light. In the second year, buds emerge in the center and produce stems that grow rapidly into deep-yellow flowers. These mature quickly into lacy tops with small seeds embedded on the bottom of the fluffy "down." The latter is scattered by winds to germinate in new places. The root is long and deep, making it a nightmare to dig out of lawns.

To grow dandelions, collect or buy seed. Press it into finely worked soil as soon as possible in spring. Keep it moist until germination, which generally occurs within 14 days. Keep consistently moist until growing well, and then thin, eating the thinnings. Either eat the plants, or let them grow for a full season, removing all blossoms in the second year. To reduce bitterness, cover the more mature dandelions with an overturned pot in late fall. In spring lift the pot, harvesting the leaves when they have grown to a suitable size. They will be blanched to a whitish yellow but less nutrient rich.

All parts of the dandelion are edible but should be picked from areas where no pesticides have been used. The leaves are edible raw or cooked. Pick them in the first year, or just before buds begin to form, no later, in the second year. The older growth is admittedly bitter. Remove the leaves from the stems, and tear them into small pieces. Just a small amount adds bite to fresh salads. Cooking reduces bitterness but also results in a loss of nutrients. Most common cooking methods include boiling, frying, sautéing, and steaming the greens. Chopped leaves or new buds are delicious in quiche.

The flowers are edible raw and worth a try—at least once. Pick them just as they open. Consider sprinkling petals over cooked rice. Or dip whole flowers or buds in batter to be fried like tempura. The flower petals with stems removed can be made into dandelion wine. The peeled roots can be boiled in salted water and eaten like other root crops or sliced thinly and added to stir-fries.

Dried and ground roots are used as a coffee substitute. Let plants get really large to form long, thick roots. Remove flower buds immediately if any begin to form. The larger the plant, the bigger the root. Grow these for more than a year if necessary, never allowing to go to flower. Wash the roots, and let them dry out for a couple days, unless you are in a hurry. Slice them into thin slivers, place them on a cookie sheet in an oven at 220°F for about an hour until they become brittle. Let them cool down before grinding into small pieces. Place these back on the sheet in an oven at 320° to 350°F. Cook for 20 to 30 minutes, but watch them carefully. They are ready when they turn dark brown and begin to smoke a bit. Place several tablespoons into 2 cups of boiling water. Let them boil until the liquid turns a deep brown. The intensity of the taste increases with the length of

Dandelion Nutrition Facts

Serving size: 100 grams (3.5 ounces)

	AMOUNT PER RAW SERVING	% DV	AMOUNT PER COOKED SERVING	% DV
Calcium	185 mg	20%	14 mg	14%
Calories	45	2%	33	2%
Carbohydrates	9 g	3%	6 g	2%
Copper	0.2 mg	10%	0.1 mg	6%
Dietary fiber	4 g	14%	3 g	12%
Iron	3 mg	17%	1.8 mg	10%
Magnesium	35 mg	9%	24 mg	6%
Manganese	0.3 mg	17%	0.2 mg	10%
Phosphorus	65 mg	7%	42 mg	4%
Potassium	400 mg	10%	230 mg	7%
Protein	3 g	5%	2 g	4%
Riboflavin	0.3 mg	15%	0.2 mg	10%
Thiamin	0.2 mg	13%	0.1 mg	9%
Vitamin A	10,200 IU	205%	14,545 IU	290%
Vitamin B6	0.3 mg	13%	0.2 mg	8%
Vitamin C	35 mg	60%	18 mg	30%
Vitamin E	3.5 mg	15%	0.6 mg	2%
Vitamin K	780 mcg	975%	360 mcg	450%

Allowed to overwinter, dandelions produce numerous flowers and large, elongated roots, which can be used to make "coffee."

boiling. The amount of grounds needed varies by individual taste. Pour the liquid through a sieve. I like mixing the brew with vanilla almond milk. The taste is reminiscent of coffee but distinct. You can do this with the other roots mentioned as coffee substitutes in this guide.

Dandelions may have originated in Europe. Do not confuse dandelions with Italian dandelions, which are a type of chicory.

Endive
Cichorium endivia var. *crispum*

Escarole
Cichorium endivia var. *latifolia*
Aster, Daisy, or Sunflower Family (Asteraceae, formerly Compositae)

Endive and escarole are two closely related endives. They are hardy to very hardy, cool- to cold-season biennials grown most commonly as annuals. Endive, a succulent green crop, adds a special flavor all its own to a salad. Escarole, also an endive, tends to be more upright with broader leaves and an overall form somewhat similar to butterhead lettuce. Both have outer green leaves with a distinct, somewhat bitter taste, and inner, creamy-white leaves with a buttery texture and more delicate flavor. The foliage of both types is edible raw or cooked. Endives are not as easy to grow as lettuce, but they do well in warm periods when lettuce often goes to seed.

The seed of endives is tiny (about 17,000 to 20,000 seeds per ounce) and when magnified, looks like a tan tooth. Depending on the variety, it matures into plants with frizzy, deeply serrated edges or broader leaves with less prominent indentations. The outer leaves tend to be much darker than the inner ones, which are often creamy or light yellow. Plants may flower in the first year if they bolt, but more commonly produce lovely, daisy-like, blue flowers in the following year, which go to seed. Plant after the last chance of frost when the soil has reached 55°F. Planting earlier is possible but a bit of a gamble. Plants may go to seed if exposed to temperatures below 40°F for more than a couple of weeks. Plant again in midsummer for a fall harvest. Endives taste best when maturing in cool weather. Keep the soil evenly moist until plants are growing vigorously. Once plants get larger, soak the soil but not the foliage. Never let these endives suffer stress from lack of moisture. The foliage will become even more bitter than it already is. Lots of moisture

Endive
Nutrition Facts
Serving size: 100 grams (3.5 ounces)

	AMOUNT PER RAW SERVING	% DV
Calories	17	1%
Carbohydrates	3.5 g	1%
Dietary fiber	3 g	12%
Folate	135 mcg	35%
Manganese	0.4 mg	20%
Potassium	315 mg	10%
Protein	1.3 g	3%
Vitamin A	2,200 IU	45%
Vitamin C	6.5 mg	10%
Vitamin K	200 mcg	250%

time varies by variety but may take up to 3 weeks. Blanching takes less time in warm weather, more time in cool. Check plants regularly to see whether they meet your criteria of being blanched "enough." To reduce the chance of rot, consider placing small rocks under the base of the pot or bucket to allow fresh air to circulate. Some gardeners pull and tie dry leaves together as a way of blanching. Avoid tying leaves too tight—tie them just tight enough to exclude light. There should be some air circulation. This method is fine, except when it rains. Undo the leaves, let them dry, then tie them up again. This reduces the chance of leaf rot. Blanch only one or two plants at a time. This extends the blanching period over a longer period of time. Many people regard blanching as a waste of time and energy.

Endive has foliage with a bitter taste, a combination of chicory and dandelion, but the texture is nice and crunchy. If it matures in cool weather, the taste is more mild. The inner leaves may be eaten raw in salads, one of the most popular being Lyonnaise salad. In this recipe leaves are tossed in warm vinaigrette and topped with a poached egg and pieces of bacon. The outer leaves are baked, braised, broiled, grilled, sautéed, or steamed. Sautéing them with garlic and hot peppers is one of the more popular ways of cooking them. Also consider chopping the leaves and adding them to soups and stews. It is often used in "wedding soup," an

makes the plant grow quickly, and the more rapidly endive matures, the better it tastes.

Although it destroys many vitamins, some people prefer endive blanched to make it more tender and a little less bitter. When all the leaves are dry and the plant is close to harvest time, cover it with a large pot or bucket. When using a pot, cover the drainage hole to exclude light. Clay pots are recommended because they breathe. Blanching

The frilly leaves of endive add a distinctively bitter touch to a fresh salad.

Escarole, also an endive, looks like butterhead lettuce and is eaten both fresh and cooked.

Italian American dish that has as many recipes as there are Italian American cooks. Escarole also has bitter leaves and is best used young. It too is used sparingly in salads, often mixed with other greens. Older leaves are treated much as endive, braised or tossed into soups and stews.

Both endive and escarole are endives, sometimes referred to as chicories. The type labeled endive is sometimes called chicory endive, curly endive, or frizzy (frisée) endive. In England it is referred to as chicory or curly chicory, while in France it is called chicorée frisée. There are dozens of varieties. Try the heirlooms 'Cour d'Oro', 'Rhodos', and 'Très Fine Maraîchère' for starters. Escarole plants tend to be more upright with broader, thicker, and less curly leaves. Most of the plants have a buttery center. Common names for escarole are Batavian endive, broad-leaved endive, grumolo, scarola, and scarole. As with endive, there are numerous varieties. Try 'Batavian Full Heart' (AAS-1934) and 'Blond Full Heart', both heirlooms. Start with these, and branch out from there. Note that the roots of these can be dug up and forced like Belgian endive.

Endives probably originated in India or along the Mediterranean.

Garden Cress
Lepidium sativum ssp. *sativum*
Upland Cress
Barbarea verna
Cabbage Family or Mustard Family (Brassicaceae, formerly Cruciferae)

Garden and upland cress are in the same family, but they are in two different plant groups (genera). *Garden* cress is a hardy, cool-season annual. It produces peppery, parsley-like leaves used to add bite to salads and sandwiches. *Upland* cress is a hardy, cool- to cold-season biennial grown commonly grown as an annual. The plant produces rosettes of glossy, green, rounded leaves eaten raw or cooked. It makes an excellent substitute for watercress, which is considerably harder to grow. These plants may have originated elsewhere but are most commonly associated with Great Britain.

Garden cress seed is very small, elongated, and often reddish (about 11,500 seeds per ounce). It produces short plants with lacy, deeply cut, green leaves on stiff, little stems. If allowed to go to seed, a garden cress plant will form a long, barely leaved stem that shoots upward from the foliage to form a "candelabra" of branches bearing tiny white to pinkish flowers. These in turn mature into flat, disklike seedpods. These produce enough seed so that the plant commonly self-sows. Upland cress seed is tiny, irregular, and round (about 17,000 seeds per ounce). The plants hug the

Garden Cress Nutrition Facts
Serving size: 100 grams (3.5 ounces)

	AMOUNT PER RAW SERVING	% DV
Calcium	80 mg	8%
Calories	32	2%
Carbohydrates	5.5 g	2%
Dietary fiber	1 g	4%
Iron	1.3 mg	7%
Magnesium	40 mg	10%
Manganese	0.55 mg	25%
Niacin	1 mg	7%
Phosphorus	75 mg	10%
Potassium	605 mg	17%
Protein	2.5 g	5%
Riboflavin	0.25 mg	20%
Thiamin	0.08 mg	7%
Vitamin A	6,900 IU	138%
Vitamin B6	0.25 mg	15%
Vitamin C	70 mg	115%
Vitamin K	549 mcg	515%

Garden cress tastes as good as and is prettier than upland cress but tends to go to seed.

Upland cress is tasty, prolific, easy to grow, and very hardy, often surviving through the winter.

ground in rosettes of attractive deep-green, rounded leaves. The plants are remarkably hardy and in the second year will send up long stems that produce bright-yellow, four-petaled flowers. These in turn will form seed-filled pods and self-sow.

Both types of cress grow well in containers. They grow so rapidly that many gardeners keep pots indoors for year-round enjoyment. They are then sprouted and allowed to grow into microgreens to be harvested regularly. This is most commonly done with garden cress. The sprouts themselves can be slimy, but the young plants cut in the early stage of growth are delicious. Plant garden cress seed ½ inch deep in sandy soil, or not so deep in heavier soils. Cover the tan, almost kidney-shaped seed, and firm it in place. Or scatter the seed over a narrow bed. Rake it lightly into the soil. Press into soil surface. It may germinate in as little as 2 days at 60° to 80°F but typically takes 5. Germination of upland cress seed can be erratic. Sow in blocks or short rows to use as little space as possible. Barely cover the dark-brown, round seed when planting. It usually germinates within 7 days at 70°F *if kept evenly moist.* Some people place seed on a wet sponge or inside a damp cloth. As soon as the seed shows signs of growth, they plant it immediately in

the garden. I have never found presprouting necessary. Both cresses can be planted as soon as the soil can be worked in spring. Successive plantings every 14 days make sense since you do not need a lot of cress all at once. Stop planting as the weather gets hot. Begin planting again 5 weeks before the first expected fall frost. Upland cress will make it through the winter in most years. Garden cress will die out. Plant all year long indoors in shallow trays for microgreens. Garden cress speeds through the growth process. To help it along, keep the soil consistently moist. Upland cress needs lots of water and evenly moist soil at all times for best growth. It stands up to heat much better than garden cress.

Thinning cress is optional. If harvesting garden cress regularly, consider thinning to 2 inches. Eat any thinnings. Let upland cress seeds form several leaves before thinning. Eat the thinnings. When growing vigorously, thin to 6 to 12 inches apart in all directions if you want the plants to form uniform rosettes. Pinch out the growing tip of garden cress to create branching. This gives you a little more plant to harvest. If seeding regularly, this is certainly optional. Definitely snip off any stems if the plant begins to bolt. Do not do this if you want the plant to self-seed. Upland cress is a tidier plant and rarely gets gangly until the second year when it goes to seed. Consider growing garden cress indoors. Generally, upland cress is frost tolerant and can be picked until late in the season. These plants do not tolerate hot, dry conditions. Keep them moist. Shear garden cress at 2 to 4 inches. It will send up new shoots. The leaves get bitter if allowed to mature. Pick the leaves of upland cress at whatever stage you prefer, young or older. Taste varies with age, but what taste is preferred is a personal choice.

Cresses are delicious as microgreens harvested at just a few inches tall. Their tangy, peppery taste adds bite to salads and sandwiches. Chop up leaves into fine bits, and add to humus, omelets, or quiches. When leaves are more mature, cook like mustard greens. Upland cress makes a good substitute for watercress and is much easier to grow. The leafy green may be used in egg and cress sandwiches, as at British high teas. Its leaves are also used as a main ingredient for soups. Cress roots are edible and a bit like horseradish. Seeds can be used as a seasoning.

Garden cress has many other common names, including broadleaf cress, curly cress, extra curled cress, garden pepper cress, mustard cress, peppergrass, pepperweed, pepperwort, and Persian cress. It may have originated in Iran. It's a lovely cress but tends to bolt as soon as the weather warms up. There are a number of excellent varieties. A few worth comparing are 'Broadleaf', 'Cressida', 'Garden Cress', and 'Wrinkly Crinkly Cress'. The latter is delightful and lives up to its name. Garden cress typically goes to seed quickly.

Upland cress is known by numerous common names, including American cress or watercress, bank cress, Belle Isle cress, black wood cress, Bermuda cress, cassabully, creasy greens or salad, dry land cress, early winter cress or wintercress, early yellow rocket, land cress, Normandy cress, and scurvy cress. Some of these common names are used to describe other species, so check the Latin name when buying this plant. This cress stays a lovely deep green throughout the entire season. Admittedly, leaves become tough with age. It will go to seed the following summer. It has survived to -30°F in my garden. It is sold by its generic name. It probably originated in southwestern Europe.

Hanover Salad
Brassica napus var. *pabularia*
Cabbage or Mustard Family
(Brassicaceae, formerly Cruciferae)

Hanover salad is also known as Hanover kale, Hanover turnip, Siberian kale, and spring kale. It looks somewhat like collards or edible rape with purplish to white stems. The plant forms a rosette of curly leaves but does not form a thick root. Pick young, and eat like kale.

Italian Dandelion
Cichorium intybus
Aster, Daisy, or Sunflower Family
(Asteraceae, formerly Compositae)

Italian dandelion is a very hardy, cold-season biennial typically grown as an annual. It is not a dandelion at all but a leafy endive (large-leafed chicory, sometimes called dandelion chicory). The plant forms a rosette of deep-green leaves with serrated edges. These leaves are picked to be eaten raw or cooked. The plants are easy to grow but considered invasive in a few states. In most gardens the plant is harvested before it can form seed, and while it has the potential to naturalize, this can easily be curbed by removing the plant once it begins to flower. These are larger and better-tasting plants than the true dandelions carpeting lawns in spring.

The seed of Italian dandelion is light to dark tan, small and pointed (about 16,000 to 23,000 seeds per ounce). They look a bit like grayish-brown teeth. The seed grows into a plant with dark-green, heavily notched leaves and stems that vary in color by variety. If the plant matures in its second year of growth, it will form numerous blue, daisy-like flowers. The clear-blue flowers often fade by the middle of the day. If allowed to mature fully, they will form copious amounts of seed. Get the seed into ground as soon as possible. Rub it between your thumb and forefinger as you move along a ⅛-inch-deep furrow or depression in the soil.

Italian Dandelion Nutrition Facts
Serving size: 100 grams (3.5 ounces)

	AMOUNT PER RAW SERVING	% DV
Calories	8	0.5%
Carbohydrates	2 g	1%
Calcium	103 mg	10%
Dietary fiber	2 g	7%
Iron	2 mg	10%
Potassium	220 mg	7%
Protein	1.5 g	2%
Vitamin C	20 mg	35%
Vitamin K	115 mcg	125%

Italian dandelion is a chicory that forms colorful blue flowers if allowed to overwinter.

Cover and firm the soil in place. Keep evenly moist at all times. Seed should sprout within 14 days. Endive seed can be erratic, so better to sprinkle more seed in the furrow than less. Starting endive seed indoors is more commonly done with other types of endive. Italian dandelions mature relatively rapidly, so there is not a lot to be gained by getting a jump on the season. Furthermore, endive does relatively well in higher temperatures compared to crops such as lettuce. Since this is actually an endive, not a dandelion, keep the soil consistently moist throughout the growing season. This moisture helps the plant to mature quickly, reducing the natural bitterness of the leaves. Water regularly a little rather than a lot at one time.

Blanching by covering plants with pots or containers is possible. Leaves become pale and less bitter but also lose nutrients. Part of the fun of Italian dandelion is its unique taste, admittedly a bit bitter. If it doesn't suit you, grow lettuce instead. Begin harvesting when the leaves are only a few inches tall. The young leaves are more tender and less bitter than older ones. They are also better in cool weather. After cutting, the plants will often sprout new leaves, so this is a good "cut and come again" crop.

Both the leaves and tender stems are edible, raw or cooked. Leaves are delicious in sandwiches or in salads with a basil dressing. Slice stems with leaves attached, and soak in cold water before making a frilly Caesar salad with olive oil, garlic, vinegar, and anchovies. Even when Italian dandelion greens are picked young as microgreens, they can still be a bit bitter. Some people enjoy this, others not so much. Mix them with other greens to tone down the taste. Bits of bacon, garlic, onion, and hot peppers may also be mixed in. The varieties with red stems and veins add a splash of color to any dish. Older leaves are often soaked in salt water before being cooked lightly, usually sautéed in hot oil seasoned with garlic. Consider tossing these greens over pasta and topping with grated cheese. The long taproots harvested in fall can be ground into a coffee substitute (see "Dandelion," for directions).

A number of varieties are available. 'Clio' is a nice green, but I like 'Garnet Stem' because of its rich-red stems and leaf veins. 'Romanesco da Taglio' is an endive often placed in this category, but whether it is an escarole or Italian dandelion is debatable. It's simply a good choice.

Italian dandelions are native to Europe.

Lamb's Quarters (Lambsquarters) and Quinoa
Chenopodium species
Amaranth or Goosefoot Family (Amaranthaceae, formerly Chenopodiaceae)

Lamb's quarters *(Chenopodium album),* Aztec Red Spinach, also known as Red Aztec Huauzontle (pronounced wah-ZONT-lay) *(Chenopodium berlandieri* ssp. *nuttalliae),* 'Magentaspreen' *(Chenopodium giganteum),* and 'Brightest Brilliant Rainbow' *(Chenopodium quinoa)* are all in the same genus and available as seeds in the marketplace. Lamb's quarters is a prolific common weed. Plants sprout from tiny, dark, brownish-black seeds (about 55,000 or more seeds per ounce) and if allowed, will mature into a many-branched and very tall "shrub" with green "goosefoot-shaped" leaves that appear to have a waxy, whitish powder underneath.

'Magentaspreen', a colorful version of lamb's quarters, is tasty and deep green when cooked rapidly.

Quinoa is suited primarily to cool, high mountain areas and is marginally ornamental in warmer ones.

The powder washes off when rinsed in water. Sometimes, there are purplish dots on the leaves, but these are nothing to worry about. The plant may be called fat hen, goosefoot, pigweed, or wild spinach.

Most commonly eaten are young leaves and emerging stems gathered when the plant is less than 6 inches tall. Pick them just before eating, since they wilt very fast. The leaves do contain oxalic acid and if eaten raw, should be consumed in small amounts. Shoots and leaves are more often boiled lightly, the water removed, and then cooked some more, either sautéed or added to other dishes. Cooked, they are a bright green. Sautéed in olive oil, they are delicious and tender. Spice with garlic, lemon, onion, or peppers for additional flavor. Or sauté, and use as a side dish with vinegar, salt, and butter. Boil young leaves lightly, chill, and add to salads, or add them to sauces, soups, or omelets. The plant does well in cold climates and multiplies prolifically if allowed to go to seed. Lamb's quarters probably originated in Europe.

Aztec red spinach comes from Mexico and is not truly a cold-climate plant. 'Magentaspreen' is also called "Giant Tree Spinach," which makes no sense to me since the common lamb's quarters gets just as big. This plant has leaves with a purplish hue at their base near the stem. It grows well in cold climates and is more ornamental than lamb's quarters. As it matures fully, it often loses its dramatic coloring and looks identical to lamb's quarters. Grow it as an edible ornamental. Once cooked, it turns the same deep green as lamb's quarters. It too self-seeds prolifically.

'Brightest Brilliant Rainbow' is one variety of quinoa (KEEN-wah). Quinoa is native to the the Andes region in South America, possibly Peru, so it is suited only to areas with consistently cool summer weather. While its seeds (technically pseudo-cereals) are extremely nutritious, getting many is difficult, as is the harvesting and cooking. My suggestion is to buy, not grow, this highly nutritious seed. Promoted as a lovely ornamental, it produces some limited coloration but overall is disappointing—at least to me. I have grown it both from seed and transplants with equally poor results. The young leaves and pink stems are edible and should be picked at the same time as you would lamb's quarters.

Malabar Spinach
Basella alba and *Basella rubra*
Madeira Vine Family (Basellaceae)

Malabar spinach is a tender, tropical perennial grown as an annual in cold climates. This short-day plant may sulk a bit or a lot in the long days of summer. On the plus side

Lamb's Quarters (Lambsquarters) and Quinoa Nutrition Facts
Serving size: 100 grams (3.5 ounces)

	AMOUNT PER COOKED SERVING	% DV
Calcium	260 mg	25%
Calories	32	2%
Carbohydrates	5 g	2%
Copper	0.2 mg	10%
Dietary fiber	2 g	8%
Manganese	0.5 mg	25%
Potassium	2,909 mg	8%
Protein	3 g	6%
Riboflavin	0.3 mg	15%
Vitamin A	7,820 IU	155%
Vitamin B6	0.2 mg	9%
Vitamin C	37 mg	60%
Vitamin K	495 mcg	620%

its thick leaves, commonly cooked before eating, are high in nutrients. The plant is also known as Ceylon spinach, climbing spinach, country spinach, Indian spinach, libato, Malabar nightshade, Pasali, Pu-tin-choi, and vine spinach. Neither its taste nor texture is like spinach. The seeds of Malabar spinach are medium sized (roughly 950 seeds per ounce), hard, round, irregular, and whitish tan on one end. They produce thick, firm stems that turn into a vine with tuberous roots. The leaves are fleshy and succulent, glossy green or tinged red, depending on the variety. Rounded, white to pinkish-white flowers may be produced in clusters on mature plants and eventually turn into purplish-black fruits once fully mature. Each berry contains one seed.

To get a jump on the season, plant seed indoors 6 to 8 weeks before the last expected frost. Plant several seeds in individual 4-inch pots approximately ¼ to ½ inch deep. Use bottom heat to keep at 85°F if possible. Seed may take up to 3 weeks to germinate. Soaking the seed in water as hot as your hand can stand may help break dormancy. Or soaking the seeds for up to 24 hours may do the same. If seeds begin to swell, plant them immediately. Since germination is erratic, plant seeds quite close together—roughly 1 inch apart. Harden off, and plant outdoors next to a good support when temperatures hit 75°F. Begin harvesting plant tips once plants begin growing well. This will create side shoots.

Some cooks add small amounts of young leaves to fresh salads. Their taste has been described in many ways. They remind me a bit of beets, but others describe them differently.

Malabar Spinach Nutrition Facts

Serving size: 100 grams (3.5 ounces)

	AMOUNT PER RAW SERVING	% DV	AMOUNT PER COOKED SERVING	% DV
Calcium	125 mg	12%	125 mg	12%
Calories	23	1%	23	1%
Carbohydrates	3 g	1%	3 g	1%
Dietary fiber	2 g	8%	2 g	8%
Folate	140 mcg	35%	115 mcg	30%
Iron	1.5 mg	8%	1.5 mg	8%
Magnesium	65	16%	50 mg	12%
Manganese	0.75 mg	30%	0.3 mg	13%
Potassium	330 mg	8%	255 mg	6%
Protein	3 g	6%	3 g	6%
Riboflavin	0.15 mg	12%	0.1 mg	8%
Thiamin	0.5 mg	4%	0.1 mg	7%
Vitamin A	2,500 IU	50%	1,160 IU	23%
Vitamin C	6 mg	10%	6 mg	10%

Malabar spinach spirals upward if given support and produces glossy leaves that are gelatinous when cooked.

They also have a slimy texture if you chew on them for awhile. The best part of the plant is the stem tips with young leaves. Most people prefer these cooked as briefly as possible until tender. Malabar spinach is commonly steamed or stir-fried by itself or with meat, seafood, and other vegetables. The leaves and stems do have a gelatinous texture. They may be used in soups as a thickener. The older leaves can get quite tough. Green varieties stay green when cooked; red varieties are lovely on the vine but lose color once cooked. Note that medical warnings do exist, especially for people with kidney problems.

There are two varieties: the green leafed (var. *alba*) and the red leafed (var. *rubra*). Both produce rather limited amounts of foliage. Stem cuttings can be rooted and grown indoors over the winter as a house plant.

Malabar spinach probably is native to Africa, India, or Southeast Asia.

Malva
Malva verticillata var. *crispa*
Hibiscus or Mallow Family (Malvaceae)

Malva is a mild-season annual or biennial grown as an annual in cold climates. All plant parts are edible, from the root to the seed. The plant grows from an irregularly shaped, tannish-brown seed (about 935 seeds per ounce) into a potentially large, branching plant—up to 72 inches. The plant is easy to grow. To speed germination, nick the seed coat

Although somewhat difficult to find, the seed of malva produces a plant with many edible parts.

(scarification), or soak overnight in water. Plant the seed about ⅛ inch deep. It germinates best at 68°F. The plant does well in sun to partial shade. Its lobed leaves have frilly edges. Harvest some leaves as the plant begins to mature, more as it gets larger. Never denude the plant, or it will die.

Use small portions of raw leaves in green salads. Leaves can also be boiled, fried, roasted, or sautéed. If boiled, the leaves can be a bit slimy, like okra. Consider drying them for teas. If the plant produces pinkish flowers, use these for color in salads. Seed heads are also edible raw or cooked. Seeds are nutritious but difficult to harvest. Supposedly, the fleshy taproots can be boiled and beaten into an egg white substitute.

The plant can be highly invasive if the fruit (seedpods) are not removed. If you are worried about the plant spreading, snip off all flower heads. The formation of fruits is not all that common in a short season.

Malva is sometimes referred to as cheese weed, the name derived from the shape of wedges in the pods. The plant likely originated in China and is often referred to as Chinese mallow.

Note that the plant may be toxic to livestock.

I could find no reliable information on this plant's nutritional value.

Mibuna (Mibu Greens)
Brassica rapa var. *japonica*
Cabbage or Mustard Family
(Brassicaceae, formerly Cruciferae)

Mibuna is a cool-season plant that matures quickly, usually within 40 days. It grows from tiny, purplish-brown black seeds (11,500 per ounce) into a 12-inch or taller plant with long, slender, strap-like, rounded leaves with a mustardy flavor. Individual leaves can be picked, but leave the main portion of the plant alone. Or make successive sowings.

Harvest young leaves for salads. Steam and season older ones for a side dish, stir-fry quickly, or use in traditional dishes such as sukiyaki. Older leaves are more pungent. Leaves are delicate and easily damaged by slugs. New growth is resistant to frost and can stand temperatures down to 20°F.

Mibuna is sometimes called Mibu greens, *dento yasai* in Japanese, and *Ren sheng cai* in Chinese. 'Early Mibuna' is a popular open-pollinated variety. Mibuna is closely related to mizuna. For that reason, the nutritional information duplicates that of mizuna, although I could find no reliable information specifically on this plant.

Mibuna has been grown for centuries in Japan, which may be its country of origin.

Mibuna (Mibu Greens) Nutrition Facts
Serving size: 100 grams (3.5 ounces)

	AMOUNT PER RAW SERVING	% DV
Calcium	100 mg	11%
Calories	27	1%
Carbohydrates	4.7 g	1%
Dietary fiber	3.2 g	12%
Iron	1.5 mg	8%
Magnesium	35 mg	8%
Potassium	385 mg	10%
Protein	2.9 g	5%
Vitamin A	2,960 IU	60%
Vitamin B6	0.2 mg	10%
Vitamin C	60 mg	115%

The leafy "tongues" of mibuna, with their mustardy flavor, are essential to many Japanese dishes.

Miner's Lettuce (Claytonia)
Montia perfoliata, formerly *Claytonia perfoliata*
Purslane Family (Portulacaceae)

Miner's lettuce is a short-lived, cool-season perennial grown as an annual in cold climates. This weed grows from minuscule, very shiny black seeds (about 78,500 seeds per ounce) and may have saved the lives of many miners during the gold rush. Its other common names are claytonia, Cuban spinach, Indian lettuce, spring beauty, and winter purslane. As a wild plant, it appears in early spring. It will grow in full sun to light shade but lasts longer in shade. Heart-shaped leaves encircle the stems like an umbrella and are followed by tiny, delicate, white, five-petaled flowers that fade and mature into brown seed capsules. The plant self-seeds prolifically. It matures quickly into a very short plant, and its oval to lance-shaped young leaves are juicy and eaten fresh in salads when only 2 inches tall. Treat it as a "cut and come again" plant.

Older leaves become slightly bitter, but stalks and flowers are edible. Cook it lightly as a side dish, like spinach, or stir-fried with vegetables. Some people prefer it puréed and added to cream soups or added as a green to smoothies. Consider planting it in fall rather than spring since it is hardy to 20°F. Also, consider growing it in a pot where you can enjoy it more fully.

The plant is native to the western United States.

I could find no reliable source on the nutritional value of this plant. It is supposed to be high in iron (10% of RDA per 100 grams, or 3.5 ounces, raw), vitamin A (22% of RDA), vitamin C (33% of RDA), and protein. Claims are made that it is high in beta-carotene.

Minutina
Plantago coronopus
Plantain Family (Plantaginaceae)

Minutina is a cold-season perennial most commonly grown as an annual for salad greens. In Europe it is called buckshorn (buckhorn) plantain or star herb *(erba* or *herba stella),* or staghorn. The plant grows from ultratiny, black, spearhead-like seed (108,000 seeds per ounce) into a rosette of bladelike, deep-green, serrated leaves. Direct seed in full sun in well-pulverized soil just below the soil surface. It generally germinates in 10 to 21 days and is a fast-growing plant as long as you keep it consistently moist. Pick it when it is young and tender, roughly between 4 to 5 inches. It never gets par-

Miner's lettuce forms delicate stems encircled by edible leaves. It is best grown in a container unless you want it to self-seed rampantly in the garden.

The feathery leaves of minutina have a distinctive look and can be cut back for a new round of growth.

ticularly high and will sprout a few bare stems with elongated and edible grain-like flower heads. Although it can be a "cut and come again" crop, planting small crops a week or two apart is more highly recommended. It is said to have a "mild, sweet" flavor, though perhaps its main charm is its shape and appearance. Its taproot is about 3 inches long and shoots out from what looks like a little white bulb, from which spring a dozen or more long leaves. These tend to flop over, but as long as the plant is well watered, it seems to go on and on. It is cold tolerant and will survive light frosts.

Minutina most likely originated in Eurasia or North Africa.

I could find no reliable source on the nutritional value of this plant.

Mitsuba (Japanese Parsley)
Chryptotaenia japonica
Carrot or Parsley Family
(Apiaceae, formerly Umbelliferae)

Japanese parsley is a somewhat tender, perennial, woodland plant grown as an annual in cold climates. It looks a bit like Italian parsley, with long stalks and aromatic leaves. It is sometimes referred to as Japanese or white chervil. The combination of the two names describes how these plants both look and taste. Its seeds are thin and elongated (about 14,000 seeds per ounce). Plant them in a finely screened soil at a depth of roughly ¼ inch when temperatures are at least 68°F. Plants mature in 50 to 60 days and are ready for harvest when only 6 inches tall. Make successive plantings to extend the harvest. It is said to be hardy to -20°F, but that is probably pushing it. Being a woodland plant, it thrives in partial shade and consistently moist, but not soggy, soil.

Direct seed it in the garden, or grow it in a pot; the latter is probably easier. Keep the soil moist and make sure the pot drains freely. The plant will form attractive stalks with three-leaflet leaves and will eventually go to seed, producing tiny, white, star-shaped flowers and delicate, thin stems. These are hermaphroditic, both male and female organs on the same plant, and self-fertile, although usually pollinated by insects. Normally, plants are kept trimmed to stop flower formation. The plant self-seeds in warmer climates.

Like parsley, the stems make a lovely garnish. Chop leaves and stalks fresh for use in salads and soups. Or use them to season or add body to hot dishes or stir-fries, but add at the last moment since the flavor is lost quickly if overcooked and may even become bitter. The leaves and stems can be cooked like spinach, briefly or just until tender. It is popular in Japan in a cooked dish called *ohitashi*. All parts

Mitsuba (Japanese Parsley) Nutrition Facts
Serving size: 100 grams (3.5 ounces)

	AMOUNT PER RAW SERVING	% DV
Calories	18	1%
Carbohydrates	4 g	1%
Dietary fiber	2.5 g	10%
Folate	40 mcg	13%
Potassium	640 mg	18%
Protein	1 g	2%
Vitamin C	8 mg	10%
Vitamin K	65 mcg	70%

Mitsuba grows well in partial shade. Its leaves, shredded into bits, flavor salads and cooked dishes.

of the plant are edible, from the root, usually fried, to the seed, used as a seasoning.

Mitsuba is sometimes sold as Japanese hornwort in catalogs. It is, as its common names indicates, of Japanese origin.

Mizuna
Nutrition Facts
Serving size: 100 grams (3.5 ounces)

	AMOUNT PER RAW SERVING	% DV
Calcium	100 mg	11%
Calories	27	1%
Carbohydrates	4.7 g	1%
Dietary fiber	3.2 g	12%
Iron	1.5 mg	8%
Magnesium	35 mg	8%
Potassium	385 mg	10%
Protein	2.9 g	5%
Vitamin A	2,960 IU	60%
Vitamin B6	0.2 mg	10%
Vitamin C	60 mg	115%

Mizuna mustard forms edible serrated leaves and bright-yellow blossoms that attract beneficial insects.

Mizuna
Brassica rapa var. *nipposinica*
Cabbage or Mustard Family
(Brassicaceae, formerly Cruciferae)

Mizuna is a hardy, cool-season annual. Its Japanese name means "watery or juicy vegetable." It is grown for its feathery leaves, which have a mild, peppery flavor. Mizuna may be sold under the names cai, California peppergrass, Japanese greens, Japanese mustard, kyomizuna, kyona or kyoto greens in Japan, mizuna in Japanese, mizuna mustard, potherb mustard, shui cai in Mandarin Chinese, spider mustard, water greens, and xue. The seeds of mizuna are very small, round, and tan to brown (roughly 9,000 to 12,000 seeds per ounce). As the plant matures quickly to a height of 18 inches or less, it forms a lovely rosette of deeply cut leaves, with white petioles and veins. The leaves look somewhat like oak leaves, with their jagged edges. Plants bolt as they mature, forming lovely clusters of tiny, cross-shaped, yellow flowers at the end of thin stems, which are a magnet for beneficial insects. These mature into thin, pointed pods, which point up as they dry out. Once dry, they crack open easily to reveal tiny seeds inside. The plant self-sows freely.

Begin planting as early in the season as possible. Seeds will germinate in temperatures as low as 40°F. Make a shallow ¼- to ½-inch groove in the soil, sprinkle seed about 1 inch apart, firm the soil, and water well. Plants germinate in a wide range of temperatures, typically within 5 days. Mizuna is a bit unpredictable, so make successive plantings every 2 weeks. Continue until the end of summer since plants have been known to survive extremely cold weather once growing well. The taste of the plant may vary a bit ac-

cording to growing conditions. Avoid using seeds as sprouts, since they can be slimy. However, definitely harvest them as microgreens when plants are just 2 to 3 inches tall. If the seeds are planted thickly, this harvest is a form of thinning. Then when plants get about 5 inches tall, cut, or "prune," them back, or snip off leaves as needed. When cutting, leave the smaller inner leaves intact. This is a great "cut and come again" plant, which may regenerate several times.

Young leaves are the most tender and succulent. They are excellent raw in salads and can be quite decorative since there is a wide range of colors in different varieties. Older leaves become a bit tough as they mature, but they are still tasty in soups and stir-fries. If plants get away from you, pull them up, or eat the flower stems. Successive plantings early in the season make discarding older plants less painful. Consider growing this plant in a large container protected with a row cover early in the season to deter flea beetles and slugs.

Try several varieties for a full array of color and form, such as 'Dark Purple Hybrid', 'Red Mizuna', and 'Ruby Mizuna', to name but a few of the many available.

The plant probably originated in China.

Mustard
Brassica species
Cabbage or Mustard Family
(Brassicaceae, formerly Cruciferae)

Mustard greens are hardy to very hardy, cool- to cold-season annuals and biennials grown primarily as annuals. Although these fast-growing greens are commonly cooked, the small leaves add a peppery taste to salads when picked

Mustard Nutrition Facts

Serving size: 100 grams (3.5 ounces)

	AMOUNT PER RAW SERVING	% DV	AMOUNT PER COOKED SERVING	% DV
Calcium	105 mg	10%	75 mg	7%
Calories	25	1%	15	1%
Carbohydrates	5 g	2%	2 g	1%
Dietary fiber	3 g	13%	2 g	8%
Folate	185 mcg	45%	75 mcg	18%
Iron	1.5 mg	8%	0.7 mg	4%
Magnesium	32 mg	8%	15 mg	4%
Manganese	0.5 mg	24%	0.3 mg	14%
Potassium	355 mg	10%	200 mg	6%
Protein	3 g	5%	2 g	5%
Vitamin A	10,500 IU	210%	6,325 IU	125%
Vitamin B6	0.2 mg	9%	0.1	5%
Vitamin C	70 mg	115%	25 mg	45%
Vitamin E	2 mg	10%	1.2 mg	6%
Vitamin K	500 mcg	625%	300 mcg	375%

Mustard greens are easy to grow and add a bite to fresh salads or a side dish of greens.

young. Mustard makes a good early spring and late fall crop. Mustard seed is very small, round, and dark reddish-brown to almost black (about 10,500 to 15,000 seeds per ounce). Mustard grows much like lettuce, with upright leaves of varying color depending on the variety. If allowed to, plants form clusters of yellow, cross-shaped flowers that mature into narrow ½- to ¾-inch pointed pods with seeds inside. These seeds are edible or can be used to plant the following season's crop. Plants self-seed readily.

Get seed into the ground as early as possible in the spring as soon as the ground can be worked. The soil temperature can be as low as 40° to 45°F. Plant again in late summer for a fall crop. Make successive sowings in spring. Ideally, the plant will mature in cool weather. Plants will take heat and even some drought but may go to seed under these conditions. This is an easy plant to grow. Just keep it well watered.

There are two common methods of harvesting mustard greens. The first is to snip off a few leaves from different plants before they are longer than 4 inches. Remove leaves from the outside, allowing the inner leaves to continue growing. A scissors works well to do this. A second method is to shear off the plants in crew-cut fashion when most leaves are 4 to 6 inches tall. Plants will often regenerate as a "cut and come again" plant. Young leaves are more tender than and not as pungent as older leaves. Note that fall crops often taste best after a mild frost. In fact, some gardeners plunge just-picked leaves into a pan filled with ice water to preserve flavor and a more crisp texture. Mustard does not store for a long time. Roll leaves in a paper towel so that each leaf is sandwiched between paper. Place the rolled-up leaves in a plastic bag in the crisper of the refrigerator. Use the leaves as soon as possible since they become tougher with age—certainly within 4 days.

For a peppery tang, add young leaves to salads or sandwiches. Older leaves are best cooked. Some people find older leaves to be too bitter or pungent. Washing them several times, discarding the water with each washing, reduces some of this bitterness. Removing the midribs of older leaves may also help. Stir-fry or sauté leaves for 1 to 2 minutes, boil lightly, or steam briefly. Add them cooked to soups. For a side dish, cook them as you would spinach by placing them in a pan with just a little butter and water. Cook them just until tender, and expect the leaves to shrink dramatically. To freeze leaves, choose young leaves or remove stems from older ones, wash, blanch for 2 to 3 minutes in boiling water, chill immediately in ice water for the same time, place in a plastic freezer bag, label, and freeze.

The bright flowers are edible as are the young seedpods and the flower shoots. Add them to salads for a real bite. The seed is also edible. Use them for sprouts, or grow them for microgreens. Add them whole to dishes, or use them whole for pickling, as in sauerkraut. Mustards as a condiment are powders made from ground seed of various species,

Mustard Spinach Nutrition Facts

Serving size: 100 grams (3.5 ounces)

	AMOUNT PER RAW SERVING	% DV	AMOUNT PER COOKED SERVING	% DV
Calcium	210 mg	20%	160 mg	16%
Calories	22	1%	16	1%
Carbohydrates	4 g	1%	3 g	1%
Dietary fiber	2.8 g	11%	2 g	8%
Folate	160 mcg	40%	75 mcg	18%
Iron	1.5 mg	8%	0.8 mg	4%
Manganese	0.4 mg	20%	0.3 mg	13%
Potassium	450 mg	12%	285 mg	8%
Protein	2.2 g	4%	1.7 g	3%
Vitamin A	9,900 IU	200%	8,200 IU	165%
Vitamin B6	0.2 mg	10%	0.1 mg	5%
Vitamin C	130 mg	215%	65 mg	110%

Mustard spinach is a magnet for flea beetles and should be protected with row covers.

identified primarily by the color of the seed. Brown seed is more pungent than white. Powders turn spicy when mixed with other ingredients, including vinegar, wine, and salt. Other popular additions are honey, horseradish, and a wide variety of spices. There are hundreds of varieties of mustard preparations throughout the world. Note that true Dijon mustard must come from Dijon, France. Imitations are labeled Dijon-style.

Most varieties recommended in this section are called broad-leaved mustards (*Brassica juncea* var. *rugosa).* Many plants listed as mustards in catalogs are closely related but not true mustards. Following are some good cold-climate varieties: 'Florida Broad Leaf' (fairly tall plant with smooth, broad, green leaves on the milder side), 'Green Wave' (AAS-1957, a shorter plant with very frilly, green leaves), 'Red Giant' or 'Giant Red' (thick, crinkly, bronzy-purple leaves), 'Southern Giant Curled' (AAS-1935, bright-green, curly, crumpled leaves, mild), 'Tatsoi Mustard' (also sold as Chinese cabbage under *Brassica rapa* var. *rosularis,* forming rosettes of mild leaves and best planted for a fall harvest), and the unique 'Wasabina' (midgreen, ruffled leaves that have the taste of wasabi). The Asian seed suppliers have a vast selection of other mustards and their relatives, but the ones listed here are a good start for the home gardener.

Mustard is high in vitamin K. If you are on a blood thinner such as warfarin (Coumadin), talk to your doctor.

Mustard probably originated in the Mediterranean area.

Mustard Spinach
Brassica rapa var. *perviridis*
Cabbage or Mustard Family
(Brassicaceae, formerly Cruciferae)

Mustard spinach is a hardy, cool-season annual. Although related to turnips, it is strictly grown for its greens. The leaves are edible at any time. Mustard spinach grows from a dark-brown, hard, rounded seed (a little more than 11,000 seeds per ounce) into a leafy, upright plant with large, generally smooth, oblong, rounded leaves. It grows rapidly and will begin to form flower stems as soon as the weather gets really hot. These rise above the foliage and blossom with small clusters of bright-yellow, four-petaled flowers. Shortly after flowering, very thin, pointed pods begin to form and will produce seed if allowed to mature. Plants may be damaged by a hard frost or freeze when emerging in late spring, but take the gamble. Plant small, successive plantings in early spring, then again in mid- to late summer for fall harvests. Mustard spinach can often withstand temperatures down to 10°F. Extending the season with row covers or tunnels is possible but rarely done in the home garden except by ardent gardeners.

Mustard spinach is a good "cut and come again" crop. Pick young for microgreens. As plants mature, pick individual leaves, or cut the tops of plants to about 2 inches above the soil line. Plants normally resprout. Typically you can get two cuttings before the taste of leaves begins to deteriorate. The name *mustard spinach* implies that the taste is either like mustard or spinach. In fact, it is like neither. It is not bland nor pungent but almost sweet when picked young. While milder than true mustard, the greens do get a bit "hot" as they mature, providing a bit of a bite to salads but less of a bite when cooked. Young leaves are best used in salads. For a special flare, add newly emerging flowers to salads as well. Cook young or older leaves in stir-fries, or steam as a side dish. Sautéing them lightly in sesame oil with added spices or soy sauce is another option. When cooking leaves, consider slicing them into thin strips. If leaves are older, separate leaves from stems. Note that leaves can be pickled. To freeze, use young leaves, or remove stems from older ones, wash, blanch for 2 to 3 minutes in boiling water, chill immediately in ice water for the same time, place in a plastic freezer bag, label, and freeze.

Although there are many named varieties, try 'Komatsuna' or 'Tendergreen'. 'Green Boy Hybrid' is often recommended but bolts quickly, so if you want flowers, this is a good choice. 'Senposai' is a hybrid of cabbage and Komatsuna. Names may be listed in different ways in catalogs. For example, 'Torasan Hybrid' may appear as *Brassica rapa* var. *komatsuna* 'Komatsuna Torasan'. The plant is often called Japanese mustard spinach, since it probably originated in Japan.

Nettle
Urtica dioica
Nettle Family (Urticaceae)

Stinging nettle is a cool-season perennial that is considered by many a noxious weed to be uprooted immediately. That point of view is not shared by everyone. In other countries it is considered a healthful cooked green. It is also commonly dried and used to make tea. The plant is easy to grow, and while it can become invasive, it is simple to uproot and eradicate if you do not share the love that others have for this unusual potherb. Nettle grows well in evenly moist areas in partial shade. Plants have medium- to dark-green leaves that look like serrated spearheads, pointed on the end and heart shaped at the base. Stems are square, hollow, but strong. Tiny, hypodermic-like needles (trichomes) stick up and out from their surface. At the base of each needle is a little swollen area that contains a substance containing a number of chemicals, including formic acid, the same substance that gives ant bites or stings their painful punch. The acid is carried up the needle and into your skin when you brush against it lightly. As the plant matures, it forms brownish-green clumps of tassel-like flowers at the tip of the plant and from leaf axils (places where leaves join the stem).

Nettle Nutrition Facts

Serving size: 100 grams (3.5 ounces)

	AMOUNT PER COOKED SERVING	% DV
Calories	42	2%
Carbohydrates	6.5 g	2%
Dietary fiber	7 g	28%
Iron	1.6 mg	9%
Magnesium	57 mg	14%
Manganese	0.8 mg	40%
Phosphorus	70 mg	7%
Potassium	335 mg	10%
Protein	2.5 g	5%
Vitamin A	2,010 IU	40%
Vitamin K	500 mcg	14%

Nettle is not only edible but also draws up nutrients from the subsoil to make topsoil more fertile.

These then form seed, which helps the plant form colonies. The plant also spreads out at its base, forming plantlets off to the side of the mother plant.

Stinging nettle is most commonly eaten when plants are about 6 inches tall. Pull up the young plants, or pick tender, young leaves and growing tips as the plant gets larger, but no taller than your knees. Don't forget to protect exposed skin with gloves and a long-sleeved shirt. *Do not pick leaves after the plant flowers. At this stage they may cause digestive and urinary problems.*

Although the leaves are edible raw, only masochists eat them this way. If harvested when young, cook both the leaves and stems (if still tender). Wash. Pat dry. Then sauté in butter, or butter and oil, or in oil alone. If you plan on steaming the greens, do not pat dry. Cook them just until tender. Once wilted, they will not sting and will become a brilliant bright green. While often listed as a "spinach" substitute, the taste is most commonly described as salty and "earthy." To disguise this earthiness, sprinkle bits of hard-boiled eggs, bacon dressing, or grated cheese over the steamed greens. Stinging nettles are better known in Great Britain, where they are used in puddings and soups. They are commonly combined with chicken stock, cream, onions, potatoes, and assorted seasonings before being served this way.

Dried leaves are often used to make tea and may be mixed with a wide assortment of herbs to make special "blends" that appeal to individual tastes. The tea is believed by many to be extremely healthful. Place leaves in a single layer on a screen, and air-dry in a well-ventilated area. The leaves should not be touching. If there is no wind, dry them in the sun. Or place them in a dehydrator. To make a hot tea from fresh (1 cup) or dried leaves (1 tablespoon), drop them into water, and bring to a near boil. Reduce the heat, and let simmer for a few minutes. Simmer longer for a stronger tea. Remove the leaves from the brew by pouring it through a strainer. Adjust the amount of leaves to taste. The brew can be sweetened with sugar or honey to taste.

Some organic gardeners cut back mature plants, place pieces of stems and leaves in water, and let them ferment for 2 to 3 weeks. They then run the mixture through a sieve, pour it around the base of plants, or use it as a foliar spray. Normally, the nettle "tea" is diluted to 1/15th its original strength. Compost the material caught in the sieve. This "tea" is often mixed with fermented comfrey for an additional boost. If this is all too much, cut the plant back each year, and toss the stem and leaves into the compost pile as a nitrogen-rich booster.

The origin of stinging nettle is disputed. Stinging nettle may be native to northern Africa, Asia, Europe, or North America.

New Zealand Spinach
Tetragonia tetragonioides, formerly *Tetragonia expansa*
Fig Marigold Family (Aizoaceae)

New Zealand spinach is a tender, warm-season perennial grown as an annual in cold climates. It is considered a good warm-season replacement for spinach. Although it can be eaten raw, it is almost always cooked. It also is called Botany Bay spinach, Cook's cabbage, everbearing spinach, everlasting spinach, kohiki, Native Australian bushtucker, sea spinach, summer spinach, and warrigal greens. The seed of New Zealand spinach is thick and irregular (about 425 seeds per ounce). The vining plant produces thick, green, succulent, triangular leaves on rather fragile, sprawling stems. The silvery grains on leaves are calcium oxalate. Once mature, it will produce small, 3/16-inch, yellowish-green flowers and seed capsules, which are hard-horned fruit pods that contain several seeds.

Germination can be erratic. Soak seeds for a full day, or file through the outer seed coating before planting immediately. Or soak in hot water for 4 hours. Make several small, successive plantings starting several weeks before the last frost. Why a warmth-loving plant may germinate in cool soil is somewhat of a mystery, but it sometimes does. Seed may germinate quickly or take up to a month. Be patient. Just keep the area moist. Do not mulch until weather warms up. Mature New Zealand spinach will tolerate dry spells, but consistent watering results in more tender leaves.

Keep cutting off new growth once the plant is growing vigorously. This is a "cut and come again" crop, but it should be fertilized lightly after each cutting. Lack of fertilizer may result in the plant going to seed. Begin harvesting when the plant is young. Remove the growing tip to force lateral branching. Make successive harvests rather than denuding the plant. This encourages the plant to get ever bushier for additional harvests of new growth, which is the only part of the plant that is good to eat. It is rarely bothered by leafminers, as is spinach.

Strip the fleshy leaves from the harvested tips. Eat these only. In small amounts they are fine fresh in salads, although rather bland. The use of these leaves raw is limited, not like those of true spinach, which have a completely different taste. Leaves do contain relatively high amounts of oxalates, which can be a problem for some people, especially those with kidney problems. To remove these, blanch for 1 minute, and dispose of water. Then braise or sauté the leaves whole or chopped into pieces. They can also be puréed and added to sauces. To freeze, wash, remove stems, place in a sieve, plunge into boiling water for 30 seconds to a minute,

New Zealand Spinach Nutrition Facts

Serving size: 100 grams (3.5 ounces)

	AMOUNT PER RAW SERVING	% DV	AMOUNT PER COOKED SERVING	% DV
Calcium	58 mg	6%	48 mg	5%
Calories	15	1%	12	1%
Carbohydrates	3 g	1%	2 g	1%
Dietary fiber	minimal		minimal	
Magnesium	39 mg	10%	32 mg	8%
Manganese	0.6 mg	32%	0.5 mg	25%
Protein	1.5 g	3%	1.3 g	3%
Vitamin A	4,400 IU	88%	3,625 IU	72%
Vitamin B6	0.3 mg	15%	0.2 mg	12%
Vitamin C	30 mg	50%	16 mg	27%

The young leaves of New Zealand spinach taste best if cooked briefly.

lift up, drain, place into ice water for 2 minutes, then into airtight freezer bags, and freeze. Note that leaves do lose vitamins when blanched. Some people prefer cooking it for less than a minute in the microwave instead of plunging it into boiling water.

There is a variety named 'Maori', but it is difficult to find. Instead, buy seeds labeled New Zealand spinach. The plant probably originated in Australia or New Zealand.

Orach (Mountain Spinach)
Atriplex hortensis
Amaranth or Goosefoot Family (Amaranthaceae, formerly Chenopodiaceae)

Orach is a fairly hardy, cool-season annual, but it is often referred to as a warm-season plant because it can tolerate drought and heat better than spinach. It was popular in the seventeenth and eighteenth centuries but is now rather rare in the home garden. It is grown for its edible leaves and flower buds, both of which are an acquired taste. Its other common names are butter leaves, French spinach, garden orach, giant lambsquarters, marsh orach, mountain spinach, musk weed, salt bush, and sea purslane. The last two names give a hint to its tolerance of salty soils. Flat, tan seeds are located inside teardrop-shaped coverings called husks (about 8,000 seeds per ounce).

Plant seed directly in the garden. The seed is finicky, and once growing, the plants have flimsy, needlelike stems that topple over easily. Place mulch around them so that if they do tumble over, they don't stick to the soil. Seed grows into plants with soft to crinkly textured, arrow-shaped, somewhat hairy leaves, often serrated on the edges. Leaf col-

ors vary according to the variety. These upright plants can get fairly tall if allowed to mature and will form spikes of greenish-red, inconspicuous flowers. Fertile seed is enclosed in translucent, papery bracts.

Pick young leaves, or eat the young tips of more mature plants, which can get really tall. Harvest when no more than 2 inches tall for microgreens. For side dishes and stir-fries,

Tender, young orach leaves will be eaten by deer if your garden is not surrounded by a good fence.

pick or shear back leaves at 4 to 6 inches to 2 inches above the soil. Plants often regenerate as a "cut and come again" plant. If plants get away from you, pick only growing tips. Most people agree that leaves taste best when harvested in cool weather. Unlike spinach, however, the leaves are good to eat even after the plant goes to flower. In fact, some gardeners eat leaves until the plant is killed off by a hard frost.

Orach has a mild, slightly salty taste and, occasionally, mealy texture. Some cooks serve leaves on a plate under other foods. Young leaves are colorful in salads and usually used in small amounts. Leaves may be added to soups and stews, which they tend to thicken. Sauté, steam, or stir-fry young leaves briefly in butter for a side dish. 'Fire Red' has arrow-shaped, purple leaves with pink stems, which make it a favorite as a microgreen in salads. However, most red or purple varieties with the exception of 'Red Orach' lose their bright color once cooked. While opinions vary, green orach has a more pleasing taste to some, but, of course, reds appeal to the eye as much as the palate. In Europe the yellow or golden orachs referred to as whites, such as 'Golden' are prized. Seeds are edible and can be used in baking.

Plants can be invasive, so don't let them go to seed unless you are saving seed for next year's crop. Plants can usually withstand a light frost.

Plantain is a common weed whose leaves and flower stalks are best eaten as young as possible.

The plant probably originated in Europe in the Mediterranean region or in western Asia.

I could find no reliable information on the nutritional value of this plant. I have been told that it is extremely high in vitamin C.

Plantain
Plantago major
Plantain Family (Plantaginaceae)

This broadleaf weed is extremely common in cold-climate areas. It grows wild in many fields and lawns. You have probably pulled this weed from your yard dozens of times. It is considered an excellent plant to draw up nutrients from deep in the soil. The plant is a dark-green rosette and produces spiky shoots covered in seed capsules as it matures. Seeds are tiny, vary somewhat in shape and color, and are available through Richters Seeds. Pick the leaves when only a few inches long. Sauté them quickly in oil. Do the same with the seedy shoots, but pull the stem through your teeth to eat the seeds.

This plant is considered medicinal and may not be compatible with some medications. This species of plantain may have originated in Europe.

Purslane
Portulaca oleracea var. *sativa*
Purslane Family (Portulacaceae)

Purslane is a cool-season annual, popular as a salad green or potherb in other countries, where it is appreciated for what some call a tart, peppery, somewhat lemony taste. In my opinion that is an overly generous description. Some say that it is the most common weed in the world. It is called *carti-choy* in Chinese, *pourpier* in France, *portulaca* in Italy, and *verdolaga* in Latin America. In the United States it may be called duckweed, fatweed, pigweed, little hogweed, pusley, and pussley. You have probably already removed it from your garden without knowing what it was or its food value. Gardeners jokingly call it an "herb gone wild" since it can become invasive and will even grow in cracks of asphalt or cement.

There are two species of purslane. The wild and some cultivated varieties are *Portulaca oleracea,* and the golden types are *Portulaca sativa*. The wild types hug the ground and spread out quickly. In fact, they grow rampantly throughout cold-climate regions. Let nature take its course, and you can eat as much of this as you want. The cultivated golden varieties are prettier than the green. Gourmets and most gardeners, including me, insist the golden types have a better

Purslane Nutrition Facts

Serving size: 100 grams (3.5 ounces)

	AMOUNT PER RAW SERVING	% DV	AMOUNT PER COOKED SERVING	% DV
Calcium	65 mg	7%	78 mg	8%
Calories	16	1%	16	1%
Carbohydrates	3 g	1%	3 g	1%
Iron	2 mg	11%	0.8 mg	4%
Magnesium	68 mg	17%	68 mg	17%
Manganese	0.3 mg	15%	0.3 mg	15%
Potassium	495 mg	15%	495 mg	15%
Protein	1.3 g	3%	1.3 g	3%
Riboflavin	0.1 mg	7%	0.1 mg	7%
Vitamin A	1,320 IU	25%	1,825 IU	37%
Vitamin C	21 mg	35%	10.5 mg	18%

Golden purslane produces crisp, juicy leaves with a richer color than the common weed of the same name.

flavor. They grow more upright and have thicker leaves, but they don't produce as much foliage. Consider growing the golden varieties in a container with extremely close spacing, since their overall growth is upward. Both types have paddle-shaped leaves that are a bit crunchy and have a rather unusual flavor. For pure volume, gather wild purslane wherever it emerges, but for beauty grow one of the golds, such as 'Goldberg Golden', 'Golden', or 'Goldgelber'.

The plant grows from minute, round, brown seeds (65,000 to 78,000 seeds per ounce) into spreading or upright plants, as mentioned. Plant in airy, sifted soil to a depth of ¼ inch as soon as possible in spring after any threat of frost. Or press the seed into the soil since seed responds best to some light. It will germinate in temperatures as low as 40°F. The named varieties must have consistent moisture during germination or will die off. Wild plants seem to appear overnight and seem to take any amount of abuse. Stems and leaves are best in all types when young. Consider several plantings of the named varieties a few weeks apart.

Add young leaves to fresh salads, or sauté them in butter and sprinkle with Parmesan cheese. Pick older leaves before the plant flowers. Boil for a few minutes, then add to stir-fries. Purslane can be used as a thickener, like okra, in soups and stews. It can also be added to sauces, as is done in the Middle East for tzatzike (tsadziki), a sauce or dip made most often with yogurt, cucumbers, and garlic. Some gardeners even pickle the older stems.

This weed is especially high in omega-3 fatty acids, which are hard to get in anything but fish such as salmon. Purslane, both wild and cultivated types, will self-seed pro-

lifically if allowed to mature and go to seed. Do not confuse this plant with spurges (*Euphorbia* species), which exude a milky sap.

Purslane probably originated in India, although some sources say Europe.

Rape
Brassica napus
Cabbage or Mustard Family (Brassicaceae, formerly Cruciferae)

Specific varieties are grown for their edible leaves and stems, while others are grown for seed, which is pressed into canola oil. For information on an edible rape called Hanover salad, see the section on kale. This variety is sometimes called spring kale. Also, see Chinese cabbage.

Sorrel
Rumex species
Buckwheat or Knotweed Family (Polygonaceae)

Sorrel is a hardy, cool- to cold-season perennial that produces tart, lemony-flavored leaves that are delicious in soups, salads, and herb butters. It is commonly grown as an annual in cold climates, although it may survive depending on the severity of the winter. It is easy to grow and lovely to look at. It is extremely popular in France and is sometimes referred to as an herb vegetable or potherb. Common names include little vinegar plant, sour grabs, sour suds, gowke-meat, sourgrass, and green sauce.

Sorrel
Nutrition Facts

Serving size: 100 grams (3.5 ounces)

	AMOUNT PER RAW SERVING	% DV	AMOUNT PER COOKED SERVING	% DV
Calories	24	1%	24	1%
Carbohydrates	2.4 g	0.5%	2.9 g	0.7%
Dietary fiber	0.8 g	3%	0.7 g	3%
Magnesium	103 mg	25%	90 mg	22%
Potassium	390 mg	10%	320 mg	8%
Protein	2 g	4%	1.8 g	4%
Vitamin A	2,400 IU	48%	2,080 IU	42%
Vitamin C	48 mg	80%	26 mg	45%

Sorrel is a durable plant with lush leaves that adds a lemony flavor to dishes, especially to sorrel soup.

Dark-brown to black sorrel seed is shiny, pointed, and oval (roughly 30,000 to 40,000 seeds per ounce). Sorrel forms a rosette of large, fleshy leaves varying from 8 to 16 inches long or longer. The arrow- to shield-shaped leaves vary in color and thickness according to variety, and give the plant a soft, sprawling look. The creeping roots penetrate the soil fairly deeply and look a bit like parsnips. Plants send up tall flower stalks with bell-like, reddish-pink flowers, which form seed once fully mature. Remove the flower stalks immediately once they appear. Flower production reduces leaf formation and size. Plants often send up flower shoots early in the season. If the plant blooms and withers, cut it back to the soil line. It may resprout. Sorrel grows best in slightly acidic soil and will become bitter if underwatered. It can be finicky about light. If your summers tend to be hot, place sorrel in partial shade. If your summers tend to be cool, then place it in full sun. Sorrel has the potential to last for a number of years, so choose the spot carefully from the start. If planted in the right spot, it will resist bolting better and have a milder taste.

Let plants begin to grow well before picking any leaves. Once plants are growing vigorously, begin harvesting. Pick regularly. If plants survive the winter, begin picking sooner than in the first year. Always pick leaves before the plant begins to send up flower shoots. Leaves tend to have the best taste when picked young but not too young. If the leaf tastes lemony, it's at the right stage. As plants mature, the lower leaves are often the best, the upper leaves somewhat bitter. Stems in general are stringy and tough. Stick to leaves.

Sorrel is edible fresh or cooked. Once cooked, sorrel loses its bright-green color and becomes a dull green. For fresh use, pick leaves when very small. Add to salads, or use in sandwiches in small amounts. They are tangy and tart. Or place young leaves next to sliced tomatoes. Use older leaves to wrap fish, especially salmon. Cover the fish with foil, and grill. Before using larger leaves in sauces, soups, and cooked dishes, break off the stem and pull backwards to remove the stringy portion from the center of the leaf. Then chop or purée leaves, depending on their intended use. Add chopped leaves to au gratin potatoes, omelets, and potato and other vegetable soups. Sauté chopped leaves in butter until they go limp. Spread over fish or veal. Cook chopped or whole leaves in bouillon for 5 to 6 minutes. Serve as greens. Make sauces for fish, fowl, and meats. Typical ingredients include butter, cream, onions or shallots, wine, and, of course, lots of fresh sorrel. These are cooked and blended together. For a really simple sauce, add puréed sorrel to yogurt, or mix with sugar and vinegar. Sorrel soup *(germiny à l'oseille)* is often referred to as the "Queen of Soups": sauté 6 cups of sliced sorrel in several tablespoons of butter. The sorrel appears to melt as you do this. This is blended with chicken or vegetable broth, egg yolks often whipped into cream, and spiced with onions, ramps, or shallots. Don't waste leaves toward the end of the season. Pick, cook, and purée before freezing.

Plants die back each fall. Remove all dead leaves and

any remaining mulch around the plant. Water the soil well until the first hard freeze. Then cover with a 12-inch winter mulch of loose straw. The plant may come back in spring. Many plants will survive to 20°F or occasionally colder with protection. If plants begin to weaken, divide the clump in early spring as you would rhubarb.

French or garden sorrel *(Rumex acetosa),* with arrow-shaped leaves, and True French sorrel *(Rumex scutatus),* with shield-shaped leaves, are most commonly used in the kitchen. Red-veined sorrel *(Rumex sanguineus)* should be considered an edible ornamental. Few varieties are available to the home gardener. Start seed sold as sorrel, or try the named variety 'De Belleville'.

Sorrel probably originated in Asia and Europe.

Tyfon Holland Greens
Brassica rapa 'Tyfon', technically *Brassica rapa* ssp. *pekinensis* × *Brassica rapa* var. *rapifera*
Cabbage or Mustard Family
(Brassicaceae, formerly Cruciferae)

'Tyfon Holland greens' also known as 'Tyfon greens' or 'Holland greens' are a cross between Chinese cabbage (Wong Bok) and stubble turnips. They are a hardy, cool-to cold-weather annual that you can get into the garden as soon as the soil can be worked. The plants grow rapidly from round, purplish-black seed (approximately 8,500 seeds per ounce), producing a lush crop of relatively mild leaves within 40 days. Give these plants full sun, ample nitrogen, and regular watering. Begin harvesting outer leaves when young, or shear back to 1 inch or so when larger, as this is a good "cut and come again" crop. Do this several times if possible.

Use young leaves raw in salads for a bit of a bite, or cook as a side dish as you would spinach: cut into strips, boiled in a little water, sautéed, steamed, or stir-fried. Bits of cooked leaves are delightful used in dips. The shredded leaves are delicious in lasagna. Consider juicing the leaves with other vegetables for added nutrients. Plants can get quite bulky. If they do get overgrown, cut them off, and add to the compost pile. Till in the roots as a green manure.

I could find no reliable information on the nutritional value of this plant or its origin.

Watercress
Nasturtium officinale, also known as Rorippa nasturtium var. aquaticum
Mustard Family
(Brassicaceae, formerly Cruciferae)

Watercress is a hardy, cool-season perennial grown as an annual or as a perennial under ideal conditions. Watercress grows wild along the banks of cool, fast-moving streams in many parts of the United States. It can be grown from hard, ultratiny, reddish-tan, round seed (about 142,000 seeds per ounce), but most home gardeners buy a plant from a local nursery or create their own by sprouting purchased watercress stems in a glass of water. Change the water every day. Plants hug the soil and spread, producing tender stems with irregularly rounded leaves. Plants will produce small, four-petaled, white flowers if allowed to mature. It is better to keep pinching the plant back than to let it flower. It will become bushier and produce more foliage. The plant tends to do poorly in the garden and dies out for unknown reasons, although some speculate it is from lack of oxygen. It grows much better in a container as long as it is kept consistently moist. It will overwinter in running water. Consider bringing a potted plant indoors in cold climates, where you can keep the plant moist at all times.

Watercress has a sharp, peppery taste. Americans use it most frequently as an ingredient in salads or as a garnish. The Chinese usually serve it cooked. It is commonly used in watercress sandwiches, consisting of bread and butter with watercress on top. Add it to soups to spice them up, or make a watercress soup as you would sorrel soup. Mix fine bits

Tyfon Holland greens are not well known, but they are easy to grow, resilient to heat and insects, and quite mild.

Watercress
Nutrition Facts
Serving size: 100 grams (3.5 ounces)

	AMOUNT PER RAW SERVING	% DV
Calcium	120 mg	12%
Calories	11	1%
Carbohydrates	1 g	minimal
Dietary fiber	0.5 g	2%
Manganese	0.2 mg	12%
Phosphorus	60 mg	6%
Potassium	330 mg	9%
Protein	2 g	5%
Riboflavin	0.1 mg	7%
Thiamin	0.1 mg	6%
Vitamin A	3,200 IU	64%
Vitamin B6	0.1 mg	6%
Vitamin C	43 mg	72%
Vitamin K	250 mcg	310%

Watercress grows wild along rapidly moving streams and thrives in pots kept consistently moist.

Wheatgrass, a highly nutritious green, must be broken down in a juicer to be absorbed by human bodies.

into butter for a a slight bite. There are several varieties on the market, but none stands out, and all must be grown from seed. For generic watercress, propagate it with stem cuttings. Frankly, garden and upland cress are much easier to grow and have a similar taste.

Watercress may have originated in Europe along the Mediterranean or in Asia.

Wheatgrass
Triticum aestivum
Grass Family (Poaceae, formerly Gramineae)

Wheatgrass is a fast-growing, warm-season annual "crop" grown not for flavoring but for its nutritional value. The grain, or hard winter wheat berries, vary in color but are fairly large, oblong-pointed cylinders indented on one side (about 500 seeds per ounce). Some gardeners insist that red wheat is better than white because it has more protein, but wheatgrass from any type of wheat is fine. Before planting, you want the seed to germinate (sprout). How much seed you need will vary by the size of the growing container, which is usually a shallow tray with a ½ inch of sterile starting mix laid on the bottom. You need just enough sprouts to cover the mix in a single layer.

There are many methods for getting seeds to sprout, but all begin by soaking them in room-temperature water for at least 12 hours. Drain off the water. Place the seeds in a sprouting jar or colander over a bowl. Rinse and thoroughly drain at least two to three times a day before covering each time with a towel. Keep at about 70°F. When the seed begins to form little white tails, it is ready for planting.

Place the sprouts over the thin layer of mix. Spray them with a mister until thoroughly moist. Keep the tray covered with a moist towel. Spray every morning and night for a few days. The tray or container should rest on a plate or metal tray to collect excess water, which should be drained off after each watering. Keep evenly moist and humid until seeds begin to send up little green shoots, which usually takes place within a few days.

Remove the moist towel covering the flat or container. Mist thoroughly each day so that water runs out of the holes in the container. Your crop will grow fine in indirect light at 70°F. Sterile starting mix and good air circulation reduce the chance of mold.

Begin harvesting the grass by snipping it back with scissors before it reaches 6 inches and just as individual blades barely start to form a second leaf. Often, you can do this several times, although the nutritional value apparently dips with each cutting. The grass is edible as a green, but some insist *the grass must be juiced for maximum nutrition.* Juicing grasses requires high-end juicers, which are expensive. The juice is bitter and often mixed with apple, carrot, or orange juice to make it more palatable. This is one of the simplest and quickest greens that the home gardener can grow. Note that wheat seeds can also be eaten as sprouts, just as the roots emerge in the jar. Otherwise, they become tough. Make sure any seed used for wheatgrass or sprouts is organic. Check for seed sold in local health food stores or through mail-order sources. Consider growing wheat outdoors as a cover crop.

Wheat probably originated in Egypt.

Wheatgrass Nutrition Facts

Serving size: 100 grams (3.5 ounces)

	AMOUNT PER RAW SERVING, JUICED	% DV
Calories	20	1%
Carbohydrates	2 g	1%
Dietary fiber	0.0 g	
Folate	28 mcg	7%
Iron	2.3 mg	13%
Magnesium	28 mg	7%
Phosphorus	74 mg	7%
Potassium	147 mg	5%
Protein	3 mg	6%
Vitamin A	420 IU	8%
Vitamin B12	1.0 mcg	42%
Vitamin C	3.5 mg	7%
Vitamin E	3 mg	15%

HERBS

This section contains descriptions of herbs and flowers that are commonly used in the kitchen and have similar growing needs. They can be grown in beds, borders, containers, gardens, and planters on windowsills. Most of these herbs thrive in full sun. Chervil prefers cool conditions, so it does better in shade. All grow well in loose soil amended generously with organic matter for good drainage and moisture retention. Their nutritional needs are met by typical garden soils, and they do not demand high fertility. If they demand nutrition (fairly common if potted), feed them lightly with fish emulsion or a similar organic fertilizer. They all grow well in mildly acidic to neutral soils ranging in pH from 6.5 to 7. If grown in pots, they should be potted up each year with new potting soil. If gangly, cut herbs back and feed. Regular harvesting amounts to the same thing. If plants begin to flower, cut off flower stems unless flowers are desired for culinary use. Most of these herbs taste best grown with consistent moisture, but a few such as oregano, lavender, sage, sweet marjoram, tarragon, and thyme tolerate dry spells between deep waterings. The fragrant oils that make these plants so delicious are usually at their best just after dew evaporates in the morning. Most of these herbs are best used fresh, but many dry well. The culinary use of these herbs is varied.

Herbs are often promoted for their health benefits, but warnings must be noted about possible side effects of some herbs if overused, if used at all by specific individuals, and if taken with certain medications. This topic is both controversial and often undocumented. If you are taking medications, ask your doctor for medical advice. If you have never eaten a specific herb, test your tolerance by eating a little at first. Admittedly, most people have been using the majority of these herbs for years without any apparent ill effects, probably because their use is limited to tiny amounts in comparison to other plants.

If possible, grow herbs as close to the kitchen as possible, either in an herb garden or in pots. Use is often directly proportional to distance from the stove. Nutritional information is not included with herbs, since so little of each is typically used in any given dish.

Three common French culinary terms regarding herbs show up frequently in recipes. *Bouquet garni* is herbs tied and wrapped in cheesecloth to be added to soups, stocks, and stews, then removed before serving; herbs most commonly used are basil, bay leaf, chervil, parsley, salad burnet, rosemary, savory, tarragon, and thyme. *Fines herbes* (pronounced "feen-erb") typically consists of finely chopped chervil, chives, parsley, and tarragon. *Herbes de Provence* almost always includes dried basil, fennel seed, marjoram, oregano, rosemary, savory, and thyme (optional are bay, Italian parsley, lavender, and tarragon).

This section includes two plants grown primarily for their flowers: marigolds and violets. The flowers of many vegetables and herbs are edible. When this is the case, the information is provided in the descriptions of specific plants, ranging from chrysanthemums to squash, and for the herbs in this section. Generally, the flowers of herbs taste similar to the foliage. In some instances, the entire flower is edible; in others only the petals are. The base of some flowers may be quite bitter and should be removed. Wash most flowers gently before eating, or at least check for insects. Never eat any flowers sprayed with a pesticide. If you are growing plants by a road, check that pesticides are not sprayed in that area.

While many flowers are edible, others are toxic. For example, never eat asparagus, eggplant, pepper, potato, or tomato flowers.

Borage
Borago officinalis
Borage Family (Boraginaceae)

Borage is a hardy, cool-season annual. Buy a plant if possible since the growing season is short. If preferred, start it from seed (about 1,500 seeds per ounce) indoors (preferred), or direct seed outdoors. The seed is indented and looks a bit like the rough bottom of a sock. If planting outdoors, wait until the soil warms up to about 60° to 65°F, although it is worth a gamble to plant some several weeks before the last expected frost. Germination usually occurs within 14 days. Borage tends to be less gangly if grown in full sun. Soil should be loose, drain well, and be mildly acidic with a pH of 6 to 7 to encourage the plant to form a long taproot. Plants may reach a height of up to 36 inches. Stems are bristly, hollow, and huge once fully grown. Fuzzy drooping buds burst into blue or white, five-petaled, star-shaped flowers that hang down in clusters. If allowed to go to seed, the plant may self-sow freely.

Eat flower petals raw, sautéed, or steamed. As soon as the flower opens, pull it away from the little, green leaves, actually sepals, holding them in place. The flower pops out. Float flowers in drinks such as lemonade. Flowers can be candied or added to vinegar. The plants are a favorite of bees and are nicknamed "bee bread." The plant comes with

Both the blue and white varieties of borage attract a wide range of beneficial insects.

medical warnings—use it sparingly, especially the first time you try it.

Borage probably comes from the Mediterranean area, specifically in what is now Syria.

Caraway
Carum carvi
Carrot or Parsley Family
(Apiaceae, formerly Umbelliferae)

Caraway is a hardy, cool-season biennial. Start it from the light-brown, indented, "boomerang-like" seeds (about 10,000 seeds per ounce) directly in the garden at about the frost-free date. Plant the seed about ⅛ inch deep. Germination generally takes place within 2 weeks. The plant produces a swollen taproot that looks a bit like a parsnip and a rosette of bright-green, ferny foliage in the first year. Plants that make it through the winter will produce tall stems with umbrella-like clusters of creamy-white to pinkish flowers. Seeds (technically one-seeded fruits called *achenes*) will begin to form and are ready to harvest just before the plant dies.

In the first year snip off a few young leaves to add to a

Although caraway is difficult to overwinter for its seeds, its young leaves are delicious.

Catnip intoxicates cats, who are drawn to it both fresh in the garden or dried, stuffed in toys.

salad, but do not strip the plant bare, since you are growing it mainly for its seeds, although some gardeners pull up the plant at the end of the first season to eat the root. Place a thick straw mulch over the plants after the ground begins to freeze in fall. Remove it immediately as the weather warms up in spring. Hope that the plant survives to produce flowers and the much sought-after seed. Let the seed mature to its brown stage on the plant, then cut off seed heads into a paper bag. Crunch the heads with your hands, and remove all debris. Some people boil the seeds in case they are infested with insects and then dry them for several days before storing them in airtight glass jars. Caraway is commonly used in cheeses and sausages as well as a flavoring for breads and cakes.

The plant likely originated in central Europe but may have come from Asia or the Middle East.

Catnip or Catmint
Nepeta cataria
Mint Family (Lamiaceae, formerly Labiatae)

Catnip is a tender, warm-season perennial, although it may die out in cold winters without snow. Catnip grows from an ultratiny, hard, rounded to oblong, brown seed (about 35,000 to 45,000 seeds per ounce) into a rather coarse, upright plant with flower spikes of light- to medium-blue, tubular flowers. Plant after any chance of frost about ¼ inch deep in well-prepared soil. Seed may take from 14 to 21 days to germinate. The scent is unique and easily recognizable and comes from an oil exuded from stems and foliage. Most cats are drawn to the distinctive lemon, minty, pheromone-like scent and will rub against and roll around the foliage to get a good whiff, which acts as a mild narcotic.

Although some people eat the downy young leaves in salads or boil leaves to make a tea, in my opinion, this plant is for the cats. Harvest and dry leaves for cat toys. Once the plant is in flower, cut off or pull up, and hang upside down in a warm, dry, airy place until the plant dries out thoroughly. If it is hot and sunny, foliage dries well on a screen. Stuff toys with the leaves and flowers. Cats will play with them for hours.

This perennial self-seeds like crazy and is considered invasive, but the heavy-stemmed plants are easy to grab onto and pull up from the soil whenever they become a nuisance.

Catnip probably originated in the Caspian Sea area, although authorities suggest other possible areas as well.

The charming white flowers of chamomile attract bees, but medical warnings are associated with their use.

The French adore chervil on its own or as an ingredient in the seasoning fines herbes.

Chamomile (Common or German Chamomile)
Matricaria recutita
Aster, Daisy, or Sunflower Family
(Asteraceae, formerly Compositae)

Chamomile is a tender, warm-season annual grown for its dainty, daisy-like flowers used primarily to make tea. Consider buying a plant rather than growing it from light-tan, grain-like seed (300,000 seeds per ounce). If you like the challenge, start seed indoors 4 to 6 weeks before planting outdoors after all chance of frost. Press the seed into a sterile starting mix, but do not cover, since light enhances chances of germination. Keep moist, and vary day- and nighttime temperatures by as much as 20 degrees. The plant forms tall stems with lacy foliage and numerous white flowers with raised, yellow cone centers. Stems tend to topple over. New growth should emerge when you cut back stems to harvest flowers at peak bloom. The plant self-seeds if allowed to mature completely.

Either use fresh, or dry on a screen in full sun. Boil 1 cup of fresh flowers in a pint of boiling water, or 2 tablespoons of dried powder per cup. Always strain the solution before drinking. Do not drink this tea if you are taking allergy medications, anticonvulsants, antidepressants, birth control pills, blood thinners, pain medications, sedatives, sleeping pills, or statins. Never drink with alcohol or if you are pregnant. Instead, add dried flowers to potpourris for their sweet, fruity scent.

Chamomile probably originated in Europe.

Chervil
Anthriscus cerefolium
Carrot or Parsley Family
(Apiaceae, formerly Umbelliferae)

Chervil is a hardy, cool-season annual. Chervil grows from long, thin, dark-brown seeds that look a bit like caraway (about 12,500 seeds per ounce). Plant 3 weeks before the last expected frost in spring. Some gardeners have success sowing it in late fall for spring germination. Chervil grows best in loose soil that drains freely but retains moisture well, conditions that encourage the growth of a long taproot. It is an excellent container plant, but pots must be at least 12 inches deep. Plants grow best in filtered light or partial shade where it tends to stay cooler than in full sun. Chervil grows best in cool weather. For successful germination, presprout by placing seed in a moist towel in the refrigerator. Press the seed into the soil surface. Keep consistently moist, and make successive plantings. Seeds usually germinate within 10 days.

The plant produces finely cut leaves reminiscent of Italian parsley. The ferny leaves are aromatic and have a subtle taste of licorice or anise. As it matures, the stems form delicate candelabra-like clusters of lacy, white flowers. Although dried as one of the ingredients of fines herbes, chervil is best used fresh. It will keep for about a week wrapped in a moist paper towel in the refrigerator. It does not freeze well. It is excellent added to salads and as a flavoring for butter, cream cheese, egg dishes, fish, sauces, soups, vegetables, and vinegar. Always add late in the cooking process for full flavor.

Let a plant go to seed, either to collect seed or to encourage self-seeding. Or dry for use in a floral arrangement. Seeds are edible and can be added to baked goods or sprinkled into juices, such as tomato juice. If only leaves are desired, pull up and compost plants just as they begin to flower since the taste of the foliage changes at this stage.

The plant is also sold as annual French parsley, gourmet parsley, and Brussels winter chervil. Note that there is both a plain ('Vertissimo') and a curly-leafed variety ('Crispum').

Buy a young chive plant, and let it mature over the years to self-seed prolifically.

Turnip-rooted chervil *(Chaerophyllum bulbosum)* is in a different plant group (genus), is a biennial, and is not covered in this guide. Apparently, the root of the plant resembles a carrot and can be harvested, kept cool for several months to increase its sugar content, and then boiled. The French describe the flavor as that of a chestnut.

The chervil described here probably originated in southeastern Europe, the Middle East, and southern Russia (possibly in the Caucasus mountains).

Chives
Allium species
Onion or Amaryllis Family (Alliaceae or Amaryllidaceae), formerly Lily Family (Liliaceae)

Chives are a hardy, cold-season perennial. Chives may well be one of the easiest garden plants to grow. And it's a fun plant to have around all year; bring it in during the winter in a pot, but wait until the first frost. Seeds are small, hard, black, and irregular (roughly 6,000 to 7,500 per ounce). Chives germinate and sprout from the ground as thin, reed-like leaves that thicken as they mature into rounded, hollow leaves. However, it makes sense to start off with potted plants since they are relatively inexpensive and more mature. Common chives will blossom with pinkish-lavender globes composed of small flowers. These fade and dry into crinkly seedpods, which will scatter seed around the mother plant to increase the size of the original planting over a period of years. The flowers of garlic chives, sometimes referred to as Chinese chives, are bright-white, starry clusters and will also form copious amounts of seed if allowed to. The stems of both types of chive do not have bulbous bases like onions but form a tight clump of stems. Garlic chive stems are wider than those of regular chives.

Let the chives take root and start to grow before you begin any serious snipping of leaves. Use a sharp knife or scissors to snip off the tender leaves. If cutting individual leaves, start with the outer ones first and cut down to the bottom. Some gardeners prefer to cut smaller clumps flush with the ground or back to 2 inches. The plant regrows to form new tender leaves. In Asia garlic chives are sometimes blanched by cutting them back, covering with a pot, and waiting until the leaves turn a soft yellow.

It is a good idea to divide mature clumps of chives every few years. Amend the soil and replant. Divided plants seem to do better in the long run.

The leaves, flower buds, and flowers of both varieties are edible. Common chives have a mild onion taste that comes from a sulfur-based oil. Garlic chives taste as you would expect from the name. The leaves make wonderful micro-

The name garlic chives *describes its taste but does not indicate the beauty of its white blossoms.*

Russian comfrey draws up nutrients from the soil, an important consideration to organic gardeners.

greens for fresh salads. More mature leaves can be cut into small pieces and added to egg dishes, pastas, sandwiches, and soups, such as vichyssoise. Whenever adding chives to hot dishes, always add at the end just before serving. When overcooked, as in stir-fries, much of their fragrance is lost. Bunches of longer stems are good for tempura. Consider adding bits of chives to butter, cheese dishes, and sauces. Pick flowers just as they are opening. Don't wait too long or they become papery. Since the flowers are pungent, pick off petals, and add these to salads or hot dishes. They add color as well as taste. They do the same when added to white vinegar, which turns a light pink.

Some interesting varieties of common chives *(Allium schoenoprasum)* include 'Fine Leaf' for its thin, grassy leaves; 'Forescate' for lovely rose flowers; and 'Purly' or 'Staro' for thicker leaves. Generic garlic chives *(Allium tuberosum)* are just fine. For fun, try the dwarf 'Silver Corkscrew', a type of curly chive *(Allium senescens* var. *glaucum),* to add silvery gray-blue foliage to your herb garden. Note that Chinese leeks are often sold as garlic chives but are technically a different species *(Allium ramosum)* and have a more bulbous base.

Common chives originated in northern Europe, while garlic chives probably came from China, Japan, or Nepal. Chinese leeks originated in China and parts of Russia.

Comfrey (Russian Comfrey)
Symphytum × *uplandicum* (possibly *Symphytum asperum* × *Symphytum officinale)*
Borage Family (Boraginaceae)

Russian comfrey (Bocking cultivars #4 and #14) is a sterile, long-lived, hardy, perennial plant with large, wide, pointed leaves and thick stems. Purchase it as a plant, propagated from division or root cuttings. When planting, give it plenty of water until it begins growing well. It tends to go limp otherwise since it loses so much water from its broad leaves. Over a period of years it will reach a height of 48 inches or taller and produce purplish blue-pink, elongated, bell-shaped flowers that hang down in clusters in the summer.

Organic gardeners grow comfrey in the garden for several reasons. First, it has a deep taproot that breaks up soil and brings nutrients to the soil surface. Some claim roots penetrate soil to a depth of 10 feet. Let the plant mature for at least a year, removing any flowers that form before using it for its second purpose: its abundant foliage (biomass), which can be cut several times a season. Add the stems to the compost pile. Brew the leaves with stinging nettle into a type of "compost" tea used at the base of plants or as a foliar spray, or place leaves on the soil around plants as a mulch and fertilizer (3.5-0.5-5.8). Cut the foliage with shears just before the plant begins to flower. If the rough, bristly foliage bothers you, wear gloves and a long-sleeved shirt. Russian comfrey is also believed to attract beneficial insects.

Comfrey thrives in any type of soil in both sun and partial shade, is rarely bothered by insects or disease, can be planted off to the side of the garden where it will not take up too much space, and can be planted as soon as the ground can be worked in spring. Expect it to die back to the ground in winter, remove and compost the foliage, and wait for it to regrow. Note that once comfrey has been growing for several years, you can dig up most of the plant in spring, cut the exposed roots into sections, and plant them for a patch of comfrey. Or divide the plant into sections just as it begins growing in spring as you would rhubarb.

While some people do eat comfrey, it is not advised. It has been reported to cause severe liver damage and possibly even death. That said, people have been consuming small amounts or making teas from it for centuries.

The Bocking strains were developed in England.

Dill
Anethum graveolens
Parsley or Carrot Family
(Apiaceae, formerly Umbelliferae)

A very hardy, cool- to cold-season annual, dill (whose foliage is called dill weed) is just that—a weed. There is no mystery to growing it. The feathery plant exudes a wonderful odor when you brush against it in the garden, making it a delightful plant for its scent, beauty, and taste. Dill seed is light, flat, and indented (roughly 27,000 seeds per ounce). It is typically brown with light-tan edges. Once growing, the plant forms stiff, hollow stems with numerous branches covered in feathery leaves. As it matures, it produces umbrella-like clusters (umbels) of tiny, yellow blossoms. These develop into seeds that will self-sow freely if allowed to.

If you have no plants already growing and self-seeding, plant seed in early spring about 2 weeks before the last expected frost directly in the garden about 1/16 inch deep or merely pressed into the soil surface. It grows best if exposed to some light. Keep the soil moist until seedlings emerge. Dill is popular in the kitchen for its leaves, flowers, and seeds. Pick the feathery leaves (dill weed) whenever you need them for cooking. They have the most flavor in early morning. Leave most of the plant intact each time, taking a few leaves from several plants rather than most of the leaves from one.

The foliage of dill (known as "dill weed") is used similarly as the seed.

The seeds of dill are essential to flavoring pickles and many dishes.

The foliage can be dried or frozen, but it is best fresh. And it is better frozen than dried. If necessary, you can keep it for a short time wrapped in a moist paper towel in the refrigerator. Here is a delicious dill weed dish: Slice fresh tomatoes on a plate, cover with chopped dill, let rest for a couple of hours before serving. It can be eaten plain or seasoned and oiled if you prefer. Chop up leaves for a wonderful aroma in potato salads, especially with parsley and chives added as well. Place dill leaves over seafood on a platter. Mix bits of dill weed into butter, cream cheese, salad dressings, and sauces. Add flowers, which are milder than seeds, to fish, omelets, and vegetables.

Dill flowers are not only edible but are gorgeous in bouquets. Cut stems as the delicate sprays first burst into bloom. Get the base of stems into water immediately. The foliage of 'Fernleaf' complements a wide range of flowers. Adding sugar and lemon to the water may increase their shelf life, or you can buy floral food from a floral shop.

Pickling recipes vary in their use of foliage, flowers, or seed. Some gardeners insist that the optimal flavor for pickling is when seeds are just beginning to mature or are almost, but not completely, mature. Others let the seed dry on the plant before gathering it. As the flower heads turn brown, shake the top of the plant over a paper bag. If seeds drop out, snip the entire head into the bag. Leave the bag open. Let the tops dry for a couple of days or longer indoors. Shake the bag. The seeds will drop off and lie on the bottom of the bag. Save the seed, and compost the remaining debris. Some use the dry seed as is, while others place it in the oven at 200°F for 30 minutes for a thorough curing. Store seed once thoroughly dry in an airtight opaque jar. Whole seed is used for pickling, while crushed seed may be used to flavor vinegar and bread.

Dill grows so easily that many gardeners try different varieties to come up with their own favorite. Good varieties include 'Bouquet', 'Dukat', 'Fernleaf' (AAS-1992), 'Grandma Einck's', 'Hercules' or 'Herkules', 'Long Island Mammoth', 'Tetra', and 'Vierling'. 'Tetra' and 'Fernleaf' produce lots of foliage. 'Hercules' is excellent for seeds. Compact 'Fernleaf' makes a good container plant.

Dill probably originated in southern Europe, southern Russia, or western Asia.

Note: Black swallowtail butterflies may lay their yellow eggs on dill and other members of the parsley or carrot family. Let the eggs mature. In later stages of development (instars) the larvae do feed on the plant, so grow enough for you and the immature swallowtails, should you be so lucky to have them.

Leaf fennel exudes the scent of anise and explodes in a fireworks of umbrella-like clusters of yellow flowers.

Fennel (Leaf or Sweet)
Foeniculum vulgare ssp. *vulgare* var. *dulce*
Carrot or Parsley Family
(Apiaceae, formerly Umbelliferae)

Leaf fennel is a hardy, cool-season biennial or perennial grown as an annual in cold climates. Press seed into the soil surface at about the time of the last expected frost. The brown to gray seed with a scent of licorice is elongated and grooved (about 9,500 to 11,000 seeds per ounce). Each seed grows a long taproot and forms a clump of hollow, bluish-greens stems with numerous feathery leaves that give the plant a smoky effect. The leaves are more delicate but similar to dill. If the plant is allowed to mature completely, it will form rayed or umbrella-like flower heads with dozens of little, yellow flowers that produce copious amounts of seed.

All parts of the plant have an anise flavor and exude a fragrant licorice scent. They can be used either fresh, frozen (vacuum sealed), or dried. Some cooks delight in the young shoots. For these, plant several plants, and cut back one plant at a time. Water well to encourage regrowth from the sheared plant. Stalks and foliage are preferred by others. These can be roasted or smoked fresh or dried with meats and seafood or used as a bed for fresh bread to give it a unique flavor. Add fresh bits to salads, including egg, green, or tuna fish. Use the plant's flowers to season desserts, fish, meat, soups (especially cold cucumber or potato), and vegetables.

Let plants mature fully until they begin to form seeds. Immature seeds have a nice flavor. For mature seeds, cut the heads off into a paper bag, and allow to dry thoroughly. Then rub the foliage between your thumb and forefinger to dislodge the seeds. Seeds are used in a number of ways, including roasted and coated with sugar for a snack, added to pickles and chutneys, mixed into cheese and sausage, and even brewed into a tea.

Varieties include both green and bronze types. The most common green is 'Dulce'; bronze types may be sold as 'Nigra', 'Purpureum', or 'Rubrum'. These are as beautiful as they are delicious and often used in floral arrangements. Some floral arrangers boil or char the base of stems to seal them.

The plant is said to attract beneficial insects, including the syrphid fly (hoverfly) and tachinid fly. The former attacks aphids, the latter caterpillars. It also apparently serves as a food source for black swallowtails, although I have not observed this.

Fennel is native to northern Asia and the Mediterranean area.

Horseradish
Armoracia rusticana, also known as *Cochlearia armoracia*
Cabbage or Mustard Family
(Brassicaceae, formerly Cruciferae)

Horseradish, a prolific, very cold-hardy perennial, is one of the easiest of all plants to grow and ideally suited to cold-climate gardening. The grated root makes a biting condiment rich in vitamin C. The present name may be a spinoff of an earlier name, "coarse radish." Horseradish grows from root cuttings, known as thongs, into a vigorous upright plant with large, scalloped or serrated leaves. The plant forms an extensive root system. The main taproot enlarges and grows deep into the ground. The tannish side roots are narrower and tapered, usually 6 to 12 inches long. These are a light tan with white flesh and if separated from the mother plant, can be grown as a new plant or used as a food crop. Older plants may produce clusters of tiny, fragrant, four-petaled, white flowers on the tops of stems rising above the lush, deep-green foliage below.

Prepare a separate bed off to the side of the main garden, a place where horseradish can stay for years. It is not nearly as invasive as many publications say. The main

plant enlarges, but it doesn't shoot off in all directions like a Jerusalem artichoke, a plant that is truly invasive. The irregular and bumpy roots sold in supermarkets and in catalogs are cuttings from larger roots. Buy firm roots that are not at all shriveled, ideally thick at the top where the leaves were cut off. Avoid roots with any mold or soft spots. Contrary to what many publications say, the plants do not have to be planted at a 45° angle. Plant the thickest part of the root up so that it is roughly 2 inches from the soil surface. Sometimes roots are evenly thick from top to bottom. If you don't know which is the top portion of the root, lay the root horizontally in the planting hole. It will still grow. Catalogs sell horseradish as both crowns, the top portion of the root, or more commonly as cuttings, portions of roots broken or cut off from the lower portion of the root. Plant as soon as the ground can be worked in spring, 2 weeks before the last expected frost if possible. This may be the only time certain catalogs will offer roots for sale. If you can find roots in the fall, get them in as soon as possible so that they can form a root system before the soil freezes. Water frequently to encourage vigorous growth, especially early in the season. Then water deeply during hot, dry spells during the summer. Late-season watering is especially important. Water the plants well until the leaves die back in late fall. Horseradish roots can become bitter, sour, or woody if stressed by drought.

As mentioned, horseradish is said to be invasive. It certainly is if you till an area where it has been growing and spread bits of root around the garden. Each piece of root will grow into a new plant. This is why most gardeners plant it in its own designated spot. If space is really tight, it is often suggested to buy a large plastic garbage can, cut out the bottom, dig a hole as deep as the can, place the can in the hole, fill it with soil, and plant root cuttings there. This is a lot of work—and unnecessary in my opinion. If plants are spreading too much for your liking, dig up the entire plant, cut off the side shoots from the main taproot, replant the smaller shoots, and use the taproot. Do this in early spring or early fall.

Harvest horseradish roots only after a bed is fully mature with many plants growing well. This may mean leaving the plants alone the first year as you would for rhubarb. Harvest roots in early spring before new growth emerges or in late fall after a frost has killed off the foliage, which should be removed and composted. Fall is the more common harvesting time. Ideal roots are about 8 inches long and perhaps ¾ inch around. The frilly leaves when barely emerging in the spring are delicious added to salads and soups. A few, very few, gardeners dig up several roots in fall and pot them up for indoor growing. They place the pot in

Snip small roots of horseradish in spring or fall; grate into salads, or grind to mix with vinegar.

The scent of white horseradish flowers is surprisingly sweet and appealing to beneficial insects.

a cool, dark room. Moistening the soil causes new leaves to sprout. These are harvested at 3 to 4 inches and are usually cooked like mustard greens.

The easiest way to harvest roots and protect the mother plant is to dig a hole off to the side of the plant. The large main root may reach 2 feet down or farther. Cut or break off some of the outer, tapered side roots, leaving the innermost taproot in place. Push the soil back, and water immediately. Or dig up the plant. Use the main root for food, and replant the laterals. Older roots can become woody, so this is a good option on any aging plants. In fact, digging up a patch every 3 to 4 years to remove older roots and plant younger ones is commonly recommended.

Peel the root using a potato peeler, and grate for immediate use. Protect your eyes when working with the root as you would with onions. Peeling it under running water may help. Or peel and cut into small cubes before blending roots in an electric blender or food processor—preferably outdoors since the fumes are so powerful. Add some water if necessary to get a smoother mixture. Don't get your face close to the lid of the blender or processor as you open it. The more you grind the root, the hotter it will likely get.

Add the root to white vinegar (some people use wine) mixed with water. Experiment with the ratio of water to vinegar to see how it affects the taste and "spiciness" of the mixture. Some people prefer a little water (10 percent); others, a lot (90 percent). Adding salt, sugar, or lemon will also change the flavor. Note that the longer you wait to add the horseradish to the vinegar-water solution, the hotter the mixture may get. Just a few minutes can make a tremendous difference. Keep the mixture refrigerated in a glass jar. When mixed with vinegar, horseradish may last almost indefinitely in the refrigerator. Note that horseradish can also be cut into thin strips (or grated), dehydrated, and kept in an opaque airtight jar.

Horseradish root adds bite to barbecue and cranberry sauce, butter melted on meat and greens, chicken or egg salads, deviled eggs, dips made with yogurt, sour cream, whipped cream, hash browns, hot sauce for seafood, marmalades, mustard, omelets, pickles, soy sauce, scalloped or mashed potatoes, soups, sour cream (for fish, potatoes, and meats, especially beef), stews, and so on. Horseradish tastes best when raw or barely cooked. Grate or shave it directly on to food. Add it toward the end of any cooking process since cooking destroys its nutrients. Some people claim that you can wrap roots in foil and freeze them. I prefer to peel and grate the root, flash freeze, then place in an airtight plastic bag. Vacuum sealing helps retain flavor and pungency. Grated root can also be dried and then ground into a powder, much like garlic. While relatively long-lasting, flavor is affected.

As many as thirty named varieties of horseradish may be available in the United States, but only a few are sold in garden catalogs. 'Maliner Kren' is generally available. It is sometimes referred to as 'Common Horseradish'. It has crinkly leaves. The variety called 'Big Top' has smoother leaves. Many times horseradish is sold by its common name. If you want only a root or two, check farmers' markets, Asian food stores, and supermarkets. Ask when roots will be available, since they are often not stocked throughout the year. Commercial growers are less interested in leaf type than disease resistance, which varies considerably from one variety to another. However, the home gardener rarely has to worry about this.

Horseradish probably originated in southern Russia or eastern Ukraine.

Japanese Horseradish (Wasabi)
Wasabia japonica, also
known as *Eutrema japonica*
**Mustard or Cabbage Family
(Brassicaceae, formerly Cruciferae)**

The common name fools people into believing that this plant is a horseradish. It is really more like a mustard. One type is grown in cold, running water; another, in moist soil. *It is extremely difficult to grow and not suited to cold climates.* Chinese mustard mixed with horseradish makes a good substitute and is commonly referred to as wasabi in most restaurants, although it is not. A little green coloring may be added to make it appear more authentic. Also, note that there is an arugula variety that may be used to make wasabi paste. Naturally, the variety is called 'Wasabi'. And there is a mustard called 'Wasabina' that mimics the flavor as well.

Lavender
Lavandula angustifolia
Mint Family (Lamiaceae, formerly Labiatae)

Lavender is a half-hardy perennial often listed as hardier than it really ends up being. It is very slow growing and doesn't bloom the way you might hope, with glorious clouds of blue, as seen in photos from Provence, France. It may survive to -20°F and even colder, but don't count on it. It

tends to live for several years and then die out even though it has already made it through tough winters. It can be grown from hard, elongated, black to brownish seeds (about 25,000 seeds per ounce) into a multistemmed plant with blue flowers. But since seeds produce variable results, I suggest buying a plant grown from a cutting if possible. Plant it in *soil with exceptionally good drainage.* During the growing season, allow the soil to dry out between deep waterings.

Lavender is hard to overwinter not only because of its sensitivity to cold but also because it often dies out in overly wet soils. The most commonly recommended choice for kitchen use and chance of survival in cold climates is 'Hidcote'. Another lavender sometimes suggested for cold-climate gardeners is 'Munstead'. Cover plants with a thick, loose layer of straw once the ground freezes, and add a second protective layer of pine boughs after Christmas. Remove these as soon as the weather warms up in spring. Many branches may die back, but give the plant lots of time to regenerate before removing any of them. It is slow to come back to life.

Lavender is just one of many potential herbs that can be used in *herbes de Provence.* The flowers and leaves are most commonly used fresh, while the stems and buds are often dried. The latter have a more powerful flavor. Plant parts are

Lavender 'Hidcote' produces sparse blooms and limited growth but often survives in cold climates.

used for flavoring bread, desserts, jellies, sauces, stews, and teas. Lamb either fed or flavored with lavender is considered a delicacy in France.

When harvesting flowers, pick them just as the dew evaporates in the morning. Use them as soon as possible. Flowers are sweet with citrusy overtones. Use them in drinks and sweets such as cakes, custard dishes, and ice cream and sorbets. Just as the leaves are, flowers are often used to flavor meats and vegetables either directly or in sauces. Add them early in the cooking process for greatest effect. Dried buds and flowers add an exquisite scent to potpourris and sachets.

While lavender does not grow well indoors, it is worth a try. Start it out in a pot, bring indoors in late fall, keep cool in bright light, and water lightly until spring. Whether grown indoors or outdoors, expect plants to stay small with limited flowering, as already mentioned.

Lavender is native to the Mediterranean.

Lemon Balm
Melissa officinalis
Mint Family (Lamiaceae, formerly Labiatae)

Lemon balm is a tender perennial grown as an annual in cold climates. Some say it is hardy to -20°F, but I find that overly optimistic. Consider growing it in a container to be brought indoors in the winter. Its seed is small, pointy, and blackish brown (about 40,000 seeds per ounce). When sowing seed indoors, keep it close to the soil surface since it needs light to germinate. Germination is erratic. Soaking the seed in hot water for a couple of hours may help. But getting plants from seed may take up to 200 days. Lemon balm may also be propagated by division or cuttings taken from spring through summer. Clearly most gardeners find it easiest to buy a plant rather than starting from seed.

Plants grow best in warm soil that drains freely but is kept evenly moist. They will tolerate partial shade. In fact, gold lemon balms may turn brownish in overly intense sun. Plants will get up to 24 inches tall with lush, crinkly, green to golden foliage depending on the variety. Shear plants back to stop the formation of small, white flowers unless you want to add them to salads, soups, or stuffings. Do this often enough to keep the plant bushy, since it has a tendency to become gangly over time.

The lemon- to lime-scented, green leaves are popular fresh or dried in desserts, marinades, salads, sandwiches, sauces for fish and meat, teas, vinegar, and so on. They can be dried, preferably in a dehydrator, for culinary use and for a potpourri. The most popular varieties are 'Aurea', also known as 'Golden', 'Citronella', and 'Lime'.

Lemon balm forms a gorgeous, bushy plant with deep-green, lemon-scented leaves.

There are warnings that the use of this plant with thyroid medication may be ill advised. Check with your doctor if wary.

The plant is native to southern Europe.

Lemon Verbena
Aloysia triphylla
Verbena Family (Verbenaceae)

Lemon verbena is a tender, warm-season perennial best grown in a container in cold climates, where it can be kept alive indoors during the winter. The soft foliage of this plant exudes an incredible scent appreciated on a patio or deck, especially in the evening. It is not grown from seed but from softwood cuttings taken in midsummer. These cuttings must be planted in a sterile starting mix and kept misted to root. So buy a plant.

The plant itself thrives in full sun in a soil that retains moisture but drains freely. Outdoors, place little feet under the container so that the pot will drain quickly after a rain. Indoors, use a saucer lined with pebbles instead. The plant

If allowed to mature, lemon verbena forms tough stalks showered in leaves and has a haunting citrus scent.

The long, weeping leaves of lemongrass are bundled and added to cooked dishes for flavoring.

goes dormant during the off-season, loses its leaves, and regrows in spring. Cut it back in fall. The stems can get thick and hard. Once spring arrives, water the plant more generously, and place it in the sun after hardening off. Over several years the plant will become shrubby; just as new growth starts in spring, trim and shape it. Pruning will cause the plant to become full and bushy.

Always harvest leaves before the plant produces pale lavender to white flowers. Consider drying leaves for culinary use and as an addition to a potpourri. Use fresh or dried foliage to flavor desserts such as custards and sorbets. Leaves add a delightful flavor to drinks, dressings, tea, and vinegar. Cook chicken with sprigs of this aromatic herb to give it a unique taste. The tiny, cream-colored flowers are also edible if the plant gets away from you.

If spider mites become a problem, spray them off with a jet of water. Liquid seaweed is excellent to keep the plant nourished over a period of years, although periodic repotting is recommended.

The plant likely originated in Argentina or Chile.

Lemongrass
Cymbopogon citratus
Grass Family (Poaceae, formerly Gramineae)

This is a tender, warm-season perennial grown as an annual in cold climates. Buy a plant, and consider growing it in a large container to be brought indoors as a houseplant in winter. Or if started in the garden, pot up a plant at the end of the growing season, and bring it indoors in a reverse process of hardening off. It needs heat, sun, and consistent moisture to thrive. Place it in partial shade during heat waves.

Seed looks like thin, little, tan sticks (about 78,000 seeds per ounce). Start seed in a sterile starting mix at 68°F kept consistently moist and humid in a plastic tent. Or start directly in the garden once weather is 55°F, to be potted up when growing well. Germination may take longer than a month, so consider buying a plant, or start from fresh lemongrass purchased at a store. Place the base of the stems in water in a warm window. Change water daily. Roots should sprout within a few weeks. When roots are about

1 inch long, cut off the top portion of the stem, and plant the base in a pot. Place outdoors only after weather warms up to 55°F or higher.

Plants can get large with their long, weeping leaves. These can be cut back to keep in check. If you bring plants indoors during the winter, keep the soil barely moist. Do not fertilize. Give lots of sun and warmth. Place the pot on a plastic tray so that any excess water can drain out. The goal is survival, not rampant growth. Consider dividing larger plants if space is at a premium, but division is difficult on mature plants.

Different parts of the plant are used in curries, salads, soups, stuffings, teas, and so on. The roots of this plant can be used like garlic. Peel, bruise to release flavor, slice fine, then use. The lower portion of the stem (culm) up to where the leaves branch out is often cut or chopped into pieces. It is sometimes referred to as "white bits." If they are tough, they can be removed before serving. The long leaves have sharp edges and are like "razor" grass. Many cooks wear gloves when working with them. These can be tied in bundles, wrapped in cheesecloth, added to dishes, and then removed before serving. The leaves can be dried or frozen. The taste of lemongrass has been described as lemony ginger. The flavor combines particularly well with fish and seafood.

Citronella grass *(Cymbopogon nardus)* is similar to lemongrass but not the same. It is commonly called citronella root because it produces citronella oil, a minimally effective (at best) mosquito repellent.

Lemongrass may have originated in the coastal areas of Southeast Asia.

Lovage
Levisticum officinale
Carrot or Parsley Family
(Apiaceae, formerly Umbelliferae)

Lovage is a tall, cold-season perennial hardy to -30°F with adequate snow cover. The light-tan seed looks somewhat like an indented spearhead, flat on one side, indented on the other (about 8,700 seeds per ounce). Seeds mature in time to what appears to be an oversized flat-leaf parsley plant. The deep-green, toothed leaflets, the sturdy, smooth, hollow stems, the long, tapered taproot, and the seeds are all edible. Bloom stalks, if not pruned off, get thick and produce flowers that look like an umbrella or "fireworks" of tiny, yellow flowers, which if allowed to mature, will form seeds. Cutting these stalks off is recommended to prevent yellowing of leaves and to promote new shoots from the base of the plant. Plants mature in approximately 3 years to reach a height and width of 3 to 5 feet, so plant them in the corner of the garden or back of a border.

Start seed indoors 6 to 8 weeks before the last expected frost, or direct seed after the frost-free date or in late fall for germination the following spring. Press into soil, or barely cover, and transplant young seedlings to their permanent location once they have formed four true leaves. Or buy a plant, since one is usually enough for a family. Harvest leaves lightly in the first year, more heavily once additional shoots and branches form in the second year. Some gardeners trim back the outer stems on larger plants several times a season to encourage new and more tender growth.

Young leaves chopped finely are favored by cooks to add a unique but pungent flavor (anise-celery-parsley) to salads, sauces, soups, and stews. The stalks can be cooked like celery or peeled, blanched lightly, and added to salads, but not many people do this. Use them instead for stir sticks in Bloody Marys. The peeled taproot of more mature plants can be braised or cut into pieces for stews, or into thin strips for stir-fries. Thin, dried pieces of root are used as a flavoring for cooked dishes and brewed into tea. Flower stems can either be snipped off or allowed to form seed, which is used to add a bite to baked dishes, bread, and pickles. It can also be powdered as a salt substitute.

Lovage tastes like celery and comes back year after year with little maintenance.

The tiny flowers of the marigold 'Tangerine Gem' are eye-catching when added to salads.

The plant dies back each year. Cut off the old growth. New growth will appear in spring. Divide mature plants if desired. Also, if foliage yellows during the growing season, cut off the stem to its base. New growth will emerge from the crown.

The plant probably is native to the Mediterranean area and possibly from Afghanistan or Iran.

Marigold
Tagetes tenuifolia, also known as *Tagetes signata*
Aster, Daisy, or Sunflower family
(Asteraceae, formerly Compositae)

Marigolds are hardy, cool-season annuals. They brighten beds, borders, and vegetable gardens with their colorful blossoms, which come in single, semidouble, and double forms. They also make delightful container plants. The seed looks like little sticks, whitish tan on one end, deeper brown on the other (about 29,000 to 39,000 seeds per ounce). Start indoors 4 to 6 weeks ahead of the last expected frost. Barely cover seeds in a starting mix kept evenly moist at 70° to 75°F. Seeds should germinate within 14 days. Place in a sunny location once sprouting. Harden off before planting outside after all danger of frost in full sun. Or direct seed in the garden just under the soil surface when it reaches about 55°F. Or buy plants from a local nursery. Most plants will end up taller than 12 inches and showered with brilliantly colored, five-petaled or more blossoms. Keep removing spent blossoms to encourage bloom over a long period of time. During intense summer heat, plants often stop blooming (stall). Be patient, as they will begin blooming again when temperatures moderate, often blooming into fall.

Marigolds are believed by many organic gardeners to discourage damage by marauders and insects, something not proven by my experience. All of the yellow and golden varieties, whether singles or doubles, are preferred for culinary use. The two marigolds most commonly mentioned for this use are 'Lemon Gem' and 'Tangerine Gem'. Both are brightly colored singles with very small flowers. These are not commonly sold in nurseries and may have to be grown from seed.

Remove the petals from the flowers, and use them fresh in desserts, salads, and seafood to take advantage of their citrusy flavor. The petals of 'Lemon Gem' are sometimes used as a substitute for saffron. Many gardeners have found them to be weak growers and also Japanese beetle magnets. Luckily, that has not been the case for me, although they have taken a long time to bloom.

Marigolds are among plants considered toxic, the harm related to the amount eaten. Eating a few of the gem petals is unlikely to cause any problem. Start with a few. Dried marigold petals are often added to chicken feed to brighten yolks.

Marigolds are native to Mexico, though they are often listed as African or French marigolds.

Marjoram (Sweet Marjoram)
Origanum majorana
Mint Family (Lamiaceae, formerly Labiatae)

All marjorams are oreganos but not vice versa. Sweet marjoram is a tender, perennial grown as an annual in cold climates, although it may survive cold winters with good snow protection or be grown in a pot to be brought indoors during the winter. It can be grown from tiny, irregularly round, medium- to dark-brown seed (about 360,000 seeds per ounce). Start seed indoors 8 weeks before the last expected frost. Press seed onto the surface of an alkaline (no peat) starting mix, and keep moist at 70°F. They need light to germinate. Or plant directly in the garden after any danger of frost in free-draining, alkaline soil. Place in a sunny location. Buying a plant is more highly recommended, however, since seed may be of many types. Plant out in a container after any danger of frost.

To keep the plant bushy, harvest young leaves of sweet marjoram, and trim off any flowers that begin to form.

The key to success with spearmint is consistently moist soil and enough patience in spring to let it regrow.

Plants have thin, gray-green leaves and produce edible, knot-like, pale lilac to white flowers along stems. Flowers can be used like leaves but are milder. Best flavor comes from foliage cut just before the plant flowers. Trim to keep the plant bushy, and prevent flowering if possible. Harvest regularly, starting when the plant is young. The mild, delicately flavored, young leaves may become bitter as the plant matures. For this reason, start new plants periodically from stem cuttings or division.

Sweet marjoram is a delight either fresh or dried. Use in omelets, pizzas, soups, sauces, stews, and stuffings. Mix some into butter, or place in vinegar to take advantage of its mild, sweet flavor. Add a whole sprig to spaghetti sauce, or lay it on top of chicken or lamb while it is cooking. Add the herb toward the end of any cooking process for the strongest flavor. Dry and store whole stems, rather than leaves, in airtight containers. Dried leaves can be added to potpourris.

Bring one of your newly started cuttings indoors in late fall for wintertime use or to extend the life of the original plant. Most plants if kept on the dry side will do well indoors.

Sweet marjoram probably originated in the Mediterranean region, possibly from Greece or Turkey.

Mint
Mentha species
Mint Family (Lamiaceae, formerly Labiatae)

The mints recommended in this section are hardy perennials. The impression by some is that mint is hard to grow. That results from trying to grow a type of mint that is not truly hardy. Mint is not hard to grow, but it has a similar disposition to African violets in that it lets you know right away if it is happy. Once it is happy, it grows like a weed. Most mint is grown from plant divisions or stem cuttings from mother plants. These are sold as potted plants at local nurseries. It is possible to grow mint from hard, round, light-tan, minuscule seed (225,000 or more seeds per ounce), but since you need only one plant of each type, this is rarely done by the home gardener. If you want to try, either direct seed it well after the last chance of frost, or start it indoors. Press the seed into the the surface of a sterile starting mix 8 to 10 weeks before planting outdoors. Keep moist. Prick out, and pot when seed has two pairs of true leaves. Harden off before setting outdoors.

As the plants mature, they become bushy and spreading with four-sided, upright stems covered in deliciously fragrant leaves. They expand by sending out new growth underground (rhizomes) or on the soil surface (runners). These in turn produce additional stems. The plant starts taking off like a weed and can become invasive. As each plant matures, it produces slightly curved flower heads at the tip of the stem or from leaf axils just below. These heads are made up of clusters of tiny, tubular, lavender, pink, to white flowers, which have a subtle beauty and can be added to flower arrangements. For a wonderful mint patch, get a plant into the ground as soon as it is available in spring. Plant it in moisture-retentive soil, and keep it well watered until the first freeze in fall. If it appears to die out over winter (common for spearmint), water and wait. What appears to be a dead zone springs back to life as little shoots emerge from the soil often several feet away from the mother plant.

Mint also grows well in large containers, ones either above- or belowground. Use a 5-gallon or larger plastic pot when growing mint in the ground. Cut off the bottom of the pot, and place it into a hole as large as the pot. The edge of the pot should be 2 inches above the soil line. Cut off any branches of the plant that hang over the pot. If they are allowed to touch the soil, they will often take root and begin to spread. If you leave mint in clay or ceramic pots over winter, the soil may expand and break the pot. Consider double potting by placing a plastic pot inside a more attractive and larger pot, then taking out the plastic pot to sink into the ground in late fall or to bring indoors.

Develop a small, vigorous patch of mint before harvesting leaves. If too impatient, you will stunt the growth of younger plants. Once the patch is well established, you will have more than enough mint. The best time to pick mint is early in the morning, when leaves are rich with aromatic oil. Snip off the top 7 to 10 inches of the growing stems. Young plants have tender stems. As they mature, the stems get increasingly woody. The easiest way to strip off leaves is to pull the stem through your closed hand from top to bottom. Once a patch is mature, harvest regularly throughout the season.

Mint has a strong flavor. Mint leaves and flowers are used to flavor cakes and ice cream, jelly, meat (especially lamb), fruit salads, rice, tea, vegetable dishes (particularly carrots, peas, and new potatoes), and vinegar. For a special summer drink, strip leaves off five to six stems of spearmint, toss into a blender with two cans of frozen lemonade and one can of frozen limeade, blend until leaves are pulverized, and strain. Fill a glass with ice, pour 1 to 2 ounces of the mint mixture into the glass, and add plain or carbonated water. Add vodka for a hard drink. Mint julep is a traditional summer drink consisting of bourbon, sugar, spearmint, and crushed ice traditionally served in silver or pewter cups that have been prechilled until frosty. Mojito, actually a spearmint variety, is the name of a Cuban rum drink flavored with mint. Mint flowers are edible and may be added to both fruit and green salads. Break them up, and sprinkle them over chocolate desserts. Some cooks do the same to flavor lamb dishes.

There are dozens of mint species and named varieties within those species. Cold-climate gardeners most commonly grow two types of mint: peppermint and spearmint. Many other varieties are hardy to -20°F and offer flavors varying from lemon and lime to chocolate. Although I have grown many of these, peppermint and spearmint are, in my opinion, the hardiest and the best for cold climates. There are some named varieties of peppermint and spearmint, so when buying a plant, ask what variety it is. Herb specialists will know, but most nurseries won't. Grow both peppermint (Mentha × piperita) and spearmint (Mentha spicata) to compare flavors. Generally, spearmint is more popular but farther spreading. Both have mildly serrated leaves, but spearmint's are larger and more "crinkly," while peppermint's are a deeper green. With proper care these will last in a garden for decades. The mint I am presently growing has been in the family for half a century.

Mint is believed to be native to southern Europe.

Oregano
Origanum vulgare
Mint Family (Lamiaceae, formerly Labiatae)

Oregano is a tender perennial. Some varieties may survive to -25°F with protection, but the more tender plants listed here have to be grown in pots and brought indoors during the winter. While there are many edible and ornamental oreganos, one of the most popular is Greek oregano (*Origanum vulgare* ssp. *hirtum,* formerly *Origanum heraclites* or *heracleoticum).* It is also known as rigani (REE-gah-knee). This herbaceous, bushy perennial has pungent light- to dark-green, oval, pointed leaves with wavy edges. Its flavor is bolder than that of sweet marjoram. Do not start this plant from its ultrafine seed (about 300,000 rounded brown seeds per ounce), since seed is often incorrectly labeled. Instead, purchase a plant (these should be grown from cuttings, which you can do as well). Grow in a container with excellent drainage. It thrives in full sun but tolerates partial shade. Water only when the soil dries out. Snip off the ends of growing stems regularly to force the plant to form lateral

Of the many varieties of this herb, Greek oregano is one of the best and should be picked before the plant blooms.

Red perilla is more beautiful than green perilla, but green perilla grows more vigorously and self-seeds like crazy.

branches and become bushy as well as eliminate the chance of flowering. True Greek oregano has white flowers.

One other good, and perhaps better, choice is 'Hilltop', *Origanum × majoricum*. The plant is a cross between oregano and marjoram. It is commonly referred to as Italian oregano, noted for its excellent flavor. If you don't cut the plant back, stiff tan stems shoot up from its base. Little branches form at intervals and produce small, green, ball-like clusters with tiny, pointed, white flowers. The leaves of both varieties have a poor taste if the plant is allowed to bloom. So snip the stems back to the point where flowers are beginning to form, which is often right to the main clump of leaves. Some gardeners dry these stems before stripping off the mild tasting blooms, which they then use in cooking.

The leaves and flowers of both varieties are edible and can be dried. Oregano, fresh or dried, is used in bread, added as a flavoring to butter, and used in a wide variety of Italian dishes, including flavored toppings for pizza.

Bring pots indoors in winter. Keep plants cool and in bright light, water lightly, and let them limp through winter. Begin more consistent watering in spring. Harden off before placing outdoors.

Species of oregano are native to Europe and the Middle East.

Perilla
Perilla species
Mint Family (Lamiaceae, formerly Labiatae)

Perilla is a tender, warm-season annual that produces lush and long-lasting foliage. It is one of the loveliest plants in the garden and could be raised for its ornamental appeal alone. It is sometimes referred to as beefsteak plant (now obsolete), Chinese or Japanese basil, gee so, purple mint, sesame leaf, shiso (shi-so), wild coleus, and wild sesame (the seed). It grows from tan to gray, round to irregularly round, hard seed (varying from 8,000 to 27,000 seeds per ounce) into a tall plant with feathery, frilly, green or purple leaves depending on the variety planted. As the name Japanese basil implies, it too has a wide range of scents, including anise (more common in red perilla), basil, cilantro, cinnamon (more common in green), citrus (lemon), clove, ginger (more common in green), licorice, and mint. Plants may form clusters of dainty, white to purplish, tubular flowers, a favorite of bumblebees, and eventually seedpods.

Before planting, perilla seed has a tendency to need a long dormant period. Buy seeds well in advance, and place them in moist sphagnum peat moss in a plastic bag in the refrigerator for 3 to 4 months before planting. After this moist chilling (stratification), soak seeds for 24 hours before planting. Note that many gardeners skip this process and still get seeds to germinate. Even so, this process is recommended. Whether planting seed indoors 6 to 8 weeks before the frost-free date or direct seeding outdoors when the soil is 70°F, press the seed into the soil surface. Seeds grow best if they "sense" light. It is critical to keep the soil evenly moist until seed germinates and plants are growing vigorously. Don't grow mixtures of green and red perilla seed. The reason is that the green overwhelms the red. Grow them in different rows. Also, most seed packet mixtures contain far more of the green than the red perilla seeds.

Perilla can be used in many stages of growth: the seed for sprouts, the young plants for microgreens, and the mature leaves raw or cooked in numerous ways. Raw leaves can be cut into bits to flavor salads and cooked dishes, wrapped around meats during cooking, and used to flavor and color ginger, sake, and vinegar (especially the purple types). The fresh leaves are considered most desirable when picked from newly emerging plants or from the tips of more mature plants. The red types are rarely used raw. The green types are commonly used with sashimi, sushi, and tempura. Perilla is considered a good replacement for nori (seaweed) in Japanese dishes. It is commonly sautéed and stir-fried with vegetables, often spiced with garlic or ginger. The leaves can be dried for tea. They can be used as an optional ingredient in the seven spices of Japan (shichimi togarashi), which translates into "seven-flavor chile pepper." The seven spices (nine with optional ingredients) are citrus peel, garlic, ginger, hemp seeds, nori (seaweed), perilla, poppy seeds, sancho (sichuan pepper), and sesame seeds. The leaves and flower buds can be pickled. The flowers themselves can be added to numerous dishes as flavoring, and if they have a chance to go to seed, the seed whole or ground into a powder can be sprinkled on fish, rice, salads, and seafood.

If plants have a chance to flower and form seed, they are potentially invasive. *Note that perilla can be toxic to horses and cattle and that a few people have an allergic reaction (dermatitis) to the perilla aldehyde in the leaves.* Perilla is sold as *Perilla* (often green and purple mixes), *Perilla* var. *crispa*, and 'Hojiso'. The later has lovely leaves, green on top and purple underneath.

Perilla probably originated in China or Japan but may have come from India as well.

Rosemary
Rosemarinus officinalis
Mint Family (Lamiaceae, formerly Labiatae)

Rosemary is a very tender perennial. Consider it an indoor plant to be grown over the summer outdoors. Buy as large a plant as you can afford. It is extremely slow growing. Check to make sure the plant has not been newly potted. Give it a light tug. If it resists, it is well established. Roots coming out of the drainage holes are another sign that the plant has not been planted recently. If not in a clay pot, pot it up in one. Grow it in light, almost airy, alkaline soil that drains freely. The plant should have a nice, even bushy look from the start since it is difficult to shape later on. The narrow, pointed leaves should be an even green.

Rosemary can be grown from rounded, oblong, brownish-tipped tan seeds (about 17,500 to 21,000 seeds per ounce) but is most often propagated by stem cuttings. If you have a deep-green thumb and are dying for a challenge, start seed indoors 10 weeks before the last spring frost. Plant ⅛ to ¼ inch deep in starting mix that contains no peat moss, and keep evenly moist at 70° to 80°F in day, cooler at night. Germination generally occurs within 21 days but is highly erratic. Harden off young plants before setting them outdoors for the summer. Never place outdoors if there is any chance of frost. The plant thrives in hot, sunny places. In warm climates it literally covers hillsides, *but in cold climates it tends to sulk.*

This evergreen has an incredible scent, almost medicinal, which clings to your fingers if you touch the elongated, spiky, narrow needlelike leaves. The plant gets woody at its base with age, more tender at its tips. Water and fertilize the plant regularly. Harvesting stem tips will make the plant bushier, although a nice specimen is quite bushy on its own. Clip tips off stems as needed for seasoning, but don't overdo it, especially on younger plants. Do not cut off any stems in winter. Hang stems upside down to dry the leaves, then use or strip off leaves and store in a tightly sealed container. Stems of rosemary can be flash frozen and placed in airtight freezer bags, but drying is preferred.

Rosemary is delightful for roasts, most commonly used with lamb but nice with pork and chicken as well. It can be added as flavoring for bread, marinades, salad dressings, sauces, soups, and stuffings (especially chicken).

This is not a cold-climate plant, since most varieties die out at temperatures below 17°F. Two specific varieties, 'Arp' and 'Madeline Hill', also known as 'Hill Hardy', have shown

Rosemary will die out in winter unless brought indoors, but it is worth the effort for its unique aroma.

If sage survives a winter, cut back the woody stems to live growth to harvest leaves later in the season.

greater hardiness, even from 0° to -10°F. This is still not hardy enough to be left outdoors during the winter. Bringing it indoors and having it survive is challenging but possible. At the end of the season bring the plant indoors for part of each day over several weeks to acclimate it to the higher temperature, lower humidity, and lower light conditions indoors. Do not stop watering, but let the top inch or so of the soil dry out between waterings. Once it starts to get really cold outside, bring the plant inside. Give it as much sun as possible on a south-facing windowsill or under grow lights. Water the plant well as soon as the soil begins to dry out, typically every other day. You want the soil surface to dry out between deep waterings but not stay soggy—especially around the roots, which will rot out if they rest in water too long. Make sure there is good air circulation around the plant. *If not given enough light, warmth, and water, this plant can turn on a dime and die.* If kept alive for several years , these plants may form small, delicate, light-blue, five-petaled, edible flowers, although this is rare in cold climates. I can only recommend this plant if you have a greenhouse, a south-facing windowsill, or are content to view it as an annual.

Rosemary is native to the Mediterranean coast.

Sage
Salvia species
Mint Family (Lamiaceae, formerly Labiatae)

Although there are many edible varieties, the following perennial sages grown as annuals in cold climates are commonly suggested for culinary purposes: *Salvia officinalis* (common sage) with light-blue flowers, *Salvia officinalis* var. 'Purpurea' (purple sage) with purple flowers and leaves, and *Salvia elegans* (pineapple sage) with striking, flaring, red flowers. Although you can grow these plants from small, dark-brown seed (about 7,000 to 3,400 seeds per ounce), buying plants makes more sense. Even seed sources often sell plants rather than seeds. Common and purple sage may survive to -20°F and, occasionally, colder, but if soil is compacted and moist, they will die out. If they die back but show signs of growth at the base, cut back the dead stems to that part of the plant. You will need pruning shears to cut through the stiff stems. Pineapple sage is hardy only to 20°F. Consider growing them all in pots to winter over indoors if you would like to keep them from year to year.

All grow well from cuttings, and these can be started in pots and brought indoors. Place in full sun. Keep evenly moist until growing well, and then cut back on watering. Sages demand good drainage but need deep waterings once the soil dries out. In the summer cut plants back if they get gangly, but avoid trimming in winter if possible.

Plants are grown primarily for leaves, but the flowers are edible and used in salads, mustards, and vinaigrettes. Some gardeners mash them into pesto sauce. The leaves have a haunting scent. Although you can pick leaves at any time, many gardeners believe they have the best flavor just before the plant begins to flower. Common or garden sage has gray-green, downy, oblong leaves, while purple sage has elongated, pointed, green leaves with lovely purple tones. The leaves of pineapple sage look like green spearheads. Add sparingly to salads, mix bits with butter, add fresh right at the end to cooked dishes. Common or garden sage is often used to flavor breads, cheeses, pork, poultry, and sausage. Pineapple sage is used primarily as a flavoring for lemonade and tea, although its gorgeous tubular flowers make a stunning statement when added to cream cheese.

Most people prefer fresh sage, although it does dry reasonably well. To dry, hang upside down in a dry, well-ventilated area. Strip off the leaves once thoroughly dry. The taste does change but is still agreeable. Store in an airtight container. Add to omelets, sausage, soups, stews, and stuffings.

Common and purple sage are native to the Mediterranean area, while pineapple sage comes from Mexico.

Young leaves of salad burnet contribute a cucumber-like flavor to salads.

Salad Burnet
Sanguisorba minor ssp. *minor (Poterium sanguisorba)*
Rose Family (Rosaceae)

Salad burnet is an herbaceous perennial hardy to -30°F in the garden, less so in containers. In warmer climates it can be an evergreen. The seeds look like small, bumpy shields (about 2,800 to 3,900 seeds per ounce). They form a clump or rosette of lacy, rounded leaves with pinked edges. The plants grow best on the edge of sunny areas in dappled light and make good edging plants along pathways. Plant seed ⅛ inch deep about 2 weeks before the last expected spring frost. Keep the soil consistently moist, which helps keep the area around the plants on the cool side. The edible leaves have a mild cucumber taste and should be picked young before they become bitter with age. Remove them from the stems. Begin regular harvesting when the plants are no more than 4 inches tall. Keep plants trimmed back, forcing them to produce regular rounds of young leaves.

Add fresh leaves to salads, or cut them into small pieces, and mix them into dressings, as in herb vinegar, and sauces—delightful mixed with yogurt. Or toss a few whole leaves into iced tea or lemonade. If used to flavor cheese spreads, cooked dishes, or soups, chop finely, and add at the last moment for best flavor. Salad burnet does not dry well but does freeze. To freeze, wash young and tender leaves, mince, place in ice cube trays, and freeze. Remove from trays, and place in airtight freezer bags. Toss cubes into sauces, seasonings, and soups.

If plants are allowed to mature, they will eventually form small, pinkish-purple, ball-like flowers. Stems at this stage are sometimes woven into wreaths. If flowers are not removed, the plant may self-seed. The base of the plant, a clump of rhizomes, can also be divided to produce additional plants. *Sanguisorba officinalis,* greater burnet, is larger and boasts red, ball- to cone-shaped flowers.

Salad burnet is native to parts of Asia and Europe.

Savory (Summer and Winter)
Satureja species
Mint Family (Lamiaceae, formerly Labiatae)

Summer savory (*Satureja hortensis*) is an annual. It can be started indoors, but since it grows rapidly, seeding it directly in the garden is common. The deep-brown, oval seeds (47,000 seeds per ounce) should be planted ¼ inch deep after all danger of frost in spring. The seedlings usually germinate within 21 days and grow rapidly into tall, lanky plants with pinkish stems and narrow, pointed leaves. The leaves are spread far apart along these stems. Little branches shoot out

Winter savory, with its shiny, bright leaves used to season meats, survives the winter cold.

The leaves of stevia, fresh or dried, can serve as a sugar substitute.

from mature plants, forming a cuplike cluster of leaves with tiny, lilac, tubular flowers inside. It is best to harvest leaves from young plants less than 6 inches tall rather than from taller stems that have already begun to flower.

The minty flavor of summer savory is milder and more subtle than that of winter savory. The young leaves can be used fresh or dried. They are most notably used to flavor beans, from which comes the common name "the bean herb." They also make a good addition to breads, dressings, egg dishes, herb vinegar, marinades, rolls, sauerkraut, soups, stews, and stuffings. The flowers are edible and often described as spicy, even peppery, while in reality they taste much like the leaves and, in my opinion, have a poor texture. Flowers will form seed, which can be collected and used the following spring.

Winter savory *(Satureja montana)* is a perennial hardy to 10°F, although some sources claim it is hardy to -20°F or colder with winter protection. Mine has survived colder temperatures completely exposed. Consider wintering it over indoors in a pot if you are not a gambler. The plant has wider, glossier, and deeper-green leaves than summer savory. Its leaves are also more pungent. The plant tends to hug the ground and not become as gangly as summer savory.

Its young stems are green, tender, and close together. They do become woodier with age. Mature plants will flower in a cloud of small, white flowers dotting individual stems. However, the plant can be kept cut back to encourage young and more desirable growth.

Start seed indoors 6 to 8 weeks before the last expected frost. Seed is tiny (59,000 seeds per ounce) and will germinate within 14 days. The average gardener needs only one plant, so more commonly buys a plant from a nursery. Dividing mature plants or taking stem cuttings will provide additional plants.

Winter savory is used to flavor fish, meat, and poultry. It can also be used to flavor cheeses. Younger sprigs and side shoots produce the most suitable leaves for drying.

Both types probably originated in southern Europe, probably along the Mediterranean.

Stevia
Stevia rebaudiana
Aster, Daisy, or Sunflower Family
(Asteraceae, formerly Compositae)

Stevia is a very tender, short-lived perennial that will grow to a height of 36 inches or higher. The raw or dried leaves are roughly fifteen times as sweet as sugar and contain no calories. The lack of calories is appealing, but only processed stevia has been approved by the Food and Drug Administration. *Whether the plant is dangerous in its natural state is still unknown.* The raw leaves taste sweet at first but leave an awful aftertaste. Nevertheless, it has been used to sweeten drinks, and some people dry it as a sugar replacement for uncooked foods. Whole leaves are said to retain their sweetening capacity longer than powder. The latter is not as sweet as processed commercial products available at health food stores. As with any herb, consult with a doctor before using this as a sugar replacement.

I grew stevia because I had never grown or tasted it in its natural state. Now I have, and I will never grow it again. To experiment on your own, buy a plant locally or through mail order.

The plant probably originated in Paraguay and possibly other South American countries.

Tarragon (French)
Artemesia dracunculus var. *sativa*
Aster, Daisy, or Sunflower Family
(Asteraceae, formerly Compositae)

French tarragon is a perennial hardy to -30°F. It has narrow, thin, pointy, green foliage with a wonderful aroma of lico-

To get the flavor of true French tarragon, buy plants grown from cuttings.

rice or anise. Always buy plants grown from divisions, not from seed, to get true French tarragon, which is sterile. Buy plants with at least three, preferably more, shoots. If a plant seems a bit weak, continue to grow it in the original pot for an additional 2 to 3 weeks until it has formed a strong root system. Preferably, plant directly in the garden. Tarragon will grow in large containers but generally not as well. Place it in full sun in well-prepared soil that drains freely. Let the soil dry out somewhat between deep waterings.

Leaves can be dried and are a main ingredient in fines herbes, but most home gardeners prefer it fresh. To dry, snip off stem tips, remove leaves, and dry. Store as pulverized leaves in an airtight container, or add one part tarragon to two parts white vinegar. It is safer as a flavoring for vinegar than oil. Tarragon leaves can also be frozen, preferably using vacuum sealing.

French tarragon is an essential component of béarnaise sauce, often used in marinades and salad dressings, and wonderful on chicken and seafood. The leaves of older plants may lose some of their flavor. Rejuvenate older plants every 3 to 5 years by division, root cuttings, or stem cuttings. Division is usually the preferred method.

The exact origin of tarragon is unknown but is probably western Asia.

Thyme
Thymus species
Mint Family (Lamiaceae, formerly Labiatae)

The thymes included here are perennials most commonly grown as annuals in cold climates unless brought indoors during the winter. When you bring plants indoors, keep them cool and in bright light, and water lightly until spring, when you bring them back to "life."

There are hundreds of species of thyme and numerous named varieties. All have a wonderful scent and attract bees. The two covered here for culinary purposes are common or French thyme (*Thymus vulgaris*) and lemon thyme (*Thymus citriodorus*), of which there are many varieties. Grow common thyme from ultrafine, black, round seed (about 170,000 seeds per ounce). Either buy a plant, or start seed in a sterile starting mix in a pot. Press the seed into barely damp starting mix. Keep the soil at 65°F, and expect germination to take up to 21 days. Plant outdoors when temperatures reach 75°F. Buy lemon thyme as a plant, or start it from a cutting for best flavor.

Common thyme grows up to 10 to 12 inches tall and equally wide. Stems are woody at the base and produce small, green leaves with a lovely scent. Flowers are purple to white and will appear quite early in the season if plants are not sheared back. Plants are potentially hardy to about -25°F

French thyme is a shrubby plant with sprigs that go well with many types of meat.

Lemon thyme, a plant that varies in hardiness, has many different uses.

or a bit more with good winter protection but frequently die out. Lemon thyme creeps along the ground, forming a mat about 3 to 4 inches tall. Leaves also tend to be small and vary greatly in color by variety. The tiny, five-petaled flowers are typically light lilac or pink. Plants are hardy to about -15° or a bit more with good winter protection but also may die out.

Harvest sprigs and leaves just before the plant blooms. Cut plants back to about 4 inches. Do not do this late in the season if you want to try to winter plants over in the garden. Containers can be brought indoors. Or take stem cuttings to start a new plant in a sunny windowsill.

Some cooks prefer fresh leaves, others dry. The latter are more potent, and smaller amounts are needed for seasoning. Fresh leaves can be used whole, cut into bits or strips, or even crushed to release the essential oils. Common thyme is excellent with meats (especially lamb), poultry, sauces, seafood, soups, stews, and a wide range of vegetables. Blend bits of leaves into butter or cream cheese. Or add to vinegar. Use the stems in potpourris. Lemon thyme adds a unique flavor to desserts, such as cakes, custard, and muffins. It may also be used to flavor teas and fruit drinks. Place over chicken and fish while cooking. Flavor honey with it as well.

Thyme stores well either frozen or dried. To freeze, strip off leaves, flash freeze in a single layer on a flat pan in the freezer, place in airtight bags, and keep frozen. To dry, cut stems just before the plant begins to flower, hang stems upside down in a paper bag. Let dry completely. Or place on a screen in full sun. Keep whole dried sprigs or individual leaves in airtight containers in a cool, dry place.

Thyme is probably native to the western Mediterranean area, especially southern Italy.

Violet (Pansy)
Viola species
Violet Family (Violaceae)

Violets are hardy to very hardy, cool- to cold-season annuals or short-lived perennials that come in a wide variety of colors and sizes. There are more than five hundred species. The small seed is typically a pointed oval (about 24,000 seeds per ounce). Plant these as soon as the soil can be worked, or start indoors to get a jump on the season. Start 4 to 6 weeks or longer ahead of the last expected spring frost. Species vary in their growing requirements and may need moist chilling

Cooks feature violets as an edible garnish, sprinkle petals over salads, and crystallize them as colorful candy.

(stratification) to germinate well. Follow directions on the seed package. Harden off, and plant out as seedlings with final spacing about 8 inches apart or more. Snip off blossoms (deadhead) regularly to encourage new bloom.

Violet flowers make edible garnishes and delightful additions to salads, either whole or chopped into finer pieces. They are delicious added to or popped on citrusy drinks, fruit salads, and sweet deserts. Bits of *Viola tricolor,* with its ever so subtle taste of wintergreen, may be added to cheese. Crystallized (candied) flowers of most violets make striking toppings to cakes, cookies, and custard dishes. To crystallize, cover with egg whites from pasteurized eggs, and dust with superfine sugar. Let dry for a day.

Tastes do differ by species, varying from a light to a strong floral flavor. Pick flowers when at their peak, rinse lightly, and use as soon as possible. Particularly popular are *Viola cornuta* (horned pansy), *Viola odorata* (sweet violet), *Viola tricolor* (Johnny-jump-up or heartsease), and *Viola × wittrokiana* (pansy). The leaves of *Viola odorata* and *Viola × wittrokiana* may be used as edible greens added to salads when young and to stir-fries when more mature. Taste the whole flowers with the base intact and then the petals alone. The base may have a metallic or bitter flavor and can be cut off before use.

Violets frequently self-seed and come up freely the following season. They transplant easily when immature. Stem cuttings often root well to produce a greater number of plants. Larger violets can be divided as well.

Many of these plants are native to Asia, Europe, and North Africa.

KALE

'Redbor Hybrid' pleases the eye as much as the palate and tastes best after a fall frost.

***Brassica* species**
Cabbage or Mustard Family (Brassicaceae, formerly Cruciferae)

Kale is a very hardy, cold-season biennial grown as an annual. Kale, like other members of the cabbage family, likes it cool. Once growing, kale is a tough plant that can put up with a lot of abuse, including hard frosts and heavy freezes. It produces a crop of relatively tough, coarse leaves. It is a fine winter green. Common names for kale are borecole, Hanover salad, and peasant's cabbage. It probably originated in the eastern Mediterranean, Asia Minor (Turkey), and possibly along the Atlantic coast of Europe as a primitive form of cabbage.

How Kale Grows

Kale grows from a small, round, hard, purplish-tan seed (about 6,000 to 10,000 seeds per ounce). It forms firm, thick leaves that spread out from a fibrous stalk. Leaves vary in color, shape, and size according to the variety. If the plant is able to survive cold winters, it will bolt and form yellow, cross-shaped, four-petaled flowers. These mature into sickle-shaped pods containing seeds to complete the plant's life cycle.

Where to Plant Kale

Site and Light

Kale thrives in full sun but needs to mature in cool weather for best taste. If you live in an area with cool summers, you will be able to extend the harvest period for seed planted in spring. If you live in a hot area, plant in early spring in partial shade or later in the season for a fall harvest.

Soil and Moisture

Kale grows well in loose soil that drains freely but retains moisture during dry spells. By adding lots of organic matter to the soil, you provide ideal conditions. If soil is compacted, build a raised bed. Add organic fertilizers, especially those containing nitrogen. Go easy from the start, and add more later in the season only if necessary. Adding a fertilizer high in calcium often results in lush growth. The ideal soil pH is mildly acidic, around 6.5 to 6.8, but can be more alkaline if clubroot has been a problem in your garden. Reduce the chance of this disease by adding lime to the soil in fall.

Nutrition Facts

Serving size: 100 grams (3.5 ounces)

	AMOUNT PER RAW SERVING	% DV	AMOUNT PER COOKED SERVING	% DV
Calcium	135 mg	14%	72 mg	7%
Calories	50	2%	28	1%
Carbohydrates	10 g	3%	6 g	2%
Copper	0.3 mg	14%	0.2 mg	8%
Dietary fiber	2 g	8%	2 g	8%
Folate	30 mcg	7%	13 mcg	3%
Iron	1.7 mg	9%	0.9 mg	5%
Magnesium	35 mg	8%	18 mg	5%
Manganese	0.8 mg	40%	0.4 mg	20%
Potassium	450 mg	13%	230 mg	7%
Protein	3 g	7%	2 g	4%
Riboflavin	0.1 mg	8%	0.05 mg	4%
Thiamin	0.1 mg	7%	0.05 mg	4%
Vitamin A	15,375 IU	310%	13,625 IU	275%
Vitamin B6	0.3 mg	14%	0.1 mg	7%
Vitamin C	120 mg	200%	40 mg	70%
Vitamin K	820 mcg	1,020%	820 mcg	1,020%

Container

Kale grows well in large containers. Unless you eat a lot of kale, this is a highly recommended way to grow it. Start the seed in full sun in spring, but move the pot into partial shade if temperatures soar. Pots tend to heat up quickly and dry out fast. This is a plant that really likes it cool. Dwarf varieties are preferred for containers. Consider growing lettuce in a second container, harvesting it as long as possible, then switching it to kale to be harvested in fall.

Planting

Seed

Sow seed ¼ to ½ inch deep about 3 inches apart in rows 18 inches apart. Or scatter seed over a wide band for wide-row gardening. Cover the seed with vermiculite or sifted soil. Moisten immediately. Seed should sprout within 7 to 10 days. Plant a little more seed than you really need. Thin as needed later.

Transplants

Some ardent kale fans start plants indoors, either in spring for an early planting or in midsummer for a fall harvest. Sow seed in a moist starting mix at 70°F. Ideally, transplants should be no more than 3 to 4 inches tall when trans-

planted. Some gardeners don't even let them get that tall. When planting transplants, set plants in holes up to their lowest leaf, and firm the soil around them before watering immediately. Note that flowering or ornamental kales should be started indoors since they rarely develop as fast as edible varieties. They are commonly sold as transplants in local nurseries.

Spacing

Most gardeners space plants 12 to 15 inches apart, a little less if entire plants are harvested early in the season. Place farther apart if growing larger plants late in the season. Some varieties will spread out to 18 to 24 inches.

When to Plant

Some gardeners start seed indoors to get transplants into the ground as early as possible, usually 1 to 2 weeks before the last expected spring frost, or they direct seed as soon as the soil can be worked in spring when temperatures are around 40° to 45°F. Once seedlings are growing vigorously, they may survive temperatures down to 25°F. Still, you may have to plant small, successive plantings since a hard frost or severe cold spell may destroy an initial planting if not fully protected. For the fall planting, sow seeds 10 weeks before the first expected frost. Again, some gardeners start seed indoors since outdoor temperatures can be extremely hot. Seeds germinate best at 60° to 70°F. Others direct seed in much hotter weather, making sure that seedlings stay moist and well mulched to keep the soil cool. The later planting often produces the best-tasting leaves, as they mature in cold weather when covered with frost or snow. Although it's a gamble, some gardeners plant seeds just before the ground freezes in the hope that they will sprout the following spring when the soil warms to exactly the correct temperature for germination.

How to Care for Kale

Water

Providing the right amount of water for kale is a bit tricky. Keep soil consistently moist while seedlings develop into young plants. As plants mature, let the soil dry out a bit. Water less frequently but deeply around the root zone. If plants are stressed by drought, leaves often get tough and bitter.

Mulch

Kale has a shallow root system. By mulching around the plants, you avoid weeding and cultivating the soil. The mulch keeps the soil moist and cool, both conditions favorable to rapid growth. Mulch also keeps soil from splashing onto leaves. Straw is the ideal mulch, but grass clippings and pulverized leaves work fine.

Fertilizing

Kale grown in fertile soil often grows well without additional fertilizer during the growing season. Let the vigor and color of the leaves be your guide. Fertilize only if necessary. Some gardeners insist that too much nitrogen makes leaves overly frost sensitive in the fall. So when fertilizing, feed lightly.

Weeding

Weed carefully. If you hoe, avoid damaging the shallow root system. Pull any weeds by hand as soon as they appear. Handpick any weeds that pop up through the mulch. Do not cultivate close to the plants, or you will damage their shallow root system.

Thinning

If you have planted seed close together, then thin to 4 inches as seedlings emerge. Let them get tall enough to eat. Thin again depending on how often and hard you harvest.

Pruning

Old kale is tough and stringy. Remove older leaves to stimulate new growth—young, tender, and tasty new leaves. Or let the outer leaves grow, and harvest only the smaller ones inside, making sure to leave the terminal bud and a few small leaves underneath it alone.

Special Considerations

Kale does get tough and more bitter and may bolt in hot weather when temperatures reach 77°F. Even so it is both nutritious and edible. Work with it to make it palatable.

Consume a moderate amount of kale. It is highly nutritious, but eating too much has been associated with thyroid problems and allergies. Be particularly cautious if you are juicing vegetables. If you are on a blood thinner such as warfarin (Coumadin), talk to your doctor. Kale is high in vitamin K.

The variety 'Giant Walking Stick' is a novelty but rarely grown because it takes a full 6 months to mature. Many varieties of kale are sold as ornamentals, mixed into perennial borders and even used in wedding bouquets. The varietal chart includes the lovely, red-purple 'Red Chidori Flowering Kale Hybrid'.

Extending the Season

Most varieties of kale are hardy to 5°F. 'Red Russian' is said to have survived temperatures down to -10°F. 'Ripbor',

'Starbor', and 'Winterbor' are also cold resistant. If you want to harvest the crop during winter, cover the plants with a thick layer of mulch, such as 12 inches of loose straw. Hope for lots of snow and a lack of fluctuating temperatures. Of course, you can protect plants with individual cloches or a plastic tunnel for even more effective protection.

Problems

Insects

Although not as commonly bothered as other crops in the same family, kale is susceptible to attack by aphids, cabbage loopers, cabbage root maggots, cabbage worms, cutworms, flea beetles, leafminers, nematodes, slugs, and snails.

Disease

Kale is not as commonly affected by disease as some of the other members of its family. *Brassica oleracea* is mildly susceptible to clubroot, while *Brassica napus* is less so. Unfortunately, the disease lingers in garden soil for years. Rotate crops regularly.

Propagation

Kale plants are hard to overwinter. Cutting plants back to the ground and covering them with a thick straw mulch may work. Do not count on it. To preserve genetic diversity, you need a minimum of ten plants, some would say fifty. Digging up and storing the roots at just above freezing for replanting in spring is more reliable but an incredible chore. If you are able to overwinter plants, allow them to bolt. Long flower stems will produce numerous branches and clusters of yellow flowers that mature into thin 2- to 3-inch seedpods. Let the pods dry and turn brown on the plant. Cut them off with scissors into a paper bag, and allow to dry for several more weeks. Pinch the pods to release the seeds. Remove the debris, and keep the seed in an envelope in a cool, dry, dark place.

Brassica oleracea will cross with broccoli, Brussels sprouts, cabbage, cauliflower, collards, and so on. *Brassica napus* will cross with rutabagas and rape but not with the previously mentioned plants. Of course, both species will cross with other varieties in that same species. Flowers are both male and female on same plant and pollinated by bees. Seed lasts up to 4 to 5 years.

Harvesting

Many gardeners dislike the taste of kale, probably because they pick it during the heat of summer when leaves can get

'Dwarf Blue Curled Vates' is as nutritious as it is beautiful and has been on the market for years.

tough and bitter. Kale tastes best if harvested really young in cool weather in spring or after a frost when mature in fall. In the spring pick new leaves when no longer than a thumb for salads. Snip off small, outer leaves with a scissors. Small leaves are more tender than larger ones. For greens as a cooked side dish, pick the outer, larger leaves first, leaving the inner leaves alone. The inside of the plant has a terminal bud. Avoid damaging this, or the plant may stop producing leaves. Pick early in the day, and plunge the leaves into a pan filled with ice water. Harvest kale in the fall after a frost. The latter improves the flavor by turning starch into sugar. Kale is extremely cold resistant. You can harvest it even after a snow.

Storing

Store kale in the garden by covering it with a thick winter mulch. A 12-inch covering of loose straw is the easiest to work with. A winter mulch of whole leaves is another option, but they tend to mat down after the first snow.

Once picked, kale does not store for a long time. That's why market gardeners often pull up the entire plant for sale. Keep it cool while picking. As with other leafy vegetables, it may collect a little coating of soil. Rinse it under cold running water, and shake off excess moisture. Roll leaves in a paper towel so that each leaf is sandwiched between paper. Place the rolled-up leaves in a plastic bag in the crisper of the refrigerator. Use the leaves as soon as possible since they become tougher with age—certainly within 4 days. Keep as close to freezing and 100 percent humidity as possible.

To freeze, pick young leaves, or remove stems from older leaves, blanch small amounts at a time for 1 to 2 minutes depending on thickness of leaves, plunge into ice water, drain, chop into pieces or leave whole, pack into airtight freezer bags, and freeze. Note that greens do lose vitamins when blanched. Some people prefer cooking them for less than a minute in the microwave instead of plunging them into boiling water.

Culinary Uses

The leaves, flowers, and seeds are all edible. The leaves are usually eaten cooked, but young leaves less than finger size can be gathered for fresh salads. Try this with 'White Russian'. For color, use 'Winter Red'. Raw kale also makes a lovely garnish.

Rinse before chopping, cutting, or shredding leaves for cooking. Some people remove the stems and larger ribs from leaves, but this is optional. To cook, barely cover in boiling water, sauté in a pan with a little butter or olive oil (add garlic just at end of cooking), microwave in a little water, steam lightly, or add to stir-fries. Note that greens do lose vitamins when cooked. Cook just until tender. For side dishes, some cooks splash with vinegar, add some lemon juice mixed in melted butter, or top with bits of hard-boiled egg. 'Winterbor' is excellent cooked as a side dish.

If plants bolt, allow them to form buds. Sauté the top budding portion of the flower stem like broccoli raab, or sprinkle the buds alone on salads. If plants survive the winter, do the same. Also, allow some flower stalks to form seed, which can be sprouted and added to salads or sandwiches for a mustardy bite.

Consider making a Portuguese soup called *caldo verde*. Add potatoes and water to onions and garlic cooked in olive oil for a few minutes, and then cook until tender. Add kale toward the end of the cooking process. 'Lacinato' is the traditional kale used in this dish. Recipes abound.

For a nutritious snack, cut leaves into thin strips, brush with oil, place on a cookie sheet, and bake at 375°F until brittle and dry. Salt if desired. These chips actually appeal to children.

Varieties

Kale varieties come from a diverse group of species. Many are crosses. Determining the origin can be difficult. The form of plants varies from mounded to upright. The texture of the leaves may be tightly curled resembling parsley or more open and less curly, almost smooth. Leaf color varies by variety. Colors are blue, blue gray, gray green, light to deep green, red, and purplish. Tastes are also quite different, varying from relatively mild to pungent and peppery. For flavor, start with 'Lacinato' and 'Winterbor', and span out from there, perhaps adding 'White Russian' to compare tastes. Note that 'Lacinato' has a reputation for being more difficult to grow than 'Winterbor'.

Depending on the source, varieties of kale may be listed as *Brassica napus*, *Brassica napus* var. *pabularia*, *Brassica oleracea* var. *acephala* or Acephala group, and *Brassica rapa* var. *ruvo*. *Brassica napus* var. *pabularia* may be a cross between *Brassica rapa* ssp. *chinensis* (Asian mustard) and *Brassica oleracea* var. *acephala* (kale/collard). Individual varieties may also be crosses. 'Pentland Brig' may be a cross between *Brassica oleracea* and thousand-headed kale *Brassica oleracea* var. *fruticosa,* commonly used as animal fodder. 'Red Ursa' may be a cross between 'Red Russian' and 'Siberian'. In many ways the leaves and flower stalks of varying varieties are similar to cabbage, collards, rape, and even turnips. To add to the confusion, plants may be labeled Scotch (borecole) or Siberian (Russo-Siberian) kales, and different varietal names may be used for identical plants. The term *European kale* may refer to black Italian types, such as 'Lacinato'. 'Hanover Salad' is listed in many catalogs as a type of rape but may be called Hanover turnip. And Siberian kales are also sometimes referred to as rapes. Actually, any *Brassica napus* can be called a rape. 'Nero di Toscano' is essentially the same as 'Lacinato', which is listed as a cabbage in some catalogs. Scotch types *(Brassica oleracea)* have very curly and wrinkled leaves, while Russian (or Siberian) types *(Brassica napus)* are almost flat with finely divided edges and blue or reddish hues. Finally, the Italian heirloom 'Lacinato' is in a class of its own and sold by many different names.

VARIETIES	DAYS	SPECIES	LEAVES	HEIGHT (INCHES)
'Black Cabbage' (see 'Lacinato')				
'Black Kale' (see 'Lacinato')				
'Black Palm (Cabbage)' (see 'Lacinato')				
'Black Tuscan' (see 'Lacinato')				
'Blue Curled Scotch' (see 'Dwarf Blue Curled')				
'Blue Curled Vates' (see 'Dwarf Blue Curled Vates')				
'Blue Ridge Hybrid'	60	*Oleracea*	Very curly, dark blue green	18
'Cavolo Nero' (see 'Lacinato')				
'Cavolo Pamizio' (see 'Lacinato')				
'Darkibor Hybrid'	75	*Oleracea*	Very curly, dark blue green	18
'Dazzling Blue' (OP)*****	60	*Oleracea*	Very curly, dark blue green with pink midribs	24–36
'Dinosaur Kale' (see 'Lacinato')				
'Dwarf Blue Curled' (heirloom)	60	*Oleracea*	Very finely curled, blue green	12–15
'Dwarf Blue Curled Scotch' (see 'Dwarf Blue Curled')				
'Dwarf Blue Curled Vates' (heirloom)*****	55	*Oleracea*	Curly, blue green	12–15
'Dwarf Green Curled' (heirloom)	65	*Oleracea*	Wrinkled, curly, yellow green with white ribs	18
'Dwarf Siberian Improved' (heirloom)	65	*Napus*	Frilly edged, gray green tinged purplish	14–16
'Early Curled Siberian' (see 'Siberian')				
'Early Hanover' (heirloom)	65	*Napus*	Smooth, medium, green scalloped edges	12–14
'Early Siberian' (see 'Siberian')				
'Fizz' (heirloom)	40	*Oleracea*	Soft green, mildly lobed, oak leaf-like	24 (eat when immature)
'Greenpeace' (OP)	65	*Napus*	Frilly, green blue with red stems	12–16
'Hanover Salad' (see 'Early Hanover')				
'Improved Dwarf Siberian' (Heirloom)	55	*Napus*	Frilly, dark green, white-stemmed rosette	24

VARIETIES	DAYS	SPECIES	LEAVES	HEIGHT (INCHES)
'Lacinato' (heirloom)*****	80	*Oleracea*	Dark green, blistered, long, strap-like	24–36
'Lacinato Rainbow Mix' (OP)*****	60	*Oleracea*	Blue green tinted red and purple	24
'Nero di Toscana' (see 'Lacinato')				
'Palm Tree' (see 'Lacinato')				
'Pentland Brig' (heirloom)	65	*Oleracea*	Curly, smooth, green leaves and side shoots	24
'Premier' (see 'Early Hanover')				
'Ragged Jack' (see 'Red Russian')				
'Redbor ('Red Bor') Hybrid'	65	*Oleracea*	Curly, purple burgundy leaves	18–24
'Red Chidori Flowering Hybrid'	50	*Oleracea*	Ultra-curly red with green to purple edges	12
'Red Ruffled' (OP)	60	*Napus*	Flat, ruffled margins, gray green with purple stem	24
'Red Russian' (heirloom)*****	60	*Napus*	Oak-like, blue gray green with purple veins	30
'Red Ursa' (OP)	60	*Napus*	Gray green, frilly with red purple veins	24–30
'Red Winter' (see 'Winter Red')				
'Ripbor Hybrid'	60	*Oleracea*	Dark blue green, ruffled	16
'Russian Red' (see 'Red Russian')				
'Semi Dwarf Westlandse' (heirloom)	55–60	*Oleracea*	Very curly, green	32–40
'Siberian' (heirloom)	55	*Napus*	Huge oak-like or feathery, blue green	18–24
'Siberian Curled' (see 'Siberian')				
'Siberian Dwarf' (see 'Dwarf Siberian Improved')				
'Starbor Hybrid'	55	*Oleracea*	Very finely curled, blue green	18
'Tronchuda Beira Hybrid'	55	*Oleracea*	Blue green, paddle-shaped	12–18
'True Siberian' (see 'Siberian')				
'Tuscan Black Cabbage' (see 'Lacinato')				
'Tuscan Black Palm' (see 'Lacinato')				
'Tuscan Kale' (see 'Lacinato')				
'Vates' (see 'Dwarf Blue Curled Vates')				
'Vates Blue Curled' (see 'Dwarf Blue Curled Vates')				
'Westland Winter' (heirloom)	60	*Oleracea*	Very frilly, blue green	18
'White Russian' (heirloom)*****	60	*Napus*	Oak-like, blue green with white stem	36
'Winterbor Hybrid'*****	60	*Oleracea*	Very curly, green blue with frilly edges	36
'Winter Red' (heirloom)*****	50	*Napus*	Oak-leaf, frilly, dark green with red veins	24–30

Kalette (Flower Sprout) (Brusselkale™) (Lollipops)
Brassica oleracea

This is a cross between kale and brussels sprouts. It appears to be a tiny cabbage but with frilly leaves streaked purple. They are edible raw or cooked, normally grilled, roasted, or sautéed.

Giant Walking Stick Kale
Brassica oleracea var. *longata*

This is grown as an oddity, not for food. The stem may get up to 7 feet tall to be cut and dried in fall. It is not really a cold-climate plant unless you start it indoors and hope for warm weather in fall through early winter. It's a gamble and grown for fun. The giant leaves that form on top are part of the amusement.

KOHLRABI

Brassica oleracea var. *gongylodes* or Gongylodes Group
Cabbage or Mustard Family (Brassicaceae, formerly Cruciferae)

Kohlrabi, sometimes referred to as stem or turnip cabbage, is a very hardy, cold-season biennial grown as an annual. Kohlrabi produces an edible, swollen stem, often referred to as a "bulb," which it is not. It's an odd-looking plant, with an outer-space aura. Good either raw or cooked, it is finally beginning to be appreciated for its mild, turnip-like taste and water chestnut texture. It is fairly easy to grow, takes up little space, and has few problems compared to other members of its family. Kohlrabi may have originated in an area along the Atlantic coast of Europe or in the Mediterranean.

How Kohlrabi Grows

Kohlrabi seed is small, round, hard, and dark brown to black (about 6,000 to 9,000 seeds per ounce). It produces small plants similar to cabbage. As the plant matures, the stem swells. The swollen portion looks like a "bulb" floating above the soil surface. Bluish-green leaves hover on sparsely spaced stems, which is why it is often referred to as looking like an alien spaceship. It is highly unlikely in cold climates for the plants to survive winters and produce delicate, yellow flowers in the shape of a cross the following year.

Where to Plant Kohlrabi

Site and Light

Kohlrabi grows best in full sun but will tolerate partial shade.

Soil and Moisture

Kohlrabi thrives in a cool, moist soil that drains freely. Loosen the soil well, then add plenty of organic matter. Mix in well-rotted manure if available. If not, use organic fertilizers, since kohlrabi is a heavy feeder. A soil pH of 6.5 is ideal; pH between 6 and 7 is fine.

Container

Plants grow well in containers. Plant them more thickly than you might think necessary, and harvest young.

Nutrition Facts

Serving size: 100 grams (3.5 ounces)

	AMOUNT PER RAW SERVING	% DV	AMOUNT PER COOKED SERVING	% DV
Calories	27	1%	27	1%
Carbohydrates	6 g	2%	7g	2%
Dietary fiber	4 grams	14%	1 g	4%
Manganese	0.1 mg	7%	0.1 mg	7%
Potassium	350 mg	10%	350 mg	10%
Protein	2 g	3%	2 g	3%
Vitamin B6	0.2 mg	8%	0.2 mg	8%
Vitamin C	60 mg	105%	55 mg	90%

Planting

Seed

Sow seed directly in the garden about ¼ to ½ inch deep. Presoaking is OK. Consider placing a thin layer of compost or sphagnum peat moss in the furrow, and cover the seed with fine soil. Press firmly in place, and water immediately. Some gardeners plant seed under a row cover to keep temperatures even and prevent insect damage.

Transplant

Transplanting is not really necessary for the typical home gardener but perhaps worth it for professional growers. Start seed indoors 6 to 8 weeks before the spring frost-free date. Plant seed in a sterile starting mix, and keep them at 60° to 70°F. Seed should germinate within 9 days. Always harden off seedlings for 7 to 10 days before planting them out. When planting, avoid damaging the growing tip.

Spacing

Spacing depends on the variety and how soon you will begin to harvest the "bulbs." Your initial planting of just a few inches apart allows you to harvest some plants early, leaving the rest to mature later. For most varieties, 6 inches between plants is fine as they mature. For larger varieties, a foot apart makes sense.

When to Plant

Get transplants into the garden 3 to 4 weeks before the frost-free date in spring. Cover with a cloche if frost threatens. Direct seed as early in spring as possible, usually about 4 to 6 weeks before the last expected frost or as soon as the soil can be worked. The soil temperature should be at least 50°F. Plant seed again later in the summer to mature in the cool weeks of fall. Count back from the first expected frost date to decide on a good date for summer planting. Kohlrabi is best if it matures in cool spring or fall weather. Note that plants occasionally bolt if exposed to temperatures under 50°F for too long.

How to Care for Kohlrabi

Water

The faster kohlrabi grows, the more tender it is. Keep the soil consistently moist. This also helps keep the soil more uniformly cool.

Mulch

Kohlrabi has rather shallow and fragile roots. As soon as the plants pop up, mulch around them. Pulverized leaves or grass clippings work well. Start with an inch or so of mulch, and add more as the season progresses. Do not place mulch against the stem. Again, this helps keep the soil moist and cool—just the way kohlrabi prefers it.

Fertilizing

Kohlrabi is a heavy feeder. Pour a transplant solution around the plants when they are a few inches tall. Feed every few weeks with an organic fertilizer. Feeding is important as leaves form and as the stem begins to swell. Blood meal, fish meal, and cottonseed meal are good choices since they are high in nitrogen.

Weeding

Avoid cultivating around the base of the plants. The roots are sensitive to disturbance. If you mulch, you don't have to cultivate. If a few weeds sprout, pull them out by hand.

Thinning

Thin the plants so that they are not closer than 6 to 8 inches. One simple way of thinning is to begin harvesting at a young age. This is especially true for a spring planting. For larger varieties that typically are planted in summer for a fall harvest, you can do the same, but leave a foot or so between plants if they are "giant" types.

Extending the Season

Many people feel that kohlrabi tastes better when touched by frost. Protect late plantings with a mulch to extend the harvest as much as possible, but don't expect your plants to withstand temperatures below 10°F. Without protection they may freeze at 30°F.

Problems

Insects

Cabbage worms and loopers, cutworms, and flea beetles have been known to attack kohlrabi but less so than other members of the cabbage family. Handpick worms, and cover young plants with row covers to prevent damage early in the season. Root maggots are more of a problem with other members of this family.

Disease

Prevent most problems with disease by planting kohlrabi in a new spot each year and by pulling up and composting all plant debris in the fall. If you have a problem with black rot, buy a resistant variety such as 'Grand Duke Hybrid'.

Marauders

Animals will eat just about anything if they are hungry enough, but other crops tend to be preferred over kohlrabi.

Physiological

The swollen stems may split if they are left to mature too long. Begin harvesting early to extend the season over a period of weeks.

Propagation

Plants are hermaphroditic, having both male and female organs, but must be insect pollinated. Plants rarely go to flower in the first year. For propagating biennials, see chapter 5. Seed stored in an envelope in a cool place is typically good for up to 4 years.

Harvesting

Begin harvesting knobs (swollen stems) when they are the size of a golf ball. Harvest all of the quick-maturing varieties before they are wider than 2 inches. Some varieties can get a bit larger, but most will become increasingly bitter, stringy, tough, and even woody if too mature. The later-maturing varieties, such as 'Gigante' and 'Kossak Hybrid', can get much larger, even up to 8 to 10 inches. These are typically grown for a fall harvest. Begin harvesting these when smaller, and continue harvesting to find the point at which they begin to deteriorate.

Storing

Remove roots and leaves from the "bulb." Place unwashed in a plastic bag with holes. Keep as close to 32°F as possible.

They may last for up to 1 month stored in this way but are better used well before that time.

To store plants maturing in late fall for a longer period of time, trim off leaves but not the roots. Dig a shallow trench in the garden, and line it with straw. Place the swollen stems in the trench, cover them with 12 inches of straw and 6 inches of soil. Then cover the mound with whole leaves. Even if you have to dig through snow, you may be able to use these over a period of several months. 'Kossak Hybrid' stores well. A second option is to store them in moist sand in a large box. In this case remove both leaves and roots. The bulbs should not be touching. The ideal temperature is 34°F, but do not let them freeze.

To freeze, cut off tops, wash, peel, dice, or cut into ½-inch sections, blanch for 1 to 2 minutes, plunge immediately into ice water, drain, package, label, and freeze.

To pickle, cut into cubes, splash with olive oil and vinegar, season with salt and pepper, and place in the refrigerator for up to 1 week. Tweak the ingredients to taste. You can also pickle for long-term use in glass jars as you would other vegetables.

Culinary Uses

If you harvest young plants, snip off the young leaves, and cook them as you would spinach. They are also tasty added to stir-fries. Older leaves are less appetizing. They are often discarded, but a few people do eat them as they would collards, especially if growing the Czech heirloom 'Gigante'.

Kohlrabi is sometimes referred to as "stem turnip" because the swollen stem has a bit of a mild turnip taste, sometimes with a little "radishy" bite. The bulbs are good raw or cooked, although many people feel strongly that they are better raw. Peel off the outer layer of tissue. Then chop, cube, grate, shred, slice, or sliver the flesh for fresh use in salads. Some people eat them just like an apple, although this is an acquired taste.

Boil, broil, butter steam, roast, sauté, steam, or stir-fry the whole or sliced knobs for a delicious side dish. Try kohlrabi au gratin, creamed, or covered with Hollandaise sauce. Add chunks to soups. Cook just until tender; do not overcook.

Varieties

Despite varying skin colors, the flesh of all varieties is creamy white. Do not be afraid to try some of the really large kohlrabies. They usually taste good even when mature.

VARIETIES	DAYS	COLOR OF SKIN	SHAPE
'Aventino Hybrid'	65	Light green	Round to mildly flat
'Azur Star' (OP)*****	60	Purple	Round to flat
'Delicacy Purple' (OP)	65	Purple	Rounded
'Delicacy White' (OP)	65	Light green	Rounded
'Dyna' (OP)	60	Reddish purple	Large round oval
'Early Purple Vienna' (heirloom)	60	Purple	Round
'Early White Vienna' (heirloom)	55	Light green	Round
'Eder Hybrid'	40	Light green	Flat round
'Express Forcer Hybrid'	45	Light green	Flat round
'Giant White' (see 'Gigante')			
'Gigante' (heirloom)	80–100+	Light green	Huge round oval
'Grand Duke Hybrid' (AAS-1979)*****	50	Light green	Round
'Kolibri Hybrid'*****	45	Purple	Flat round
'Kolpak Hybrid'	45	Light green	Flat round
'Kongo Hybrid'	50	Light green	Flat round
'Korist Hybrid'	50	Light green	Flat globe
'Korridor Hybrid'	40	Light green	Globe
'Kossak Hybrid'	80	Light to deeper green	Very large flat to globe
'Olivia Hybrid'	65	Light green	Round to flat
'Purple Vienna' (see 'Early Purple Vienna')			
'Quickstar Hybrid'	55	Light green	Flat to round
'Superschmelz' (see 'Gigante')			
'Sweet Vienna' (OP)	50	Light green	Flat rounded
'Winner Hybrid'	55	Light green	Semi-globe

Bright and beautiful red kohlrabi is crisp and crunchy raw or cooked.

To eat leeks over a longer period of time, begin to harvest them when they are much smaller than those sold in stores.

LEEKS

Allium ampeloprasum* var. *porrum,* also known as *Allium porrum
Onion or Amaryllis Family (Alliaceae or Amaryllidaceae), formerly Lily Family (Liliaceae)

Leeks are very hardy, cold-season biennials typically grown as annuals. Relatively few gardeners grow leeks, similar to elongated onions with a milder taste. Leeks, the "gourmet's onion," are a favorite of French cooks, truly a prized vegetable that is expensive in most stores. Leeks are easy to grow, stand up well to cold fall weather, and are well worth trying. Leeks may have originated in Egypt.

How Leeks Grow

Leeks grow from hard, black, irregular seeds (9,500 to 10,000 seeds per ounce) into thin, upright seedlings. Each small seedling looks like a chive or immature onion plant. It forms a strong root system with roots that look like thick threads. Instead of forming a bulb aboveground, the leek produces a fleshy, cylinder-like stem that cut in half looks like a rolled-up newspaper. The stem or stalk is really a bundle of leaves. The bottom of the plant is a pale white, while the long, fleshy leaves are a rich green. As the plant matures,

the white stem thickens and elongates, looking like an oversized green bunching onion. It is this lovely stem that is the edible portion of the plant.

Where to Plant Leeks
Site and Light

Leeks grow best in full sun but will grow reasonably well even in partial shade.

Soil and Moisture

Leeks grow best in rich, loose soil that drains freely. Loosen soil by adding lots of organic matter to it. If your soil is compacted, build a raised bed. If possible, create the bed in fall. Mix in organic fertilizers containing phosphorus and potassium at that time. Mix fertilizer high in nitrogen in spring. Dig a trench 12 inches deep where you want to plant the leeks in spring. Fill in the bottom 6 inches with compost or sphagnum peat moss mixed with some soil. Leeks grow best in soil with a pH ranging from 6 to 6.5, which is slightly acidic.

Nutrition Facts
Serving size: 100 grams (3.5 ounces)

	AMOUNT PER COOKED SERVING	% DV
Calories	30	2%
Carbohydrates	8 g	3%
Dietary fiber	1 g	4%
Folate	24 mcg	6%
Iron	1.1 mg	6%
Manganese	0.2 mg	12%
Protein	1 g	2%
Vitamin A	810 IU	16%
Vitamin B6	0.1 mg	6%
Vitamin C	4.2 mg	7%
Vitamin K	25 mcg	32%

Container

It is possible to grow leeks in containers with the idea of harvesting them young, almost like scallions. If you allow a few leeks to mature in a large, deep container, you may get a few to match those grown in the garden.

Planting
Seed

Some gardeners plant seed directly in the garden. Prepare the bed in fall. Plant seed 4 weeks before the last expected frost, which is usually as soon as the soil can be worked in spring. Sow at a depth of ½ inch, and cover with sifted soil. Firm the soil with your fingers, and water immediately. Do not expect to get as large a leek as one grown from a transplant. For microgreens or small plants, plant seed close together.

Transplants

To ensure getting large plants late in the season, either buy plants from a local nursery, or start seed indoors. Leeks can be hard to find, so starting seed may be your only option. Start seed indoors 12 to 14 weeks before the appropriate planting time, which is 2 to 4 weeks before the frost-free date in your area. You want to get plants into the garden as early as possible. Sow seeds in a large pot or flat filled with sterile starting mix. Plant them ¼ to ½ inch deep and about 1 inch apart in all directions. Keep moist at 70°F until seed leaves emerge, generally within 12 days. Tighter planting often works out fine, since some of the seeds may not sprout and seedlings shoot straight up like chives or onions.

Once the planting time is at hand, gently tease the plants out of the mix. It would be ideal to keep some mix around the roots, but this often doesn't happen. Immediately plant each seedling in the bottom of the prepared trench. Poke your finger into the compost, slide the base of the seedling into the hole, firm the plant in place with your fingers, and water immediately. Do not fill up the trench. The seedlings should end up 8 inches or so below the surrounding soil about 3 inches apart. If a hard frost or freeze is expected shortly after planting, cover the trench with row covers or a sheet. Once leeks take root, they can withstand cold.

As the plants mature, fill in the trench a little at a time to just below the leaves. By covering the stem, you are producing tender, white stalks. The longer the white portion, the better the vegetable. Some gardeners think trenching is a waste of time and blanch the stems by pulling soil up around them as the season progresses. I think that for the home gardener, trenching is the simplest and most effective way to grow leeks.

Spacing

Leeks grow well in either rows or blocks, a series of trenches alongside each other. Close planting, even as close as 6 inches between the trenches, works out fine as long as you pull up some of the younger leeks as the season progresses.

When to Plant

Get transplants into the garden as early as possible. The daytime temperature doesn't have to be any higher than 45°F. This is usually about 2 to 4 weeks before the last expected frost. For direct seeding, start as soon as the soil can be worked.

How to Care for Leeks
Water

If rain is insufficient, soak with a garden hose to maintain soil moisture. In well-drained soil, it is almost impossible to overwater leeks. The more water, the more rapid the growth. The more growth, the bigger and better the lower edible section of the plant.

Mulch

If you are planting leeks on level ground, not in a trench, mulch the area around the young plants up to the first leaf. Straw and pulverized leaves work well. As the plant grows, keep adding mulch but never higher than the bottom of the lowest leaf. In short, cover only the lower, white portion of the stem. Mulch keeps soil from splattering on the leaves. It also keeps the soil moist and cool while blanching the lower portion of stem.

Fertilizing

Add side-dressings of fertilizer throughout the growing season. Any organic fertilizer high in nitrogen is recommended. Fish emulsion is excellent, but so are others. Do this at least 3 weeks after planting and again another 3 weeks later. If your soil is already fertile, this may be unnecessary. Let the plants' growth guide you.

Weeding

Nip weeds as soon as they begin to invade the rows. Pull out any weeds that pop up through the mulch. Do this carefully when the plants are young. As they get older, they get anchored in the soil and rarely are pulled up during weeding.

Thinning

When plants reach 8 inches, thin them to 6 inches apart. Plant the thinned seedlings the same distance apart in another row, or eat them. As the plants mature to scallion size, you may want to thin them out again, but this is optional. Eat the young plants, leaving 9 inches between the remaining plants.

Pruning

Leeks may go to seed. They produce ball-like clusters of small, white to pinkish flowers. If seed heads are allowed to develop, leeks are no longer good. Cut out seed heads, or harvest plants going to seed. Or if open pollinated, let them form seed to plant the following season.

Special Considerations

Blanching means excluding light from the stem so that it turns white instead of green. Proper trenching and pulling up soil around maturing plants have already been discussed. If you pull up soil, mound it only up to, but not onto, the developing green leaves themselves. Other blanching methods include putting paper or cardboard collars around the base of the stem, but these are unnecessary if seedlings are planted deep into the soil from the start. See also "Mulch" earlier in this section.

Dried leek flowers are lovely additions to floral arrangements. Cut the flowers before they begin to form seed, and hang them upside down in a warm, well-ventilated area until completely dry.

Problems

Insects

Onion thrips and root maggots are potential threats. If these are a problem, cover seedlings with row covers at time of planting.

Disease

Diseases include white tip, a fungus that causes leaves to yellow and the plant to die; downy mildew, which looks like a purplish mold over leaf spots; neck rot, generally caused by improper cultivation that damages the plant; pink rot, where the plant turns color, wilts, and dies; and smut, or black spots on leaves, which is much more common on onions. These are not common in the home garden.

Propagation

The plant forms delicate white to pink, spherical blossoms that will produce hard, black seeds if allowed to mature. Leeks usually bloom in their second year of growth, but it is not uncommon for them to bloom in the first year if grown from transplants. Let some leeks produce flowers and go to seed. Let the seed heads dry on the plant. When dry, cut them off over an open paper bag. Let the seed head hang down in the bag. Bring it indoors, and let it dry for several weeks. The small, black seeds will fall out. Separate the seed from the debris, and store it in an envelope in a cool, dark place. Seed may last from 1 to 3 years.

Leeks apparently may form little bulbs at their base when flowering. These can be eaten or planted. Some people call these bulblets, cloves, or corms. Since I have never seen these, a proper description would be secondhand information, which is conflicting.

Harvesting

Begin harvesting leeks when only 6 to 8 inches tall. Smaller leeks are excellent raw in salads. Keep pulling at different levels of maturity throughout the season. Trim most of the roots off. As plants reach maturity when their stems are 1 to 2 inches thick, snip off the leaves so that the top looks like a Christmas tree. This fan of leaves is not good to eat but is highly decorative. Removing foliage also reduces water loss from the stems. Leeks continue to mature into late fall. They can withstand severe frosts. Leave them in the garden as long as you can. To harvest, loosen the soil around the base of the plant with a spading fork, or yank the plants out. A firm twisting motion often works well.

Storing

Some gardeners "store" leeks in the garden. Just before the soil freezes, cover leeks with a 12-inch layer of straw or whole leaves, and continue the harvest into the winter. Early snows provide excellent protection. Or place them upright in a cold frame, and cover them with moist sand, peat, or soil. When doing this, leave the roots and leaves on. Trim these off only when ready to use. If the leeks freeze, they will begin to rot. Compost them.

To store in the refrigerator, do not wash or trim off the last few roots. Place in a plastic bag in the refrigerator. Check regularly, and use as quickly as possible. If kept close to freezing at high humidity, they may last for 2 to 3 weeks but do deteriorate the longer they are stored. To freeze, keep only the white portion and tender green areas, cut lengthwise, wash well, chop into small pieces, blanch for 2 minutes (optional), cool in ice water, pack in airtight freezer bags, and freeze.

Culinary Uses

Leeks make excellent microgreens when pulled very young. Chop them into pieces, and add to omelets and salads. Wash off the soft, pliable leaves of younger leeks. They are extremely tender and have a mellow, earthy flavor. Use them fresh in salads, or cook quickly for a side dish.

On more mature leeks the lower white portion is the part of the plant that is the most tender and sought after. In homegrown leeks a good portion of green is also quite tender. Pick older leeks just before using if possible. Swish the leaves in a pot of water. If not trimmed in the garden, cut off the tough upper portion of the leaves, creating a fan shape. Trim off the roots. Cut the leek in two lengthwise. Wash again. If necessary, pull out one portion of outer "skin" to get rid of soil. Boiling, broiling butter steaming, microwaving, sautéing, steaming, and stir-frying—all are good ways of cooking leeks. Boil leeks until tender, cut in two lengthwise, place in single layer in a shallow pan, drench in butter flavored with fresh tarragon, cover with shredded cheese, and broil for several minutes until cheese melts. Cut the lower white portion of the plant into ¼-inch slices, and butter steam until tender. Cut leeks in two, and microwave. Or place halved stems on a rack, and steam until tender. Sauté with lemon juice and herbs. For stir-frying, cut the lower portion into thin slices and cook quickly, or add to other vegetables. Cut into pieces, and add to soups and stews during the last few minutes of cooking. Or make vichyssoise, the famed potato-leek soup served chilled. In the second year, pick flowers just as they bloom, snap off florets, and add to salads for taste and color. Leeks do not always survive cold winters but sometimes do.

Varieties

Elephant garlic is not a garlic but a leek (*Allium ampeloprasum* var. *ampeloprasum*). It produces a large bulb with five to six cloves and can weigh up to a pound. Normally available only in fall, it usually dies out over the winter. It is often listed as hardier than it really is. Its true hardiness is highly debated but may only be 10°F.

Pearl onions (*Allium porrum* var. *sectivum* or *Allium ampeloprasum* var. *sectivum*) are closely related to leeks. They are sometimes referred to as perennial leeks or miniature elephant garlic. The name *pearl onion* is often used incorrectly to describe small onions. True pearl onions form tiny bulbs (offsets) to the side of the mother plant. These in turn form clumps of plants if left to mature. The variety 'Perlzwiebel', pearl onion in German, is included in the table below. It is hardy only to -20°F.

Kurrat (*Allium ampeloprasum* var. *kurrat*), or Egyptian leek, is grown primarily for its leaves. *It is not cold hardy and mentioned only because it is in the marketplace.*

The following varieties represent a range of early- to later-maturing varieties and varying plant heights. Some catalog companies offer both seed and plants. If buying plants, ask how many are in an order and how thick they are. Ideally, they should be as wide as a pencil, but that may not be the case. Or ask how old they are if the person doesn't know thickness.

VARIETIES	DAYS FROM TRANSPLANT	HEIGHT (INCHES)
'American Flag' (see 'Broad London')		
'Bandit' (OP)	110	20
'Belton Hybrid'	110	20
'Bleu de Solaise' (see 'Blue Solaise')		
'Blue Solaise' (heirloom)*****	110	20
'Broad London' (heirloom)	130	18
'Carlton Hybrid'	100	22
'Dawn Giant' (OP)	100	16
'Electra' (OP)	110	24
'Giant Musselburgh' (heirloom)	110	18
'Kenton Hybrid'*****	110	24
'King Richard' (OP)	85	24
'Lancelot' (OP)*****	85	18
'Large American Flag' (see 'Broad London')		
'Lincoln Hybrid'	110	20
'Lyon' (see 'Prizetaker')		
'Magaton Hybrid'	90	22
'Musselburgh' (see 'Giant Musselburgh')		
'Pancho' (heirloom)	80	16
'Prizetaker' (heirloom)	125	36
'Scotch Flag' (see 'Giant Musselburgh')		
'Tadorna' (OP)	110	24
'Titan' (OP)	110	30
'Vitaton Hybrid'	110	24

If you're a seed saver, let a few leeks flower to form copious amounts of seed.

The heirloom 'Black Seeded Simpson' is a fine selection of an easy-to-grow leaf lettuce.

LETTUCE

Lactuca sativa **species**
Aster, Daisy, or Sunflower Family (Asteraceae, formerly Compositae)

Lettuce is a hardy to very hardy, cool- to cold-season annual grown for its delicious foliage. It takes up little room in the garden and produces well throughout much of the season. It grows quickly, is generally easy to care for, and comes in a variety of forms and flavors. Most types probably originated in Asia Minor and the Mediterranean area.

How Lettuce Grows

Most lettuce seed is tiny, spear-shaped, tan, and firm (about 25,000 to 30,000 seeds per ounce). Stem lettuce seeds are a little wider and very dark. Once the seeds germinate, they form leafy plants that vary in growth habits according to the variety but generally have fairly large leaves. Parts of the plant may exude a milky sap when wounded. During the heat of midsummer, the plants begin to send up flower shoots topped with small, yellow flowers that form downy seed heads. Each plant can produce thousands of seeds on these strands of "silk."

Where to Plant Lettuce
Site and Light

Lettuce likes it cool but grows best in full sun. If temperatures soar, it does better in partial shade. Most lettuce varieties grow well intermingled with flowers in the border, or in the shade of other, slower-growing vegetables, such as cabbage, cauliflower, or broccoli.

Soil and Moisture

The ideal soil for lettuce is loose and fertile with good drainage but the ability to maintain moisture during dry spells. Mixing organic matter such as leaf mold or sphagnum peat moss into the soil along with organic fertilizers high in nitrogen is recommended. If the soil where seed is to be planted is lumpy, work it through a fine screen or sieve. The ideal pH is 6.5 to 6.8, but lettuce will do fine in soils more acidic or alkaline than this.

Container

Lettuce is a great container plant. Containers are often close to kitchens, and newly planted seeds seem to get all the attention they need. Since its roots are shallow, lettuce grows well in a wide variety of containers, including hanging baskets, planters, strawberry jars, and so on. The main problem in growing lettuce in containers is that they tend to dry out quickly, and lettuce demands consistent watering from the time it is planted until it is harvested. One good variety for containers is 'Tom Thumb'.

How to Plant Lettuce

Seed

Most types of lettuce are direct seeded in the garden either in rows or in broad bands. Lettuce is notorious for erratic germination. Sometimes, it pops right up; other times seed seems to languish.

If you have had trouble getting lettuce seeds to germinate, here are some methods used by various gardeners to deal with this problem. Place the seeds in a shallow dish without water in the refrigerator for 24 hours, and sow immediately. Sprinkle seeds in a moist towel, place it in the refrigerator for up to 10 days, check each day until seeds sprout, and sow immediately. Put seeds in a plastic bag filled with moistened vermiculite, check each day until they sprout, and sow immediately. Or soak the seed in a 10 percent bleach solution for a couple of hours to weaken the seed coat, and sow immediately. These treatments are rarely needed if you plant fresh seed at the correct depth and keep it consistently moist. The latter is usually the main problem for home gardeners with a hectic schedule.

Lettuce seed is very small. Pour a small amount of seed into one hand, and grip the seed between the forefinger and thumb of the other hand. Plant the seed as if sprinkling salt on corn at a depth of ⅛ inch or less since seed should "sense" light. Or sprinkle the seed lightly on the soil surface. This works best if you have sifted the soil so that it is extremely fine. Water the soil immediately, and keep it consistently moist at all times. Seeds typically germinate within 10 days but sometimes take longer. If frequent watering is difficult to achieve, consider covering the area with a light layer of mulch or wet fabric. The goal is to keep the soil moist at all times until germination. If using wet fabric, remove it immediately once seedlings begin to sprout. Seedlings will often work their way through a thin layer of mulch, such as finely pulverized leaves. Seed-starting mix is another option but costs money.

Transplants

Few people start lettuce indoors, with the exception of crisphead lettuce, which needs a longer growing season. Start seeds of crisphead varieties 6 to 8 weeks before the frost-free

Nutrition Facts
Serving size: 100 grams (3.5 ounces)

	AMOUNT PER RAW SERVING OF ICEBERG	% DV	AMOUNT PER RAW SERVING OF ROMAINE	% DV
Calories	14	1%	17	1%
Carbohydrates	3 g	1%	3 g	1%
Dietary fiber	1 g	5%	2 g	8%
Folate	30 mcg	7%	135 mcg	35%
Manganese	0.1 mg	6%	0.2 mg	8%
Protein	1 g	2%	1 g	2%
Vitamin A	500 IU	10%	8,710 IU	175%
Vitamin C	3 mg	5%	24 mg	40%
Vitamin K	24 mcg	30%	105 mcg	130%

date, setting the seedlings into the garden 4 to 6 weeks before that date. Plant several seeds in small containers. Keep moist and cool, preferably around 65°F. Harden off transplants before placing them in the garden. Transplant them on a cloudy day or in the evening. When root systems are disturbed, the plants go into shock. Sun does not help them recuperate quickly. Coolness and moisture do. Plant them just deep enough so that the soil barely touches the lower leaves. Firm the soil around the roots, and use a mild transplant solution to get them off to a good start. Place mulch around the plants. Water well. If a heavy frost threatens before the transplants have taken root and are growing well, protect them with row covers, individual cloches, or a piece of cloth.

A second form of transplanting works extremely well for the other types of lettuce. Direct seed in the garden as early as possible. When the seedlings are growing well and have two sets of true leaves, dig up small clumps of plants, and place these immediately in already prepared planting holes. Fill in the area around the clumps with soil. Firm the soil with your fingers, cover the soil with mulch, and water immediately. These transplants wilt and look almost dead. They often topple over. As long as they land on mulch, and not soil, they will recover. If they land on soil, they may get stuck and die. If you keep them moist for a couple of days, they spring back to life by popping up off the mulch in an erect position. Snip off any dead leaves. Once they have recuperated and are growing well, snip off all but the healthiest plant in each small bunch of plants moved. If you are really skilled, you can pull clumps apart and plant bare-root seedlings individually. This is done by experienced growers all the time but requires planting quickly, watering properly, and getting a thin layer of mulch around them immediately.

Spacing

Spacing depends on the type of lettuce you are growing and also your garden style. Head lettuce needs plenty of space to form solid heads. It does best with good air circulation, so plant transplants roughly 14 to 18 inches apart. Space the other types according to how you intend to harvest them—farther apart for heads, closer together for leaves. Leaf lettuce can be planted extremely close together if harvested regularly. Lettuce does well planted with other crops that take a longer time to mature or provide shade as they grow. In short, you don't have to plant lettuce in rows or broad bands as a single crop.

When to Plant

Start head lettuce indoors 6 to 8 weeks before the frost-free date with the goal of setting out transplants 4 to 6 weeks before that date. Plant all other types of lettuce, including stem lettuce, as soon as you can work the ground in spring. Most lettuces do well in fluctuating temperatures, but they all like it cool. Most lettuces will germinate at temperatures ranging from 30° to 70°F. Still, once seedlings have sprouted, play it safe by covering young plants with row covers or fabric, such as a sheet, if a hard freeze threatens. Plant several small plantings every 14 days to extend the season. Stop spring planting when temperatures reach 77°F or higher. Most lettuce varieties will become bitter and unusable if maturing during hot midsummer weather, but don't let that stop you from sowing seeds again in early August for a good-tasting fall harvest. Plant leaf types at that time to mature in cool to cold fall weather.

How to Care for Lettuce

Water

All types of lettuce need consistent watering throughout the entire growing season. Plants need to grow fast and continuously for best taste. Early in the season, water the base of the plants early in the morning if possible. Consistent, rather than deep, watering is preferred. The foliage of leaf lettuces tends to spread out as the season progresses. If the area is well mulched, don't worry about getting water on the leaves. The plants will dry off and do just fine.

Mulch

Just as seedlings break through the soil surface, place a thin layer of organic mulch along the side of the row. Lettuce plants like a cool, moist root run. Mulch helps provide this and stops many weeds from growing. The few weeds that do pop through are easy to pull from moist earth. Mulch also prevents soil from splashing up on leaves. This reduces the chance of disease and definitely makes washing leaves easier.

Fertilizing

Lettuce is a heavy feeder. The soil should be rich with organic fertilizers from the start. As the season progresses, fertilize with frequent, light applications of organic fertilizers high in nitrogen. Never sprinkle solid fertilizer on the leaves, although you can feed the plants with foliar sprays up until 14 days or so before harvest. The goal is abundant leaf growth. If you cut plants back, encourage regrowth with a light application of fertilizer at that time. Some gardeners feel that overfeeding results in bitterness. They also feed heading types less than leaf lettuces. Let the growth of your plants guide you. Note that a few gardeners sprinkle rabbit pellets (alfalfa) right into the drill. Better than this is to dissolve them in water, stir them around, and use the liquid as either a transplant solution or liquid fertilizer.

Weeding

Lettuce has shallow roots. Weeding is most difficult when the tiny seedlings begin to emerge. Let them grow a little larger, then gently pull up weeds by hand. If you pull up some seedlings, transplant them immediately if you feel you aren't growing enough already.

Thinning

Thinning depends on the type of lettuce you are growing. Give plants that form loose or fairly tight heads enough space to mature into their natural form. Thin leaf lettuce when plants are roughly 4 inches tall, although there is no set rule. These young plants transplant well as long as you work quickly and water them well. Of course, you can also eat them.

Special Considerations

Some gardeners blanch romaine lettuces by tying the leaves together as the plants are maturing. The leaves are succulent as they turn pale, but much of the nutritional value of these leaves is lost in the process.

If you buy romaine lettuce, pull off all of the outer leaves. Leave the bottom of the stem intact with several immature leaves attached. Plant the stem as you would a transplant in a pot with the base of the leaves just at the soil surface. These stems will sometimes mature into a nice, but smaller, head of lettuce.

Extending the Season

There are numerous ways to extend the growing season for lettuce. The first is to get seed into the garden as soon as the soil can be worked. You are gambling that there won't be a hard frost, but the risk is worth it. Cover the plants with a sheet in a sudden cold spell. Plant it again in the summer for a fall crop. For even a longer season, protect plants in spring and fall under cloches or plastic tunnels. Or plant it in cold frames. Don't let the plants freeze, but definitely push the envelope.

Problems

Insects

Aphids, cutworms, flea beetles, leafhoppers (which transmit disease), and slugs can be problems. The home gardener usually can grow enough lettuce to share a bit with the bugs. If you can't, use row covers.

Disease

Disease is not usually a major problem in the home garden. Prevent problems by spacing plants for good air circulation, controlling weeds, and growing plants vigorously. Also, by controlling insects, you stop the spread of disease. If you have a problem with disease, check catalogs for disease-resistant varieties the following year.

Marauders

Rabbits are often far more of a problem in the home garden than insects and disease. A good fence is the only practical solution. If rabbits eat the tips off plants, give the plants a chance to regrow. Most varieties will.

Physiological

The main problem with lettuce is that it tends to go to seed when temperatures soar. Some varieties are more resistant to this than others. Because the problem is so common, catalogs emphasize bolt resistance in their listed varieties. The best way to deal with bolt resistance is to get plants or seeds into the ground early in the season and to grow an assortment of lettuces, rather than to rely on just one type or variety.

Propagation

Lettuce is self-pollinating. Varieties have been known to cross. Each lettuce flower opens briefly each morning, but the daisy-like flowers open sequentially, creating a good opportunity for pollination. Cut off stems when seed heads mature and turn fuzzy. Hang them upside down in a paper bag when half of the flowers have reached this stage. Seeds are attached to tiny "parachutes." Collect seed, and store in an envelope in a dry, cool, dark place for up to 3 to 6 years. To practice, start with 'Black Seeded Simpson'.

Harvesting

How and when you harvest lettuces is a matter of personal choice. Even varieties that form heads can be used early on as leaf lettuces. Here are a few general tips. Take a large bowl of ice water into the garden with you. Harvest leaves at the coolest time of day. Cut or pinch off leaves at their base. When cutting off individual leaves, take the outer leaves only, leaving the inner leaves to mature. If cutting back plants for regrowth as "cut and come again" crops, cut back to 2 inches from the crown, leaving the inner growing tip intact with a few tiny, developing leaves around it. Following are the most common methods of harvesting the main types of lettuce.

Cut Batavian lettuces off at the base once they form a nicely shaped head. Butterheads form small, loose heads. You can cut off individual leaves or cut the entire plant back to 2 inches above the crown. A new head will often form. Let crisphead lettuces develop as fully as possible before cutting them. If heads don't develop, harvest the leaves. Leaf lettuce is sweet and crispy when leaves have just reached 4 to 6 inches. Cut off the outer leaves as you need them. Let the smaller, inner leaves mature. Or cut the entire plant back to 2 inches with a knife. Most leaf lettuces will regrow. You can do this several times before the new leaves begin to get bitter later in the season. Let romaine lettuces mature into loose or fairly tight heads. Remove the heads by cutting off the entire plant at soil level with a knife. Don't wait too long, or romaines will go to seed.

Stem lettuce is different. This plant is grown for its swollen edible stem. Always harvest the stems when they are about the thickness of a pencil. Or pull up the plants. Leaves are edible, but the stem is what you are after.

Storing

To store in the refrigerator, keep head lettuces close to freezing at high humidity. For leaf lettuce, remove leaves, rinse under cold running water, shake off excess moisture, roll in barely damp paper towels so that the leaves are not touching, place in a large plastic container with the lid on in the crisper of the refrigerator. Use the leaves as soon as possible since the leaf edges turn brown and even rot in time. A few people pull up whole plants of heading lettuce by the roots, place these in water, and keep that way. To freeze, cook with other vegetables as soup, cool, and freeze. Otherwise, do not freeze.

Culinary Uses

Lettuce is most commonly eaten raw in salads in the United States. Handle leaves as gently as possible to avoid bruising them. Keep leaves cool, and eat them as soon as possible. Wash leaves well since a thin layer of soil may have splashed on them. A spinner is helpful, but not essential, in removing excess moisture from the leaves. Either cut or tear into pieces before use. The controversy over whether to cut or tear leaves is silly. What counts is that the lettuce is young and fresh, not turning old and somewhat bitter. Some cooks remove the midribs on older leaves. Romaine lettuce is the preferred type for Caesar salad. For those on a specialized diet, use lettuce to replace bread (lettuce wraps).

Not as well known is how good lettuce is cooked. Try butter steaming iceberg lettuce. Sauté romaine lettuce in olive oil, or boil it for a few minutes as a side dish. Experiment, and give this a try with different types of lettuce. Particularly popular is cream of lettuce soup. Cook the lettuce before putting it into a blender. Then follow your favorite recipe for making creamed soups.

The leaves, stalks, and flower stems of stem lettuce are also edible raw or cooked. The raw stems are crisp and crunchy. The leaves are good in salads and cooked as greens as long as they are picked when young. If they get too old, they turn milky and bitter. To eat stems cooked, peel the stems, especially removing tissue at the nodes (places where leaves join the stem). The outer layer can be bitter. Boil them for 3 to 4 minutes. Set them in a shallow dish. Sprinkle them with parmesan cheese and bread crumbs before baking until slightly brown. Or cut into thin strips, and sauté in seasoned oil or butter. The stems are also delicious in "cream of celtuce" soup.

Varieties

It's easy to get in a rut growing just one variety of lettuce. Try several new varieties each year until you come up with four or five favorites. Below are some growing tips for the major groups of lettuce: Batavian, butterhead, crisphead, leaf, romaine, and stem lettuce. These vary in form, leaf shape, leaf color, leaf texture (crispy to tender), and taste (buttery to sweet). The red and purplish tones are most intense in cool weather with plenty of sunlight. The red color comes from anthocyanin and is a dominant trait that growers bred out and now realize is trendy. Some cooks like the red color but find the leaves to be a bit more bitter. Others disagree, saying the red leaves are more "complex" in taste and texture. They are particularly high in antioxidants.

Batavian (also known as French crisp or summercrisp) are European-style crispheads. They look like leaf lettuce when first growing, then begin to mature into tighter heads. Each variety has a somewhat different form, leaf shape, and color. They are becoming increasingly popular because of their "nutty" flavor and crunchy texture as well as their ability to stand heat and cold.

Butterhead (also known as Bibb, Boston, limestone) describes the loosely formed, soft heads of this succulent and delicious lettuce. The hearts of many varieties self-blanch into a soft, buttery yellow. They are heat tolerant in general and prized for their soft, pliable leaves with a buttery flavor reflected in their color.

Celtuce is the name given to stem lettuce by Burpee. It is really a variety rather than a category of lettuce (see "stem lettuce," below).

Crisphead (also known as cabbage, head, iceberg) is supposed to form a tighter head than loose leaf. In many cold-climate areas, summers get hot, and this type of lettuce takes a long time to mature. Often, you must be satisfied with somewhat loose heads. The variety 'Iceberg' listed in the table is not necessarily the iceberg lettuce sold by the millions each year in grocery stores, or so I have been told. Crisphead lettuces are popular for mild, watery, crisp leaves with limited nutritional value. These lettuces should be

The color of 'Merveille des Quatre Saisons', a butterhead, makes this heirloom especially popular.

started indoors and have a tendency to rot out if moisture gets into their core during hot weather.

Leaf lettuce (also known as bunching, cutting, loose-leaf, rosette, salad bowl, or sundial) is by far the easiest lettuce for the home gardener to grow. Try several short rows of different varieties. Don't plant more than a few feet of each variety. Save the seeds, and plant more lettuce every 2 or 3 weeks. These successive plantings keep fresh lettuce on the table for an extended period of time. Leaf lettuce has more nutrients than iceberg and makes an excellent "cut and come again" crop. When leaves are edged, speckled, splotched, or tinted with red, the depth of coloration is strongly affected by sunlight.

Romaine (also known as cos) forms loose, upright heads that usually grow well and stay clean in the home garden. The long leaves are broad on the top and have firm, central midribs. Leaves have a crisp but tender texture and sweet taste. Note that 'Little Gem' is sometimes sold as this type, although I have listed it as a butterhead. Try a late-season planting of 'Rouge d'Hiver' or 'Winter Density'.

Stem lettuce (also known as asparagus, celery, Chinese lettuce) is grown for its swollen stems, although the leaves are also edible. Do not let the stems get thicker than a pencil or a bit larger, or they lose their sweet juiciness and become stringy. The plant does not taste like asparagus.

Note that there are comments in some cases under leaf color in the chart. Leaf color is highly subjective and is related to weather conditions. The amount of sunshine is especially important to develop red coloration. *Heat resistant* means that plants do not bolt (go to flower) easily, but that does not mean they won't. *Good for fall* indicates plants ideally suited for late-season planting. Days to maturity are rough approximations and vary by source by up to 5 days or more.

VARIETY	DAYS	LEAF COLOR
Batavian, French crisp, or summercrisp		
Lactuca sativa **var.** *capitata*		
'Arianna' (OP)	50	Mint green
'Blush' (OP)	55	Green tinted red
'Cardinale' (OP)*****	50	Red green
'Cherokee' (OP)	50	Deep red
'Concept' (OP)*****	45	Light green
'Loma' (OP)	45	Apple green, scalloped
'Magenta' (OP)	50	Green tinged red
'Merlot' (OP)	55	Ruby, crinkled
'Nevada' (OP)*****	50	Medium green, ruffled
'Red Grenoble' (see 'Rouge Grenobloise')		
'Rouge Grenobloise' (OP)*****	55	Green red
'Sierra' (OP)	50	Green tinged red
'Victoria' (OP)	50	Deep green (some classify this as butterhead)
Butterhead, Bibb, or Boston lettuce, loose head		
Lactuca sativa **var.** *capitata*		
'Adriana' (OP)	48	Medium green
'Arctic King' (OP)	75	Light to medium green (good for fall)
'Ben Shemen' (OP)	65	Light to medium green
'Besson Rouge' (see 'Merveille des Quatre Saisons')		
'Bibb' (heirloom)	55	Medium green to golden
'Big Boston' (heirloom)	70	Medium green
'Brune d'Hiver' (OP)	65	Green tinged red (good for fall)
'Burpee Bibb' (OP)	75	Dark green
'Buttercrunch' (heirloom) (AAS-1963)*****	60	Medium green to pale core (heat resistant)
'Butter King' (OP) (AAS-1966)	65	Light green to pale yellow (heat resistant)
'Carmona' (OP)	55	Bronzy outer leaves with pale center
'Dark Green Boston' (OP)	70	Medium green, wavy
'Four Seasons Lettuce' (see 'Merveille des Quatre Saisons')		
'Italian Red Perella' (heirloom)		Olive green with red bronze tones

VARIETY	DAYS	LEAF COLOR
'Limestone' (see 'Bibb')		
'Little Gem' (OP)	65	Bright green (small; heat resistant)
'Little Red Riding Hood' (see 'Merveille des Quatre Saisons')		
'Merveille des Quatre Saisons' (heirloom)	55	Magenta outer leaves with paler core
'Mignonette Bronze' (heirloom)	60	Medium green to bronze
'Nancy' (OP)*****	50	Medium green
'Red Cross' (heirloom)	55	Green-tinged red
'Sugar Cos' (see 'Little Gem')	50	Green red
'Sangria' (OP)*****	55	Green-tinged red
'Summer (Baby) Bibb' (OP)	60	Light green (heat resistant)
'Susan's Red Bibb' (heirloom)*****	60	Ruffled, green-edged red
'Tom Thumb' (heirloom)*****	65	Light green (miniature)
'White Boston' (heirloom)	70	Light green (almost crisphead)

Crisphead or iceberg lettuce
Lactuca sativa var. *capitata*

VARIETY	DAYS	LEAF COLOR
'Burpee's Iceberg A' (heirloom)	85	Light to medium green
'Crispino' (OP)*****	70	Medium green
'Great Lakes' (heirloom) (AAS-1944)	70	Medium green
'Ice Queen' (see 'Reine des Glaces')		
'Iceberg' (heirloom)	80	Medium green
'Igloo' (OP)	75	Medium green
'Ithaca' (heirloom)*****	80	Medium green (heat resistant)
'Reine des Glaces' (heirloom) *****	80	Medium green
'Saladin' (heirloom)	75	Medium green
'Salinas' (see 'Saladin')		
'Summertime' (heirloom)	70	Medium green
'Webb's Wonderful' (heirloom)	70	Frilly, dark green (heat resistant)

Leaf or looseleaf lettuce
Lactuca sativa var. *crispa*

VARIETY	DAYS	LEAF COLOR
'Amish Deer Tongue' (heirloom)	60	Light green, triangular wavy
'Black-Seeded Simpson' (heirloom)*****	45	Light green, frilly
'Bronze Arrow' (heirloom)*****	45	Green red bronze, oak-leaf
'Cardinale' (OP)*****	50	Bronze brilliant red
'Deer or Deer's Tongue' (see 'Matchless')		
'Flame' (heirloom)*****	50	Inconsistently bright red
'Grand Rapids' (heirloom)	45	Light green, wavy
'Green Ice' (heirloom)*****	45	Varied green, ruffled, wavy
'Green Salad Bowl' (see 'Salad Bowl')	55	
'Matchless' (heirloom)	60	Light green, triangular, wavy
'Merlot' (heirloom)	55	Red purple, frilly, puckered
'New Red Fire' (OP)*****	55	Red, ruffled (tart)
'Oakleaf' (heirloom)*****	50	Pale to medium green, oak-leaf (heat resistant)
'Prizehead' (heirloom)***** (AAS-1958)	50	Light green, frilly-edged red
'Red Sails' (heirloom) (AAS-1985)*****	45	Crinkly, bronze red (heat resistant)
'Red Salad Bowl' (heirloom)	50	Red frilly, wavy
'Royal Oak Leaf' (OP)	50	Medium green, oak-leaf
'Ruby' (OP) (AAS-1958)*****	50	Very frilly, medium to deep red
'Salad Bowl' (heirloom) (AAS-1952)*****	50	Light green, wavy, oak-leaf (heat resistant)
'Salad Trim' (OP)	55	Bronze red, crinkly, oak-leaf
'Simpson Elite' (OP)*****	50	Lime green, ruffled

VARIETY	DAYS	LEAF COLOR
'Slobolt' (heirloom)	50	Light green, frilly
'Sunset' (OP)*****	50	Vivid red, frilly

Romaine or cos lettuce
    Lactuca sativa var. *longifolia*

VARIETY	DAYS	LEAF COLOR
'Cimmaron' (see 'Rouge d'Hiver')		
'Craquerelle du Midi' (see 'Winter Density')		
'Green Towers' (heirloom)	75	Dark green, wavy (good for fall)
'Jericho Hybrid'	60	Bright green (heat resistant)
'Little Gem' (heirloom)*****	50	Light green (semi-cos; small)
'Lobjoits Cos' (heirloom)	60	Dark to medium green (small)
'Majestic Red' (heirloom)	60	Green red, frilly
'Paris White' (heirloom)	70	Light green, rumpled edges, white heart
'Parris Island Cos' (heirloom)*****	70	Medium green
'Red Leprechaun' (heirloom)	70	Highly ruffled, purple green (heat resistant)
'Red Rosie' (OP)	55	Green to red
'Red Winter' (see 'Rouge d'Hiver')		
'Rouge d'Hiver' (heirloom)*****	65	Bronze green red (good for fall)
'Sucrine' (see 'Little Gem')		
'Vivian' (heirloom)	70	Medium green, upright, rounded
'Winter Density' (heirloom)*****(semi-cos)	55	Dark green like tall 'Buttercrunch'

Stem, asparagus, celery, or Chinese lettuce
    Lactuca sativa var. *asparagina, augustana, or angustata*

VARIETY	DAYS	LEAF COLOR
'Celtuce' (generic)	45	Light green

It is remarkable how many varieties of lettuce can be grown in a small place.

Muskmelons need really good soil that drains freely, lots of sun, and regular heat to grow well.

MUSKMELON

Cucumis melo species
Cucumber or Gourd Family (Cucurbitaceae)

Muskmelons are a very tender, warm-season annual crop. They have a wonderful aroma and taste but require a long season of warm, bright days to mature properly. Improved varieties and growing techniques put a reasonable harvest of muskmelons within the reach of cold-climate gardeners. Most muskmelons probably originated in Africa.

How Muskmelons Grow

Muskmelon seed is relatively large (1,000 to 1,200 seeds per ounce) and looks somewhat like a tan spearhead. The young plant forms leaves that are easily identifiable as they emerge from the soil. As the plant matures, it sends off vines that begin to spread out. Sticking out from the vine are broad, hairy leaves. Yellow flowers begin to appear, typically male at first. Then both male and female flowers form. The females have a slight bulge at their base. These are round, green ovaries that need to be pollinated by insects to form fruit. Once pollinated, they swell and balloon over time into muskmelons. Mature melons contain seeds to continue the life cycle.

Where to Plant Muskmelons
Site and Light

Basically, the more sun and water, the faster the growth. The faster melons grow, the better they taste—that's the underlying rule. Choose a warm, sunny spot protected from prevailing winds. A southern slope is ideal. Placing plastic over the planting area several weeks before planting heats up the soil. Permeable fabric also works well if you intend to plant through it.

Soil and Moisture

Muskmelons grow best in a light, loose soil, preferably sand. They will grow in a wide range of soil types, however, if amended with lots of organic matter, such as sphagnum peat moss, rotted manures, and leaf mold. Add organic fertilizers to the soil as well. Highly recommended are granite dust for boron, and bonemeal for phosphorus. Work the soil well to loosen it. Work in the organic matter and fertilizer, preferably the year before planting. Soil should drain freely but retain moisture during dry spells. The preferred pH is from 6.0 to 7.0.

If your soil is compacted, build a raised bed. Or dig a 2-feet-deep pit, fill it with organic matter, then place another 4 to 6 inches of soil on top to form a hill. Raised beds and hills help water drain freely and also increase soil temperature in spring.

A practice that is hardly ever mentioned is to plant seeds in a compost pile, one that has aged for at least a year or longer. Dig a hole in the pile, fill with loose soil, and plant seeds. I am not sure why this works so well. But compost is still breaking down and so provides bottom heat; it holds lots of water and provides a nutrient-rich environment for vining plants. Keep the pile moist, and let the seeds do the rest.

Container

Grow a type like 'Amy' or 'Minnesota Midget' in a 5-gallon container. Sink a trellis into the potting soil before planting seeds or transplants. Any container should drain freely and will need to be watered frequently. Expect the best melons to be produced at the base of the plant. See "Support."

Planting
Seed

Muskmelons need warm soil above 60°F but also require a long growing season to mature. Warm up the soil in spring by covering it with clear or black plastic. Plant seed through slits in the plastic. Once plants emerge, cover each plant or plant group with an individual cloche, such as a plastic ice cream bucket or milk jug with the bottom cut out. Leave the lid or top on during the night, and remove it during the day.

Or let the soil warm up naturally, and plant varieties that mature relatively quickly. Plant seed ½ to 1 inch deep in hills, mounds of soil with lots of organic matter mixed in. The hill should be at least 4 inches high and several feet wide if possible. Plant five seeds in the hill. Place seeds on the soil surface in a circle with a seed or two in the center. Press the seed into the soil. Firm the soil over the seed, and water immediately. Seed should germinate within 10 days or less.

Transplants

Muskmelons really dislike being transplanted. Root disturbance sets plants back. However, most varieties take a long time to mature, so starting them indoors helps you get a jump on the season. You have to trick the melons into believing that they are growing in the tropics.

Prepare the soil for planting well in advance. Covering the soil with black plastic or permeable landscape fabric is optional. It definitely increases soil temperature by as much as 5° to 10°F, so many gardeners do use these materials for

Nutrition Facts
Serving size: 100 grams (3.5 ounces)

	AMOUNT PER RAW SERVING	% DV
Calories	34	2%
Carbohydrates	9 g	3%
Dietary fiber	21 g	4%
Potassium	270 mg	8%
Protein	1 g	2%
Vitamin A	3,340 IU	70%
Vitamin C	35 mg	60%

warmth-loving plants and get them into place 10 days to several weeks before the expected planting time. Do not plant until the soil temperature reaches at least 60°F. When using inorganic mulches, soak the soil thoroughly before laying them down.

Start seeds indoors about 3 to 4 weeks before your expected outdoor planting time. Don't start them too early, because they have deep roots, grow quickly, and don't like being disturbed. Plant several seeds ½ to 1 inch deep in sterile starting mix in 4-inch peat pots. Keep the seeds moist and warm. Provide bottom heat to get soil temperature to 80°F if possible during the day with a drop of 5 degrees at night during germination. Once the seeds are germinating, provide seedlings with 16 hours of light per day. As they mature, snip off all but the healthiest plant in each pot. Ideally, you want each plant to be 4 to 6 inches high with at least two to four true leaves when you plant it outdoors. Typically, plants take about 3 weeks to reach their ideal height. Harden off the plants.

If possible, plant them outdoors just before a rain when the soil reaches the correct temperature. If using plastic, cut slits through it. Plant the pots in the prepared soil so that the rim of the pots is barely covered. Roots will grow through the sides of the pot. Place metal hoops over the planting area, and cover with white row covers at a height of roughly 18 inches above the plants. Make sure the ends are closed. The row covers keep temperature and humidity uniform. Just as important, they keep insects from damaging the young plants. The row covers allow filtered light and rain into the planting area. Remove the row covers as soon as foliage begins to touch the fabric. Never place row covers directly on foliage since it can damage it badly.

Alternatively, use a 32-ounce plastic container. Yogurt containers, just a bit wider than 4 inches, are ideal for this use. Keep the lid, cut out the bottom, set the container on the lid. Fill it with a sterile starting mix. Plant and grow the seeds as described. After hardening off and at the correct planting time, make a hole in the soil large enough to hold the container. Set the container off to the side of the hole. Slide the plastic lid out from under the container. Cover the bottom where the lid was with your hand, and place the container in the hole. Push soil lightly around the container, and then lift it up and away from the plant. Firm the soil around the plant. Water immediately. If the weather is not stable, protect the plant until it warms up with row covers or cloches. Or leave part of the container in the ground with the upper part exposed and snap on the lid at night for a few days. Using a large container and planting carefully to avoid root disturbance are the critical elements of this method.

Since it is sometimes impossible to predict when warm weather will come, you may want to start several pots of plants a week apart for 3 weeks. Seeds are relatively inexpensive. A half-dozen plants grown properly is all the average home gardener needs.

Spacing

If direct seeding, plant a number of seeds to be thinned later. If planting transplants, plant about 18 to 24 inches apart; even farther is fine. Settle for two to three plants per hill. Each plant needs lots of water and nutrients. Muskmelons are vining plants and like to spread out, taking up a lot of space in the garden. Even if you pinch back the growing tips, the plants still cover a lot of territory in a short time. Proper spacing provides good air circulation and may help prevent disease.

When to Plant

More than anything, muskmelon needs heat to develop good fruits. Do not direct plant seeds before the soil temperature has reached 60°F, preferably 70° to 75°. Transplants can go into the garden as early as 2 weeks after the last frost if the soil has been warmed up and if the plants will be covered in a tunnel or by a row cover. Planting through a black, permeable fabric also helps heat up the area around the seedlings.

Support

For gardeners with little space, the solution is to grow muskmelons on a sturdy trellis covered with mesh or chicken wire. Always have the support in place before planting seeds or transplants. As the plant grows, attach each vine to the support with pieces of cloth. Use a figure-eight knot when doing this. Get the vine growing up, not out. Begin doing this when the vine is young. As it matures, tie it as often as necessary. Be careful. Vines become brittle and may break if you bend them too much.

The problem with this method is that as the fruit matures, it must be supported, or it may drop off. Use onion or citrus fruit bags (the netted mesh kind that are open and not enclosed with plastic)—anything open and airy but strong. These have to be attached to the support so that pressure is on the bag and not on the stem of the fruit. Get your support in place when melons are about the size of an egg but no larger than a tennis ball.

Keep the base of the plants mulched and moist since vines trained in this way are heavy drinkers. The exposed leaves lose moisture rapidly in hot dry spells, especially if windy.

How to Care for Muskmelons

Water

Muskmelons have deep roots but need consistent watering. If on exposed ground (no plastic), water the base of the plants. Soak the planting area, not the foliage, to reduce the chance of foliar diseases. Depending on rainfall, water once or twice a week. Deep watering is critical during early growth until fruit is just beginning to form. Once the fruit has enlarged, water deeply once a week if there is no rain. During the last week before harvesting, do not water. Hope for hot, dry weather at this time. This will concentrate sugar in the fruit, intensifying its aroma and flavor.

If using plastic as a mulch, consider drip irrigation underneath it. Water collects on the bottom of the plastic instead of evaporating into the air. This reduces the need for watering. If it rains and water pools up on plastic, punch holes through the depressed areas to let water soak into the soil.

If a plant is wilted either in the morning or in the evening, it's showing signs of stress. Water it immediately.

Some gardeners find that placing a milk jug right into the hill at planting time acts as a reservoir for water. Punch holes in the bottom. Fill as necessary throughout the growing season. This water gets right to the roots, where it is needed the most.

Mulch

If growing plants on bare soil, mulch heavily around the plant as soon as the soil is warm. Vines will reach out from the planting hill and cover quite a bit of ground. Mulch the entire area. This keeps the soil moist, prevents weed growth, and reduces fluctuations in soil temperature. The ideal mulch is straw, because it is so easy to spread out quickly in a thick layer. Vines creep over and through it easily. Mulch between the soil and fruit reduces the chance of rot.

If using black plastic or fabric as a mulch, get it in place at planting time. Leave it exposed early in the season to keep the soil warm, but consider covering it with organic mulch to keep it in place and a bit cooler later in the season. Black plastic can be folded, stored, and used again year after year. Weeds often penetrate landscape fabric, and it can be a hassle pulling it up at the end of the season. However, it does allow for easy watering and allows the soil to "breathe."

Fertilizing

Muskmelons are heavy feeders. Prepare the soil properly with organic soil amendments and appropriate organic fertilizers, especially bonemeal. Pour a transplant solution around transplants as they are set into the garden. Then fertilize as the vines begin to run, again during bloom, and at least one more time 3 weeks later. Kelp and fish emulsion are excellent fertilizers. Use diluted solutions from the time of transplanting until fruits begin to swell. Blood meal is also excellent as a source of nitrogen. Use it to stimulate lush foliage growth, but avoid it after blossoms form. Otherwise you will be producing foliage at the expense of fruits.

To make fruit sweeter, add boron and magnesium to the soil directly around the roots of the plant. In a gallon of water put 2 tablespoons of Epsom salts (for magnesium) and 1 tablespoon of borax (for boron). Give several cupfuls of this solution to each plant, once when the plants are growing vigorously, and once when the fruit is 2 inches in diameter. This is optional since many soils have ample amounts of magnesium and boron.

Weeding

Ideally, you want to weed around the plants as little as possible. When plants are sprouting or are just beginning to vine, make sure that all weeds are removed. Do not cultivate near the plants. Pull out the weeds carefully by hand. On bare ground around the hill remove all weeds where vines will run. Then cover the area with a deep mulch to prevent additional weed growth. If an occasional weed pops up, try to pull it before vines wrap around it. Once vines are sprawling and covering a wide area, stay out of the patch. If vines get entangled with weeds, leave them alone. Besides, if you try to weed, you may step on vines and break them.

Thinning

After seedlings are up and have developed three to four true leaves, thin them to stand two to three plants per hill. Better a few vines carefully nurtured than lots of vines neglected.

Pruning

There is no one right answer to the question of pruning. You will have to experiment. For the home gardener, pruning may be dictated by available space. Here are a few options regarding the removal of flowers, foliage, and fruit.

If space is limited, pick off all flowers once a few fruits are developing. If fruits are growing on a support, keep only a few fruits closest to the bottom of the support. This increases the chances of getting a few good fruits to mature early in the season.

With lots of space, some gardeners do not prune vines at all, just letting them ramble to form fruits as they will. Others employ various pruning methods. Some gardeners snip off the growing tip, the very end of the vine, when the plant is 3 to 5 feet long. This encourages the growth of lateral shoots. Another method is to snip off the growing tip of a vine when the fifth or sixth leaf forms. Generally, this will result in two or more side shoots from the original one. When five to six new leaves form, the growing tip of each shoot is cut off again. The plant is then pruned to the four sturdiest shoots. Others wait until any vine forms three fruits about the size of an egg, and then snip off the growing tip. The idea of any pruning method is get the plant's energy directed into fruit rather than foliage formation. Also, some gardeners snip off a few leaves closest to the fruit as it matures.

Foliage is necessary, however, for fruits to form sugars. Removing leaves might reduce the sweetness of ripe fruits. This is why some gardeners insist that any removal of foliage, particularly in cold climates, is a mistake. Experiment and make up your own mind.

Most gardeners do agree that as frost approaches, remove fruits that have little chance of maturing. Pick these off, and use them.

Special Considerations

Muskmelons are pollinated by insects, often bumblebees. If pollination is not taking place, hand pollination is possible but rarely successful. To increase the odds, hand pollinate early or late in the day. Pollen needs to be sticky, not dry.

Do not move vines. Let them spread out naturally. Vines often wilt or grow poorly if you lift them with the goal of getting them to grow in a different direction.

The flavor of muskmelons is affected by temperature, water, variety, health, and maturity. Melons need to mature rapidly in high heat, have consistent watering, and be picked at the right time. Flavor may also be affected by a lack of boron or magnesium in the soil.

Deeper orange types contain more vitamin A than green- and white-fleshed varieties. Melons vary in their nutrient content by type. However, they are all rich in vitamin C.

Extending the Season

Get plants into the garden early in the season using the strategy of starting plants indoors and getting them out under row covers when soil temperatures reach 60°F or higher. At the end of the season, if frost threatens, cover with light fabric, such as a sheet, at the warmest part of the day if possible.

Problems

Insects

Aphids, cucumber beetles, flea beetles, leafminers, squash bugs, and squash vine borers may damage muskmelon vines. Striped and spotted cucumber beetles are a major concern because they also carry bacterial wilt. Row covers are good deterrents. They should be supported above the vines and removed once foliage begins to touch the cover.

Disease

By controlling insects, you reduce the chance of disease. A number of diseases may affect your patch. These include alternaria leaf spot fungus, anthracnose, bacterial leaf and fruit spots (especially angular leaf spot), bacterial wilt, cucumber mosaic virus, downy mildew, fusarium (several races), nematodes, and powdery mildew. Avoid growing members of the cucumber family in the same area two years in a row, clean up all vines at the end of the season, and, most importantly, buy disease-resistant varieties.

Physiological

Male flowers form first, so if they drop off, don't worry.

Marauders

Muskmelons are not the favorite crop for most animals until melons mature. Cover nearly mature fruits with crates or row covers to stop animals from nibbling on them. Deer have an irritating habit of taking little nibbles out of many fruits rather than devouring one.

Propagation

Muskmelons are cross-pollinating. Grow only one kind of muskmelon but at least five plants of that variety. Note that some people believe that older seed is better, claiming it produces shorter vines and more intensely flavored fruit. So they save seed for as long as possible as long as it remains viable. Also, some people believe that seed from the first melon to ripen is best. I cannot confirm either belief.

Muskmelons do not cross with cucumbers, pumpkins, squash, and watermelons. Although sold as cucumbers, Armenian cucumbers are really melons and so will cross with muskmelons.

Let melons ripen for as long as possible on the vine, at least until skins are hard. Bring indoors, and store in dry place for an additional 3 weeks. Scoop out the inside. Mash the pulp in a bowl, adding a few tablespoons of water. Let the pulp ferment for at least 3 days to kill germs. At this point spoon off the surface. The viable seeds sink. Add water, and carefully pour out any debris. Keep doing this, making sure not to lose the seeds in the rinsing process. Tap or push the seeds into a sieve. Wash the seeds thoroughly. Then lay them out on a plate to dry. Since they dry best if they are not touching, push the seeds around until they are in a single layer and separated from each other. Let them dry until they slide around easily when pushed lightly. This can take a week or longer. Place them in a paper envelope. Keep them dry, cool, and dark until planting time. Seeds will last 4 to 5 years and in some cases up to 10.

An alternative is to scoop out the seed from a ripe melon, and place it where the pulp can dry. Seeds will often pop off the flesh once dry. This method is messy and requires a protected spot where it is hot and dry.

Harvesting

Most muskmelons (*Cucumis melo* var. *reticulatus*) are ripe when netting becomes tight or thick, the fruit begins to turn tan, the fruit gives off a fragrant odor, and the little stem attached to the fruit will slide off easily with pressure (will slip). Muskmelons will ripen a bit more if kept at room temperature after harvesting.

Varieties of so-called winter melon (*Cucumis melo* var. *inodorus*) give off different signals when ripe. Their skin color changes, often turning white, yellow, or golden depending on the variety. The blossom end, the lower portion of the fruit, will often feel slightly soft to the touch. Press on it to see whether it gives a bit. The stems do not push off (slip), so this is not a helpful way to gauge maturity. And the rind may even begin to crack slightly, depending on the variety being grown.

No matter what type of melon you are harvesting, never pull on the vine. Either the fruit will slip or it won't. If it won't and it is the type of melon that doesn't slip, cut off the fruit from the vine with pruners or scissors. Each gardener develops a sixth sense about how to tell when melons are ripe. This comes with experience, and so you will pick a few melons that may not be fully ripe. Everyone does. See "Varieties" for additional tips on harvesting.

Storing

Muskmelons will keep for about 4 days at room temperature. If cut into, the flesh will last for a few days if kept in a sealed bag in the refrigerator.

To freeze, cut into 1-inch balls or cubes, cover with sweet syrup (3 cups sugar to 1 cup water), place in a container, and freeze. Lemon juice and honey are also good. When needed, eat while still partially frozen for best consistency. To make a sorbet, place frozen cubes into a food processor with lemon or lime juice. Blend until the right texture. Freeze the mix if necessary to get the right consistency.

Culinary Uses

Most netted muskmelons are best when just picked. Some winter melons will last longer, but this varies considerably by variety and storage conditions. Slice the melon in two, or remove melon balls from the flesh after removing any seeds from the seed cavity. It is popular in many countries to serve melon with honey, lemon or lime juice, liqueurs, prosciutto, or salt. Some people dry and toast the seeds. This is often done if fruit is picked by accident when overly mature. Small fruits pruned from young vines can be cut into thin slices to replace cucumbers in salads or into thin strips to add to stir-fries. They can also be made into chutneys that combine vinegar with assorted spices sweetened with sugar.

Varieties

Seed catalogs commonly use some descriptive terms. *Sutures* are grooves in the rind running from one end to the other. *Netting* refers to the crisscrossing, typically tan, lines on the rind. The term *slip* means the fruit drops off the stem either naturally or with a gentle push. Some melons slip, others don't.

The varietal table includes a number of plants from different species. Varieties listed as *Cucumis melo* var. *reticulatus* are usually easier to grow in cold climates and usually have netting on their skins and will slip off the vine. Varieties listed as *Cucumis melo* var. *inodorus* generally have smooth skins and don't always slip from the vine. One oddity, usually sold as Armenian cucumber, is actually the melon *Cucumis melo* var. *flexuosus*. Do not confuse muskmelons with cantaloupes, which are rarely grown in the United States. The latter, *Cucumis melo* var. *cantalupensis,* are better suited to other areas, although a few are included in the varietal list.

When growing later-maturing varieties, use all of the strategies described in this section to get them to mature before a fall frost. These include starting plants indoors, planting them out as early as possible on a plastic or fabric soil covering, and protecting them with a row cover to keep them evenly warm and moist.

The varietal list includes open-pollinated (heirloom) and hybrid varieties. Hybrids are developed to produce earlier in the season and to be vigorous, more disease resistant, relatively uniform in size, more productive, and more drought tolerant. The taste, including sweetness, varies by variety. Sugar content is measured by a Brix number, which occasionally is listed in catalogs. The higher the number, the sweeter the fruit. Each person has their own idea of what tastes good, but melons grown properly and picked at the right time will always be good at worst and exquisite at best.

The ten groups of melons described below are represented in the varietal table. Other types do exist but are either extremely hard to find or not suited to cold-climate growing conditions. *Some of the following varieties are difficult to grow and included in this guide as "challenge" plants for the green-thumb gardener.* Climatic conditions over which you have no control may result in either a good or poor crop. If in doubt, choose some of the varieties that mature sooner, rather than later, in the season. The fruit may be small, but a few totally mature small fruits are better than unripe larger ones. Dates to maturity are somewhat misleading. To be safe, add 14 to 21 days to the days listed in the chart.

There are many classifications of melons, and these are confusing. Rather than getting bogged down in details, I have arbitrarily divided muskmelons into the following ten groups.

Armenian cucumbers (also known as snake cucumber or melon, uri melon, metki, mikti, and yard-long cucumber) *(Cucumis melo* var. *flexuosus)*: These "cucumbers" are actually very long melons. The fruits are ribbed with a thin, pale-green skin. They are good eaten raw up to a foot long and are often not peeled. They can be pickled when small (up to 6 inches) or cooked like summer squash when larger. They are often sold as "burpless cucumbers."

Bitter melons: See the section "Gourds" in "Unique Plants."

Canary (or Spanish melon) *(Cucumis melo* var. *inodorus)*: This melon is oval-shaped, bright yellow to orange beige when mature, and has smooth skin turning wrinkly with age. The cream-white flesh has the texture of a juicy pear. The taste is somewhat hard to describe but mildly sweet and aromatic. These melons generally do not slip from the vine.

Cantaloupe/Charentais *(Cucumis melo* var. *cantalupensis)*: What are sold as cantaloupes in the United States are usually muskmelons. Cantaloupes are a different species altogether and are rarely grown here but quite common in Europe. Their skin is rough, not netted. Fruits may be ribbed or sutured on some varieties. Flesh color varies by variety from orange to green. They must be picked at just the right moment for full flavor and fragrance before they turn tan or the stem begins to break (slip) from fruit. *These plants are extremely challenging for the home gardener.*

Crenshaw *(Cucumis melo* **var.** *inodorus)*: This melon is shaped a bit like a teardrop with a rough, waxy rind, typically turning a deep yellow to gold color when fully mature. The flesh is pink to peachy colored and is often described as a bit "spicy." *These take skill to grow in cold climates.*

Galia (a cantaloupe-honeydew cross often referred to as a "honeyloupe"): Developed in Israel, this melon has a netted, golden yellow, green, or white-orange rind. The flesh is pale green or orange depending on the variety. The flesh tends to be sweet but a bit spicy with a lovely scent. These are fairly easy to grow in cold climates.

Honeydew *(Cucumis melo* **var.** *inodorus)*: This round melon has a nearly white rind and green (usually), mild flesh. It may have gold, orange, or white flesh, especially when crossed with other melons. The green to whitish rind tends to be smooth and waxy, turning a creamy yellow when mature. This type will not slip and tends to crack around the stem when ripe.

Mediterranean *(Cucumis melo* **var.** *inodorus)*: Admittedly, this is an artificial grouping of rather unique melons popular in Europe. Christmas melons (also known as Santa Claus melons) are very similar to Piel de Sapo melons and sometimes listed that way. These elongated fruits have green rinds mottled yellow and flesh that varies from green to light orange. The rind varies as well, from smooth to netted depending on the variety. They can weigh up to 8 pounds. These will keep for a few months if stored in a cool place. Occasionally, these may be called Rochet melons. Piel de Sapo melons (also known as Toad Skin melons) are noted for a thin, bumpy rind, small seed cavity, and pale-green to orange flesh that is both sweet and juicy. It looks a bit like an oval watermelon with green skin mottled yellow. Although often sold as a watermelon, it is not. It stores well if kept cool. Christmas and Piel de Sapo varieties generally do not slip from the vine.

Mixed parentage: These are interesting melons with backgrounds that are not clearly defined. Banana melons are large, banana-shaped melons up to 24 inches long. They have a yellow, smooth but sutured rind and spicy, salmon-pink flesh. They are tough to grow in cold climates because they take a long time to mature. 'Gourmet' and 'Sensation' are called specialty melons by the breeder. The flesh is creamy white and crispy when the rind is turning from green to yellow, but it is sweeter and softer once the fruit is completely mature. These must be picked at exactly the right time. Follow instructions on the seed package.

Muskmelon *(Cucumis melo* **var.** *reticulatus)*: This general category covers various types of melons: ones with varied netting, with or without ribs (sutures), with small or large seed cavities, with orange or green flesh, and having a wide range of sizes. Muskmelons may give off a lovely "musk" scent when fully ripe. Athena melons are oval, densely netted orange tan, and mildly sutured. These are noted for their ability to stay on the vine, even once fully ripe. The seed cavity is small; the flesh, firm and sweet yellow orange. Italian (Tuscan) melons are those muskmelons apparently developed in Italy, such as 'Bella Tuscana Hybrid'. Nutmeg melons, such as 'Green Nutmeg', have fruit with a thin, netted rind, sweet green flesh, and a strong noticeable scent. All muskmelons tend to slip off the vine.

Oriental *(Cucumis* **species)**: These melons come from Japan and Korea. They are often small, weighing between 1 and 3 pounds. The rind color varies but is often yellowish gold and may be netted or smooth. The sweet flesh may also vary in color but is most commonly white to pale green and very fragrant. Some people eat the whole melon, rind and seeds included. Eat 'Ginkaku Hybrid' in this way. 'Golden Honey Hybrid' is of Korean origin and favored for its sweet, white flesh.

Winter melon: See the section "Gourds" in "Unique Plants." Note that the generic term *winter melon* is often used loosely to describe any melons with smooth skins that take a long time to mature. These include melons in the *Cucumis melo* var. *inodorus* group. This group includes casaba, Crenshaw, honeydew, Persian, and crosses of these, some of which are not covered in this guide.

VARIETIES	DAYS	RIND/FLESH/SHAPE	LBS.
'Alaska Hybrid' (muskmelon type)	80	Netted cream/orange salmon/round	4
'Ambrosia Hybrid' (muskmelon type)*****	85	Heavy netted cream tan/salmon pink/round	4
'Amy Hybrid' (AAS-2004) (canary type)*****	70	Golden yellow/white/round	2–3
'Angel Hybrid' (AAS-2003) (mixed parentage)*****	80	Yellow with netting/white/round	2
'Aphrodite Hybrid' (muskmelon type)	70	Mildly netted tan/orange/round oval	6
'Armenian' (heirloom) (Armenian type)	65	Pale green/green white/long curved	1
'Athena Hybrid' (muskmelon type)	75	Netted/yellow orange/oval	6
'Atlantis Hybrid' (muskmelon type)	75	Mildly netted tan/orange/round	6
'Banana' (heirloom) (mixed parentage)	95	Yellow sutured/salmon pink/banana "squash"	6
'Bella Tuscana Hybrid' (muskmelon type)	80	Netted tan sutured/orange/rounded oval	4
'Burpees Hybrid' (muskmelon type)*****	85	Coarse netted tan/orange salmon/round oval	4
'Burpees Early Hybrid Crenshaw' (Crenshaw type)	90	Dark green to yellow/peach pink/round	3
'Burrell's Jumbo Melon' (heirloom) (muskmelon type)	85	Tan netted sutured/salmon orange/round oval	4
'Charentais' (heirloom) (cantaloupe/Charentais type)	85	Smooth cream/light orange to salmon/round	4
'Classic Hybrid' (muskmelon type)	85	Heavily netted sutured/deep orange/round	5
'Collective Farm Woman Melon' (heirloom) (honeydew type)	85	Yellow gold/white/nearly round	2
'Delicious 51' (heirloom) (muskmelon type)*****	80	Netted cream green sutured/salmon orange/round oval	2
'Diva Hybrid' (cantaloupe/Charentais type)	85	Mildly netted/orange/rounded oval	6
'Earlichamp Hybrid' (muskmelon type)	75	Heavily netted/light orange/rounded oval	4
'Earli-dew Hybrid' (honeydew type)*****	90	Smooth/lime green/rounded	3
'Earliqueen Hybrid' (muskmelon type)*****	75	Coarse netted tan/bright orange/round	3
'Earlisweet Hybrid' (muskmelon type)	70	Netted tan/salmon orange/rounded	2
'Early Hanover' (heirloom) (muskmelon type)	80	Netted tan sutured/pale green/round	2
'Emerald Gem' (heirloom) (muskmelon type)	85	Ribbed netted green/light orange green/globe	2–3
'Extra Early Hanover' (see 'Early Hanover')			
'French Orange Hybrid' (cantaloupe/Charentais type)	75	Netted gray green/orange/round	2
'Galia Hybrid' (Galia type)	70	Netted green to yellow/green/round	2–3
'Ginkaku Hybrid' (Oriental type)	80	Deep gold striped white/white/oval	1
'Golden honey Hybrid' (Oriental type)	80	Smooth gold/white/round	2
'Gold Star Hybrid' (muskmelon type)*****	90	Netted tan/deep orange/oval	4
'Gourmet Hybrid' (mixed parentage type)	85	Orangish/greenish white/round	4
'Green Nutmeg' (heirloom) (muskmelon type)	80	Netted tan/green/round	½
'Hale's Best Jumbo' (heirloom) (muskmelon type)	90	Gold netted over green/salmon orange/oval	4
'Harper Hybrid' (muskmelon type)	85	Netted tan/light orange/round	2
'Hearts of Gold' (heirloom) (muskmelon type)	90	Netted sutured/gold to salmon orange/round	3
'Honey Rock' (AAS-1933) (heirloom) (muskmelon type)	85	Tan netted/dark salmon orange/round	3
'Honey Bun Hybrid' (muskmelon type) (bush)	75	Tan netted/medium orange/round	3
'Ichiba Kouji Hybrid' (Oriental type)	90	Netted tan green/green/round	3
'Iroquois' (heirloom) (muskmelon type)	90	Tan netted/deep orange/rounded oval	6
'Jenny Lind' (heirloom) (muskmelon type)*****	75	Netted pale tan/lime green/rounded turban	1–2
'Lambkin Hybrid' (AAS-2009) (Mediterranean type)	75	Green mottled yellow/pale white green/oval	3
'Melemon Hybrid' (AAS-2013) (Mediterranean type)	80	Green mottled chartreuse/white/round	3
'Minnesota Midget' (heirloom) (muskmelon type)*****	65	Tannish green/golden yellow/round miniature	1
'Montreal Market' (heirloom) (muskmelon type)	85	Green ribbed/green/round	4–5
'Passport Hybrid' (Galia type)	85	Tan netted/green/round	5
'Petit Gris de Rennes' (heirloom) (cantaloupe/ Charentais type)*****	85	Gray green sutured/orange/rounded	2
'Pride of Wisconsin' (heirloom) (muskmelon type)*****	95	Bluish tan/light orange/football	4

VARIETIES	DAYS	RIND/FLESH/SHAPE	LBS.
'Pulsar Hybrid' (muskmelon type)	85	Netted tan/light orange/round	4
'Riviera Sweet Hybrid' (cantaloupe/Charentais type)	70	Greenish yellow sutured/orange/round	2
'Roadside Hybrid' (muskmelon type)*****	85	Tan heavily sutured/salmon orange/round	6
'Sarah's Choice Hybrid' (muskmelon type)	75	Tan netted/orange/round	3
'Savor Hybrid' (cantaloupe/Charentais type)*****	80	Grayish green sutured/deep orange/round	2
'Schoon's Hard Shell' (heirloom) (muskmelon type)	95	Netted/pale apricot orange/round	6
'Sensation Hybrid' (mixed parentage type)	85	Smooth white/ivory/round	5
'Scrumptious Hybrid' (muskmelon type)	85	Finely netted/salmon orange/round oval	5
'Spanish Moon Hybrid' (mixed parentage type)	90	Creamy textured/white to pale green/round oval	5
'Superstar Hybrid' (muskmelon type)*****	90	Heavily netted sutured/orange/round	8
'Sweet Delight Hybrid' (honeydew type)	90	Greenish white/light green/oval	6
'Sweet Granite' (heirloom) (muskmelon type)*****	80	Lightly netted/light orange/oblong	3
'Sweet 'N' Early Hybrid' (muskmelon type)*****	75	Netted sutured/salmon orange/rounded oval	6
'Top Mark' (heirloom) (muskmelon type)	90	Netted tan/salmon orange/round oblong	3
'Tuscan Melon' (see 'Bella Tuscana Hybrid')			
'Vedrantais' (heirloom) (cantaloupe/Charentais type)	80	Blue green to orange/reddish orange/rounded	3
'Venus Hybrid' (honeydew type)	90	Netted pale tan/green/oval	4

For a change of taste, experiment by growing different varieties, such as this lovely golden Canary melon

NASTURTIUM

The leaves, flowers, and pods of sweet-smelling nasturtiums are all edible.

***Tropaeolum* species**
Nasturtium Family (Tropaeolaceae)

Nasturtiums are hardy, cool-season annuals in cold climates. The plants produce dense foliage and an abundance of five-petaled or more, fragrant flowers. Both leaves and flowers are edible. Nasturtiums grow quickly and easily from seed, filling any void with a riot of color. Nasturtiums are sometimes called Indian cress. Nasturtiums most likely originated in South America, possibly Peru.

How Nasturtiums Grow

Nasturtium seeds (210 seeds per ounce) are large and typically tan and have a highly irregular surface. The stems tend to be thick and solid on mature plants. The growth pattern varies by variety; some form bushes, and others form trailing plants, although the bush types often have a few trailing stems as well. Although foliage of different varieties does vary, it generally looks somewhat like a water lily pad. Stem and leaf coloration also vary by variety, from light green to greenish red or even mottled green and white. The brilliant, exquisitely scented flowers come in a range of colors, shapes, and

sizes. They mature into green, caper-like seeds that shrivel and turn brown at the end of the season.

Nutrition Facts

Although touted as a good source of vitamin C (12 percent of RDA for a serving of 100 grams, or 3.5 ounces), nasturtium actually has only about one-quarter the amount of vitamin C that spinach does. It is reputed to be high in antioxidants and believed to reduce the risk of cancer and heart disease. Specific information about its mineral and vitamin content are elusive. Most people will eat only a few blossoms at a time, either stuffed or added to a salad, so the nutritional value is moot.

Where to Plant Nasturtiums
Site and Light

Nasturtiums grow best in full sun. They will tolerate partial shade. The trailing types are often planted along the edge of timber or rock walls where they can cascade over the edges.

They also look lovely in hanging baskets. Trailing types can also be trained up trellises. The bush types are delightful right in the vegetable garden or placed along borders or in flower beds.

Soil and Moisture

Nasturtiums thrive in a wide range of soils. Soil does not have to be fertile but must drain freely. Adding organic matter to the soil is highly recommended because it helps retain moisture throughout the growing season but improves drainage as well.

Container

Many home gardeners grow nasturtiums in pots or hanging baskets. The scent is easiest to appreciate when plants are close by on a deck or patio. Consistent watering is critical for plants grown in any type of container.

Planting
Seed

Soaking the seed up to 24 hours or nicking the outer seed coat with a file (scarification) may result in faster germination. Neither are necessary to get good germination as long as the seed is planted in firm contact with the soil. Place seed ½ inch deep or a little more, press down on the soil with your hands, anchoring the seeds in place, then water immediately. Seeds should germinate within 14 days. But germination is erratic and, occasionally, disappointing depending on the seed source.

Transplant

Nasturtiums resent transplanting. Still, you can start them indoors about 3 to 4 weeks before the last expected frost if you really want to get a jump on the season. Plant two seeds per pot in sterile starting mix. Seeds will germinate at a temperature of 65°F or above. Keep moist, and place in high light once growing. Seedlings often vary greatly in vigor, so snip out the weakest plant in each pot. Harden off before planting outdoors when temperatures are at least 50°F. Disturb the roots as little as possible when planting out. Transplanting is not recommended by most growers.

Spacing

Plant two seeds in each spot 3 to 4 inches apart. Not all seeds germinate, and some plants tend to be weak. Spacing does depend on the variety being grown, since some get much larger than others.

When to Plant

Plant directly in the garden 1 to 2 weeks after the last expected frost in spring. Spreading out the seeding time ensures the earliest possible germination. Frost may delay or damage new growth, but this is rare. The plants self-seed freely and seem to "know" when to sprout.

Support

The trailing types can be trained up any type of support you prefer for a spectacular floral display. Fences, trellises, and tripods are most commonly used.

How to Care for Nasturtiums
Water

Keep the soil moist but not soggy until seedlings emerge. Once plants are growing well, soak the soil deeply with each watering. Then let the soil dry out before watering again. The plants are said to be drought tolerant. However, if you let them dry out too long, they do not perform well. At the same time, overwatering is not a good idea either, since it encourages foliage growth at the expense of flowering. So let the plants guide you. Water immediately if leaves begin to wilt.

Mulch

Place a light layer of organic mulch around the young seedlings. Increase the depth as the plants mature. Get lots of mulch under the trailing types early since mulching becomes difficult once the plants spread out. Mulch reduces fluctuations in soil temperature but more importantly helps keep the area around the roots weed-free. Good organic mulches include grass clippings and pulverized leaves. The latter makes a more attractive background to the foliage of these flowering plants.

Fertilizing

Nasturtiums generally thrive without additional fertilizer in the growing season. Since leaves vary greatly in color, there is no easy signal for nutrient deficiency. As long as plants form lots of healthy foliage and plentiful blossoms, let them be. If plants have lots of leaves and few flowers, the soil usually contains too much nitrogen. Stop fertilizing.

Weeding

If you use mulch, weeding is generally easy. Hand pull any weeds that appear through the mulch. The plants are delicate when young, so weed carefully. As they mature, their rambling stems get much thicker. Even so, hand pull weeds from around the base.

Thinning

The bush types can get fairly wide and take up more space than might be expected. Thin them to about 12 inches apart once growing vigorously. The trailing types look lovely climbing up trellises, hanging over rock walls, or cascading from hanging baskets. Thin enough so that the plants are not overly crowded. When doing this, thin out the weaker plants. If you thin early in the season when plants have only one or two sets of true leaves, you can transplant them. Keep as much soil around the roots as possible. They resent this, but will bounce back if you keep them uniformly moist until they are growing well.

Pruning

If plants get too gangly and start roaming where you don't want them, snip them back. Pruning doesn't hurt them at all. Removing spent flowers (deadheading) promotes more bloom. However, plants bloom profusely, and deadheading is a poor idea if you want to save seed.

Special Considerations

The vining types do not have clinging tendrils. Tie these types to supports to get them heading in the right direction. You may have to do this several times if the plants flop down. Gently tie soft fabric around the stems and the support in a loose figure-eight knot.

Short stems with foliage and flowers attached are wonderful in a small vase. Place them where you can enjoy the fragrance, which can fill a small room.

Finally, some varieties seem to lack vigor. I have grown 'Empress of India' several times and find it a weak plant. Still, it's worth growing for its blue-green foliage and bright, if sparse, red blooms. The foliage is particularly lovely in arrangements with more free-flowering varieties.

Extending the Season

Extending the season is not really practical. If an early fall frost threatens, cover them with a sheet. A hard frost will eventually kill the plants. They are remarkably durable, however, and usually last well into fall.

Problems

Insects

These plants are rarely bothered by most insects. In fact, they are believed by some to repel insects.

Disease

Diseases are not common. However, it is not unusual for younger plants to have some blotchy spots on the leaves. These usually disappear as plants mature. Some say that this is caused by overwatering. Experiment by watering deeply and letting the soil dry out well before watering again.

Marauders

Animals are rarely interested in nasturtiums. Some gardeners claim they repel rabbits and deer from the garden. That has not been my experience.

Physiological

Curling leaves are caused by inconsistent watering and are most common early in the season when plants are still immature. Scent and vigor are related to good seed.

Propagation

If you plant the seed early in the season, nasturtium will often form mature seed by late fall. Let plants die down naturally at the end of the season. Mature seeds often drop onto the soil. Shake lightly to dislodge additional mature seeds. Collect seed, and dry it longer indoors. Place in an envelope, and keep in a cool, dark, dry place. Or scatter them where you would like plants to grow the following spring. Nasturtiums frequently self-seed when you do nothing at all—it just depends on winter weather.

You can also root tip cuttings. Bring these indoors, and keep in bright light over the winter. Bright light in cold climates is a problem unless you have a greenhouse or provide supplemental lighting. This is only worth the trouble if you find a plant that stands out in flower color or form from the others.

Harvesting

Do not remove foliage until plants are fairly mature and beginning to flower well. Remove blossoms at any time. Pick seedpods when still light green for a caper substitute. If you let them mature too long, they become hard and eventually turn brown with hard seeds inside.

Storing

Cut flowering stems, and place them in a floral arrangement. They will often last a few days or longer if you change water daily. Some people place individual flowers in ice cube trays, one flower covered in water in each well, and use the cubes in drinks. The flowers are colorful but turn soggy once they thaw.

Culinary Uses

The leaves, flowers, and immature seed pods are all edible. The leaves taste a little like watercress, and the flowers have a spicy bite reminiscent of radishes. When immature, the large, light-green, round, ridged seedpods are often pickled as a caper substitute. There is no taste advantage of one variety over another, as far as I know.

Use young leaves in salads, and older ones as a bed for other dishes. Also, just as you can stuff grape leaves, you can stuff older nasturtium leaves. The leaves are sometimes substituted for basil in making pesto.

Wash the flowers well since insects sometimes hide inside the blooms. Removing pistils and stamens is optional. Use the flowers in egg, green, or tuna salads. Shredded or sliced petals are excellent in butter, cheese spreads, guacamole, omelets, and scrambled eggs. Fill individual blossoms with any stuffing of your choice for lovely hors d'oeuvres. Add buds or flowers to stir-fries.

Flavor and color butter, oil, vinegar, and wine with the delightfully colored and often sweetly scented flowers.

To pickle seedpods as a caper replacement, pick seeds when green, soak in salt water (couple tablespoons per quart) for up to 2 days, rinse, drain, place in glass jar, cover with vinegar brought to boiling point, and seal. Spice with garlic, peppers, or shallots. Add salt and sugar to taste. Let age for a month or more. Do not eat seeds raw, as they are reported to contain oxalic acid (used to clean decks).

Varieties

Several species of nasturtium are suited only to warmer climates. These are extremely long trailing types. The varieties listed below are in two major species: *Tropaeolum majus* and *Tropaeolum minus*. In warmer climates the taller varieties can reach 10 to 12 feet. Most of the plants have single flowers with five petals. Some are spurred, and a few are semidouble (SD) or double (D) with a greater number of petals. The 'Whirlybirds' hold flowers well above the foliage, as do a few of the others. Nasturtium flowers often have a heavenly scent. Admittedly, scent does vary by variety, season, and seed source.

Seed source is important and difficult even for suppliers to control. For this reason, always grow a mix of different varieties, or grow several distinct varieties to avoid disappointment. To my knowledge, these are all open pollinated, and many not listed as heirlooms may qualify for that distinction.

VARIETIES	BLOOM COLOR	TYPE (INCHES)	FOLIAGE
'Alaska Mix' (heirloom)*****	Cream, gold, orange, red, salmon	12	Green splashed cream
'Amazon Jewel'	Yellow, peach to red	48–72	Green splashed cream
'Black Velvet'*****	Very deep burgundy	16	Medium blue green
'Buttercream'	Cream yellow (SD)	10	Medium green
'Cherries Jubilee'	Rose red	12	Blue green
'Cherry Rose'	Rose pink	12	Light green
'Copper Sunset'	Bright red	12	Medium green
'Creamsicle'	Pink to orange salmon	12	Light green
'Cup of Sun'	Yellow to orange tones	10	Medium green
'Double Dwarf Jewel' (heirloom)	Mix: orange, red, yellow (D)	12	Medium green
'Double Gleam'	Mix: orange, red, yellow (SD, D)	36	Medium green
'Dwarf Cherry'	Rose red (D)	12	Medium green
'Dwarf Jewel Mix'*****	Orange, salmon, red, yellow	12	Medium green
'Empress of India' (heirloom)	Scarlet red	12	Dark blue green
'Flame Thrower' (heirloom)	Unique split yellow petals with brown base	12	Ivy shaped green
'Fordhook Mix'	Orange, red, yellow	36+	Medium green
'Glorius Gleam Mix' (AAS-1935)	Gold, orange, red (SD, D)	36	Medium to deep green
'Jewel Mix'*****	Orange, red, yellow (D)	10–12	Medium green
'King Theodore'	Mahogany red	16	Medium green
'Ladybird Gold'*****	Bright yellow gold with red spot	10–12	Medium to dark green
'Mahogany'	Deep red	10–12	Medium green
'Milkmaid'	Close to white	12	Medium green
'Moonlight'	Primrose yellow	72	Bright green
'Papaya Cream'	Mix: orange red/cream yellow spotted red	12	Blue green
'Peach Melba' (heirloom)	Salmon/raspberry throat	10–12	Light green
'Salmon Baby'	Salmon (SD)	12	Deep green
'Scarlet Gleam' (AAS-1935)	Bright red (SD)	12–15	Medium green
'Spitfire'	Scarlet orange	48–72	Medium green
'Strawberries and Cream'	Yellow/throat splashed red (SD)	10	Deep green
'Tall Trailing Mix'	Orange, rose, yellow	48–72	Medium green
'Tip Top Mix'	Apricot, gold, mahogany, scarlet	8–10	Light green
'Vanilla Berry'	Yellow cream/orange red throat	12	Light green
'Vesuvius' (heirloom)	Orange salmon	12	Blue green
'Whirlybird Mix'*****	Cream, gold, orange, red, rose (SD)	16	Medium to deep green

Okra will grow in cold climates as long as it receives plenty of sun and is kept consistently moist and warm.

OKRA

Abelmoschus esculentus, **formerly** ***Hibiscus esculentus***
Hibiscus or Mallow Family (Malvaceae)

Okra is a very tender, warm-season annual. The plant, sometimes called "gumbo" or "lady's fingers," has long been popular in the South for Creole dishes and spicy soups. It prefers hot, humid weather but does surprisingly well in cold climates. Not only does it produce interesting edible pods but also has gorgeous flowers, making it an edible ornamental. Okra most likely originated in West Africa.

How Okra Grows

Seeds are fairly large, round, greenish, and indented on one end (about 500 to 700 seeds per ounce). Plants are usually erect and bushy with bold stems and crinkly, lobed or serrated leaves. Much of the plant may be covered with annoying spines. Okra is a member of the hibiscus family and produces stunning, if fleeting, flowers with dark centers. Bees pollinate the flowers, which produce pods, normally eaten when they are immature. Pods may be smooth or covered with bristly "hairs." The pod color and size vary by variety. Pods may be elongated or rounded, smooth or indented with ridges. Pods will form seed if allowed to mature throughout the growing season.

Where to Plant Okra
Site and Light

Place okra in full sun, ideally on a south-facing slope, or in lots of light in a protected location where warmth and humidity are high.

Soil and Moisture

Okra grows well in a wide range of soils as long as they retain moisture and drain freely. If soil is compacted, build a raised bed. Add lots of organic matter to the soil. Sphagnum peat moss is an excellent soil amendment since it acidifies the soil slightly. Okra thrives in soil with a pH of 5.8 to 6.5, which is mildly acidic. Okra needs fertile soil with sufficient nitrogen but not lots. Prepare the bed with a variety of organic fertilizers. A combination of blood meal, bonemeal, and greensand are good sources for a balanced amount of major nutrients.

Container

The smaller varieties will grow in containers. Use a large container, support the plant, and keep well watered and fertilized for best results.

Planting

Seed

Okra is most commonly planted directly in the garden, but it can be grown from transplants. When planting in the garden, make a furrow about 1 inch deep. Place three to four seeds per foot, cover with sifted soil, firm, and water immediately. Seed germination is erratic but usually occurs with 21 days at the most. The key to more uniform and rapid germination is to keep the soil moist around the seed at all times. Consider planting through black plastic for increased warmth, but remove it after 3 to 4 weeks.

There are several pretreatments believed to induce more rapid germination: freeze the seed (stratification), soak the seed overnight in tepid water, soak the seed overnight in cold water in the refrigerator, wrap in a moist towel in a refrigerator overnight, or soak in pure bleach for 2 hours and rinse. Plant the seeds *immediately* after any of these treatments. All of these are optional and possibly unnecessary if you keep seed planted directly in the garden consistently moist and warm.

Transplant

Start seed indoors 6 to 8 weeks before the frost-free date in your area. Use individual 3- to 4-inch pots to avoid disturbing roots at time of transplanting. Okra really resents root disturbance. Fill pots with sterile starting mix; plant three to four seeds ¼ to ½ inch deep; provide bottom heat for high soil temperature, if possible (80° to 90°F); keep moist; and place in a hot, sunny spot once germination has taken place, usually within 14 days. Once true leaves form, cut out all but the strongest plant in each pot.

Spacing

Sprouting in the garden may be uneven, so plant seeds about 2 inches apart. If most seeds sprout, thin to 6 inches when several inches tall. Then thin to 12 inches or more later in the season. Keep only the strongest plants. Place transplants at least 12 or more inches apart.

When to Plant

Direct seed no sooner than 3 weeks after the last expected frost when both soil and air temperature are at least 65°F. If the soil is too cool, seed usually rots. If you expect nighttime temperature below 55°F, cover young plants with row covers or individual cloches. Or surround plants with homemade or purchased Wall O' Water "cloches." The temporary use of black plastic to warm up the soil may be helpful.

Nutrition Facts

Serving size: 100 grams (3.5 ounces)

	AMOUNT PER COOKED SERVING	% DV
Calcium	75 mg	8%
Calories	28	1%
Carbohydrates	5 g	2%
Dietary fiber	3 g	10%
Folate	45 mcg	11%
Magnesium	35 mg	9%
Manganese	0.3 mg	15%
Potassium	235 mg	7%
Protein	2 g	4%
Thiamin	0.1 mg	9%
Vitamin A	285 IU	6%
Vitamin B6	0.2 mg	9%
Vitamin C	16 mg	25%
Vitamin K	40 mcg	50%

The stunning buds of okra open to beautiful, hibiscus-like flowers.

Support

If your area is prone to windstorms, avoid planting taller varieties. Staking all stems is highly recommended. Get your support into the ground early to avoid disturbing roots. Attach the stem loosely to the support in a figure-eight knot. You can also gamble. If a plant falls over, prop it up, and hill soil around its base as you would corn. Hilling works, but supports are better.

How to Care for Okra

Water

Okra demands heat and moisture. Water whenever the soil dries out. Water provides the plant with nutrients but also keeps humidity high. Warmth, moist soil, and high humidity are ideal.

Mulch

Place a 4-inch layer of mulch around individual plants once the soil has heated up thoroughly. If using grass clippings, build up mulch over a period of a few weeks. Too thick an initial layer may produce an off odor. If using shredded leaves, place a thick mulch around the plants from the start. Mulch is important to keep soil uniformly moist and to help increase humidity around the plants.

Fertilizing

Okra is a heavy feeder. Place organic fertilizers, such as fish emulsion, off to the side of the plant after thinning, as flowers begin to develop, and several weeks later to encourage regular pod formation. Watch how fruit is setting. If there is little fruit and lots of foliage, stop fertilizing with nitrogen-rich fertilizers.

Weeding

Keep after weeds, never allowing them to interfere with seedling growth. Hand pull any weeds that pop through mulch, especially around the base of growing plants.

Pruning

Pruning is common in the South, less so in cold climates. Experiment. Just as a plant begins to bloom, remove one-third of the leaves. Snip off the leaves closest to the stems, not the ones farther out on the branches. Prune some plants, leave others alone. This will give you an idea whether pruning is increasing pod production.

On taller plants, consider pinching out the growing tips to encourage lateral branching. This is typically done just as the first pods begin to form. You can even cut plants back to 18 inches if they get too tall or gangly. Pruning is optional and, again, more common in the South.

Special Considerations

While flowers are ephemeral, the pods can be lovely once fully mature. Let a plant or two form silvery-tan pods for floral arrangements. Pods are at their peak just as they begin to crack.

When working with okra, wear gloves. Some people are allergic to the plant; others just itch some from the spines.

Extending the Season

Okra is extremely frost sensitive. Get it into the garden earlier than normal by placing black plastic on the soil to warm it up. Then plant through the plastic. Grow shorter varieties to be able to cover individual plants with a sheet in fall to protect from an early frost.

Problems

Insects

Okra is not particularly prone to problems with insects and disease. However, aphids, corn earworms, cutworms, flea beetles, Japanese beetles, and stink bugs can be a problem. Protect young plants with row covers. As plants mature, pick off any worms or beetles.

Disease

Fusarium wilt (plant yellows from bottom up, wilts, and dies) and verticillium wilt (plant wilts and dies) are known to infect okra, but they are rare in the home garden. If a plant dies back, dig up and burn it.

Physiological

Flowers dropping off may be caused by variable weather patterns, over which you have no control. They can also drop off from inconsistent watering, which you can control. Take care of your plant, and it will rebloom again.

Propagation

Okra is commonly pollinated by insects, although it can be self-fertile. Varieties will cross-pollinate. Let pods mature until they begin to crack. Pick at this time, break open, remove seed, and dry. Okra seed is viable from 2 to 4 years, although best fresh.

Harvesting

The pods of almost all varieties are delicious when 2 to 4 inches long. Pods are often this length within 5 days of pollination. The pods on longer-podded varieties may be tender and tasty when larger. If the tip of a pod snaps off when pressed, the pod is still tender. If left on the plant too long, pods can turn woody. Pick pods at different sizes to see which you prefer. Note that vitamin C content tends to decrease as pods get larger.

Pick when plants are dry, not wet from watering or a recent rain. Pods are usually most tender in humid weather. Pick early in the day after dew evaporates if possible.

Wear gloves when harvesting pods. Do not pull pods off the plant, since tugging can hurt the plant. On some varieties just pushing on pods will snap then off. If this doesn't work, use pruners or scissors to snip off pods. Snip through the stem, not through the pod. Avoid wounding the pod, since it exudes a sticky (mucilaginous) substance. Cutting should be easy; if not, the pod is overly mature. Handle the pods as gently as possible.

Remove pods regularly to stimulate new production, at least every other day. If you allow pods to go to seed, the plant will have accomplished its task in life and quit producing. Some people cook seeds like peas.

Storing

Okra does not store well. Young pods are perishable. If at all possible, do not refrigerate or place in a closed container. Cover with a moist towel, and use immediately. If this is not possible, place pods unwashed in a plastic bag in the crisper of your refrigerator for no more than a few days. If you can't use pods within that time, freeze them.

To freeze, remove stem and blossom (if still attached), wash, scald 3 minutes, chill in ice water, drain, place in airtight freezer bags, and freeze. Blanched pods can be frozen whole or sliced. If slices will be fried later, consider coating them in cornmeal or flour. Place them in a single layer on a flat pan, and flash freeze before placing in freezer bags.

To pickle, pick when smaller than 4 inches. Follow your favorite pickling technique. If done properly, okra is crunchy, not slimy, when pickled.

Culinary Uses

Okra is grown primarily for its tender pods. These pods become slimy only if cut or pierced, so avoid both during preparation, leaving a small portion of stem with each pod. If okra has spines, rub them off with a wet rag.

Boil pods whole until tender, and serve as a side dish with hollandaise sauce or melted butter, pepper, and salt. To fry or stir-fry, blanch pods briefly, cool, and cook in oil. Or dust with cornmeal or flour before sautéing. Or boil until tender, drain, place in a baking dish, sprinkle with grated cheese, and broil until the cheese melts. Add pods to soups and stews for a natural thickener. Brass, copper, and iron pots may discolor the pods, but this is strictly cosmetic.

Although the flowers are edible, they are more beautiful than tasty. Young pods are tender and edible raw. When they are harvested very small, cut them into thin slices like cucumbers, and add them to salads.

Some growers let the pods mature to eat the seeds inside like peas, but this is rare. Mature dried seeds can be ground into a coffee substitute if for any reason you are not able to pick the pods when you would like to.

Varieties

Since okra germinates erratically, the days to maturity is difficult to assess accurately. Plant height is also variable depending on growing conditions. While many of the varieties will produce large pods, it is best to pick them at a much smaller stage. The term *spineless* is somewhat misleading, since some plants listed this way may produce some spines. Red okras are highly decorative and often used as ornamentals. Okra tends to be long and slender or a bit rounded and fat. Ease of picking varies by variety depending on density of foliage and overall height. 'Evertender' has long been appreciated for easy access to its pods. Choose varieties by time to maturity, size of plants, and types of pods.

VARIETY	DAYS	HEIGHT (INCHES)	PODS (LENGTH IN INCHES)
'Annie Oakley II Hybrid'	60	48	Almost spineless, medium green to 9
'Beck's Gardenville Okra' (heirloom)	80	36	Fat, green tinged red, ribbed to 3
'Beck's Big Buck' (heirloom)	80	60	Fluted, green to 5
'Burgundy' (heirloom) (AAS-1988)	80	48–60	Elongated, deep red, mildly ribbed to 8
'Burmese' (heirloom)	60	18–36	Elongated, green to cream to 10
'Cajun Delight Hybrid' (AAS-1997)*****	60	40–48	Spineless, dark green to 5
'Cajun Jewel' (heirloom)	55	36–48	Elongated, spineless, medium green to 7
'Chant Hybrid'	55	60	Elongated, medium green, mildly ribbed to 6
'Choppee' (heirloom)	70	40	Almost spineless, elongated, medium green to 7
'Clemson Spineless' (heirloom) (AAS-1939)*****	65	36–60	Elongated, almost spineless, medium green, mildly ribbed to 8
'Clemson Spineless 80' (heirloom)	60	48–60	Almost spineless, medium green, mildly ribbed to 7
'Cow Horn' (heirloom)	70	48–96	Elongated, almost spineless, light green to 14
'Dwarf Green Long Pod' (heirloom)	55	24–30	Spineless, dark green, ribbed to 7
'Eagle Pass' (heirloom)	65	48–60	Fat, green splashed red, ribbed to 4
'Emerald' (heirloom)*****	60	30–48	Elongated, medium green, ribbed to 9
'Emerald Velvet' (see 'Emerald')			
'Evertender' (heirloom)*****	70	60–72	Elongated, spineless, light green to 5
'Fife Creek Cowhorn' (heirloom)	55	48–96	Elongated, light green, cowhorns to 7
'Hill Country Red' (heirloom)*****	70	48–72	Fat, green ribbed red to 3
'Jade' (heirloom)	70	36–48	Elongated, spiny, dark green to 6
'James Hopper' (heirloom)	70	36–40	Elongated, green to 5
'Jimmy T's' (heirloom)	65	48–60	Elongated, green (harvest to 4)
'Jing Orange' (heirloom)	60	48–60	Spineless, bright red, ribbed to 6
'Lee' (heirloom)*****	55	30–36	Spineless, dark green, mildly ribbed to 7
'Louisiana Green Velvet' (heirloom) (AAS-1941)	60	48	Spineless, dark green to 8
'Mammoth' (heirloom)	65	60–72	Fat, bright green, ribbed (eat at 5)
'Millionaire Hybrid'	50	24–36	Elongated, dark green to 4 (edible flowers)
'North & South Hybrid'	45	36	Elongated, rounded, light green to 7
'Old Fashioned Okra' (see 'Star of David')			
'Penta Dragon' (heirloom)	60	24	Elongated, light medium green, ribbed to 6
'Perkins Dwarf Long Green' (heirloom)	55	48	Elongated, medium green to 9
'Perkins Mammoth Long Red' (heirloom)	55	60	Elongated, red to 6
'Pentagreen' (heirloom)	70	30	Elongated, green to 7
'Red Burgundy' (see 'Burgundy')			
'Red Okra' (heirloom)*****	70	60–90	Elongated, ribbed, deep red to 6
'Red River' (heirloom)	70	90	Elongated, maroon red to 7
'Red Velvet' (heirloom)	65	48–60	Elongated, scarlet red, mildly ribbed to 6
'Silver Queen' (heirloom)	80	72–86	Elongated, cream green to 7
'Snapping Okra' (see 'Beck's Big Buck')			
'Star of David' (heirloom)	70	60–96	Fat, medium green, ribbed to 7
'Stewart's Zeebest' (heirloom)	80	40–48	Elongated, spineless, light green to 7
'White Velvet' (heirloom)	60	60	Spineless, white from 8 to 12

The sooner you get an onion planted, the larger it will be by the time it is harvested.

ONION

Allium species
Onion or Amaryllis Family (Alliaceae or Amaryllidaceae), formerly Lily Family (Liliaceae)

Onions and their close relatives are hardy to very hardy, cool- to cold-season annuals, biennials, or perennials. They are one of the easiest vegetables to grow. They do extremely well in colder climates if planted early in the season. They produce large yields in a relatively small space. There are dozens of varieties, some so unique that they make great conversation pieces. Onions may have originated in Asia or the Middle East, possibly in Iran or Pakistan.

How Members of the Onion Family Grow

Varying types of onions grow in different ways as outlined in "Varieties." However, all of the onions listed in this section grow best in the long summer days typical of cold-climate regions. "Short-day" varieties would be suggested if you were living in the South. Intermediate day onions overlap the two areas, and a few of these are suggested in the varietal table.

Where to Plant Onions
Site and Light

Members of the onion family generally thrive in full sun. Plant them in the brightest light available, ideally a southern or western exposure. The more light, the larger the leaves. These larger leaves are responsible for larger bulbs or bulb clusters.

Soil and Moisture

All members of the onion family thrive in loose, fertile soil with good drainage. Add lots of organic matter to all soil types. The organic matter in the soil also retains moisture during dry periods. Good soil amendments are fully rotted manures or sphagnum peat moss. Good fertilizers include blood meal, bonemeal, and compost. Peat contains few nutrients but does make soil slightly acidic, which helps the plants take in needed food supplies. If you have clay or rocky soil, build a raised bed. These provide better drainage and heat up more quickly in the spring for an early start. The soil should have a pH of 6 to 7.

Nutrition Facts

Serving size: 100 grams (3.5 ounces)

	AMOUNT PER RAW SERVING	% DV	AMOUNT PER COOKED SERVING	% DV	AMOUNT PER RAW SERVING OF LEAVES	% DV
Calcium	23 mg	2%	22 mg	2%	60 mg	6%
Calories	40	2%	42	2%	25	1%
Carbohydrates	9 g	3%	10 g	3%	6 g	2%
Dietary fiber	2 g	7%	1.4 g	6%	4 g	14%
Folate	19 mcg	5%	15 mcg	4%	14 mcg	3%
Iron	0.2 mg	1%	0.2 mg	1%	2 mg	11%
Manganese	0.1 mg	6%	0.2 mg	8%	0.15 mg	7%
Potassium	145 mg	4%	165 mg	5%	260 mg	7%
Protein	1.2 g	2%	1.4 g	3%	2 g	4%
Riboflavin	0.0 mg		0.0 mg		0.1 mg	8%
Vitamin A	0.0 IU		0.0 IU		4,000 IU	80%
Vitamin B6	0.1 mg	6%	0.1 mg	6%	0.1 mg	6%
Vitamin C	7.4 mg	12%	5.2 mg	9%	45 mg	75%
Vitamin K	0.0 mcg		0.5 mcg	1%	165 mcg	210%

Container

These plants can be grown in large containers. The soil should be loose and drain freely through drain holes in the bottom of the pot.

Planting

Seed (Outdoors)

Planting seed outdoors is only suggested for green bunching onions. Plant it in ½-inch furrows. The seeds germinate and pop through the soil as very thin spikes. It can be hard to see the miniature plants, so mark the area well on both ends.

Seed (Indoors)

The big advantage of starting some members of this group from seed is that you can select the exact variety you want from a catalog. Onion seeds are small but quite easy to work with. Start them 10 to 12 weeks before the frost-free date in your area. Press them ¼ inch deep into a growing mix of damp peat, perlite, sand, or vermiculite. Plant seed close together. Keep the plants at 70° to 75°F under grow lights to encourage healthy growth. Lights should be about 6 inches above the plants. Move the lights up as the plants grow. These onions, crowded together, will grow well in the early stages. You divide them into individual plants only when you transplant them to the garden. When you divide these plants, they will be 4 to 5 inches tall. Note that some growers snip off the top inch of the plant before planting. This is said to help them snap back after the shock of transplant-

ing. This is not necessary. However, if plants get gangly and begin to topple over while still indoors, snip them back to 3 to 4 inches. This shearing does them no harm. Harden off and plant outdoors when the average temperature is 50°F.

Plant each seedling 2½ to 4 inches apart in each direction. Poke a hole into the soil with your finger or a pencil. Gently place the roots and lower (white) portion of the seedling into the hole. Firm the soil around the seedling. Water immediately, and keep moist at all times.

Note that onions grown from seedlings rarely form seed stalks, but with some types bolting may occur after unexpectedly cold weather.

Seedlings (Transplants)

Purchase transplants from a local nursery or from a southern source. Plants purchased from areas farther south are usually larger and more likely to produce more foliage to support enlarged bulb growth. Ideally, transplants are about as thick as a pencil. Get them into the ground immediately with stems buried at least an inch deep to support the foliage.

Sets

Sets are small, dormant bulbs that can be purchased locally or from mail-order sources. It is important to know the varietal name. Purchase only long- or intermediate-day sets (see "Varieties" for an explanation of this). Small sets are better than larger ones. They produce better onions and rarely go to seed in the current growing season. Sets are often sold by weight or volume. Pick through the sets, taking the smallest ones available. Choose sets no larger than a marble or a dime. They should be firm, not soft or mushy. Choose sets that have no green sprouts showing.

The earlier you get sets in, the larger the growth of leaves and the bigger the onions produced. This is the single most important secret to large yields. When planting sets, make sure the pointed end is up. Plant them so the tip of the set is just above the soil line. Do not plant deeper than this, since this may reduce bulb size and cause stems to be thick—according to some growers. Onions with thick stems store poorly. Water immediately.

When to Plant

Most onion family members are planted as early as possible in spring. (Garlic, covered in its own section, is planted in the fall.) However, if extreme cold threatens young plants, cover them with a sheet. They are very cold hardy, but a hard frost can damage them before they have taken root and are growing vigorously.

Spacing

Plant green bunching onion seeds very close together since you will be pulling them out regularly throughout the season. Space bulb onion seedlings and sets according to how you will be using them. Plant them 2 to 3 inches apart if you intend to pull bulbs up before they reach maturity. If planning to leave the plants or bulbs in place until the end of the season, plant them 4 to 6 inches apart. Plant onions that form numerous bulbs around their base at least 12 inches apart. These unique onions need space for their foliage to spread out as they mature.

Support

Support is not needed. Egyptian onions topple over as they mature, but that is part of the way they reproduce. The bulblets on top of the stems take root when they touch the ground, and produce new plants.

How to Care for Onions

Water

Keep onions well watered. Water is essential for quick growth, lush foliage, and large bulbs. It also improves flavor. Onions have a shallow root system, which can dry out very quickly if neglected. Water deeply around the base of the plant when the bulbs are forming. Do this consistently throughout the main growing season. When leaves begin to topple over toward the end of the season, stop watering. Watering at this time may reduce storage life. Note that if onion bulbs split

and form two bulbs or if onions have a strong sulfuric taste, you are underwatering during active growth or overwatering once stems are dying back. Overwatering is almost impossible if soil is loose and drains freely.

Mulch

Most onions are surface growers, so the entire onion will be exposed by the end of the growing season. A light, not heavy mulch, is ideal early in the season to keep the soil evenly moist. Place mulch around the onions without touching the bulb itself when plants have leaves 3 to 4 inches tall. If mulch touches the bulb during moist weather, it may cause rot. Mulch is less important as bulbs swell later in the season.

Fertilizing

Overall, onions are heavy feeders. Feed them well during the main part of the season with fish emulsion, ocean kelp, or other organic fertilizers. Do not place the fertilizer close to the bulb but several inches away. Watering and rain will carry the nutrients into the soil where roots are actively growing. The goal is to stimulate heavy foliage growth. Toward the end of the season, check the necks of the onions. If they are beginning to soften, stop feeding. Bulbs are beginning to cure at this stage. Too much nitrogen late in the season is believed to reduce storage life.

Weeding

Onions develop two sets of roots during the growing season. Both are extremely shallow. Pull all weeds closer to bulbs by hand. Shallow cultivation away from the plant is helpful in keeping the soil loose. If you use a tool to help you weed, be careful not to disturb the roots. Use a thin layer of mulch between the plants to suppress weeds. The few weeds that do pop through come up easily when pulled by hand. Weeding is easiest when the soil is moist (not wet). Onions compete poorly with weeds.

Thinning

Thin according to the size of onion you want to eat. Unless you want onions strictly for storage, begin eating some when ½ inch thick. The stems are good at this stage as well.

The onion maggot fly is believed to be attracted to onion odors during thinning. Row covers are a good deterrent.

Special Considerations

If an onion starts to form a flower, either let it go to seed if you want to collect seed, or pull up the onion and use it immediately. Once onions have formed flowers, they are not good for storage. While onions are very cold tolerant, unexpectedly cold temperatures early in the season may cause plants to bolt. Most onions do not flower until the second season of growth.

Problems

Insects

Onions are sometimes attacked by onion maggots, which are the larvae of the maggot fly. These ⅜-inch white worms burrow into bulbs and make them mushy. Dust wood ash around the base of onion plants if maggots are a threat. If some onions are infested, pull up and destroy them immediately. Thrips, almost invisible to the naked eye, will cause leaves to be distorted and discolored, somewhat bleached in appearance. They occur in hot, dry weather and may spread certain blights.

Disease

Prevent disease by buying disease-resistant varieties. Resistance to botrytis, downy mildew, fusarium, pinkroot or rot, and white rot is covered in most seed catalogs. Choose firm, healthy sets or plants. Plant onions in a different place each year. If the soil drains freely, if there is plenty of space between each plant, if weeds are pulled regularly, and if you avoid injuring bulbs by hand weeding, you will rarely have problems. If a plant shows signs of disease, dig it up and dispose of it immediately.

Marauders

Mice and moles can sometimes cause problems. Trap them with mouse traps baited with peanut butter. If you have a severe problem, use wire mesh under a raised bed and traps designed to kill underground marauders.

Physiological

Plants that bolt should be pulled and eaten immediately. Even if you cut off the stalk, the onions will not store well. Bolting may be caused by varietal selection or any kind of stress. Reds are particularly vulnerable to fluctuating temperatures.

Propagation

Propagation is directly related to how a specific type of onion grows. This is covered in the varietal table. Onions that produce flowers and seed in the second year are cross-pollinating. So grow only one variety of a type that flowers if you intend to collect seed. Let the plant flower, let the flower produce seed, cut off when the seed heads dry, and save the hard, black seed. Do not save seed from an onion that flowers the first year it is planted, as this is not a desirable trait.

Harvesting

Pick green onions or scallions throughout the entire growing season. They are best tasting when less than 10 inches tall. Leave ¼ inch of roots on until just ready to serve, which should be as close to immediately as possible. Harvest pickling onions when they are small. They taste better and are more tender when tiny. Use the bottom portions of Egyptian onions early or very late in the season much as you would leeks. They are most tender and mild at these times of year. Use the bulblets that appear at the end of each stalk in the second year for pickling onions.

At the end of the season, bulb onion stalks wilt and turn brown. They then collapse to one side. This signals the end of the growing season, and the onions are as large as they are going to get. When all the tops are dry, the onions are ready to be picked. This wilting and drying period often takes several weeks. All of the onions may not mature at the same time.

Some books suggest pushing the tops of onions over at the end of the season. This is known as "lodging." In theory, it speeds up the maturation process. In reality, it stops the onion from growing to full maturity and drying out naturally. Natural drying is preferred because onions will store better if they are allowed to dry out naturally.

Sometimes, if it rains frequently toward the end of the season, the natural drying process of the tops is delayed. Use a spading fork to loosen the onions slightly. This will break some of the shallow roots, causing the tops to die off more quickly. This technique is rarely necessary. Do harvest onions before a heavy frost.

When all stalks are dry and their necks have shriveled, pull up the onions on a bright, sunny day. Spread them out on the ground with their roots up to dry for several days. Brush off any loose dirt once it is dry. Avoid bruising or cutting the onions. The wounds will get infected and cause rot during storage. If you expect a rain, delay this process. Bring the onions into an area that is cool, dry, and dark. Spread them out on a rack or screen so that air circulates around them freely. The onions should not be touching each other. Cure them in this way for a minimum of 10 days up to several weeks. This natural curing process is essential for good storage. Onions have cured when the roots on the bottom of the bulb are brittle.

Once onions have cured, cut off the stems 1 inch above the bulb. Leave stems on if you intend to braid them. Many times the stems will shrivel and die off completely, so cutting them is unnecessary and braiding impossible. If the stem is moist or oozes water after it has been severed, use this onion right away. It will just rot in storage. If all of the onion stems are "bleeding," stop cutting them off. The onions have not cured long enough. Bleeding rarely takes place after a few weeks except on onions with thick stems.

Storing

In general, pungent onions last longer than sweeter ones. If the necks are thick on any storage onion, eat it as a fresh onion. These do not store well. Never allow storage onions to freeze, since they will rot once frozen. Leave the dry skins on since these papery outer layers contain an enzyme that prevents sprouting during storage. In short, don't attempt to have onions that are completely clean.

If onions can be kept cool and dry with good air circulation, they may last several months or longer. Air circulation is particularly important to prevent rotting. Hang onions from rafters in mesh bags or old nylon stockings. If you use the latter, place a knot between each onion to keep them apart. This helps avoid spoilage. Or you can braid the stalks (if present), if you keep them on the onions, as you would garlic. In modern homes providing the ideal temperature and humidity for storage is difficult. Any place where temperatures do not get above 50°F will work but not as well as cooler areas. Even in rooms with higher temperatures, a number of onions will store reasonably well. If roots appear on stored onions, it is too humid. Eat these bulbs before they rot. If onions start to sprout new stems, then it is too warm. Eat these as well.

To refrigerate green onions, store them unwashed in a plastic bag, close to freezing; remove outer leaves as they wilt or turn yellow; use as soon as possible. To freeze onions, peel and chop, dice, slice, or break into rings. Do not blanch. Place directly in airtight plastic bags and freeze. Use in hot dishes only. Onions are better stored dry. To dry, wash, peel off papery skins, slice off top and root ends, slice into sections ¼ inch thick, and dry in a dehydrator. They may last up to 2 months. To pickle, use your favorite recipe.

Culinary Uses

The members of the onion family have edible roots, stems, and flowers. Each type of "onion" is noted for particular uses. Green bunching onions are picked for their edible stems and typically sliced or julienned to be added to salads or cooked dishes. However, the sprouting stems of most onions are delicious as microgreens. Few onions are grown for their flowers, but the latter are edible and can be broken into florets to be added to salads.

It is the bulb that most cooks are after. Before peeling onions, refrigerate or freeze them for 30 minutes. Then trim stem and root ends off, before peeling them under cold, running water. Or boil them briefly before peeling. Onions contain syn-propanethial-S-oxide, which burns your eyes but is controlled somewhat by using either of these two methods. Peeled bulbs are delicious raw or cooked. Slice raw into salads, slide into burgers, and dice and add to hot dogs. Place on a platter with sliced tomatoes topped with mozzarella cheese, splashed with olive oil, and flavored with basil. Bulbs can be baked (peel, cook at 350°F until tender, basting with butter several times), boiled (white onions are best; cut an X in the base to keep the bulbs from falling apart), braised, broiled, butter steamed (¼-inch slices cooked until tender crisp), creamed, grilled (cut into sections, placed on skewers, cooked until tender), french fried (slice, batter, and deep-fry), microwaved (sliced or quartered), roasted, sautéed, steamed (mainly white onions), and stir-fried (¼-inch slices). Cooked onions are delicious covered with cream and cheese sauces or coated with an orange-honey glaze. And where would we be without onions for casseroles, pizzas, quiches, soups, and stews?

Varieties

The following information will help you distinguish between onion types in the marketplace. The descriptions will help you decide which ones to grow and how to use them.

Bulb Onion (Common or Garden Onion)
Allium cepa var. *cepa*

Bulb onions are the large onions found in most grocery stores. Onion varieties are divided by color (red, white, yellow, called brown in Great Britain), use (fresh or stored), flavor (mild, pungent, sweet), shape (flagon, flat or disc, globe or round, torpedo), and growth pattern related to day length (short: 10 to 12 hours of light per day; intermediate: 12 to 14; and long: more than 14 hours). There are some varieties that are considered day neutral. Short-day onions are best grown in the South, whereas long-day onions are better suited to the North. Intermediate-day onions overlap the two regions.

Red (purple) or Italian onions are mild and sweet. They are among the best onions to eat raw. They are delicious sliced and added to sandwiches or salads. They are also excellent grilled. In cold climates it is hard to get them to grow to a large size. They will store for awhile but are not known for this. White onions are mild to fairly pungent tasting. When picked the size of a golf ball, they are added whole to stews or cooked and served with a cream sauce. Used this way, they are referred to as boiling or creaming onions. 'Southport White Globe' is excellent for this use. White onions become mild and sweet when sautéed for French onion soup. Yellow onions have a tough, tan skin, produce lots of foliage, and are the easiest to grow. The flavor of their white flesh can be pungent, but it often mellows with cooking. They are often cooked by themselves or used in a wide variety of dishes. They keep well in a cool, dry place for several months or longer.

Bulb onions grow best from sets or transplants, available locally or through mail-order catalogs. The earlier you get these into the ground, the better. The more leaves they produce, the larger the bulbs. It is difficult for cold-climate gardens to get bulbs the size of those grown in the South, but many will be about the size of a baseball.

The following onions are not suited for growing in cold climates: Bermuda onions (flat, mild-flavored onions with white flesh); granex onions (the sweet Vidalia from Georgia is derived from this type); grano onions (another type of sweet onion imported from Spain and improved in Texas); and any extra sweet onions with little sulfur content, such as Maui from Hawaii and the already mentioned Vidalia. Bermuda, Maui, and Vidalia are sometimes called Spanish onions. Replace all of these with 'Walla Walla', which has been bred to do well in longer-day areas.

The varieties in this chart are well suited for growing in cold climates. Some may be available only as seed or plants, while a number are also sold as sets. After each name in parenthesis is a letter denoting whether the onion is a long-day (L) or an intermediate-day (I) type. If available only as seed, be prepared to start them indoors. Days to maturity is from transplants or sets. Size is tough to determine, since it is related to planting date and type of growing season. Storage is approximate as well and not consistently reported.

VARIETY	DAYS	TYPE	SHAPE/SIZE (INCHES)	STORAGE (MONTHS)	TASTE
'Ailsa Craig' (heirloom) (L)	100	Yellow	Globe to 8	Fresh	Sweet
'Australian Brown' (heirloom) (I)	100	Yellow	Oval to 5	5+	Pungent
'Candy Hybrid' (I)*****	100	Yellow	Globe to 6	3	Sweet
'Copra Hybrid' (L)*****	110	Yellow	Globe to 4	3½	Mildly pungent
'Dark Red Beauty' (see 'Red Wethersfield')					
'Hylander Hybrid' ('Highlander') (L)	90	Yellow	Flat globe to 4	4	Sweet
'Kelsai Sweet Giant' (see 'Ailsa Craig')					
'Long Red Florence' (heirloom) (L)	110	Purple red	Flagon to 4	Fresh	Mild to sweet
'Red Candy Apple' (Hybrid) (I)	95	Red	Globe to 3	3	Mild to sweet
'Red River Hybrid' (I-L)	100	Red	Globe to 4	3+	Sweet
'Red Wethersfield' (heirloom) (I)	100	Red	Flat globe to 4	2	Slightly pungent
'Red Zeppelin Hybrid' (L)	105	Red	Globe to 4	6+	Mildly pungent
'Ringmaster White Spanish' (heirloom) (L)	105	White	Globe to 5	4	Mild
'Rocca' (see 'Southport White Globe')					
'Ruby Ring Hybrid' (L)	110	Red	Globe to 3	3+	Slightly pungent
'Silver Ball' (see 'Southport White Globe')					
'Snow White Hybrid' (I)	90	White	Globe to 4	Fresh	Mild
'Southport Red Globe' (heirloom) (L)	120	Red	Globe to 3	3+	Mild
'Southport White Globe' (heirloom) (L)	120	White	Globe to 3	4	Pungent
'Sterling Hybrid' (L)	95	White	Globe to 5	6	Mildly pungent
'Stuttgarter' (see 'Yellow Stuttgarter')					
'Superstar Hybrid' (I) (AAS-2001)*****	95	White	Globe to 4	2	Mild to sweet
'Walla Walla' (heirloom) (L)	100	Yellow	Flat globe to 6	Fresh	Sweet
'White Rocca' (see 'Southport White Globe')					
'White Sweet Spanish' (heirloom) (L)	115	White	Globe to 3	3	Sweet
'Yellow Ebenezer' (heirloom) (L)	85	Yellow	Globe to 3	2	Pungent
'Yellow of Parma' (heirloom) (L)	110	Yellow	Oblong globe to 6	4	Mild to sweet
'Yellow Sweet Spanish' (heirloom) (L)*****	110	Yellow	Globe to 6	4	Mild
'Yellow Stuttgarter' (heirloom) (L)*****	115	Yellow	Flat globe to 4	4+	Pungent

The bulblets at the tips of Egyptian onion stems will take root whenever the stems topple over and touch soil.

Scallions are easy to grow from hard, black seed and produce green leaves and elongated white stems.

Cipollini
Allium cepa

Cipollini (pronounced CHIP-oh-LEE-nee), meaning "little onions" in Italian, are disk-shaped gourmet onions somewhat larger than boiling onions. Mild and sweet, they are delicious chopped and added to salads; baked, grilled, or roasted whole; or added to shish kebabs. The white 'Borettana' has a thin, tan skin and produces well in cold climates. Although they can be stored for a couple of months, they are usually eaten fresh. If planted 1 to 2 inches apart, they tend to be small and can be used as pearl or pickling onions. These are sometimes referred to as button onions since they are more flat than round.

VARIETY	DAYS	TYPE	SHAPE/SIZE (INCHES)	STORAGE	TASTE
'Borettana' (heirloom)*****	60	White	Flat to 4	Fresh	Sweet
'Red Marble Hybrid'	75	Red	Flat to rounded 2	Fresh	Sweet

Egyptian Onion
Allium × proliferum (Allium cepa var. vivaparum)

The Egyptian onion (also known as topset, tree, walking, or winter onion) is a fascinating perennial plant that produces little bulblets or topsets at the end of its stems, usually in clusters of three to six onions. These little bulbs are a bit bitter and strong but good for pickling. A mature plant will topple over, allowing the topsets to take root and form new plants—hence, the name walking onion. The main onion also multiplies at the base of the stalk. These are fun to grow as a novelty and are winter hardy.

VARIETY	DAYS	TYPE	SHAPE/SIZE	STORAGE	TASTE
'Egyptian Onion' (heirloom)	Sets	Greenish white	Marble size	Pickled	Pungent

Green Bunching Onion
(Allium fistulosum, Allium cepa var. cepa, and Allium fistulosum × Allium cepa)

Bunching onions (also known as green onions, green tails, scallions, salad, or spring onions) get their name from the fact that they are pulled and tied together in bunches for sale. Do not confuse them with multipliers, which produce numerous bulbs around the base of the plant. Bunching onions are easy to grow from seed but take a long time to mature fully. Most gardeners plant seed thickly 4 to 6 weeks before the last expected spring frost, begin harvesting when the plants are only a few inches tall and look like long, green hair, and keep harvesting regularly until the season ends when the onions are fully mature. Both the green hollow leaves and white lower portions of stem are delicious in salads and on vegetable platters.

To get plants with superlong, tender, lower portions of stem, dig a deep, flat-bottomed trench before planting. Plant seeds in the base of the trench. As plants mature, fill in the trench a little at a time so that the soil ends up just below the upper, green portion of the leaf. This produces onions with up to 12 inches of white stem tissue. When harvesting, keep the roots on to prevent water loss from the stems. Store these unwashed in a plastic bag in the refrigerator, and keep no longer than 1 week. They are juicier, milder, and sweeter than sets of bulb onions planted early and pulled just as green leaves form, which is what many gardeners do to replace them. Most people eat these onions raw, but try them once grilled—just for the fun of it. Some people think the flavor of the white, lower portion has a strong resemblance to that of a shallot.

It may be possible to overwinter some of these plants, especially 'Evergreen Hardy White', with a thick layer of loose straw mulch. I have even overwintered them without any mulch at all, but hardiness may vary by variety, so play it safe with a winter mulch. Days to maturity is on the generous side.

VARIETY	DAYS	COLOR OF LOWER STEM (LENGTH IN INCHES)
'Deep Purple' (OP)	65	Purple red to 4
'Evergreen Hardy White' (OP)*****	65	White 3–4
'Evergreen Long White' (heirloom)	65	White to 4–5
'Evergreen White Nebuka' (heirloom)	65	White to 3
'Ishikura Improved' (heirloom)*****	65	White to 20
'Lillia' (OP)	65	Red to 2–3
'Tokyo Long White' (heirloom)*****	65	White to 3–5
'Parade' (OP)	65	White to 2–3
'Red Beard' (heirloom)	65	Red to 4–5
'White Lisbon Bunching' (heirloom)*****	65	White to 2–3

Pearl Onion
Allium ampeloprasum var. sectivum, Allium ampeloprasum var. perlzwiebel, Allium porrum var. sectivum

This is the true pearl onion (also known as cocktail onion or perennial leek), but there are many bulbs or bulblets used as substitutes. The plant can be started in spring if bulbs are available. Plants will form little bunches of tiny bulbs, each with a single stem. Plants are hardy only to -20°F. Unfortunately, they may be sold only in the fall. It may be worth a gamble to try to overwinter them. Look for the variety 'Perlzwiebel' (the German word for "pearl onion") in seed catalogs. True pearl onions have a mild, sweet flavor, so their substitutes may be poor representatives of this name. One of the standard substitutes is a short-day onion, an onion good for the South, grown in the North, where it tends to stay small.

Potato Onion
Allium cepa var. aggregatum

Once extremely popular, potato onions (also known as hill, mother, multiplier, or pregnant) form clusters of bulbs from each bulb planted. Usually, one bulb will become four or five, rarely more, and look like a nest of onions once mature. They are not as big as bulb onions. Many shallots sold in this country are really multiplier onions. There were at one time red, white, and yellow potato onions. These onions have nothing to do with potatoes and do not grow like them, so the name is misleading. The 'Yellow Potato Onion' is the easiest to find.

Potato onions are planted exactly like bulb onions, with just the tip above the ground. The best planting time is spring, although the bulbs are most often sold in fall. Growers claim they are hardy to -30°F if covered with a thick, winter mulch of loose straw. If they don't winterkill, harvest as with other onions. However, if purchased in the fall, save a few bulbs, and store in a cool, dry, dark place. Plant these the following year *in spring,* just in case the fall-planted bulbs rot out.

Ramps
Allium tricoccum

Ramps are often referred to as wild onions. They are essentially a woodland plant, a spring ephemeral with broad, pointed leaves. They have a strong onion-garlic flavor in both their green tops and bulbous bottoms. The species is endangered in some parts of the country. They are difficult to grow from seed or plants, and many suppliers do not recommend them for cold-climate areas.

Shallot
Allium cepa var. *aggregatum* or Aggregatum Group, formerly *Allium cepa* var. *ascalonicum*

The true shallot *(Allium oschaninii)* is considered the queen of all onions and an essential part of French cooking. It is called *l'échalote traditionnelle,* and the French are not happy that many bulbs sold as shallots are not shallots at all. The true shallot can be grown only from bulbs since it does not produce a flower. However, many bulbs are being grown from seed and sold in the market as shallots. The true shallot has a thick, gray skin that is difficult to cut. Its flavor is delicate, with undertones of garlic and onion. It is difficult to find and may not overwinter in cold climates. The shallots that are readily available are essentially potato onions, at least, according to the French. Whatever you call them, they have a great taste. They are generally sold in the fall, but I prefer to start them in spring. That leaves me with a limited selection from health food stores, local nurseries, and an occasional catalog. Call local sources ahead in fall so that you can buy them *early in the season the following spring.*

Get them into the ground immediately. They form ground-hugging clusters of bulbs similar to the one planted. Despite what some packages say, do not break the bulb apart unless it is already splitting in two. Plant the whole bulb. My shallots have on occasion flowered, proving the French right. Build a 6-inch mound, and cover it with leaf bags collected the previous fall. Cut holes about 12 inches apart

Most shallots may be a form of multiplier onion; they add subtle flavor to cooked dishes.

in the bag or bags, large enough to insert the bulb with the pointed end up. Keep consistently moist until leaves start to turn yellow later in the season. The mound provides good drainage, stops most weeds from competing with the bulbs, and holds moisture in the soil.

Harvest when the stems turn brown. Cure by laying out on a dry, flat surface. The bulbs should not be touching. Store in mesh bags. Mince into vinaigrette, sauté in butter, caramelize, or cut in half and braise. Or use as you would an onion. To freeze, remove papery skin, chop into bits, and freeze for up to 3 months. Do not unfreeze before adding to a cooked dish. Add them at the end, giving them just enough time to cook and add the desired flavor. Freezing is not commonly recommended.

There are about a dozen varieties available in the marketplace. One of the most common is 'Santé'. Whatever variety you find, make sure it is available as a set, which is much easier to grow than from seed. If you are going to gamble with a fall planting, try 'Gray'. Cover it with a thick layer of mulch, and hope it survives. Sources selling it claim that it is the true French shallot, supposedly hardy to -20°F. I have not grown it, since I live in an area where temperatures get much colder than that.

The round, pinkish-white flowers on Welsh onions are typical of almost all types of plants in the onion family.

Welsh Onion
Allium fistulosum

Welsh onions (also known as ciboule, everlasting onion, negi, or spring) have nothing to do with Wales and are grown from seed to form numerous leek-like stalks rather than bulbs. The stalks can replace green bunching onions, and, in fact, green bunching onions are often interconnected with Welsh onions in catalogs. The plant is a perennial and is normally winter hardy. Two varieties worth trying are 'Franz Bunching' (heirloom) and 'Siberian Everlasting' (OP). The flowers of Welsh onions are lovely, as are those of most plants in the onion family.

PARSLEY

Flat-leaf parsley is a favorite of cooks.

Petroselinum species
Carrot or Parsley Family (Apiaceae, formerly Umbelliferae)

Parsley is a hardy to very hardy, cool- to cold-weather biennial grown as an annual in cold climates. Although parsley is inexpensive in most stores, it doesn't compare to fresh parsley with its strong, earthy flavor. It is an easy plant to grow from transplants and will produce prolifically once mature. Leaves are easy to pick and incredibly nutritious. Hamburg parsley is grown primarily for its parsnip-like roots, although its leaves are edible. Parsley probably originated in the eastern Mediterranean, possibly in Sicily.

How Parsley Grows

Leaf parsley grows from tiny, indented, tan seeds (about 9,400 to 18,000 seeds per ounce) into plants that are fragile early on, sturdy and vigorous once growing well. Leaf shape varies by variety from indented and curly to flat. Hamburg parsley grows much like a carrot, forming an edible root. If protected during the winter, the leaf types may spring back to life the following year and continue to produce edible leaves. During the second year these plants will often send

up flower stalks with rays of tiny gold blossoms in nearly flat heads. These produce copious amounts of seed.

Where to Plant Parsley
Site and Light

Parsley grows best in full sun but tolerates partial shade where summer temperatures soar. If possible, grow it close to the kitchen so that it is used almost daily. It is a lovely plant and blends well into flower beds and borders.

Soil and Moisture

Parsley likes soil that is loose, drains freely, but retains moisture during dry spells. Add lots of organic matter to the soil. Compost and manure work well. Parsley prefers a pH of 5.5 to 6.5, which is slightly acidic, so sphagnum peat moss is an even better soil amendment. Mix in a blend of organic fertilizers. Adding these will promote quick and healthy leaf growth. The more leaf growth, the better the plant. If your soil is compacted, either build a raised bed or grow parsley in a container.

Nutrition Facts

Serving size: 100 grams (3.5 ounces)

	AMOUNT PER RAW SERVING	% DV
Calcium	138 mg	14%
Calories	36	2%
Carbohydrates	6 g	2%
Dietary fiber	3 g	13%
Folate	152 mcg	38%
Iron	6 mg	34%
Magnesium	50 mg	12%
Niacin	1.3 mg	9%
Pantothenic acid	0.4 mg	8%
Phosphorus	58 mg	8%
Potassium	555 mg	16%
Protein	3 g	6%
Riboflavin	0.2 mg	17%
Thiamin	0.1 mg	9%
Vitamin A	8,425 IU	168%
Vitamin B6	0.1mg	8%
Vitamin C	133 mg	222%
Vitamin K	1,640 mcg	2,050%

Container

Many home gardeners have good luck growing leaf parsley in pots. Make a light, almost airy potting mix that drains well. Keep it consistently moist, and water with light feedings every few weeks if leaf color begins to fade. Harvest lightly at first, more as the plant matures. Consider growing both a curly and flat-leaf (Italian) variety in separate pots. It is possible to grow Hamburg parsley in pots, but few people do. This is a root crop and must have a deep container.

Planting
Seed

Direct seeding leafy varieties makes little sense in cold climates, but there is a strategy described under "When to Plant" that may appeal to some. Do direct seed Hamburg parsley. Loosen the soil, and remove any debris. In a shallow furrow, sift the soil. Plant the seed ½ inch deep, and keep consistently moist. Thin as necessary as you would for other root crops.

Transplant

If you want a specific variety of leaf parsley, you may have to start it from seed. There is an old saying that "parsley seed goes seven times to the Devil and back" before it sprouts. In short, it may not sprout for weeks even when properly planted. Tricks to overcome its natural dormancy include moist chilling the seeds in the freezer for 3 to 5 days, scalding seed briefly in boiling water, soaking seed for up to 24 hours or longer in tepid water, laying seed out on a moist paper towel in the refrigerator until seeds break open and begin to sprout, and so on.

Plant seed 8 to 10 weeks before the frost-free date. Fill an 8-inch pot with sterile starting mix. Press more seeds than you need into the mix before sifting ⅛ inch of mix over the seeds. Keep moist, dark, and cool until seeds sprout. Then move them into light in a cool place. Keep only one or two plants per pot once they are growing well. Harden off and plant as soon as the ground can be worked. If a sudden cold snap occurs, cover the plants with a cloche.

The simplest way to add parsley to your garden is to buy a young plant from an organic grocery store or garden center. The hardest part of the growing process has already been done by someone else, and you have "instant" parsley. Buy both curly and flat-leaf types for a taste comparison. However, you will not know the variety in most instances.

Spacing

Parsley grown for its leaves can be grown fairly close together, but most home gardeners space plants about 12 to 18 inches apart. Only a few plants are really needed by most families.

Hamburg parsley is generally sown thickly to ensure that there are enough plants for a good harvest (see "Thinning").

When to Plant

A good strategy for growing leaf parsley is to both direct seed and plant transplants into the garden very early in the season as soon as the soil can be worked. The idea is to have plants at a different stage of growth. Some gardeners plant seed just as the soil begins to freeze in fall. It often germinates the following spring as if a mature plant had self-seeded. This doesn't always work but is well worth the gamble. Mark the planting area well. While you want to plant seed early, protect young plants from frost either with a sheet or individual cloches.

Hamburg parsley seed also should be planted early in the season. The earlier you get it in the better, since it needs plenty of time to form elongated roots.

How to Care for Parsley
Water

All forms of parsley grow best with consistent watering. Feel the soil with your hand. Water whenever the top few inches are dry. Leaf parsley stays green and vibrant with regular watering. The roots of Hamburg parsley may split or become deformed if stressed by lack of water.

Mulch

Surround parsley with a 3-inch layer of grass clippings, shredded leaves, straw, or pine needles—whatever is readily available and inexpensive. Avoid touching the base of the leaf stems with the mulch, but reapply it regularly as it is eaten by worms and soil microorganisms throughout the growing season.

Fertilizing

All types of parsley benefit from regular, small feedings of organic fertilizer. This helps stimulate lush foliage. This is particularly important for Hamburg parsley. The more lush its foliage, the larger its roots. The larger its roots, the better its taste.

Weeding

Keep the area around each seedling or plant weed-free. If a weed is close to a seedling, snip it off with a cuticle scissors, or pull it up with a tweezers. As plants get larger, pull up weeds by hand.

Pruning

It is common for newly planted plants to have some outer leaves turn yellow. Snip these off with a scissors. Unless you are growing a plant for seed, snip off any stems that start to flower. This puts emphasis on stem and leaf growth— the part of the plant you want to eat for weeks to come. Parsley usually goes to seed in the second, not the first, year of growth.

Thinning

If you direct seed parsley, then dig up small clumps that emerge, and plant as individual plants. Once they take, snip out all but the healthiest plant. Thinning is important with Hamburg parsley. Generally its seeds are sown close together to ensure enough plants for a decent harvest. However, begin thinning early on if plants are crowded. Thin first to 2 inches, then to 4, and finally to 6. Do this over a period of weeks. Do not expect roots to be as big as parsnips.

Winter Protection

As the weather begins to turn cold in late fall and the ground is about to freeze, cover plants with a thick layer of loose straw. Remove the mulch in spring as soon as it gets warm to prevent rot. Plants may survive. If they don't, dig up and compost them. Use the same method with Hamburg parsley. If the plants survive, dig the roots up in spring as needed, and use the new greens like regular parsley.

Special Considerations

Parsley may act as a host for black swallowtail butterfly larvae (*Papilio polyxenes*). The larvae go through stages of growth. In the final stage they are about an inch long, black and green, with yellow dots on their body. While they do damage plants, many gardeners consider the loss worth it.

Parsley is high in vitamin K. If you are on a blood thinner such as warfarin (Coumadin), talk to your doctor.

Extending the Season

Leaf varieties planted directly in the garden stand up well to fall cold. If temperatures are dropping temporarily, cover the plants with a sheet during the day. Once temperatures rise, remove the sheets. If winter is setting in, cover the plants with a thick layer of loose straw. This may get them through the winter, but there is no guarantee. Bring potted plants indoors, either temporarily during a cold snap or permanently once winter sets in. Do not expect a lot of foliage. Just keeping them alive is an accomplishment.

Problems

Insects

Parsley is not bothered by many insects. Occasionally, larvae may be a nuisance (see "Special Considerations").

Disease

Hamburg parsley is susceptible to parsnip canker, but this is not common. Dig up and destroy infected plants.

Marauders

Rabbits can, but don't always, nibble on parsley depending on what else is available. Deer will also damage plants early on as they roam the area looking for tender greens. However, parsley can be sheared and still spring back to life. As parsley plants mature, they seem to be less attractive to wildlife.

Physiological

Occasionally, parsley plants may bolt in hot weather.

Propagation

Parsley is a biennial. To help it survive into its second year of growth, cover it with a thick layer of loose straw as soon as the ground begins to freeze in late fall. If well protected, plants often spring back to life once the snow melts, produce

Curly-leaf parsley makes an attractive border and is popular as a garnish or deep-fried as tempura.

new leaves, and then produce tall flower stalks tipped with umbrella-like blossoms pollinated by insects. Let the seed heads dry thoroughly on the plant. Once seeds have formed, remove mulch around the plant, and scratch the soil to loosen it. Let the plant self-seed. Keep the soil moist until the first freeze. Seedlings will often emerge in spring and can be transplanted once growing well. This is much easier than seed saving, although seed savers can get a jump on the season by planting them indoors as transplants.

Harvesting

Let the parsley start to grow vigorously before you begin to pick off any stems. If you want some right away, grow several plants—one for instant gratification, the others for growing. Snip off only a few leaves from the outside of the plant. Snip these off at ground level. Let the inner leaves grow. As the plant matures, harvest more heavily.

Harvest Hamburg parsley after a frost, but do not let it freeze. The frost changes starches into sugar and gives the root a better flavor. Use a garden fork, rather than a spade, to dig up the roots, which can be deep. Cut off the leaves. If you are able to get flat-leaf parsley to survive the winter, try eating some of its roots if you have enough plants.

Storage

The easiest way to have fresh parsley all winter long is to grow it in a pot that you bring indoors. Cut the plant back, place it in a sunny spot, and keep it well watered. Providing enough light is often difficult, but since parsley likes it cool, it can be placed next to an outside window.

To keep harvested leaves fresh indoors, wash, shake off excess water, place leaves spaced apart in a single layer on a damp paper towel, cover with a second damp paper towel, roll loosely, and slide into an open plastic bag in the crisper of your refrigerator.

To dry, air dry in bunches hanging upside down in an area with excellent circulation and low humidity. Or cut into pieces, and place on parchment on a metal tray in the oven set at 200°F. Drying may take 2 to 3 hours or longer. Flat-leaf (Italian) parsley types dry better than their curly cousins, but drying affects their flavor.

To freeze, place whole stems or individual leaves chopped into pieces on a metal tray. Flash freeze. Place the leafy stems or chopped leaves into freezer bags, and keep frozen. Or place chopped leaves into the small compartments of an ice cube tray. Add water and freeze. Pop out the cubes, and keep frozen in freezer bags, and add to cooked dishes at the last moment. Curly-leaf types are best suited to freezing.

Consider making a parsley pesto. It takes up little space and lasts for months.

Place the roots of Hamburg parsley in moist peat or sand if you want to store them for awhile. Keep cool and moist but not soggy. Pot up and force a root whenever you would like some fresh "greens."

Culinary Uses

The tops of all types of parsley are edible and used in a variety of ways. The curly type is often used as a garnish but is excellent battered and cooked as tempura or simply sautéed in oil at 375°F. Both curly and flat-leaf varieties may be chopped up and added to casseroles, salads, soups, and stews. An easy way to cut parsley is to put sprigs in a measuring cup and cut them into bits with a scissors. Keep snipping until you have pieces the right size for sprinkling over hot dishes. Parsley seed is edible and excellent in cheeses. The French seasoning known as fines herbes consists of chervil, chives, parsley, French tarragon, and sometimes marjoram.

It can be used either fresh or dried. If used fresh, add it to any dish at the last moment for the best flavor. The main ingredients of the Italian condiment *gremolata* are lemon rind, garlic, and parsley. It is also one of the main ingredients in tabbouleh.

Hamburg parsley is grown primarily for its long, swollen, carrot-like roots, although its leaves are also flavorful. The roots have a nutty taste, are white, and are rather dry. Some gardeners insist the taste has hints of carrot, celeriac, celery, kohlrabi, parsnip, and turnip. Peel, cut into crisp strips, and eat with a dip. Grate and add the raw flesh to salads or slaws. Slice and fry them like french fries. Boil and mash them like parsnips or potatoes. Roast wedges along with meats, as you would carrots or potatoes. Cut into pieces, dip in batter, and fry. Or add chunks of flesh to soups and stews, which you can also do with the foliage for an interesting flavor.

If you are growing 'Giant of Italy' from seed, let it mature to the point that you can eat some of its stems like celery. This is quite a bit of work. The plant is closely related to celery and mimics leaf celery somewhat.

Varieties

There are two basic types of leaf parsley: curly and flat-leaf (Italian). The curly has a strong taste, while the flat-leaf is milder and preferred by many cooks. Neither is really better than the other, just different. Hamburg parsley does produce edible leaves and is worth trying for comparison. Not included in the following table is Japanese parsley, which, despite its name, is not a parsley. Also not included is Cilician parsley, with its unique citrus flavor. This ancient herb is a true parsley and is slowly being reintroduced to seed catalogs. Although French parsley is sometimes used to describe either curly or flat-leaf parsley depending on the source, it is most often used as common name for chervil.

VARIETY	DAYS	HEIGHT (INCHES)	LEAF COLOR	FORM OR COMMENT
Parsley, curly-leaf, common, curled leaf				
Petroselinum crispum var. (ssp.) *crispum*, also known as *Petroselinum hortense*				
'Banquet' (OP)*****	90	18–24	Dark green	Tightly curled
'Champion Moss Curled' (OP)*****	75–80	24	Dark green	Finely curled
'Darki' (OP)*****	80		Very dark green	Super curly
'Double Curled' (OP)	70	14	Dark green	Dense closely curled
'Evergreen' (heirloom) (AAS-1940)	70	12	Dark green	Finely cut, tight curls
'Extra Curled Dwarf' (OP)	40–60	10–12	Dark green	Curly, finely cut
'Extra Triple Curled' (see 'Champion Moss Curled')				
'Favorit' (OP)	75	15	Bright green	Tight curls
'Forest Green' (heirloom)*****	75	12	Bright green	Deeply cut leaves
'Green River' (OP)	70	18	Bright green	Double curled
'Krausa' (heirloom)*****	75	12	Medium green	Delicious stems and leaves
'Moss Curled' (heirloom)*****	70	12	Very dark green	Thick mass of curled leaves
'Pagoda' (OP)*****	75	12	Dark green	Rounded triple curled
'Paramount' (heirloom) (AAS-1936)	85	15	Dark green	Triple curled
'Triple Curled' (heirloom)	70	18	Dark green	Finely curled
Parsley, flat-leaf or Italian or celery-leaved or plain-leaved				
Petroselinum crispum var. *neapolitanum*, also known as *Petroselinum crispum* var. *latifolium*				
'Dark Green Italian' (heirloom)	80	12–15	Dark green	Wide, smooth leaves
'Giant of Italy' (heirloom)	60–90	18–36	Dark green	Large leaves and thick stems
'Plain Italian' (heirloom)*****	60–80	18–24	Dark green	Deeply serrated
'Single Italian' (see 'Plain Italian')				
'Titan' (OP)	75	12–15	Dark green	Extra small leaves
Parsley, Hamburg, turnip-rooted, or parsley root				
Petroselinum crispum var. *tuberosum*, also known as *Petroselinum crispum* var. *radicosum*				
'Hamburg Rooted' (heirloom)	85–90	24	White roots	Carrot-like to 12 in
'Hamburg Half Long' (OP)	85	18	White roots	Carrot-like wedges to 6 in

Don't be afraid to dig up parsnips before they are fully mature. They often develop hard cores with age.

PARSNIP

Pastinaca sativa
Carrot or Parsley Family (Apiaceae, formerly Umbelliferae)

Parsnips are hardy to very hardy, cool- to cold-season biennials grown as annuals and ideally suited to cold-climate gardening. Mature parsnips developing in the fall become sweeter with hard frosts. While they take patience to grow, they are relatively disease- and insect-free. Their flavor is pleasant, and this root crop is often overlooked by the home gardener. Parsnips probably originated in the Mediterranean area.

How Parsnips Grow

Parsnip seeds are light, flat to rounded (about 5,000 to 7,000 seeds per ounce). The young leaves are frilly, small, but easy to distinguish from surrounding weeds. As the plants mature, the attractive foliage gets increasingly larger. The growth of the roots continues over a period of months until harvest in late fall. The roots vary in length but can be up to 18 inches long depending on the variety and the growing conditions. Plants that survive a winter may produce flowers in the second year. These appear as clusters of tiny flowers in what appears to be a yellow umbrella from a distance. The umbrella turns light brown as the seeds mature.

Where to Plant Parsnips
Site and Light

Plant parsnips in full sun. They will grow in partial shade but develop more foliage in full sun. This provides the roots with the nutrients necessary to increase to full size.

Soil and Moisture

Since parsnips can reach a depth of 15 inches or more, they grow best in loose, rich soil that drains freely. Sand enriched with organic fertilizers is ideal. Prepare a deep bed of less desirable soils by loosening them with a spade or tiller. Add lots of sphagnum peat moss, compost, or rotted manure to the bed, and mix in organic fertilizers. Some gardeners add a little wood ash to the soil, believing that it helps deter disease and insect infestations. Remove all debris such as rocks, sticks, or large clumps of earth. Obstacles in the soil may cause the roots to fork. Working the soil through a screen makes it fine and easy for roots to penetrate. The pH should be approximately 6 to 6.8.

Some gardeners use posthole diggers to dig deep holes for individual parsnip plants. They then fill each hole with soil amended exactly the way they want.

If you have compacted soil, it is often easier to build a raised bed 8 to 12 inches high. In this way you have the same control over the soil as someone digging individual holes. If you can dig easily a foot down into your soil with your bare hand, then it is loose enough. This loose soil will also drain freely. If water collects after a rain, the roots of parsnips may rot.

Container

It is possible and a bit offbeat to grow parsnips in a deep container on a deck or patio. Get pots as big as the ones large shrubs are sold in. Keep the soil evenly moist throughout the season. Dump the pot over to gather the roots at the end of the season. This works for other deep-rooting plants as well, which often snap off as you try to dig them up.

Planting

Seed

Parsnip seed can be finicky. Always use fresh seed each year. It may take up to 21 days or even longer to germinate. Seed must stay moist to germinate properly. Soaking the seed overnight may help. Do not soak seed for more than 24 hours.

Plant the seed directly in the garden. The soil should be loose and fine. Some gardeners mix sifted compost, sphagnum peat moss, or vermiculite into the soil at the planting site. Place seed ¼ to ½ inch deep. Plant more seed than you really need. Firm the soil over the seed so there is good contact. Mist the soil until it is uniformly moist. A ¼-inch layer of pulverized leaves, compost, or grass clippings placed over the seeds helps prevent crusting, which may prevent seeds from sprouting. Its other advantage is that it keeps the soil moist.

Skillful gardeners may cover the area with a damp cloth, which helps retain moisture in the soil. However, the cloth must be removed immediately when seedlings emerge. For this reason, most home gardeners do not use this method. Instead, they water frequently with a gentle mist to keep the soil consistently moist. This may mean watering the soil twice a day.

Transplant

Root crops do not transplant well. Some people do presprout parsnip seeds by laying them between sheets of moist paper towels. Keep them cool. If you are lucky, the seeds will begin to germinate. When the little white roots are less than ¼ inch long, gently plant them outdoors as you would regular seed. A few gardeners insist on indoor planting. Start seed indoors 6 weeks before the last expected spring frost. Fill cardboard tubes from the inside of toilet paper rolls with a sterile starting medium. Plant seeds in these. Keep the mix moist at 65°F until seeds germinate, which can take as long as 21 days. Slide these into outdoor planting holes when seeds have formed true leaves and have been hardened off for 10 days.

Spacing

Traditional planting is to place seeds about 1 inch apart along a row, or to place three seeds about an inch apart in individual holes. The holes should be about 4 to 8 inches apart. A less conservative approach is to plant more thickly with the idea of thinning at a later date. Since germination is so erratic, thicker planting makes sense.

When to Plant

Plant seeds as soon as ground can be worked, which is usually about 2 to 4 weeks before the last expected frost in spring. Or plant seed just as daffodils begin to bloom. The minimum soil temperature is 35°F. Get seeds in before the ground reaches 60°F. Plant again later in the summer for a harvest the following spring. Parsnips are incredibly hardy.

How to Care for Parsnips

Water

Keep the soil moist at all times to prevent young seedlings from drying out. Water the plants frequently when immature, and regularly during the main season. Although the plants are drought tolerant, dry spells can cause roots to have a woody core. So water consistently.

Mulch

Mulch around the young plants after thinning them to stand several inches apart. Use mulch along the parsnip row to keep the soil moist and cool. This is especially important in the high heat of midsummer. Good mulches include grass clippings, pulverized leaves, and straw.

Fertilizing

If you have added rotted manure or compost and some organic fertilizer to the soil before planting, that is normally all the plants will need. Some gardeners sprinkle a little more fertilizer around the plants when they reach 3 inches. Water immediately after fertilizing, and avoid getting any fertilizer on the leaves. Fertilize according to the plant's growth. Add more nitrogen if foliage appears weak.

Weeding

Remove all weeds immediately around seedlings. If parsnip seeds are planted close together, some of them may pop up with the roots of the weeds. This is fine in the case of overly close planting. Otherwise, snip off the weeds with a scissors if you find it difficult to weed with your fingers. Later in the season remove weeds by hand as they emerge through the mulch.

Thinning

Never allow parsnips to mature close together. Close planting encourages bushy top growth but poor root formation. Enough space encourages the formation of larger roots. After the parsnips have grown for 3 weeks, thin out the seedlings so that there is a plant every 4 inches along a row. If you have planted too many seeds, gently pull a garden rake through the seedlings. Do this lightly so that the rake penetrates the surface of the soil about ¼ inch down. This will leave seedlings roughly an inch or so apart. If necessary,

further thinning by hand is now much easier. If planting in groups, thin to the strongest plant per hole. Snip off all but one plant with a scissors if plants are really close together. This will help the survivors. Water immediately after thinning to settle soil around the roots of the young plants. Do not bother with transplanting uprooted seedlings unless you have too few plants developing well. Do this when seedlings are about 4 to 6 inches tall.

Special Considerations

Never eat wild plants with roots resembling parsnips. These may be poisonous. And do not eat the stems or foliage of cultivated parsnips. Whenever handling parsnips, wear gloves, and do not let foliage come in contact with your skin. Not everyone experiences an "allergic" reaction from these plants, but some do. Play it safe with gloves, long-sleeved shirts, and pants unless you have already worked with the plants and experienced no reaction.

Extending the Season

By getting plants in early, you can begin harvesting tender, small roots whenever they are large enough for your taste. Admittedly, parsnips do taste best after a few fall frosts when temperatures dip down to at least 34°F. The starches in the roots turn sugary at this time. Parsnips can be harvested from late fall and into early winter if covered with a thick winter mulch of straw or loose leaves. Parsnips generally survive into spring, sometimes without any protection at all other than snow. At that time dig up and eat them before or just as they show new growth.

Problems

Insects

Flea beetles may attack seedlings and nibble small holes in the leaves. This is not a common problem with this vegetable. Parsnips are vulnerable to carrot fly maggots and a few other insects, but these problems are rare. For control, cover young plants with row covers, or just put up with less than perfect early growth.

Disease

Canker shows up as rot in the upper portion of the root. Too much nitrogen and too early planting may encourage canker. Reduce the chance of rot by planting canker-resistant varieties, such as 'Andover', 'Gladiator', 'Javelin', and 'Lancer'.

Propagation

Parsnips tend to winter over well. As they grow in the second year, they form long flower stalks with lovely clusters (umbels) of yellow flowers that produce copious amounts of seed. Let these dry on the plant. The stalks often become so heavy they topple over. Provide them with support if you want the seed to dry thoroughly on the plant before harvesting. Once the seed is dry, cut off the tops of the plant into paper bags. Scrunch up the seed heads, remove the seeds, and keep them in an envelope in a cool, dark, dry area until planting the following season. Plants self-sow freely if allowed to. Seed typically lasts 1 year.

Harvesting

Unless your soil is extremely loose, do not try to pull up parsnips, since the roots can break off underground. Dig off to the side of the plant with a garden fork. Loosen the soil all around the root as deeply as you can. Now pop them out of the ground with the fork. Try parsnips young as well as mature. Many gardeners prefer them after they have been exposed to a frost. Note that they get limp quickly once dug out of the ground.

Storing

Only store roots that have no bruises or cuts. If they are damaged, they tend to rot. Use these right away. Parsnips can be stored briefly unwashed in a plastic bag in the crisper for about 10 days. If not in bags, they will tend to shrivel. Do not store the roots near apples, which give off ethylene gas, which can make them bitter. If you can keep them close to freezing in high humidity, it is possible to store them for up to 6 months.

There are several methods for long-term storage. To "store" them in the garden, leave the parsnips in the ground. Remove foliage. Cover the bed with a 10- to 12-inch layer of straw. Hope for a good snow, which acts as excellent insulation against winter cold. Dig up roots as needed. In spring remove the mulch before the soil warms to avoid root rot. By setting mulch off to the side of the bed, you can put it back on if there is an unexpected cold spell. Dig the roots as soon as possible and *definitely before new growth emerges*. If the plants begin to grow, the outer portion of the root turns leathery.

Other gardeners prefer to harvest all of the roots at once. Dig up parsnips on a dry day. Take only the best of the lot for storage. Eat the rest. Let the parsnips dry out for a couple of hours in shade outdoors. Much of the loose soil will drop off, but don't wash or brush the parsnips. Snip off the foliage to within 1 inch of the top of the root. If you cut into the parsnip by accident or damage it any way, don't store but eat it. The roots will store well in a plastic garbage can filled with moist sawdust, sphagnum peat moss, sterile sand, or whole maple or oak leaves. Place the can in an unheated, but insulated, garage where temperatures range from 35° to 40°F, close to, but above, freezing. If they freeze, they will rot. Place each root with 1 inch of stem upright or lying flat in the packing material. Parsnips should not be touching one another or the side of the container. Cover each parsnip completely. Place the parsnips in layers until the container is full. The insulating material should keep any roots from touching. Cover the top of the insulation with plastic to keep humidity high, as close to 95 percent as possible. The moisture will keep the parsnips from drying out. Parsnips may last for up to 3 months stored in this way.

If you don't have a root cellar or an insulated garage, freeze the parsnips. Cut off tops, wash, peel, soak in lemon water, slice lengthwise, remove core, slice or dice, scald 2 to 3 minutes, sprinkle with the juice of a whole lemon, cool, drain, pack, seal, label, and freeze.

Culinary Uses

Only eat parsnip roots, which have a sweet, nutty flavor. *Do not eat leaves or stems.* Eat the raw roots grated, julienned, shredded, or sliced into salads. The flavor is more pungent than that of cooked roots. Raw parsnip is a bit more nutritious than cooked, but the taste is an acquired one. Parsnips are eaten far more often cooked.

When ready to eat raw or cooked, wash and cut off the top and bottom tip of the root. Scrub young roots, and peel older ones with a vegetable peeler until the flesh is fully exposed. Eat young roots whole, and cut mature roots in two lengthwise, then cut in two again. If the roots have a tough inner core, remove this by running your knife lengthwise along each quarter between the core and the outer tender portion of the root. Soak the roots in lemon water (3 tablespoons lemon per quart of water) to prevent discoloration.

You can cook them in a number of ways, but do not overcook them. They are good baked, boiled, broiled, butter steamed, fried, grilled, microwaved, roasted, sautéed, steamed, and stir-fried. Bake whole sprinkled with brown sugar or glazed with honey or drenched in butter. Boil and mix them in with mashed potatoes, or mash them, shape into patties, dip in flour, and sauté in butter until both sides are golden brown. Cut them into strips to be cooked in oil like french fries. Slice and sauté in butter. Stir-fry ¼-inch slices by themselves or with other vegetables.

Varieties

The inside of the root (flesh) of most varieties is white to creamy white. All require a long time to mature. The shape of the root does vary by variety. In theory, there are three forms: bulbous (shorter), wedge (thick on top and then tapered), and bayonet (long and narrow). The reality is there is a lot of crossover between the types, so that the following chart is a loose approximation at best.

VARIETY	DAYS	LENGTH (INCHES)
'All American' (heirloom)	115	Wedge to 12
'Albion Hybrid'	110	Broad wedge tapered to 10–12
'Andover' (heirloom)	120	Carrot-like to 12
'Arrow' (heirloom)	120	Bayonet to 8
'Cobham Improved Marrow' (heirloom)	120	Broad wedge to 8–10
'Gladiator Hybrid'*****	115	Wedge to 12
'Guernsey Half Long' (heirloom)	125	Stubby wedge to 8
'Harris Model' (heirloom)*****	115	Broad wedge to 12
'Hollow Crown' (heirloom)******	110	Bayonet to 12+
'Hollow Crown Improved' (heirloom)	125	Broad wedge to 10
'Javelin Hybrid'	110	Broad wedge to 8
'Lancer' (heirloom)*****	120	Carrot-like to 10–12
'Turga' (heirloom)	105	Stout to 5–7
'White Gem' (heirloom)	105	Bulbous irregularly shaped

Stems of parsnips produce beautiful umbrella-like blooms, which mature into deep-brown seed heads.

Shelled peas picked at just the right moment are one of the sweetest and most memorable fresh vegetables.

PEAS

Pisum sativum
Legume or Pea Family (Fabaceae, formerly Leguminosae)

Peas are very hardy, cold-season annuals. They are green gold to gardeners. Fresh shelled peas are like a different vegetable compared to their frozen or canned cousins. Nothing is better than fresh peas prepared within minutes of picking—nothing! Peas may have originated in Southeast Asia, possibly from India and Pakistan.

How Peas Grow

Pea seeds are large and either smooth or wrinkled (about 50 to 125 seeds per ounce). They sprout into easily recognizable seedlings with small, bluish-green leaves. They grow quickly, sending up shoots with larger, rounded leaves and delicate tendrils that will cling to any nearby support. Flowers vary in color by variety but are lovely, looking a bit like tiny orchids or small butterflies. Pea pods develop and typically hang down. If allowed to mature, the pods turn brown and brittle with seeds rattling about inside.

Where to Plant Peas
Site and Light

Peas like lots of light and cool temperatures. Plant them in full sun if possible. They will grow in partial shade but prefer bright light.

Soil and Moisture

Since you will be planting seed extra early in the growing season, prepare your bed in fall. Work the soil until it is loose. Add lots of organic matter such as compost, leaf mold (rotted leaves), rotted manure, or sphagnum peat moss. This keeps the soil "fluffy" but capable of retaining moisture during dry spells. If your soil is compacted, build a raised bed. Good drainage is critical since seeds will rot out in cold, soggy soil. The pH should be 6.5 to 6.8.

Container

Peas are not known for their plentiful pod production when planted in containers. With support, a few are worth growing

Nutrition Facts

Serving size: 100 grams (3.5 ounces)

	AMOUNT PER RAW SERVING	% DV	AMOUNT PER COOKED SERVING	% DV	AMOUNT PER DRY SERVING	% DV
Calories	80	4%	80	4%	120	6%
Carbohydrates	15 mg	5%	15 g	5%	20 g	7%
Copper	0.2 mg	9%	0.2 mg	9%	0.2 mg	9%
Dietary fiber	5 g	20%	5 g	20%	8 g	35%
Folate	65 mcg	15%	65 mcg	15%	65 mcg	15%
Iron	1.5 mg	8%	1.5 mg	8%	1.3 mg	7%
Magnesium	33 mg	8%	40 mg	10%	35 mg	9%
Manganese	0.4 mg	20%	0.5 mg	25%	0.4 mg	20%
Niacin	2 mg	10%	2 mg	10%	1 mg	5%
Phosphorus	110 mg	10%	110 mg	10%	100 mg	10%
Potassium	245 mg	7%	270 mg	8%	360 mg	10%
Protein	5 g	10%	5 g	10%	8 g	17%
Riboflavin	0.1 mg	8%	0.1 mg	8%	0.1 mg	8%
Thiamin	0.3 mg	20%	0.3 mg	20%	0.2 mg	13%
Vitamin A	765 IU	15%	800 IU	15%	0.0	0%
Vitamin B6	0.2 mg	8%	0.2 mg	10%	0.05 mg	2.5%
Vitamin C	40 mg	65%	15 mg	25%	0.4 mg	1%
Vitamin K	25 mcg	30%	25 mcg	30%	5 mcg	6%
Zinc	1.2 mg	8%	1.2 mg	8%	1.0 mg	7%

if you don't have a garden. 'Sugar Ann' has been around for a long time and can be eaten either as a flat pod or filled with peas. It's worth a try in a large pot filled with loose soil kept consistently moist. If you want shelled peas, try 'Tom Thumb'.

Planting

Seed

Plant early-, mid-, and late-season varieties. While it is suggested to get peas into the soil as early as possible, seed may rot out in cold, wet soil. Wet soil tends to be sticky. If soil is loose, plant seeds 1 to 2 inches deep depending on your soil type. Plant either in rows or in broad blocks. When planting seed in rows, place seeds about 1 to 2 inches apart. Plan to thin a bit later. If planting in a block, scatter seed over a loose soil surface. Then rake over the area, but do not walk on it. If planting vining types, place seed either along or around the support at the same depth and spacing as in rows. It is often suggested to use an inoculant, but I never have. It is also suggested to soak seed for several hours or longer before planting. I never have.

The easiest way to plant bush peas is in double rows. Cut two 1-inch furrows into loose soil 6 inches apart. Cover the seeds with soil, firm the soil, and water thoroughly. If the soil is moist, don't walk on it. Just pat it down with your hand. Vining plants will need support, a subject covered in detail later.

Transplant

Few people start peas from seed indoors. Admittedly, the soil is warm in later summer for a fall planting. But peas seem to do well anyway most of the time. Still, if you don't want to take a chance with hot summer weather, start seed 4 weeks in advance of your planned planting date.

Spacing

Plant seeds 1 to 2 inches apart in each of two parallel furrows. If planted in a wide row or block, scatter the seeds 1 to 2 inches apart. Peas like to be planted thick. They give each other shade and support. Forming a thick mat of peas is fine, as the vines intertwine. Peas take up a lot of space but mature quickly. Replace peas with a different crop shortly after harvest.

When to Plant

If your fingers aren't numb, you are planting too late. Get peas in as soon as soil can be worked in your garden. Light frosts won't hurt seedlings. If an unexpected frost is predicted *once plants are flowering,* cover them with sheets in the middle of the day. If you don't like numb fingers, plant a bit later. But get peas into the ground as early as you can. Slightly later plantings may do as well or even better than a superearly planting—it all depends on the season. Plant some early-, mid-, and late-season varieties. Successive plantings of a single variety is an option but not as good as the one just mentioned.

Planting seed for a fall crop is tricky. Count back from the first expected fall frost to figure out a good planting date. Plant seed that tolerates heat (see "Varieties" for suggestions). Remember that flowers are not frost tolerant. Hope for cool autumn temperatures. Many gardeners forget about this planting and miss out on an additional crop. Admittedly, spring plantings are much more reliable since high temperatures and lack of rainfall are always possible in late summer and early fall.

Support

Shorter varieties of peas are self-supporting if you plant two rows side by side. Plants intertwine and connect themselves to each other with tendrils. Harvesting is easy. You flip the plants to one side, harvest, then flip the plants in the opposite direction, and harvest some more.

If you prefer to support bush varieties, place 3-foot branches (pea brush) at an angle above the plants to form an elongated tepee. Plant seeds at the base of both sides of or directly underneath the brush. As the young peas surface, they will cling to the brush. This method gives easy access to pods during harvesting but takes time to set up and is no more effective than planting rows close together. Furthermore, entangled vines and brush are a pain to handle once peas have been harvested.

Chicken wire works well as a replacement for brush and takes up less space. Support the wire with metal stakes no farther than 4 feet apart. The peas climb up the wire, and the pods dangle openly for easy harvest. Dealing with wire and cleaning debris from it at the end of the season are also a pain—in my opinion. Fences along the outside of the garden also make good vertical supports. They do not have to be set up each year, which is an advantage.

Taller varieties clearly need taller supports, including tall fences, poles, and bamboo tepees. Some of these varieties get a lot larger than published heights. Sometimes, you need to help plants get attached to supports by tying earlier growth to them with synthetic twine. Be gentle. Don't wait too long or vines will get really hard to deal with. You end up breaking them. Any support in full sun and with good air circulation will help cut down on disease.

Some gardeners take the time to set up intricate twine supports between poles. These are a lot of work and tend to blow around if peas are planted in an open area. Vines are like a sail in the wind.

How to Care for Peas

Water

Keep plants moist at all times. To reduce the chance of disease, water only the base of plants. This is especially important in hot weather, when wet foliage may result in mildew. Consistent watering helps peas mature quickly. Water is essential as flowers and pods first appear.

Mulch

As soon as seedlings emerge, place a 2-inch layer of organic mulch around the base of each plant. Do not touch the stems. Add more mulch as the plants mature.

Fertilizing

In fertile soil, there is no need to add additional fertilizers throughout the growing season. Peas are in the legume family and fix nitrogen in the soil. Fertilizing with nitrogen-rich fertilizers often results in an abundance of tender foliage that attracts insects at the expense of pod production. Since nitrogen may not be available early in the season, foliar feeding 6-inch plants with seaweed or a similar product may help plants get off to a good start. After that, leave them alone.

Add pea tendrils and flowers to your cooking repertoire for color and taste.

Weeding

Pull all weeds as soon as they sprout. Do not cultivate close to the plants, as pea roots are extremely fragile. Hand pull or snip off weeds instead. Try to disturb the soil as little as possible. Note that stems are easy to break, so be careful. Mulch should stop many, but not all, weeds from sprouting. Peas produce tendrils that get wrapped around weeds if you do not remove them quickly. Weed when plants are dry.

Special Considerations

Once peas have stopped producing, pull up and compost the plants. Or till or spade them into the ground, letting them decompose in the soil over the next few weeks. Peas are legumes and will add nitrogen to the soil. Once plant tissue has broken down, plant another crop in that area.

Extending the Season

Plant several plantings in spring. Use seed from varieties with different maturation dates. Plant again in late summer for a fall crop. Peas past the flowering stage withstand frost well, so don't skip the second growing season.

Problems

Insects

While several insects may attack peas, the most common is aphids. Spray them off plants with a hose. If a single plant part is heavily infested, snip it off and burn it.

Disease

Peas are susceptible to several diseases including mildews, wilts, and viruses. Reduce the chance of disease by getting seed into the garden early; by watering only the soil around the base of plants, not the foliage; and by choosing disease-resistant varieties. Resistance is noted in most catalogs.

Marauders

I have read about, but never experienced, birds eating newly planted seeds. Rabbits are a serious problem and will nibble off emerging growth. Deer also will do the same. The advice is always the same: fence in your garden. If chipmunks are a problem, trap them.

Physiological

If plants produce lots of foliage but few flowers, there may be too much nitrogen in the soil. Try snipping off the growing tips of the plants. This may induce pod formation.

Propagation

Peas are self-pollinating. Grow an open-pollinated variety. Allow pods to dry completely on the vine. The seeds will rattle in the pods. Harvest when dry, not moist, to prevent mold. Open pods, but leave seed in place. Dry indoors for several days. Check for insects. Remove any infested pods. Now slide the seeds out of the pods. Place thoroughly dried seed in an envelope in a cool, dry, dark place. Seed will store for up to 2 to 3 years.

Harvesting

Garden peas are the candy of the garden world—a treat to be eaten now, not later. Pick garden peas just before eating them—the closer to mealtime, the better. They lose much of their sugar content within a few hours at room temperature. Garden peas take attention and care when harvesting. Once pods of garden peas begin to form, check the plants daily so that the peas do not become overripe. The surface of the pod will swell and feel firm but not hard. Pick one or two pods to check the size of the peas. They should be small and tender but not tiny. A pea squeezed between your thumb and forefinger will exude juice. Picked at just the right stage, they are extremely sweet. If you let them grow too big, they begin to change color and become harder. At this stage the sugars turn to starch, and the peas taste mealy. *This can happen in as little as a day in hot or humid weather.* When picking pods, hold onto the vine with one hand, and pinch off the pod with the other. Do not pull on the pods, as this could damage the vine, often brittle and easily broken. Try to pick pods when the foliage is dry to reduce the spread of disease. Toss them into a pan filled with ice water to keep them cool. Not all the pods fill in at the same rate. Most of the pods do mature at close to the same time. Some gardeners pick them all at once. Others do this over a period of a few days. This means you should pick every day as the peas come in. If you have a small patch, then you will get enough peas for a meal each day. If you have a larger patch, you can invite guests over for a feast or freeze the surplus. If peas get away from you, let them dry on the vine. Use them to make pea soup. Note, however, that the plant will stop producing pods regularly if you let any mature at all.

Snap peas are ready to pick when they are plump. Pick them before they begin to turn color. Harvest snap peas when pods begin to bulge. As with garden peas, pick them just as they reach maturity. Sample them daily if necessary. If bent, they should snap like a mature bean.

Harvest snow peas when the pods are thin and flat with minuscule immature peas barely beginning to form inside. At this stage the pod is tender and juicy, and the tiny peas extra sweet.

To harvest dried peas, let mature on the vine until peas rattle in the pods. Bring indoors, place in a freezer for 30 hours to kill insects if present, then dry longer at room temperature in a single layer in a dry, warm, airy place for at least 3 weeks. Bite into one pea, or hit it with a hammer and see whether it shatters. If there is no tooth mark or if the bean flies into tiny fragments, it is dry. Place in an airtight container. Keep as cold as possible, checking regularly for mold.

Storing

If you can't eat peas right away, place the pods immediately in ice water to cool them down. Dry and place in a refrigerator for as few days as possible.

To freeze garden peas, shell as soon after picking as possible, blanch for 1 to 3 minutes depending on size, immerse in ice water, drain, pat dry, place in airtight freezer bags, label, and freeze. It's best to do this in small batches. Many home gardeners flash freeze peas by placing them on a plate in the freezer before putting them into airtight freezer bags.

To freeze snap and snow peas, wash, remove string along spine, leave whole, blanch for 2 to 3 minutes, cool in ice water, drain, pat dry, place in airtight freezer bags, and freeze.

Culinary Uses

The flowers, young tendrils, peas, and pods are edible. The colorful flowers taste like peas and are added to salads for color and flavor. The flowers are often candied for decoration on cakes. The tender shoots and tendrils of peas are edible raw or cooked. Snip off 4- to 6-inch pieces. Add them to salads. Sauté or stir-fry them in sesame oil seasoned with fresh garlic. 'Sugar Lace II' is one example of a pea grown more for its edible tendrils than its peas. 'Novella' and 'Novella II' are unique in that they are almost leafless with most pods on top of the plant. They too are grown for delicious tendrils.

Garden peas picked at just the right stage are edible raw or cooked. Shelling garden peas takes time. The longer your fingernails, the better. Open the peas on the thinner side of the pod where a ridge runs down the center. The pod pops open as you use both thumbs to crack the ridge. Push the peas out with your thumb. To cook, blanch 1 to 2 minutes, drench in butter, and flavor with mint if desired. Do

the same with petits pois, which are just a little smaller but succulent. Both go beautifully in dishes combining boiled onions, new potatoes, and sautéed mushrooms.

Snow peas, grown for their edible pods, are best if you break off both ends and pull off the string along the spine like a zipper. Eat them raw or cooked. Steam the pods lightly before unstringing and placing in salads. Or place them uncooked on a vegetable platter after removing the spines. They are delicious in stir-fries when cooked briefly for about 2 minutes. Add them to any number of Asian dishes, but never overcook. Keep them bright green, crisp, and juicy. Batter and deep-fry them for tempura.

You can also remove the string on snap peas. These peas are unique in that you can eat both the peas and the shell, raw or cooked. Steam until done. Splash the pods with butter and soy sauce. Or dip the pod in butter, and pull the pod between your teeth to pop out the peas. Stir-fry pods in oil with garlic and onions.

Both snow and snap peas are sometimes referred to as *mangetout* peas, which is French for "eat the whole thing." Eat either the whole pod or the whole pod with its peas inside.

Warning: Do not confuse the pea flowers of edible varieties with those of sweet pea flowers (*Lathyrus odoratus*). The latter are toxic.

Varieties

The following table has been divided into four types of peas: garden, petits pois, snap, and snow peas. Garden peas form large, swollen pods with peas inside. You eat only the peas, since the pods are chewy and unappetizing. Garden peas may be listed in catalogs as English, green, shell or shelling, or standard peas. Picked at the right time, they are tender and incredibly sweet. Petits pois is French for "small peas." They are essentially tiny garden peas. Again, only the peas are eaten, the pods discarded. They are tedious to pick and shell. Snap or sugar snap peas created a sensation in the garden world when first introduced in 1979, because both the peas and the pods are eaten together, just as you would a green "snap" bean. They can be eaten at any stage, even allowed to form dry peas. Snow peas are grown for thin, succulent pods picked when peas are barely forming inside. They may be called Chinese or sugar peas in catalogs. These often produce the best tendrils for cooking.

Shorter bush varieties usually produce pods that mature at about the same time. Taller plants tend to produce pods over a longer period of time. When choosing varieties, consider the type of pea, the days to maturity, the overall height, and disease resistance, which is noted in most catalogs. Shorter varieties are often referred to as bush peas, growing to about 24 inches. Semi-dwarf may grow up to 36 inches, while tall or vining varieties may reach a height of 72 inches. This is a somewhat deceptive in that bush varieties can climb and cling to support with tendrils.

When you buy peas, they appear either wrinkled or smooth. Some people say that wrinkled varieties taste better but are less cold resistant, while smooth germinate better in cool soils. Having grown both types, I have no idea whether it makes any difference. Maybe I have just been lucky. Some of the wrinkled varieties of garden peas include 'Early Frosty', 'Green Arrow', 'Kelvedon Wonder', 'Legacy', 'Lincoln', 'Little Marvel', 'Thomas Laxton', and 'Wando'. Wrinkled varieties of snow peas include 'Dwarf Gray Sugar' and 'Snowbird'. One variety with wrinkled seed does stand out: 'Wando', which is heat resistant and also excellent for fall planting. 'Maestro' is another good choice for fall planting. In general, bush varieties are best for early crops, and vines better for overall production.

VARIETY	DAYS	HEIGHT (INCHES)	PODS (LENGTH IN INCHES)
Pea, garden *(Pisum sativum)*			
'Alderman' (see 'Tall Telephone')			
'Bikini' (see 'Novella')			
'British Wonder' (heirloom)	55	36	4, in pairs
'Burpeena Early' (heirloom)	65	24	3, often in pairs
'Champion of England' (heirloom)	65	72	3
'Dark Green Perfection' (heirloom)	70	30	3–5
'Early Frosty' (heirloom)	65	36	3½, in pairs
'Freezonian' (heirloom) (AAS-1948)	65	36	3
'Green Arrow' (heirloom)*****	70	28	4–5, in pairs
'Homesteader' (see 'Lincoln')			
'Improved American Wonder' (see 'Little Marvel')			
'Kelvedon Wonder' (OP)	60	18	3½, in pairs
'Knight' (heirloom)*****	60	24	4, singly or in pairs
'Laxton's Progress #9' (heirloom)	65	20	3½
'Legacy' (OP)	70	24	3½, in pairs
'Lincoln' (heirloom)*****	70	32	3½
'Little Marvel' (heirloom) (AAS-1934)	65	18	3
'Maestro' (heirloom)*****	60	26	4
'Main Crop' (see 'Wando')			
'Mayfair' (heirloom)*****	75	40	4, in pairs
'Misty' (OP)	55	24	3, in pairs
'Mr. Big' (OP) (AAS-2000)	60	28	5+
'Novella' and 'Novella II' (OP) (few leaves)	65	24	3, in pairs at top of plant
'Premium' (OP)	50	30	2–3
'Progress #9' (OP)	65	18	4
'Sabre' (OP)	65	24	3½, in pairs
'Strike' (OP)*****	50	24	2¾
'Tall Telephone' (heirloom)	85	72	4–5
'Thomas Laxton' (heirloom)*****	60	32	5
'Tom Thumb' (heirloom)	55	10	2
'Wando' (heirloom)*****	70	28	2½

VARIETY	DAYS	HEIGHT (INCHES)	PODS (LENGTH IN INCHES)
Petits pois *(Pisum sativum)*			
'Charmette' (OP)	65	24	3
'Petit Provençal' (heirloom)	65–70	18	3
'Waverex' (OP) (for freezing)	65	24	3
Pea, edible podded, snap *(Pisum sativum* var. *macrocarpon)*			
'Cascadia' (heirloom)*****	70	36	3
'Sugar Ann' (heirloom) (AAS-1984)	60	24	2
'Sugar Daddy' (heirloom)	65	28	3
'Sugar Lace II' (heirloom) (semi-leafless)	65	16	Eat tendrils
'Sugar Snap' (heirloom) (AAS-1979)*****	70	72	3
'Sugar Sprint' (heirloom)	60	26	3
'Super Sugar Snap' (heirloom)	70	72	3
Pea, edible podded, snow *(Pisum sativum* var. *macrocarpon)*			
'Carouby de Mausanne' (heirloom)	65	60	5–6
'Dwarf Gray Sugar' (heirloom)*****	65	24–30	3
'Golden Sweet' (heirloom)	70	72	Variable yellow
'Little Sweetie' (heirloom)*****	60	16	2½
'Norli' (OP)*****	60	60+	2
'Oregon Giant' (heirloom)	70	36	4+
'Oregon Sugar Pod' (heirloom)	70	28	4
'Oriental Sugar Pod II' (OP)	70	28	4–5, in pairs
'Snowbird' (heirloom)	60	18	3, in pairs
Pea, dry *(Pisum sativum* species)			
'Alaska' (smooth) (heirloom)	60	24	2½
'Blauwschokkers' (see 'Blue Pod Capucijners')			
'Blue Pod Capucijners' (heirloom)	85	48+	3, purple with brown seeds

'Pusa Jwala', a favorite pepper in India, is at its hottest when fruit turns bright red.

PEPPERS

Capsicum species
Nightshade Family (Solanaceae)

Peppers are very tender, subtropical to tropical perennials grown as warm-season annuals. They are beautiful garden plants with lovely leaves and flowers. Some gardeners grow them not only for edible but also for ornamental fruit. Somewhat finicky, peppers need even temperatures and uniform moisture to develop fully. In cold climates bell peppers are much easier to grow than hot peppers, which require a long growing season. Peppers may have originated in a variety of places including Bolivia, Brazil, Central America, Mexico, and the West Indies.

How Peppers Grow

Pepper seed is thin, flat, and light tan with a little notch in it (about 3,000 to 4,500 seeds per ounce). Seedlings respond to warmth, sun, and moisture by growing into vigorous plants with attractive arrow- to spade-shaped leaves, often a rich dark green. The plants produce delicate starry flowers, which are self-pollinating. Fruit develops over a period of weeks, starting off green and then typically maturing into a

different color as it ripens. The fruit on most varieties hangs down from the plant (pendant), while on others it points up from the top of the plant.

Where to Plant Peppers
Site and Light

Plant peppers in full sun in a protected area. Peppers need warmth and are easily damaged by winds. Ideal locations in areas with cool summers are on the side of a south-facing fence or wall, in a pot placed in full sun in a sheltered location, or even in a flower garden where there is lots of light. If you live in an area where summer temperatures often soar, your peppers may actually benefit from some shade during the day. Planting near tall-growing plants that block sun in the afternoon is one solution. The other is to grow peppers that do well in containers, so that you can move them around.

Soil and Moisture

Peppers do best in fertile soils that are loose, drain freely, but retain moisture during dry periods. If possible, prepare the planting bed in fall with at least 8 to 12 inches of loose soil. Add organic matter, such as compost or well-rotted manure, to the planting bed. Then mix in small amounts of bonemeal and gypsum (calcium sulfate). In early spring mix blood meal or any organic fertilizer high in nitrogen into the soil before planting. The nitrogen helps the plant form a thick canopy of foliage. Bonemeal and gypsum provide nutrients that may help prevent blossom-end rot. Adding peat to the soil as a substitute for compost will help lower the soil pH if it is a little too high. Peppers like an acidic soil ranging from 5.5 to 6.5 pH. Raised beds are excellent for peppers since they warm up early in spring and drain freely compared to level or more compacted soil. To increase the soil temperature temporarily, cover the bed with clear or black plastic. Remove just before planting.

Container

Growing peppers in containers is one of the most popular ways to grow these plants. Choose varieties suited to this purpose. Use a large container, at least a 5-gallon black plastic one. Fill it with a mix of sphagnum peat moss, perlite, and soil in equal parts. Move containers as necessary to provide plants with the optimum amount of warmth and protection from prevailing winds. Be very attentive to watering since peppers react badly to stress caused by dry soil. Containers will dry out quickly in summer heat waves. Place a stake next to the stem for support. Good sweet peppers for this use are 'Cute Stuff Red Hybrid', 'Gypsy Hybrid', and 'Tequila Sunrise'. For hot peppers, try 'Super Cayenne Hybrid' and 'Super Chili Hybrid'. These are both ornamental and productive.

Planting

Seed

Do not plant seed directly in the garden.

Transplants

Nurseries sell a limited number of varieties, although more each year as the popularity of peppers has risen. If you buy a pepper plant locally, get a short, stocky plant if possible. If in flower, remove the flowers. Get it into the ground as soon as the soil warms up to roughly 60°F. The planting hole should be larger than the size of the pot. Plant up to the first set of true leaves if the plant is small. If gangly, remove the lower leaves and plant to the top set of leaves. Firm in place and water immediately.

You may have to grow less well-known varieties by starting them from seed indoors. Plant two to three seeds ¼ inch deep or less in a 4-inch container filled with sterile

Nutrition Facts
Serving size: 100 grams (3.5 ounces)

	GREEN PEPPERS		RED SWEET PEPPERS	
	AMOUNT PER RAW SERVING	% DV	AMOUNT PER RAW SERVING	% DV
Calories	20	1%	30	2%
Carbohydrate	5 g	2%	6 g	2%
Dietary fiber	2 g	7%	2 g	8%
Folate	45 mcg	11%	45 mcg	11%
Potassium	175 mg	5%	210 mg	6%
Protein	1 g	2%	1 g	2%
Vitamin A	370 IU	7%	3,130 IU	63%
Vitamin B6	0.2 mg	10%	0.3 mg	15%
Vitamin C	80 mg	135%	130 mg	210%
Vitamin E	0.4 mg	2%	1.6 mg	8%
Vitamin K	7.5 mcg	9%	5 mcg	6%

starting mix. Or start in smaller pots, and prick out and pot up when the first set of true leaves form. Plant seeds 6 to 8 weeks (sweet) and up to 10 weeks (hot) before the last expected frost in your area. The soil needs to be kept at 80°F or higher for good germination. Use a heating mat if necessary. This is particularly important for hot pepper varieties. A drop of 10 degrees at night is fine. Place the pot in a plastic tent to keep humidity high. Germination of bell peppers usually occurs within 8 days, but hot peppers may take up to 21 days or longer. Germination is erratic, so be patient. Moisten the soil. Let it dry out a little, then moisten again. Peppers do not need a lot of moisture to germinate. Never get the soil soggy. Once seedlings appear, do not let them get overly dry. It's a tricky balance. Some gardeners prefer bottom watering. Once plants germinate, uncover the tent a bit more each day, reducing the humidity over time. Once plants form true leaves, begin feeding them with a highly diluted organic fertilizer. Cut out all but the healthiest plant per pot. Seedlings need bright light, warmth, and consistent moisture to thrive. Your goal is compact, vigorous plants about 5 inches tall with three to four true leaves. Harden off gradually over a period of weeks. Temperatures at night should not be below 55°F. If colder than this, bring the plants indoors. This chilling process (vernalization) will help, not hurt the plants. If you have a cold frame, this process is much easier.

Spacing

Generally, sweet (bell) peppers grow quite well when planted close together because they prefer humid conditions. There is

Peppers are fussy and need lots of light, warmth, and moisture to form fruit, whose nutrition increases with age.

a saying that "peppers like to stay in touch." Spacing should be done with the mature plant size in mind. For most varieties, this means roughly 12 inches apart or more. Close planting is highly recommended in raised beds, which tend to stay warm but lose more moisture than level beds. On the other hand, hot (chili) peppers prefer somewhat drier conditions. Space them farther apart to increase air circulation and cut down on the incidence of disease. A spacing of up to 24 inches may be necessary.

When to Plant

Ideally, you want to plant peppers in warm soil that is at least 60°F in early morning. Do not plant any earlier than 2 to 3 weeks after the frost-free date in your area. Frost can kill young plants. The temperatures should not fall below 55°F at night or below 70°F in the day. You can cheat some by protecting transplants from wind and cold with cloches, plastic tunnels, floating row covers, or Wall O' Water plant protectors. These keep the air temperature higher around the young plants. Keep the young plants moist and warm. During the growing season, plants do best between 70°F and 90°F. Plants flower and form fruit according to the temperature. Hot peppers need lots of heat over a longer period

of time to fruit well. This can be difficult to provide in cold climates.

Support

Fruit combined with lush foliage can get quite heavy. Individual staking of stems from the time of planting is recommended for any variety that can get tall. You can surround bushy plants with a cage if necessary. By planting peppers in a protected location and by picking fruits as soon as they mature, you can often get by without support. However, pepper plants have brittle stems and branches and a relatively shallow root system. So many home gardeners don't take a chance, and provide support from the time of initial planting.

How to Care for Peppers
Water

Peppers need consistent watering to create luxuriant foliage and abundant fruit. Let the soil dry out somewhat, then soak the soil around the base of each plant. Do not wet the leaves. Peppers can tolerate some dry spells, but be careful. Once flowering, they need a steady supply of water. Not enough water can cause the plants to drop blossoms and may be a partial cause of sunken brown spots on the fruit. A drip irrigation system (soaker hoses) is a good option if your time is limited. When growing peppers in containers, you may have to water frequently, sometimes twice a day, if it is hot, dry, and windy outside. Note that hot peppers may be drought tolerant but do better with regular watering.

Mulch

While peppers thrive in relatively high air temperatures, they like a moist, cool root run. A 2- to 3-inch-deep organic mulch around the base of the plants ensures just that. Avoid placing the mulch against the stems of the plants. Organic mulch also increases the humidity around the peppers, and they love this. Good mulches include grass clippings and pulverized leaves. Increase the depth of mulch to 6 inches in the heat of summer.

Fertilizing

Place some well-rotted manure or compost around the base of the plant. Work it lightly into the soil at planting time. Fertilize with an organic fertilizer high in nitrogen when plants are 6 to 8 inches tall, again when fruit begins to form, and every 4 weeks after that. Place the fertilizer a foot or so away from the stem. If the plant forms lush foliage but little fruit, stop fertilizing. Fish emulsion and seaweed products are highly recommended. Note that too much nitrogen may cause blossom drop. Some gardeners supply peppers with magnesium through foliar feeding with a spray consisting of 1 teaspoon Epsom salts to 1 quart water. They spray both the tops and bottoms of leaves just as blossoms appear and repeat the application 2 weeks later. Experiment with fertilization. Let your plants guide you with foliage color, number of blossoms, and fruit set.

Weeding

Avoid cultivating around the base of the plants, because their root system is shallow. Hand weed instead. By using mulch, you inhibit weed growth. The few that sprout up are much easier to pull.

Pruning

Pruning is strictly optional and recommended primarily for larger fruiting varieties. One commonly recommended technique is to pinch out growing tips when the plants reach 6 inches. This may cause plants to get bushy. Another method is to remove blossoms for 2 to 3 weeks after placing a transplant in the garden. Some gardeners do this even longer. All of the energy of the plant will then go into growth, rather than fruit formation. Another option is to do this only after your first harvest. Not only do you remove blossoms for 1 to 2 weeks, but you also pinch off the tips of side branches. Yet another option is to leave only six to eight fruits on each plant. Pick off extra fruit when it reaches ¼ inch. Experiment on your own.

Special Considerations

The spiciness of a hot pepper is directly related to the variety you choose, the length of time the pepper is allowed to mature on the plant, and any kind of environmental stress. If the weather is particularly hot and dry, the peppers may become hotter (contain more capsaicin). For this reason the spiciness of any given pepper is often related to where it is grown. Do not worry about cross-pollination affecting flavor. It is only a concern for seed savers.

Capsaicin (cap-SAY-sin), the substance that makes peppers hot, is potentially dangerous. Wear rubber gloves and protective glasses when working with hot peppers that contain high amounts of the chemical, which can affect your eyes, lungs, and skin. While working with hot peppers, keep your gloved hand away from your face. Wash your hands thoroughly.

The longer fruits mature, the more nutritious they are. However, fruit set can be poor at temperatures over 86°F. Hot peppers may be a bit more tolerant of high temperatures. Consider shading bell peppers in extreme heat.

Extending the Season

To get a jump on the season, warm soil with black plastic. Get plants in earlier by protecting them with cloches, plastic tunnels, row covers, or Wall O' Water plant protectors, as mentioned earlier. Without proper protection from frost, they will die. In the fall, cover plants with a sheet or row cover if a cold snap is predicted. Do this during the day to trap heat. Take the covering off as soon as it warms up and when the sun is out. This simple procedure may extend the growing season for several weeks. If you are growing pepper plants in containers, bring them indoors until it warms up again.

Problems

Insects

Up to thirty-five insects are known to bother peppers. Over a number of years the home gardener will run into a few. Don't let this stop you from growing peppers. Protect plants with row covers if necessary. Once the plant is flowering, remove these while insects are active in the day for proper pollination necessary to produce fruit.

Disease

Peppers are also susceptible to a variety of diseases, including leaf spots, rots, viruses, and wilts. Prevent disease by buying disease-resistant varieties, controlling insects as best you can, and growing peppers in a different spot each year.

Marauders

Holes in pods are generally caused by birds. Remove damaged fruit. If this is a major problem, protect the plants with netting. Although larger marauders, including rabbits and deer, will eat just about anything if they are hungry enough, other vegetables are higher up on their hit list.

Physiological

The blossoms may drop off plants when temperatures at night drop below 60°F or rise above 70°F. They may also drop off if daytime temperatures are higher than 90°F. Uneven watering, too much nitrogen, and cool, rainy spells may also cause blossom drop, which is a temporary condition.

Watch for light-colored (papery) spots on the blossom end of the fruit. Prevent this condition by watering whenever the soil starts to dry out. Mulch is also effective. Fertilizer containing calcium may help (gypsum). Cut back on the use of nitrogen.

Sunscald, sudden exposure of fruit to sun, may cause whitish blisters or papery patches to form on the fruit.

Exposure may result from leaf drop caused by disease or over pruning by a zealous gardener.

Pepper plants with too much fruit may shed some of it. Pick fruit regularly so that this is less likely to happen.

Propagation

Flowers are perfect, having both male and female organs. Peppers are self-fertile. However, peppers within the same species can cross-pollinate, which is more of a problem with hot peppers than sweet. Hot pepper genes are dominant. Save seed from open-pollinated varieties. Let the fruits mature and dry on the plants. Cut open, scrape out seeds, rinse in cool water, clean, set on a plate, and dry in a warm, dark, well-ventilated place for no less than 2 weeks, longer if possible. Place seed in an envelope, and keep cool and dry. If working with hot peppers, protect yourself from burns by wearing rubber gloves and eyeglasses. Wash off all utensils well. Seed usually is good for about 2 to 3 years. Some gardeners bring pots in during the winter and then take cuttings in spring from the mother plant.

Harvesting

Harvest peppers at any stage you prefer. Do not pull peppers from the plant. Snip them off with a scissors, leaving ½ inch of stem on each pod. Pulling the stem off acts like a wound and encourages decay. Peppers do ripen somewhat after picking. Removing fruit stimulates continued pepper production. Allowing fruit to ripen lessens overall production. As sweet peppers mature, they become sweeter. As hot peppers mature, they become hotter. Many peppers change color as they mature; however, some stay green, such as jalapeños.

Wear gloves and eyeglasses when picking hot peppers. Pick all peppers before a frost. If you are expecting a snowstorm, not a cold snap, tear up the plants by their roots. Hang them upside down indoors in a cool place. Some of the fruit will still mature.

Storing

Store bell peppers preferably at room temperature or in the warmest area of the refrigerator. Do not wash them until ready to use. Placing them in a plastic bag is optional. Although they may last up to 2 weeks, they are best used within a few days.

To freeze sweet peppers, wash, remove the stem but not the skin, and cut open and remove seeds. Dice, halve, quarter, slice, or leave whole. Place on a tray in a freezer for 30 minutes, place in airtight freezer bags, label, and freeze. Blanching is optional but done by many from 1 to 3 minutes depending on the size of pieces. Add pieces later to sauces and stews. Let whole peppers thaw, then stuff and bake.

To dry fresh peppers, wash, cut out the stem, remove seeds, cut into desired size and shape, and dry. Peppers may last up to 8 months.

To freeze hot peppers, broil or grill peppers until the skin becomes evenly blistered but still stays intact. Place the peppers in a paper bag and let "sweat" for anywhere from 5 to 30 minutes. Then, wearing gloves, plunge the peppers into ice water. Cool, and then make a slit from the stem end down with a knife under running water. Remove the skin, and open to remove seeds and the membrane inside. Blister but leave the skin on ancho and Anaheim types. Blanch jalapeños and serranos for 3 minutes. Place in freezer bags, and flatten. Remove all air from the freezer bags to preserve nutrients. Frozen peppers lose more flavor than ones that are dried.

Dried hot peppers are especially nutritious, as vitamins get concentrated in the drying process. Where it is really hot and dry, the peppers can be hung out to dry in strings (ristras) or placed on screens. In cold climates oven drying or using a dehydrator makes more sense. Peppers can be dried whole or cut into thin strips. They can be dried with or without seeds. Some cooks remove the skins of specific varieties. Blanching or steaming for 10 minutes is also recommended for specific varieties. If you intend to grind peppers into powder or smash them into flakes, they retain color better if seeds are removed. Seeded peppers are known as capones (castrated peppers). Dry peppers on a cookie sheet covered with parchment paper in an oven set at warm. Slow drying is usually the most effective and may take several hours. To bring peppers back to life, just soak in water. Note that some peppers, like jalapeños, are excellent smoked. Once smoked they are called chipotle.

To pickle, wash, puncture fruit, soak in salt water for 24 hours (use pickling salt), remove, rinse, boil for 3 minutes, rinse, drain, spice to taste, fill sterile jars with spice mixture and boiling white vinegar, seal, and let soak for several weeks. Jalapeño and serrano peppers are excellent for pickling, as are any of the cherry peppers. Specific varieties recommended for pickling include 'Big Bomb Hybrid', 'Golden Greek Pepperoncini', 'Hungarian Yellow Wax', and 'Santa Fe Grande'.

Cayenne peppers are the type most commonly used for flakes, pepper, or powders. Dry and grind these in a coffee grinder. Store ground peppers in an airtight container, preferably in the refrigerator. In the varietal list are three excellent varieties for this use: 'Cayenne Long Red Slim', 'Super Cayenne Hybrid', and 'Super Chili Hybrid'.

Culinary Uses

Do not eat pepper flowers or foliage—just the fruit. Sweet or bell peppers can be eaten raw or cooked. As bell peppers mature from green to red or gold or purple, the nutritional value goes up dramatically. The sweet taste often intensifies as well. Preparation is easy. Wash, and remove the stems and pithy interior with seeds. Slice into thin strips for salads or vegetable platters.

Sweet peppers are delicious fried, grilled, puréed after cooking, roasted in the oven, sautéed, stir-fried, and stuffed. For frying and roasting, try 'Bulgarian Carrot', 'Chervena Chushka', 'Golden Marconi', 'Jimmy Nardello's', and 'Sweet Banana', although many others are very good. Great stuffing varieties include, but are not limited to, 'Big Bertha PS Hybrid' and 'Chinese Giant'. Almost any sweet pepper is delicious when cut into ¼-inch strips to be sautéed in butter. Cooked pieces or strips are often added to omelets, pizzas, soups, and stews. A particularly popular dish is chiles rellenos, which is stuffed peppers, often Anaheim varieties, battered and deep-fried.

Hot peppers are far more versatile in the kitchen than sweet peppers, but they do require some specialized knowledge since they are often referred to as "the only vegetable that bites back." Hot peppers usually get sweeter and hotter as they mature. Always wear gloves and eye protection when dealing with hot peppers. Some people even wear masks and work only in a well-ventilated area. Play it safe with any hot pepper with a high amount of capsaicin, measured in Scoville units (given in the "Varieties" table). The membrane (placenta) inside hot peppers contains roughly 90 percent of the capsaicin in each fruit. Seeds contain the rest. Capsaicin is not water soluble.

Hot peppers can be eaten raw, as in guacamole and salsas. Types most commonly used for salsas are cayenne, habañero, jalapeño, and serrano. Specific varieties worth trying are 'Bulgarian Carrot', 'Cajun Belle Hybrid', 'Fish', 'Fresno Chile Grande', and 'Santa Fe Grande'. Chop and mix with bits of cilantro, onion, and tomato.

Hot peppers are used in Mexican sauces known as moles, for which there are numerous recipes. The most common peppers used are ancho and mulato (dried poblanos), chipotle (smoked jalapeño), and pasilla (dried chilaca).

Hot peppers are also dried to be made into flakes or powders, grilled, puréed once cooked, roasted, sautéed, stir-fried, stuffed, and added to a wide variety of cooked dishes.

To clean hot peppers, rinse in cold water, slit, remove seeds, and rinse again. Wash thoroughly all utensils and anything that the pepper touches. Wash your gloves, and then remove them. Never let any capsaicin get on your skin, into a wound, or into your eyes!

Varieties

There are thousands of varieties of peppers. The following list offers a nice range of colors (chocolate, gold, green, lavender, orange, red, yellow, white), flavors, shapes (banana, heart, round, tapered), spiciness (none to burning hot), sizes (from berry to foot long), and use (chiles rellenos, drying, fresh, frying, pepper, pickling, roasting, salsas, stuffing). It contains some old standbys as well as fine new varieties.

The list is divided into two sections. The first covers sweet peppers; the second, hot peppers. The varieties are either hybrids or open pollinated (heirloom). The seed from the latter can be saved and will reproduce the mother plant. Hybrids may have better disease resistance or tolerance, flavor, and higher yield per plant. Sweet peppers are not usually hot, although a few can be spicy.

Hot peppers get their name from the burning sensation they cause when eaten. After each variety of hot pepper listed in the varieties table is the *approximate* Scoville units for that pepper in parentheses. The higher the number, the hotter the pepper. The unit represents a midrange from immature to mature fruits, which get hotter with age and with drying. The word *chili* describes a hot pepper plant. When that plant is used for food, it becomes "chile" as in chile relleno (stuffed pepper). *Note that the name of a pepper may change according to whether it is used fresh or dried.* For example a poblano pepper becomes an ancho when dried, a mirasol becomes a guajillo, and a jalapeño becomes a chipotle when fully smoked and dried.

Color is not a reliable guide to flavor. The spiciness of hot peppers does depend on the climate. Some fiery peppers grown in cold climates will be less hot than if grown in Texas or Mexico. There is always a race on for breeders to create the hottest pepper in the world. Varieties have already gone over the two million Scoville units mark. Who knows where it will end?

In the list "days" stands for the time it takes for each variety to mature from a transplant, typically already grown indoors for 6 to 10 weeks. In cold climates direct seeding is next to impossible. The number of days is approximate because the weather affects the plants so dramatically. Also, the plants mature over a period of weeks. So "days" stands for the appearance of the first fruit. If your growing season is really short, you are limited to fewer choices.

VARIETY	DAYS	HEIGHT (INCHES)	COLOR	WALL/SHAPE/SIZE (INCHES)
Pepper, sweet or bell, also known as banana, bull's horn, cubanelle, pimiento, or cherry _Capsicum_ **species**				
'Ace Hybrid'*****	60	18	Green to red	Thick walled, lobed bell to 2½ by 4
'Aconcagua Giant' (see 'Giant Aconcagua')				
'Alma Paprika' (OP)	80	24	Cream to orange to red	Cherry-like
'Bell Boy Hybrid' (AAS-1967)*****	75	24	Green to red	Thick walled, blocky to 4½ by 3½
'Better Belle Hybrid Improved'	65	30	Green to red	Thick walled, blocky to 3½ by 3½
'Bianca Hybrid'	70	18	Creamy white to orange to red	Thick walled, blocky to 4½ by 3½
'Big Bertha PS Hybrid'	75	30	Green to red	Thick walled, elongated to 7 by 4
'Biscayne Hybrid'	65	18–24	Light yellow green	Thin walled, elongated to 7 by 2½
'Buran' (heirloom)	90	18–24	Green to red	Thick walled, blocky to 4 by 3
'Chervena Chushka' (heirloom)	85	18	Green to brown to red	Thick walled, tapered to 6 by 2
'Carmen Hybrid' (AAS-2006)	75	28	Green to red	Horn shape to 6 by 2½
'Chinese Giant' (heirloom)	75	24	Green to red	Thick walled, blocky to 6 by 5
'Cubanelle' (heirloom)	75	18–24	Yellow green to red	Thin walled, lobed, tapered to 6
'Cute Stuff Red Hybrid'	60	18–24	Green to red	Apple-like to 3
'Early Sunsation Hybrid'	75	18–24	Green to gold yellow	Thick walled, blocky to 4 by 4
'Fat 'n' Sassy' (see 'King Arthur Hybrid')				
'Giant Aconcagua' (heirloom)	70	36	Green to red	Indented oblong to 12 by 2½
'Golden Calwonder' (OP)	75	24–30	Golden yellow	Thick walled, blocky to 4 by 4
'Golden Marconi' (heirloom)*****	90	24–36	Deep yellow to orange	Thin walled, tapered to 7
'Gypsy Hybrid' (AAS-1981)*****	65	18–24	Pale yellow to orange to red	Thick walled, wedge shaped to 5 by 3
'King Arthur Hybrid'	75	22	Green to red	Thick walled, blocky to 4 by 4
'Jimmy Nardello's' (heirloom)*****	100	20–24	Green to red	Wrinkly bullhorn to 10
'Lady Bell Hybrid'	70	18–24	Green to red	Thick walled, blocky to 4
'Large Red Cherry Sweet' (heirloom)	75	20	Green to red	Medium thick, oversized, cherry-like
'Lipstick' (OP)	55	20	Green to red	Thick walled, tapered to 4
'Long Sweet Hungarian' (see 'Sweet Banana')				
'Miniature Chocolate Bell' (heirloom)	90	16	Green to chocolate	Thick walled to 2½
'Orange Bell' (OP)*****	80	24–36	Green to orange	Thick walled, blocky to 4 by 3½
'Orange Blaze Hybrid' (AAS-2011)	75	30	Green to deep orange	Thick walled, blocky to 4 by 1½
'Orange Sun' (heirloom)	80	24	Green to deep orange	Thick walled, blocky to 4 by 3
'Pimiento L' (OP)	95	18	Green to red	Large, heart tapered to 4½
'Purple Beauty' (heirloom)	75	24–36	Purple to blackish red	Thick walled, blocky to 4
'Red Beauty Hybrid'	75	24–36	Green to red	Thick walled, blocky to 4 by 3
'Red Knight X3R Hybrid'*****	75	24	Green to red	Thick walled, blocky to 4 by 4
'Roumanian Rainbow' (heirloom)	75	24	Ivory to orange to red	Blocky to 5 by 4
'Socrates X3R Hybrid'	75	20–24	Green to red	Thick walled, blocky to 4 by 4
'Super Red Pimento' (OP)	70	18–24	Green to red	Ribbed bell to 3 by 5
'Sweet Banana' (heirloom) (AAS-1941)	75	18–24	Green to yellow to orange red	Indented, tapered, jalapeño-like to 6
'Sweet Chocolate' (heirloom)	70	18	Green to chocolate brown	Thick walled, elongated block to 4
'Sweet Spot X3R Hybrid'	75	18–24	Yellow, orange, red	Tapered carrot-like to 8
'Tequila Hybrid'	80	18–24	Lavender to orange to red	Blocky to 4½ by 4
'Tequila Sunrise' (heirloom)	80	16	Green to golden orange	Carrot-like to 5 and lovely
'The Big Early Hybrid'	70	18–24	Green to red	Thick walled, elongated to 8 by 4½
'Yellow Banana' (see 'Sweet Banana')				
'Yolo Wonder' (heirloom)	75	24–28	Green to red	Thick walled, blocky 4 by 3½

VARIETY	DAYS	HEIGHT (INCHES)	COLOR	WALL/SHAPE/SIZE (INCHES)
Pepper, hot, also known as chili, cayenne, hot cherry				
Capsicum annuum species				
'Alma Paprika' (OP) (600)	85	36	Pale yellow to red	Thick walled, blocky to 2
'Anaheim TMR' (OP) (1,500)	75	48	Green to dark red	Skinny, jalapeño-like to 7
'Ancho' (see 'Poblano')				
'Ancho San Martin Hybrid' (2,000)	75	46	Deep green	Thick walled, tapered bell to 5
'Big Bomb Hybrid' (2,500)	80	18	Green to red	Thick walled, cherry to 2
'Bulgarian Carrot' (heirloom) (3,500)	80	18	Green to yellow to orange	Carrot-like to 4
'Cajun Belle Hybrid' (AAS-2010) (500)	60	24	Green to deep red	Blocky to 3
'Caribbean Red Habanero' (heirloom) (to 445,000)	110	30	Green to red	Indented, round to tapered end to 2
'Caribe' (see 'Santa Fe Grande')				
'Cayenne Large Red Thick' (OP) (30,000)	75	24	Green to red	Wrinkly, carrot-like to 6
'Cayenne Long Red Slim' (OP) (30,000)	80	24	Green to red	Twisted, thin, carrot-like to 6
'Chichen Itza Hybrid' (180,000)	85	24	Orange	Indented, tapered bell to 3
'Chichimeca Hybrid' (4,000)	70	30	Green	Rounded, fat, banana-like to 4
'Chipotle' (see 'Jalapeño M')				
'Finger Hot Indian Pepper' (see 'Pusa Jwala')				
'Fish' (heirloom) (30,000)	80	24	Striped cream to orange to red	Tapered to 3
'Fresno Chili Grande' (heirloom) (2,000)	85	36	Green to red	Tapered to 3
'Garden Salsa Hybrid' (3,500)	75	30	Green to red	Jalapeño-like to 9
'Golden Greek Pepperoncini' (OP) (350)	65	36	Green to yellow gold to red	Indented fingers to 4
'Guajillo' (see 'Mirasol')				
'Habanero' (heirloom) (350,000)	100	18–24	Orange to red	Rippled lantern to 2
'Hot Red Cherry' (see 'Red Cherry Hot')				
'Hot Paper Lantern' (OP) (200,000)	90	24–36	Green to red	Crinkly, elongated to 4
'Hungarian Yellow Wax' (heirloom) (10,000)	85	18–24	Light yellow to red	Banana-like to 8
'Jalapeño M' (OP) (4,000)	75	30–36	Green to red	Thick walled, oblong to 3
'Jaloro Hybrid' (20,000–25,000)	70	18–24	Yellow to orange to red	Thick walled, cone shape to 4
'Long Red Cayenne' (see 'Cayenne Long Red Slim')				
'Lemon Drop' (heirloom) (up to 50,000)	100	36	Bright yellow	Crinkly cones to 2½
'Lucifer's Dream' (see 'Habanero')				
'Mirasol' (OP) (3,000–5,000)	90	18–24	Green to red	Upward-facing, tapered to 4
'Mucho Nacho Hybrid (5,000)	85	20–24	Green to red	Jalapeño shape to 4
'New Mexican Chile' (see 'Anaheim TMR')				
'Pimiento de Padrón' (OP) (1,500)	65	36	Green to red	Indented, jalapeño shape to 3
'Poblano' (heirloom) (1,500)	65	24	Green to red	Heart shaped to 4
'Poblano L' (heirloom) (1,500)	80	24–36	Dark green to chocolate	Indented, heart tapered to 5
'Pusa Jwala' (OP) (30,000–50,000)	85	36	Light green to bright red	Bumpy, elongated, thin to 5½
'Red Cherry Hot' (heirloom) (up to 15,000)	80	24–36	Green to red	Cherry shaped to 1½
'Ring of Fire' (OP) (55,000)	60	24–36	Green to red	Slightly curved, thin, carrot-like to 4
'Romanian Hot' (OP) (800–1,400)	85	24–36	Green to yellow to orange red	Thick walled, cone to 4
'Santa Fe Grande' (heirloom) (5,000–8,000)	80	36	Bright yellow to red	Thick walled, cone shape to 3½
'Scotch Bonnet Yellow' (heirloom) (up to 300,000)	100	20	Green to yellow	Crinkled bonnets to 1½

VARIETY	DAYS	HEIGHT (INCHES)	COLOR	WALL/SHAPE/SIZE (INCHES)
'Serrano del Sol Hybrid' (7,500)	75	32	Green to red	Thick, carrot-like to 3
'Super Cayenne Hybrid' (AAS-1990) (up to 50,000)	85	28	Green to red	Thin to 6
'Super Chili Hybrid' (AAS-1988) (60,000)	85	16–24	Green to orange to red	Upward-facing, elongated to 2½
'Tabasco' (heirloom) (40,000)	100+	24–36	Yellow green to orange to red	Upward-pointing fingers to 2
'Tam (Mild) Jalapeño' (heirloom) (1,000–1,500)	70	24–36	Green to red	Pendant, oblong to 3 or less
'Thai Hot' (heirloom) (25,000–40,000)	85	8	Green to red	Upward-pointing, ½ to 1
'Volcano Hybrid' (2,000–4,000)	90	48	Green to yellow to red	Indented, tapered to 6

If you allow peppers to mature, they become increasingly nutritious and sweet, but plants will produce fewer fruits.

Harvest potatoes working from outside the patch in to avoid cutting the tubers in two.

POTATO
(IRISH OR WHITE POTATO)

Solanum tuberosum
Nightshade Family (Solanaceae)

Potatoes are hardy to very hardy, cool- to cold-season perennials grown as annuals in cold climates. This vegetable is often referred to as an Irish potato to distinguish it from a sweet potato, in a different family of plants. While the potato is the number one–selling vegetable in North America, it is often overlooked by the home gardener. The reason may be that potatoes are inexpensive to buy, but this misses an important point. There are hundreds of varieties of potatoes with different shapes, colors, and tastes. Harvesting new (small, young) potatoes fresh from the garden is a special moment. These small potatoes are almost skinless and incredibly delicious. Potatoes are also easy to grow depending on what method you use. They are one of the best plants for children to grow, as I did at the age of eight—an experience that turned me on to gardening for the rest of my life. Potatoes probably originated in Peru or in the overall region of the Andes.

How Potatoes Grow

Potatoes grow from seed potatoes or slices of seed potatoes with eyes on them. The eyes, little indentations in the potato, sprout into stems, which push up through the soil and have puckered, deep-green leaves. As the plant grows, a number of small tubers begin to form to the side of the underground stem. These tubers are not roots but swollen stem tissue that acts as food storage units for foliage. Plants may form clusters of flowers just as these new potatoes begin to form. Flowers will form fruit that looks a bit like a cherry tomato with small, round, tannish seeds inside. The plant continues to grow above- and belowground until the lush foliage dies down at the end of the season, when it turns yellow to brown. The underground tubers vary in size, the oldest being large, the youngest as small as a pea. The easiest way to understand the growth pattern overall is to visualize a small tree growing from a potato underground. Roots grow downward from the buried potato. Above the potato a stem grows up (imagine a trunk) with many branches (stolons).

Nutrition Facts

Serving size: 100 grams (3.5 ounces)

	AMOUNT PER COOKED SERVING	% DV
Calories	95	5%
Carbohydrates	21 g	7%
Dietary fiber	2 g	9%
Folate	28 mg	7%
Iron	1.1 mg	6%
Magnesium	28 mg	7%
Manganese	0.2 mg	11%
Niacin	1.4 mg	7%
Phosphorus	70 mg	7%
Potassium	535 mg	15%
Protein	2.5 g	5%
Vitamin B6	0.3 mg	16%
Vitamin C	10 mg	16%

At the end of the "branches" are potatoes. Aboveground is the tip of the tree with additional "branches" covered in foliage and bearing flowers.

Where to Plant Potatoes

Site and Light

Plant potatoes in full sun. Keep them out of low-lying frost pockets or areas where the soil stays wet. Potatoes rot out in wet areas. They like open, breezy sites with good air circulation, which cuts down on the incidence of disease.

Soil and Moisture

Traditionally, potatoes are planted deep in loose garden soil that drains freely. Ideally, prepare your planting bed in the fall. Loosen the soil to a depth of 12 inches. If you have compacted or rocky soil, consider building a raised bed or growing potatoes in a nontraditional manner, as described later. Add lots of organic matter to the soil; a combination of sphagnum peat moss and compost is ideal. Enrich with cattle manure (not other manures, believed to induce scab), and mix in some bonemeal and a little sulfur to acidify the soil slightly. Acidic soil may actually help prevent scab. Another possible addition is gypsum (calcium sulfate), which provides nutrients without raising the soil pH, which should be roughly 5.5 to 6.5 or lower.

Container

Potatoes are lovely plants and do grow well in large containers that drain freely. Place 6 to 8 inches of soil in the base of the container. Mix in appropriate fertilizers for a good balance of nutrients. Now place seed 8 inches apart in all directions. Cover with 4 inches of soil. As the stems shoot up, keep adding soil around them. Keep the soil consistently moist throughout the growing season until plants die back. Tip the container over at that time, and harvest the potatoes easily.

Planting

Seed (True Seed)

Potato plants do flower and produce "true seed." So it is possible to grow potatoes from seed. The process is so time-consuming and impractical that it is usually done only by professionals trying to breed a new variety of potato.

Seed (Potatoes)

A seed potato is a small to larger potato sold by nurseries or mail-order companies. These are planted instead of "true seed." Purchase certified disease-free seed potatoes, which can be planted whole or cut into pieces. Seed potatoes the size of eggs are ideal. Companies selling seed potatoes also sell eyes with just a little piece of potato flesh attached. When buying potatoes, understand that whole potatoes and eyes are not the same but still considered "seed." Some varieties will only be available as eyes, which are easier to produce than whole potatoes.

Seed potatoes, often called sets, will sprout once planted in the garden. And they will produce a nice number of potatoes. Still, the process known as "presprouting" often results in a greater number of potatoes. This is also known as "chitting," "green sprouting," and "pipping." Place your seed potatoes, if small, into an egg carton in bright, but not direct, sunlight at 50° to 70°F (a lower temperature of 40°F is even better but difficult to provide in a home setting). Place the end with the most eyes up (rose end). Fingerlings have eyes scattered on the tuber. Just lay them on their side. Within a week or two, stems may begin to sprout from the "eyes" or indentations on each small potato. Each gardener has an opinion about how long you should let the stems grow. Some say no more than a few inches; others insist that stems up to 12 inches are best. Since potatoes develop from stems, not roots, the argument for longer stems seems solid but only if starting with really large potatoes. Chitting results in later planting unless you get seed potatoes well in advance of the growing season. Most gardeners do agree that you should limit the number of stems per potato to two to four. Pinch off unwanted sprouts with your fingers just as they emerge; they snap off easily. The number is related to the size of the seed potato, more for larger, fewer for smaller.

Whether you should cut your seed potatoes into pieces or plant them whole is also debated. Both ways work fine, although whole potatoes are somewhat less prone to rot. If you cut potatoes into pieces, each section should have at least one eye, preferably two. The eye is the area from which sprouts form. Sections should be no smaller than an egg, so if your seed potatoes are small to begin with, plant them whole. Make as few cuts as possible to get sections. You can plant these immediately or allow them to "cure" for two days. This simply means letting the cut form a corky layer or skin (callus) over the wounded area. Curing is more important early in the season when the soil may still be cool.

Potatoes sold in grocery stores are treated with an anti-sprouting compound. However, they sometimes sprout and can be used for seed potatoes. These potatoes are not certified; they are fine for eating but may bring disease into your garden. However, they are big, and when cut into pieces, they provide lots of seed potatoes at a low price.

Described here are a number of methods of using seed potatoes to get a plentiful crop.

Hilling: The traditional method is to plant seed in rows. Dig a furrow 6 inches deep. Place the seed about 8 to 12 inches apart at the bottom of the furrow with eyes up. Cover with 2 inches of soil. If seed has been cut into sections, place the cut end down, eyes up. Press firmly on the section to eliminate any air pockets. As the seeds sprout, fill in the trench around the emerging stems. When the stems are 4 to 6 inches tall, mound up soil around them. Do this several times until the mounded soil is about 12 inches high. If you presprout seed, dig a deeper trench so that the top of the stem is 4 inches below soil level. Fill in around the stem. Then follow the same procedure of hilling up soil around the stems as they mature.

A variation of this method is to build a long, 12-inch mound on the soil surface right from the start. Plant the seed at the base of the raised mound. Follow the same directions regarding covering the stem as it grows. Add additional soil to the sides of the hill throughout the season if necessary to keep the hill intact and the emerging tubers covered with soil.

Holes: A furrow or trench is not necessary if you prefer to plant seed in individual holes, usually 8 to 12 inches deep. This works fine as long as the entire bed has been loosened thoroughly. Otherwise, the holes may act as little miniature holding ponds, and your seed may rot. Place the seed in the base of the hole. Do not plant too early, as soil at this depth tends to be cool and moist. Warm and moist is better. Cover the seed 1 inch above any sprouted portion, and fill in as the stem grows. Deep planting takes up little space and results in a good crop, but getting at new pota-

toes is difficult, and digging up the mature ones is a chore at the end of the season.

A variant of the hole method is to dig up a bed as long and wide as necessary to plant the available seed. This block planting takes up little space, but digging a deep and large bed is a lot of work. Lining the bed and covering seed with whole leaves under a layer of soil often results in potatoes with thin skins—wonderful for fresh eating (new potatoes), not so good for storage (mature potatoes). A variation of this method is to loosen soil, build it up into a 12-inch, 4-feet-by-4-feet raised bed while adding lots of organic matter. Then place the seed potatoes at the base of the bed, and fill in as just described.

Mulching: Till or loosen the soil as already described. Place seed potatoes directly on top of the soil. Now cover them with at least 12 inches of straw as a thick mulch. Whole leaves also work well and have the advantage of being cost-free. Let the potatoes grow up and eventually through the top of the mulch. Mulch will break down during the growing season. Replenish it as needed to keep the base of the plants, not the upper leaves, covered at all times. Mulch dries out much faster than soil, so pay close attention to watering.

Compost bed: In the fall, cover the planting bed for a potential potato patch with 3 feet of leaves. That sounds like, and is, a lot of leaves, but they will settle under winter snow. Keep the leaves moist until the first freeze to stop them from blowing around. The following spring lay seed potatoes directly on the bed of leaves, and cover with a mulch 12 inches deep. Add mulch throughout the growing season as necessary, covering only the base of the plants where tubers are forming. Some gardeners insist that potato beetles rarely disturb plants grown in mulch. Again, the skins of potatoes grown in this way may be thin. This and the previous method make harvesting new potatoes a breeze. Just push the mulch aside, and look for small potatoes. Snip these off, and push the mulch back in place.

Spacing

If you are going to hill plants, place the sets up to 12 inches apart. This makes the job of drawing soil up around the plants easier. If you plan on mulching the plants, a closer planting of 6 to 8 inches is possible. Spacing is also related to the number of sprouts left on the seed. The more sprouts, the wider the spacing recommended.

When to Plant

Plant nonsprouted whole seed potatoes as much as 2 to 4 weeks before the last expected frost in your area. If frost threatens after the plants have begun to sprout, mound soil over the stems and leaves. This won't harm the plant. They will grow right up through the soil as if nothing had happened. While potatoes can take a frost, they may rot buried in cold (45°F or less), wet soil for too long.

If planting cut-up or presprouted potatoes, let the soil dry out and warm up a bit—to 50° or 60°F. This can be 1 to 3 weeks before the last expected spring frost, typically when dandelions begin to sprout freely.

How to Care for Potatoes

Water

How you water depends on your growing method. When planting in soil, water frequently and deeply after the plants begin to sprout. Allow the soil to dry out briefly between soakings. Regular watering is critical during early growth until flower formation. After that, it can be a little more sporadic. If planting under mulch, keep the mulch consistently moist at all times. Don't let it dry out. The more water, the nicer the potatoes. No matter what method you are using, stop watering as soon as plants turn yellow toward the end of the growing season.

Mulch

If planted in the soil, place mulch around the emerging shoots. Any readily available organic mulch is fine.

Fertilizing

When plants are about 4 inches tall, fertilize lightly. Fertilize several more times at 2-week intervals. Fish and seaweed emulsion are excellent organic fertilizers to use during the growing season. If you apply too much fertilizer, the plants may form lush foliage but relatively few tubers. Potatoes are heavy feeders, but the overuse of nitrogen may cause hollow heart (see "Physiological").

Weeding

If you are growing potatoes in a traditional manner, keep the bed free of weeds by frequent cultivation. Mound soil regularly up the hills. Weeds occasionally pop up through mulch. Pull them by hand.

Pruning

Gardeners differ on their views about removing potato flowers. Not all plants produce flowers, but many do. I have never bothered to remove flowers and have had excellent crops. Whether they would have been even better with deadheading is next to impossible to determine. Of course, seed savers should leave flowers on the plants, but growing potatoes from seed is primarily of interest to plant breeders, not the average home gardener.

Special Considerations

Every part of the potato plant is toxic with the exception of the tubers. Occasionally, tubers are exposed to light and turn green on their shoulders. Cover any exposed portions of potato to keep them from turning green. This is a problem more with mulched potatoes than ones grown underground. The green areas contain an alkaloid called solanine, which can be toxic if eaten. So stop its formation in the first place.

Extending the Season

Keep the potatoes in the soil until the threat of a hard frost. Dig up potatoes as needed once foliage has died down. This will give you an extended harvest.

Problems

Insects

Potatoes are susceptible to invasions by flea beetles and Colorado potato beetles and are occasionally bothered by aphids, which carry disease. Spray off aphids with a forceful jet of water. Cover plants with row covers if flea beetles have caused damage in previous years. Colorado beetles, both in the larva and adult stage, can do a lot of damage by defoliating a plant. Some gardeners believe mulch helps keep their population down. Handpick the adults, and squish the yellowish-orange to brick-red egg masses you find on the undersides of leaves. Rye planted in fall and tilled into the garden in spring may reduce attacks by these beetles.

Disease

Listing all of the fungal and bacterial infections possible in a potato patch might discourage you from growing this crop. In fact, disease is rarely a problem in the home garden *if you buy certified disease-free seed potatoes;* if you keep the soil mildly acidic (avoid the use of lime and wood ash); if you keep the area free of weeds; if you avoid planting potatoes in the same spot for 3 years; if you avoid planting potatoes where eggplants, peppers, or tomatoes were grown in the past 2 years; and if you stay out of the potato patch when foliage is wet. Also, check the disease resistance of any seed potatoes you purchase. Resistance, particularly to late blight, scab, and verticillium wilt, is covered in detail in seed catalogs.

Physiological

Unusual growing conditions, possibly overly cold and wet soil, overwatering after flowering, or too much nitrogen may cause potatoes to develop hollow heart, nothing more than a dark hole in the center of the tuber. Cut this area out. The potato is fine to eat.

Sometimes when you wash a potato, a blackish area remains on the skin. This may be the result of a fungal infection called black scurf. Remove it without worrying about it harming you.

Propagation

Potatoes do produce flowers and then swollen seedpods. Few people collect seed. Sometimes seed is available for unusual varieties, but seed growing is an obscure practice. Start plants from seed potatoes, either saved from a previous crop or purchased. Note that some varieties are being grown using tissue culture to produce disease-free stock.

Harvesting

Eat potatoes fresh from the garden starting as soon as you can. Extend the harvest season from just after the plant flowers for new potatoes to after its foliage dies down.

When the plant begins to flower, you will often find new potatoes under the surface of the soil or mulch. If in soil, dig carefully from the outside in to find these. If growing in mulch, simply push the mulch aside. Collect these tiny, nearly skinless potatoes by twisting gently or snipping them off with a scissors. Try not to damage the main root system and underground stem. Cover the area with soil or mulch, and let the plant continue to produce other potatoes.

The top growth of potato plants dies at the end of the growing season. When the growth goes from green to yellow to shriveled and brown, the potatoes are ready for harvest. Leave unneeded tubers in the ground as long as possible. You are essentially storing them in the soil. But do harvest them before a hard frost. Cut off and compost the dead foliage.

Try to harvest potatoes on a dry, sunny day. This will cut down on spoilage. If the seed potatoes have been planted in soil, use a spading fork to dig them up. Start well off to the side of the plant, and work your way in. As you pull up soil, break it apart. The smaller potatoes have a way of hiding. You will sometimes hit a potato, causing a wound. Eat these potatoes immediately. A bad potato, like a bruised apple, can spoil the others around it. If potatoes were mulched, move the mulch aside to expose potatoes growing from the

stems. Let the tubers dry out in the sun for 2 to 3 hours and up to a full day if the weather cooperates.

Storing

For storage, grow appropriate varieties. They must have skins that won't rub off. Don't wash until you are ready to use them. Dry the potatoes in a dark place at room temperature for a week. Darkness keeps skins from turning green. Brush off any loose soil without damaging the skin. Hang potatoes in a mesh bag or spread them out on a large table. Avoid putting them on the floor, where they can get damp and rot. Store potatoes in a cool, dark, and dry spot. Air must be able to circulate around them freely. Do not put them in a paper or plastic bag. They should not be touching each other. They store quite well in the bottom of a large cardboard box. Ideal storage temperature is 45° to 50°F. Potatoes that freeze will rot. Potatoes stored below 40°F develop a sweet taste. Return to room temperature of 70°F for 2 weeks, and the taste disappears. Potatoes stored at a higher temperature may begin to sprout, usually within 2 months but sometimes considerably longer.

Most people store potatoes in a refrigerator drawer. This does change the taste, making them slightly sweeter. It also has the potential to darken the flesh.

To freeze new potatoes, wash, blanch for 4 minutes, drain, and pack. To freeze older potatoes, grate for hash browns, or cut into french fries. Fry in oil for 4 minutes before cooling and packing. An optional method for hash browns is to cook whole and grate before freezing. Cook potatoes peeled or unpeeled, mash, cool off, then pack, preferably in plastic containers.

To dry, wash, peel, remove blemishes and eyes, cut into ¼-inch slices, soak in ice water with lemon juice to prevent discoloration, steam or boil for 4 to 5 minutes, cook until translucent but firm, rinse under cold running water to remove starch, drain, and dry in a dehydrator according to instructions. These may last up to 4 months in an airtight container.

Culinary Uses

Do not eat potato flowers or foliage. The underground tuber is the edible portion of the plant. The skin is especially rich in nutrients.

Potatoes grown in the home garden often have thinner skins than those purchased in stores. Handle them carefully since they bruise easily. Wash just before preparing, and cut off any green portions of the tuber. Do the same with any black spots or scabs. The rest of the potato is safe to eat. Always eat any damaged potato right away—the ones speared or sliced by mistake in harvesting. Once washed, they are fine to eat. Wash new potatoes, cook them skin and all, drench them with butter, and sprinkle with parsley. Older potatoes are delicious baked, boiled (and mashed), french fried, microwaved, panfried, or steamed.

To bake, preheat oven to 400°F, gently clean skins, pierce to prevent the potato from exploding, oil red potatoes for better coloration, and cook until done. Potatoes are ready when they give way to gentle pressure. Bake uncovered. If you cover with tin foil, potatoes tend to get mushy—all a matter of personal preference. When boiling, bring water to a rolling boil, add potatoes, and cover the pan. Thin-skinned potatoes are best and excellent for potato salads. Mash boiled potatoes that have been cut into pieces and cooked until done. Follow your favorite recipe, but never overmash or they will turn slimy.

Russets, commonly called Idaho potatoes, are among the best for french frying. Slice to desired size, plunge into cold water to retain color, pat dry, place in vegetable oil at least 4 inches deep and heated to 380° to 390°F, cook until golden or crispier, drain, and pat dry. French fries are delicious with skins on.

To panfry, cut into desired shape and thickness, and cook in oil one side at a time. To microwave, pierce the potato to stop from exploding, and cook until done. To steam, place in a steaming basket over 1 inch of boiling water. Choose small, round reds with thin skin, and steam whole or cut into pieces.

To make chips, slice as thin as possible (skin on or off), place in ice water in a refrigerator until very cold, dry on a paper towel just before tossing into hot oil. Be careful. The chips cook quickly, often ballooning as they do. Salt to taste.

To make hash browns, bake the potatoes the day before, and refrigerate. Peel an onion, grate coarsely or shred, then sauté. Add potatoes, parsley, salt, and pepper. Never pack potatoes down, and cook one side at a time.

Popular dishes made with potatoes are potatoes au gratin, scalloped potatoes, potato pancakes (mix grated cooked potato with flour and egg before frying, or form patties from mashed potatoes mixed with onion and seasoned with pepper), and vichyssoise (a cold, cream-based soup made with leeks, onions, and potatoes). Potatoes cooked with roasts are delicious, as are twice-baked potatoes. If you are on a gluten-free diet, check into potato flour and potato starch.

Varieties

Different varieties of potatoes are best for different uses in the kitchen. Grow varieties that match your needs: baking, boiling, french frying, making potato chips, roasting, and so on.

More than 5,500 varieties are stored at the International Potato Center in Lima, Peru (Centro Internacional de la Papa). These include many types not typically sold or grown in North America. The three main categories of potatoes grown here are red, russet, and white. Within these broad categories, many varieties have been developed, and some of the best are listed below.

Following are some potato terms.

Fingerling: A small potato with an unusual shape like a distorted or contorted finger. These are often colorful with a waxy texture and a sweet, nutty taste. Most mature late in the season.

German: Same as fingerling.

Idaho: A potato raised in Idaho, although most are russets.

Irish: Same as white potato.

New potato: This is any potato harvested when young. It can be any type or variety. New potatoes are known for having thin skins and should be used immediately on harvesting.

Purple (blue or black) potatoes: Good for most uses as long as they are not overcooked.

Red potato: These waxy potatoes, usually round, have red skins that vary in intensity by variety. The flesh is usually white but may be tinted or marbled pink or red. The size of the tubers also varies greatly by variety. These are superb potatoes for boiling, since the flesh stays firm—excellent for potato salads or scalloped potatoes but not good for mashing.

Russet potato: Oblong russet potatoes have brownish skins with a fine netting. The term *russet* refers to the netting, not the color. They are often quite large with a nutty taste and a starchy flesh suited to numerous uses but best for baking, French fries, and mashed potatoes; they are not as good for potato salads or scalloped potatoes, and they are poor for chips.

White potato: White potatoes are listed as white, but the skin color is really light cream colored to tan. The mild flesh is usually white and suited to almost any use. These potatoes vary in size from quite small to very large and in shape from round to oblong. The flesh is dry and is especially good for chips and fries.

The following table includes a wide variety of potatoes suited to home use. The main criteria important to the home gardener are skin and flesh color, the potential use of the potato, the days to maturity, and overall resistance to disease. Color is less important than taste, and the following varieties are among the most flavorful available. However, for aesthetic reasons, color plays a role. We eat with our eyes as well as our taste buds. The use of a potato depends on the specific gravity of the flesh, which defines how soggy or dry it is: less than 16 for frying and salads (very soggy); 16 to 18 for frying, salads, and marginally for boiling (soggy); 18 to 20 for boiling and mashed potatoes (waxy); 20 to 22 for baking, mashing, chips, and french fries (mealy); and 22 to 24 for baking, chips, and french fries (very mealy).

Potatoes mature at different rates. In the table *early* means 65 to 80 days; *mid,* up to 80 or a bit longer; *late,* 90 to about 115; and *very late,* a bit later than that. This characteristic is quite variable depending on your soil and the season. Comments include information on disease resistance, flavor, shape, size at maturity, and yield. 'Bintje' is pronounced BEN-jee, and 'Caribé' is pronounced kah-REE-bay. Note that hybrid seed potatoes are planted just like heirlooms. I have distinguished them as hybrids simply because they are newer introductions.

VARIETIES	SKIN/FLESH COLORS/ SHAPE	USE	SEASON	COMMENTS
'All Red' (heirloom)	Cranberry/rose/rounded oblong	BO, PS	Mid	Yields well, lovely flesh
'Austrian Crescent Fingerling' (heirloom)	Tan/yellow/elongated irregular	BO, PS, R	Late	Yields well
'Bake King' (heirloom)	White russet/white/oblong	BA, FF, M, S	Early	Yields well, eat skin
'Banana Fingerling' (heirloom)	Yellow/yellow/elongated irregular	BO, PS, R	Very late	Excellent flavor
'Bintje' (heirloom)	Yellow/yellow/long	FF, R	Very late	Excellent flavor
'Caribé' (heirloom)	Lavender purple/white/rounded oblong	BO, M	Early	Eat fresh
'Charlotte' (OP)	Golden yellow/golden yellow/oblong	BO, PS	Early	Eat fresh
'Cherry Red' (OP)	Bright red/white/round to oblong	N	Early	Yields well, easy to harvest
'Chieftain' (heirloom)	Red/white/oval to oblong	All, S	Mid	Yields well
'Cranberry Red' (see 'All Red')				
'Dark Red Norland' (heirloom)	Burgundy red/white/round to oblong	BO, PS, R	Early mid	Disease resistant
'Defender' (OP)*****	Tan/white/oblong	BA, FF, R, S	Late	Disease resistant
'French Fingerling' (heirloom)	Rose/pale yellow/elongated	R, S	Very late	Thin skin, lovely flesh
'German Butterball' (heirloom)	Gold yellow/yellow/oblong	All, S	Mid	Excellent flavor
'Kennebec' (heirloom)*****	Pale yellow white/white/oblong	All, S	Mid late	Yields well, heat resistant
'Purple Majesty' (heirloom)	Purple/purple/rounded oblong	All	Mid	High in antioxidants
'Purple Peruvian Fingerling' (heirloom)	Purple/purple/round to oblong	All	Late	Large, many eyes, sweet
'Purple Viking' (heirloom)	Dark purple/white/round to oblong	BO, M, S	Early	Yields well, large
'Red LaSoda' (heirloom)	Red/white/rounded oblong	PS, S	Mid	Great taste
'Red Norland' (heirloom)*****	Red/white/round to oblong	BO, N, PS	Early	Yields well, thin skin
'Rose Finn Apple Fingerling' (heirloom)	Pink/yellow/elongated oblong	BO, PS, R	Very late	Yields well
'Russet Norkotah' (heirloom)	Reddish brown/white/long to oblong	BA, BO, S	Early	Uniform
'Russian Banana Fingerling' (heirloom)	Yellow/yellow/elongated irregular	BO, PS, R	Very late	Excellent flavor
'Viking Purple' (see 'Purple Viking')				
'Warba' (heirloom)	Spotted golden/white/round to oval	BO, N	Early	Excellent flavor
'Yellow Finn' (heirloom)	Yellow white/deep yellow/pear	All, S	Late	Creamy, sweet flesh
'Yukon Gem Hybrid'*****	Light yellow/yellow/round to oval	All	Mid	Yields well, blight resistant
'Yukon Gold Hybrid'	Tan yellow/yellow/rounded oblong	BO, M, N, PS	Early to mid	Do not overcook

Note: Abbreviations under the column "Use" mean the following: All = good for all uses; BA = baking; BO = boiled, steamed; FF = french fries; M = mashed; N = new; PS = potato salad; R = roasting; S = good storage.

Ground Nut (Indian Potato)
Apios americana
Pea or Bean Family
(Fabaceae, formerly Leguminosae)

Ground nut, or Indian potato, is not a potato at all but the name of a perennial vining plant that produces swollen portions of root most commonly called tubers (technically rhizomes), which vary in size but are rarely larger than a golf ball with some notable exceptions. The tubers spaced along the long roots like a beaded necklace are very high in protein and were a staple in the diet of Native Americans and early settlers. Generally started from tubers, rather than seed, the plant is invasive and best grown on the edge of a woods where it can climb up branches and be out of the way. The plant grows best in sun to partial shade in soil that is kept evenly moist. It produces colorful clusters of maroon, pealike flowers that mature into seedpods where the season is long enough. Once the plant is established, which may take 2 to 3 years, the tubers can be dug up at any time, although most gardeners wait until fall after a frost, which tends to sweeten their taste.

They are eaten cooked: peel, then cut up, and use as you would a potato. Note that some people have an allergic reaction to ground nut but not necessarily the first time they eat it. If this were not the case, it would be far more popular in the home garden. It does, however, fix nitrogen in the soil. Consider growing it as an oddity, rather than a staple food crop.

Ground nut is supposed to be hardy to -40°F, but reports are not uniform, suggesting that where plants are originally gathered may play an important role in cold sensitivity. Despite considerable research and efforts to get it on the market, it remains essentially unknown, probably because of its potential allergic reaction, the time it takes to mature, its tendency to be invasive, and variable hardiness.

Let pumpkins mature until deep orange, but harvest them before a hard frost, or the fruit will turn to mush.

PUMPKIN

Cucurbita species
Cucumber or Gourd Family (Cucurbitaceae)

Pumpkins, all of which are technically squash, are tender to very tender, warm-season annuals. Most varieties grow into large, spreading vines that quickly cover a wide area and require more space than the average gardener can afford. They can tolerate some shade, so you might find an unused area where they can roam freely. Or grow bush varieties instead. They are fun, easy to grow, and a good way to introduce children to home gardening, especially with the Halloween connection. Pumpkins are native to North America.

How Pumpkins Grow

Pumpkins grow from large, flat seeds (about 150 to 200 seeds per ounce) into husky plants that quickly produce vines with broad leaves. The plant may crawl for up to 2 months before producing broad, lovely, bell-shaped, yellowish-orange blossoms. The male flowers die after producing pollen, carried into the female flowers, which once fertilized, swell into pale-green fruits. These expand throughout the remainder of the growing season into pumpkins, which turn first deep green, then orange (or other colors) as fall approaches. Frost then kills off the vines, which signals harvest time.

Where to Plant Pumpkins
Site and Light

Pumpkins are remarkably adaptable plants. Although they grow best in full sun, they tolerate partial shade.

Soil and Moisture

Prepare a good bed for pumpkins, which need lots of moisture and rich soil. Mix compost, rotted manure, or sphagnum peat moss into the planting area. The soil should drain freely. Also add organic fertilizer high in nitrogen. Pumpkins seem to grow especially well in 6-inch-high hills approximately 2 to 3 feet wide. This is the base for their strong root system. The vines spread out from the hill in all directions. Pumpkins also grow well in compost piles that have been in place for at least a year. Toss some soil into a large hole in the pile, and plant as you would in a hill. I have been growing pumpkins this way for years. A pH of 6 to 6.5 is fine.

Nutrition Facts

Serving size: 100 grams (3.5 ounces)

	AMOUNT PER COOKED SERVING	% DV	AMOUNT PER SERVING OF ROASTED SEEDS	% DV
Calcium	15 mg	1%	55 mg	6%
Calories	20	1%	445	22%
Carbohydrates	5 g	2%	54 g	18%
Copper	0.1 mg	5%	0.7 mg	35%
Dietary fiber	1 g	4%	0.0 g	0%
Iron	0.6 mg	3%	3.3 mg	18%
Magnesium	9.0 mg	2%	265 mg	65%
Manganese	0.1 mg	4%	0.5 mg	20%
Phosphorus	30 mg	3%	92 mg	9%
Potassium	230 mg	7%	920 mg	25%
Protein	0.7 g	1%	30 g	37%
Vitamin A	5,000 IU	100%	60 IU	1%
Vitamin C	5.0 mg	9%	0.3 mg	0%
Zinc	0.2 mg	2%	10 mg	70%

Containers

You can grow the miniature pumpkins in containers. Grow just one plant per container. Containers should be at least 18 inches deep and as wide as possible. You may need space for the vines to cascade over and out from the pot. Or supply them with support.

Planting

Seed

Pumpkin seeds are easy to plant. Most home gardeners plant six seeds in each mound of soil. Lay the seeds on top of the soil about 12 inches apart. Create a circle with the seeds. Place a seed or two in the center. Press the seed about ¾ to 1 inch deep into the loose soil with your finger. Then press down on the soil with your hand to make it firm. Water immediately. Seed should germinate within 10 days. Note that varieties grown primarily for their seed germinate poorly and should be started indoors if possible. They may rot out if planted too soon.

Transplants

Pumpkins really dislike being transplanted. Root disturbance sets plants back. However, if you want to grow a pumpkin variety that takes a long time to mature, then getting a head start by planting seed indoors makes sense.

Start seeds indoors about 2 to 3 weeks before the last expected frost. Don't start them too early, because they have deep roots, grow quickly, and don't like being disturbed. Use a 32-ounce plastic container. Keep the lid, cut out the bottom, set the container on the lid. Fill it with a sterile starting mix. Plant two to three seeds in it 1 inch deep. Keep the mix moist and warm, preferably 75°F or above. Seeds should germinate within 10 days. Snip out all but the one healthiest plant. Seedlings ideally will have two to three true leaves before being transplanted.

Harden the plants off. Make a hole in the soil large enough to hold the container. Set the container off to the side of the hole. Slide the plastic lid out from under the container. Cover the bottom where the lid was with your hand, and place the container in the hole. Push soil lightly around the container, and then lift it up and away from the plant. Firm the soil around the plant. Water immediately. If the weather is not stable, protect the plant until it warms up with row covers or cloches. Using a large container and planting carefully to avoid root disturbance are the critical elements of this method.

Spacing

Correct spacing is directly related to the number of pumpkin plants, their position in the garden, the planting method (horizontal or vertical), and the variety planted. In general, pumpkin vines are vigorous and sprawling. Place your plants accordingly. Good air circulation around the vines helps prevent powdery mildew—common with pumpkins. If space is at a premium, choose a "bush" or semivining pumpkin variety.

When to Plant

Plant seeds in the garden at least 2 weeks after any danger of frost is past. The soil should be thoroughly warm, preferably 65° to 70°F. Consider warming it up for a few weeks before planting with black plastic. Transplants should go in at the same time, although they can be planted earlier, at 55°F, if protected by row covers or cloches. For proper pollination, be sure to remove row covers when blossoms appear. Naked seeded varieties have extremely poor germination rates in cool soils.

Support

If space is extremely limited, you can grow the mini or smaller pumpkins up supports such as A-frames, trellises, and tripods. Pumpkins have been known to weigh up to 25 pounds without breaking off their vines, although supporting fruit with slings may be worth the extra effort. Let larger varieties roam freely.

How to Care for Pumpkins

Water

Keep the root zone consistently moist until plants are growing vigorously. Some gardeners punch holes in the bottom of gallon milk jugs and then place them deep into the hills before planting. The purpose is to release moisture slowly and continuously to stimulate rapid growth. You still have to fill the milk jugs regularly, so it may be just as easy to water the base of the plants by hand.

Once growing vigorously, pumpkins are remarkably resilient. Still, if there is a prolonged dry spell, water the plants deeply around the root zone. You can just let the hose flood that area. Deep watering is especially important once fruit begins to develop.

Mulch

Mulch around the plants to retain moisture in the soil. Spread mulch around seedlings as they sprout. Then apply a thick 3- to 4-inch layer over the area where vines will run. Good mulches include grass clippings, pulverized leaves, and straw. Do this right away. You do not want to have to lift up vines to place mulch underneath them, as they can be quite brittle. Lifting vines also disturbs roots growing from leaf nodes. This is one time when wood chips are effective, but get them spread out as far as you think the vines will roam. It's a lot of work and probably unnecessary, but it does keep the area weed-free.

Fertilizing

Pumpkins like lots of water and are heavy feeders. As the vines begin to run, fertilize the base of the plant with organic fertilizer. Do this again about 3 weeks later. It is better to apply moderate amounts a couple of times than lots all at once. Diluted fertilizers are effective at any stage, but especially so just as plants begin to form true leaves. The more leaves, the better the fruit.

Weeding

Disturb the soil surface early in the season. After the first growth of weeds, remove them. Once seedlings emerge, hand pull all weeds that sprout around them. Keep the surrounding area weed-free. Once pumpkins are several feet long, they take off on their own and will snake their way through weedy or grassy areas. Let the vines meander through them. One of the best pumpkins I ever grew was in an abandoned field full of grass and weeds. If this is unappealing to you, mulch the area where the vines will run well in advance of their spreading growth. Never pull up weeds entangled in vines. You may break the stems.

Thinning

When seedlings are several inches tall, thin them to two to three of the healthiest seedlings per hill. Once pumpkins are a foot or so long, they take off on their own.

Pruning

If your pumpkins seem to be maturing slowly and if you are satisfied with a specific number, keep only the larger or largest on each vine. Snip off the less mature fruit. If you are growing pumpkins in a weedy or grassy area, check the entire length of the vine. Developing fruit often gets camouflaged in this situation.

Special Considerations

When pumpkins get the size of muskmelons, gently turn them so the stem is directly on top of the fruit. Be careful not to damage the stem of the vine when you turn pumpkins upright. If you don't do this, pumpkins will grow on their sides and may become misshapen. You can slide a board under it at the same time. Only do this for pumpkins intended for use as jack-o'-lanterns. All of this is optional. The shape of a pumpkin has no effect whatsoever on its taste.

Growing pumpkins is as much for fun as for food. Let kids scratch their names into the sides of immature (green) pumpkins in the middle of the season. The scratches will heal, and the kids will know which pumpkin is theirs at the end of the season as the name expands and heals over in time.

If you want huge pumpkins, buy seeds which specify this trait. Start indoors and transplant. Once growing well, remove several of the first female flowers, then allow one to be pollinated. Allow only one pumpkin to grow on each plant. Snip off all other female flowers on the vine. Keep all of the foliage growing vigorously with heavy doses of fertilizer. Lightly dislodge any roots that start to grow from the vine into the soil close to the pumpkin to stop it from breaking off the stem.

Dislodging roots for monster pumpkins is one thing—don't do it for others. These roots can be important, especially if your plant is infested with borers. In fact, they appear to supply water and nutrients to the vine when the main stem is compromised at its base. Cover the damaged base of the plant and any areas forming roots along the stem with soil. This stopgap measure occasionally works.

As the organic movement gains steam, the restrictions on raising chickens in populated areas have become increasingly fewer. Feed pumpkin or marigold flowers to chickens for great yolk color. Note that pumpkins are extremely high in beta-carotene.

Extending the Season

Plant seeds indoors for later-maturing varieties. Protect them when transplanting with a cloche or plastic tent. At the end of the season, cover with cloth in the middle of the day if an early frost threatens. Pumpkins are extremely frost sensitive. Pumpkins will take a mild frost, but the vines often wilt and begin to die.

Problems

Insects

Flea beetles, striped or spotted cucumber beetles, which carry bacterial wilt disease, squash vine borer, and squash bugs can be a problem. Infested pumpkins have a way of withstanding these fairly well. Protect young plants with floating row covers. Pick off any insects you see.

Disease

Prevent disease by rotating crops, giving vines plenty of space for good air circulation, destroying diseased plants, getting rid of refuse at end of season, planting resistant varieties, getting rid of weeds, killing insects, and working in the patch only when it is dry. Bacterial wilt and powdery mildew are the two main problems. Wilt, carried by insects, is the more serious of the two. If powdery mildew is a recurring problem, plant a resistant variety, such as 'Charisma PMR' (Powdery Mildew Resistant).

Marauders

Marauders can be a problem at different stages of growth. Deer seem to do the most damage as fruit is ripening. This varies by year. They have refined taste and will munch on butternut squash before pumpkins. And then they will start nibbling on the pumpkins, disfiguring or devouring them in the process.

Physiological

Poor fruit set is generally caused by lack of pollination in cold, rainy, or cloudy weather. If you experience this kind of weather while plants are blooming, hand pollinate.

Propagation

Varieties of squash and pumpkin from the same species can cross-pollinate. Cover female blossoms with a bag just before they open. Pollinate them by hand the next day. Cover the bloom again with a bag. Remove the bag as soon as the fruit starts to develop. Once fully mature, remove the fruit from the vine. Store it in a cool, dry place for 2 weeks before cutting open. Use an axe if you have to. Save only plump, not flat, seed. Wash and dry. Place in paper envelopes. Seed stays viable for up to 4 to 5 years if stored in a cool, dark, dry place.

Harvesting

Allow pumpkins to mature on the vine for as long as possible. Do not pick them while still green unless absolutely necessary. A light frost will kill the vines but not hurt the pumpkins. A heavy frost or deep freeze, however, will damage these fruits, causing them to rot and turn mushy. Pick all pumpkins before this happens. When harvesting, cut the stem about 6 inches above the fruit. Pumpkins store better with stems attached. Avoid scratching, nicking, or bruising the fruit if possible, to prevent rot. Let the pumpkin sit outside for a few days in the sun to cure if possible. This makes the rind even harder than it first appears. However, if you have a deer problem, do not leave them in the field. Never carry the pumpkin by the stem since it may break off, inducing rot. Bring them inside, and store for 2 weeks in high temperature (75°F) to finish the curing process.

Storing

Never let pumpkins freeze. They will store for up to 2 months in a cool (50° to 55°F) and humid (50 percent relative humidity) room. Furnace rooms are often suggested and worth a try, but they tend to be too warm and dry. A better alternative is to cook and freeze.

To freeze, cut off the stem, wash, slice the pumpkin in two, scrape out the seeds and stringy material on the inside, and cook. You can bake at 350°F, boil, or microwave while resting in water. Remove pumpkin from skin, mash, purée, or cut into pieces. Push through a sieve if mashed or puréed but still stringy, then cool and freeze.

Culinary Uses

Pumpkin blossoms are edible. Remove the bristly leaves at the base and the sex organ in the center. Dip them in batter, and deep-fry as in tempura. Or stir-fry them with young pumpkin leaves (bristly middle vein removed) and stems stripped of bristly outside "strings." Pumpkins can be eaten like summer squash when only 2 to 4 inches wide. A good choice for this is 'Autumn Gold Hybrid' or 'Kumi Kumi'. Once mature, the flesh of cooked pumpkins can be used for bars, bread, cookies, custard (crème brûlée), pies, soups, and stews. Use 'Chinese Miniature', really an acorn squash, for soup.

To prepare for pumpkin pie, quarter, remove seeds and stringy pith, cut in 1-inch strips, peel off skin, slice into thin strips, and steam for up to 15 minutes until soft but not sticky. Or cut in half, scoop out seeds, place covered in a microwave, cook until tender (usually about 20 minutes), peel, then purée or blend. Or slice off the bottom of the pumpkin, trim off skin from top to bottom, slice open, clean out seeds and fiber, cut flesh into chunks, stew until tender, and purée.

The roasted seeds are nutritious, loaded with protein, and reasonably tasty. They are vaguely similar to sunflower seeds in taste and crunch. Clean the seeds, and let them dry for a few days. Soak 3 to 4 cups of seed overnight in 1 gallon of water with ¼ cup salt. Dry again for a day. Coat seeds by mixing 1 cup of seed with 1 teaspoon oil. Spread them out in a single layer on a cookie sheet. Salt again if desired. Then cook at 300° to 350°F for 15 to 40 minutes or until evenly golden brown. Remove them from the oven as soon as they swell and crack or begin to pop. Stir them off and on. Or cook them more slowly at 250°F, usually for up to 1 to 1½ hours. Never let them get scorched. Scrape off onto a paper towel, and let dry. Some people prefer them sugared rather than salted after roasting. Or you can fry them in oil. These are popular in Mexico, where they are called "pepitas."

Plants that produce seeds with thin seed coats are known as naked seeded pumpkins. Each seed actually has a seed coat; it is simply much thinner than on other varieties. Cook seeds from naked seeded (hulless) varieties in the same way but for only 3 to 5 minutes.

Varieties

There are four main species represented in the varietal table: *Cucurbita maxima,* with rounded stems; *Cucurbita argyrosperma,* formerly *Cucurbita mixta,* with hard, hairy stems; *Cucurbita moschata,* with pentagonal smooth, stems; and *Cucurbita pepo* var. *pepo,* with pentagonal, prickly stems. If you are saving seed, choose varieties from different species since plants within the same species can cross-pollinate.

Pumpkins are really a form of winter squash. The following list includes a few squash varieties that either make excellent pumpkin pies or are particularly decorative. The time to maturity is long on some varieties, so get these in as soon as the weather warms up in spring, or trick the plants with row covers or tunnels into believing that it is warmer than it really is. These vining plants take up quite a bit of space. Even the ones listed as semivining are not that compact. Colors and weights are approximate. Even if green, bring pumpkins indoors if a freeze is expected. They will often turn color over a period of days. 'Long Pie' doesn't look like a pumpkin at all and should be harvested as soon as any orange shows up on the fruit. 'Autumn Gold' has the precocious yellow gene, which makes its fruit turn color early. The plant is not sick. Plants suited for pumpkin pies are divided into four groups in the varietal table according to species. They make good jack-o'-lanterns as well.

VARIETY	DAYS	HABIT	COLOR	WEIGHT (POUNDS)
Pie, pumpkin				
Cucurbita maxima				
'Amish Pie' (heirloom)*****	105	Vining	Creamy orange apple	30–60+
'Cinderella' (see 'Rouge Vif d'Etampes')				
'Rouge Vif d'Etampes' (heirloom)	110	Semivining	Scarlet orange furrowed	8–20
'Sweet Meat' (heirloom) (squash)	115	Vining	Creamy gray	10–15
Pie, pumpkin (cushaw squash)				
Cucurbita argyrosperma, formerly known as ***Cucurbita mixta***				
'Green Striped Cushaw' (heirloom)	105	Vining	Cream with green markings	8–12
'Tennessee Sweet Potato' (heirloom)	100	Vining	Cream pear faint green	10–20
Pie, pumpkin				
Cucurbita moschata				
'Autumn Buckskin Hybrid'	105	Vining	Tan orange flattish	10–15
'Dickinson (Field)' (OP)*****	115	Vining	Buff tan furrowed oval	20–40
Pie, pumpkin				
Cucurbita pepo				
'Autumn Gold Hybrid' (AAS-1987)	90	Vining	Orange gold ribbed	8–15
'Baby Pam Hybrid' (Oz)	95	Semivining	Bright orange	2–5
'Big Red California Sugar' (heirloom)	85	Semivining	Deep orange	3–4
'Early Sweet Sugar Pie' (heirloom)	110	Vining	Bright orange	6–7
'Kumi Kumi' (heirloom)	50–100	Vining	Green yellow ribbed	3

VARIETY	DAYS	HABIT	COLOR	WEIGHT (POUNDS)
'Long Pie' (heirloom)	100	Vining	Orange zucchini-like	5–6
'New England Pie' (heirloom)	105	Semivining	Dark orange flattened	4–6
'Small Sugar' (see 'New England Pie')				
'Spirit Hybrid' (AAS-1977)	95	Semivining	Medium orange	8–15
'Spookie' (heirloom)	100	Semivining	Dark to medium orange	5–6
'Spooktacular Hybrid'	90	Vining	Bright orange ribbed	2–5
'Sugar Pie' (see 'New England')				
'Triple Treat' (heirloom)	110	Vining	Dark orange	4–6
'Winter Luxury' (heirloom)*****	95	Vining	Light orange gold netted	5–7
'Young's Beauty' (heirloom)	105	Vining	Dark orange	8–10

Jack-o'-lanterns
   Cucurbita species

VARIETY	DAYS	HABIT	COLOR	WEIGHT (POUNDS)
'Big Tom' (see 'Connecticut Field')				
'Charisma PMR Hybrid' *(C. pepo)*	115	Semivining	Deep orange	14–18
'Connecticut Field' (heirloom) *(C. pepo)*	115	Vining	Yellowish orange	15–25+
'Ghost Rider' (OP) *(C. pepo)*	115	Vining	Dark orange	10–15+
'Hijinks Hybrid' (AAS-2011) *(C. pepo)*	100	Vining	Bright orange	6–7
'Howden's Field' (OP) *(C. pepo)*	110	Strong vining	Dark orange ribbed	10–15+
'Jack O' Lantern' (heirloom) *(C. pepo)*	105	Vining	Yellowish orange elongated	8–15
'Kentucky Field' (heirloom) *(C. moschata)*	110	Vining	Yellow orange ribbed	10–15
'Lumina' (heirloom) *(C. maxima)******	100	Vining	White	10–20
'Orange Smoothie Hybrid' (AAS-2002) *(C. pepo)*	90	Semivining	Medium orange	5–8
'Pankow's Field' (heirloom) *(C. pepo)*	110	Vining	Dark orange	20–30
'Sorcerer Hybrid' (AAS-2002) *(C. pepo)******	110	Semivining	Dark orange	15–20
'Turner Family' (heirloom) *(C. pepo)*	90	Vining	Deep orange ribbed warted	6–7

Jumbo
   Cucurbita maxima

VARIETY	DAYS	HABIT	COLOR	WEIGHT (POUNDS)
'Atlantic Giant' (heirloom)*****	115	Vining	Pink orange ribbed	100–900+
'Big Max' (heirloom)	120	Vining	Reddish orange pink	30–75+
'Big Moon' (OP)	110	Vining	Medium orange	40–200+
'Dill's Atlantic Giant' (see 'Atlantic Giant')				
'Mammoth Gold' (heirloom)	110	Vining	Golden orange	40–50+
'Prizewinner Hybrid'*****	115	Vining	Bright orange	50–200+
'Wyatt's Wonder Hybrid'	115	Vining	Deep orange	70–150+

Miniature
   Cucurbita pepo

VARIETY	DAYS	HABIT	COLOR	WEIGHT (POUNDS)
'Baby Bear Hybrid' (AAS-1993)	105	Semivining	Mid orange	1–2+
'Baby Boo' (OP)	95	Semivining	White to pale yellow ribbed	1+
'Chinese Miniature' (heirloom)*****	100	Semivining	Light orange ribbed	⅓–1
'Jack Be Little' (see 'Chinese Miniature')				
'Munchkin' (see 'Chinese Miniature')				
'Wee-B-Little' (OP) (AAS-1999)	90	Semivining	Bright orange	¾

Seed (naked seed varieties)
   Cucurbita pepo

VARIETY	DAYS	HABIT	COLOR	WEIGHT (POUNDS)
'Lady Godiva' (heirloom)*****	110	Vining	Yellow striped green	3–10+
'Snack Jack Hybrid'	90	Semivining	Deep orange	2–3
'Streaker' (see 'Lady Godiva')				
'Trick or Treat Hybrid'	105	Semivining	Bright orange	10–12
'Triple Treat' (see Pie, Pumpkin: *Cucurbita pepo*)				

Get spring radishes into the ground early to mature quickly before turning woody in high heat.

RADISH

Raphanus sativus species
Cabbage or Mustard Family (Brassicaceae, formerly Cruciferae)

Radishes are a diverse group of plants. Most are cool- to cold-season annuals, but others are biennials. They are commonly labeled spring, summer, and winter radishes depending on when they are typically planted. Most radishes are eaten raw, but a number are cooked in other cultures. They take up relatively little space and mature rapidly. Most radishes are believed to have originated in China.

How Radishes Grow

Radish seeds are small, round, and usually tan to reddish brown (about 2,500 to 3,000 seeds per ounce). The two little seed leaves are easy to spot and look a bit like a green butterfly. The plant then produces true leaves, which are much larger. As leaves develop, the roots begin to swell and are easily visible at or above the soil line. If allowed to mature well past the normal harvesting stage, the plants will form thick flower stalks. On the ends of these are clusters of tiny buds opening into four-petaled flowers. These flowers de-velop into slender, pointed pods that will eventually produce seed similar to that originally planted.

Where to Plant Radishes
Site and Light

Although radishes will grow in a wide variety of light conditions, they prefer full sun. Keep the area cool with consistent watering and a layer of mulch. Bright light is never a problem, but high temperature is. Provide partial shade when over 80°F, already too hot for spring radishes.

Soil and Moisture

Radishes need loose soil that stays moist but drains freely. If the soil is compacted, it will stunt root growth. Add lots of organic matter to the soil. Compost is excellent, as is leaf mold. They retain moisture and help the crop mature quickly. Mix in some green sand or wood ash for potassium, and bonemeal for phosphorus in the fall. If you have rocky soil, build a raised bed. A pH of 6 to 7 is preferred.

Nutrition Facts
Serving size: 100 grams (3.5 ounces)

	SPRING RADISH		WINTER RADISH (DAIKON)	
	AMOUNT PER RAW SERVING	% DV	AMOUNT PER RAW SERVING	% DV
Calories	16	1%	18	1%
Carbohydrates	3 g	1%	4 g	1%
Dietary fiber	2 g	6%	1.5 g	6%
Folate	25 mcg	6%	28 mcg	7%
Potassium	235 mg	7%	225 mg	6%
Protein	1 g	1%	0.5 g	1%
Vitamin C	15 mg	25%	22 mg	37%

Container

Growing radishes in containers makes a lot of sense, even if you have plenty of space for them in the garden. Radishes can be replanted frequently or with other vegetables that mature more slowly. Keep the soil consistently moist. A good combination for two colors is 'Early Scarlet Globe' and 'Hailstone'. Some gardeners even grow radishes indoors.

Planting
Seed

Place some seeds in the palm of your hand, allowing them to slide down between your thumb and forefinger as a way to control them as you drop them in the furrow. Sow them thinly about ¼ to ½ inch deep. If seeds drop together, just flick them apart. Plant spring radishes in short rows. Plant one row each week for 4 consecutive weeks in the spring. Do the same thing in the fall. Seeds usually germinate within 10 days, often much faster. Some gardeners prefer broadcasting seed over a wide bed and raking the seed under. This is fine as long as you can reach the plants easily from the sides of the bed.

Many gardeners mix spring radish seeds with slower-maturing crops such as carrots and parsnips. The radishes mark the location of the other root crops. As you harvest the radishes, you will be thinning out the young carrots and parsnips. Radishes mature quickly (25 to 50 days), and their harvest lasts only 10 days or so.

Spacing

Spacing depends on the potential size of the radish. Start by planting seeds closer together than needed, roughly 1 to 2 inches or less for spring and summer types, 3 to 4 inches for winter radishes. Spacing is important for proper growth. See "Thinning."

When to Plant

Most people say that radishes are really easy to grow. They can be, but it depends on the season. Different varieties are sensitive to day length and temperature. Catalogs rarely give accurate information on exactly when to plant a specific variety. I can't do it either, but here are some hints. Get the small, rounded varieties, such as 'Champion', into the ground 4 to 6 weeks before the last expected frost in spring. Radishes similar to this one like it cool, roughly around 45°F, so get them into the garden early. If they are planted too late, they often produce poorly and may go to seed. Then a bit later plant the more-oblong types, such as 'French Breakfast'. Just a bit later, try long-rooted spring varieties, such as 'White Icicle'. The winter varieties should be planted in midsummer, generally in July. By planting small amounts of seed over a period of a few weeks, you will learn the preferences of each variety. Having said that, no one can predict the weather, which can stay cool over a period of weeks in spring or flip from winter to summer almost overnight. *Weather patterns do affect radishes.* While it may be true that radishes sprint into growth, try other plants to turn kids onto gardening—totally contrary to what most other sources would say.

Support

Support is needed only for edible-podded types grown in containers. They get large and flop over. Tying them to a piece of bamboo keeps them in place.

How to Care for Radishes
Water

Water immediately after seeding. Keep the soil moist until seeds begin to germinate. Keep the young plants consistently moist to encourage the roots to mature rapidly. The faster the roots form, the more tender and less woody they will be. Consistent watering may also prevent splitting. You can get by with somewhat shallow watering for smaller-bulbed varieties, but water deeply for varieties with long roots.

Mulch

Place a razor-thin layer of mulch over the furrow to keep the soil from forming a crust. Radish seedlings are quite vigorous and will break through the mulch. Once they have germinated and are about 1 inch tall, place a thicker layer of mulch along the edges of the row. Pulverized leaves and grass clippings are excellent. The mulch keeps the soil moist and cool, just the way radishes like it.

Fertilizing

If you have prepared the soil with enough compost or other organic matter, you won't need to fertilize. Avoid any fertilizer with a high concentration of nitrogen since this will just make the plants leafy and stunt root growth.

Weeding

Spring radishes mature quickly, but it is still a good idea to hand pull any small weeds that appear along the row as soon as they appear. Once the ground has been mulched, weeds should be a minor problem.

Thinning

If you plant spring radishes a little too close, thin them when an inch or so tall. This is really a form of weeding since weeds compete with the radishes for moisture and nutrients. Crowded radishes do the same. You may get a few good radishes in a crowded row, but you won't get many. Thin radishes to 2 inches apart. Otherwise, you get all tops and thin roots useful only for microgreens. By giving the winter and daikon types more space to begin with, thinning may not be needed until roots are fairly large. However, some winter varieties get really big and need enough space to grow to maturity.

Special Considerations

Grow radishes quickly and uniformly, or they may split, get woody, or bolt. Water consistently, and pick radishes as soon as they are mature. If you have lots of foliage and poor roots, you may have planted the seed too late, too thickly, in too much shade, or with too much nitrogen. Radishes can get spicy hot if picked past their prime. Also, in areas where cool springs are short, you often get better radishes by planting late rather than early in the season. Radishes need to mature in cool weather. Radishes have little nutritional value and even less if cooked.

Extending the Season

It is possible to get early and late crops by planting under tunnels in spring and in cold frames in fall.

Problems

Insects

Flea beetles often damage young leaves, which begin to look like they have been shot with a shotgun. This is unsightly but does little damage in the long run to the edible roots. Radishes are the target of root maggots on occasion. Uproot and discard the infected plants. Scatter ashes around young

Summer radishes, including daikon, can be planted later and are suited to many culinary uses.

plants. Plant a new crop in a different location. Consider covering young plants with row covers if flea beetles get out of hand. Radishes are occasionally bothered by slugs. Pick these off.

Physiological

High heat will cause spring radishes to become hot and woody. Sometimes, radishes will split if allowed to mature too long. Splitting may also be caused by inconsistent watering.

Propagation

Radishes are hermaphroditic, having both male and female organs, but they must be insect pollinated. They do not cross with other members of their family. They will cross with other radishes. Most gardeners do not eat all of the radishes they grow. Some of the plants may bolt, forming long stems with tiny flowers. These are typically pollinated by bees. If pods form, let them dry on the plant. As soon as they are dry, break them open to collect the seeds. Pods do have a tendency to shatter, so don't wait too long. Radish seeds last 4 to 5 years if kept in a cool, dark, dry place. Moist chill seed if it fails to germinate.

Harvesting

Pick spring radishes early. Do not go by days to maturity listed in the varietal table. Begin pulling up spring radishes when the size of a marble. Harvest every day if necessary. After reaching 1 inch in diameter, roots often get woody or hot. Squeeze them. If they are firm, they are still probably good to eat. A few spring radishes can get much larger or longer and still be excellent to eat, but these are the exception. Once a plant begins to send up flower shoots, the roots deteriorate, and plants should be composted.

Harvest winter radishes when they mature at the end of the season. They often taste best after a frost. Use a spading fork for monster varieties. Let the radishes dry out for several hours. Then eat or store.

Harvest emerging shoots, leaves, flowers, and seedpods according to taste and texture.

Storing

Cut or twist off the tops of spring radishes, place in a perforated plastic bag in the crisper of your refrigerator, and use them as quickly as possible, certainly within 2 weeks. Cutting off tops prevents moisture loss from the roots of all varieties of radish.

Winter radishes will store for about 1 week when treated like spring radishes. They will sometimes last in the garden under a 12- to 18-inch layer of mulch, usually whole leaves or straw, that gets covered with snow. When you uncover these, eat them as soon as you pull them since they rarely last. They can also be stored in moist sand or sphagnum peat moss in an insulated garage for up to 2 months as long as they are fully covered, do not freeze, and do not touch each other in the storage material. Before storing them in this manner, pull them up, remove the greens about an inch from the root, do not wash, and use before they begin to sprout in spring if they survive the winter and do not rot out.

Radishes do not freeze well, although the leaves and roots of winter types can be pickled. Daikons can be dried: slice into long, thin strips; lay out thinly in a dehydrator. Boil in water for several minutes to rehydrate, and use in dishes.

Culinary Uses

All parts of spring radishes are edible. The tiny leaves and roots are excellent as microgreens in salads. More mature greens are edible but not very appetizing if they have been marred by flea beetle activity. The roots are delicious as long as they are tender and juicy. They are most commonly cut into small pieces and added to salads or placed on platters to be dipped in sour cream sprinkled with bits of green onions or chives, but large roots can be carved into flowers and salted to taste. Try wrapping radish slices in bread and butter for a snack. The flowers taste like radish and add color to salads or sprinkled over cooked vegetables. Seedpods are also edible. 'Rat Tail' is grown just for its pods—crisp, juicy, and hot before they become fibrous and tough with age. They are typically chopped up and added to salads, although when thin, they can be added to stir-fries. If any radish flowers and forms seed, the seed can be eaten fresh or sprouted like alfalfa sprouts. Once seeds have sprouted, separate the sprouts from their hulls by swirling them in cold water.

Winter radishes have varied flavors from mild to quite pungent and a crunchy dense texture. Some prefer them to spring types for their overall versatility. Both the leaves and roots of winter radishes are edible. Pick early for microgreens. Cut older leaves into thin strips, salt, and let stand for an hour to remove excess water, then add to soups and stir-fries. Sauté young leaves in olive oil, and splash with lemon juice. Cook them for a side dish of greens. The roots are most often, but not always, peeled before being used raw or cooked. When small, the roots can be grated into salads, dips, or tempura sauce. Splash thin slices of raw daikon with olive oil, and sprinkle with salt. Slices often accompany sashimi or sushi. Winter radishes can be diced, sliced, or shredded for cooking in soups, stews, and stir-fries. They are delicious sautéed in butter or steamed like carrots. Roots can be sliced and battered for tempura. Some cooks use them for a replacement in recipes that call for turnips.

Varieties

Spring and Summer Radishes
Raphanus sativus, Raphanus sativus var. *sativus,* and *Raphanus sativus* var. *radicula*

This group of radishes is the one most familiar to gardeners. They are grown for their edible roots, eaten raw. The seedlings are excellent as microgreens.

VARIETY	DAYS	COLOR/SHAPE/SIZE (INCHES)
'Amethyst Hybrid'	30	Pale purple/round/to 1
'Brightest Breakfast' (heirloom)	30	Scarlet red-tipped white/oblong/to 2
'Champion' (heirloom) (AAS-1957)*****	25	Red/round/to 2
'Cherriette Hybrid'	25	Bright red/round/to 2

VARIETY	DAYS	COLOR/SHAPE/SIZE (INCHES)
'Cherry Belle' (heirloom) (AAS-1949)*****	25	Deep red/round/to 1
'Crimson Giant' (heirloom)	30	Red/round/to 2
'Crunchy Royale Hybrid'	30	Red/round/to 1
'D'Avignon' (OP)*****	25	Red with white tip/tapered/to 4
'Early Scarlet Globe' (heirloom)	25	Bright red/round/to 1
'Easter Egg Hybrid' (heirloom)	30	Mixed/oval/to 2
'French Breakfast' (heirloom)*****	30	Red tipped white/oblong/to 3
'German Beer' (heirloom)	50	White tan/tapered bulb/to 6 (plant summer)
'German Giant' (heirloom)	30+	Deep red with white flesh/round/marble to baseball size
'Hailstone' (heirloom)*****	25	White/round/to 2
'Icicle' (see 'White Icicle')		
'Pink Beauty' (heirloom)	25	Light pink/round/to 1
'Pink Summer Icicle' (heirloom)	30	Pink/cylindrical/to 5
'Ping Pong Hybrid'*****	30	White/round/to 2
'Plum Purple' (heirloom)	25	Magenta/round/to 2
'Rover Hybrid'	20	Dark red/round/to 3
'Rudolf' (heirloom)	25	Bright red/round/to 2
'Sora' (heirloom)*****	26	Bright red/round/to 2
'Short Top' (see 'White Icicle')		
'Sparkler White Tip' (heirloom)*****	25	Red pink tipped white/irregular rounded/to 2
'Tinto Hybrid'	25	Bright red/round/to 1
'White Globe' (see 'Hailstone')		
'White Icicle' (heirloom)	30	White/long/tapered to 6 (decent pods; plant in summer)

Winter Radishes
Raphanus sativus var. *longipinnatus,* also known as *Raphanus bipinnatus; Raphanus sativus* var. *niger*

For the sake of convenience, this group contains varied plants from different species, which are eaten raw or cooked depending on the variety. Included are plants that may be labeled by different catalogs as black radish, Chinese, daikon, Japanese, mooli, and Oriental radishes. They do have different shapes (cylindrical, elongated, oblong, spherical with tapered roots) and sizes. Unlike spring radishes, some can get huge and still be good to eat. *Daikon* means "great root" in Japanese. The flavor of these is unique and worth trying. Some are best planted in summer to mature in fall. Follow seed package directions for the best planting time. These plants probably came from Iran or Southeast Asia.

VARIETY	DAYS	COLOR/SHAPE/SIZE (INCHES)
'April Cross Hybrid'	60	White/carrot-like/to 8+
'All Seasons' (OP)	70+	White/cylindrical/to 18
'Black Spanish' (heirloom)	60	Black with white flesh/round/to 4
'Black Spanish Long' (heirloom)	60	Black with white flesh/thick carrot-like/to 10
'China Rose' (heirloom)*****	55+	Rose with white flesh/stocky carrot/to 5 (good sprouts)
'Chinese White' (heirloom)	65	White/tubular/to 8
'Japanese Minowase' (heirloom)	55	White/cylindrical/to 24
'Mino Early' (heirloom)	50	White with white flesh/irregular tube/to 16
'Misato Rose' (heirloom)	65	White green with pink flesh/turnip-like/to 4+
'Miyashige' (heirloom)	70	Pale green to white/cylindrical/to 18
'Nero Tondo' (heirloom)	55	Black with white flesh/round/to 4
'Summer Cross No. 3 Hybrid'*****	55	White/tapered/to 16
'Tama Hybrid'	70	White/cigar shaped/to 18
'Tokinashi' (see 'All Seasons')		

Edible Podded Radish
Raphanus sativus var. *caudatus*

VARIETY	DAYS	COLOR/SHAPE/SIZE (INCHES)
'German Beer Radish' (see 'Münchner Bier')		
'Münchner Bier' (heirloom)	55	White/oval/to 4 (roots and pods good)
'Rat (Rat's) Tail' (heirloom)	50	For seedpods up to 6

Let a few radishes bolt to form edible, bright-white flowers and deep-green pointed pods.

Consider growing more than one type of raspberry to extend the harvest of this delectable fruit.

RASPBERRY (BLACKBERRY, BOYSENBERRY)

Rubus species
Rose Family (Rosaceae)

Raspberries are hardy woody plants. For the sake of simplicity, raspberries and blackberries are referred to as brambles in this section. Brambles are easy to grow, produce offspring year after year for decades, form delicious and nutritious fruits in abundance, and, in my opinion, should be a part of every home garden if possible. Brambles do require frequent watering and may be damaged by disease and rabbits. Different species originated in Asia, Europe, and North America.

How Raspberries Grow

Brambles are fast-growing, shallow-rooted plants that are generally quite tall and prickly. While individual stems or canes last no more than 2 years, each plant forms suckers, or new growth, from its base to replace older canes that die off. In this way the plants will live for decades with proper care. Brambles that grow the first year only to produce berries in the second year are listed as summer-bearing fruits, whose shoots are known as floricanes. They produce lots of berries in one major flush during the summer. The exact time varies with variety and season. Not only do they form berries but also new growth at the base of the plant. That new growth will produce berries the following season. So, it takes two growing seasons for summer-bearing brambles to produce berries. Brambles that produce berries the first year are listed as fall or everbearing types, whose shoots are known as primocanes. They too form new plantlets off to the side or stems at their base. And these may form berries by the end of the season.

Where to Plant Raspberries
Site and Light

Brambles grow best in full sun, although they do tolerate partial shade as long as they get at least 6 hours of sun a day. Avoid planting them in low-lying areas. These act as frost pockets and often have poor drainage. While brambles thrive in moist soil, they may rot out in soggy areas. Avoid planting brambles in areas affected by strong summer winds. These dry out soil and can even whip canes back and forth, causing considerable damage. By planting brambles

Nutrition Facts

Serving size: 100 grams (3.5 ounces)

	AMOUNT PER SERVING	% DV
Calories	50	3%
Carbohydrates	12 g	4%
Dietary fiber	6.5 g	27%
Manganese	0.6 mg	33%
Protein	0.8 g	1%
Vitamin C	25 mg	45%
Vitamin K	8 mcg	9%

along fences, edges of roads, or in patches, you can keep them more easily in check. They grow quite well on mild slopes, as water drains away from the roots.

Soil and Moisture

Brambles grow best in loose, fertile soil that drains freely but retains moisture during dry spells. They like cool, moist, but not soggy, root runs. If your soil is compacted or rocky, build a deep raised bed. Add lots of organic matter to the soil to keep it loose but moisture retentive. Compost, rotted manures, and sphagnum peat moss are excellent; the latter is especially good since it is slightly acidic. Add some bone-meal as well. Brambles thrive in mildly acidic soils with a pH of 6.5 or slightly lower. If possible, prepare your raspberry bed in fall. That's a good time to loosen soil and add organic fertilizers, which take time to break down and enrich the soil. Consider planting a green manure in the area to provide nutrients the following spring.

You don't have to prepare a raspberry bed as you would your general garden area. Clean the area, and mow it before planting. Dig planting holes from 12 to 24 inches apart. Into the soil mix in a few handfuls of compost or peat moss. Then fill the hole back up. Mark the holes so that you know exactly where to plant in spring. Surround the holes with a thick layer of mulch, roughly 8 to 12 inches deep. The mulch will kill grass and weeds, encourage worms to work the area, and promote the growth of suckers from the parent plants in subsequent years. This no-till method works well in all but compacted or rocky soils as long as you keep adding mulch to the bed as it disappears. If soil is overly compacted, it collects water and will rot out the roots.

Planting

Transplants

Neighbors or friends will often offer home gardeners young plantlets or suckers from varieties that multiply in this fash-

ion. People who grow raspberries usually have a surplus of these. In fact, they may even uproot and throw away suckers to keep an established bed in check. Rarely do they know the variety, but they usually know whether plants produce berries on new or old cane.

If digging up young plants to the side of the mother plant, try to keep some soil around the roots. If the soil drops off, wrap moist newspaper around the roots and get them into the ground as quickly as possible. Never let roots dry out! Try to dig these up as early in the season as possible, even before leaf buds are beginning to turn green. Although they can be transplanted later, keeping them alive and thriving is harder.

If you are particular about varieties, find a local commercial grower, and ask for their advice. Sample some berries to know what kind of fruit you like the best. That way you will know the name of the variety you want to grow and that it is hardy in your area.

Plants are available for purchase as bare-root plants or in containers. Bare-root plants are usually far less expensive. This is how most mail-order plants are sold. As soon as you get them, take them out of the package. Soak the roots for 2 hours before planting. Get them into the garden as soon as possible. Most come with directions on exactly what to do. The most critical point is not to let the plants dry out. When planting, spread the roots out or lay them in one direction. Cover the roots with soil, and firm in place. This removes air pockets. Water the plants well. If the soil sinks, add some more soil and water again. Roots need to be firmly anchored. Keep the young plants moist at all times. Water the plants every day if necessary until they "take." At that stage leaves are unfolding and firm.

If you buy potted plants, slide them out of the container into the planting hole, keeping the soil around the roots intact. Good potted plants should have a network of roots forming a solid root ball. If soil easily falls off the roots, you are basically buying a bare-root plant that has been potted up simply to keep it alive. Local nurseries may have bare-root plants available early in the season before being potted up. Call ahead to find out when they are coming in.

Brambles are propagated in a variety of ways. Buy plants certified to be disease-free. If plants have been grown by tissue culture, they are unlikely to be diseased. However, they are more demanding than others. Plant them after all danger of frost, and keep the soil moist at all times until they are growing well. They may have to be watered twice a day in dry spells.

Spacing

Spacing depends on your gardening style. Many home gardeners like bramble patches. They plant bare-root or potted plants without any support from 12 to 24 inches apart in a cluster.

Others make hedgerows out of brambles, placing individual plants 24 inches apart in long rows about 3 to 4 feet apart. These are allowed to sucker and fill in the space between plants. Hedgerows may be on the edge of a garden or along a road leading to the home. As with the bramble patch, no support is provided.

The style preferred by commercial growers and a number of home gardeners is to create rows of plants with enough space in between to walk around the plants easily when it comes time to pick berries. Each plant is supported as described under "Support."

When to Plant

Get your plants into the ground as early as possible. If buying bare-root plants, they should be dormant with no growth showing. If they have leafed out, the leaves may or may not die off. Potted plants often have already leafed out and can be planted later than bare-root stock. *Keep the soil around the roots intact as you plant them.*

Support

Brambles are naturally untidy. In the wild, they are self-supporting and produce prolifically. A number of gardeners plant them in patches or as hedge rows without any support at all. They do nothing but remove dead cane. It typically takes 2 to 3 years to form a patch or thick hedgerow. The advantages are that you do not have to mess with stakes and wires, you have less wasted space, and birds are reluctant to plunder the inner areas of tangled growth, where they feel vulnerable. The disadvantage is that most raspberries have prickers (thorns) and are harder to pick grown this way.

Tying plants to tall, single stakes is a popular method of support. Space stakes far enough apart to walk between mature plants easily. Plant five plants around the stakes about 6 inches from its base. As plants grow, tie them to the support. A variation of this is the tepee method, where you plant six to eight plants about a foot apart in a circle and tie the growing canes together at 3 feet and again higher up.

Other gardeners prefer growing plants in rows supported by wires. Place posts 10 feet apart, anchoring them firmly in the ground. Then stretch wire tightly between the posts. Stretch one wire between the posts at a height of 4 feet. Then space your plants in a row on alternate sides of the wire. Tie them to the wire when the canes are tall enough. For even more support, stretch two wires between the posts at 36 inches and another two at 60 inches. Guide the growing cane between the wires. Tie each cane to the wire at two heights.

Supporting brambles takes time, money, and energy, but it does result in larger berries, potentially less disease, and definitely easier picking and pruning. I did this for years until the loss of berries to birds led me to the more casual "patch" method of growing.

How to Care for Raspberries

Water

Consistent moisture is critical to lush growth. As long as your soil drains freely, it is difficult to overwater these plants. Watering is particularly important for young plants trying to establish themselves for the first time. Continue watering right up to the first freeze.

Mulch

Mulch around plants right away, but avoid touching the base of the plants. Good mulches include grass clippings and pulverized leaves or straw. Add mulch regularly throughout the season as it is eaten away by worms and soil microorganisms.

Fertilizing

Any kind of natural fertilizer will help brambles become thick and lush. Any organic fertilizer high in nitrogen is recommended, one of the best being aged poultry manure. Also good is horse, cow, or rabbit manure. Add organic fertilizers in early spring and again in late fall after plants go dormant. During the season foliar feeding with liquid fish emulsion is effective. Stop feeding once flowers form. Whenever you use pulverized leaves or straw as mulch in a garden, add extra nitrogen.

Weeding

Kill all perennial weeds before planting. Prepare the planting bed well, preferably in fall. Brambles, more appropriately their offspring, last for decades. Weeds compete for nutrients and moisture and also harbor insects that may transmit disease. Get rid of them. Avoid deep cultivation around plants, since they have a shallow root system. Hand pull weeds, and use mulch.

Pruning

A really oversimplified method of pruning works for both types of raspberries. Remove all dead cane or dead portions of cane. Do this in late winter just as snow melts or very early spring before plants begin to sprout. Dead cane has a grayish look and breaks easily if you push against or bend it. Cut completely dead canes off at the base of the plant with

Ripe raspberries slide easily into your hand with a light pull.

cut them right down to the base of the plant before growth starts in spring. This discourages "double cropping"—no summer berries but larger and more berries in fall. Many home gardeners do not do this, preferring two crops over an extended season. In either case, if canes are bunched close together, which is not always the case, thin them out for good air circulation to reduce the chance of disease. I have found these berries to be nearly self-thinning with most canes growing roughly 6 or more inches apart.

Winter Protection

Buy raspberries that can stand up to the potential low temperature in your area. For more tender berries, including black and purple raspberries and true blackberries, bend canes over and protect them with a thick mulch of straw or whole leaves. Pin the growing tips to the ground, and cover with soil. Avoid bending the base of the cane severely, since crimping cane damages the plant.

Special Considerations

Remove all wild brambles close to the area where you will be planting your raspberries or blackberries. They may be carrying diseases that will infect your new planting.

Problems

Insects

Aphids, beetles (especially Japanese), borers, fruit worms, raspberry sawfly, and spotted wing drosophila pose potential problems to a bramble patch. Wash off aphids with a hose, handpick Japanese beetles, and cut off cane infested with borers. See "Insects" in chapter 6 for information on spotted wing drosophila.

Disease

Most home gardeners will have few problems with disease, but when it occurs, it can be discouraging. Potential diseases include anthracnose, botrytis (gray mold), cane blight, phytophthora root rot, powdery mildew, raspberry leaf curl, raspberry mosaic, rust, spur blight, tomato ringspot, and verticillium wilt. If there are any brambles growing wild in your yard, remove these unless they are producing beautiful crops on their own. Grow only these. Otherwise, buy disease-free plants. Plants grown through tissue culture, although finicky to get started, are often disease-free. Stock certified to be disease-free often is but occasionally is not. If already growing a bramble, segregate new plantings from old. In an existing patch, remove any diseased cane immediately. If entire plants become diseased, remove them. If necessary, start a new patch in a new location. Otherwise,

pruning shears. If only the top portion of a cane has died back, cut it back just above a bud on remaining live cane. Wear protective glasses, gloves, and a long-sleeved shirt when working with brambles.

More fastidious and professional growers prune summer- and fall-bearing types in specific ways to control the size of plantings, get more berries, and make picking easier. For summer-bearing plants (floricane brambles), remove all cane that flowered and produced berries in the previous season, which translates into dead cane, as mentioned above. Then cut out all but five or six of the remaining live canes from each plant, if there are more canes than this per square foot of row or patch. Cutting these remaining canes back by ¼ is optional. *Never remove all of the new growth around the base of the plant, since you will be removing the cane that will produce berries the following year!*

The pruning of fall-bearing types (primocane brambles) can be more complicated depending on your goal. Fall-bearing types, often called everbearing brambles, will form fruit more than once in a season. They are not truly everbearing but produce fruits in a summer flush and then over a number of weeks late in the season—sometimes, right up to the first freeze. Since these plants produce fruit on the present season's growth (new wood), some gardeners follow all the cultural recommendations described earlier to reduce the chance of disease.

Marauders

Rabbits can be a problem. During the winter they will eat as much of the cane as possible, down to the snow line or farther if there is little snow. This is not a problem for fall-bearing (primocane) varieties, since they produce berries on new wood, but it can eliminate or reduce crops of summer-bearing (floricane) types dramatically. When growing summer-bearing varieties of brambles, protect the plants with appropriate fencing. Note that deer will eat the foliage off plants, particularly in the fall.

Birds are allies to the organic gardener but can feed voraciously on ripe raspberries. Having grown both summer- and fall-bearing brambles in a number of ways, I have found the patch method clearly the best in protecting berries from birds, although it is the method least commonly recommended to the home gardener. I don't know why they shy away from patches, they just do. The other growing methods may require covering all plants with netting, both time-consuming and expensive to do.

Physiological

If berries on a plant are crumbly, it is probably caused by a virus. There is no cure, but some gardeners dig up unaffected plants and place them in a new location in the hope that they are not infected. If the problem is widespread, remove all plants, and start with new stock in a different site.

Propagation

Brambles are self-propagating. A number of varieties produce plantlets or suckers at the base or off to the side of the mother plant. These can be dug up in early spring and planted like a bare-root plant.

Blackberries and black raspberries have long, arching stems that bend over and touch the ground. Where the tips touch the ground, plants begin to form. This is the classic way that blackberries expand in the wild. Once the plantlets form roots, snip them off, and plant as you would a bare-root plant.

Brambles can also be propagated from cuttings (bud and stem), tip layering, and tissue culture. For information on these methods, see chapter 5.

Harvesting

Berries should be harvested when fully ripe, when it is warm and dry, and early in the day if possible. They have the best flavor and contain the most vitamins at this stage. Fully ripe berries slide off the plant easily. If they are immature, they resist picking. If they are too ripe, they begin to shrivel. To get them at the right stage, check berries daily. They do not ripen all at once. Berries often turn color before they are fully ripe. So let them mature until the color is rich, and the taste sweet.

Ripe berries will bruise easily and become mushy if handled roughly. When picking berries, place them in a shallow container since the weight of berries placed on top of others may damage them.

Storing

Eat berries as soon as possible after picking them. If you don't eat them right away, spread them out on a plate in a single layer and put them in the refrigerator for as short a time as possible. Wash them only when you are ready to eat them. Soak them briefly, and remove the rare "intruder."

To freeze, lay them out on a cookie sheet in a single layer, and flash freeze them. Wash or don't wash, but freeze dry. Slide them into freezer bags once frozen, removing as much air from the bag as possible. Label and freeze.

Culinary Uses

Fresh raspberries are one of the great delights of a home garden. But their firmness and texture are fleeting even when placed in the refrigerator. Use them immediately after picking. Purée and strain berries for a scrumptious sauce (coulis). Frozen berries are almost as good as fresh for jams, jellies, pies, sauces, and smoothies.

Varieties

Following is a list of brambles often mentioned in books, catalogs, and magazines. The varieties have been chosen with hardiness in mind. Other characteristics are mentioned but are only relevant if plants will survive in your area. If you live in the far north, choose a variety that will bloom well before a hard freeze.

The most highly recommended bramble for any area other than the far north is a red fall-bearing raspberry. This produces some berries the first year but abundant berries the following year. If you have room, grow one summer-bearing and one fall-bearing variety to begin with but in separate areas so you know which are which (label them). Depending on how you prune them, fall-bearing types produce berries either twice a year or over an extended period in fall. Summer-bearing produce lots of berries over

Blackberry plants are extremely spiny with bright-white flowers and succulent black fruits.

a relatively short period of time. The combination of the two is ideal.

Black, purple, and yellow raspberries (albino red raspberries) tend to have more "issues" than straightforward red berries—reduced hardiness and less tolerance to disease. For that reason, only one black ('Jewel'), two purples ('Brandywine' and 'Royalty'), and three yellow raspberries ('Anne', 'Fallgold', and 'Honeyqueen') are included in the table. 'Jewel', while a great black raspberry, is only marginally hardy. 'Royalty' tends to be more disease resistant than 'Brandywine', although some gardeners would dispute this. Although 'Anne' falls into this group, it is an excellent-producing plant. 'Fallgold' has good-tasting berries, but they tend to crumble, according to some growers. 'Honeyqueen' has an unusual floral taste that some describe as that of an apricot.

Red and yellow raspberries generally sucker freely, while black and purple varieties produce an abundance of canes from the base or crown of the plant. Some varieties grow more upright than others, while different varieties bend over or arch. The growth habit may dictate your preferred method of support or lack of it. Note that all named varieties are crosses. Consider them hybrids. I have also mentioned a few other plants in the *Rubus* genus because they are sometimes offered in catalogs. The comments will help you decide whether they might be worth growing.

Raspberries (Black, Purple, Red, Yellow-Red, also known as Albino)
Rubus idaeus, Rubus idaeus ssp. *strigosus, Rubus occidentalis, Rubus leucodermis*

VARIETY	COLOR	TYPE	HEIGHT (INCHES)	THORNINESS	FLAVOR	HARDINESS
'Anne'	Pale yellow	Fall	60	Quite thorny	Unusual; fruity	-30°F
'Autumn Bliss'	Dark red	Fall	72	Slightly thorny	Very good	-40°F
'Boyne' (early)	Dark red	Summer	60+	Quite thorny	Good	-40°F
'Brandywine' (late)	Purple red	Summer	72+	Very thorny	Good	-20°F
'Caroline'	Medium red	Fall	60	Quite thorny	Very good	-20°F
'Double Delight'	Medium red	Fall	60	Slightly thorny	Good to very good	-35°F
'Encore' (late mid)	Medium red	Summer	60	Slightly thorny	Very good	-25°F
'Fallgold'	Yellow	Fall	36+	Thorny	Unique (crumbly)	-20°F
'Heritage'	Red	Fall	60+	Quite thorny	Very good	-30°F
'Honeyqueen' (mid)	Amber gold	Summer	48	Quite thorny	Good; aromatic	-30°F
'Jewel' (mid)	Black	Summer	72+	Very thorny	Very good	-20°F
'Joan J'	Red	Fall	60	Thornless	Good to very good	-20°F
'Killarney' (early mid)	Light red	Summer	60+	Quite thorny	Very good	-30°F
'Latham' (mid)	Deep red	Summer	60+	Almost thornless	Good	-30°F
'Nova' (mid)	Light red	Summer	48	Slightly thorny	Very good	-40°F
'Polana'	Medium red	Fall	72	Slightly thorny	Fair to good	-30°F
'Polka'	Deep red	Fall	72	Slightly thorny	Good to very good	-30°F
'Royalty' (late)	Purple red	Summer	72+	Very thorny	Good to very good	-20°F

Blackberry
Rubus fruticosus

Blackberries, not to be confused with black raspberries, are very thorny, form lovely clusters of white flowers, and produce berries either in their first or second year of growth depending on the variety. If you live on the southern edge of the cold-climate region, you may want to gamble with 'Chester', 'Darrow', 'Triple Crown', or 'Ouachita'. The following two berries grow best on supports. Although said to be hardy to -30°F, that seems overly optimistic to me. They are self-fertile, but plant several plants to improve pollination and berry size.

VARIETY	COLOR	TYPE	HEIGHT (INCHES)	THORNINESS	FLAVOR	HARDINESS
'Prime Jan®'	Black	Fall	60+	Quite thorny	Good to very good	-20°F
'Prime Jim®'	Black	Fall	60+	Quite thorny	Good	-20°F

Boysenberry
Rubus idaeus (European raspberry) × Rubus fruticosus (blackberry) × Rubusloganobaccus (loganberry)

This dark-maroon berry is very good tasting, but the canes need lots of winter protection to survive in cold climates. Since they are not truly hardy, they are not recommended.

Cloudberry
Rubus chamaemorus

This low-growing (9-inch) bramble spreads through rhizomes and is extremely hardy (-40°F). Both male and female plants must be grown together, and the plant is demanding in its cultural needs: marshy conditions, acid soil with a pH of 5 or below, and afternoon shade if possible. Plants produce white flowers with a red blush and raspberry-like berries that are pale red turning to golden yellow. They are tart when young, and sweet when mature. They are used in Scandinavian countries for jams, juices, and liqueurs. The most commonly recommended are 'Apollo' (male), 'Fjellgull' (female), and 'Fjordgull' (female), but sources are difficult to find.

Dewberry
Rubus caesius, Rubus alleganiensis

Dewberries produce fruit on old wood, which is susceptible to dieback in cold climates. The berries tend to be larger than raspberries. Some blackberries are sold as dewberries. Consider them a gamble if your winter temperatures can dip below -15°F, although catalogs often list them as hardier than this.

Loganberry
Rubus × loganobaccus

This is probably a cross between a blackberry and raspberry. While delicious, the plant forms berries on old wood that is not reliably hardy in cold climates. It can be grown with extreme winter protection and is available.

Tayberry
Rubus fruticosus × idaeus

This is another blackberry-raspberry cross noted for its huge, tart berry, which many consider better than the loganberry. However, it is not reliably hardy in cold climates and demands winter protection in areas where winter temperatures dip below -15°F.

Tummelberry
Rubus cross

This is a hybrid, similar to a tayberry. Exactly what crosses were made to breed it remains controversial. While a nice berry, it too is really not suited to cold-climate gardening.

Wineberry
Rubus phoenicolasius

This Asian plant is available but generally not recommended for the home gardener. It has survived in some cold-climate areas, but there are better alternatives. If it survives, it can become invasive.

Once a rhubarb plant matures, harvest stems regularly and enjoy delicious treats such as rhubarb upside-down cake.

RHUBARB

Rheum rhabarbarum
Buckwheat or Knotweed Family (Polygonaceae)

Rhubarb is a perennial, very hardy, cold-season plant. Prized for its flavorful stalks, it grows prolifically in cold climates because it does best where the ground freezes each year. Rhubarb is easy to grow and demands only limited attention from the home gardener. These attractive plants appear unfailingly in the early spring of each year. Once rhubarb takes, it is a remarkably tough plant. Rhubarb is a vegetable that likely originated in China.

How Rhubarb Grows

Rhubarb grows from thin, light-tan seed edged dark brown (32,500 seeds per ounce) into a plant that forms a large, somewhat woody crown (rhizome) with roots and several buds. The buds ("eyes") develop into leaf stalks (petioles) with broad, green, elephant-ear leaves or into flower stalks with tiny, white flowers maturing into seeds. The leaves nourish the crown, which enlarges to produce yet more buds, so that the plant increases in size each year until it may be several feet tall and equally as wide or even larger. At the end of the season, the leaves die back. The following season in early spring the buds once again emerge to produce new leaves. With proper care the plant can last for decades, although it typically needs to be divided or placed in a new location every 5 to 7 years for best growth.

Where to Plant Rhubarb
Site and Light

Rhubarb prefers full sun, where it will produce the largest stalks, but it will tolerate some shade. Rhubarb is a perennial plant, so choose your site carefully. Once it is growing well, you don't want to be forced to move it, although you can. Plant it in an unused corner of the garden where the plants will not be bothered by yearly cultivation. Or plant it any location where it can grow undisturbed. It fits nicely into large perennial beds.

Soil and Moisture

Rhubarb thrives in rich, loose soil with a pH of 6 to 6.5. The soil should drain freely but stay moist in hot weather.

Prepare the bed by digging a 2-feet-deep and 3-feet-wide hole. Fill it with compost, rotted manure, or sphagnum peat moss mixed into the soil. Peat is slightly acidic and holds moisture well. However, it does not provide the nutrients of compost or rotted manure, so the combination is ideal.

Planting

It is possible, but generally not recommended, to start rhubarb from either purchased or collected seed. Seed is less reliable than purchasing plants since it may produce plants different from the parent. It takes 3 years to produce edible stems this way. Still, it can be fun. The light, flat seeds do well planted ¼ inch deep in humus-rich soil kept continually moist. They can take a long time to germinate. Some gardeners soak them for 2 hours before planting. You can either plant seed directly in the garden as soon as the ground can be worked in spring or start it indoors 6 to 8 weeks before the frost-free date. Typically, you want to get plants into the garden as soon as the soil can be worked. If started indoors, give seedlings planted in the garden some protection for 1 to 2 weeks until they take root and are growing vigorously.

Divisions (Potted Plants), Crowns

If you have a neighbor or friend with the kind of rhubarb you like, ask them for a division. Dividing plants helps them retain vigor. Most gardeners will gladly give you a little rhubarb. This way you will know exactly the type of rhubarb you will be growing.

Place the root division with the buds pointed up in the hole. The buds, or "eyes," should be 1 inch below the soil surface or barely protruding from it with larger divisions. The larger the division, the better. Divisions, or "crowns," are available through mail-order sources. *So are small budded pieces; when ordering, ask for a crown.* Press the soil into place, and water to remove air pockets. If gaps appear, fill in with soil.

Potted plants may be available at a local nursery. Prepare a planting hole, and slide the plant from the pot. Plant as you would a division. Keep the soil line the same as in the pot.

Spacing

Rhubarb plants can get remarkably large. Give them space to develop 3 to 4 feet in all directions. Often, one mature plant provides enough stems each year for a family of four.

When to Plant

Get your rhubarb into the garden as early in spring as possible. You can plant it later, but early planting is preferred. This gives the roots plenty of time to spread and for stems to begin maturing.

Nutrition Facts
Serving size: 100 grams (3.5 ounces)

	AMOUNT PER SERVING, COOKED WITH SUGAR	% DV
Calcium	145 mg	14%
Calories	116	6%
Carbohydrates	31 g	10%
Dietary fiber	2 g	8%
Vitamin K	21 mcg	25%

How to Care for Rhubarb
Watering

Rhubarb does well in consistently moist soil. Water the plant with a deep watering whenever the top few inches of soil dry out. The plant can withstand some drought when mature, but it tends to deteriorate and produce fewer leaves when stressed.

Mulch

Place a 4- to 6-inch layer of organic mulch, such as grass clippings or shredded leaves, around young plants as a 2- to 3-feet-wide collar. The mulch should not touch the base of the plant. As the plant matures, you can use less mulch each year since the thick leaves shade the ground. But adding a little mulch regularly is still a good idea to keep soil moist and cool, especially in hot or dry periods in midsummer.

Fertilizing

Side-dress with organic fertilizer once early in the season and again in late summer. Place well-rotted manure or a similar organic fertilizer around the base of each plant. Do not place it directly against the base of the stems. Nutrients will get to the roots with each watering.

Weeding

If any weeds appear, pull them immediately so that the young plants can establish themselves without competition. As plants mature, they form a canopy of leaves that deters most weed growth. Still, some weeds sprout underneath. Just reach under the plant and sweep your hand along the soil surface to feel and pull them out.

Pruning

Rhubarb will produce flower stalks. These often appear early in the season. Slide your hand down to the base of the stalk and yank upward. It will pop out. Do this with every flower stalk that appears. Most flower stalks appear early in the season, but a few will surprise you later on. Removing flower stalks keeps all of the plant's energy going into the crown rather than into seed production. Of course, if you want to save seed to start new plants from scratch, let one stalk mature to the seed stage. 'Chipman's Canada Red' and 'Valentine' are at least two varieties that produce few flower stalks, if the process of flower stalk removal bothers you. Also, pull off all mushy or yellow leaves throughout the season. It is easy to neglect plants some, but don't worry, the plant is constantly generating new growth.

Winter Protection

Rhubarb does not need a winter mulch, although providing one in the first year is playing it on the safe side. The use of a thick winter mulch, such as straw or whole leaves, stops the plant from producing growth as early as it normally would the following spring. Remove the mulch as soon as the weather warms up. If you leave it on, it could cause the crown to rot out.

Special Considerations

Note that the leaves of rhubarb are technically toxic, but you have to eat a lot of them to get really sick. Eat only the stems. Like sorrel, this plant contains high amounts of oxalic acid, which can be a problem for people with gout, kidney problems, or rheumatoid arthritis. Compost all leaves. The acid breaks down in the compost pile and causes no problems.

There are many different species of rhubarb plants. Some are highly valued as ornamental plants for the perennial garden. The flowers of garden varieties can be used in dried floral arrangements. Let one or two flower stalks emerge and go to seed. Cut the flowers as the seeds begin to dry. Hang them upside down in a dry, airy place. Once completely dry, mist them with hair spray and combine with other dried flowers.

Extending the Season

It is possible to force rhubarb indoors by planting a portion of crown in a pot after the plant dies down, letting it freeze for 3 weeks, and then bringing it indoors. With the large green types, taking a division does little harm, and the stalks produced indoors are light pink and delicious. However, freezing individual stems throughout the growing season makes this extra work a bit pointless.

Problems
Insects

Insects are not a common problem with rhubarb. I have heard reports of Japanese beetles feeding on rhubarb. I grow rhubarb next to raspberries covered with Japanese beetles and have never seen one on the rhubarb. You may see a few holes appearing in the leaves, but this rarely interferes with the production of juicy, tart stems. Sometimes, slugs will cause minor damage. Just squish them with your fingers. They feed at night.

Disease

Prevent disease by starting with healthy stock. Plant rhubarb in well-drained soil to prevent root rot. If leaves show signs of disease, just pull them off. Lower leaves touching soil often turn slimy and mushy. Remove these immediately. Then place mulch around the plant to keep the leaves off the ground. Clean up all debris at the end of the season, leaving the crown bare. If the crown of the plant rots out or if the plant dies back completely, dig up the plant and burn. This is rare. Plant a new plant in a different spot.

Physiological

Stalks left on the ground turn mushy and slimy. Remove and compost any yellowing stems before this happens. This is primarily an aesthetic problem, but why tempt fate.

Propagation

Many gardeners divide rhubarb plants every 5 years. If your rhubarb plant is healthy and producing lots of stems, this is certainly not necessary. Some plants last longer than a decade before needing renewal. However, plants may begin to get weak as time goes by. They produce fewer and thinner stalks. In this case, dividing the plant and renewing the soil with organic material makes good sense.

Dig up the entire plant early in the season as soon as the ground thaws. Some roots may break off. Don't worry about this. With a spade cut the crown into several pieces. Each part of the crown should have roots and at least two, preferably more, buds. The buds are bulges on top of the crown. On smaller divisions, pull away the dark-brown sheath (ocrea) at the base of the stem. Plant each division (thong) immediately in a separate hole filled with a mixture of compost, rotted manure, and peat. The buds, or eyes, should be about 1 inch below the soil surface or closer to the surface on larger divisions. Soak the plants with water.

If you ask in advance, an acquaintance, neighbor, or family member may want a division. Have them present to take it home just after you divide the crown. It should be planted right away. It's a gift that can last for decades with proper care.

It is possible to grow rhubarb from seed. If you want seed, let one stem bloom and form seed. Let seed dry on the stem. Cut off the tip of the stem into a bag, and dry. Seed lasts up to 1 year. Seedlings show great variability in the color of stalks produced. Seed of 'Glaskin's Perpetual' is sometimes sold, but it too produces a wide range of plants. Keep only the most desirable plants, culling the rest.

Harvesting

Do not harvest during the first year. Rhubarb needs time to build up a healthy root system. If you pull stems on young plants, you stunt the plant's growth. However, if any leaf turns yellow, it should be removed. Let all the stems with healthy green foliage grow throughout the entire season.

During the second year, harvest lightly for several weeks. Pick only a few stems. Let the others mature. In subsequent years, harvest heavily for 6 weeks or so in the beginning of each season. Each year the first rhubarb is always the best. You can harvest lightly later in the season; just pay close attention to how the plant is growing. If stems are weak or spindly as the season progresses, don't harvest at all!

Rhubarb is grown for its stems. To harvest these, slide your hand down to the base of the stem and pull up with a sharp twisting motion. The base of the stem normally pops out. If a stem breaks, keep the upper portion, but reach down and pull again until the lower part of the stem pulls free. Cut off the base of each stem and the upper leaf portion. Never eat any portion of the plant other than the stem, since the leafy areas contain poisonous oxalic acid (calcium oxalate). Warn children about this. They can suck on the bitter stems but must not chew the leaves.

Always pull out the largest leaves first. These are the ones closest to the ground. Regular harvesting stimulates the plant to create new stalks (petioles). Always leave at least half of the leaves on the plant.

Storing

Stalks will store for about 1 to 2 weeks in a plastic bag in the crisper of your refrigerator.

To freeze, remove leaves and tough ends from stems. Freeze these whole, cut into 1-inch pieces, or cook and purée. Use within a few months. Blanching for 1 minute is optional before cooling, draining, and placing in airtight freezer bags. Or cook and cover with honey or sugar syrup before packing. The latter method is more long lasting but time-consuming.

To dry, slice into 1-inch diagonal pieces, steam for up to 2 minutes, then dry in a dehydrator. These may last for up to 4 months.

Culinary Uses

Rhubarb is sometimes called "pie plant," an indication of how commonly it has been used in strawberry-rhubarb pie. Rhubarb upside-down cake is another favorite. Red rhubarb tastes better than green, but the two mixed together are still delicious. Young stems are preferred, but older are larger and give you more rhubarb. Though optional, some people peel larger stems.

Use rhubarb in breads, cakes, cobblers, jams, muffins, and pies. Strawberry rhubarb jam is always a hit. Strawberries often ripen soon after rhubarb is maturing. If your strawberries ripen at a different time, simply freeze rhubarb stems until ready for use.

To make a simple sauce, boil 4 cups of clean rhubarb cut into 1-inch pieces in a little water with 1 cup sugar. To make rhubarb juice, chop up a number of stalks, and boil them in water. Strain to separate the pulp. Let the bright juice cool down. Mix a few tablespoons into a cool glass of water for a refreshing drink. Few people eat rhubarb raw, since it is quite sour and bitter.

Varieties

The best-tasting varieties produce lovely, deep-red stalks, red from the crown right up to the base of the leaf. The green varieties produce more and thicker stalks. Growing one variety of each is highly recommended. Although only two green varieties are listed below, you can often find green rhubarb plants locally. Start from plants, not seed.

VARIETY	STALK COLOR
'Canada Red' (see 'Chipman's Canada Red')	
'Cawood Delight'	Red
'Chipman's Canada Red'*****	Red
'Crimson Cherry' (see 'Crimson Red')	
'Crimson Red'	Red
'Crimson Wine' (see 'Crimson Red')	
'Glaskin's Perpetual'	Green with red base
'MacDonald'	Red
'Starkrimson'®	Red
'Strawberry'	Pink red
'Valentine'	Red
'Victoria'	Green with red base

Give this root crop a try. It can be eaten raw or cooked and was once a staple in home gardens.

RUTABAGA

Brassica napus var. ***napobrassica*** or Napobrassica Group
Cabbage or Mustard Family (Brassicaceae, formerly Cruciferae)

Rutabagas are hardy to very hardy, cool- to cold-season biennials grown as annuals. Rutabagas are similar to turnips, but some would say they have a more delicate flavor. They are an excellent fall crop in cold climates, prolific and good for storing. They do take a long time to mature. Rutabagas and turnips are often confused, and the following common names for rutabagas don't help: Canadian turnip, mangel-wurzel, Russian turnip, swede, Swedish turnip, table turnip, turnip-rooted cabbage, winter turnip, and yellow turnip. Rutabagas probably originated in Russia and Scandinavia.

How Rutabagas Grow

Rutabagas are a cross between a cabbage and a turnip. They grow from a small, hard, round, brownish purple-black seed (about 9,500 to 10,000 seeds per ounce). Plants produce ever-larger, bluish-green leaves as they mature. The smooth, waxy leaves are thick, resembling those of cabbage or kale to some degree. The foliage provides nutrients to develop an enlarged root below. The upper portion or neck of this "root" is really stem tissue. Just below is a true root, which expands rapidly in cool weather, often producing many side roots and a long taproot. If plants were to survive a winter, they would produce stalks with small, yellow flowers shaped like a cross in the following season.

Where to Plant Rutabagas
Site and Light

Rutabagas grow best in sunny, cool locations. Place them in full sun. If you live in an area with cool summers, fine. If not, the cool part of the equation is difficult to provide, so time your planting for the roots to mature in fall.

Soil and Moisture

Rutabagas grow best in loose soil that drains freely but retains moisture during dry weather. Add compost, sphagnum peat moss, or well-rotted manure on the bottom of the planting row unless you have enough to mix into the entire bed. If your soil is compacted or rocky, build a raised bed. The soil should have a pH of roughly 6.5 to 7. Mix organic fertilizer into the soil to encourage rapid root growth. Good fertilizers include bonemeal, gypsum, and wood ash or dolomitic limestone applied in fall. These provide calcium, phosphorus, and potassium—all helpful for this plant's growth. The plants need some nitrogen, but go easy on it. It may cause misshapen roots. Boron and magnesium (found in Epsom salts) are also important in tiny amounts. Most garden soil amended with organic matter contains enough of these micronutrients.

Container

Growing rutabagas in containers is not recommended but is certainly possible in large, 10-gallon containers. Soil must be loose, drain freely, but retain moisture. Do not let the soil dry out. In my opinion, this is not worth the bother.

Planting
Seed

The hard, black seed of rutabagas is very small and round. Plant it about ¼ to ½ inch deep depending on your soil type—deeper in sand, more shallow in loam. Rub the seed between your thumb and forefinger, trying to space it an inch or so apart. Firm the soil in place, cover with an ultra-thin layer of mulch, and water immediately. Germination generally occurs within 10 days, often sooner.

Transplants

It is possible to start seed indoors, but this makes little sense since you want the roots to mature in cool fall weather. These plants resent root disturbance.

Spacing

Plant close together initially. Then follow the guidelines described under "Thinning."

When to Plant

Rutabagas need to mature in cool weather. In cold climates that means planting them roughly 75 to 120 days before the first expected fall frost, depending on the variety planted. Rutabagas often taste better after a good frost. If you plant rutabagas too early, they may mature in high heat, which makes them woody and bitter. In most cold-climate areas the majority of varieties are planted as soon as the soil can be worked when soil temperature reaches 50°F, or approximately in early July for quicker-maturing varieties.

Nutrition Facts
Serving size: 100 grams (3.5 ounces)

	AMOUNT PER COOKED SERVING	% DV
Calories	39	2%
Carbohydrates	9 g	3%
Dietary fiber	2 g	8%
Manganese	0.2 mg	9%
Potassium	325 mgs	9%
Protein	1 g	2%
Vitamin C	19 mgs	31%

How to Care for Rutabagas
Water

During the early stage of growth, water consistently. As the plants mature, cut down on watering, but do not let the soil dry out completely, to prevent roots from splitting and possibly to reduce the incidence of powdery mildew. Also, rutabagas need to develop quickly to taste good. However, they do have a long taproot and are more resistant to drought than turnips.

Mulch

Place a very thin, ⅛- to ¼-inch mulch over the soil at seeding. This keeps the soil moist and cool and helps germination. Once seedlings are growing vigorously, apply a thicker mulch around the outer edges of the developing plants. This continues to keep soil temperature even as well as reducing the need for watering and weeding.

Fertilizing

If you have added organic matter and organic fertilizers to the soil at planting time, rutabagas do not need much additional feeding. Kelp fertilizer applied to the soil 4 to 6 weeks after planting may give roots a boost. However, too much nitrogen may create lush foliage growth at the expense of good root development.

Weeding

Weed carefully to stop all competition for water and nutrients. Don't cultivate, but hand weed around the base of plants to avoid damaging the developing roots. This is especially important around seedlings. Continue to pull weeds from mulch as the season progresses.

Thinning

Thinning is important. Rutabagas can get much larger than turnips. If young seedlings are crowded, thin the plants to

3 inches apart. When they are about 2 to 4 inches high, thin to 6 inches. When they are 6 inches high, you may want to thin to 10 inches. Look at the tops. Leaves should barely touch. This may be a bit extreme, but rutabagas do not form large roots if they are too close together. If plants form mostly tops and poor roots, they have not been thinned enough. Although edible, few people eat the greens. In this way rutabagas are different from turnips, whose greens are delicious.

Problems

Insects

Rutabagas are susceptible to aphids, flea beetles, and root maggots. Cabbage loopers, cutworms, and imported cabbage worms are other potential threats. You can avoid most problems with mechanical barriers and floating row covers.

Disease

Clubroot can be a problem. Calcium in the soil helps prevent the formation of these distorted roots. Adding a little lime or wood ash in the fall also helps prevent this by increasing the soil pH to a slightly alkaline level. There are more than a dozen races of clubroot. Read catalogs carefully to see whether the variety you are ordering is resistant. 'Marian' and 'York' claim to be resistant to some races. Problems like black leg, black rot, downy mildew, powdery mildew, rhizoctonia rot, scab, and turnip mosaic virus are relatively rare in the home garden. Dig up and destroy any diseased plant to stop the spread of an infection.

Marauders

Rutabagas are rarely bothered. The oxalates in the greens are bad for rabbits.

Physiological

Brown heart describes a condition where the inside of the roots rot out. This may be caused by a boron deficiency in the soil. The addition of compost and kelp fertilizer to the soil should provide enough boron to prevent brown heart. Boron is less available to plants at a higher pH, but the latter helps prevent clubroot. That puts the home gardener in a quandary. Don't worry about either until they are actually a problem. Brown heart is sometimes called water-core.

Roots may crack if watering is inconsistent, if plants are over fertilized, and if weather is particularly hot and humid. Water well during hot, dry weather.

Bolting or flowering in the first season is uncommon but usually caused by planting seed very early in the season. If young plants are exposed to prolonged periods of cold, they are stimulated to produce flowering stems. This would only be a plus for seed savers, not for the average gardener looking for a good edible crop.

Propagation

These are biennials and form seed in their second year of growth. Rutabagas are hermaphroditic, with each plant having both male and female organs. The plants must be insect pollinated. It is difficult getting plants through cold winters. A heavy straw mulch and lots of snow may protect them, but usually they rot out unless pulled up and stored in a cool, humid area where they will not freeze. However, you may get some roots to flower if you plant them very early in the year. Hot weather may result in their bolting. Seed lasts roughly 4 to 5 years.

Harvesting

A fall crop is usually better than a summer crop in cold climates. Cool weather enhances the roots' flavor by converting starches in the roots to sugar. Pick the roots after a couple of frosts, but harvest before the ground freezes and when the soil is dry. Always try a few smaller roots as well as larger ones to see which flavor you prefer. Flavor varies from "peppery cabbage" to "nutty."

Pulling up roots is sometimes possible, but digging them up is easier. Twist or cut off the leaves about 1 inch above the top of the root. Cut off long taproots. Roots should feel heavy for their size. If they feel light, the flesh is often woody.

Storing

For short-term storage, place unwrapped roots in the crisper of your refrigerator. They may last for up to 14 days but are best used within 7.

Rutabagas store extremely well, better than turnips. Root cellars are the best place for storage, but few gardeners have them anymore. Indoors, they will last for about 2 months if kept at 50°F in a dry, dark, well-ventilated area. These conditions are also hard to find in homes. Since they can give off an unpleasant odor, consider outdoor storage instead.

Place them in a container filled with moist leaf mold, sand, sawdust, or sphagnum peat moss. The roots should not touch. Or set them in a plastic basket filled with dry oak leaves. Keep them in the garage. Ideally, temperatures should be between 32°F and 40°F. They may last up to 3 months stored in this way as long as they do not freeze.

Or gamble by leaving the roots in the ground. Cover them with a 12- to 18-inch of loose leaves or straw, and dig them up, even through snow, as you need them throughout late fall and early winter. If the roots freeze, they will rot out.

To freeze, remove tops, wash, peel, slice or dice, scald 2 to 3 minutes, cool in ice water, drain, seal, label, and freeze.

Culinary Uses

Few people eat rutabaga greens, although they are edible. If you want greens, harvest very lightly before leaves are a few inches tall. Harvest only one or two leaves from each plant. Or plant seeds late enough so that young leaves emerge to be sweetened by fall frosts. When roots are packed for storage, the sheared tops may begin to sprout. This new, rather delicate growth appeals to some more than leaves produced during the regular growing season.

Rutabagas are denser and sweeter than turnips. Peel the roots before use. They are edible raw and have a "nutty" taste. They can be shredded, grated, or julienned and added to salads and slaws or even sliced for dips.

More often they are cooked for a peppery cabbage flavor. Their texture makes them a good substitute for potatoes. Dice, quarter, or slice. Steam whole or sliced, and butter. Boil and mash with potatoes, add in chunks to vegetable soups and stews, or slice into thin strips and mix into stir-fries—delicious.

In some countries rutabagas are used in cakes with sugar and lemon to replace apples.

For fries, cut into ¼-inch strips, fry in 300°F oil for a couple of minutes, cool briefly, then place for several minutes in an oven at 375°F.

For roasting, peel, cut into wedges, cover in oil, and roast whole at 325°F until done. They can be placed alongside meats as you would sliced carrots or other vegetables during baking.

Varieties

Most rutabagas have yellow to light-orange flesh. Some have white, which often turns yellowish when cooked. 'Gilfeather' and 'York' are often listed in catalogs as turnips but are actually rutabagas. Root colors vary by variety. The top portion of the root, or "shoulder," is often another color. These colors do not affect taste but help in identifying the variety. Note that rutabagas may be a cross between *Brassica oleracea* var. *acephala* (collards and kale) and *Brassica napa* var. *rapifera* (turnip).

VARIETY	DAYS	ROOT/SHOULDER/FLESH
'American Purple Top' (heirloom)*****	90	Tan yellow/purple/cream yellow
'American Purple Top Yellow' (heirloom)	90	White/purple/yellow
'Burpee's Purple Top' (heirloom)	90	White to yellow/purple/light yellow
'Champion A Collet Rouge' (heirloom)	100	Yellow/purple red/yellow
'Collet Vert' (heirloom)	75	Yellow/green/light yellow
'German Green Top' (see 'Wilhelmsburger')		
'Gilfeather' (heirloom)	90	White/slightly green/white
'Helenor Hybrid'	90	White tan/purple/light orange yellow
'Improved American Purple Top' (see 'Laurentian')		
'Joan' (heirloom)	95	Yellow/purple/yellow
'Laurentian' (heirloom)*****	95	Tan yellow/purple/cream yellow
'Macomber' (heirloom)	90	White/light green/white
'Marian' (heirloom)	90	White/purple/yellow
'Melford' (heirloom)	100	Tan/green/yellow
'Nadmorska' (heirloom)	90	Whitish tan/green/yellowish gold
'Norfolk Green' (heirloom)	85	White/medium green/yellow
'Norfolk Red' (heirloom)	85	White/pink red/yellow
'Purple Prince Hybrid'	55	White/purple/yellow
'Wilhelmsburger' (heirloom)	90	Tan/green/cream yellow to gold
'York' (heirloom)	115	White/purple/cream yellow

Spinach is a great cool-season crop; some varieties survive well into winter with adequate snowfall.

SPINACH

Spinacea oleracea species
Amaranth or Goosefoot Family (Amaranthaceae, formerly Chenopodiaceae)

Spinach is a very hardy, cool- to cold-season annual. Grown quickly in ideal conditions, it takes up very little space and produces some of the most delicious greens in the garden. It is a tough plant, able to withstand cold in both spring and fall. It is the ideal plant for interplanting, especially with later-maturing crops, such as broccoli or Brussels sprouts. Spinach probably originated in Persia, mainly in Iran, and some varieties are possibly from Southeast Asia.

How Spinach Grows

Spinach seed is moderately small, smooth or prickly, and typically tan to dark brown (about 2,500 to 3,000 seeds per ounce). The seedlings have elongated leaves. As the plant grows, leaves fill out and get increasingly large. The oval, pointed, or rounded leaves may be smooth or crinkly (savoyed). As the plants mature, they send up a long central stem. Leaves appear to swirl around it, getting ever smaller toward the tip. Yellow-green flowers bloom, maturing into elongated pods that eventually turn dry and brittle. Each pod contains several seeds.

Where to Plant
Site and Light

Spinach can grow in various light conditions but prefers full sun in spring, partial shade in summer, then full sun again in fall. It often bolts during the long, hot days of summer. When exposed to 14 to 16 hours of light, the uppermost leaves produce a hormone (florigen) that signals the plant to bolt. Providing shade at this time helps somewhat. Consider placing spinach in the shade of plants being grown on a vertical support.

Soil and Moisture

Spinach grows best in loose, fertile soil that drains freely but retains moisture during dry spells. Sand is ideal, but if you have another type of soil, mix in lots of organic matter. If your soil is compacted, build a raised bed. These warm up quickly in spring, allowing for and demanding superearly seed planting. In the fall before spring planting, adding a little lime for magnesium or wood ash for potassium helps. Lime also creates a more alkaline soil. Don't go overboard—just a little of each. The soil should have a pH of 6.5 to 6.9, which is slightly acidic to neutral. In spring, mix into the soil any organic fertilizer high in nitrogen.

Container

Spinach grows well in containers. Planting in containers is a good way to handle a rabbit problem. Keep plants consistently moist and well fed in a *large* pot with loose soil that drains freely through holes in the bottom of the pot. Large pots require less frequent watering. The baby-leaf types listed in the varietal list, such as 'Baby's Leaf Hybrid', are particularly recommended for this use.

Planting

Seed

Plant spinach in rows or wide beds. Make a shallow furrow for rows, planting seed ¼ to ½ inch deep depending on the type of soil. Cover seed with sifted soil. Firm and moisten immediately. Place an ultrathin layer of mulch over the soil to keep it from crusting. Keep consistently moist at all times. Fresh seed usually sprouts within 14 days. Broadcasting seed over a wide bed also works well. Cover the seed with a thin layer of soil, or rake it into soil if it is loose enough.

Spinach seed is really an enclosed fruit (utricle). It will sometimes germinate faster, especially if old, if you soak it overnight but no longer than 24 hours, if you freeze it for a few days (stratification), or if you place it in a moist towel in the refrigerator until it begins to sprout. After any of these treatments, plant seed immediately in the garden.

Transplant

Start seed indoors only for late-summer plantings when the soil outdoors can be extremely hot. Plant in individual pots about 3 weeks before you intend to plant outdoors. Keep moist and humid until germination occurs. Move into brighter light. Keep consistently moist. Plant out when temperatures begin to drop. This does not always work out well, since fall temperatures are hard to predict.

Spacing

Plant seed about 1 inch apart in spring. In fall, plant even closer since germination is erratic in warmer soil.

Nutrition Facts
Serving size: 100 grams (3.5 ounces)

	AMOUNT PER RAW SERVING	% DV	AMOUNT PER COOKED SERVING	% DV
Calcium	100 mg	10%	135 mg	15%
Calories	23	1%	23	1%
Carbohydrates	4 g	1%	4 g	1%
Dietary fiber	2.5 g	10%	2.5 g	10%
Folate	195 mcg	50%	145 mcg	35%
Iron	2.7 mg	15%	3.6 mg	20%
Magnesium	80 mg	20%	80 mg	20%
Manganese	0.9 mg	45%	0.9 mg	45%
Potassium	560 mg	15%	465 mg	13%
Protein	3 g	6%	3 g	6%
Riboflavin	0.2 mg	15%	0.2 mg	15%
Vitamin A	9,375 IU	190%	10,480 IU	210%
Vitamin B6	0.2 mg	10%	0.2 mg	10%
Vitamin C	28 mg	47%	9.8 mg	15%
Vitamin E	2 mg	10%	2 mg	10%
Vitamin K	485 mcg	605%	485 mg	605%

When to Plant

Spinach grows best during the cooler temperatures of spring and fall. The ideal growing temperature is 40°F over a period of 7 weeks. That's a large bill to fill in some areas. As soon as you can work the soil in spring, plant seed directly in the garden. That is roughly 4 to 6 weeks before the last expected spring frost. Sow seed at 10-day intervals until warm weather arrives. This successive planting gives you fresh leaves more continuously. Some people see this as a nuisance and grow one large crop to be harvested and frozen all at once.

Spinach seed does not germinate well in soil warmer than 75°F. Spinach planted in the middle of the summer often bolts and goes to seed. The leaves are small and unappetizing when this happens. Plant a bit later, roughly 4 to 6 weeks before the first expected fall frost, typically in middle to late August, depending on where you live. Plant seed more thickly at this time, since germination will be erratic in warmer soil. Keep the soil as cool as possible with consistent watering and the use of organic mulch.

Some gardeners plant a short row of spinach seed just before the ground freezes with the hope that new growth will appear in early spring when the soil becomes just warm enough for germination. This is a gamble but worth a try. Even if seed begins to sprout, it may winter over with good snow cover. If in doubt, cover the row with a thick layer of loose straw. Be sure to remove the straw very early the following spring.

How to Care for Spinach

Water

Quality and quantity of the spinach crop depend entirely on the amount of moisture and nitrogen available to the plants. Keep the plants well supplied with water. Consistent watering helps develop foliage and prevents bolting to some degree. Spinach has a limited root system. Sprinkling in midday may also delay bolting some. Drip irrigation is also effective since it provides even watering over a period of weeks. If possible, do not spray foliage unless you do it early in the day to give it a chance to dry out.

Mulch

As soon as seedlings germinate in spring, place organic mulch along the row but not against the stems of the young plants. Mulch is the easiest way to create a good growing environment for the plant. It also stops soil from splashing on leaves, which helps prevent disease and makes cleaning leaves less of a chore at harvest time.

In late summer, place a thick layer of mulch over the area where you intend to plant seeds for a fall crop. Just before planting, push the mulch aside. The soil will be moist and relatively cool. Plant seed immediately, and push mulch up close to where it has been planted.

Fertilizing

The secret to lots of spinach is quick growth. Moisture, fertile soil, and cool weather—that's the ideal combination. Once the plant has grown four leaves, pour dilute fish emulsion around the base. Fertilize again after the first few weeks of growth with fish emulsion, blood meal, or cottonseed meal. The goal is to stimulate plants to form abundant foliage. Each time you harvest lots of leaves, apply some more fertilizer to the soil.

Weeding

Handpick all weeds before they get large and compete with the seedlings for nutrients and water. If weeds sprout close to or within germinating seeds, snip them off with a scissors. This prevents pulling up seedlings along with the weeds. Do not cultivate close to the base of spinach plants, since they are shallow rooted. Let your mulch prevent weed growth.

Thinning

When leaves are about 4 to 6 inches long, thin tightly planted seedlings to about 4 inches apart. This is usually about 4 to 6 weeks or so after planting. Use the plants removed from the row in salads.

Pruning

Extend harvesting somewhat by cutting off flower stems just as they begin to appear. Cutting plants back to 2 inches is also a form of pruning with the same goal. Plants often resprout.

Winter Protection

A fall crop may survive to spring with winter protection. Water the plants just before the first expected freeze. Cover them with a 12-inch layer of winter mulch, such as straw or whole leaves, as soon as the soil actually begins to freeze. Remove the mulch immediately when the weather gets warm in spring to avoid rot in newly emerging foliage.

Special Considerations

Spinach tends to bolt as days get longer and hotter. Once plants begin forming flower stems, leaves become more bitter. Varieties do vary in their bolt resistance.

Spinach contains oxalic acid. This can be a concern for people with gout, kidney problems, or rheumatoid arthritis. The oxalic content does drop somewhat when leaves are cooked. If you are on a blood thinner such as warfarin (Coumadin), talk to your doctor. Spinach is high in vitamin K.

Extending the Season

To extend the season in spring or fall, grow plants under plastic tunnels or in cold frames. Spinach tolerates hard frosts and temperatures down to 25°F and a bit lower for some varieties. It does not tolerate high heat, which can be generated under plastic even when it is cold outside. So the use of protection demands attention. Ideally, plants should be growing well before there is 10 hours of daylight.

Problems

Spinach is a tough plant and has only a few problems. Since you will be eating the leaves, avoid the use of chemicals. Prevent problems, and use simple cures whenever possible.

Insects

Control aphids by washing them off with a jet of water. Spinach leafminers cause brown blotches to appear on leaves, while flea beetles make tiny holes. Both are best prevented with row covers.

Disease

Spinach is vulnerable to cucumber mosaic virus, downy mildew (many races), fusarium, and white rust. If you experience a problem, choose disease-resistant varieties. Keep your soil "airy" and loose so that it drains freely to cut down on disease, especially in clay soils. Space plants for better air circulation, and rotate crops regularly.

Marauders

The main enemy of spinach is rabbits. Deer can also nibble off the tops at the oddest of times. Fence them out of the garden.

Physiological

If leaves begin to turn yellow (chlorosis), the soil may be too alkaline. On the other hand, if soil is too acidic, the tips and edges of leaves may turn yellow. Generally, if you have added lots of organic matter to the soil before planting, it should be in the correct pH range. High heat often causes plants to bolt or flower.

Propagation

Most spinach plants are either male or female (dioecious). Relatively few are both male and female (monoecious). If you want to keep seed, grow only one open-pollinated variety. Let a number of plants go to seed, the more the better. Flowers are wind pollinated. Let seeds dry as long as possible on the plant. Then hang upside down in a dry place. Cover the seed heads with a paper bag. Remove all debris, keep seeds, and store in an envelope in a cool, dry, dark place. Seed may be either smooth or prickly depending on the variety. Seed deteriorates each year. It is always best to use fresh seed. Seed may be viable for up to 3 years, but germination becomes more erratic and less likely. Some gardeners place seeds in a plastic bag filled with moist peat and chill them in the refrigerator for 3 months.

Harvesting

Harvest outer leaves when just 2 to 3 inches long. Keep harvesting as needed, leaving the central bud alone. Or harvest the whole plant when it is 6 to 8 inches tall, either by pulling it up or cutting it back to 2 inches. If you cut it back, it will often sprout again. Spinach is considered a good "cut and come again" crop. As warmer weather arrives, leaves become increasingly bitter with a more metallic taste. Some gardeners notice that spring and fall plantings of the same variety have a bit of a difference in flavor. This may be the result of sugars building up after cold fall weather. Whenever you pick spinach, plunge it into ice water.

Storing

To store in refrigerator, rinse leaves under cold running water, shake off excess moisture, roll in barely damp paper towels so that the leaves are not touching, place in a large plastic container with lid on in the crisper of the refrigerator. Use the leaves as soon as possible since the leaf edges turn brown and even rot in time. Do not store with apples in the refrigerator, since they emit ethylene gas.

To freeze, wash, remove stems from older leaves, place in sieve, plunge into boiling water for 30 seconds to 1½ minutes depending on thickness of leaves, lift up, drain, place into ice water for 2 minutes, then into airtight freezer bags, and freeze. Note that spinach does lose vitamins when blanched. Some people prefer cooking it for less than a minute in the microwave instead of plunging it into boiling water. Leaves can be frozen whole, chopped up, or puréed.

Culinary Uses

Spinach is edible raw or cooked. For fresh use, wash all leaves carefully, especially if they are a crinkly variety, since they can hide bits of sand and dirt. Plunge into ice water if at all wilted, and pat or spin dry. Try to avoid bruising the leaves. Remove pithy stems on older leaves. Leaves can be used to make pesto or can be combined with artichoke for a dip. They also make a good bed for other dishes.

Cook leaves cut, shredded, or whole. Cook them as quickly as possible, either boiling, microwaving, steaming, or stir-frying. If washed, simply cook spinach in a pan by itself. Steam briefly, no longer than 1 minute, with a little butter if desired. Leaves shrink dramatically. Ten cups of fresh leaves will cook down to 1 cup of cooked spinach, about enough for two to three people. Serve with melted butter, and season with salt and pepper. Or splash with lemon juice or vinegar. Or cover with bits of bacon, boiled egg, or shredded cheese. Add it to any number of dishes, including lasagna, omelets, and soups. Or sauté it quickly in garlic butter or olive oil (dry the leaves in this instance) for a side dish or topping to pasta. Add it to stuffings for a little added flavor and a lot of extra nutrients.

Varieties

There are two main types of spinach: crinkly (savoy) and smooth-leaf. The crinkly types tend to produce lots of thick, rich-green leaves. They are harder to clean but very flavorful. The smooth-leaf varieties appeal to commercial growers and restaurants because they wash more easily. For some, shape and color are also important. Shapes vary from arrowhead (Asian) to rounded, and color is usually mid to deep green. To brighten fresh salads, choose 'Red Kitten Hybrid' with its magenta stems.

Other factors in choosing varieties include days to maturity, the leaf texture, resistance to disease, and whether they tend to bolt easily. The term *long-standing* equals "slow to bolt."

Faster-growing types mature best in cool weather and include the term *baby* in the following table. Slower-maturing types can withstand heat better. For example, 'Olympia' and 'Tyee' hybrids do reasonably well as summer plantings. 'Avon', 'Carmel', 'Indian Summer', 'Melody', 'Racoon', 'Razzle Dazzle', and 'Tyee' hybrids are good choices for a fall crop. The heirlooms 'Bloomsdale Long Standing' and 'Winter Bloomsdale' as well as the hybrids 'Avon' and 'Tyee' may survive winters with winter protection.

VARIETY	DAYS	LEAF FORM/COLOR	COMMENT
'America' (heirloom) (AAS-1952)	50	Crinkly/dark green	Bolt resistant
'Avon Hybrid'	45	Semicrinkly/dark green	Somewhat bolt resistant
'Baby's Leaf Hybrid'	30	Smooth/light green	Good baby
'Benton No. 2 Hybrid'	45	Semicrinkly/dark green	Bolt resistant
'Bloomsdale' (heirloom)	45	Crinkly/dark green	Good spring and fall
'Bloomsdale Long Standing' (heirloom)*****	50	Crinkly/medium to dark green	Bolt resistant
'Carmel Hybrid'	30	Semicrinkly/medium green	Good baby
'Charger Hybrid'	35	Smooth/medium green	Good baby
'Early Hybrid No. 7'	45	Semicrinkly/medium green	Somewhat bolt resistant
'Emu Hybrid'	45	Mildly crinkly/mid green	Very bolt resistant
'Galilee' (heirloom)	40	Frilly/light green	Heat tolerant
'Giant Noble' (heirloom) (AAS-1933)	45	Mildly crinkly/dark green	Huge pointed leaves
'Harmony Hybrid'	45	Very crinkly/dark green	Bolt resistant
'Indian Summer Hybrid'*****	40	Semicrinkly/dark green	Bolt resistant
'Lorelay' (heirloom)	55	Mildly crinkly/bright green	Bolt resistant
'Melody Hybrid' (AAS-1977)*****	45	Semicrinkly/dark green	Good spring and fall
'Monnopa' (heirloom)	45	Smooth/medium green	Low oxalic acid and bolt resistant
'Olympia Hybrid'	45	Smooth/dark green	Bolt resistant
'Palco Hybrid'	40	Semicrinkly/glossy green	Bolt resistant
'Picasso Hybrid'	35	Semicrinkly/dark green	Good baby and bolt resistant
'Racoon (Raccoon) Hybrid'	35	Smooth/dark green	Good spring and fall
'Razzle Dazzle Hybrid'	30	Smooth/medium green	Arrow-shaped leaves
'Red Kitten Hybrid'	35	Smooth/green with red veins	Good baby
'Regal Hybrid'	35	Semicrinkly/bright green	Good baby
'Regatta Hybrid'	45	Mildly crinkly/dark green	Bolt resistant
'Renegade Hybrid'	35	Mildly crinkly/dark green	Arrow-shaped leaves
'7-Green Hybrid'	35	Mildly crinkly/medium green	Fairly bolt resistant
'Samish Hybrid'	40	Very crinkly/dark green	Not bolt resistant
'Skookum Hybrid'	40	Mildly crinkly/dark green	Good spring and fall
'Space Hybrid'*****	40	Smooth to barely savoyed/dark green	Bolt resistant
'Teton Hybrid'	45	Mildly crinkly/medium green	Bolt resistant
'Tyee Hybrid'*****	40	Crinkly/dark green	Bolt resistant
'Viroflay' (heirloom)	45	Mildly crinkly/dark green	Baby to giant leaves
'Winter Bloomsdale' (heirloom)	50	Crinkly/dark green	Bolt resistant

Enjoy zucchini when the flower is still attached to the fruit.

SQUASH, SUMMER

Cucurbita pepo
Cucumber or Gourd Family (Cucurbitaceae)

Summer squash are tender to very tender, warm-season annuals. They are easy to grow, mature rapidly, and produce abundantly. Depending on the variety, they take up relatively little to a moderate amount of space in the home garden. You can eat them raw or cooked. They probably originated in Mexico.

How Summer Squash Grows

The firm seeds of summer squash are large, flat, and a bit swollen (about 150 to 225 seeds per ounce). They are typically light tan with one end pointed like a spear. Once growing, the seeds open into easy-to-identify seed leaves to be followed by true leaves. The plant forms prickly pentagonal stems that are often fairly brittle. The foliage enlarges and matures into broad leaves sending energy into the plant, which then produces lovely yellow flowers. Each plant has both male (staminoid) and female (pistillate) flowers. The early flowers are all male and ephemeral, but shortly after both male and female flowers appear. Insects transfer pollen from the male to the female flowers, which have a bulge

(embryo) at their base. Once fertilized, these swell and eventually form mature fruit containing seed for the next generation of plants.

Where to Plant
Site and Light

Summer squash thrive in full sun. They love heat. If possible, plant them in a protected location.

Soil and Moisture

Moisture and heat—those are the two secrets to growing summer squash. Properly prepared soil will provide even moisture throughout the season. If possible, prepare the growing bed in fall. Raised beds are especially effective since they warm up quickly in spring. You can also make 6-inch mounds or hills several feet wide in the planting area. Add lots of organic matter to the soil. Compost, peat, and rotted manures are excellent soil amendments. Work the soil until it is loose. Add organic fertilizers to enrich it. You want the soil to be rich, loose (drain freely), and moisture retentive.

Nutrition Facts

Serving size: 100 grams (3.5 ounces)

	AMOUNT PER RAW SERVING	% DV	AMOUNT PER COOKED SERVING	% DV
Calories	16	1%	16	1%
Carbohydrates	3 g	1%	3 g	1%
Dietary fiber	1 g	5%	1 g	5%
Folate	30 mcg	10%	20 mcg	6%
Manganese	0.2 mg	9%	0.2 mg	9%
Potassium	260 mg	7%	170 mg	5%
Protein	1 g	2%	1 g	2%
Riboflavin	0.1 mg	8%	0.05 mg	3%
Vitamin B6	0.2 mg	10%	0.1 mg	5%
Vitamin C	17 mg	28%	5.5 mg	9%

Once you have made the bed, don't walk on it. Avoid compacting the soil that you have worked so hard to keep aerated. With all of the organic matter added to the soil, it probably will be mildly acidic with a pH close to 6.0 to 6.5. That's ideal for squash.

If you are not in a hurry for compost, consider planting seeds directly in an older pile. Dig a hole, fill it with soil, and plant the seeds. Heap fresh compost in a different pile or the center of a Japanese tomato ring.

Containers

Many varieties of zucchinis grow well in large containers. While they may not be strong vining plants, they get tall and wide once mature. They are far less susceptible to squash borers when grown this way. Container-grown zucchini does require frequent watering. On really hot, dry days watering twice a day may be advised. Or you can place the container in a wide and deep saucer filled with water. However, to avoid root rot, let the water in the saucer dry out regularly between waterings.

Planting

Seed

Most gardeners plant seed directly in the garden. The soil temperature should be at least 70°F, but warmer is better. If the soil is too cold, the seed may rot. Even so, it is worth a gamble to plant a few seeds before the weather cooperates. Summer squash sometimes surprises us by defying conventional wisdom. Place six seeds up to 12 inches apart on top of the hill. Seeing them on the soil surface makes spacing easy. Press them down into the loose soil with your finger to roughly 1 inch below the soil surface. Then firm the top of

the hill with your hand. Water immediately. Seeds usually sprout within 14 days.

A common misconception is that the soil must be mounded, but this is a matter of choice. The advantage of raised hills is that they drain well and dry out quickly in spring, like miniature raised beds. Planting on a level surface is fine as long as you have prepared the soil as you would for a hill or raised bed. The spacing of hills, raised or level, depends on the potential size of the plant. Typically, a few feet is fine for bush types; farther apart, for vining varieties.

Transplants

Squash really dislikes being transplanted. Root disturbance sets plants back. When transplants and seeds are planted in the same hill at the same time, the seeds often do as well or outperform the transplants. If transplants are set in the garden and kept artificially warm with plant protectors, they do get a head start. Since summer squash matures rapidly, this extra work makes sense only to the avid home gardener or someone living in areas where summers are especially short (see "Squash, Winter" for indoor planting tips).

When to Plant

Squash thrives in hot weather. Be patient, and let the soil warm up. Air temperature should be at least 70°F in the

'Early Prolific Straightneck' produces copious amounts of fruit on a bushy plant.

day. This is usually close to the time when late irises are in bloom. Plant transplants 2 weeks after the last expected frost with protection.

Spacing

How far the plants should be set apart depends on the variety and its growth pattern. Tight planting is possible for bush types. For example, you could plant three zucchini plants in a single mound. The plants themselves become large, but the combination takes up less space than if they were planted farther apart. Vining types can be allowed to roam or be grown vertically. Again, spacing is based on the growing method. So there are no set rules.

How to Care for Summer Squash

Water

Summer squash need lots of moisture in the soil to thrive. Keep the soil consistently moist by watering around the base of the plants regularly. To cut down on disease, avoid watering the leaves. Even watering may help prevent powdery mildew. Watering is especially important when plants are forming fruit. Summer squash requires more water than winter squash. Drip irrigation is effective.

Squash leaves may wilt in the middle of the day. However, if they wilt in early morning or late evening, water immediately. Wilting after watering is an indication that a plant is suffering from a disease or insect attack. This is most noticeable when only one plant in a large group wilts. Dig up and destroy it if diseased. This may prevent disease from spreading to other, nearby plants. If insects are the problem, use floating row covers early in the season the following year.

Mulch

When your plants are growing well and the soil is thoroughly warm, apply a thick layer of organic mulch around their base. The mulch should not touch the stems but can reach out several feet. Mulching keeps moisture in the soil and increases overall yield. The use of mulch around yellow summer squash is somewhat controversial. Some gardeners believe that squash bugs thrive in mulched areas. Mulch until you actually have a problem.

Fertilizing

Squash are heavy feeders. When they are several inches high, pour 1 or 2 cups of diluted fertilizer around them. Side-dressings of organic fertilizer every 10 days encourage healthy growth. Fertilize when fruits are forming. A combination of organic fertilizers is effective. However, if your plants are producing lots of foliage and little fruit, you are applying too much nitrogen. Often, with properly prepared soil fertilizing isn't necessary at all.

Weeding

Early in the season hand weed around the base of plants. Pull up weeds carefully to avoid root disturbance. Once you have placed mulch around the plants, it is easy to pull up any weeds that appear. If you don't use mulch, cultivate the plants frequently and lightly. Shallow cultivation is best. As plants mature, they can compete more successfully with weeds, but still remove any that appear close to the base of the plant. But do not walk on or disturb the vines.

Thinning

After the seedlings emerge, let them grow until they get stocky. Thin to two or three healthy plants per hill. If you leave too many plants, they compete with each other for water and nutrients as if they were weeds. Crowding reduces vigorous growth and fruit formation.

Pruning

Any type of pruning is optional. Don't remove foliage, but do consider pinching off the growing tip of any vining type of squash to keep it in check, to create lateral branching, or to hasten fruit ripening at the end of the season. In general, removing foliage is less recommended than snipping off late-developing fruit to send energy to the remaining larger squash to mature.

Special Considerations

Occasionally, gardeners have to help nature out by pollinating flowers if insects are not doing their job. The easiest way to pollinate flowers is to strip off the outer petals of a male flower and swirl it around the inside of a female flower. The male flower has a protrusion (stamen) in the center and a thin stem (peduncle). The female flower has a small, swollen ovary at its base. You can also do this with a cotton swab or an artist's paintbrush. You may have to repeat this several times with different flowers over a series of days. Note that the first flowers on a plant may all be male. They will drop off, so you may want to eat them instead. The best time to pollinate female flowers is in the morning just as blooms open up. They may last only a day.

Extending the Season

Spring planting with protection with cloches or row covers is possible. Fall protection is difficult since the plants have gotten much larger. If you expect a frost, cover the plants in midday with cloth, such as a sheet.

Problems

Insects

Unfortunately, squash are insect magnets. Having said that, summer squash often produces abundantly even when severely damaged by insect activity. There's an old saying, "Plant one for the insects, one for the deer, and one for me." Here are the primary insects that will take one for themselves: squash bugs, squash vine borers, and striped cucumber beetles, which carry mosaic virus and bacterial wilt disease.

Floating row covers help protect young plants but must be lifted at least several times a week when plants start to flower for proper pollination. Squash bugs lay reddish-brown eggs on the undersides of leaves. Look for these, and squish them with your fingers. Place boards by plants at night, and turn them over in the morning. Kill any squash bugs taking refuge there. The squash vine borer drills into the lower part of stems, leaving behind what looks like sawdust (frass) beneath the hole. Cut into the stem, and stab the borer with a straightened-out paper clip. If low enough, cover the hole with soil after killing the insect.

Different types of squash are more or less susceptible. For example, zucchini is commonly damaged by squash vine borers, while summer crookneck is less so. Even so, heavily infested zucchini may produce copious amounts of fruit.

Disease

Your best defense against disease is insect control. They spread mosaic virus (mottled yellow leaves) and bacterial wilt (plant wilts and sometimes dies). Powdery mildew can also be a problem. It looks like a plant is covered in a white dust or film. If it appears early in the season, it is a problem; late in the season, not so much. If you spot it on a few leaves early, cut them off. Avoid evening or late night sprinkling if powdery mildew shows up. To reduce problems with disease, plant resistant varieties, plant squash in a new area each year, and keep your garden weed-free.

Marauders

Deer are more of a problem with winter squash. They love nibbling on them.

Physiological

Occasionally, the blossom end of a fruit rots. This may be caused by inconsistent moisture or a calcium deficiency. If you are adding organic matter to the soil and watering regularly, this is uncommon.

A good reason for planting more seeds than you will need is that some seeds will outperform others. They may come from the same seed package, but some may be weak and on occasion distorted.

Propagation

Summer squash is monoecious in that male and female flowers are on the same plant. Occasionally, a flower with both reproductive organs (perfect) occurs. Flowers are insect pollinated. If you are growing open-pollinated plants, save the seed as long as different plants of the same species are not growing nearby. Squash will not cross with cucumbers, muskmelons, or watermelons. They will cross with pumpkins in the same species (*Cucurbita pepo*).

To save seed, let the fruit mature on the vine. Store for several weeks indoors, scoop out seeds, put in water, let the good seeds sink, remove, dry in a single layer as long as it takes (when they will break in two if bent), and place in an envelope in a cool place. Seed lasts up to 4 to 5 years.

If concerned about cross-pollination, cover a budding female flower with a bag. Pollinate it as described earlier, just as it opens. Then cover it again. As the fruit swells, remove the bag.

Harvesting

Summer squash is at its best when picked very young. Often, at this stage the flower will still be attached to the fruit. Crookneck should be no longer than 4 inches; pattypan, no larger than a quarter—at most a silver dollar; straightneck, no longer than 5 to 8 inches; zucchini, under 6 inches. The fruit is best at this stage. Constant picking is essential. If you allow squash to mature on the vine, it will give off a hormone that causes the plant to shrivel and die. If you miss a larger fruit, pick it immediately. Zucchini is especially quick growing. Check plants every day. Summer squash fruit is easy to miss, so circle the plant when harvesting.

Some plants are prickly, having numerous foliar spikes (trichomes). Wear a long-sleeved shirt and a pair of gloves if sensitive to this. Gloves not only protect you but the fruit as well. Carry pruners or scissors into the garden to cut off the fruits. Cut off a little portion of stem with each squash. Don't yank squash off the plant. It's not a tug of war. Pulling at squash may damage the stems or vines, which can be brittle.

The buds and blossoms of summer squash are edible. Pick them just as they start to unfold. Since male flowers drop off early in the season, don't let them go to waste.

Storing

Summer squash stores poorly. The fruit dries out quickly once picked. Wash, dry, place in a plastic bag in the crisper of the refrigerator, and eat as soon as possible. Summer squash lasts from 5 to 14 days treated in this way.

To freeze, peel or not depending on preference, slice

or leave whole, remove or leave seeds in, blanch 1 to 3 minutes or until slightly cooked, cool rapidly in ice water, drain, place in airtight freezer bags, and freeze. Alternatively, cook and mash or purée before freezing.

To dry, wash, peel, slice into 1/8-inch pieces, and dry in a dehydrator. The squash usually keeps less than a month. Squash can also be pickled using your favorite recipe.

Culinary Uses

Pick buds and blossoms (*flor de calabaza*) in early morning before they open or as soon as possible before eating. Don't wash. Snip off the base, pull out pistils or stamens, and check for insects. Dip them in tempura batter, or stuff them with cheese and deep-fry. Add sliced to omelets, pasta dishes, and soups. Sauté or add to stir-fries. They make a lovely edible garnish.

Squash comes from the Indian word *askutasqush,* which means "eaten raw." Summer squash has thin skin and barely noticeable seeds when picked at an early age. It is commonly diced, grated, or sliced and eaten raw in salads. It even makes a good slaw. Place crunchy, thin strips on a platter for dips.

Picked at the right stage the skin does not have to be removed. Trim off the ends. Eat whole or diced, julienned, or sliced. Squash can be baked, boiled, grilled, microwaved, roasted, sautéed, steamed, stir-fried, and stuffed. Cut open, and cover with cheese to be broiled. Cooked squash can be blended for cold or hot soups, commonly seasoned with basil, dill weed, oregano, or thyme. If zucchini gets overly mature, which seems to happen overnight, use it for breads or ratatouille.

Varieties

Summer squash are varieties of *Cucurbita pepo*. These can be further divided into two subspecies. Crookneck, pattypan, and straightneck are varieties of *Cucurbita pepo* ssp. *texana,* while zucchinis are *Cucurbita pepo* ssp. *pepo*. Most varieties of summer squash tend to be bushy rather than vining. Although some people will tell you they all taste the same, they really don't. The ability of a person to taste is DNA dependent. Choose varieties by type (shape), days to maturity, and color. The latter can make a difference in spotting fruit that needs immediate picking.

Note that through hybridization breeders have been able to mask two viruses primarily in straightneck squash with the "precocious yellow gene." This makes them more attractive. They are not genetically modified. And whether they are more nutritious is not certain. The presence of the gene is included after the flower color in the varietal chart.

A crookneck squash looks like the neck of a swan on a bulbous base. The neck can be abbreviated or long. Pattypan has crimped edges. Pattypan is sometimes listed in catalogs as custard marrow, custard squash, cymling, pâtisson, scallop squash, or white squash. The most common synonym is scallop squash. Straightneck has a tapered neck and and looks like a cylinder although it can be bent a bit at times. This is especially true for 'Multipik Hybrid' and 'Saffron', which could be called semi-straightnecks. Summer pumpkin is a common name for a round squash from France. Zucchini is typically tubular but can be round or curved. Zucchini may be called courgettes (pronounce with a soft *g*), cocozelle (say the *z* as if there is a *t* in front of it), or vegetable marrow (marrow). Technically, zucchini is none of these, but it is commonly sold this way. 'Alfresco' is a courgette; 'Costata Romanesco', a cocozelle; and 'Caserta', a marrow.

Note that the variety 'Sure Thing Hybrid' will set fruit without pollination, making it a good choice in cool, cloudy areas where insect activity may be limited. If left on the vine, 'Ronde de Nice' (listed as a zucchini) will develop into a green pumpkin, which technically it may well be. However, most people eat it when young. 'Butterblossom' was developed for its abundant production of edible flowers. Finally, 'Zucchetta Rampicante' is a vining plant and a *Cucurbita moschata,* not a *Cucurbita pepo*. Eat it young as a summer squash; mature, as a winter squash.

VARIETY	DAYS	FRUIT COLOR
Crookneck		
'Early Yellow Summer Crookneck' (heirloom)*****	55	Buttery bright yellow
'Gentry Hybrid'*****	45	Yellow
'Summer Crookneck' (see 'Early Yellow Summer Crookneck')		
'Sundance Hybrid'	50	Bright yellow
'Sun Drops Hybrid' (AAS-1990)	55	Cream yellow (oval shape)
'Yellow Crookneck' (see 'Early Yellow Summer Crookneck')		
Marrow (see Zucchini)		
Mediterranean or Middle Eastern (see Zucchini)		
Pattypan (Scallop) (Cymling)		
'Bennings Green Tint' (heirloom)	55	Pale green
'Early White Bush' (OP)	55	Pale green to white
'Golden Bush' (heirloom)	65	Yellow
'Peter Pan Hybrid' (AAS-1982)	50	Lime green
'Scallopini Hybrid' (AAS-1977)	55	Bright green
'Sunburst Hybrid' (AAS-1985)*****	50	Bright yellow
'White Bush Scallop' (see 'Early White Bush')		
Straightneck (Semi-Straightnecks)		
'Cougar Hybrid'	45	Yellow (precocious)
'Early Prolific Straightneck' (heirloom) (AAS-1938)*****	50	Cream yellow (bush)
'Enterprise Hybrid'	45	Light yellow (precocious)
'Fortune Hybrid'	45	Bright yellow (precocious)
'Goldbar Hybrid'	50	Gold yellow (bush) (precocious)
'Lioness Hybrid'	50	Light yellow (precocious)
'Multipik Hybrid'	50	Yellow (precocious)
'Saffron' (OP)	45	Golden yellow
'Seneca Prolific Hybrid'	50	Cream yellow (precocious)
'Sunray Hybrid'	50	Buttery yellow
'Superpik Hybrid'	50	Bright yellow (precocious)
'Zephyr Hybrid'*****	55	Yellow with green end
Summer Pumpkin (See 'Ronde De Nice' under Zucchini)		
Zucchini, green		
'Aristocrat Hybrid' (AAS-1973)	50	Medium to dark green
'Black Beauty' (OP) (AAS-1957)*****	55	Greenish black
'Burpee's Fordhook' (heirloom) (AAS-1942)	60	Dark green
'Burpee Hybrid'	50	Dark green
'Butter Blossom' (OP)*****	45	Dark green (for flowers)
'Chefini Hybrid' (AAS-1965)	55	Glossy medium green
'Classic Hybrid'	50	Medium green
'Elite Hybrid'	50	Glossy medium green
'Embassy Hybrid'	50	Medium green
'Fordhook' (heirloom) (AAS-1942)	60	Deep green
'President Hybrid'	50	Dark green flecked light green
'Raven Hybrid'	50	Dark green
'Spacemiser Hybrid'	50	Green speckled white green
'Spineless Beauty Hybrid'	50	Medium to dark green (not prickly)
'Sure Thing Hybrid'	45	Medium green speckled

VARIETY	DAYS	FRUIT COLOR
Zucchini, yellow		
'Butterstick Hybrid'	50	Yellow (precocious)
'Golden Zucchini' (OP)*****	55	Yellow gold
'Gold Rush Hybrid' (AAS-1980)*****	50	Rich yellow gold (for flowers)
Zucchini, round		
'Eight Ball Hybrid' (AAS-1999)*****	40	Deep glossy green round (container)
'Gourmet Globe Hybrid'	50	Dark green with stripes
'Nano Verde di Milano' (OP)*****	45	Dark green
'Papaya Pear Hybrid' (AAS-2003)	40	Yellow (pear shape)
'Ronde de Nice' (heirloom)*****	60	Green speckled white (perfect for stuffing)
'Round Zucchini' (see 'Eight Ball')		
Zucchini, Lebanese or Mediterranean (Italian)		
'Alfresco Hybrid'	50	Pale green
'Caserta' (heirloom) (AAS-1949)*****	65	Grayish green striped green
'Cocozelle' (heirloom)	55	Dark green striped medium green
'Costata Romanesco' (heirloom)*****	60	Medium gray green ribbed
'Tromboncino' (see 'Zucchetta Rampicante')		
'White Bush Vegetable Marrow' (heirloom)	55	Cream green
'Zucchetta Rampicante' (heirloom)	70	Green to tannish curved up to 3 feet

Squash flowers are prized in many cultures as a culinary treat when dipped in batter and deep-fried.

Turk's turban adds a splash of color to the garden and is sometimes sold as a gourd.

SQUASH, WINTER

Cucurbita species
Cucumber or Gourd Family (Cucurbitaceae)

Winter squash is a very tender, warm-season annual. Most varieties take a long time to mature. However, the wait is worth it for the wide range of tastes. Some varieties will store for several months, offering feasts in late fall into early winter. Most winter squash create vines that require a fair amount of space and may crawl over you if you stand in the way. Winter squash probably originated in Mexico.

How Winter Squash Grows

Winter squash grows from large, firm seeds, typically light tan with one end pointed like a spear (about 150 to 200 seeds per ounce). The seeds open into fairly large seed leaves to be followed by even larger true leaves. The stems vary in shape, texture, and density according to the species being grown. Most stems spread out along the ground and form foliage along the entire length of the elongated stem. As plants mature, flowers emerge along the stem as well, first closer to the base of the plant, and later farther out. Each plant has both male and female flowers. The early flowers are male, but

shortly after both male and female flowers appear. Insects transfer pollen from the male to the female flowers, which have a bulge (embryo) at their base. Once fertilized, these develop into fruit that matures to form seed for the next generation of plants. The mature fruit has a tough rind that varies in color, size, and shape according to the species grown.

Where to Plant
Site and Light

Winter squash need warmth and lots of light. Plant them in full sun. A gentle, south-facing slope is ideal. The vining varieties need space to roam, so consider planting them on the edge of the garden where they can spread out. If space is limited, grow some varieties on a vertical support. Face these south to take advantage of the sun. Or plant bush or semibush varieties.

Soil and Moisture

Winter squash need consistent watering but are more drought tolerant than summer squash. Properly prepared soil will provide even moisture throughout the season. If possible, prepare the growing bed in fall. Raised beds are especially effective since they warm up quickly in spring. You can also make 6-inch mounds or hills several feet wide in the planting area. Add lots of organic matter to the soil. Compost, leaf mold, sphagnum peat moss, and rotted manures are excellent soil amendments. Work the soil until it is loose. Add organic fertilizers to enrich it. You want the soil to be rich, loose (drain freely), and moisture retentive. Once you have made the bed, don't walk on it. Avoid compacting the soil that you have worked so hard to keep aerated. With all of the organic matter added to the soil, it probably will be mildly acidic with a pH close to 6.0 to 6.5. That's ideal for squash.

To provide additional warmth you may want to cover the area with black plastic or black landscape fabric either in fall or early spring. Do this at least 10 days before the expected planting time. This will help warm up the soil early in the planting season. Seed or plants can be placed in slits made in the plastic, although some gardeners prefer to remove it before planting. Experiment with both options to see which you prefer or to compare the two methods.

Planting
Seed

Direct seeding winter squash in the garden is more of a gamble than it is for summer squash. It all depends on the season. It also depends on the variety of squash being grown. Still, many gardeners get decent crops if the weather cooperates and insect invasions are limited. Plant seeds only when the soil temperature reaches 60°F or warmer. If the soil is too cold, the seed may rot. Even so, it is worth a gamble to plant a few seeds before the weather cooperates. Place six seeds 12 inches or more apart on top of the hill. Seeing them on the soil surface makes spacing easy. Press them down into the loose soil with your finger to roughly 1 inch below the soil surface. Then firm the top of the hill with your hand. If you have covered the area with black plastic or fabric, plant seeds through slits made in these materials. Water immediately.

A common misconception is that the soil must be mounded, but this is a matter of choice. The advantage of raised hills is that they drain well and dry out quickly in spring like miniature raised beds. Planting on a level surface is fine as long as you have prepared the soil as you would for a hill or raised bed. The spacing of hills, raised or level, depends on the potential size of the plant. Typically, a few feet is fine for bush types; much farther apart, for vining varieties. Vines can intermingle without any problem.

A trick that is hardly ever mentioned is to plant seeds in

Nutrition Facts
Serving size: 100 grams (3.5 ounces)

	AMOUNT PER COOKED SERVING	% DV
Calories	40	2%
Carbohydrates	10 g	3%
Dietary fiber	2 g	5%
Folate	20 mcg	5%
Magnesium	30 mg	7%
Manganese	0.2 mg	9%
Niacin	1.2 mg	8%
Potassium	285–350 mg	8–10%
Protein	1.0 g	2%
Vitamin A	10,650+ IU	225–300%
Vitamin B6	0.1 mg	6%
Vitamin C	15–20 mg	25–35%
Vitamin E	1.3–1.5 mg	6–10%

a compost pile, one that has aged for at least a year or longer. Dig a hole in the pile, fill with loose soil, and plant seeds. Why this works so well, I am not completely sure. But compost is still breaking down so provides bottom heat, holds lots of water, and provides a friendly environment for vining plants. Keep the pile moist, and let the seeds do the rest. It

'Waltham Butternut' may be one of the finest heirloom squashes.

is amazing how large plants grow, how disease resistant they are, and how many fruits may be produced this way. Vines do roam and take up a lot of space.

Transplants

The varieties that take the longest to mature and are most vulnerable to insect attack are better started indoors. Admittedly, winter squash really dislikes being transplanted. Root disturbance sets plants back. The following method, also described in the muskmelon section, works equally well for winter squash.

Prepare the soil for planting well in advance. Covering the soil with black plastic or permeable landscape fabric is optional. It definitely increases soil temperature by as much as 5° to 10°F, so many gardeners do use these materials for warmth-loving plants and get them into place 10 days to several weeks before the expected planting time. Do not plant until the soil temperature reaches at least 60°F. When using inorganic mulches, soak the soil thoroughly before laying them down.

Start seeds indoors about 3 to 4 weeks before your expected outdoor planting time. Don't start them too early, because they have deep roots, grow quickly, and don't like being disturbed. Plant several seeds ½ to 1 inch deep in sterile starting mix in 4-inch peat pots. Keep the seeds moist and warm. Provide bottom heat to get soil temperature to 80°F if possible during the day with a drop of 5 degrees at night during germination. Once germinating, provide seedlings with 16 hours of light per day. As they mature, snip off all but the healthiest plant in each pot. Ideally, you want each plant to be 4 to 6 inches high with at least two to four true leaves when you plant it outdoors. Typically, plants take about 3 weeks to reach their ideal height. Harden off the plants. If possible, plant them outdoors just before a rain when the soil reaches the correct temperature. If using plastic, cut slits through it. Plant the pots in the prepared soil so that the rim of the pots is barely covered. Roots will grow through the sides of the pot. Place metal hoops over the planting area, and cover with white row covers at a height of roughly 18 inches above the plants. Make sure the ends are closed. The row covers keep temperature and humidity uniform. Just as importantly, they keep insects from damaging the young plants. The row covers allow filtered light and rain into the planting area. Remove the row covers as soon as foliage begins to touch the fabric. Never place row covers directly on foliage, since it can damage it badly.

Alternatively, use a 32-ounce plastic container. Yogurt containers, just a bit wider than 4 inches, are ideal for this use. Keep the lid, cut out the bottom, set the container on the lid. Fill it with a sterile starting mix. Plant and grow the seeds as described. After hardening off and at the correct planting time, make a hole in the soil large enough to hold the container. Set the container off to the side of the hole. Slide the plastic lid out from under the container. Cover the bottom where the lid was with your hand and place the container in the hole. Push soil lightly around the container and then lift it up and away from the plant. Firm the soil around the plant. Water immediately. If the weather is not stable, protect the plant until it warms up with row covers or cloches. Or leave part of the container in the ground with the upper part exposed and snap on the lid at night for a few days. Using a large container and planting carefully to avoid root disturbance are the critical elements of this method.

Since it is sometimes impossible to predict when warm weather will come, you may want to start several pots of plants a week apart for 3 weeks. Seeds are relatively inexpensive. A half dozen plants grown properly is really all the average home gardener needs.

Spacing

Start off with as much space between plants as possible, even up to 24 inches apart in the hill itself. Guide the new growth in varied directions. Vines will wander far and fast. Give them room to roam. The bush types will spread out 6 feet or more; the vining types, double that or more.

When to Plant

Squash thrives in hot weather. Be patient and let the soil warm up. Air temperature should be at least 70°F in the day. This is usually close to the time when late irises are in bloom. Plant seed in warm soil. Plant transplants 2 weeks after the last expected frost with protection or several weeks later without.

Support

Small-fruited types such as acorn can be grown on supports to save space. A tepee made from bamboo stakes or an A-frame trellis at least 4 feet tall works well. Heavy-fruited varieties should be allowed to roam and mature on the ground.

How to Care for Winter Squash
Water

Watering varies by the method used to start plants. If you are using black plastic as a mulch, place drip irrigation underneath it. Water collects under the plastic and keeps soil moisture even.

If plants are not covered by row covers, keep the soil consistently moist by watering around the base of the plants regularly, especially when they are young. Avoid watering the leaves to cut down on disease. Even watering *may* help prevent powdery mildew. Watering is especially important when plants are forming fruit.

Squash leaves may wilt in the middle of the day. However, if they are wilted in early morning or late evening, water immediately. Wilting after watering is an indication that a plant is suffering from a disease or insect attack. This is most noticeable when one plant in a large group wilts. Dig it up if diseased. This may prevent disease from spreading to other, nearby plants. If insects are the problem, use an organic insecticide if you cannot bear the loss.

Mulch

The use of black plastic mulch is especially effective in areas with cool summertime temperatures. Black plastic traps water under it and suffocates weeds. Landscape fabric also works well. It allows both water and light to penetrate it.

Once the soil is thoroughly warm, some gardeners apply a thin layer of organic mulch over the area where vines will spread. This has good and bad points. Mulch does reduce weed growth. However, vines take root at leaf nodes, and they do this best on bare ground, although they will penetrate thin layers of mulch. Even if the main crown of the squash plant is damaged by insects, the roots at the nodes will help the plant take in moisture and nutrients, especially if fruits have already begun to form. Never pull up the vines where they have taken root—never.

Fertilizing

Squash are heavy feeders. When they are several inches high, pour 1 to 2 cups of diluted fertilizer around their base. Side-dressings of organic fertilizer every 10 days encourage healthy growth. Fertilize when fruits are forming. A combination of organic fertilizers is effective. However, if your plants are producing lots of foliage and little fruit, you are applying too much nitrogen. Often, with properly prepared soil fertilizing isn't necessary at all. Occasionally, young leaves may appear distorted, most commonly caused by cucumber mosaic disease. The cause may also be a lack of boron, which can be applied lightly as a mist in foliar feeding.

Weeding

Early in the season, hand weed around the base of plants. Pull up weeds carefully to avoid root disturbance. Spreading a layer of mulch out wherever you think the vines will roam is optional. If vines get to the edge of the mulch, expand it farther. Winter squash are spreading plants and really don't mind "hiding" in weeds. Let them do their thing. Definitely allow them to take root at their nodes. *If pulling weeds far away from the original seeding area, avoid damaging the vines.* The vines may attach themselves to weeds with their tendrils. Let nature take its course, and skip late weeding altogether.

Thinning

After the seedlings emerge, let them grow until they get stocky. Thin to the two or three healthiest plants per hill. If you leave too many plants, they compete with each other for water and nutrients as if they were weeds. Crowding reduces vigorous growth and fruit formation.

Pruning

Never prune winter squash—at least not until the end of the season. The idea at that time is to get all of the plant's energy flowing to the production of the remaining fruit. Alternatively, once enough fruits are forming, snip off developing fruits farther out on the vine. Keep only the number you need. Do not damage the vine or foliage.

Special Considerations

The first flowers on a plant may be all male. They will drop off, so you may want to eat them instead. They often stay open for no more than a day. To get fruit, you may have to hand pollinate flowers if there is not enough insect activity. See "Propagation."

Winter squash are a good source of beta-carotene. The richer and deeper colored the flesh, the better. The amount of nutrients in the chart is simply an approximation since varying squashes contain a wide range of vitamins and minerals. Still, all are excellent for your health.

Extending the Season

Spring planting with protection is possible, as described earlier. Fall protection is difficult since the plants have gotten much larger. If you expect a frost, cover the plants in midday with cloth (sheets).

Problems

Insects

Winter squash are attacked by the same insects as summer varieties. Insects that may cause significant damage are squash bugs, squash vine borers, and striped cucumber beetles, which carry mosaic virus and bacterial wilt disease. Squash varieties do vary in their resistance to these insects. For example, Hubbard squash are highly susceptible to squash vine borers, while butternut are more resistant. 'Early Butternut Hybrid' is particularly resistant. Row covers work well to prevent insect damage. Support them with hoops that keep the fabric well above the growing plants. Remove them when the foliage barely begins to touch the supported fabric, or you will damage the foliage. Note that insect problems vary from year to year and from one region of the country to another in any given season. So some years you can have a great crop without doing much of anything, while in others the plants suffer an invasion.

Disease

Your best defense against disease is insect control. Insects spread mosaic virus (mottled yellow leaves) and bacterial wilt (plant wilts and dies). Powdery mildew can also be a problem. It looks like a plant is covered in white dust. If it appears early in the season, it is a problem; late in the season, not so much. If you spot it on a few leaves early, cut them off. Avoid evening or late night sprinkling if powdery mildew shows up. To reduce problems with disease, plant resistant varieties, plant squash in a new area each year, and keep your garden weed-free.

Marauders

Deer love to nibble on maturing fruit. They may take just a taste or eat nearly the whole thing.

Physiological

Sometimes, winter squash don't set fruit well. Hand pollination may be helpful or necessary in some instances. See the section on "Propagation."

Winter squash on vining plants can lie on the ground for a long time. Some gardeners set them on boards. Do this when the squash are very small, and be careful not to damage the vine. This is said to reduce the chance of rot. I have never done this.

Propagation

Winter squash have male and female flowers on the same plant (monoecious). Flowers are insect pollinated, but in some seasons you may have to pollinate flowers yourself. Strip off the outer petals of a male flower, and swirl it around the inside of a female flower. The male flower has a protrusion (stamen) in the center and a thin stem (peduncle). The female flower has a small, swollen ovary at its base. You can also do this with a cotton swab or an artist's paintbrush. You may have to repeat this several times.

You can save seeds of open-pollinated varieties. Seed will come true as long as they are not planted by gourds, squash, or pumpkins of the same species. Occasionally, *Cucurbita argyrosperma* (*Cucurbita mixta*) and *moschata* may cross. If squash of the same species are grown in gardens within 1 mile, crosses may also occur. Squash does not cross with cucumber, muskmelon, or watermelon.

Let fruit ripen as long as possible on the vine. Then bring them indoors, and let dry for an additional 3 weeks. Cut open. Scoop out seed, place it in water, and keep only the seeds that sink. Rub each of these seeds between your fingers, removing any sticky substance clinging to it. Place on a plate in a single layer. Seed should not be touching. Let dry thoroughly at room temperature. Once dry, place in an envelope in a cool, dark area. They may last for up to 4 to 5 years.

Harvesting

Let winter squash ripen on the vine as long as possible, picking it just before the first expected hard frost. This allows the flesh to form more sugars, which affect both taste and storing capacity. At the end of the season, stems begin to dry, die off, and wither. Many winter squash begin to become dull in color. Ripe fruit is heavy for its size. Cut the fruits from the vine with a sharp knife or pruners, leaving 1 to 2 inches of stem attached to each squash. Do not carry squash by these stems. If they break, they may rot if not eaten right away. Avoid wounding or bruising the squash. If damaged, eat the fruit as soon as possible.

Storing

The following information about storing applies to all winter squash. Store squash whole, do not wrap, do not refrigerate, place in a dry, dark area, keep as cool as possible, and let air circulate around them freely. Some squash need curing for the best taste. The curing process allows starches to turn into sugar. Squash lose weight in this process but become increasingly sweet.

To cure, place squash in a sunny, dry location for several days if possible. The ideal temperature is 80°F with humidity up to 80 percent, but this is difficult to provide in cold climates late in the year. If necessary, bring them indoors. Wipe them off. Now put them inside in a warm, dry area for at least 10 days. Curing hardens the rind and prevents spoilage. After that, keep them cool until ready to eat.

Acorn squash does not need curing and and is best eaten within 1 month but can be stored for up to 3 months. Ambercup stores well. Buttercup is best cured for 1 to 2 months and eaten within 3 or fewer. Butternut is best cured for 2 months and eaten within 6. Cushaw does not store well so eat as soon as possible. Delicata does not need curing and should be eaten within 1 to 2 months. Hubbard is best cured for 1 month and eaten within 4. Cure kabocha for 1 month and eat within 4. Spaghetti does not need curing and should be eaten within 3 months. Sweet dumpling does not need curing and should be eaten within 3 months.

To freeze, cut flesh into large pieces or chunks, cook until tender, cool off, remove skin, and freeze. Cutting into pieces is much easier than trying to purée it before freezing, and the pieces are suited to more uses. However, puréed squash is excellent for squash soups. Or puncture the rind, bake, cool, remove skin, chunk or purée, and if really stringy, push through a sieve.

The fruit can be canned in chunks but not if mashed or puréed. Winter squash flesh is dense, and if mashed or puréed, it may not allow enough heat to get to the center of the canning jar.

Culinary Uses

Pick buds and blossoms (flor de calabaza) in early morning before they open or as soon as possible before eating. Don't wash. Snip off the base, pull out pistils or stamens, and check for insects. Dip them in tempura batter, or stuff them with cheese and deep-fry. Add sliced to omelets, pasta dishes, and soups. Sauté or add to stir-fries. They make a lovely, edible garnish. Since male flowers drop off early in the season, eat these without worrying about loss of fruit. Some varieties of immature fruit can be eaten raw or lightly steamed when just a few days old, such as 'Eat It All', 'Jersey Golden Acorn', and 'Table Gold'.

Most winter squash are eaten cooked either with the skin on or cut into cubes, slices, or spears. They can be baked, boiled, broiled, microwaved, or steamed. To bake, cook whole or cut in two and cook at 400° to 450°F (usually cut side down on a pan). To boil, cut into ½-inch pieces, and cook in a covered pan. To microwave, cut in two and cook (usually cut side up). To steam, cut into 1-inch cubes or slices. The flesh is excellent puréed for a side dish or made into soups. The sweet flesh is often used to make bread, cookies, muffins, pies, and puddings. The seeds can be toasted and eaten like pumpkin seeds. Pumpkins are really a form of winter squash.

Varieties

Most winter squashes produce long vines. Some are semivining or bush varieties—both terms are rather vague, meaning vines are not as long as on the vining types. If space is a concern, grow the more compact plants.

Try different kinds of winter squash over a period of years.

Unlike summer squash, they have distinctive flesh colors and tastes. Four main considerations in choosing varieties are the space needed, days to maturity, yield, and disease resistance. There are four main species represented in the varietal table: *Cucurbita maxima,* with rounded spongy stems; *Cucurbita argyrosperma* (formerly *Cucurbita mixta*), with hard, hairy stems; *Cucurbita moschata,* with pentagonal, smooth stems; and *Cucurbita pepo,* with pentagonal, prickly stems.

If you are saving seed, choose varieties from different species since plants within the same species can cross-pollinate. 'Gold Nugget' and 'Sweet Mama Hybrid' are both listed in two places because that is how you will find them in catalogs. 'Red Kuri' and related 'Hokkaido' varieties are listed under kabocha (Japanese pumpkin squash), although some would classify them as a subspecies of Hubbards.

This is a complicated group of plants. General categories follow with descriptions and possible culinary uses:

Acorn: These small, varied-colored squash are shaped like a furrowed acorn with a splotch on the bottom where it rested on the soil. It has a very hard rind when mature, although it is one winter squash that is tasty eaten immature as a "summer squash." Cut in half lengthwise, or pierce whole before cooking. The yellow flesh is grainy but sweet and fairly moist. Melt butter and brown sugar in the center. Purée flesh for soups. 'Festival' (listed under acorn squash) has golden flesh and is often sold as, but is not, an acorn squash. It has a similar shape but different rind and flesh color; it also has a hint of delicata in its flavor. 'Carnival Hybrid' (listed under acorn squash) is like an acorn squash with a thick, cream-yellow rind etched green. Its yellow flesh has a distinctive flavor similar to a butternut. Bake or steam. It is very similar to 'Festival'.

Ambercup: This squash looks like a small, deep-orange buttercup. Peel off the rind to reveal orange flesh. It is dry with a slight sweet-potato taste and very sweet. Cube and cook. Ambercup may be a buttercup-kabocha cross.

Banana: This squash looks like a large banana with blue, gray, pink, and orange skin tones. Its gorgeous golden-orange flesh is mildly sweet and creamy. Slice into pieces before cooking. Purée flesh for soups.

Buttercup: This is a hard-shelled, dark-green, drum-shaped squash with a creamy orange, somewhat dry flesh with a hint of sweet-potato flavor. It can be cooked in many ways but is commonly cut in half. It can be used for pie filling. 'Sweet Mama Hybrid', often listed as its own type, is commonly sold as a buttercup or kabocha squash (and listed in the varietal table under both).

Butternut: This squash looks like a tannish-beige bell. The rind is relatively easy to peel off, although it is technically edible. Its deep-orange, creamy flesh is sweet and nutty with a hint of sweet-potato flavor. It is one of the best winter squash for soups and "pumpkin" pie.

Cushaw: Labeled pumpkins by some, these tend to be tough to grow in cold climates, as can some of the later-maturing squash. I list two, including 'Green Striped Cushaw', noted for its use in custards and pies.

Delicata (pronounced dell-ee-KAH-tuh): This squash is also known as Bohemian, delicatessen, peanut, and sweet potato. An elongated squash with a thin, cream-colored rind striped green, its unique creamy flesh has a hint of corn and sweet-potato flavor—it is very sweet. Bake or steam, whole or cut in half lengthwise. Some people eat the skin.

Hubbard: This is usually a large squash with varied shapes. The rind is blue gray, red, striped, and often warted. It can be eaten at an immature or mature stage. Its moist, yellow flesh is moderately sweet and creamy. Pierce the rind, and bake whole with skin on, or cut into smaller pieces. The flesh can also be boiled, roasted, sautéed, or steamed. It is excellent in pies and soups.

Kabocha (pronounced kuh-BOW-chuh): This squash is also known as Japanese pumpkin. It is round with varied mottled skin colors. Its yellowish-orange, nearly fiber-less flesh is very sweet and dry with hint of sweet-potato flavor. Pierce the rind, and bake (some cooks cut the top off first, like a lid), or cut in half lengthwise. 'Tetsukabuto' is a cross between *Cucurbita maxima* and *moschata* and has a custardy flesh, eaten baked or used in pies. This variety does best planted near a *Cucurbita maxima* pollinator, such as a buttercup or Hubbard.

Spaghetti squash: This squash is also known as calabash, cucuzza, Manchurian squash, and vegetable spaghetti. The more golden and larger the squash, the better. Pierce the rind, bake for 45 minutes at 375°F, remove seeds, and scoop out the spaghetti-like strands. It is a low-calorie substitute for spaghetti, but the taste is not comparable, although it is sweet and mild. It is delicious served with herb butter and grated Parmesan cheese or with your favorite tomato-based spaghetti sauce.

Turk's turban: This squash is also known as Turk's cap. Of varied size, it looks like a bowl with a bumpy cap painted green, orange, and white. Eat it like a butternut, or cut in two and roast. 'Turk's Turban' is commonly hollowed out and filled with soup or placed on the table as an ornate decoration. Many sell it as a gourd.

VARIETY	DAYS	HABIT	FRUIT	POUNDS
Acorn				
Cucurbita pepo				
'Bush Acorn Table King' (heirloom) (AAS-1974)	80	Bush	Dark glossy green	2
'Carnival Hybrid'	85	Semivining	Gold yellow etched green	1–2
'Cream of the Crop Hybrid' (AAS-1990)	85	Bush	Creamy white	3
'Ebony Acorn' (heirloom)	85	Vining	Green black	2–3
'Festival Hybrid'*****	100	Bush	Green golden orange	2
'Fordhook Acorn' (heirloom)*****	85	Vining	Cream	2
'Honey Bear Hybrid' (AAS-2009)	100	Bush	Deep green	1–1¼
'Jersey Golden Acorn' (heirloom) (AAS-1982)	85	Bush	Orange gold	1½–2
'Royal Acorn' (heirloom)	90	Semivining	Black cream	2
'Sweet Dumpling' (heirloom)*****	95	Bush	Cream striped green sutured	½
'Table Ace Hybrid'	75	Semivining	Black green	1–2
'Table Gold' (heirloom)	90	Bush	Gold orange	1½
'Table King Bush' (heirloom)	85	Semivining	Dark green black	1½
'Table Queen' (heirloom)	90	Vining	Dark green black	1½
'Table Queen Bush' (heirloom)*****	80	Bush	Dark green	¾–1
'Thelma Sanders Sweet Potato' (heirloom)*****	90	Bush	Creamy light orange	2
'Tay-Belle (Taybelle) Hybrid'	70	Semivining	Dark green to black	2

VARIETY	DAYS	HABIT	FRUIT	POUNDS
Ambercup				
Cucurbita maxima				
'Kindred' (heirloom) (AAS-1969)*****	90	Semivining	Reddish gold marked green	3–5
'Mooregold' (heirloom)	100	Vining	Orange	4–7
'Sun Spot Hybrid'	75	Vining	Orange with light striping	2
'Sunshine Hybrid' (AAS-2004)	95	Semivining	Orange	3–5
Banana				
Cucurbita maxima				
'Blue Banana' (heirloom)	105	Vining	Blue gray	5–8+
'Guatemalan (Blue) Banana' (heirloom)	105	Vining	Blue gray green striped cream	5–8
'Jumbo Pink Banana' (heirloom)	105	Vining	Pink orange	10–70+
'Sibley' (heirloom)*****	100	Vining	Green gray blue	6–8+
Buttercup				
Cucurbita maxima				
'Autumn Cup Hybrid'	95	Semivining	Deep green	2½
'Bonbon Hybrid' (AAS-2005)	95	Semivining	Dark green with gray button	4–5
'Burgess Strain Buttercup' (heirloom)	95	Vining	Dark green with gray button	3–5
'Emerald Strain' (OP)	95	Bush	Blue green	3–5
'Gold Nugget' (OP) (AAS-1966)	95	Bush	Dull red orange, pumpkin-like	1–3
'Sweet Mama Hybrid' (AAS-1979)*****	90	Semivining	Dark gray green	3–5
Butternut				
Cucurbita moschata				
'Burpee's Butterbush' (OP)	75	Bush	Tan	1–2
'Canada Crookneck' (heirloom)*****	110	Vining	Creamy yellow	2–4
'Early Butternut Hybrid' (AAS-1979)*****	85	Vining	Tan	2–3
'Greek Sweet Red' (heirloom)*****	95	Vining	Reddish tan	2–3
'Pilgrim Hybrid'	90	Semivining	Tan	3
'Ponca' (heirloom)*****	90	Bush	Tan	2+
'Rogosa Violina Gioia' (heirloom)*****	105	Vining	Tan, violin shape	4
'Ultra Hybrid'	90	Bush	Tan	6–10
'Sucrine du Berry' (heirloom)	110	Vining	Dark green to yellowish tan	3–6
'Waltham Butternut' (heirloom) (AAS-1970)*****	105	Vining	Tan (resists borers)	4–5
'Zenith Hybrid'	90	Semivining	Tan	2–3
Cushaw				
Cucurbita argyrosperma (formerly *Cucurbita mixta*)				
'Green Striped Cushaw' (heirloom)	110	Vining	Cream with green markings	8–12
'Tennessee Sweet Potato' (heirloom)	100	Vining	Cream pear faint green	10–20
Delicata (Sweet Potato)				
Cucurbita pepo				
'Bush Delicata' (OP) (AAS-2002)	95	Semivining	Pale green cream stripes	2
'Delicata (Peanut)' (heirloom)	100	Semivining	Cream striped dark green	1½–2½
'Honey Boat' (OP)	100	Semivining	Tan striped dark green	½–1½
'Sugar Loaf' (OP)	100	Semivining	Tan striped green	1+

VARIETY	DAYS	HABIT	FRUIT	POUNDS
Hubbard				
Cucurbita maxima				
'Baby Blue' (OP)	95	Vining	Blue	5–7
'Blue Ballet' (OP)	95	Vining	Blue gray	4–6
'Blue Hubbard' (heirloom)	105	Vining	Blue gray	10–30
'Delicious' (see 'Green Delicious')				
'Gold Nugget' (OP) (AAS-1966)	95	Bush	Dull red orange, pumpkin-like	1–3
'Golden Delicious' (heirloom)	105	Vining	Red orange, teardrop	8–14+
'Golden Hubbard' (heirloom)*****	105	Vining	Red orange with white stripes	6–12
'Green Delicious' (heirloom)*****	100	Vining	Dark green	4–10
'Sugar Hubbard' (heirloom)	110	Vining	Blue gray	15–20
'Sweet Meat' (heirloom)*****	110	Vining	Slate gray	10–15
'Warted Green Hubbard' (heirloom)	110	Vining	Dark green, warted	10–12
Kabocha (Chinese or Japanese Pumpkin)				
Cucurbita maxima				
'Baby Red Hubbard' (see 'Red Kuri')				
'Black Forest' (heirloom)	95	Vining	Dark green striped green gray	3–4
'Blue Hokkaido' (heirloom)	105	Vining	Blue green, ribbed	2–3
'Blue Kuri' (see 'Blue Hokkaido)				
'Hokkaido' (sometimes listed as 'Red Kuri')	105	Vining	Deep green spotted red	6–12
'Orange (Red) Hokkaido' (see 'Red Kuri')				
'Potimarron' (heirloom; French version of 'Red Kuri')	105	Vining	Scarlet red orange, teardrop	4–7
'Red Kuri' (heirloom)*****	105	Vining	Scarlet red orange, teardrop	4–7
'Sunshine Hybrid' (AAS-2004)	95	Semivining	Orange	3–5
'Sweet Mama Hybrid' (AAS-1979)*****	90	Semivining	Dark gray green	3–5
'Tetsukabuto Hybrid'	100	Vining	Blackish green, ribbed	4–6
Spaghetti				
Cucurbita pepo				
'Orangetti Hybrid'	85	Semivining	Dark orange	2–3
'Hasta Pasta Hybrid'	85	Bush	Yellow gold orange	2–3
'Stripetti Hybrid'	95	Vining	Cream striped green	4
'Trifetti Hybrid'	90	Semivining	Orange green yellow striped	4–6
'Tivoli Hybrid' (AAS-1991)	90	Bush	Creamy tan to yellow	3–5
'Vegetable Spaghetti' (heirloom)	90	Vining	Ivory turning deep yellow	2–5
'Vermicelli Hybrid'	90	Semivining	Ivory gold	2–3
Turk's Turban				
Cucurbita maxima var. *turbaniformis*				
'Turk's Turban' (heirloom)*****	110	Semivining	Bright orange, green, white	3–5
'Marina di Chioggia' (heirloom)	100	Vining	Bluish green, warted	8–10
'Chioggia Sea Pumpkin' (see 'Marina di Chioggia')				

Eating fresh strawberries when they are still warm is a delicious summer activity.

STRAWBERRY

Fragaria species
Rose Family (Rosaceae)

Strawberries are hardy to very hardy, cool- to cold-season herbs. One of the most delicious fruits in the garden, strawberries require care but are relatively easy to grow if you get good stock right from the start. The productive life span of most varieties of strawberry plants is roughly 3 to 4 years. Since parent plants of many varieties produce runners, referred to as daughter plants, these can be used to start new beds each year. With proper care you may never have to buy or borrow plants again. Strawberries have been found wild in many areas of the world. Some of the varieties originated in Chile and eastern North America. Many crosses have resulted in named varieties.

How Strawberries Grow

Although alpine strawberries grow from seed, most varieties grow from runners or are propagated through tissue culture. These plants consist of a shallow root system connected to a crown made up of woody stem tissue, from which leaves sprout. The crown, located at the soil line, is important because it supports the plant and stores food produced by the leaves. This food is used to create foliage and fruit. The more leaves, the more fruit. Leaves spring up from the crown, spread out, and are followed by the production of stems that produce white-petaled flowers. When pollinated, these form fruits or berries that change color from green to white to deep red. The fruit is not really a fruit at all but an enlarged stamen, the male reproductive organ of the plant. But most people still call these berries or fruits. Little seeds form on the outside, not on the inside, of the "berry." As the berries ripen, the white petals fall off, leaving a portion of green stem (calyx) that looks like a series of small leaves at the base of the fruit. In reality, the tiny seed capsules (achenes) are the fruit. As the mother plants mature, some varieties send off runners or daughter plants. These are attached to the mother by stiff, stringy stems. The little daughter plants take root to form a mother plant by the following season. This cycle continues from year to year, making many varieties of strawberries perennial plants in nature.

Nutrition Facts

Serving size: 100 grams (3.5 ounces)

	AMOUNT PER RAW SERVING	% DV
Calories	32	2%
Carbohydrates	8 g	3%
Dietary fiber	2 g	8%
Folate	24 mcg	6%
Manganese	0.4 mg	19%
Protein	1 g	1%
Vitamin C	59 mg	98%

Where to Plant Strawberries

Site and Light

Strawberries grow best in full sun. Alpine strawberries, however, do better in partial shade. Avoid low-lying areas as they are prone to late spring frosts, which will destroy the flower buds of early-blooming varieties. Avoid south-facing slopes, where buds may mature early and also be hit by a late spring frost. Definitely plant strawberries in their own bed or on the edge of the garden.

Soil and Moisture

Strawberries thrive in fertile, well-drained soil that retains moisture during hot, dry spells. Add lots of organic matter, such as compost, rotted oak leaves, rotted manures, or sphagnum peat moss. The latter is excellent since it is slightly acidic. Strawberries prefer mildly acidic soil ranging in pH from 6 to 6.5. Drainage is very important. That's why the plants thrive in sandy soil as long as it is watered and fertilized regularly. If your soil is compacted, build a raised bed. Once your bed is completed, do not walk in it. The soil needs to stay loose. Raised beds have the advantage of better drainage, the disadvantage of getting hot and dry easily, requiring more water and more fertilization. Adding organic fertilizers to the soil from the start is highly recommended. Bonemeal, high in phosphorus, is particularly important.

Containers

Strawberries adapt well to container planting if you have a sheltered place to overwinter them. Any large 3- to 4-gallon container will grow enough plants for a small harvest in spring. Tiered circular metal rings or square timbers arranged in a vertical pattern take up a small amount of space but produce nice crops. Hanging baskets are effective for a small number of plants, and the dangling runners are decorative. Container-grown plants are more susceptible to die-off in winters. 'Tristar' makes a good container plant.

Planting

Seed

It is possible to start alpine strawberries from seed. In fact, it is sometimes the only way to get specific varieties. It is geared more to the specialist than the average home gardener. Start 12 weeks before outdoor planting in a sterile, moist starting mix. Press seed gently into the surface so that they are exposed to light. Keep the surface of the starting mix damp at 70°F but not wet at all times. Place pots or flat in a plastic tent to keep humidity high. Germination is erratic and may take 21 days. Once seeds begin to sprout, remove the tent, and move the pot or flat into light, keeping the temperature on the low side. As seedlings grow, prick them out, and move into small pots. If easier, move small clumps into a pot. Then let them begin to grow before snipping off all but the healthiest plant with cuticle scissors. This is a lot of work for plants that are hardy only in the southern area of the cold-climate region.

Transplants

Most strawberry plants are started from runners. These are small plants separated from a mother plant. They produce few berries in the first year but a plentiful crop the year after. You can get runners from neighbors or friends, at local nurseries in spring, where they should be kept refrigerated, or from mail-order companies.

If you get plants from a friend, try to keep some soil around the roots. If the soil drops off, as it often does, don't let the roots dry out. Sprinkle them with water, and keep them moist until the plants are in the ground. Do this as early in the season as possible.

If you get plants from a nursery or mail-order source, they may be small and are sold bare root with no soil around their roots. Check the plants to make sure that they are healthy. This can be difficult to do, since viable plants may look dry, shriveled, and nearly lifeless with little green, if any, showing on the top of the plant. Soak the roots after taking them out of the packaging for 30 minutes.

Get these plants into the soil immediately. If the soil is still frozen, take them out of the package. Put them in the refrigerator with the roots in moist (not wet) sphagnum peat moss. Correct planting is critical to survival but actually easy. Study the plant. The roots are obvious. Just above the roots is the crown. It may have a few shriveled leaves sticking up from it. You want the roots to end up below the soil, the crown just at soil level, and the few leaves sticking up above the crown in the air.

If there are just a few roots, stick your finger into the loose soil of the planting bed to make a little hole. Place the roots into the hole making sure the crown is not buried but level with the soil. Now press the soil around the roots, and firm them in place. Water immediately.

If the roots are longer, spread them out over a cone of soil or lay them off to one side. I prefer spreading them out. Do not snip off any portion of root unless it is clearly damaged. Again, the crown should be level with the surrounding soil. Cover the roots, and firm the soil in place. Water immediately.

If you bury the crown, the plants may rot out. If you plant the crown too high with portions of the roots exposed, the plant may dry out and die. This sounds difficult, but once you study the little plant, these directions will be simple. Correct planting depth and consistent water in the first weeks is the key to success with strawberries.

If the plants you buy look really rough from the start, let the company know. Tell them you will give them a try, and if they do not grow, ask for your money back. But call them immediately on receipt of the plants so they cannot blame you for the problem. It amazes me how small and shriveled some of these plants sold are, and yet, when planted, they do remarkably well within a few weeks. Assume nothing without giving them a chance.

Spacing

There is little agreement among home gardeners about how to space strawberry plants. Some people plant individual plants 12 to 18 inches apart and remove runners as they appear (called "hilling"). This is a popular method for everbearing strawberries. Others space plants at the same distance but allow a few runners to develop (called "hedgerow"), while still others allow all of the runners to develop into an ever-expanding mat (called "matting"). The latter is commonly done with June-bearing strawberries. Air circulation does help reduce the chance of disease. Still, I prefer matting to reduce the time dealing with the plants and limiting bird damage. Some fruits do rot out because getting fresh mulch into mats is difficult. Also, picking strawberries in a mat is a game of hide-and-seek.

When to Plant

Get regular strawberry plants into the ground as soon as the ground can be worked. This can be as early as 3 to 4 weeks before the last expected spring frost when the soil may be no warmer than 40°F. Ideally, plant strawberries in the evening or on a cloudy day. Set alpine strawberry transplants into the garden later, after the frost-free date. Protect them if a cold snap threatens.

Strawberry flowers add beauty to the spring garden and can be candied for an edible treat.

Support

The individual plants do not need support. However, a thick layer of straw placed around the plants keeps the berries off the ground, where they tend to rot out.

How to Care for Strawberries
Water

Consistent moisture is critical after initial planting. Water every day if necessary in the first 2 to 3 weeks. Drip irrigation is effective if strawberries are planted in long raised beds, since soil in these dries out quickly. Just flooding a flat bed with a hose works fine. The main concern is that plants do not like drought and need deep and frequent watering throughout the entire growing season. Day-neutral strawberries are especially sensitive to drought. If you use sprinklers to water plants, do this early in the day to give the strawberries a chance to dry off.

Mulch

It is common for commercial growers to build long raised beds, cover these with black plastic, and have extensive drip irrigation systems to water the plants under the plastic. This method is effective but expensive and labor intensive.

Some home gardeners plant transplants through slits in black fabric or plastic. This helps prevent the growth of weeds, which can be a real nuisance in a strawberry bed. Some use drip irrigation; others don't. Often this synthetic mulch is covered with a thick layer of organic mulch, such as straw. This keeps the area cooler and the strawberries raised off the ground to prevent rot. Also, runners have no place to take root and are usually snipped off as they appear. However, plastic can get really hot, is fairly expensive, and somewhat of a pain to work with.

The most common and simplest method of mulching is to surround young plants with a ½-inch layer of organic mulch a few weeks after they are planted, just as the soil begins to warm up a bit. Good mulches early in the season include grass clippings, pulverized leaves, and shredded straw. These keep the soil moist, prevent weed growth, and keep the soil at an even temperature. As the season progresses, tuck a loose layer of whole straw under the developing leaves as the plants begin to flower. As the berries form, the mulch keeps them off the ground, where they may rot.

Fertilizing

Plant new plants in already well-fertilized soil. Fertilize June-bearing varieties in mid-July. Fertilize all everbearing (fall) berries in the fall after they have stopped producing. Good organic fertilizers include fish emulsion and seaweed. Cottonseed and soybean meals are fine where available. Spread fertilizer around the base of the plants, and water it in well.

Weeding

Strawberry plants compete poorly with weeds. It is easy enough to keep weeds out of a newly planted area, but if you allow strawberries to form a thick mat over a period of years, things can get out of hand. At this point the overabundant strawberry plants are in themselves weeds.

One way of handling this problem is to start a new bed. Dig up enough healthy plants, and plant them in early spring as you did when you started your original patch. Then scrape off the remaining weeds and intermingled strawberry plants, toss them into the compost pile, and till the soil until it is loose and ready to be planted with another crop.

Another way of handling a weed-choked strawberry bed is to mow it with a lawn mower set at a high level. The thought of this scares most gardeners. The idea is to cut down the weeds and the strawberry plants to a level just above their crowns. Rake up the debris. Dig up weeds, and leave space between healthy strawberry plants. The mower

has cut these back to the tip of the crown, which will re-sprout. Mulch between the plants. You will not believe how quickly these plants come back to full growth, especially June-bearing varieties.

One other method is to till all but 2 to 3 feet of the bed. Let this strip produce runners off to the side. Let these mature and start producing. Then till in the original bed that produced the runners. The idea behind any of these methods is to destroy weeds but also cut down on the number of strawberry plants so that they are not competing for moisture and nutrients as weeds would. This is a form of bed renewal that really works well since plants often deteriorate after a few years.

Pruning

Pruning in the first year consists of removing flowers and runners (daughter plants) that form off to the side of the mother plant. You can pinch off flowers, but use scissors to cut the wiry stem between the mother and daughter plants.

To prune June-bearing strawberries, pinch off all flowers as they develop early in the season. This is optional. However, flower removal directs energy into the mother plant and encourages the growth of runners. Some gardeners remove all, some, or none of these runners in the first season. Most gardeners leave some to ensure a steady supply of new mother plants in the following and subsequent years.

If flowers on everbearing strawberries blossom in the first year, remove all of them for the first 6 to 8 weeks. Again, this is optional. Additional flowers may develop later in the season, and few gardeners remove these. Everbearing strawberries produce far fewer runners than June-bearing types. Most gardeners leave these on, again for additional plants in the coming season.

Remove the flowers of day-neutral (everbearing day-neutral in this guide) for 6 to 8 weeks, and keep flowers on for the rest of the season. As for other types of strawberries, this is optional. Runners are relatively restrained, so runner removal is not a concern.

In subsequent years, you do not have to remove flowers, but you may want to thin out runners, especially on June-bearing varieties. Left on their own, these berries can form a thick, sprawling mass of plants.

Consider planting June-bearing and everbearing strawberries in two different locations. This spreads out the yield of strawberries over the summer months. Experiment with flower and runner removal. I do neither, with the exception of using runners as a way of propagating new plants each year. Plants do deteriorate with age, so this strategy makes sense to me.

Winter Protection

Snow is your best winter protection. Unfortunately, you can't count on it. During the first year after planting, cover the bed with a thick layer of straw after a few hard frosts. Oat straw is ideal since it will not mat down. Long pine needles are also good. Whole leaves work but may mat down. They are known as "junk mulch" by some strawberry growers, but they do work. Timing is important. If you protect the plants too early, they may rot out or be damaged by rodents using the winter cover as a home. If you wait too long, plants may be damaged or heave out of the soil. As soon as the soil freezes hard at night, apply the mulch. In spring remove the mulch over a period of days until plants are fully exposed. If it gets too warm, the covered plants may rot out. If a severe frost or freeze is predicted after you have removed the mulch, cover the area with a sheet. Strawberry plants are quite durable. The winter mulch can be used around the plants as a summer mulch, or you can toss it into a compost pile. After strawberries have gotten through their first winter, winter protection is rarely needed.

Fabric row covers also provide good winter protection but must be anchored down to stop them from blowing around in wind gusts. Although expensive, they are easy to put on and take off as temperatures fluctuate.

Special Considerations

When overall harvests begin to diminish, it is time to renew your bed. Or you can root runners in an entirely different location, starting a new bed from scratch. Enrich and loosen the soil well before doing this. You will have a beautiful crop the following year.

Extending the Season

The everbearing varieties sometimes have small berries maturing late in the season. Covering these with sheets or row covers is an option.

Problems

Insects

Occasionally, you will see tiny patches of foam on strawberry plants. These are made by spittlebugs. Cut off the leaves and discard them. If your berries are small and misshapen, known as "nubbins," this could be the work of the tarnished plant bug. Occasionally, grubs, such as June beetle larvae, will attack the roots of strawberries, usually in areas where sod was growing in the previous year.

Disease

If you pick all of the ripe berries each day, your patch will rarely be bothered seriously by fungal infections. Pick and discard the bad berries that may be mushy or fuzzy whenever you see them to stop the spread of the disease. Problems are most common in wet seasons, and very common if you do not use a straw mulch to keep the berries off the ground. Overcrowding and competition with weeds can also be a cause of infections.

Marauders

Exposed berries are sometimes bothered by birds. In the matted berry patch this is rarely a problem. If your berries are completely exposed, use netting. Deer will eat the tops off strawberries in both spring and fall, less commonly in midseason. While frustrating, plants usually recuperate and produce a reasonable crop of berries. If chipmunks are a nuisance, either accept the damage or trap them.

Physiological

On rare occasions berries will be hollow inside. The berry is still edible. Cut down on your use of nitrogen.

Propagation

Most strawberries are propagated from runners, the little daughter plants that form off to the side of the mother plant as the season progresses. Pull up gently on one of the runners. If it resists, then it has formed roots. Cut the stem joining the mother plant to the runner. Dig up the small plant with some soil around its roots. Plant it as you did your initial planting—no deeper, no higher in the soil.

Note that you can save seed from mature alpine strawberries. Let the fruit mature and dry, then rub it between your fingers to separate the seed. Or place overly mature fruit into a blender to separate pulp from seed. Store the seed in an envelope in a cool, dry place.

Harvesting

If you remove flowers in the first year, there will be no harvest. Some immature plants will produce no flowers or very few. Begin harvesting the following year. Strawberries tend to mature first where the sun is brightest. So look for ripe berries on the edge of beds first. Berries in the inside of the patch almost hide under a thick canopy of leaves. Lift leaves up gently and really search for all of the ripe berries.

Pick berries only when they are a deep red with no green color on their tips. This often means waiting a day or two after they first turn red. These will be fragrant and juicy because they are fully ripe. Less ripe berries will continue to ripen if you pick them a bit too early, but the sweetness will never be the same. Sugars are at their peak just as the berries are picked, which is why some sampling usually goes on during harvesting. Strawberries do not store well, and they bruise easily. Take a plate or platter into the garden, and set the berries in a single layer on these. Never stack them. Too many berries? Take them inside, and freeze them immediately.

If possible, pick the berries when the foliage is dry to stop the spread of disease. They are most fragrant if warm, although they may last a little longer if picked on a cool or cloudy day early in the morning. Pick them with their green caps on, just as you see them in the grocery store. Wash the berries only when you are ready to eat them.

If your strawberries are in a large patch, try not to damage plants or fruit as you walk into it. A thick layer of mulch also helps prevent soil compaction as you make your way from one plant to the next.

Storing

As soon as you pick strawberries, get them into your refrigerator. Do not wash these until ready to use. Spread them out evenly on a large plate. They usually last 2 to 3 days if handled gently from the start.

To freeze, wash and remove green caps, pack whole or slice, freeze on trays. If whole, pack dry; if sliced, consider sweetening with honey or sugar. Sugar can either be sugar syrup, consisting of 3 cups sugar to 1 cup water, or dry sugar. Or make a purée in a blender, and freeze. With alpine strawberries, try adding a little claret, a red wine from Bordeaux.

To dry, wash, slice into thin pieces, dip into water with lemon juice (ascorbic acid), and dry in a dehydrator. Alternatively, dry in an oven on a metal tray covered with parchment paper. Set the oven at its lowest setting, and flip the slices over in about 2 hours. Continue until the slices are completely dry. They may last for up to 6 months.

Culinary Uses

Most people use freshly picked strawberries right away on cereals, in fruit cups, or as a dessert. Frozen berries are delicious in smoothies. They are favorites for jams, jellies, and pies. The flowers are sometimes candied and are both lovely and tasty.

Varieties

Following is a good selection of strawberries for cold climates. They have proven themselves over a period of many years. Buy certified plants of any specific variety. Choose varieties by type, hardiness, and overall resistance to disease, which is covered in most catalogs. Despite hardiness ratings, strawberries do better in specific regions, so ask locally for advice. More than likely several of those will be in the following list.

June-bearing strawberries tend to come in early- to mid-season in one big flush. Flower buds on some varieties can be damaged by a late spring freeze. They produce runners prolifically. 'Honeyoye' and 'Sparkle' are commonly recommended for storing as frozen berries.

Day-neutral strawberries were developed from everbearing plants, and I choose to call them everbearing day-neutral. They produce more or less continuously throughout the season. If temperatures get above 90°F, they stop flowering. Over time they may revert to everbearing plants. They may not produce runners or produce only a few. Use the limited number of runners to create a new bed (see "Propagation").

Everbearing is a bit misleading. These berries produce fruit in flushes, just the way many roses bloom. They may also be called perpetual fruiting or *remontant*—French for repeat blooming. Typically, they produce two main flushes in spring to midsummer and again in fall. If you want just one large, late crop, pick off all early blossoms. They will produce runners but not as freely as June-bearing varieties.

VARIETY	TYPE	BLOOM TIME	HARDINESS
'Albion' (disease resistant)	Everbearing day-neutral	Off and on	-30°F
'Allstar'	June-bearing	Mid	-30°F
'Annapolis'	June-bearing	Early	-40°F
'Cabot'	June-bearing	Mid to late	-30°F
'Cavendish'	June-bearing	Early mid	-40°F
'Earliglow'*****	June-bearing	Early	-30°F
'Fort Laramie'	Everbearing	Mainly late	-30°F
'Honeyoye'	June-bearing	Early mid	-40°F
'Jewel'	June-bearing	Mid to late	-30°F
'Kent'	June-bearing	Late mid	-40°F
'Ogallala'	Everbearing	Mainly late	-30° to -40°F
'Ozark Beauty'	Everbearing	Mid to late	-30°F
'Seascape'	Everbearing day-neutral	Off and on	-30°F
'Sparkle'	June-bearing	Mid to late	-30° to -40°F
'Tribute'	Everbearing day-neutral	Off and on	-20° to -25°F
'Tristar'	Everbearing day-neutral	Off and on	-30°F

Strawberry, Alpine
Fragaria vesca var. *semperflorens (sempervirens)*

Alpine strawberries are small plants with tiny berries that have an exquisite scent and flavor. However, they are not reliably hardy. Most varieties produce strawberries throughout much of the growing season. They produce few, if any, runners. Wild or woodland strawberries, known as *fraises des bois* in French, are similar. There are named varieties, but they are most commonly sold by their generic name. Grow them only on the southern border of the cold-climate region with a thick winter mulch.

The vines and lustrous leaves of sweet potatoes are edible—in case tuberous roots form poorly.

SWEET POTATO

Ipomoea batatas
Morning Glory Family (Convolvulaceae)

Sweet potatoes are very tender, warm-season perennials grown as annuals. Sweet potatoes grow best in the South, where summers are long and hot. Even so, breeders have introduced varieties that will mature in the shorter growing seasons of cold-climate areas. Sweet potatoes are not yams (*Dioscorea* species) but may be sold under that name. Sweet potatoes probably originated in South America.

How Sweet Potatoes Grow

Sweet potatoes grow from slips, portions of stem, cut from sprouting tuberous roots. Once planted, each slip develops an extensive root system as the foliage aboveground matures into long vines with attractive heart-shaped leaves. While the root system develops, the aboveground growth may be slow. Sweet potatoes are pieces of root, not stem tissue as are Irish potatoes, and often develop within a short distance from the base of the stem. The planted stems may produce no, a few, or many swollen portions of root, and these swollen portions may vary greatly in size. Occasionally, a lucky gardener will have plants produce a morning glory–like flower, but this is uncommon. Sweet potatoes usually develop by fall and are harvested at that time.

Where to Plant
Site and Light

Sweet potatoes like it hot and dry. Choose the sunniest spot available in the garden. The vines will roam, so keep that in mind. To heat up the soil, consider laying black plastic on the planting area 30 days before planting. If you live in the far north, use clear plastic, but be aware that if temperatures soar in the middle of summer, clear plastic can get so hot that it damages the vines lying on it. Placing hoops over the area before covering these with clear plastic is fine. If temperatures soar, remove the tunnel.

Soil and Moisture

A moderately fertile, sandy loam is ideal. Soil should be loose and drain freely. If your soil is compacted, loosen it, and make an 18- to 24-inch-high ridge 2 to 4 feet wide. Or build an enclosed raised bed. Add compost, sphagnum peat moss, or well-rotted manure to the soil as well as organic fertilizer, especially bonemeal for phosphorus and any organic fertilizer high in potassium except wood ash. Ideally, do this in the fall for spring planting. Sweet potatoes like a pH of 5.8 to 6.2, which is slightly acidic, so adding peat is helpful.

Container

It is possible to grow sweet potatoes in a large pot, but this is more for fun than a large crop. The vines are attractive and can be snipped back to keep them trimmed and tidy. It is possible to bring pots indoors, where plants can limp through the winter to be placed outdoors the following summer. This is a lot of work but does give you a chance to take slips off the mature plant the following spring.

Planting
Transplants (Slips)

Most sweet potatoes are started from slips purchased from mail-order sources. The slips, anywhere from 5 to 18 inches long depending on the variety, are portions of stem slid off sprouting sweet potatoes. They will have some small roots already growing from the base of the stem. These are packed in a moist material and will continue to grow during shipping. The slips may be called draws, stem or vine cuttings, or starts. If you cannot plant them immediately, do not place them in water or soil. In both cases the slips form a thick mat of roots. Planting slips with too many roots results in transplant shock, which may stunt the plant's growth. Instead, place them in moist sphagnum moss in an ice cream bucket, and store for as little time as possible (not in the refrigerator) before planting. Buy your slips from a northern source familiar with correct planting times.

In cold climates it makes sense to plant sweet potatoes in ridges at least 18 inches high. These ridges warm up quickly in spring and allow for extensive root growth. The entire ridge can be covered with black plastic to raise the soil temperature by as much as 10°F. Plastic should be in place at least several weeks before the last expected frost in your area. Always anchor the plastic in place.

Make slits in the plastic when you are ready to plant. Get the roots deep into the soil. If leaves turn yellow, snip them off, but do not remove any healthy leaves.

Slips grown from sweet potatoes purchased at a grocery store may be from a variety poorly suited to cold climates and may also harbor disease. Still, many home gardeners do grow their own slips.

Nutrition Facts
Serving size: 100 grams (3.5 ounces)

	AMOUNT PER COOKED SERVING	% DV
Calories	90	5%
Carbohydrates	21 g	7%
Copper	0.2 mg	8%
Dietary fiber	3 g	13%
Magnesium	27 mg	7%
Manganese	0.5 mg	25%
Phosphorus	54 mg	5%
Potassium	475 mg	14%
Protein	2 g	4%
Vitamin A	19,200 IU	385%
Vitamin B6	0.3 mg	14%
Vitamin C	20 mg	33%

There are several ways to grow sweet potatoes purchased from an organic grocery store or co-op. Buy a firm, healthy potato. Roots grow from the lower pointed end, while slips or sprouts grow from the stem end, which usually has a scar from where the tuberous root was snipped off the

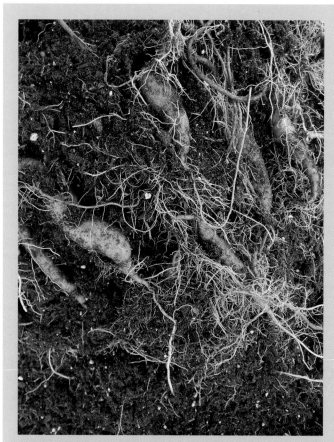

The secret of growing sweet potatoes in cold climates is heat, heat, and more heat.

mother plant. Begin working with this potato at least 8 to 12 weeks before the last expected frost in your area. Fill a pot with soil, lay the sweet potato on its side, cover halfway with potting soil, and keep moist and as hot as 80°F in good light until the sweet potato is growing well. Remove slips, and plant these individually, as described later. The advantage of this method is that you don't have to know which end of the potato is the root or stem end to be assured of getting slips. Do not plant the whole potato in the garden as you would an Irish potato, just a single slip in one spot at a time.

Alternatively, place three toothpicks into the potato about one-third from the base of the root end. Rest the toothpicks on the rim of a jar filled with water. Just the bottom of the tuber should be in the water. Put this jar in a dark area. Don't let the bottom of the tuber get above water level. Change the water daily. As soon as the sweet potato begins to sprout, bring the jar into light. The stems grow quickly and start to leaf out. When they are at least 6 inches long or longer, twist them off the sweet potato with your fingers. The best slips are thick with about six nodes, the places where leaves join the stem. Now place the base of these slips into water until they form a few short roots. Continue to change the water regularly to stop it from going stagnant.

Spacing

Plant slips about 12 to 18 inches apart along the ridge or in the raised bed. The vines will spread out in all directions, but the base of the plant is where the tubers will form.

When to Plant

Anything you can do to provide these plants with heat will help them produce good-sized, edible tuberous roots. Heat refers to both soil and air temperature. Since you can't control the weather, control the growing environment to the best of your ability. Plant slips only after the garden soil has reached 65°F. Increase soil temperature with black plastic over the planting bed. Ideally, cover the plants temporarily in a clear plastic grow tunnel. Although this takes time, money, and effort and is optional, it is almost a necessity in the far north. Get plants in by early or mid-June in most cold-climate areas to give sweet potatoes a long enough season to develop. Glenn Drowns of Sandhill Preservation Center has come up with a formula that predicts your chance of success. He claims that plants need 1,200 heat units per season to produce nice potatoes. To determine a heat unit, add the high and low temperature each day, divide by two, and subtract 55 degrees. So 80°F in the day with 70°F at night is 150; divided by two, equals 75; less 55 equals 20 heat units. Clearly the hotter it is every day, the better your chance of

reaching the critical heat unit number. Anything you can do to increase the number, the better.

Support

Although it is possible to grow sweet potato vines vertically, few people do, unless they bring a plant indoors to grow as a houseplant.

How to Care for Sweet Potatoes
Water

Water the plants heavily just after planting for 7 to 10 days. As soon as the plants take root and start to grow, water plants only every few days during dry spells. Deep watering is preferable at such times. Soaker hoses under plastic work fine, but don't overwater. Overwatering late in the season may cause cracks to form in the skin, which results in poor storage. So stop watering 3 to 4 weeks before your expected harvest. Too much rain during the season may result in poorly formed roots, but you have no control over this. Just make sure your soil is draining freely, which is usually the case in raised beds.

Mulch

Using a synthetic mulch is highly recommended, and it should be put in place as early in the season as possible. Black plastic increases soil temperature dramatically. Make sure that it is tight against the soil and well anchored on its sides to prevent air leaks. The latter can lead to weed growth under the cover.

Fertilizing

Do not feed with any nitrogen-rich fertilizer. This will just stimulate heavy foliage at the expense of the underground potatoes, which may end up long and thin. Sometimes, foliage looks weak and spindly for a week or so, possibly even longer if the temperature remains cool. This should not continue. As the season progresses, foliage should become full and lush with good color. Sweet potato vines are truly beautiful.

Weeding

Weeding during the first 6 to 7 weeks is critical. Hand pull all weeds close to the stem. If you use a plastic cover as a mulch, you won't have to worry about weeding between the vines.

Pruning

Of course, if growing in containers, cut off meandering foliage. Otherwise, most gardeners let plants create as much foliage as possible to direct food into the tuberous roots. As vines spread out, they sometimes take root at leaf nodes. Slide your hand under the vine to dislodge the roots. You want all energy directed toward the base of the plant.

Extending the Season

Get plastic on the growing area as early as possible. This will warm up the soil. Keep it in place, and plant through it for an earlier planting. Cover with a tunnel. If plants are not mature enough in fall, protect them from frost with floating row covers. Or if growing them in a large pot, bring indoors.

Problems

Insects

Watch for cutworms, flea beetles, and slugs. 'Patriot' has good disease and pest resistance.

Disease

Prevent problems by planting healthy slips from certified organic growers. Plant slips only after the soil is thoroughly warm. Otherwise, you risk rot from too cool or wet soil.

Marauders

Sweet potatoes are delicacies to deer, ground hogs, mice, moles, gophers, rabbits, voles—just about any animal that digs through the soil or attacks sprouts and greens above the soil. Plastic tunnels offer good protection along with a sturdy fence.

Physiological

It is in the nature of the plant to put most of its energy into root formation early in the season. Foliage will develop later—be patient. Slips from the same variety may produce quite different crops. Don't expect uniform yields.

Propagation

At the end of the season, plant several tuberous roots in a large pot. Lay them down half-covered in sterile soil. They will begin to sprout. Grow them as a houseplant. In the spring take slips or stem cuttings from the tubers, and continue the plant's life cycle, essentially making it a perennial vegetable.

Harvesting

You can begin harvesting tuberous roots whenever you want, but realistically cold-climate gardeners should let them ma-

ture as long as possible. Leave them in the ground as long as the soil temperature stays above 55°F and there is no threat of frost. If the soil gets too cool or if there is a frost, decay organisms may cause the tuberous roots to rot. If surprised by a frost, cut off the vines and harvest immediately, preferably in full sun when the soil is dry enough to fork up the tuberous roots easily. Dig about 18 inches from the base, and work your way into where the initial slip was planted. Be careful not to damage the thin skin, as this can lead to decay. Cold can affect the taste and storage capacity, so if vines are killed by frost, act quickly.

Storing

Unlike Irish potatoes, sweet potatoes do not taste as good fresh. They need to be cured and stored for a week or so at 75° to 85°F. Once fully dry, lightly brush off soil, but do not break the skin—better a little dirt on the tubers than damage. Do not wash. Curing creates a "second skin" that hardens the exterior of the potato and protects the tuber. Some people place them close to the furnace if it is running; others, on top of the refrigerator. If temperatures are lower, cure them longer. Avoid dropping sweet potatoes, since this can cause bruising, which leads to rot.

Once cured, the ideal storing temperature is 65°F. Sweet potatoes can stand quite high humidity, even up to 85 percent. But if the air is drier, they seem to store reasonably well anyway. The largest and most mature sweet potatoes store the longest, so eat the smaller ones first.

Do not place sweet potatoes in plastic or in the refrigerator. They tend to self-destruct in plastic, and the temperature in the refrigerator adversely affects flavor and texture. Store the potatoes with some space between them, as on a flat shelf in total darkness. Some home gardeners claim success storing sweet potatoes wrapped individually in newspaper or placed in dry peat or maple leaves. Check the potatoes frequently. Cut off minor blemishes, and use the rest of the potato immediately. If the temperature and humidity are correct, they may store from 4 to 6 months. Home storage can be difficult. If they get too cold, they will rot. If too hot, they will sprout and shrivel. If they turn moldy or start to rot, toss them, since they can become toxic. They have been proven toxic to farm animals, so why take a chance?

If skeptical about long-term storage, cook and freeze excess potatoes after curing and storing for as long as possible. To freeze, peel, bake until tender, cool, cut up or purée, place in airtight freezer bags, and freeze. Adding a little lemon juice to sweet potatoes may help prevent discoloration.

Culinary Uses

Sweet potato is edible raw, most commonly grated into salads. Tiny new leaves and shoot tips are also edible and not poisonous like those of Irish potatoes. These are steamed, stir-fried with garlic, or added to soups. Don't cut off too much foliage, since this can affect the overall size of the developing tuberous roots.

Once sweet potatoes have been cured and stored to develop sweetness, wash them for the first time. Most sources agree that it is *safer not to eat the skins as you would on a white potato.* Note that color may change if sweet potatoes are peeled before cooking. For example, purple fleshed varieties may lose much of their color if not cooked with the skin on.

To bake, pierce the skin, coat lightly with butter, and cook at 400°F until tender. The flavor tends to be best when sweet potatoes are exposed to direct heat and not covered. If microwaving, cook just until soft when squeezed. Serve with butter, lemon or orange zest, brown sugar, or chopped nuts. They are also delicious mashed with a touch of cinnamon or nutmeg, or covered with butter and honey.

Sweet potatoes may be cut up and added to soups, slivered and added to stir-fries, or cut into thin strips and cooked like french fries. Or steam strips to preserve as many nutrients as possible. Many consider sweet potato bread a delicacy, and sweet potato pie as well, which is most attractive made from the flesh of dark-orange varieties.

Sweet potatoes vary in texture. Some are firm when cooked, others soft and moist. The latter are often sold as yams.

Varieties

Most of the following varieties mature early to relatively early compared to other varieties, typically within 90 to 110 days from planted slips. Days to maturity is somewhat misleading in that development of tuberous roots varies by the intensity of heat during the season. So each variety could mature earlier or later than the time listed either here or in catalogs. There is no mention of hybrids in the list. Some varieties are referred to as improved selections by some, but that is overly technical. 'Centennial' forms excellent roots and does quite well in clay but takes up a lot of space. 'Vardaman', bred in 1981, is a better choice if your space is limited. In general, the deeper orange the color, the sweeter and more nutritious the flesh. Experiment with different varieties over a period of years. Note that 'Carolina Nugget', developed in 1954, is practically an heirloom.

VARIETIES	DAYS	SKIN/FLESH COLOR/TEXTURE	VINE LENGTH (FEET)
'Amish Bush Porto Rico' (heirloom)*****	Early	Pink/orange/fairly moist	4–6
'Arkansas Red' (heirloom)	Early	Pink red/orange/moist	6–8
'Barberman' (heirloom)	Early	Red orange/deep orange/moist	6–8
'Beauregard' (OP)	Mid	Reddish orange/orange/moist	6–8
'California Gold' (OP)	Early	Light orange/orange/dry side	6–8
'Carolina Nugget' (OP)	Early	Pink cream/orange/moist	4–6
'Centennial' (heirloom)	Early	Copper red/pale orange/moist	8–12+
'Indiana Gold' (heirloom)	Early	Gold/orange/moist	6–8
'Ivis White Cream' (heirloom)*****	Early	Cream/cream/dry side	6–8
'Japanese' (heirloom)	Early	Pink red/light orange/dry side	6–8
'Jewel' (OP)	Mid late	Copper/light orange/moist	4–6
'Korean Purple' (heirloom)*****	Early	Purple/white/dry	6–8
'Laceleaf' (heirloom)	Early	Pink/light orange/dry side	4–6
'Liberty' (OP)	Early	Magenta/white/dry side	8–12+
'Oakleaf' (heirloom)	Early	Pink/light orange/dry side	4–6
'Patriot' (OP)	Early	Pinkish orange/orange/moist side	4–6
'Pense Red' (heirloom)*****	Early	Pinkish red/pale orange/dry side	4–6
'Porto Rico Bunch' (OP)	Mid	Pale orange/pale orange/moist	4–6
'Purple' (heirloom)	Early	Deep purple/deep purple/dry	8–12
'Redglow' (OP)	Early	Pinkish red/orange/moist side	4–6
'Red Jewel' (OP)	Early	Red/orange/moist	6–8
'Red Resisto' (OP)	Early	Purplish red/orange/moist	4–6
'Scarlet' (OP)	Early	Red/orange/moist	6–8
'Topaz' (OP)	Early	Copper orange/orange/moist	6–8
'Vardaman' (OP)*****	Mid	Orange/deep orange/moist	less than 4
'Violetta' (heirloom)*****	Early	Purple/white/dry	6–8
'Wakenda' (heirloom)	Early	Dark pink/deep orange/moist	6–8
'Willowleaf' (heirloom)	Early	Light orange/orange/dry side	4–6

SWISS CHARD

Beta vulgaris ssp. *cicla,* or *Beta vulgaris* ssp. *cicla* var. *flavescens*
Amaranth or Goosefoot Family (Amaranthaceae, formerly Chenopodiaceae)

Swiss chard is a hardy, cool-season biennial grown as an annual. It is a type of beet developed for its leaves, rather than its roots. Swiss chard should be on any gardener's discover list. It grows beautifully in hot weather, can withstand some drought, and can even withstand severe frosts. It is also one of the easiest plants to grow and rarely suffers attacks from disease or insects. Swiss chard goes by a number of common names, including chard, Chilean beet, crab beet, leaf beet, mangold, perpetual spinach, Roman kale, ruby chard, seakale beet, Sicilian beet, silver beet or chard, spinach beet, strawberry spinach, and white beet. Swiss chard may have originated in the Mediterranean or Near East but is most likely from southern France or Italy.

How Swiss Chard Grows

The seed (a fruit) is tan, fairly large, and rough (about 1,500 to 1,800 seeds per ounce). Its irregular surface is similar to that of a beet, as you would expect. Each little pod contains a number of seeds. These grow like lettuce, producing deli-

cate seedlings. The outer leaves mature first, with the inner ones developing afterwards. An uncut plant gets bushy and up to 24 inches tall or more. Some varieties are so beautiful that flower gardeners grow them as ornamental plants. The leaves generally are green with thick midribs and stems that can be fairly large and come in a rainbow of colors.

Where to Plant Swiss Chard
Site and Light

Swiss chard prefers full sun but tolerates partial shade. Unlike spinach, Swiss chard is surprisingly heat tolerant. The beauty of these plants makes them attractive enough to mingle easily in flower beds and borders. Swiss chard is also one of the few vegetables that tolerates salt.

Soil and Moisture

Although Swiss chard tolerates a wide variety of soils, it thrives in moist, fertile soil that drains freely. If your soil is compacted or rocky, build a raised bed. Add lots of organic matter to the soil at planting time. Horse manure is excellent since it is slightly alkaline and holds moisture in the soil. Adding a little lime for magnesium or wood ash for potassium in the fall helps. Lime also creates a more alkaline soil. Don't go overboard—just a little of each. A small amount of bonemeal is a good source of phosphorus, which promotes healthy root growth. The soil should have a pH of 6.5 to 7.5, which is neutral to slightly alkaline.

Container

Many gardeners grow Swiss chard successfully in containers. Grow up to six plants in a 3-gallon container.

Planting

Seed

The large, irregularly surfaced seeds are really pods that usually contain three to six embryos. So when you plant a seed, you will get three or four plants in one spot. Swiss chard seeds are notorious for being unpredictable, although I have not found this to be true. Try soaking the seed in cold water for several hours up to a full day before planting. Plant them immediately after soaking.

Since germination may be erratic, plant them ½ inch deep 1 to 2 inches apart. If they all sprout, you can thin them later. Keep the soil around the seeds moist at all times. This will help germination and make it easy for the seedlings to pop through the soil surface. Ideally, seeds germinate within 14 days.

To prevent crusting of the soil surface, add a very thin layer, ½ inch or less, of grass clippings or shredded leaves over the planting row. This will also retain moisture in the soil. As soon as the plants start to pop through the soil, move the mulch just off to the side unless the seedlings are growing right through it.

Transplants

Starting plants indoors 4 weeks before planting time is possible but makes little sense unless you have extra time on your hands. Transplant into the garden when seedlings are 2 to 3 inches tall.

Spacing

Plants can be quite close if you are cutting them back regularly or harvesting the outer leaves as they get to be about 6 inches tall. However, if you are growing plants for their mature stems, space them at least 8 to 12 inches apart.

When to Plant

Swiss chard is a much easier plant to grow than spinach. It does well in both cool and warm weather. It won't bolt

Nutrition Facts
Serving size: 100 grams (3.5 ounces)

	AMOUNT PER RAW SERVING	% DV	AMOUNT PER COOKED SERVING	% DV
Calories	20	1%	20	1%
Carbohydrate	4 g	1%	4 g	1%
Copper	0.2 mg	9%	0.2 mg	9%
Dietary fiber	2 g	6%	2 g	6%
Iron	1.8 mg	10%	2.3 mg	13%
Magnesium	81 mg	20%	86 mg	21%
Manganese	0.4 mg	18%	0.3 mg	17%
Potassium	400 mg	10%	550 mg	16%
Protein	2 g	4%	2 g	4%
Vitamin A	6,125 IU	122%	6,125 IU	122%
Vitamin C	30 mg	50%	18 mg	30%
Vitamin E	1.9 mg	9%	1.9	9%
Vitamin K	830 mcg	1,040%	325 mcg	410%

in hot weather or long days the way spinach will. Plant it about 3 to 4 weeks before the last expected frost as soon as the ground can be worked. The soil temperature should be around 50°F. Swiss chard seedlings can take light frosts but will be damaged by a hard frost or freeze, so very early planting is a bit of a gamble but still worth a try. If you are not a gambler, plant after the last expected frost. Make small successive plantings for a few weeks. Then plant again in August for a fall crop.

How to Care for Swiss Chard

Water

Keep the soil evenly moist after planting seed. As the plants mature, water when the soil starts to dry out. If you cut back plants close to the ground, water immediately to encourage regrowth. If you allow plants to mature, then water whenever the soil dries out. Mature plants can withstand drier conditions, but chard still does better with consistent watering. Leaves will also turn a bit bitter if you water erratically.

Mulch

Place a 3-inch layer of organic mulch around the plants once they are several inches tall. This helps retain moisture in the soil and cuts down on watering.

Fertilizing

Fertilize lightly each time you pick leaves off a plant to stimulate new growth. If you have added organic fertilizer to the soil at planting time, fertilizing can be light or, sometimes, not necessary. If leaf growth seems weak, add a little fertilizer high in nitrogen.

Weeding

Hand weed around the young plants. If surrounded by mulch, weeds are easy to pull.

Thinning

If you keep picking or cutting the plant back, don't thin the plants—although some gardeners disagree. It depends on how many seeds you have planted close together in the row. If you want chard to mature, thin to 12 inches when 6 inches high. The size of mature plants will surprise you. Eat the thinnings.

Pruning

If a plant bolts, cut it back. It may resprout. If you want seed, let it go. You might get lucky and have some seed-pods form. Keep harvesting leaves, even if you don't want them, to keep the plant producing young leaves as long as possible.

Special Considerations

Young leaves tend to be milder than older ones. However, some people like a bit of bitterness in their greens and allow plants to mature a bit before harvesting. Hot weather also tends to turn leaves more bitter, especially if you cut back on watering.

Note that leaves contain oxalic acid, which can be a problem for some health conditions. Cooking the leaves reduces the amount somewhat. If you are on a blood thinner such as warfarin (Coumadin), talk to your doctor. Swiss chard is high in vitamin K.

Winter Protection

Swiss chard often stands up to moderate freezes in the fall. Covered with a thick mulch in winter, it may survive. But don't count on it. If it does, it will often go to seed in the second season. So start a new batch each spring.

Extending the Season

Some gardeners grow Swiss chard in cold frames in early spring. Since the leaves can be picked when immature, this can be successful. Using cold frames or plastic tunnels works just as well at the end of the season. Chard is resistant to light frosts once growing well. Place protective caps over the plants for pickings well past the first hard frost. Most varieties are hardy to 7°F.

Problems

Insects

Flea beetles may go after your Swiss chard. Leaves will have scattered holes. Leafminers create graying patches on leaves, indicating where they have been making pathways through the foliage. Slugs can also be a problem. Floating row covers help prevent damage early in the season. Pick off slugs by hand.

Disease

Blights, leaf spots, mildews, and mosaics occasionally cause problems. Pick off infected leaves, and destroy plants that are severely damaged. Start a new crop in a different place if you have to.

Marauders

When young, the plants are vulnerable to bird attack. I have not yet experienced this, but others have. As with all greens, Swiss chard is a nutritious treat to rabbits and deer. They often nibble the plants back but rarely destroy them. Let them regrow. I have had deer eat plants at three different times in one season and still ended up with plenty of Swiss chard to eat.

Physiological

When planting early, there is a small chance that very cold temperatures may cause the plant to bolt. Take the chance.

Propagation

Swiss chard has both male and female organs but is not self-fertile and is wind pollinated. Occasionally, a plant may bolt to form flowers in the first year. Let seedpods mature and become fully dry on the plant before collecting. Do not crush the pods, which contain several seeds inside. Store in a cool, dry, dark place for 4 to 5 years. If plants do not bloom in the first year, read chapter 5, "Propagation."

Harvesting

There are two methods of harvesting Swiss chard leaves. Both work well. One is to begin picking young leaves when about 4 to 6 inches tall from the outside in. They are the most tender at this stage. Never strip the plant bare; leave a number of small leaves growing in the center. The inner growing bud will continue to produce new leaves. The other method is to let the plant get a bit larger before slicing it back several inches above the ground with a knife. To allow the plant to regenerate, avoid cutting off the growing point in its center. This is an excellent "cut and come again" crop, as anyone with a rabbit or deer problem has already learned. Try both methods, and choose the one you prefer. Europeans often grow plants for their stems, not their leaves. As plants mature, they develop a thick stalk. Some people compare these to asparagus. That's pushing it, although the stalks are excellent in cooking as a crunchy, fleshy green. The varieties with white stalks are best for this use.

Storing

Swiss chard does not store well for a long time indoors. Keep leaves cool while picking. As with other leafy vegetables, they may collect a little coating of soil. Rinse them under cold running water, and shake off excess moisture. Roll leaves in a paper towel so that each leaf is sandwiched between paper. Place the rolled-up leaves in a plastic bag in the crisper of the refrigerator. Use the leaves as soon as possible, since they become tougher with age—within 2 days if possible, certainly no longer than 7.

To freeze, wash, remove stems from older leaves, place in sieve, plunge into boiling water for 30 seconds to 1½ minutes depending on thickness of leaves, lift up, drain, place into ice water for 2 minutes, then into airtight freezer bags, and freeze. Stems are edible. Treat them as you would leaves, but blanch for 3 to 4 minutes. Adding lemon juice to the water may improve the flavor. Note that stems are usually eaten fresh, rather than frozen. Leaves can be frozen whole, chopped up, or puréed.

Culinary Uses

The leaves are better cooked than eaten raw in salads. True, they can be colorful, but the taste of other greens is better. If you disagree and do serve them raw, pick leaves when small, and add dressing at the last minute to preserve the rainbow of colors. Raw they have the flavor of beets. After all, Swiss chard is really just a beet grown for its leaves.

To prepare leaves for cooking, wash and dip in ice water. Cook young leaves whole. If leaves are older or being used primarily for their stems, separate the leaves from the stems. Removing the midribs of the leaves is optional. Cook the leaves whole or shredded.

Boil the leaves like spinach with as little water as possible. For added flavor, some people season the water with bouillon. Drenched with butter afterwards the greens only get better. Cooking in butter alone is another option. The less you cook, the more vitamins you preserve. For that reason, some people cook them quickly in a microwave.

Butter steamed, sautéed in olive oil, steamed, or stir-fried, the leaves taste somewhat like spinach but have less of a metallic taste. Dipped in batter and cooked in hot oil, the leaves make a tasty tempura. Swiss chard is delicious in creamed soups and can be added to lasagna for extra flavor and nutrition.

As mentioned, many Europeans prefer to cook the thick stalks rather than the leafy greens. The stalks have a bit of crunch and a flavor somewhat similar to celery. The stalks of 'Fordhook Giant' and 'Swiss Chard of Geneva' are highly recommended. When adding leaves or sections of stems to soups, add them late in the cooking process. Experiment with your favorite herbs, but definitely play with basil, nutmeg, and oregano to enhance this vegetable's flavor.

Varieties

Perpetual spinach is in the same species as Swiss chard, but its tender leaves and thinner stems taste more similar to spinach than chard. It has the same great characteristics of chard in that it is long lasting and less likely to bolt than spinach. It is sometimes called leaf beet or spinach beet, but chard may also be listed that way as well. Perpetual spinach may be sold as a generic plant or under the varietal name of 'Erbette'. To my knowledge all Swiss chards are open pollinated with the exception of 'Red Magic Hybrid'. Some of the open-pollinated varieties are considered heirlooms. Others listed as open-pollinated varieties may also be heirlooms, but I cannot prove it. 'Bright Lights' and 'Rainbow Chard' have a similar appearance, but 'Bright Lights' is a more recent introduction.

VARIETIES	DAYS	LEAF AND STALK COLORS
'Argentata' (heirloom)	60	Deep-green, crinkly leaves with silvery-white stalks
'Bionda di Lyon' (OP)	50	Light-green, smooth leaves with pale green-white stalks
'Blonde' (OP)	60	Crinkly, green leaves with silver-white stalks
'Bright Lights' (OP) (AAS-1998)*****	60	Deep-green leaves with yellow-gold to orange-pink stalks
'Bright Yellow' (OP)	55	Dark-green leaves with lemon-yellow stalks
'Burgundy' (OP)	60	Dark-green leaves with burgundy stalks
'Canary' (OP)	60	Dark-green, curly leaves with bright-yellow stalks
'Cardinal' (OP)		Dark-green, curly leaves with rich-red stalks
'Charlotte' (OP)	60	Dark-green with red stalks
'Dark Green Lucullus' (see 'Fordhook Giant')		
'Erbette' (heirloom; a perpetual spinach)	60	Light- to medium-green with white stalks
'Fantasia Orange' (OP)	60	Dark-green with orange veins and stalks
'Five Color Silverbeet' (see 'Rainbow Chard')		
'Flamingo Pink Chard' (heirloom)	60	Green-smooth leaves with bright pinkish-red stalks
'Fordhook Giant' (heirloom)*****	60	Crinkly leaves with white stalks
'French Swiss Chard' (OP)	60	Thick green leaves with white stalks
'Geneva' (see 'Swiss Chard of Geneva')		
'Giant Lucullus' (OP)	55	Dark-green leaves with white stalks
'Gold Stem' (OP)	50	Dark-green thick leaves with golden-yellow stalks
'Italian Silver Rib' (heirloom)	50	Crinkly, deep-green leaves with silver-white stalks
'Large White Ribbed' (OP)	50	Dark-green leaves with white stalks
'Lucullus' (heirloom)	60	Yellowish-green leaves with white stalks
'Magenta Sunset' (OP)	60	Deep-green, glossy leaves with magenta stalks
'Neon Lights' (OP)	60	Deep-green, crinkly leaves with yellow gold to orange, pink-red stalks
'Northern Lights' (OP)	60	Deep-green, fleshy leaves with yellow-gold to orange, pink-red stalks
'Orange Fantasia' (see 'Fantasia Orange')		
'Oriole Orange' (heirloom)	60	Green leaves with orange stems
'Perpetual Spinach' (heirloom—generic)	50	Spinach-like leaves on thin, white stems
'Pink Lipstick' (OP)	60	Green leaves with nearly red, hot-pink stems
'Poros' (OP)	55	Dark-green, crinkly leaves with white stalks
'Pot of Gold' (OP)	60	Light-green, ribbed leaves with yellow stalks
'Rainbow Chard' (heirloom)	60	Orange, pink, red, white, and yellow stalks
'Red Magic Hybrid'	60	Red stems with deep-green, red-veined leaves
'Ruby Red' (see 'Rhubarb Chard')		
'Rhubarb Chard' (heirloom)*****	60	Deep-green, crinkly red leaves with scarlet stalks
'Rhubarb Red' (see 'Rhubarb Chard')		
'Seafoam' ('Sea Foam') (OP)	55	Crinkly, green leaves with cream-white stems
'Spinach Beet' (see 'Perpetual Spinach')		
'Swiss Chard of Geneva' (OP)*****	60	Curly, dark leaves with white stalks
'Verde da Taglio' (heirloom)	60	Large green leaves on white stalks
'Virgo' (OP)	60	Deep-green leaves with white stalks
'Vulcan' (heirloom)	60	Green leaves with purplish-red stalks
'Winterbi Mangold' (heirloom)	60	Large, dark-green leaves white veins and pale-green stalks
'Winter King' (OP)	50	Green with white stalks

Fresh tomatoes, the most popular garden vegetable, are juicy and flavorful.

TOMATO

Solanum lycopersicum species, formerly *Lycopersicon esculentum*
Nightshade Family (Solanaceae)

Tomatoes are tender to very tender, warm-season annuals. Tomatoes are the single most popular homegrown vegetable in the country, and for good reason. They grow in varied conditions, with relatively little effort, and produce many fruits (berries) in limited space. And vine-ripened tomatoes, deep red and juicy, bear no resemblance to their tough and tasteless store-bought cousins. Tomatoes are botanically a fruit but legally a vegetable. They originated in South America.

How Tomatoes Grow

Each tomato seed looks somewhat like a tiny piece of oatmeal (about 7,000 to 10,000 seeds per ounce). It is typically planted indoors until it develops several true leaves. Even when small, these indented leaves have a distinctive scent. Once planted in the garden, the tomato grows larger, producing an ever-greater number of leaves. Above specifically spaced leaves a new shoot (sucker) will emerge. It will form another main plant stem if left alone. Above other leaves little stems grow out from the main stem to form clusters of yellow flowers. When pollinated, each flower produces a fruit that starts off as a little green ball and eventually matures into a tomato. Some tomato plants will grow only so tall and then stop growing. These are called bush (determinate) tomatoes. Other tomatoes just keep growing if given the chance. These are called vining (indeterminate) tomatoes. Bush types generally produce less, but earlier, fruit over a shorter period of time. Vining types typically come in later but in greater abundance over a longer period of time. Both types produce fruits in a rainbow of colors, in a wide variety of shapes and sizes, and for an assortment of potential uses.

Where to Plant Tomatoes
Site and Light

The site should be an area with as much direct sun as possible. Protection from wind is ideal. Tomatoes like lots of sun and warmth.

Nutrition Facts

Serving size: 100 grams (3.5 ounces)

	AMOUNT PER RAW SERVING	% DV	AMOUNT PER COOKED SERVING	% DV	AMOUNT PER DRIED SERVING	% DV
Calcium	10 mg	1%	11 mg	1%	110 mg	11%
Calories	18	1%	18	1%	260	13%
Carbohydrates	4 g	1%	4 g	1%	56 g	19%
Dietary fiber	1 g	5%	1 g	3%	12 g	50%
Iron	0.3 mg	1%	0.7 mg	4%	9 mg	50%
Potassium	240 mg	7%	220 mg	6%	3,425 mg	98%
Protein	1 g	2%	1 g	2%	14 g	28%
Vitamin A	835 IU	17%	490 IU	10%	875 IU	17%
Vitamin C	13 mg	21%	23 mg	38%	39 mg	65%
Vitamin K	8 mcg	10%	3 mcg	3%	43 mg	55%

Soil and Moisture

The soil should be rich and loose to a depth of at least 12 inches. The soil should drain freely. If you have compacted or rocky soil, build a raised bed. Incorporate lots of organic matter into the soil. The soil should have a pH of 6 to 7. Beds of commercial growers are often covered with black plastic in spring to heat up the soil and to get tomatoes off to a quick start. Before applying black plastic, moisten the soil well. Getting water to the roots throughout the growing season is critical. For this reason, some gardeners use black fabric instead of plastic since it allows water penetration. The use of either is optional. Most home gardeners grow tomatoes without either.

Container

A number of tomatoes, particularly bush varieties, grow remarkably well in containers and not all of them produce tiny fruit. It's the size of the plants that make them good for container planting, and some of them produce decent-sized tomatoes. Plants may be small, but stake them anyway. One example is 'Husky Cherry Red Hybrid'.

Planting

Seed

Although some tomatoes self-seed, they produce fruit late in the season. Direct seeding in the garden makes little sense. Grow tomatoes from transplants.

Transplants

Not all of the varieties of tomatoes you may want to grow are available as plants locally. You may have to grow some from seed. Or you may prefer to. Start seed 6 to 8 weeks ahead of the last expected frost in your area. Plant several seeds ⅛ inch deep in sterile starting mix in 4-inch pots. High heat around 80°F is helpful, but plants will germinate at 70°F. Germination should occur within 14 days. Once seeds are sprouting, bottom water, and allow the starting mix to dry out between waterings. Give plants 16 hours of light to keep them stocky. Drop the the temperature by 10 degrees at night. Harden them off before planting outdoors. They should be about 6 inches tall when you plant them in the garden. Since weather is so unpredictable, consider starting seeds indoors at several different times, roughly 2 weeks apart.

If you buy plants, choose short (roughly 6-inch), stocky plants with lush green growth and thick stems. To get these, you may have to shop early in the season and protect plants from frost at home. Purchased plants should not be in flower. If you want to buy large plants that are both in flower and bearing fruit, they should be in large containers. If choosing plants in large containers, pick vining tomato plants. They are less prone to transplant shock than bush types.

When planting smaller plants, pinch off all the lower leaves. Don't remove the top three or four leaves. Dig a hole deep and wide enough to accommodate the root ball. Tap the plant out of the pot trying not to disturb the root ball. Place the root ball in the hole. Only the tip of the plant will be above the soil line. By burying the stem of the plant, you will get healthier root growth and better fruit. If you couldn't find a stocky plant and had to purchase a leggy one, just strip off the bottom leaves in the same way. Instead of digging a hole, dig a shallow trench. Place the root ball into the trench at one end and the lanky stem along the base of the trench. Now bend the top of the plant up and place a little soil, like a pillow, underneath it. Fill in the trench with soil. This encourages root growth along the entire stem, which should be barely below the soil surface. When planting this way, mark the buried portion of stem to avoid damaging it while cultivating around the plant.

If you purchased a large plant with blossoms or small fruit, strip off some of the lower leaves. Dig a hole large enough to accommodate the plastic pot and deep enough to cover the area where leaves have been removed. Cut the bottom off the pot with a utility knife and set it on the ground. Carefully set the pot on the severed bottom so that the soil doesn't spill out. Make a cut from the bottom of the pot up to within a ¼ inch of the top of the pot. Now remove the bottom gently as you set the pot into the hole. Cut through the last ¼ inch of plastic. Slide the pot out and away from the plant. Fill the hole with soil.

Some catalogs sell grafted plants. The upper portion, usually an heirloom, is grafted to the rootstock of a different tomato. The rootstock is chosen for resistance to disease and insects and often produces more vigorous plants. The upper portion (scion) is noted for its beauty and taste. Never bury any of the grafted portion under the soil. This will defeat the purpose of buying the grafted plant in the first place, since roots will grow out from the grafted portion and end up creating a tomato without the desirable characteristics of the rootstock.

Spacing

The amount of space between plants depends completely on the method chosen for growing tomatoes: either unsupported or supported. Unsupported vining tomatoes left unpruned can easily cover a 4-feet-square area. Spacing of supported plants is related to the type of support chosen.

When to Plant

The time to plant depends on what kind of special attention you want to give your young plants. Without any protection, tomato plants should go in after any chance of frost. Ideally, you want to plant on a cloudy day and give the plants a good drink to keep the soil moist while they take root.

Support

The easiest way to grow tomatoes is to let them lie on the ground and sprawl. As the plant grows, its meandering stems start to root and add vigor to the plant. The advantages are no pruning, no staking or supporting of any kind, no cost, less water loss as foliage shades the ground, and more fruit production than any other method. The disadvantages are the need for lots of space, potential for slug damage, and difficulty finding fruit. I love this method, but I always place

straw under all of the lateral growth to keep fruit off the ground and more easily visible. An even better alternative is to place brown paper from recyclable leaf or grocery bags under the mulch.

Most people, however, do support tomatoes, using Japanese tomato rings, stakes, tomato cages, trellises, wires, and so on. If you support tomatoes, tie the stems to the supports when they are young. The younger they are, the less damage you will do in working with them. Pieces of soft fabric work well for this. They are easy to use and stretch with the plant's growth. Use a figure-eight knot when doing this.

How to Care for Tomatoes
Water

Water and lots of it is important. Whenever the top few inches of soil dry out, water the plants around their base, preferably early in the day. Soak the soil until it is drenched. You have watered enough when the water begins to pool around the base of the plant. Consistent moisture is critical while the plants are flowering to ensure adequate uptake of calcium. Continue watering while fruit is forming, but water less when it is ripening. Spray the leaves only to knock off aphids or red spider mites. Drip irrigation under black plastic is effective, especially in areas with cool summers.

Mulch

Place mulch around the plants as soon as the soil is warm. This is usually about a month after planting the plants in the garden. A thick layer of organic mulch, especially straw, placed around the base of the plant, but not against the stem, will reduce the amount of water needed while keeping soil consistently moist. The mulch also draws in earthworms to aerate the soil, increases humidity around the plant to promote pollination, and prevents disease by stopping soil from splashing up onto leaves during watering. The latter is extremely important to prevent Septoria leaf spot.

Fertilizing

Feed tomatoes regularly with organic fertilizers. Spread fertilizer off to the side of the plant (side-dressing). Foliar feeding is also highly effective. Combine both to promote abundant and large fruits. Fertilize when fruit is forming and then every 2 to 4 weeks thereafter. If growing tomatoes in a raised bed covered with black plastic, place fertilizer high in phosphorus and potassium at the base of the bed, and nitrogen-rich fertilizer toward the surface before laying down the plastic.

Weeding

Pull up weeds by hand immediately as they appear. This is not difficult if you have a thick layer of mulch around the plants. Don't cultivate close to tomato plants. Roots are quite shallow, and stems are easily damaged. Wounds are an open invitation to disease.

Pruning

As tomato plants grow, they form shoots or suckers from leaf axils, the place where leaves join the main stem. As the plant matures, flower clusters emerge at intervals from the main stem above leaf axils. If nonflowering vegetative suckers are allowed to grow, they will form additional stems with leaves and suckers of their own. Some gardeners believe that if you remove all but one or two suckers, you will have better air circulation (less disease) and better fruit. In this way you are limiting growth to two or three main stems. To remove a sucker, bend it until it snaps, and pull back in the opposite direction. It will pop off. Or pinch or cut it off with a scissors. Do not confuse suckers with shoots forming flowers. *Removing suckers is optional.*

If you are growing a bush tomato, let at least one or two suckers grow. These will emerge below flower clusters. The reason is that the plant only grows so big, produces tomatoes more or less at one time, and then stops. Also, never remove the stem tips of bush varieties, because they are by nature self-topping, growing only so tall and then stopping. If you break off a tip accidentally, then let the plant form several suckers, which will produce additional stems.

With vining types, growth continues as long as weather permits. You can experiment by removing as many suckers as you want. Each sucker you leave will grow into a stem. Many gardeners leave the first sucker and remove all others that form later in the season. This is known as the "double stem" method of growing. Again, doing this is optional. Also, you can snip off the ends of stems at the end of the season to direct energy to developing fruit below. Since foliage is important to fruit production, some growers disagree with this advice and remove immature fruit instead (see below).

You do not have to remove suckers to get beautiful tomatoes, but you might experiment with different plants to compare results. Never remove foliage, just suckers. The exception is the removal of any yellowing or diseased leaves, generally at the base of the plant. Note that some gardeners disagree and do remove foliage. Again, experiment.

Another form of pruning is to limit the number of tomatoes forming on any given plant. You get fewer tomatoes, but they tend to ripen earlier and often become larger.

When tomatoes reach the size of a pea, remove all but three to four from each cluster, or leave only five to six groupings or clusters of tomatoes on the plant.

Special Considerations

Please note that a few people have an allergic reaction to tomato plants when working with them and should wear gloves and a long-sleeved shirt. If you use bare hands while working with tomatoes, avoid rubbing your eyes. In some people this can cause a great deal of pain.

Tree tomatoes are often sold as "tomatoes," but they are a different species, and they are not suited to cold climates. They are just a gimmick.

Note that tomatoes contain a high amount of lycopene, most available once cooked or processed. They do not contain as much as watermelon.

Extending the Season

Most gardeners get impatient to eat their first tomato as early in the season as possible. The easiest way to get early tomatoes is to plant a variety that matures quickly. You can help the process in varied ways. Use heat traps to get your plants in the ground before it would normally be recommended. When a plant has three or four clusters of tomatoes, grab the tomato plant by the base of the stem. Pull up until you hear some of the roots break. The plant might wilt a bit, but it will recover. This shock tricks the plant into producing fruit early. Essentially, it is afraid it is going to die. It won't. A variation of this trick is to dig your spade into the soil about 6 inches from the plant and 8 inches down. Make a half circle around the plant. If you planted the tomato using the trench method, avoid slicing the buried stem! As mentioned, other growers leave only some fruit on each plant. They selectively thin out flowers and pea-size fruits to encourage fewer, but earlier-maturing, tomatoes. Choosing an early variety and using heat traps are usually enough to get tomatoes maturing at a reasonably early time.

Tomatoes are frost tender and will wither after a severe frost. If you are warned of an upcoming frost, protect your plants with a tent of any kind of cloth. Sheets, blankets, and commercial covers are all excellent. Get the covers on during the hottest part of the day. Running a sprinkler on plants will prevent damage in a light, short-lasting period of cold (a cold night). Do not do this if you have a well, as you can burn the motor out. Container plants should be brought inside and then placed out again in full light as soon as the cold spell is over.

Problems

Insects

Many insects can damage tomato plants. Aphids are common. Hose them off with water. Pick off Colorado potato beetles. Frustrate cutworms by placing a collar around the base of the plant at time of planting. Flea beetles generally prefer nearby leafy crops. Slugs show themselves at night. Pick them off, and toss them into soapy water. Tomato hornworms chew leaves and leave behind black droppings. They are large enough to handpick and destroy. Rarely are they present in large numbers. White flies hover around plants, especially on decks and in patio gardens, creating a cloud whenever you approach. Catch them with yellow, sticky traps. If you see red spider mites, spray them off with a hose.

Disease

Most open-pollinated (heirloom) varieties have limited resistance to disease. However, disease resistance has been bred into many hybrids. The most common diseases are Septoria leaf spot, verticillium wilt (V), fusarium wilt, of which there are several races (FF), root knot nematodes (N), tobacco mosaic virus (T or TMV), and alternaria (A). When looking through catalogs check for symbols behind the plant name. For example, 'Celebrity Hybrid' VFFNTA would have resistance to most of these diseases. Prevent some disease by growing tomatoes in a new place each year. Do not plant them in a spot previously occupied by eggplants, peppers, or potatoes the year before, since they share common diseases. If you smoke, never smoke in the garden, and wash your hands before working with plants to avoid spreading tobacco mosaic virus. While this advice is highly disputed, why not err on the side of safety?

Marauders

Chipmunks will eat fruit if it is lying on the ground. Deer, if they are hungry enough, will eat almost anything. Birds sometimes peck on ripe fruit.

Physiological problems

Tomatoes have flowers with both male and female organs. They self-pollinate. Occasionally, you may have problems with flowers not producing fruit. The flowers just drop off. Blossom drop is generally caused by temperatures dipping below 55°F at night (pollen won't stick to the female organ) or rising above 85°F during the day (pollen clots at high temperatures). Blossom drop is a temporary problem. New blossoms will form. If you are having problems later in the season, tap flowers gently as they first blossom. Snap them with the end of your forefinger, or tap them lightly with a pencil. Do this several times a week, preferably at midday if possible.

If your tomatoes turn soft at their bottoms, they have blossom end rot. The sunken, watery spots often turn into black, leathery lesions or blotches over time. This problem is caused by a lack of calcium in the soil or by the inability of the plant to absorb calcium from the soil. If you have incorporated bonemeal, dolomitic limestone, pulverized egg shells, gypsum (calcium sulfate), or wood ash into the soil, the plant is not absorbing what is clearly available. As long as calcium is available, keeping the soil evenly moist and proper mulching throughout the season often overcome this problem.

It is common for a tomato or two to crack. When the cracks begin but move outward from the stem, the cause is usually quick growth from a recent rain, temperatures over 90°F, or overripening. Circular cracks around the stem or cracking on the bottom (blossom) end of the tomato is known as catfacing, usually caused by cool (50°F) nighttime temperatures while fruits are forming. There are other theories about crack formation, but since the problem is cosmetic, cut the cracks out, and eat what is left of the fruit.

Sometimes, but rarely, tomatoes develop large, white blisters (sunscald). This is caused by overexposure to the sun. Heavy pruning or loss of foliage from disease may allow too much light to hit developing tomatoes. Pick and toss these tomatoes into the compost pile.

When plants droop or wilt, they usually are short on water. Feel the soil. It is probably dry. Soak the soil thoroughly, getting water deep down to the roots. If the plant does not respond, it is probably infected with a fatal disease. Wait a day or two. If the plant doesn't look better, dig it up and dispose of it. Normal advice is to burn or toss it into the garbage.

Occasionally, the older leaves on the bottom of your plants may curl up and inward. They may become leathery. This is generally caused by overly wet conditions, as after a period of frequent, heavy rains. Other possible causes are overpruning, uneven watering, and spells of extremely high temperatures. This condition rarely affects fruiting.

If plants develop purplish coloration in their leaves, the soil is deficient in phosphorus, which helps sugars move properly throughout the plant rather than accumulating in the leaves themselves. This is rare in a garden with properly prepared soil containing lots of organic matter.

Propagation

While tomatoes can be propagated by grafting, rooting suckers, or layering main stems, these are rarely done in cold-climate gardens. Catalogs do sell grafted plants, typically heirlooms grafted to hybrid stock for greater disease resistance. Saving seed makes sense, especially for open-pollinated varieties. See the "wet method" in the section "Seed" in chapter 5, "Propagation."

Harvesting

Commercial growers pick tomatoes when they are just beginning to show some orange or yellow on the skin. These tomatoes ship better and don't get bruised as easily as ripe tomatoes. They do continue to ripen and may be exposed to ethylene to speed up the process. In the home garden always wait until the fruit is completely ripe before picking it. Let the color get really intense. The tomatoes will be firm but not hard. Vine-ripened tomatoes are tender, tasty, and incredibly juicy. This is the stage at which they contain the most sugar. They also contain far more vitamins than tomatoes picked early. But don't let them overripen. Even if you don't need more tomatoes, pick off the ripe ones, and give them away. This keeps the plant producing new tomatoes for the time when you will need them again. When picking, keep the green calyx (the stalk leaves) on the fruit. To do this, twist and lift up gently at the same time. Note that the calyx often dries before yellow and orange varieties are ready to pick.

Pick tomatoes for canning just as they start to ripen. Overripe tomatoes are not acidic enough for safe canning.

As the season ends, pick off all blossoms and small fruit at the top of the plant. This stimulates any larger fruit below to mature. When a deep freeze threatens and you can no longer protect your plants, pick off all the tomatoes, whether they are green or not. Clean them off, and wipe them dry. Store them at room temperature in a dark place, where most of them will continue to ripen. The tomatoes should not be touching each other. Some people place them in a bag with an apple. The combination of the ethylene emitted from both the apple and the ripening tomatoes combines to speed up the process.

Storing

Use ripe tomatoes immediately. This is when they are richest in vitamins. They do not store well, although some people have luck pulling up entire plants and hanging them in the basement. The green tomatoes may mature in this way over a period of weeks or longer. Keep tomatoes in a cool, shaded place, but not in the refrigerator unless you have already cut into them. They can be exposed to sun, but this increases the chance of their rotting. If not fully ripe, do not expose to sun. Place in a bag with apples that emit ethylene to speed the ripening process. Always keep them from touching each other.

To freeze, wash, place on a cookie sheet, and freeze whole in the freezer for 24 hours. Then place in a container, and keep frozen for future use. If freezing varieties with thick skins, scald 30 seconds to remove the skin before freezing. For sauce, blanch briefly, remove skin, chop up, cook for 5 minutes, cool, purée, and freeze in airtight freezer bags.

To dry, cut 'Principe Borghese' into thin slices, and dry in the sun on a screen. Or hang the whole plant upside down in the sun. Once fruit is dried, it can be used as is or crushed into flakes. Cut 'Roma' or 'San Marzano' into slices. Remove any seeds. Place in a single layer on a cookie sheet in the oven at 150°F for up to 24 hours or until leathery. Or plunge into boiling water, cool, remove skins, slice into ¼-inch slices, and dry in a dehydrator. These slices may last up to 3 months packed in airtight containers and kept in the refrigerator. Storing dried tomatoes in oil with garlic or basil for more than a few days is risky since most home growers are unable to destroy all bacteria in the drying process.

Culinary Uses

Do not eat tomato flowers. Do not eat tomato leaves. The scent produced by glands on the undersides of the leaves is distinctive, and some chefs have flavored cooked dishes with leaves for this reason. Technically, they are toxic. Old-time organic gardeners used to grind them up as an insecticide to ward off many insects, including flea beetles.

Raw ripe tomatoes are delicious whole and stuffed with egg or tuna salad over a bed of lettuce. Chop, dice, or slice and add to salads. Dice and add to chopped onion, green peppers, and cilantro for a salsa. Or add to guacamole. Slice and place on a platter with onions and drizzle with oil. Cut into thin slices for sandwiches. Use cherry tomatoes on a vegetable platter with any desired dip.

Eat with or without peel, with or without seeds. To peel, dip in boiling water for 15 to 30 seconds, plunge into ice water, and slip off skins. Or grill until skin bubbles, and remove the peel. Cut in half, remove seeds, splash with oil, bake cut side up uncovered at 400°F until cooked, cover with parmesan cheese, and broil until the cheese melts. Make tomato soup, and add to stews. Grill pieces on shish kebobs.

Green tomatoes are commonly sliced and fried fresh or made into chutneys, pickles, and relishes. Before frying green tomato slices, dip them in egg, and dust with flour or other coating seasoned to taste. Sprinkle with sugar or Tabasco sauce for two very different tastes.

To make tomato sauce, cook until soft, and push the pulp through a sieve to remove skin and seeds. The sauce can be cooked longer to reduce in half. Cool and freeze. To juice, wash, cut out stems, cut into pieces, simmer for 5 minutes, push through sieve, cool, pour into containers, seal, and freeze. Leave a little room for expansion. Or scald for a few minutes, and cool to remove skin before pushing tomatoes through a sieve.

When canning, pick tomatoes before they get fully ripe to take advantage of their higher acidity. Some cooks add a little lemon juice to canned tomatoes to increase acidity.

Varieties

The following chart indicates whether plants are D, determinate (bush types), or I, indeterminate (vining types). Growing at least one of each is a good idea to have fruit over a longer period of time. Note that 'Celebrity' falls in between these two categories and may be defined as SD, semideterminate. 'Husky Cherry Red' is a dwarf indeterminate (DI). It is technically a vining plant, but it has little space between the leaves, so it stays shorter than many other vining types.

If disease becomes a problem in your garden, then choose more-resistant varieties. That usually means choosing a hybrid rather than an open-pollinated variety. Note that all heirlooms are open pollinated; they have just been around for a longer time.

The "days" column refers to the length of time a plant will need to produce fruit from a 6- to 8-week-old transplant. Tomatoes take a long time to mature. You may want to begin with plants that mature quickly until you are skilled at lengthening the season in both spring and fall. The size (weight) of tomatoes is approximate. There can be a wide variability depending on how plants are grown and varying weather conditions.

There is a subtle difference in flavor related to the color of tomatoes. Some pinks, oranges, and yellows have a milder taste, while some blacks or near blacks have close to a barbecue flavor. However, they typically have similar acidity levels.

This list includes tomatoes that have been around for decades and newer introductions. Some of them have been included because they are excellent and widely available, but others you will have to start from seed. The tomatoes are in categories based on intended use of the fruit.

Standard Slicing Tomatoes

Most gardeners grow at least one of these varieties for fresh use. They are neither huge, like the "Beefsteak" tomatoes, nor as small as cherry, currant, and grape tomatoes. The smaller ones in this list could be referred to as salad tomatoes. A couple of slices and into the salad they go. Most of these varieties tend to be round or globe shaped.

VARIETY	DAYS	TYPE	COLOR	SIZE (OUNCES)
'Better Bush Hybrid'	70	I	Red	8
'Black Russian' (heirloom)	80	I	Mahogany brown	4–8
'Brandywine Red' (Landis Valley Strain) (heirloom)*****	80+	I	Red	8
'Bush Early Girl Hybrid'	55	D	Red	7
'Celebrity Hybrid' (AAS-1984)*****	70	SD	Red	8
'Champion II Hybrid'	70	I	Red	10
'Clear Pink Early' (heirloom)	60	D	Deep pink	3–6
'Dagma's Perfection' (heirloom)	70	I	Yellow red	12
'Early Doll Hybrid'	55	D	Bright red	4–5
'Early Girl Hybrid'	55	I	Red	4–6
'Early Wonder' (OP)	55	D	Dark pink	6
'First Prize Hybrid'	75	I	Red	10–12
'First Lady Hybrid'	65	I	Red	5
'Glacier' (heirloom)	60	D	Red	2–3
'Green Zebra' (OP)*****	75	I	Green amber	3–6
'Gregori's Altai' (heirloom)	70	I	Pink red	8–12

VARIETY	DAYS	TYPE	COLOR	SIZE (OUNCES)
'Jetsetter Hybrid'	65	I	Red	8
'Jet Star Hybrid'*****	75	I	Red	8
'Legend' (OP)	70	D	Red	8–
'Lemon Boy Hybrid'*****	75	I	Lemon yellow	6–8
'Matina' (heirloom)*****	60	I	Red	2–4
'Momotaro Hybrid'	75	I	Dark pink	6
'Moreton Hybrid'	70	I	Red	6–8
'Oregon Spring' (OP)*****	60	D	Red	4–5
'Paul Robeson' (heirloom)*****	75	I	Maroon	6
'Rose de Berne' (heirloom)	75	I	Dark pink	6–8
'Rutgers' (heirloom)	75	Both	Red	8
'Siletz' (OP)	55	D	Red	8–10
'Silvery Fir Tree' (heirloom)	60	D	Red	4–6
'Stupice' (heirloom)*****	55	I	Red	2–4
'Super Fantastic Hybrid'	70	I	Red	10
'Supersonic Hybrid'	80	I	Red	8

Large Slicing Tomatoes (including Beefsteaks)

These are big tomatoes, ideal for fresh use. This category includes a number of varieties often labeled "Beefsteak" tomatoes that can sometimes weigh more than 2 pounds. If stems protrude into the fruit, simply cut them out. 'Brandywine Pink' has potato-like leaves.

VARIETY	DAYS	TYPE	COLOR	SIZE (OUNCES)
'Aunt Ginny's Purple' (heirloom)*****	75	I	Deep pink	12–16
'Beauty' (also known as 'Ugli') (heirloom)	75	I	Red	12–16
'Big Beef Hybrid' (AAS-1994)*****	75	I	Red	10–12
'Big Boy Hybrid'	80	I	Red	10+
'Black From Tula' (heirloom)*****	80	I	Red brown	8–12
'Black Krim' (heirloom)	80	I	Dark maroon	10–12
'Brandywine Pink' (heirloom)	90+	I	Red pink	16–24
'Burpee's Supersteak Hybrid'	80	I	Red	24+
'Cherokee Chocolate' (OP)	75	I	Mahogany	10–16
'Cherokee Purple' (heirloom)*****	80	I	Purplish rose	10–12
'Delicious' ('Burpee's Delicious') (heirloom)	80	I	Red	24+
'German Queen' (heirloom)	80	I	Pink red	16
'Kellogg's Breakfast' (heirloom)	80	I	Deep orange	16
'Marianna's Peace' (heirloom)	80	I	Dark pink red	12–18+
'Mortgage Lifter' (heirloom)	85	I	Dark pink red	12+
'Orange Minsk' (OP)	75	I	Orange	12–20+
'Pruden's Purple' (heirloom)*****	75	I	Dark pink	10–16

Small-Fruited Tomatoes (Cherry, Currant, Grape)

For convenience, this group includes cherry, currant, and grape tomatoes. The names refer to the fruit shape. These plants often produce clusters of fruits in great abundance. They are most commonly used whole. Some of them do tend to crack if allowed to mature too long on the vine. 'Sweet 100' is notorious for this but a gem nevertheless.

VARIETY	DAYS	TYPE	COLOR	SIZE (OUNCES)
'Black Cherry' (heirloom)*****	75	I	Plum black	1–2, cherry
'Galina's' (heirloom)	75	I	Gold yellow	1–2, cherry
'Grape Tomato' (heirloom)	60	I	Bright red	1–2, grape
'Green Doctors' (heirloom)*****	75	I	Green	¾, cherry
'Husky Cherry Red Hybrid'	65	DI	Red	1, cherry
'Juliet Hybrid' (AAS-1999)	60	I	Red	1, grape
'Matt's Wild Cherry' (heirloom)*****	60	I	Red	1, cherry
'Riesentraube' (heirloom)*****	75	I	Red	1, elongated cherry
'Snow White Hybrid'	75	I	White yellow	1, cherry
'Sugary Hybrid' (AAS-2005)*****	60	I	Red	½, pointed
'Sun Gold Hybrid'	60	I	Bright orange	1, cherry
'Sunsugar or Sun Sugar Hybrid'	65	I	Orange	½–1, cherry
'Super Sweet 100 Hybrid'*****	65	I	Red	½–1, cherry
'Sweet Million Hybrid'	75	I	Red	1–1½, cherry
'Sweet 100 Hybrid'*****	65	I	Red	½–1, cherry
'Sweet Treats Hybrid'	70	I	Deep pink	1, cherry
'Sweet Pea Currant' (heirloom)	75	I	Red	¼, currant

Paste Tomatoes (Oxheart, Pear, Plum)

Oxheart, pear, and plum describe the fruit shapes well. While paste tomatoes can be eaten fresh (especially 'Yellow Pear'), they tend to have thicker skins and more substantial flesh than a typical slicing tomato. They are often referred to as meaty or dry. Many are nearly seedless. They are good for sauces, salsas, and tomato paste. They freeze and can well. If you want to do a lot of your processing at one time, choose a bush variety, since fruit tends to ripen in flushes (a lot of fruit at one time).

VARIETY	DAYS	TYPE	COLOR	SIZE (OUNCES)
'Anna Russian' (heirloom)*****	70	I	Red	16, oxheart
'Kosovo' (OP)	75+	I	Deep pink	12–16, oxheart
'Laroma III Hybrid'	75	D	Red	5–8, plum
'Oxheart' (heirloom)	80	I	Deep pink	16, oxheart
'Plum Regal Hybrid'	75	D	Red	4, plum
'Roma' (heirloom)	80	D	Bright red	4, pear
'San Marzano' (heirloom)*****	80	I	Bright red	4, pear
'Viva Italia Hybrid'*****	75	D	Deep red	3, plum
'Yellow Pear' (heirloom)*****	80	I	Clear yellow	2–3, pear

Dry Tomatoes

'Jaune Flamme' is a French variety that dries well. 'Principe Borghese' is small, nearly seedless, and dries well in the sun. In cold climates it's smarter to use a dehydrator whenever drying fruits (vegetables).

VARIETY	DAYS	TYPE	COLOR	SIZE (OUNCES)
'Jaune Flamme' (heirloom)	75	I	Apricot	4
'Principe Borghese' (heirloom)	75	D	Red	1–2, grape

Lycopene-Rich Tomato

This is the tomato for anyone interested in getting high levels of lycopene. It is said to have roughly 50 percent more lycopene than other varieties.

VARIETY	DAYS	TYPE	COLOR	SIZE (OUNCES)
'Health Kick Hybrid'	75	D	Red	4–6 plum

Container Tomatoes

The size of these plants make them ideal for use in containers or small places. Fruit size varies considerably and can be impressive for the size of the plant.

VARIETY	DAYS	TYPE	COLOR	SIZE (OUNCES)
'New Big Dwarf' (heirloom)	60	D	Deep pink red	8–12
'Patio Hybrid'	70	D	Bright red	3–4
'Red Robin' (OP)	55	D	Red	1, cherry
'Sprite' (OP)	60	D	Red	1, grape
'Tiny Tim' (OP)	55	D	Red	1, cherry

Novelty Tomato

Striped cavern is noted for its unusual bell shape and colorful stripes.

VARIETY	DAYS	TYPE	COLOR	SIZE (OUNCES)
'Striped Cavern' (heirloom)	80	I	Red-striped orange	8

Cherry tomato plants produce clusters of delicious small fruits over a long period of time.

Turnips, once the most popular vegetable in the country, have delicious roots and greens.

TURNIP

***Brassica* species**
Cabbage or Mustard Family (Brassicaceae, formerly Cruciferae)

Turnips are hardy to very hardy, cool- to cold-season biennials grown as annuals. At one time they were the single most popular garden vegetable. Today they have fallen out of favor, although both their leaves and roots are delicious. This dual crop is easy to grow, quick to mature, and relatively problem-free compared to other vegetables in the same family. Turnips probably originated in the Near East or South Asia but were possibly first domesticated in India.

How Turnips Grow

Turnips grow from tiny, hard, round, brown to purplish black seeds (about 9,500 to 11,000 seeds per ounce) into green leafy plants that supply nutrients to ever-expanding roots below. Leaves are fairly coarse and somewhat hairy. The roots grow partially aboveground. The plants would form flower stems with yellow, cross-shaped flowers in the second season if they were to survive cold winters.

Where to Plant Turnips

Site and Light

Turnips grow best in full sun, although they tolerate partial shade.

Soil and Moisture

Prepare a loose bed for this root crop. Clean out all old debris and rocks. Work sphagnum peat moss, manure, or compost into the soil to give it a light, airy feel. The soil should drain freely and have a smooth, fine surface. If soil is compacted, build a raised bed. Add organic fertilizers in small amounts. A pH of 6 to 6.8 is ideal but can be slightly more alkaline to prevent clubroot. Adding a small amount of lime or wood ash to the soil in fall is generally fine, as well as a balanced amount of other organic fertilizers.

Container

It is certainly possible to grow turnips in containers but is only worthwhile if space is at a premium. Turnips like lots of

Nutrition Facts
Serving size: 100 grams (3.5 ounces)

	ROOTS (COOKED)		GREENS	
	AMOUNT PER SERVING	% DV	AMOUNT PER SERVING	% DV
Calcium	33 mg	3%	137 mg	14%
Calories	22	1%	20	1%
Carbohydrates	5 g	2%	4 g	1%
Copper	0.0		0.3 mg	14%
Dietary fiber	2 g	8%	4 g	14%
Folate	9 mcg	2%	118 mcg	29%
Manganese	0.1 mg	4%	0.3 mg	17%
Protein	1 g	1%	1 g	2%
Vitamin A	0.0		7,625 IU	155%
Vitamin B6	0.1 mg	3%	0.2 mg	9%
Vitamin C	12 mg	19%	27 mg	46%
Vitamin E	0.0		2 mg	9%
Vitamin K	0.1 mcg	0%	368 mcg	460%

sun but cool temperatures. Providing sun is no problem, but containers tend to get hot and dry out quickly. Keep the soil evenly moist. It may be necessary to water more than once a day. Using this method for growing greens, rather than roots, makes more sense to me.

Planting
Seed

Plant seed about ¼ to ½ inch deep in very fine, sieved soil. Cover the seed with an ultrathin layer of pulverized leaves to keep the soil moist and cool. Keep consistently moist. Turnip seeds germinate in a wide range of temperatures, usually within 10 days or sooner. Plant the seed either in shallow rows, or broadcast it over a 2- to 3-feet band. Toss sifted soil over the scattered seed. Sow more thickly if plants will be used for greens, more precisely and farther apart if grown for roots.

Transplants

It is possible to buy young plants in some garden centers and farmers' markets. Gently tease the plant out of its container, and try to keep the root ball intact as you place the seedling into the planting hole. Firm the roots solidly in place, and water immediately. Get these into the garden as soon as possible. If a hard frost threatens, cover them with a cloche until the weather warms up. Ask what variety you are buying. Or start seed indoors 3 to 4 weeks before planting them outdoors after hardening them off. Indoor seeding only makes sense for the longer-season varieties. *Turnips do not transplant well.*

Spacing

Since turnips can be grown from seed for either greens or roots, spacing depends on the intended use. Plants grown for greens can be grown closer together. If harvesting begins young, then a few inches between plants is enough. If harvesting will be much later, then plants may have to be a foot or more apart.

If plants are grown from seed for roots, then they can be planted 1 inch apart and thinned as they mature. If grown from purchased plants, space seedlings according to the desired root size. *The latter is directly related to spacing:* less space, smaller roots; more space, larger roots.

When to Plant

Plant seed as soon as the ground can be worked, which is usually 4 to 6 weeks before the last expected spring frost. The soil temperature can be as low as 40°F. Make several plantings 7 days apart. Then plant seed once again in mid- to late summer depending on what zone you live in. Time the planting so that the roots will mature in cool weather. This improves their taste. Many gardeners prefer the fall to the spring crops. Late plantings are frost tolerant and often less prone to insect infestations.

How to Care for Turnips
Water

Consistent watering helps the roots to mature rapidly and may prevent roots from splitting. Watering along with mulch keeps the soil temperature a bit cooler, and this often results in more tender, rather than woody, roots.

Mulch

As soon as you plant turnips, place a very thin layer of mulch over the row. As seedlings emerge, place a thick layer of mulch off to the side of the row. The mulch should not touch the developing roots but can be close to keep the soil more evenly moist and cool.

Fertilizing

If the soil is prepared properly early in the season, additional fertilizing is rarely needed. However, sprinkling and watering in an organic fertilizer along the sides of the plants is recommended for types grown for their foliage, not for their roots.

Weeding

Although a bit tedious, remove any weeds that sprout close to the emerging seedlings. Some gardeners snip off the weeds with cuticle scissors or pull them up with tweezers. As the plants get larger, hand pull any weeds emerging through the surrounding mulch.

Thinning

Thinning depends on the original spacing. If growing plants for greens in a row and harvesting leaves regularly, plants can remain only 1 to 2 inches apart. If growing plants for roots, then thin more ruthlessly. Either thin by hand, or run a garden rake across the row or broad band of plants when they are a few inches tall. The prongs of the rake will pull up plants at about the right space for initial thinning. Later on just pull up the plants for additional spacing to 2 to 4 inches. Any plants you pull or rake up are delicious as young greens. Plants removed from the row can be planted, but the survival rate is moderate. Plants roughly 3 to 4 inches tall seem to take better than smaller plants. I cannot explain why, but I have tried both.

Special Considerations

Turnips may bolt in heat. By planting seeds as early as possible in the season, you often avoid this. Still, you cannot control the weather. Water and mulch to keep the soil temperature as even and cool as possible. If seeds begin to form flower stalks, pull them up, or keep if you want to save seed.

Extending the Season

In theory, it is possible to leave the roots in the garden, remove the tops, cover the plants with a 12-inch layer of loose straw, and hope for an early snow so that you can harvest turnips into early winter. Much preferred is to harvest and freeze the roots, as described under "Storing."

Problems

Insects

Turnips are susceptible to aphids, flea beetles, and root maggots. Flea beetles sometimes attack young plants and may do serious damage. Even with frayed leaves, the plants may recover and form decent roots. Spray off aphids with a jet of water if they appear. Cabbage loopers, cutworms, and imported cabbage worms are other potential threats. You can avoid most problems with floating row covers and physical barriers. Another solution is to plant a quick-maturing variety late in the season.

Disease

Clubroot can be a problem. Calcium in the soil helps prevent the formation of these distorted roots. Adding a little lime or wood ash to the soil in fall also helps prevent this by increasing the soil pH to a slightly alkaline level. Problems like black leg, black rot, downy mildew, powdery mildew, rhizoctonia rot, and scab are relatively rare in the home garden. Dig up and destroy any diseased plant to stop the spread of an infection.

Marauders

It is next to impossible to predict what animal may find turnips inviting. It depends on the year. Without proper fencing, these plants, particularly when young, are vulnerable.

Physiological

Brown heart is a condition where the inside of the roots rot out. This may be caused by a boron deficiency in the soil. The addition of compost and kelp fertilizer to the soil should provide enough boron to prevent brown heart. Or you can spray soil with a highly diluted solution of borax in fall.

Cracking is a bit of a mystery. The most commonly cited cause is inconsistent watering and fluctuations in weather conditions. Water well during hot, dry weather. This may also help prevent brown heart, sometimes referred to as water core.

Occasionally, turnips begin to form flower stalks prematurely. Get seed into the ground on time, and water consistently, especially during hot, dry weather when the temperature gets above 77°F. If a plant bolts, pull it up, as roots have already been affected, unless you are a seed saver.

Propagation

Unless plants bolt and form seed in the first season, seed saving is impractical. However, for tips on growing biennials, see chapter 5. Any purchased seed should last from 2 to 5 years. The average life expectancy is about 4.

Harvesting

Harvest greens as soon as they are 4 to 6 inches tall. Either pick off individual leaves from the smaller plants, or shear larger plants back to 2 inches or so. Avoid cutting the growing point, the central area from which new leaves are emerging. New growth will occur, so several cuttings are possible from the same plant.

The greens of varieties grown primarily for foliage can be harvested at a more mature stage. The leaves are then cooked like spinach. To preserve their nutrients, cook them just until tender and no longer.

If turnips grown for their roots were planted early in the season, then begin harvesting them when they get to the size of a golf ball. Pull or dig up roots when the soil is dry. Cut the tops off the roots immediately to reduce water loss. Harvest regularly. If these turnips are exposed to the high heat of summer when temperatures go above 80°F, they often get bitter, tough, and woody. So pick all of the earlier crop before this happens. Freeze what you cannot eat.

For turnips harvested in fall, wait until there have been several frosts. The starch in the roots turns to sugar, and the turnips have a much milder and sweeter flavor. Pull or dig up all roots before a hard freeze. Treat them as you would turnips harvested earlier in the season by removing tops. Do not clean the root if you want to try to store them.

Storing

Turnip roots need cool temperatures and high humidity to store well without drying out and shriveling. Store them in the crisper of your refrigerator for up to 1 week. It is also possible to store them for up to 3 months in moist leaf mold, sand, sawdust, and sphagnum peat moss in a plastic garbage can in a garage where temperatures stay close to 32°F. The turnips should not touch each other. If they freeze, they rot and give off a horrendous odor.

To freeze roots, harvest young, remove tops, wash, peel, dice or slice, scald 2 to 3 minutes, cool in ice water, drain, pack, seal, label, and freeze. If older, peel first.

Turnips can also be pickled. One of the favorites for this is 'Scarlet Ohno Revival'.

Turnip greens do not store for a long time indoors. Keep them cool while picking. As with other leafy vegetables, they may collect a little coating of soil. Rinse them under cold running water, and shake off excess moisture. Roll leaves in a paper towel so that each leaf is sandwiched between paper. Place the rolled-up leaves in a plastic bag in the crisper of the refrigerator. Use the leaves as soon as possible, since they become tougher with age—within 2 days if possible, certainly no longer than 7.

To freeze greens, wash, remove stems, place in sieve, plunge into boiling water for 30 seconds to 2 minutes, lift up, drain, place into ice water for 2 minutes, then into airtight freezer bags, and freeze. Note that greens do lose vitamins when blanched. Some people prefer cooking them for less than a minute in the microwave instead of plunging them into boiling water.

Culinary Uses

The small roots can be eaten just like radishes and are sometimes referred to as "salad turnips." For this use, grow 'Hakurei Hybrid', 'Market Express Hybrid', 'Oasis Hybrid', 'Tokyo Cross Hybrid', or 'Tokyo Market'. Cut roots into strips for dips on vegetable platters. Grate, julienne, or shred roots into salads, and use shredded turnips for "cole" slaw. Dip roots in lemon water before using them raw to prevent discoloration.

Use raw turnip leaves in salads when they are no longer than 6 inches. At this stage they should be brightly colored and tender. Flavor does vary by age and variety, from relatively sweet and mild to peppery and hot. Top them with any dressing, and consider using mint and lemon juice as flavorings.

Before cooking roots, rinse, remove the skin, and cut off the top and base of the root. Use a stainless steel pan to avoid discoloring the roots. Cook roots just until tender. Overcooking changes the taste. Boil small roots until tender. Cut larger roots into ¼- to ½-inch pieces to speed up cooking. Or cube, quarter, shred, or slice them as necessary. Roots are delicious baked glazed in butter and brown sugar, boiled and topped with hot butter flavored with basil or dill, butter steamed, microwaved, steamed, and stir-fried. Use them as a potato replacement for chips, french fries, and mashed potatoes. Cream them with butter, make turnip and onion au gratin, add them to stews, or make turnip and leek soup. Roast wedges with your favorite meat.

Leaves are also delicious cooked. Steam young leaves as you would any other green but as short a time as possible, certainly less than 5 minutes. Older leaves are still edible but not as delicate. Remove the center rib before chopping or shredding into pieces, These should be boiled, butter steamed, microwaved, sautéed, or steamed—again, do not overcook. Greens are often served hot with bacon bits, melted butter, lemon juice, or a splash of vinegar. Add bits of your favorite herb for seasoning. Cooked greens go well with almost any egg dish. Greens can be added to omelets and quiches, or topped with eggs cooked in a variety of ways.

Varieties

Turnips may be listed under various Latin names including *Brassica campestris* var. *rapa*, *Brassica rapa* var. *rapifera* or Rapifera Group, and *Brassica rapa* ssp. *sylvestris*. Both the root and leaves (greens) of turnips are edible. Some varieties are grown just for their greens. Closely related to these are varieties grown for their edible stems and flower buds. These are covered in the section on broccoli raab, or rapini. The leaves of varieties grown for greens may resemble oak leaves or straps similar to a dog's tongue. Varieties grown for leaves generally produce poor roots. The following varieties are grown for their greens: 'Alamo Hybrid', 'Nozawana', 'Seven Top', 'Topper Hybrid', 'Top Star Hybrid', and 'Turnip Greens Senza Testa'. 'Scarlet Queen Hybrid' is grown for both its roots and lovely green red leaves.

Most turnips are open pollinated, but some of the best are hybrids. The latter have been bred to be more uniform, disease resistant, earlier, and bolt resistant. They are often more expensive.

Note that 'York' is often sold as a turnip but is really a rutabaga. I have listed it in the varieties tables of both vegetables for that reason.

VARIETY	DAYS	ROOT/FLESH	SIZE (INCHES)
'Alamo Hybrid'	35–50	NA	NA
'Boule d'Or' (see 'Golden Ball')			
'Golden Ball' (heirloom)	45–65	Yellow tan/yellow	3–4
'Golden Globe' (heirloom)	45–65	Green tan/yellow	3–5
'Hakurei Hybrid'*****	35	White/white	2–4
'Helenor' (heirloom)	90	White purple/yellow	3–4+
'Hidabeni Hybrid'	45–50	Red/white	2
'Hinona Kabu' (heirloom)	40	Red white/white	12
'Italian White Red Top' (OP)	35–40	White red/white	3–4
'Just Right Hybrid' (AAS-1960)	30–60	White/white	3–5
'Laurentian' (OP)	90–120	White purple/yellow	
'Market Express Hybrid'	40–60	White/white	2–5
'Milan' (see 'Italian White Red Top')			
'Navet des Vertus Marteau' (heirloom)	60–65	White/white	5–6
'Nozawana' (OP)	40	NA	NA
'Oasis Hybrid'	50–55	White/white	2–4
'Orange Jelly' (see 'Golden Ball')			
'Purple Top White Globe' (heirloom)*****	45–60	White purple/white	4–5
'Red Round' (heirloom)	50	Red/reddish white	2–3
'Royal Crown Hybrid'	50–55	White purple/white	3–4
'Royal Globe Hybrid'	50	White purple/white	3–4
'Scarlet Ohno Revival' (OP)	50	White pink/bright pink	2
'Scarlet Queen Hybrid'	45	Red/white	3–4
'Seven Top' (heirloom)	30–50	NA	NA
'Shogoin' (heirloom)	30–70	Tannish white/white	4–6+
'Snowball' (see 'White Egg')			
'Tennouji Kabura' (OP)	45–50	White/white	3–4
'Tokyo Cross Hybrid' (AAS-1969)*****	30–60	White/white	6
'Tokyo Market' (OP)	25–30	White/white	2
'Topper Hybrid'	35–60	NA	NA
'Top Star Hybrid'	35	NA	NA
'Tsugaru Scarlet Hybrid'	55	Scarlet red/white	2–3
'Turnip Greens Senza Testa' (OP)	90	NA	NA
'Vertus Marteau' (heirloom)	60	White/white	5–6
'White Egg' (heirloom)	40–55	White/white	4
'White Lady Hybrid'	35	White/white	2–3
'York' (heirloom)	115	White purple/creamy yellow	4–5

UNIQUE PLANTS

This section features plants that are either unusual or difficult to grow in cold climates. It is exhilarating to have success growing one of these difficult plants! The unusual plants, whether relatively easy or difficult to grow, are not in the average home garden. Grow these for fun, to add diversity to the garden, and to experiment in the kitchen.

Artichoke
Cynara cardunculus var. *scolymus*
Aster, Daisy, or Sunflower Family
(Asteraceae, formerly Compositae)

Artichokes are tender, mild-season perennials most commonly grown as annuals in cold climates. They are said by some to contain more antioxidants than any other vegetable. Most artichokes are grown in California in the Monterey Bay area, where the conditions are just right: warm, but not too hot; moist, but not too wet. Artichokes like a long season, mild winters, and damp summers—not exactly the conditions found in cold-climate areas. Still, this gourmet's delight is worth the gamble—barely.

Grow artichokes either from seed (450 to 800 seeds per ounce) or young plants purchased through mail order. The large, oval seed is medium tan to grayish, indented slightly, and easy to work with. The silver-gray plants grow rapidly with large, serrated leaves. At the end of the season the plant produces flower buds, first at the tip of the plant, and then off to the side. These spiky buds composed of thick, fleshy scales surround a solid core known as the heart. These buds are what we know as artichokes. Ironically, years ago this plant was considered "poor man's food." Artichokes grow like large thistles and will produce beautiful, purple blue blooms if the flower buds are not picked and the season is long enough. *This is not the case in cold climates.* In fact, odds are you will grow a huge, silvery thistle and never see a bud. If this is the case, eat the stems like cardoon (see "Cardoon").

Plants are rarely available in local nurseries. Start your own from seed about 8 to 10 weeks before the last expected

Artichoke Nutrition Facts

Serving size: 100 grams (3.5 ounces)

	AMOUNT PER COOKED SERVING	% DV
Calories	53	3%
Carbohydrates	9 g	3%
Dietary fiber	5–9 g	18–34%
Folate	89 mcg	22%
Magnesium	42 mg	10%
Manganese	0.2 mg	11%
Phosphorus	73 mg	7%
Potassium	286 mg	8%
Protein	3 g	6%
Vitamin C	7.4 mg	12%
Vitamin K	15 mcg	18%

Young artichoke plants must experience a cool period in spring to form buds the first year.

frost. Place seeds in the refrigerator for 2 weeks before planting. This breaks the natural dormancy of the seed. When you do this, put the seed in moist peat moss in a plastic bag. Then plant the seed in sterile starting mix ¼ to ½ inch deep at 70°F. Seed should germinate within 14 days. Give plenty of light. Once plants are growing vigorously, set them in a cold frame or unheated portion of the house where they can remain at 50°F for up to 6 weeks. The minimum cooling-off period at this temperature is 10 days for 'Imperial Star', the most commonly recommended variety for cold-climate gardeners. This cold treatment is known as vernalization, which tricks plants into "thinking" they have already gone through one winter. This, in theory, initiates flower bud formation. I recommend starting 'Imperial Star' in a *large* pot to begin with and growing it there all season long.

Whether potted or planted as transplants, place outdoors when air temperatures stay above 60°F. Even if you buy plants such as 'Lulu Hybrid', hope for, but do not expect, success. If you get lucky, begin harvesting the largest artichokes first. Artichokes are at their best when they are young and small, roughly 3 inches wide. These are much more tender than the store-bought variety. Artichoke scales should be tight and flat. As soon as they start to stick out, the prime time for picking has passed. The stem just below the bud will be soft and pliable at this stage. Cut off the buds with roughly 5 inches of stem.

The stem just below the bud is edible. Snip off the sharp points on each of the scales with a scissors. Both the heart of the bud and the base of the scales (bracts) are delicious. Stems and leaf shoots can also be blanched and steamed. Boil the artichoke for 30 to 40 minutes in water, which can

be flavored with lemon, salt, vinegar, or varied herbs. Or microwave in water until the base is easily pierced with a knife. Drain it upside down. Pull the scales down, and dip their base in butter mixed with lemon juice or any sauce you prefer. Pull the base of the scale through your teeth. Continue doing this until you get into the center of the bud. Scales get thin at the center. Remove these. Now you are at the choke, a round mass of fuzzy fibers. Either scrape or carefully cut out these fibers with a knife, leaving behind the tender base, considered a delicacy. This too is sliced and dipped in an appropriate sauce, butter and lemon, mayonnaise, or a mustard dip.

Not well known is that the stalks and young leaf shoots, known as "chards," are also edible. Plants can be cut back to about 12 inches, tied together, and then blanched by surrounding them with black plastic. Rot is possible, so check plants daily. This is one way of salvaging something edible from a plant that has not formed buds as the season comes to an end. Also, if buds have not fully developed by the end of the season, harvest them anyway and eat them whole.

Consider overcoming "failure" with artichokes by cutting at least one plant back to 12 inches at the end of the season. Dig up the crown with as many roots as possible and plant in a 3-gallon pot. Put this pot in a cool, bright place indoors. Don't feed the plant, but do water it very lightly from time to time—just enough to keep it alive. Start to water it regularly in the spring. This will spur new growth just for the few weeks before the plant is transplanted back to the garden. This suggestion comes with no guarantee of success. Of course, if you start with a potted plant from the start, bring indoors and treat as described.

Artichokes probably originated in the Mediterranean area, most likely North Africa, spreading quickly to Italy where they are especially prized.

Asparagus Pea
Lotus tetragonolobus, also known as *Tetragonolobus purpureus*
Legume or Pea Family
(Fabaceae, formerly Leguminosae)

The asparagus pea is a somewhat obscure, tender annual grown for the beauty of its flowers and its edible pods. As a legume, it is reported to add nitrogen to the soil. This plant is sometimes referred to as a winged pea, not to be confused with a winged bean, *Psophocarpus tetragonolobus* var. *purpureus.* The latter is sometimes called asparagus pea as well, which confuses just about everyone. The latter is a plant suited to tropical areas only. Asparagus pea has no relation to asparagus, nor to peas.

The deep-tan to brown seed is fairly large and round (about 700 seeds per ounce). The plant forms a rosette of stems that spread out and up like the inside of a large cup or spokes on a bicycle wheel. The leaves are soft and medium green. Paired, butterfly-like flowers form at the tips of the stems and are a gorgeous crimson color. The plant is consid-

Asparagus peas form odd-shaped fruits and lovely, small, crimson flowers.

ered a lovely wildflower in warmer areas. Small four-winged pods that look like they have been trimmed with pinking shears form when the flowers fade.

These pods need to be picked when about 1 inch long. Otherwise, they become so fibrous as to be essentially inedible. Since each plant produces only a limited number of pods at a time, gather and collect enough over a period of days. Steam them lightly, making sure to remove the sliver of pod that was closest to the stem—it is really tough. To me, asparagus peas taste somewhat like an artichoke heart. The flowers are lovely edible garnishes. They can be mixed into cheese spreads and salads to pique the interest of gourmets. While the plant is unusual and its tiny flowers lovely, grow it mainly for fun.

Warning: Do not plant it early like garden peas. Let the soil warm up to at least 70°F.

Asparagus pea probably originated in China or northwest Africa.

I could find no reliable information on the nutritional benefits of this plant.

Belgian Endive
Cichorium intybus var. *sativum,* or *Cichorium intybus* var. *foliosum*
Aster, Daisy, or Sunflower Family
(Asteraceae, formerly Compositae)

Belgian endive is a very hardy, cool- to cold-season perennial grown as an annual for fall forcing. True Belgian endive is one of the most delicious vegetables you can grow. It is a crisp, tightly folded, succulent crown of blanched leaves. It can be eaten raw or cooked. The flavor is delicate and distinctive. Belgian endive is sometimes called Belgium chicory, blanching chicory, Brussels witloof (witloof or witloof chicory), chicon, chicory in Great Britain, Dutch chicory, endive in France, French endive, or green-leaved blanching chicory.

To grow this vegetable requires time, patience, and skill. Belgian endive seed is very small (about 13,000 to 18,000 seeds per ounce), light silver to tan, and pointed. It grows into a plant with long, broad leaves. The deep-green leaves supply food to the roots, which grow and expand for several months until they look like parsnips with secondary roots shooting off in different directions. Ideally, these roots should be 1½ to 2 inches in diameter. Now comes the difficult part.

There are several methods of forcing, which just means getting a second round of growth. Method one, for gamblers: Leave the roots in the ground. After the first frost, cut off the leafy tops back to about 1 to 2 inches above the top of the root, making sure to leave the inner growing point intact. Cover the stubs with peat and soil. Dampen lightly. Cover with a pot or bucket. Then cover either of these with a mound of whole leaves or straw. If you are lucky, the plants will begin to form new growth that can be harvested in 3 to 4 weeks. The growth looks like an elongated white flame, called a "chicon," the vegetable we know as Belgian endive. If it gets too cold, you may not get any crop at all. I do not like this method, since the ground often freezes before you get a crop.

Method two: Lay trimmed roots horizontally in damp peat in a wide container. Place it in a cool and dark place, preferably a root cellar, where the temperature remains roughly 50° to 60°F. Once a week pot up one root or more in 10-inch pots so that the crown of the root is about ½ inch above the soil. Water lightly. Cover the entire pot with a black plastic bag. Continue to keep cool. Open the bag every few days, watching for any signs of mold or decay. Remove any damaged leaves before covering again. The new growth should be tall enough to cut in 3 to 4 weeks. Cut back, leaving 1 inch of stem. Or strip off any damaged leaves, pull off the larger outside leaves, and then let the inner core continue to grow. This is my preferred way of harvesting, although I get only leaves, not whole heads. Place the pot back in the bag. Now add additional pots under the bag. Sequential potting leads to sequential harvesting.

Belgian Endive Nutrition Facts
Serving size: 100 grams (3.5 ounces)

	AMOUNT PER RAW SERVING	% DV
Calories	8	0.5%
Carbohydrates	2 g	1%
Calcium	103 mg	10%
Dietary fiber	2 g	7%
Iron	2 mg	10%
Potassium	220 mg	7%
Protein	1.5 g	2%
Vitamin C	20 mg	35%
Vitamin K	115 mcg	125%

Method three: Fill a 24-inch-deep bucket or pail with 12 inches of sand. Use sphagnum peat moss if no sand is available. Place all of the roots upright into the sand. They can be crowded together. Fill gaps in between the roots with sand. Pack them firmly in place. Cover the roots with sand. Water. Place in a cool spot. Exclude all light. The succulent crowns of Belgian endive are ready to harvest when they begin to pop through the sand or peat. Move the sand aside, and slice off the endive with a small, sharp knife. Again,

Belgian endive leaves are edible but rarely harvested, in order to create larger roots.

The roots of Belgian endive are forced indoors to induce growth of delicious, delicately colored chicons.

leave the roots in place. You may get a second crop. The second crop may be much smaller, but it is worth a try. Note that some people do not cover the roots with sand. This makes harvesting easier. Experiment with different methods to find the one that works best for you. Extend the harvest as long as you can. In this way Belgian endive really goes through two growing seasons. If plants were allowed to overwinter, they would form delightful blue flowers the following season.

Plant seed as soon as possible in spring, because the longer the growing season, the larger the roots. The larger the roots, the nicer the newly emerging growth is for eating. Do not expect your Belgian endives to be as large as the ones sold in supermarkets. The latter are grown commercially using sophisticated techniques difficult for the average home gardener to match. The small "chicons" are still delicious. Harvest only when ready to use, since new growth turns bitter when exposed to light and begins to go limp. Although the goal of growing Belgian endive is to get large roots for forcing at the end of the season, some gardeners pick a few young leaves early in the season for salads or cooked greens.

Belgian endive is edible raw or cooked. The canoe-like leaves are creamy with yellow edges, crunchy, and mildly bitter. They are often chopped and mixed into salads or filled with soft cheese spreads. A great filling is smoked salmon blended into cream cheese seasoned with finely chopped dill leaves. Belgian endive can be boiled, braised with butter and lemon, baked for 25 to 30 minutes, or fried. It is commonly topped with grated cheese in France. In parts of Europe the roots are processed after flowering in the second year and used as a coffee substitute. Dig up roots, let dry for several weeks, clean, peel, cut into ¼ inch pieces, roast at 300°F until dark brown, beat with a hammer, grind in a coffee mill, and use a smaller amount than you normally would per cup (about ¼ less).

Seed for Belgian endive has become limited over the years. 'Totem Hybrid' should be available.

There is varying opinion about the origin of this plant. Areas of possible origin include Europe (most likely), Egypt, and Indonesia.

Burdock
Arctium lappa
Aster, Daisy, or Sunflower Family
(Asteraceae, formerly Compositae)

Burdock is a hardy, cool-season biennial commonly harvested in the first year of growth, although it often survives winters in cold climates. It is grown primarily for its roots, but both its young stems and leaves are edible. It is known as gobo in Japan, where it is especially popular as a cooked vegetable. The plant is easy to grow but takes a long time to mature. It is a tough, resilient plant considered a weed in the wild.

Burdock grows from a medium-large seed that looks like a blackish-brown, rounded spearhead (about 1,700 seeds per ounce). The plant grows heart-shaped leaves that become increasingly larger as it matures. The leaves, green on top and a fuzzy white underneath, send food to roots, which are long and slender, sometimes reaching a length of 3 feet under optimal conditions. During the second season, the plant's stems rise above the foliage to produce purplish flowers that mature into burrs with tiny, hooked barbs. The seed in these can spread and become invasive, at least in the wild species.

Critical to the formation of long roots is loose soil to a depth of as much as 3 feet. Some gardeners grow burdock in extra deep pots, because harvesting the roots in regular garden soil can be quite an undertaking. Get seed into the garden as soon as possible, giving the plant a long enough season to form roots. Press seed into the soil surface. It should be able to "sense" light.

Young leaves, young shoots, and mature roots are all edible. Cut young shoots back to the ground if leaves and stems are desired. Plants may regenerate new growth, much like a dandelion, if the root is left in place. Digging up mature roots can be a chore. Do this in late summer after the first freeze or the following spring. If left in the ground too long, roots may become tough and woody. Dig a hole off to the side of the plant either with a spade or posthole digger. Then dig on the opposite side of the plant, trying to push the roots into the hole. This can prove somewhat comical but eventually works. Brush off soil, and wash only when ready to use.

Cook young leaves and tender shoots like spinach. Or steam the young stems as you would asparagus. The roots are edible raw or cooked and are easiest to harvest when less than 18 inches. They also taste best at this stage, so you don't have to wait until they are fully mature. They are usually cooked in Japan, where they are popular. Peel or scrape off the skin with the back of a knife. Place the root in water with lemon juice or vinegar to stop discoloration. Cut into large pieces to be baked or used in soups, much like carrots. Cut on the diagonal, or julienne into matchstick-size pieces. If you find the taste a bit pungent, soak the pieces in water for 2 hours, or parboil them for several minutes before further cooking. Typical cooking methods include

Burdock Nutrition Facts

Serving size: 100 grams (3.5 ounces)

	AMOUNT PER COOKED SERVING	% DV
Calories	88	4%
Carbohydrates	21 g	7%
Dietary fiber	2 g	7%
Magnesium	40 mg	10%
Manganese	0.3 mg	13%
Phosphorus	95 mg	10%
Potassium	360 mg	10%
Protein	2 g	4%
Vitamin B6	0.3 mg	14%

Select varieties of burdock produce firm, edible roots especially suited to Asian cuisine.

sautéing or steaming thin pieces with onion or carrot, coating with batter and frying as tempura, and stir-frying. The latter is often done with julienned carrots and thin slices of celery cooked quickly in sesame oil with rice wine, hot peppers, soy sauce, and sugar added to taste (a dish known as *kimpira*). Boiling pieces gently for up to an hour before using any of these methods is a common practice. To make chips, cut into ultrathin slices, and fry in oil or butter. They are firm and nutty.

Burdock can be pickled or dried and ground into a powder, the latter often sold in health food stores. Small bits of dried burdock are also used to make a tea. While studies of drug interactions are rare, there are warnings about using burdock powders as a dietary supplement if you use diuretics, medications for diabetes, or blood thinners. Another warning concerns pregnant and nursing women. They are advised to avoid burdock because of potential harm to the fetus.

'Ha Gobo' is grown primarily for its leaves and stems. 'Takinogawa Long' is the traditional choice for roots.

Burdock may have originated in Great Britain or Eurasia.

Cardoon
Cynara cardunculus
Aster, Daisy, or Sunflower Family (Asteraceae, formerly Compositae)

Cardoon is a tender perennial grown as an annual. Grow cardoon from seed (600 to 750 seeds per ounce). The large, oval, elongated seed is brownish tan. Seeds grow rapidly, producing large, silvery-green, serrated leaves on thick, grayish stems. Plants will produce flower buds, but these are not edible. If the season were long enough, they would bloom into purple seed heads that look like a cross between an artichoke and a thistle. In warmer climates these would produce seeds at the end of tiny parachutes that would be blown away to drift in the prevailing winds.

Cardoon is closely related to the artichoke. Its name comes from *chardon,* the French word for "thistle." It is grown for its stalks and the midribs of its large leaves. It is considered a delicacy by some but has a reputation for being bitter. I think that reputation is exaggerated.

Cardoon grows well if planted once the weather warms up, and will get huge in one season of growth. Grow it just like an artichoke if you want to get a jump on the season. But it will produce large plants even when direct seeded. The stems of cardoon can be blanched for 3 to 4 weeks once the weather turns cool, but this affects the limited nutrient value of the plant.

Harvest the stalks at different stages of growth to decide what size you prefer. Cut off the top leafy portions. Then slide your knife along the upper sides of the "indented" portion of the stem to remove any remaining leaves and the edge of the stem itself. Then peel the outer stem to remove the "strings" with a vegetable peeler or paring knife. Strip off the strings from the top of the stalk down. This turns the stalk from silvery to green. When stripped of their silvery coating, dip stalks into a vinegar or lemon solution to prevent discoloration.

Unlike artichokes, cardoon can be eaten raw as well as cooked, but only young stalks are typically eaten raw. More often, stalks and the midribs of leaves are cooked. Baking, boiling, and broiling take up to 30 minutes if the stems are left whole. To reduce cooking time and preserve nutrients, cut them into thin strips. Cut the stems into slices or strips either before or after cooking. To cook, boil in water (salt is optional) until tender. Add thin strips to sliced onions,

Cardoon
Nutrition Facts
Serving size: 100 grams (3.5 ounces)

	AMOUNT PER RAW SERVING	% DV	AMOUNT PER COOKED SERVING	% DV
Calcium	70 mg	7%	70 mg	7%
Calories	17	1%	22	1%
Carbohydrates	4 g	1%	5 g	2%
Dietary fiber	1.5 g	6%	2 g	7%
Folate	68 mcg	17%	22 mcg	5
Magnesium	42 mcg	10%	45 mg	11%
Manganese	0.3 mg	13%	0.1 mg	7%
Potassium	400 mg	10%	390 mg	10%
Protein	0.7 g	1%	0.8 g	2%

Large, thistle-like cardoon plants produce unique, silvery inner stems that are considered a delicacy.

and sauté in butter; cook, chill, and place in salads; cover with cheese sauce, lemon butter, or vinaigrette; cook, sprinkle with parmesan cheese, place under a broiler briefly, and top with bits of fresh parsley; dip into a batter and fry like french fries; or add to soups and stews.

'Porto Spineless' is an excellent variety and gets huge. Cardoon probably originated in the Mediterranean area.

Chickpea (Garbanzo Bean)
Cicer arietinum
Legume or Pea Family
(Fabaceae, formerly Leguminosae)

Chickpeas are referred to as cool-season annuals by many sources, but I cannot figure out why, since they are frost sensitive and thrive in subtropical to tropical areas. And they should be planted after the soil temperature reaches 65°F. Chickpeas can be a challenge to grow but worth the gamble for the gardener who wants to have grown everything. Chickpeas are also known as ceci (cici beans), garbanzo beans in Spanish, gram, and hummus in Hebrew. Chickpeas are not a pea, not a bean, but a gram, which is a legume that forms seeds. It is sometimes referred to as a pulse, plants theoretically grown just for their seeds.

A chickpea grows from a round, wrinkled seed (60 to 100 seeds per ounce) into a short "bush" with silvery hairs on its leaves and stem. Its flowers vary by variety from white to pale violet and develop into short, swollen pods typically containing two seeds. Let pods and seeds dry out before picking unless rain is in the forecast. Watch the pods, since they may crack open, releasing the seeds. Consider cutting nearly dry pods off the plant into a paper bag and continue drying indoors. Do not expect a plentiful harvest.

Chickpeas, or garbanzo beans, are favorites in making falafel and hummus. Note that some gardeners snip off tender foliage and cook as a green. Chickpeas do provide some nitrogen to the soil. Buy any variety of chickpea to see whether you think it is worth growing considering the limited number of peas produced. If you want to be different, try a black-seeded type such as 'Kabuli Black'. Some people say these are more nutritious than light-colored seed.

Chickpeas probably originated in the Middle East.

Chickpea (Garbanzo Bean) Nutrition Facts

Serving size: 100 grams (3.5 ounces)

	AMOUNT PER COOKED SERVING	% DV
Calories	165	8%
Carbohydrates	27 g	9%
Copper	0.4 mg	18%
Dietary fiber	8 g	30%
Folate	170 mcg	43%
Iron	2.9 mg	16%
Magnesium	48 mg	12%
Manganese	1.0 mg	50%
Phosphorus	168 mg	17%
Potassium	290 mg	8%
Protein	9 g	18%
Thiamin	0.1 mg	8%
Vitamin B6	0.1 mg	7%
Zinc	1.5 mg	10%

Chickpeas taste good, but individual plants typically produce few pods.

Cowpea (Black-Eyed Pea)
Vigna unguiculata ssp. *unguiculata* var. *sinensis*
Legume or Pea Family
(Fabaceae, formerly Leguminosae)

Cowpeas are very tender, warm-season annuals. They are grown primarily in the South, where they are extremely popular. Cold-climate gardeners will find them relatively easy to grow and interesting in that they are edible at many stages of growth. They also improve soil structure and fertility as an added bonus. Admittedly, they are susceptible to insect and disease, but this should not stop you from trying them. However, considering the space they take up, they are relatively unproductive, even when showered with pods containing numerous ripe seeds.

Cowpea seed is quite large (150 or more seeds per ounce), varying in shape from pea- to bean-like in a wide variety of colors. The seeds grow into bush, semivining, or vining plants with smooth, medium- to dark-green leaves and squarish stems. The flowers look like pale-pink, white, or yellow butterflies depending on the variety. The plants form 3- to 12-inch pods that look like string beans sticking up or hanging down from the stems. These pods begin to bulge with lima bean–like seeds inside, which eventually form seed similar to that planted in the first place. Let the soil warm up to 65°F before planting seed. Think of them more as "cowbeans."

Cowpeas are edible in different stages of growth. Although young leaves are edible, few people eat them. They can be added to salads or cooked like spinach for a side dish. The pods are edible at many stages of maturity. Pick them very young to eat like a snap bean. Don't wait too long, or they will be stringy. As the pods fill in, open some up, and eat the developing seeds like a lima (shell) bean. They are most commonly used as a dried bean once fully mature, although some gardeners prefer picking and drying them just before this. For mature dry beans, let the pods dry on the plants until late in the season. Pull up the plants, and hang them upside down in a dry, warm, airy place until crispy, or snip off the pods into a paper bag, and dry them indoors. Crunch the pods with your hands to separate the seed from the debris. Place the seeds in water, and remove any additional debris that floats to the surface. Swish the beans several times to get them thoroughly clean. Compost all debris. To cook, boil for 2 minutes, let soak in hot water for 2 hours, replace water, add seasoning to taste, bring back to boil, then let simmer until tender.

Cowpeas are known by a wide variety of names including black-eyed pea (light or white peas with black eyes), china bean, colored-eyed pea (light or white peas with brown, pink, or tan eyes), cornfield pea, cream or conch pea (light-colored peas), crowder pea (black, brown, or speckled peas that are "crowded" into pods), field pea (vining types

Cowpea (Black-Eyed Pea) Nutrition Facts

Serving size: 100 grams (3.5 ounces)

	AMOUNT PER COOKED SERVING	% DV
Calories	116	6%
Carbohydrates	36 g	12%
Copper	0.3 mg	13%
Dietary fiber	6.5 g	25%
Folate	208 mcg	52%
Iron	2.5 mg	14%
Magnesium	53 mg	13%
Manganese	0.5 mg	25%
Phosphorus	156 mg	16%
Potassium	275 mg	8%
Protein	8 g	15%
Thiamin	0.2 mg	13%
Zinc	1.3 mg	9%

Cowpeas are easy to grow. They have delightful butterfly blooms and pods that look like beans.

with small peas generally used to attract wildlife or as a green manure crop), pinkeye pea, purple hull pea (cowpeas with purple or purple-tinted pods), southern pea, and table pea.

To see whether you would like to grow cowpeas more than once, start with 'California Black Eye No. 5'. It is readily available and grows well in cold climates. Its "beans" grow right on top of the plant, where they are easy to pick.

Cowpeas likely originated in west Africa.

Currant
Ribes species
Gooseberry Family (Grossulariaceae)

Currants are cold-hardy perennials. Their fruits are like jewels, varying in color, flavor, shape, size, and texture by variety. Plants are most often purchased bare root, in packages consisting of stems with roots attached only. Buy older plants with as many stems as possible. Ask for pruning instructions to be sent with the plants, since these vary by variety. Although they are self-fertile, consider growing more than one variety. Always plant stems about 2 inches lower than they were growing at the nursery. Currants often take up to 4 years to fully mature, when they may produce from 2 to 8 pounds of fruit per shrub, varying with the variety—less for black, more for red.

Critical to their growth is well-prepared fertile soil, consistent watering from spring through fall, and lots of sun. With proper care they will last up to a decade or a bit longer. The plants have shallow, fibrous root systems, may be upright or spreading in their growth habit, and vary in their susceptibility to disease and insects. To provide good air circulation, which reduces the chance of disease, plant red currants at least 3 feet apart, and a little more for black currants. The shrubs bear clusters (sprigs) of pea-sized fruits. As the season progresses, currants change color but may take 2 to 3 weeks to mature fully, when they become somewhat soft and juicy. When to pick them is learned by trial and error. Cut off the drooping sprigs (not individual berries) of pink, red, and white currants for longer-lasting fruit. Pick pink, red, and white currants all at once; black, over a period of weeks, often single berries rather than sprigs. Since berries take time to mature, bird netting must be in place and anchored into the ground.

Underripe berries contain more pectin and are best for jelly. Pick berries ripe for jam and overripe for juice. Remove berries from sprigs using a fork. To freeze, sort berries, wash (optional), pack in 1 cup sugar to 8 cups fruit or without sugar, depending on intended use. Dry in a dehydrator or slowly in an oven set at 150°F. The latter method may take

Currant
Nutrition Facts
Serving size: 100 grams (3.5 ounces)

	AMOUNT PER RAW SERVING	% DV
Calories	55	3%
Carbohydrates	14 g	5%
Dietary fiber	4 g	17%
Iron	1 mg	6%
Manganese	0.2 mg	9%
Phosphorus	44 mg	6%
Potassium	275 mg	8%
Protein	1.5 g	3%
Vitamin C	41 mg	68%
Vitamin K	11 mcg	14%

Currants shine like jewels in the garden but require protection from birds.

many hours. Currants can also be cooked and made into jam, jelly, juice, or sauces.

There are dozens of varieties available in the market. For a red currant *(Ribes rubrum),* try one of the oldest and still one of the most popular, 'Red Lake', or experiment with 'Rovada', an import from the Netherlands, or 'Cherry Red'. For a black currant *(Ribes nigrum),* begin with 'Ben Sarek', and branch out from there. Black currant is a cohost to white pine blister rust *(Cronartium ribicola),* which is a nuisance to the currant but fatal to white pines. There may be restrictions on where companies can sell currants.

Currants originated in Europe and North America.

Daylily
Hemerocallis species
Grasstree Family (Xanthorrhoeaceae)

Daylilies are one of the most popular flowering perennial plants and extremely hardy. Daylilies have long been popular in Asia as edible plants as well. Their roots, their young stems, buds, and flowers are all edible. The plants are tough, durable, and easy to grow. These are considered herbs and greens. Daylilies form a thick, fibrous root system with tuberous-like structures. These roots are connected to stem tissue (a crown), from which springs a thick clump of pointed leaves. Flower stems (scapes) shoot up from the clumps and are usually leafless. Buds form on top of these long stems well above the leaves. The buds enlarge each day, finally to burst open into colorful flowers with six brightly colored petals and sepals (technically tepals). The flowers are not long lasting. They bloom, then turn limp, and wither within 24 hours or less. The plants themselves have aggres-

sive root systems that spread out to form ever-larger clumps over the years.

Not all daylilies are considered safe to eat. Do not confuse these with lilies *(Lilium* species), almost all of which are toxic. The two species, wild daylilies, most commonly used for food are *Hemerocallis fulva* (orange daylily) and *Hemerocallis liliosphodelus* (pronounced lill-ee-oh-as-foe-DELL-us). The latter is known as yellow daylily or lemon lily. The orange daylily has orange blossoms with a golden-yellow throat.

The light-yellow petals of sweetly scented Hemerocallis liliosphodelus *enliven a fresh salad.*

This is the common daylily seen on abandoned farms, in roadside ditches, and in the backyards of numerous homes throughout the country. The leaves are wider at the base, bend down from the center of the plant, and come to a sharp, narrow point at the end. The tall flower stems shoot straight up through the clump of leaves. Each stem has a cluster of buds at its tip and other buds on little branchlets just below. The buds vary in size and open one at a time over a period of days. There may be a dozen or more buds on each stem. The flowers are about 4 inches wide with six prominent stamens. Rising up from the yellow throat through the center of each petal to its tip is a light whitish-yellow streak. Identification is important because, to repeat, not all daylilies are edible. The yellow daylily is similar in form to the orange species, but its leaves are more narrow. Buds ride on top of the stem and open sequentially rather than all at once. There are numerous but a varying number of buds per stem. The flowers exude a lovely perfume.

Cut young shoots when only a few inches tall. They come up early in spring. Take only a portion of shoots from a mature clump. Pick buds on flower stalks when the indented tubular buds are roughly 2 days away from flowering. Pick flowers just as they open. Pick tubers off in fall since this gives young tubers time to form. Dig up one side of a plant, harvest a few lighter-colored young tubers, place the plant back into the soil, and water immediately.

Sauté young shoots in seasoned oil or butter. Some sources say that they are hallucinogenic if eaten in large amounts. Cooking seems to reduce the chance of any reaction. Start with a few. To prepare buds, trim off any stem tissue, and cut off the base. Rinse in cold water, and pat dry with a paper towel. Add crispy, bean-like buds raw to salads, or boil, steam, or stir-fry them for a little extra crunch in cooked dishes. Or heat oil or butter in a pan. Sauté minced onion or garlic for several minutes. Add the buds and any preferred seasoning. Cook until tender. Or dip a bud in egg, cover it with cornmeal, and panfry. The average person will eat about six buds. The flowers are edible raw or cooked. Cut off the white base, and remove the stamens and pistils from the inside of the flower. Strip off the petals, and add to salads or float in soups. Some people also sauté the petals in seasoned oil or butter. The petals are mild tasting. For tempura, dip the whole flower in batter, and deep-fry in hot oil briefly. Or stuff whole flowers like squash blossoms. Dried flowers are called "golden needles" and are used as thickeners and flavor for soups and stews. The young tubers are also edible raw or cooked. Clean and toss small pieces into salads. Use cut portions to replace potatoes in soups and stews.

The plants in this section are rarely offered in local garden centers. They are considered to be "weeds" by some, especially the orange-colored species. You may find them in your neighborhood or in farm areas, where they have been growing for years. People are often glad to give some away. Look for them in the summer, and ask whether you could dig up a clump in spring. Both tolerate temperatures to -40°F.

Daylilies are believed to be native to China and Japan.

The orange daylily Hemerocallis fulva *produces blossoms that are dried into "golden needles" for soups and stews.*

Daylily Nutrition Facts

Serving size: 100 grams (3.5 ounces)

	AMOUNT PER SERVING OF RAW PETALS	% DV
Calcium	85 mg	8%
Calories	35	2%
Carbohydrates	7 g	2%
Dietary fiber	4 g	1%
Iron	1.2 mg	8%
Phosphorus	176 mg	16%
Protein	1 g	2%
Riboflavin	0.2 mg	15%
Thiamin	0.15	8%
Vitamin A	3,000 IU	65%
Vitamin C	88 mg	130%

Elderberry Nutrition Facts

Serving size: 100 grams (3.5 ounces)

	AMOUNT PER COOKED SERVING	% DV
Calories	73	4%
Carbohydrates	18 g	6%
Dietary fiber	7 g	30%
Iron	1.6 mg	8%
Potassium	280 mg	8%
Protein	0.7 g	1%
Vitamin A	600 IU	12%
Vitamin B6	0.2 mg	10%
Vitamin C	36 mg	60%

Elderberries are toxic raw but delicious when cooked and made into jams and jellies.

Elderberry
Sambucus canadensis
Elderberry Family or Moschatel Family (Adoxaceae), formerly Honeysuckle Family (Caprifoliaceae)

Elderberries are hardy, shrubby plants that are not commonly grown in home gardens. The flowers and berries are only edible cooked. Since they are potentially toxic raw, this is not a good plant for gardeners who have young children roaming about. Plants are surprisingly tolerant of overly wet soils and, in fact, demand consistent moisture. This is a good plant for someone living by a swampy area lined with trees. *However, near does not mean in soggy soils.*

Get bare-root plants into the ground in early spring. Keep the area weed-free and well mulched, but leave the plants alone for the first 2 years. Prune off any dead tissue, but do not prune back. Do cut out older growth in the third year. Plants produce sweet, umbrella-like, white to cream flower clusters, which are used to make fritters and wine. Blossoms can be dried for tea. *Not all species produce edible flowers. Some are toxic.* Buy plants rather than searching for them in the wild.

Once flowers are pollinated, they ripen into edible berries over a period of weeks and must be protected on plants from birds. Pick in clusters, strip off fruit with your fingers, and use as soon as possible. Keep cool until ready to use. Cook for jams, jellies, juices, and pies. Note that the fruit can be dried and cooked at a later date. Or flash freeze, and then remove green stems before cooking. They can also be stored frozen in plastic freezer bags.

Buy at least two varieties to ensure proper cross-pollination. There are both American and European varie-ties. Since the American are hardier, they are mentioned here. Plant 'Adams' with 'Johns'; both can get to be as much as 10 feet tall. Plant the shorter varieties 'Nova' and 'York'. The latter are more practical for the home gardener and produce large berries. Space them within 8 feet of each other. These plants have been around for years and should be available.

Although widely spread throughout North America, the plants *may* have originated in Europe.

Garden Huckleberry
Solanum melanocerasum, also known as *Solanum nigrum* var. *guineense*
Sunberry (Wonderberry)
Solanum retroflexum, formerly *Solanum × burbankii*
Nightshade Family (Solanaceae)

The garden huckleberry and its relative the sunberry, or wonderberry, are very tender, warmth-loving annuals, not to be confused with woody huckleberries. They produce dark-black berries that when cooked, can be used much as you would blueberries. These are an uncommon crop related to peppers and tomatoes. Grow them in the same fashion, not in the way you would blueberries.

Their seed is small, flat, and light tan (roughly 25,000 seeds per ounce). This should be started indoors and treated as you would a tomato, although direct-seeded plants often do produce berries but in limited amounts. Plants are up-right with numerous branches. The plants produce very small, white flowers that mature into little clusters of green berries that turn deep purple as they mature. They are glossy

Starting garden huckleberries from transplants dramatically increases the number of berries produced.

Though best for jellies when they are immature, gooseberries are far more tasty when fully ripe.

at first and will become dull and a bit mushy when fully ripe. A light frost often improves their flavor, so leave the berries on the plant as long as possible. Note that their juice stains clothing badly.

Never eat them raw. They are not only bitter but also toxic until fully cooked for jams, jellies, or pies. Cooking does remove the bitterness, and they should be cooked until tender before adding sugar. Cooking them for 15 minutes or so and combining them with sugar makes a nice sauce.

The sunberry (also known as wonderberry) is a hybrid of the garden huckleberry and should be grown and used in the same manner. I have found the sunberry to be an insect magnet that still produces despite skeletonized leaves. Even so, I prefer it to the common garden huckleberry.

The plant probably originated in Africa.

I could find no reliable information on the nutritional benefits of this plant.

Gooseberry
Ribes hirtellum
Gooseberry Family (Grossulariaceae)

Gooseberries are hardy plants known for producing delicious round fruit. Grown properly, they will survive up to 15 years and even longer. They are offered as bare-root plants from a number of nurseries. Ask about size when ordering. You want plants with long roots and lots of stems. Get these plants in as early as possible in the growing season. Soak their roots in water for several hours. Never let roots dry out. Plant them in full sun, and give plenty of space. Stems produce inconspicuous flowers that develop into small round globes, possibly a few the first year but up to 8 to 10 pounds in 3 to 4 years, when shrubs may need support from wires or trellises.

Ask for pruning instructions to be sent with the plant. Simple pruning instructions are as follows. Gooseberries produce fruit on 2- to 3-year-old cane. Over the years keep an equal number of 1-, 2-, and 3-year-old shoots, removing any stems older than 3 years. Fruit is produced best on new wood.

dry in direct light. If a gourd develops mushiness, toss it. Pathogens on gourds can be killed by dipping them briefly in boiling water or by washing them in a bleach or borax solution, as described above. Always dry the gourds with a soft rag after disinfecting. You may have to rub or sand off a film that develops on some varieties, such as bottle gourd.

Most gourds probably originated in Asia, although the origin of some is essentially unknown.

Ground Cherry
Physalis species
Nightshade Family (Solanaceae)

Ground cherries are tender, warm-season perennials grown as annuals in cold climates. A ground cherry may be referred to as a Cape Gooseberry, cerise de terre, strawberry tomato, and yellow husk cherry. It is also sometimes called a husk tomato, but this name more commonly refers to the tomatillo. Its seed is light tan, hard, and flat (about 8,000 to 15,000 seeds per ounce). It grows into a plant quite similar to a tomato with hairy, fuzzy leaves and tiny, pale-yellow blossoms that mature into fruits covered in a papery husk (calyx) that look like a Chinese lantern. Inside is a small, round fruit, similar to, but smaller than, a cherry tomato. The plants become fairly large as they mature, spreading out to take up quite a bit of space. The fruits in their husks fall to the ground once mature, which makes the name *ground cherry* particularly appropriate.

The plants are preferably started indoors, like tomatoes, but can be direct seeded when the soil warms up. Some people plant through landscape fabric both to heat up the soil and make picking up the fallen fruit easier. This plant can begin to flower and form fruit when only a few inches tall. Pinch off early flowers and fruit to direct energy to the growing plant. Once plants are mature, they produce copious amounts of fruits until a killing frost. This is one plant "that just keeps giving."

After picking up fruits from the ground, let them stay in their husks in a dry place for a few weeks. Ground cherries tend to get sweeter that way. Of course, remove the husk before eating. The taste of the fruit is pleasant but somewhat strange. It can be eaten raw, dipped in chocolate, placed on oatmeal, pancakes, or waffles, or chopped and added to salsas. It is often cooked for jams, jellies, marmalade, pies, sauces, and tarts. It can even be dried like raisins.

Varieties have been derived from three species: *Physalis peruviana*, *Physalis pruinosa*, and *Physalis pubescens*. Available varieties include 'Aunt Molly's', 'Giant', 'Goldie', and 'Pineapple'.

Ground Cherry Nutrition Facts

Serving size: 100 grams (3.5 ounces)

	AMOUNT PER RAW SERVING	% DV
Calories	50	2%
Carbohydrates	10 g	2%
Niacin	2.8 mg	14%
Protein	2 g	4%
Vitamin A	725 IU	13%
Vitamin C	11 mg	18%

Ground cherries can be direct seeded but are incredibly prolific if planted early as transplants.

Never plant Chinese lantern (*Physalis alkekengi*) in your garden. As an edible plant, it is sometimes sold as winter cherry. It is a hardy and incredibly invasive perennial plant that spreads like a cancer through underground roots (rhizomes) and is extremely difficult to eradicate. It is just as noxious as Canada thistle *(Cirsium arvense)*.

Ground cherries probably originated in South America, possibly in Brazil or Peru.

Milkweed
Asclepias syriaca
Dogbane Family (Apocynaceae),
formerly Milkweed Family (Asclepiadaceae)

According to foragers, the young shoots and immature pods of milkweed are edible. Cut the shoots just as they emerge. Boil them. Some people say they taste a bit like green beans. They may or may not be bitter depending on the plant. Bitterness is removed by repeated boiling and removal of the water, but if this is necessary, some people suggest the plant may be overly toxic—again, plants vary in their bitterness. Later in the season, plants flower and form pointed pods. The immature flowers taste somewhat like broccoli. Immature pods with silk just forming may be added to stews or stir-fries. When the pods mature at the end of the season, they become brown, prickly, and brittle with numerous white, silky strands on the inside. At the end of each strand is a tan seed that looks like a thin tick.

Milkweed is critical to the survival of the monarch butterfly *(Danaus plexippus),* which is presently endangered. An increasing number of home gardeners protect at least a small patch of milkweed on the side or back of their garden. It may harbor some pests, but the plant provides nectar for mature butterflies and food for caterpillars.

The young shoots of milkweed are edible, but most gardeners grow the plant to sustain the monarch butterfly population.

If you want to start a patch, buy plants or seed. Or collect seed on your own. Note that seed must go through a cold treatment to germinate. Place seed in a moist towel or bag filled with moist peat moist in your refrigerator for at least 90 days. Or scatter seed outdoors in barely roughed-up soil. Mark the area with a label.

Older plants emerge in late spring with a solid stem and light-green, pointed leaves with a soft, white underside. The plant will grow up to 3 to 4 feet tall. If cut, it exudes a milky sap. What gives it away further are its lovely flowers and the pointed pods that follow with their silky interior and tick-like seeds. The seeds float in the wind like dandelion seeds and can be invasive.

I do not grow this plant to eat. There are too many conflicting warnings regarding its potential toxicity, so for me this plant is strictly for the butterflies.

Milkweed is native to North America.

Ostrich Fern (Fiddleheads)
Matteuccia struthiopteris
Wood Fern Family
(Onocleaceae, formerly Dryopteridaceae)

Ostrich ferns are perennial, cold-season plants. They are most commonly harvested in the wild but can be grown under the right conditions in the home garden over a period of years to produce a delicious edible crop. Ostrich ferns are often referred to as fiddlehead ferns because the new growth early in spring looks like the scrolls at the end of a violin. Ostrich ferns grow from spores, not seeds. The reproduction process of spores is complex, so the following description describes plant growth from the young fern stage on. Plants have shallow roots. Each plant is a clump or crown that will produce a varying number of leaves depending on its age. The leaves unfurl early in the season from tightly curled, deep-green heads covered with light-tan, papery scales. These little heads are known as fiddleheads, or crosiers. As the leaves grow, they straighten out and get quite large with a U-shaped groove on the inside of the stem and indentations along the outside portion of the leaf. The mature leaves are called fronds. Individual plants may either form fertile or nonfertile fronds. Fertile fronds turn deep brown as the season progresses. These brittle fronds look like an ostrich feather. During the growing season, plants send out underground stems (rhizomes) to produce new plants either close to or feet away from the mother plant.

Ostrich ferns grow best in partial to full shade. They seem to do particularly well in a raised bed or slope with a northern exposure. Although these plants grow well in woods in the wild, they can struggle under trees in the home yard. The reason is that the soil under upland trees tends to be quite dry as each tree sucks up as much available moisture as possible. Roots also make it difficult to dig a planting bed under trees. Find a spot in your yard that is shaded but not filled with tree roots. It also has to be large enough for the plants to form a colony if you want to grow ostrich ferns as a crop. If this is not feasible, intermingle the ferns in a perennial shade garden with the idea of picking just a few fiddleheads each year as a limited treat. These ferns thrive close to streams and rivers where the soil is rich in organic matter and stays moist throughout the growing season. Either dig or till an area to be devoted to them or build a raised bed. Adding lots of decayed organic matter to any soil is critical to success with these plants. Since ostrich ferns prefer a slightly acidic soil with a pH below 7, mixing sphagnum peat moss into the planting bed is highly recommended. The peat is particularly efficient at retaining moisture during dry spells.

Either buy bare-root or potted plants as early in the season as possible. Plant bare-root plants up to the base of the crown, firm the roots solidly in place, and water immediately. If potted, slide plants out of the pot into an individual planting hole amended with organic material. Keep the plant at the same depth as it was in the pot. Water it immediately, and keep it moist throughout the season. If you are getting plants from a friend or collecting them from the wild, dig them up just as their tops begin to show a little green as early in the season as possible. Transplanting more mature ferns is possible, but it is far more difficult to keep them alive.

Never harvest fiddleheads from young plants. Plants should have at least four fiddleheads and preferably more. If there are only four fiddleheads, snap off only two. On larger plants take no more than half of the fiddleheads. *Never harvest more than once a season.* Grab the unfurled fiddlehead between your thumb and forefinger, simply snap it off.

Rub off the papery coating on the heads. Then wash and swirl them in cold water. Check to make sure they are completely free of the papery covering. Never eat them raw. Sauté or use them in stir-fries. They are delicious when covered with melted butter and seasonings to taste. Note that a health warning from Health Canada and other agencies states that fiddleheads should be boiled for at least 15 minutes before being consumed. *This warning, presently being reviewed, may be correct in preventing disease, but it turns the ferns into mush.* If you want them to be delicious, cook them just until tender.

Ostrich ferns may have originated in Asia, Europe, and North America.

Ostrich Fern (Fiddleheads) Nutrition Facts

Serving size: 100 grams (3.5 ounces)

	AMOUNT PER COOKED SERVING	% DV
Calories	34	2%
Carbohydrates	6 g	1%
Iron	1.3 mg	16%
Phosphorus	100 mg	14%
Potassium	370 mg	7%
Protein	5 g	6%
Vitamin A	3,600 IU	70%
Vitamin C	26 mg	44%

Clip only one or two fiddleheads just as they are forming on mature ostrich fern plants.

Peanut
Arachis hypogaea
Legume or Pea Family
(Fabaceae, formerly Leguminosae)

Peanuts are very tender, warm-season annuals. They are still somewhat of a novelty in cold climates but do well despite their strictly southern reputation. Peanuts are legumes, plants that produce seeds enclosed in pods. In this case, the pods are produced underground. Peanuts are an excellent source of protein. They have the added benefit of forming nodules on their roots, which absorb nitrogen from the air, thereby enriching the soil in their growth cycle. Peanuts are also called earth almond, earth nut, goober (African word), goober pea, ground nut or pea, monkey nuts, pinda, and pinder.

The seeds vary somewhat in color from tan to brown or red and are very large (18 to 28 peanuts per ounce). The seeds produce a spreading mat of erect or creeping, deep-green, pealike foliage depending on the variety, and delicate, but inconspicuous, yellow "butterfly" flowers. The first flowers may be lovely but sterile. The second flush of flowers are lower on the plant and self-pollinate. The petals then fall off. The stalk that holds the flower is called a peg (peduncle). After the flower is fertilized, the peg begins to grow, drops down from the plant by gravity, and corkscrews its way into the soil. At the tip of the peg is an embryo, which develops into a peanut. Each plant forms many pegs, the number varying from one plant to another. Peanuts generally mature over a period of 60 days, but they do not all mature at the same time. This growth pattern is unusual in that flowers are produced aboveground while fruit develops under the soil.

Peanuts demand heat, sun, and space as well as a long enough period to develop fully. For planting, crack the shells open. Inside are nuts covered with a thin, protective "skin" (testa). Do not remove or damage the "skin," as this may reduce the chance of germination. Plant the seed 1 to 2 inches deep depending on your soil type. Plant seed in the garden after all danger of frost when the soil has reached 60°F, or better yet, 70°F. If the soil is too cold, the seed will rot. The main problem with getting peanuts off to a good start is seed robbery, usually by chipmunks and squirrels. Sometimes, they leave telltale holes after digging but not necessarily. If peanuts are not sprouting, check. You may find peanut plants sprouting in the oddest places around your garden. Be prepared to replant. And expect additional damage but usually on a smaller scale. The problem is that peanuts take a long time to mature, so the first theft reduces

The yellow flowers of peanuts produce stems that push downward into the soil, forming peanuts at their tips.

Dig up peanuts at the end of a season, and cure until fully dry.

your chance of getting a decent crop or any peanuts at all. If you have a problem with marauders, cover the planting area with netting until plants emerge.

Water regularly until the plants flower. During the flower and peg formation stage, appropriate watering is disputed. Some gardeners water frequently (I do); others stop watering altogether unless the soil dries out. The latter believe that water may slow down pollination. Gardeners agree that after pegs have penetrated the soil, moderate watering should continue until close to harvest time, when watering should be curtailed. Peanuts generally bloom within 45 days of sprouting but take longer to set pegs. Be patient. *After the flowers have sent pegs into the soil,* some gardeners place mulch around the base of the plant. In theory, this should keep peanuts closer to the surface for easier harvesting. I never mulch but pull weeds by hand. I do not want to take a chance of interfering with pegging.

If possible, harvest plants on a warm, sunny day when the soil is dry. The majority of peanuts will be mature 60 days after plants have flowered. However, peanuts do not mature all at the same time. The foliage often turns yellow toward the end of the season. Some gardeners begin harvesting at this time, but waiting longer may result in a larger harvest. Let peanuts mature until there is danger of a hard frost. This gives immature fruit as long as possible to ripen. *But do not wait until the ground freezes.* Cut off the foliage unless you intend to hang the plants for drying. Do not pull up on the plant. Instead, use a garden fork to dig it up, working from well outside the main stem inwards. Gently shake the plant to remove soil. If soil sticks to the peanuts, leave it alone. Work through the soil to pick out any peanuts that may no longer be attached to the plant. If it is likely to stay warm and dry outside, leave the plants lying on the ground with the roots up. However, these conditions are rare in cold climates in fall, and rain or a hard frost can damage the plants. It is generally necessary to hang the plants by their stems in a warm, well-ventilated area for 4 weeks. At this time, shake the plant again. The soil will be dry and drop off. Providing these conditions can be difficult. It may be easier to snip the peanuts off the plant and lay them on a screen to air-dry in a dry, well-ventilated area—not in direct sun. Space the peanuts so they are not touching each other to avoid mold. Let these cure for at least 3 weeks, or longer if possible. Ventilation is important since the goal is to reduce the moisture content of the nuts to about 10 percent.

The shell of mature peanuts is dark inside, not white. The immature or green peanuts are edible, usually boiled and eaten shell and all. The mature nuts still in their shell can be hung in mesh bags for additional curing. The bags

Peanut Nutrition Facts

Serving size: 100 grams (3.5 ounces)

	AMOUNT PER DRY ROASTED SERVING	% DV
Calcium	60 mg	6%
Calories	600	30%
Carbohydrates	15 g	5%
Copper	0.5 mg	25%
Dietary fiber	9 g	40%
Folate	120 mcg	30%
Iron	1.5 mg	8%
Magnesium	175 mg	45%
Manganese	1.8 mg	90%
Niacin	14 mg	70%
Phosphorus	400 mg	40%
Potassium	725 mg	20%
Protein	28 g	55%
Vitamin B6	0.5 mg	25%
Vitamin E	7 mg	35%
Zinc	3.5 mg	20%

used for onions and oranges are ideal as long as they are open and not covered with plastic. Hang the peanuts in a warm, dry place for up to 2 months. Check the peanuts regularly to make sure that none are going bad. Molds, especially those producing aflatoxin, on peanuts can be serious and highly toxic, so proper drying and curing is important. For home use, it is safest to shell mature, fully cured peanuts before roasting, since unshelled peanuts have a greater chance of turning moldy and potentially toxic. Leave that processing to professionals. To shell, bake for 3 to 5 minutes at 350°F, and remove shell. Or freeze for up to 24 hours, then shell. To roast in the oven, soak shelled peanuts in salted water (optional), then place on a cookie sheet in an oven at 350°F for 15 to 35 minutes. Move around for even cooking. Roasted peanuts should be light brown, and the skin should slip off easily. Begin checking at 15 minutes to see whether peanuts are as just described. Do not scorch. To roast in oil, coat with 1 teaspoon oil per cup of shelled peanuts, lay out on a cookie sheet, place in an oven at 350°F for 5 to 15 minutes or until light brown. Move the peanuts around for even cooking. Do not overcook. Salt if desired. If not eaten immediately, store these in the freezer in airtight containers. To boil immature peanuts, drop 1 pound of newly harvested "raw" whole peanuts into boiling water. Bring to boil, and then let simmer for several hours. Add salt and other spices to taste. Eat these immediately, or store for no more than a few days in the refrigerator. These are generally served warm. They are an acquired taste.

If you want to save peanuts to plant the following year, dry and store in the shell until the following season. Five varieties available to the home gardener are 'Carolina Black', 'Early Spanish', 'Improved Virginia', 'Jumbo Virginia', and 'Tennessee Red Valencia', the latter probably being the best

choice for cold-climate gardeners. It is possible to grow unshelled and *unroasted* peanuts from co-ops and health food stores, but they may not be a type ideally suited for cold-climate areas.

Peanuts make a good cover crop (green manure). If for any reason you have a crop failure, dig or till the plants into the soil. This may be second best but in a sense still a success since you have added valuable nitrogen to the soil. If you get a good crop, toss foliage and shells into the compost pile for added nutrients, but spade or till the roots into the soil.

Peanuts probably originated in Argentina, Bolivia, and Peru.

Radicchio
Cichorium intybus, Cichorium intybus ×
Cichorium endivia, Cichorium intybus
var. *foliosum*
Aster or Sunflower Family
(Asteraceae, formerly Compositae)

Radicchio (rah-DEEK-ee-oh) is a hardy, cold-season plant typically grown as an annual or biennial. Radicchio is a type of chicory. It is commonly thought of as a round, red ball, but there are both leafing and heading types noted for crunchy texture and a slightly bitter taste that adds a special touch to salads. The color varies by variety from pure green, to green with red, to red with white and green tones. Not so well known is that radicchio is delicious cooked as well as raw. Growing radicchio for leaves is easy enough, but getting it to head up is a whole different matter. So it is both an easy and difficult plant to grow, depending on your perspective. It goes by a variety of names, including chioggia, Italian red lettuce, red chicory, red leaf chicory, and red Italian chicory.

Seed is very small (about 18,000 to 19,000 seeds per ounce), light tan, and pointed. Magnified the seed looks a bit like a brown, pointed canine tooth. These grow into miniscule seedlings that mature into plants that mimic a small, rather loose cabbage or an elongated romaine. Radicchio will flower in time, often in the second year. These are beautiful daisy-like, blue blossoms that form copious amounts of seed.

Radicchio has become one of the favorite greens in fancy restaurants. Its slightly bitter taste lends a zesty bite to salads. In some European countries an entire salad may consist of radicchio "greens." These are often splashed with oil and vinegar but may taste better with oil alone salted to taste. 'Castelfranco' is an excellent choice for salads. Radicchio is surprisingly good baked, braised, grilled (cut in two and splashed with oil first), or sautéed. The dish may

Radicchio
Nutrition Facts
Serving size: 100 grams (3.5 ounces)

	AMOUNT PER RAW SERVING	% DV
Calories	23	1%
Carbohydrates	4.5 g	1%
Copper	0.3 mg	15%
Dietary fiber	1 g	4%
Folate	60 mcg	15%
Manganese	0.1 mg	7%
Potassium	300 mg	10%
Protein	1.5 g	3%
Vitamin C	8 mg	13%
Vitamin E	2.3 mg	10%
Vitamin K	255 mcg	320%

Newer varieties of radicchio can produce heads the first season but may not until the following spring.

be covered with béchamel or white sauce with herbs. The leaves of the looser-leaf types, especially 'Pain de Sucre', become sweet as they are cooked. The buds can be pickled. The pretty blue flowers taste a bit like lettuce but do not stay open long. Do not expect uniform growth or coloration.

Harvest early for leaves and later for heads if they finally form. Leave part of the crown and the roots in the ground, or dig them up and force them as you would Belgian endive. The plant often survives and produces new growth in spring. The following varieties can all be planted in early spring and will develop edible leaves and heads in summer and fall: 'Castelfranco' (also known as 'Variegata di Castelfranco'; place a bucket over this for blanching to lovely white with red tones), 'Cornetto di Bordeaux' (like a large green romaine), 'Pain de Sucre' (also known as 'Sugar Loaf', also like a large green romaine), 'Palla Rossa' (a red white ball), 'Perseo' (develops small loose heads in both the first year and following spring if left in place), 'Svelta' (elongated red with white stems), 'Variegata di Chioggia' (a red white ball), 'Red Verona' (also known as 'Rossa di Verona'; green to red, loose to tightish ball).

The species may have originated in Europe but has been bred and perfected in Italy into a maze of named varieties.

Salsify and Scorzonera
Tragopogon porrifolius and *Scorzonera hispanica*
Aster, Daisy, or Sunflower Family (Asteraceae, formerly Compositae)

While these plants have similar growth habits and cultural needs, they are from two distinct plant groups. They are placed together because they grow and are used in a similar fashion. They are considered offbeat vegetables. They do need a long growing season and may be "under appreciated" because they are not easy to grow to maturity in one season—especially in cold climates. Salsify and scorzonera are hardy to very hardy, cool- to cold-season biennials. Salsify is commonly called "oyster plant," while scorzonera is nicknamed "black salsify" or "black oyster plant" because it has darker-brown to almost black roots rather than the tan roots of salsify. Although its roots are black skinned, the flesh is cream to white with a softer and less fibrous texture than salsify. Scorzonera is also sometimes called serpent root, viper's herb, and viper's grass. Although grown mainly for their roots, the young foliage, buds, and flowers of both plants are edible. The taste and texture of the roots have given rise to their nicknames. Actually, they each have their own unique, rather bland taste, not even close to that of oysters.

These plants grow from tan to brown, ½-inch, slightly

Salsify and scorzonera are unusual root crops that produce lovely, edible flowers the following season.

curved or indented, stick-like seeds (about 2,000 to 2,500 seeds per ounce) into seedlings that resemble grass. The seed is notorious for poor germination, but if you plant it fresh and thickly, you should be successful. Both form upright leaves that supply the elongated roots with food. The leaves of salsify are bluish green, while those of scorzonera are broader and yellowish green. As the foliage enlarges, so do the long, tapered (salsify) or cylindrical (scorzonera) roots below. The longer the plants are allowed to mature, the larger the roots become. If plants are not harvested the first year and are able to survive the winter, they can be harvested the following spring. If allowed to mature, they produce frilly, rayed flowers. Salsify flowers look like purple, mauve dandelions and will form seed heads with fluffy bunches of seeds. The flowers of scorzonera are similar but yellow.

Both plants are difficult to dig up. Roots run deep and break off easily during harvesting. I have had success growing scorzonera in a large pot with holes in the bottom for good drainage. At the end of the season, I tip the container over and collect the roots easily. I have also done this with parsnips. If you plan to winter plants over, grow them in the ground.

Salsify and Scorzonera Nutrition Facts

Serving size: 100 grams (3.5 ounces)

	AMOUNT PER RAW SERVING	% DV	AMOUNT PER COOKED SERVING	% DV
Calcium	60 mg	6%	60 mg	6%
Calories	82	4%	68	3%
Carbohydrates	19 g	6%	15 g	5%
Dietary fiber	3 g	13%	3 g	13%
Folate	26 mcg	6%	15 mcg	4%
Magnesium	23 mg	6%	18 mg	5%
Manganese	0.3 mg	13%	0.2 mg	10%
Phosphorus	75 mg	7%	56 mg	6%
Potassium	380 mg	11%	285 mg	8%
Protein	3.3 g	7%	2.7 g	5%
Riboflavin	0.2 mg	10%	0.2 mg	10%
Vitamin B6	0.3 mg	14%	0.2 mg	11%
Vitamin C	8 mg	13%	4.6 mg	8%

Leaves of both salsify and scorzonera can be used raw in salads when cut at about 4 inches. These young leaves can also be steamed as a side dish. Consider covering them with béarnaise, béchamel, or hollandaise sauce. Dig up roots at any time, but for the best taste, harvest right before the ground freezes in fall or early in the second year of growth when their carbohydrates have turned to sugar. If you dig up smaller roots in summer, place them in the refrigerator for a few days to sweeten them up. In late fall of the first year, dig up roots you would like to use within a week or less unless you have the ability to store them in a moist medium kept at just above 32°F. Roots placed in a plastic bag in the crisper of your refrigerator will last about a week. Cut off the tops of the remaining roots left in the garden after they have died back in late fall. Cut just above the top of the root. Mulch the roots heavily with a thick layer of straw as soon as the ground actually freezes. When the soil thaws in spring, remove the mulch, and begin digging up the roots. Cover some roots with 8 inches of soil. Cut off the sprouts that emerge, blanch, and eat. Sprouts sometimes emerge more than once. Scrub the roots before cooking, but don't bother peeling them. You can always rub the skin off *after* cooking, if you prefer, but most gardeners leave the skin on for better flavor and nutrient value. If you do peel the roots, be careful to avoid staining your clothing. Note that roots exude a milky sap. Clean utensils immediately. Dip freshly dug and washed roots in a weak solution of lemon juice or vinegar (3 tablespoons per quart of water) to prevent discoloration.

Judging how long to cook the roots can be difficult, since they will get mushy if overcooked. Bake, boil, braise, butter steam, cream, french fry, roast, steam, or stew after cutting into desired shape and size. Cooking suggestions include adding chunks to soups or stews, grating and adding bits to omelets, battering and dipping slices of root in hot oil for tempura, simmering or steaming pieces until tender then sautéing them in garlic butter, serving them au gratin in place of potatoes, slicing roots into thin strips and french frying or baking after basting with butter in shallow pan, roasting on a grill, cooking until tender and then mashing them together with eggs before covering them with bread crumbs and frying, and rolling in melted butter before sprinkling with sugar and cooking until glazed. And, of course, you can cube, boil, and then sauté with onions before adding a cream sauce for "oyster stew." Some people chop, boil, then sauté the cubes with onion before adding milk or cream for this stew. *Do not expect these vegetables to replace oysters.* They may have a hint of oyster flavor to some gardeners, but I could detect none. Taste seems to be in the buds of the beholder. The roots may be roasted and ground into a coffee substitute. Neither vegetable freezes well. But if you are worried about losing them in the garden over winter, give it a try: wash, peel (optional), drop in lemon or vinegar water, slice, remove cores if there are any, scald in lemon water 5 minutes, cool, drain, pack, seal, label, and freeze. If you let plants go to flower in the second year, cut off a bit of stem with some flower buds. Simmer these, cool down, and place them in salads. Note that the flowers are lovely in arrangements if cut before they go to seed.

The seed of these plants is perishable. Buy fresh seed each year. If you have seed left over from a spring planting, plant it just before the ground freezes in fall. Keep the soil moist until the ground freezes. There is a good chance you will get a second crop this way, as seed germinates the following spring. There are only a few varieties of salsify. The most popular is 'Mammoth Sandwich Island'. There are numerous varieties of scorzonera because it is more popular than salsify. One that is usually available is 'Belstar Super', which may mature somewhat more rapidly than other types.

Both salsify and scorzonera originated in the Mediterranean area.

Soybean (Edamame) Nutrition Facts

Serving size: 100 grams (3.5 ounces)

	AMOUNT PER RAW SERVING	% DV	AMOUNT PER COOKED SERVING	% DV	AMOUNT PER DRIED SERVING	% DV
Calcium	200 mg	20%	100 mg	10%	140 mg	14%
Calories	150	7%	175	9%	450	19%
Carbohydrates	11 g	4%	10 g	3%	33 g	11%
Dietary fiber	4 g	17%	6 g	25%	8 g	32%
Folate	165 mcg	40%	55 mcg	15%	205 mcg	50%
Iron	3.6 mg	20%	5 mg	30%	4 mg	22%
Magnesium	65 mg	15%	85 mg	20%	230 mg	60%
Manganese	0.5 mg	25%	0.8 mg	40%	2.2 mg	110%
Phosphorus	195 mg	20%	245 mg	25%	650 mg	65%
Potassium	620 mg	18%	515 mg	15%	1,365 mg	40%
Protein	13 g	25%	17 g	35%	40 g	80%
Riboflavin	0.2 mg	10%	0.3 mg	17%	0.8 mg	45%
Thiamin	0.4 mg	20%	0.2 mg	10%	0.4 mg	30%
Vitamin B6	0.05 mg	3%	0.2 mg	12%	0.2 mg	12%
Vitamin C	30 mg	50%	1.7 mg	3%	4.6 mg	8%
Vitamin K	110 mcg	135%	20 mcg	25%	37 mcg	45%

Soybean (Edamame)
Glycine max
Legume or Pea Family
(Fabaceae, formerly Leguminosae)

Soybeans are a tender, warm-season annual crop. This is an excellent vegetable for vegetarians because the beans contain high levels of protein. The plants are equally valuable in a garden because they add nitrogen to the soil. Soybean seeds are fairly large (about 90 to 150 per ounce), smooth and rounded with a light-tan to dark-brown or black color. The rounded leaves, thick stems, and plump pods are fuzzy. Though not large, the flowers are lovely and mature into short pods that turn from green to gray, brown, or even black as they mature. Most pods contain just a few seeds similar to the ones planted.

Plant seed directly in the garden as soon as the soil warms up to 60°F or warmer. Seed germinates poorly in cool soil. Soaking seed overnight may result in faster germination, which generally occurs within 14 days of planting. However, seed will rot out in soggy soil. The use of an inoculant (*Rhizobium japonicum,* also known as *Bradyrhizobia japonicum)* is generally not necessary although commonly recommended.

Soybeans can be harvested when seeds are small and tender, a bit larger and firmer, or when fully dry and hard. The tender stage only lasts for a few days, so check plants regularly. They also have a habit of ripening all at once. Pods

Soybeans, high in protein, are a favorite when eaten immature as edamame.

change color as they ripen, and the color change indicates the need to open a pod to check on the bean inside. Pick individual pods at the stage you prefer, or simply pull up the entire plant and strip off all pods at once, unless you want to eat them at different stages of maturity. Beans still in their pods will last for a few days in the crisper of your refrigerator. If you have too many, freeze the shelled beans immediately. Wash, boil 5 minutes, plunge into ice water, drain, pop out seeds (squeeze them to shoot out one end), place in airtight freezer bag, and freeze. For dry beans, pick at the first sign of the pod splitting. If you wait too long, the pods may pop open and shoot the seeds in all directions. Place on a tray in oven set at 160°F for up to an hour depending on the size of the seed. Store in an airtight jar at as close to 32°F as possible. Check for mold regularly, and use within 1 year.

Soybeans are roughly 15 to 25 percent protein when green, and up to 40 to 80 percent when mature. They are sometimes called "meat without a bone" or "the meat of the fields." If you pick them when the pods are still green and immature, the beans taste like a cross between lima beans and peas. The immature green seeds are referred to as edamame (ed-duh-MAH-may) and are delicious either raw or cooked briefly. Pick the green pods, and drop them in boiling water or steam them. Let them boil for 2 minutes, remove, and drain. With the curved end toward you (it has a seam), squeeze the beans into your mouth. If they don't pop out, cook them longer. When the pods are a bit more mature, eat the seeds inside as a substitute for lima beans. They are firm, buttery, and a bit nutty. Roasted soybeans are eaten like nuts.

Note that there are many warnings about eating soybean sprouts or soy-based processed foods. Fermented products appear to be safe and healthful. These include miso (fermented bean paste often used in soups), natto (boiled fermented soybeans), soy sauce, tamari (like soy sauce but made with no or very little wheat), and tempeh (firm fermented soybean "cake.") As for the use of soy milk and tofu, there is nothing but scientific controversy, which also exists to some extent regarding fermented products as well. If you plan to eat significant amounts of soy, consult your doctor, since soy products can have both health benefits and risks.

Soybeans are an excellent cover crop, and once worked into the soil as a *whole* plant, act as a green manure (see "Fertilizing" in chapter 4). The mature plants can be tilled or spaded into the soil to provide added organic matter and nitrogen.

There are approximately 2,500 varieties of soybeans. There are both field and table varieties of soybeans, as there are field and sweet varieties of corn. There are two dozen or more varieties listed in catalogs, and most are open-pollinated

heirlooms. For fresh use, choose ones that mature quickly. For dried beans, match days to maturity to your growing season. A few worth considering are 'Be Sweet 292', 'Early Hakuchu', 'Envy', 'Fiskeby', and 'Shirofumi'.

The soybean probably originated in Southeast Asia.

Sunchoke
Halianthus tuberosus
Aster, Daisy, or Sunflower Family
(Asteraceae, formerly Compositae)

Sunchoke, once sold as Jerusalem artichoke, is a hardy, cool-season perennial. It is grown for its edible tubers used as a potato substitute. Its carbohydrates are in the form of inulin, not starch. The plant has nothing to do with Jerusalem and isn't even an artichoke, although its roots taste marginally similar to its namesake when boiled and sliced into small cubes and soaked in butter. Its other common names are girasole, Canada potato, lambchoke, sunflower artichoke in Italy *(girasole articiocco)*, sunroot, topinambour, and tuberous sunflower. The plant turns its flowers toward the sun, as do sunflowers in the earlier stages of growth.

Sunchokes can be grown from seed, rhizomes, or tubers. Almost everyone grows them from tubers sold at health food stores and co-ops and in catalogs. The tubers form a fibrous root system comprised of underground stems (rhizomes). These sprout coarse, stiff stems covered with a white fuzz and pointed, serrated leaves that are thick, rough, and hairy. Leaves can be up to 8 inches long in full sun. The stems vary in height according to the variety being grown, and most bloom with small, disk, daisy-like flowers, either yellow or light purple. The plant produces copious amounts of new tubers underneath the soil by fall on a thick mass of roots, which if left in the ground, will grow again the following spring. Although it is possible to plant them in rows, most gardeners prefer to plant them in a block well off to the side of the main garden. *Almost every article on these plants refers to them as highly invasive.* They really are. Even small portions of roots will sprout if left in the soil at harvest time. *I would never plant these directly in a garden but in some out-of-the-way spot where if they run wild, they won't cause a problem.*

Sunchokes can be planted in spring or fall. Spring planting as soon as the soil can be worked seems to make sense, but some growers only sell them in the fall. Try to find a supplier that will get you tubers for spring planting. That way you know whether the stock is good from the start. Although sunchokes are technically frost hardy, play it safe by planting tubers after all danger of frost. The flowers are lovely and can be used in arrangements. Cut these off

Sunchoke Nutrition Facts

Serving size: 100 grams (3.5 ounces)

	AMOUNT PER RAW SERVING	% DV	AMOUNT PER COOKED SERVING	% DV
Calories	73	4%	44	2%
Carbohydrates	17 g	6%	9 g	3%
Copper	0.1 mg	7%	0.1 mg	7%
Dietary fiber	2 g	6%	2 g	6%
Iron	3.4 mg	19%	3.4 mg	19%
Niacin	1.3 mg	7%	1.3 mg	7%
Phosphorus	78 mg	8%	78 mg	8%
Potassium	430 mg	12%	430 mg	12%
Protein	2 g	4%	2 g	4%
Thiamin	0.2 mg	13%	0.2 mg	13%
Vitamin C	4 mg	7%	4 mg	7%

Sunchokes are extremely invasive and deteriorate in summer while their roots thin and fan out widely.

to force better tuber development unless you want flowers to form seed as a way of attracting birds. Also, if you are worried about plants toppling over when they become top-heavy, snip off as much of the upper growth as necessary to avoid this. The plants can withstand the shearing. Some gardeners thin stems to two to three shoots per plant, but I have never understood why.

Let sunchokes grow for two seasons before harvesting them. Once they take root, they grow like weeds, but the first season they are vulnerable. In the second year, leave them in the ground as late as possible. Let them experience a frost or two to make them sweeter. Dig up just before the ground freezes. Let the stems die back, chop them down, and add them to the compost pile. Then, with a garden fork start digging in from the outside of the plant in. Start roughly 24 inches away from the center of the plant. Or if you are strong, pull up on the stems, and the tubers may pop out of the ground, clinging to a hefty root system. This is only possible in really loose soil. They are not like potatoes. The tubers are firmly attached to intertwining roots.

Sunchokes exposed to air will rot if wet, and dehydrate if dry. For short-term storage, roughly up to 7 days, place tubers in plastic bags in the refrigerator. Do not wash the tubers, and perforate the bag for air circulation. Diabetics should eat freshly harvested tubers, since starch will change into sugar over time. This is why refrigeration makes tubers taste sweeter. The easiest solution for long-term storage is to leave the tubers in the garden under a thick layer of straw, which stops the bed from freezing hard. Harvest the tubers throughout the winter. Sometimes, the ground does

freeze solid. At that point delay additional harvesting until a spring thaw.

Sunchokes are eaten raw or cooked. Some people just wash them off and eat them as they would a radish. Or they grate them over salads and splash the bits with lemon to prevent discoloration of the flesh. The tubers have a nutty flavor. For cooking, wash the tuber while scrubbing it lightly with a stiff brush. Cook tubers as you would a potato. Or slice or cube the tubers. Once again, to prevent discoloration, soak immediately in 3 cups water with 3 tablespoons lemon juice or vinegar added. Don't worry about the skin; it is edible. Use slices for french fries or chips and in stir-fries as a replacement for water chestnuts. Or boil briefly before sautéing. Tubers are good replacements for potatoes in au gratin dishes and creamed soups. Some people prefer them roasted on a grill or boiled and covered with butter flavored with lemon juice, parsley, and assorted spices, or topped with hollandaise sauce. Do not overcook the tubers! Also, aluminum and iron cookware may turn sunchokes black or at least an unappealing color. They are still safe to eat.

To freeze, peel (not easy and optional anyway), slice into small pieces, place in water with lemon juice to stop discoloration, blanch 2 minutes, chill in ice water 2 minutes, drain, place in airtight freezer bags, and freeze. Or cook in stock, purée, then freeze to be used in cream soups. Tubers can be roasted as a coffee substitute.

Sunchokes come in varied skin colors, may be smooth or knobby, and mature at different rates. These characteristics should be emphasized in catalogs. There are many varieties on the market. Two that are commonly available

Sunflower
Nutrition Facts

Serving size: 100 grams (3.5 ounces)

	AMOUNT PER SERVING OF DRIED KERNELS	% DV
Calcium	78 mg	8%
Calories	585	29%
Carbohydrates	20 grams	7%
Copper	1.8 mg	90%
Dietary fiber	9 g	35%
Folate	227 mg	57%
Iron	5.2 mg	29%
Magnesium	325 mg	85%
Manganese	1.9 mg	97%
Niacin	8.3 mg	42%
Phosphorus	660 mg	65%
Potassium	645 mg	18%
Protein	21 g	42%
Riboflavin	0.4 mg	21%
Selenium	53 mcg	75%
Thiamin	1.5 mg	99%
Vitamin B6	1.3 mg	67%
Vitamin E	33 mg	166%
Zinc	5 mg	33%

Larger sunflowers tower over the garden and produce numerous and highly nutritious seed.

and very good are the early-maturing 'Stampede', which is round and knobby, and the later-maturing 'White Fuseau', which is more like a smooth carrot. *I cannot emphasize enough how invasive these plants are, with underground rhizomes heading off in all directions, sometimes many feet from the original planting.*

The sunchoke is a native North American plant related to the sunflower.

Sunflower
Helianthus annuus
Aster, Daisy, or Sunflower family (Asteraceae, formerly Compositae)

Sunflowers are very tender, warm-season annuals. Grown for their bright-yellow flowers and tasty nutritious seeds, sunflowers are fun to grow and great for a kids' garden. Their seed is a favorite of poultry and wild birds, including cardinals and finches. Sunflowers are sold in a wide variety of colors, forms, and sizes. The one recommended in this section provides copious amounts of highly nutritious seed. The fruit (achene) consists of a true seed surrounded by a hull (pericarp), but for simplicity the achene will be called a seed in this section. Seeds vary in size and color, with some being striped (about 300 to 600 seeds per ounce). They look like a flattened wedge. Seeds germinate and grow rapidly, forming an extensive root system supporting the thick, tough prickly stalk and large leaves. The variety recommended in this section can easily reach 120 inches tall with giant seed heads. These heads consist of two types of flowers. The bright-yellow ray flowers (florets) fringe the outside edge of the flower head and do not produce seed, while the inside disk flowers (florets), which number in the hundreds, are pollinated, change color throughout the season, and mature into seeds. The edible part is the seed inside the hull.

Plant seeds in full sun after all danger of frost when the soil has warmed to about 70°F. However, seed is relatively inexpensive, and gambling by planting some about 2 weeks before the last expected frost often gives you a jump on the season. Wait until nighttime temperatures reach at least 50°F. A hard frost will kill emerging seedlings, so you are taking a chance. Spacing depends on gardening style. Some gardeners plant seeds in a row only about 3 to 4 inches apart. As the plants grow, they save the strongest until plants are thinned to roughly a foot apart. In this way they account for deer and rabbits nibbling off young plants. By planting more seed than necessary, they end up with enough plants in the end. Also, not all seed is created equal. Some seed just seems to be more vigorous. Culling the weak plants works well. Other gardeners plant farther apart or in hills like corn, placing several seeds in each hill. As these mature, only one seed is left remaining to develop into a mature plant.

Large sunflowers may blow over in storms, despite their strong, stiff stems. This happens when the soil gets soggy. To prevent this, plant seeds in a shallow dip. As the seedlings grow, fill the area in with soil. Then mound additional soil around the base of the expanding stem.

Deer are a problem. They especially like to nibble off the tops of young plants. Do not give up on these plants. A number will continue to grow and produce a good crop. Deer will occasionally push stems over to get to the mature heads. Keep deer away with a good fence.

The seeds in the center of the large flower mature from the edge in. There are hundreds of seeds in each head. The seeds change color as they mature, as does the seed head itself. The head is mature when its back turns yellow to brown. Birds may feed on maturing seeds. This is a plus to bird lovers! Grow some for you and some for the birds. Try to harvest seed heads before the first frost and when the seed heads are dry. If they are moist, they may develop mildew. The large stems often hang down, making harvesting easy, but if they remain upright, dig up the root system with a spade and push over. Then snip off the head with lopping pruners. Place the seed head upside down in a mesh bag with small holes or in a paper bag. Let the seeds continue to dry in a warm, dry, well-ventilated area for several weeks. The longer they dry, the easier it is to pop seeds off the seed head. However, getting the seeds off the heads can be difficult. Some people press down on the seeds and have no problem getting them to drop off. Others prefer rubbing seed heads together. A stiff brush works well. Do not wash the seeds. Keep them dry. Store seeds still in their hull in any fabric bag where they will stay warm and dry.

The buds of sunflowers are edible and a gourmet delight to deer. Steam at least one, and dip it in butter with lemon juice, as you would an artichoke heart. Buds can also be pickled. Toss some ray flowers into a salad for a splash of color. Sprout hulled seeds on a sponge. Add the sprouts to salads, sandwiches, and stir-fries. Hulled seeds, either raw or cooked, can be added to soups, scrambled eggs, or salads. To cook seeds still in their hull, spread them lightly oiled in a single layer on a metal cooking sheet, and roast them at 300° to 350°F until they are done. This usually takes 10 to 15 minutes. Seeds are ready when they begin to bulge and break open. When dry and crisp, they should crack when you bite into them. For salted seed, soak overnight in salted water before cooking. For sunflower seed butter (sunbutter), roast hulled seeds on a cookie sheet at 325°F until toasted. Keep the layer thin, and turn as needed. Once roasted and cooled, begin breaking them down in a food processor. Add olive oil, a little at a time, until the mixture is the desired consistency. Note that seeds can also be broken down into flour. Process far less than when making sunbutter.

Many people believe sunflower hulls are somehow toxic and kill grass around bird feeders. I doubt this is true. The hulls build up and act as a mulch, blocking out light. If you rake them up regularly, the grass will be fine. According to other sources, the roots of growing sunflowers emit toxins that kill nearby plants. Why then do weeds grow so freely around the base of growing sunflower stems? And why are there so many photos of sunflowers growing beautifully in the middle of a wide variety of vegetables? Sunflowers may be toxic to plants in their own species (autotoxicity), but that's another story. I have never tested this, since most of the time they are on the edge of my garden.

Breeders have developed a wide range of sunflowers varying in size from 24 to 144 inches tall, with single stems or numerous branches, with or without pollen (the latter used for cut flowers), and in an amazing array of colors. For edible seed, you can't go wrong with 'Mammoth'.

Sunflowers may have originated in North America or possibly Peru.

Tomatillo
Physalis ixocarpa, also known as *Physalis philadelphica*
Nightshade Family (Solanaceae)

Tomatillos (toe-muh-TEE-ohs) are tender to very tender, warm-season annuals. They are easy to grow, prolific, and an essential part of Mexican cuisine. Other common names are husk cherry, husk tomato, jamberry, miltomate, Mexican green tomatoes *(tomate verde),* and strawberry tomato. Grow them as you would a tomato, although the fruits are more similar to ground cherries with a completely different taste. Plants can be staked, but most people let them sprawl over a thick layer of mulch.

Tomatillo seed is a small, flat, rounded oval and usually light tan (about 16,000 seeds per ounce). It grows into a large, spreading "bush." The small, yellow flowers mature into fruit that looks like a Chinese lantern, composed of a small, shiny green "cherry tomato" inside a thin, paper-like husk (calyx). The fruits are smooth and sticky. They start out green and change color as they mature. The plant keeps flowering and bearing copious amounts of fruit until the first killing frost. Start it from seed indoors, again like a tomato, or buy plants from a local nursery. Call ahead to make sure seedlings will be available, since they are not as popular as tomatoes. However, growing your own allows you to

Tomatillo
Nutrition Facts

Serving size: 100 grams (3.5 ounces)

	AMOUNT PER RAW SERVING	% DV
Calories	32	2%
Carbohydrates	6 g	2%
Dietary fiber	2 g	8%
Manganese	0.2 mg	8%
Niacin	2 mg	9%
Potassium	270 mg	8%
Protein	1 g	2%
Vitamin C	12 mg	20%
Vitamin K	10 mcg	13%

The Chinese lantern–like fruit of tomatillos are the base of Mexico's famous salsa verde.

the plant with a sheet if frost threatens. Remove it as soon as the weather warms up again.

The fruit varies by variety from 1 inch to a little more than 3 inches; tastes fruity, tart, or sweet; and matures in 60 to 100 days from transplant. Tomatillos are edible either raw or cooked. Green fruits have a tart, lemony flavor and are quite acidic. Fully ripe fruits change color, often turning a deep yellow or purple. At this stage they are sweeter. At any stage they are much firmer than tomatoes. Before eating, remove the husk, and rinse the sticky coating from the fruit. Tomatillos are commonly used in guacamole, in moles (sauce with chile peppers and chocolate), and in soups such as gazpacho, stews, and salsas. To make a quick sauce, blend them with lime and cilantro in a blender. Raw or cooked tomatillos are an essential ingredient in salsa verde (green taco sauce), one of Mexico's most popular sauces, which includes chile peppers, cilantro, garlic, lime juice, and onion blended in a food processor and seasoned to taste with pepper, salt, and sugar. To get the best flavor, roast tomatillos over a grill, bake for 15 minutes at 500°F, or cut in half, place on foil, and char under a broiler to cook them before blending with the other ingredients.

If you can't use tomatillos immediately, leave the husks on, and place them in a paper bag. They will often last for a few weeks in the refrigerator. To freeze, remove husk, wash off sticky substance, dry, place on cookie sheet one layer deep, freeze, remove and place in airtight freezer bags, and keep frozen.

There are roughly a dozen varieties available each year in catalogs. 'Verde Puebla' matures fairly quickly and has a rich taste popular in salsa verde. For a sweeter and fruiter taste, try 'Pineapple'.

Tomatillos originated in Mexico.

Yardlong Bean
Vigna unguiculata ssp. *sesquipedalis*
Legume or Pea Family
(Fabaceae, formerly Leguminosae)

Yardlong beans are tender, warm-season annuals, more ideally suited to growing in the South. Still, they are worth a try for the adventuresome cold-climate gardener. At best, they produce a nice crop of very long beans, from which comes the common name "yardlong bean." At worst, they produce poorly and are a waste of time. Other common names are asparagus bean, Chinese long beans, Dow Gauk in Chinese, long-podded beans, noodle beans, Sasage in Japanese, and snake bean. The name *Chinese long bean* may be especially appropriate since these plants probably originated in China.

choose the variety. The fruit of each variety varies in size and taste considerably, so consider growing more than one.

Fruit continues to ripen until the first frost. They produce such copious amounts of fruit that extending the season is usually unnecessary. If fruits are developing late, cover

Seeds look like typical black or red bean seed and are easy to work with (about 200 seeds per ounce). They form an extensive root system and twining, delicate, but vigorous, if brittle, stems that blossom with beautiful white flowers tinged violet blue. The beans are pencil thin to 2 or more feet when fully mature. Beans may hang from the vines in pairs. Yardlong beans need a *solid* support to grow well since vines grow rampantly and weigh a lot. Supports should be at least 7 feet high. Good supports include fences, stakes, trellises, tripods, and so on. Tie the young plants to the support using a figure-eight knot. Do this as many times as necessary to keep the vines from toppling over. Once they intertwine with the support, they will manage well on their own.

Harvest pods at various lengths since their taste changes somewhat as they mature. Most people prefer them when about 12 to 14 inches. They are most tender when thin, about half as wide as a pencil. They should snap when bent. Snip them off the vine with a pruners or knife. Harvesting daily keeps the plants producing much longer than if pods are allowed to mature. However, some people do allow some pods to mature enough so that the seeds can be popped from the pods and eaten as shell "beans." Young leaves and stem tips can also be harvested for use in the kitchen. Avoid picking when foliage is moist. The beans tend to turn limp and wimpy quickly, so get them inside or into cold water immediately.

Yardlong beans are edible raw, although most people cook them. Use immediately, or keep in ice water for a few hours if cooking must be delayed briefly. Cook them faster than regular beans. Many cooks will not cook them in water, only in oil, claiming the taste and texture are affected by boiling or steaming. To keep beans firm and flavorful, sauté, stir-fry, or deep-fry in oil. Combining the two techniques of sautéing and stir-frying with spices is common in Chinese cooking. You can also coat them in oil and roast them in the oven. The taste is most commonly referred to as "nutty." If seeds are allowed to form, shell the pods, and cook like southern "peas."

For varieties with variously colored seeds, try 'Liana' (black seed), 'Red Noodle' (red seeds), and 'Thai White Seeded Long Bean' (cream seeds).

As mentioned, the beans probably originated in China.

Yardlong Bean Nutrition Facts

Serving size: 100 grams (3.5 ounces)

	AMOUNT PER COOKED SERVING	% DV
Calories	47	2%
Carbohydrates	9 g	3%
Folate	45 mcg	10%
Magnesium	40 mg	10%
Manganese	0.2 mg	10%
Potassium	290 mg	8%
Protein	2.5 g	5%
Vitamin A	450 IU	9%
Vitamin C	16 mg	27%

Yardlong beans rarely are a yard long, but they are big and can be eaten at many stages of growth.

WATERMELON

Citrullus lanatus var. ***lanatus,*** **also known as** ***Citrullus vulgaris***
Cucumber or Gourd Family (Cucurbitaceae)

Watermelons are very tender, warm-season annuals. The underlying rule of growing watermelons in cold climates is to provide them with sun, warmth, and water. The faster they grow, the better they taste. While these are most often thought of as a southern crop, you will be surprised at the sweet flavor and delightful texture of your own home-grown melons. Still, it should be emphasized that they can be difficult to grow and do take up a lot of space. These tropical plants probably originated in southern Africa.

How Watermelons Grow

The flat, large, broad seeds (about 250 to 500 seeds per ounce) of watermelon germinate quickly into stocky plants with broad, divided leaves. These seedlings form expansive to somewhat shorter vines depending on the variety. Vines do have tendrils for climbing. Leaves jut out from the vine and are deeply indented and bristly. Each vine produces both male and female flowers. These are five petaled and light yellow, attracting bees and other pollinating insects.

Once pollinated, the base of the female flower begins to swell into a small, pale fruit. This fruit balloons in the coming weeks into a mature melon, which in most varieties contains numerous seeds similar to those originally planted.

Where to Plant Watermelons
Site and Light

Choose a sunny site. Watermelons, originally tropical plants, like it hot. The sunnier and warmer, the better. A gentle slope to the south is ideal. Unless you intend to grow them vertically, they need space to roam. Most varieties are poorly suited to vertical gardening.

Soil and Moisture

Watermelons need loose, rich soil that drains freely. Sandy soil is ideal, but melons will grow well in most soils as long as they are loose. Mix in as much rotted manure or compost as you can. If you have hard or compacted soil, build a raised bed, or make a deep and wide mound of organic material as a planting hill. Hills are usually several feet wide. They heat up faster and drain better than level soil. If you add lots of organic matter, your soil will usually be close to a pH of 6 to 6.8. This is fine for watermelons, although they are tolerant of slightly more acidic or alkaline conditions. Mix into the soil a blend of organic fertilizers since watermelons are heavy feeders. An old compost pile makes an ideal "hill" for watermelons.

Container

It is possible, but challenging, to grow watermelons in containers. Choose a variety that produces a small melon. Plant in a large container that holds at least 10 gallons or more of growing medium, which should be loose and light. Consider using a mix of perlite, vermiculite, sphagnum peat moss, and compost as well as a blend of organic fertilizers. Hand pollinate female flowers. Fruit as well as vines need support.

Planting

Seed

Plant seed directly in the garden only after the soil has warmed to at least 70°F, preferably higher. Soil typically reaches this temperature several weeks after the frost-free date. Warm the soil artificially with black or clear plastic to get seed in earlier, but be ready to protect young seedlings with cloches or row covers if cold weather threatens. In fact, using row covers will help keep temperatures on the high side. Plant six seeds per hill about ½ to 1 inch deep. Plant individual seeds up to 12 to 15 inches apart. They should germinate in fewer than 14 days.

Transplants

Start seeds indoors about 3 to 4 weeks before your expected outdoor planting time. Don't start them too early, because they have deep roots, grow quickly, and don't like being disturbed. Since it is impossible to predict when warm weather will come in cold climates, start several pots of plants each week for 3 weeks. Seeds are relatively inexpensive. A half-dozen stocky plants is all you will end up needing. Use a 32-ounce plastic container as a pot. Keep the lid, cut out the bottom, set the container on the lid. Fill it with a sterile starting mix. Plant 2 to 3 seeds in it ½ to 1 inch deep. Keep the mix moist. Provide bottom heat if possible to get soil to 80° to 90°F in the day, lower at night, even to 65°F. Seeds should germinate within 14 days. Once seedlings have formed a true pair of leaves, snip out all but the one healthiest plant. If you pull up the weaker plants, you disturb the root system of the remaining plant, so avoid this. Provide lots of light, at least 16 hours per day.

Nutrition Facts

Serving size: 100 grams (3.5 ounces)

	AMOUNT PER RAW SERVING	% DV
Calories	30	2%
Carbohydrates	8 g	3%
Protein	1 g	1%
Vitamin A	570 IU	11%
Vitamin C	8 mg	13%

When plants are 4 to 6 inches tall, harden them off slowly. Once hardened off, plant in the garden. Make a hole in the soil large enough to hold the container. Set the container off to the side of the hole. Slide the plastic lid out from under the container. Cover the bottom where the lid was with your hand, and place the container in the hole. Push soil lightly around the container, and then lift it up and away from the plant. Firm the soil around the plant. Water immediately. Using a large container and planting carefully to avoid root disturbance are the critical elements of this method. Root disturbance results in transplant shock, which may result in slow or poor growth.

Spacing

If direct seeding, once seeds have germinated and have several pairs of true leaves, remove all but the three healthiest plants in each hill. Avoid crowding the plants. If all plants are left to mature, they will compete for available water and nutrients at the expense of forming fruit. Keep at least three plants, because some vines may not form fruit at all even though they flower prolifically. The base of each plant should end up about a foot or more apart.

When to Plant

Plant seed directly in the garden when the soil temperature reaches 70°F, which it often does several weeks after the frost-free date. You can direct seed earlier if the soil is artificially warmed up with black plastic and if the germinating seedlings are kept warm with cloches or row covers. If you start plants indoors, plant transplants at about the same time, again protecting them if necessary.

Support

Some gardeners with limited space grow the smaller melons on supports, usually A-frames or tepees large enough to accommodate vines up to 8 feet long. Have the support in place before you plant seeds or transplants. It should be solid enough to withstand winds and the weight of mature vines and fruit.

Guide the vines up the supports in the early weeks. Tie the vine to the support with pieces of cloth using a figure-eight knot. Fruits may require cloth slings to keep them from breaking off as they mature. If you see a stem starting to break from the weight of a fruit, it may be too late. So get slings on when the fruit are still small. Slings consist of loose fabric tied to the support itself. Gently place the fruit into the sling when it is the size of a baseball or smaller, but leave plenty of space for it to mature to its full size. Choose very small-fruited varieties.

How to Care for Watermelons

Water

If growing melons on soil covered with organic mulch, water the base of the plants where the seedlings originally germinated, the hill itself, rather than the vines that are forming and spreading out like a fan. Let the soil dry out some between deep waterings. However, if the plants show signs of wilting, water immediately. Once the fruit is getting close to maturity, cut back on watering. In theory, this should increase the overall sugar content of the fruit.

If growing melons through plastic, consider placing a soaker hose over the soil before planting. Otherwise, water through the slit at the base of each plant regularly. Water collects under plastic and keeps soil moist longer than soil exposed to wind and heat. Watermelons need lots of water, as their name implies.

Mulch

If you are direct seeding, place an organic mulch around the seedlings as they emerge. Do not touch the stems. Place mulch out as far as you expect vines to grow. Weeds will grow under clear plastic. Cover it with a thick layer of organic mulch several weeks after planting seeds or transplants.

Fertilizing

When planting watermelon transplants, pour a cup of starter solution around the base of each plant. During the growing season, fertilize lightly every few weeks with liquid seaweed or fish emulsion. These provide major nutrients as well as trace elements such as boron and magnesium. Also, feed at least twice with blood meal to provide these heavy feeders with enough nitrogen.

To make fruit sweeter, add boron and magnesium to the soil directly around the roots of the plant. In a gallon of water put 2 tablespoons of Epsom salts and 1 tablespoon of borax. Give several cupfuls of this solution to each plant, once when the plants are growing vigorously, once when the fruit is 2 inches in diameter.

Weeding

When seeds sprout, hand weed around them. If in doubt about damaging or loosening the seedlings' root system, snip off the weeds. Keep this area of the plant weed-free throughout the entire growing season so that the root system is never competing with other plants for nutrients and water. Remove all weeds from the area where the vines will meander, since the vines end up clinging to weeds. If you try to pull out the weeds, you may damage the fragile vines. Better to just leave the weeds alone.

Thinning

Once plants are thinned in the hill, no further thinning is necessary.

Pruning

Some gardeners clip off all but one fruit on each vine. If you have three vines, you end up with three melons. The idea is to direct all of the plant's energy into forming a few really fine melons as early in the season as possible. Whenever doing this, keep the melon closest to the hill.

Special Considerations

Avoid walking on, moving, or pulling up on watermelon vines. They are temperamental. Place melons on boards when they are the size of baseballs. Be gentle since the vines are delicate. This may reduce rot and will provide minimal protection against soil insects.

Watermelon flowers must be pollinated by insects, not wind, to get fruit. If fruits are not forming, try hand pollination. Do this in the morning. Look for female flowers with tiny, swollen bases. Just as they open up, pick a male flower, strip off the petals, leaving the protrusion (stamen) in place. Swirl the stamen in the center of the female flower. Or touch the anther (tip of the stamen) with a fine brush. This collects pollen, which you can then "paint" on the pistil (sex organ) of the female flower.

Tomatoes are touted for their high concentration of lycopene, but watermelons have much more of this phytochemical. Red-fleshed types have more than white- or yellow-fleshed varieties.

Extending the Season

Watermelon plants are extremely fragile. They will die if exposed to frost. Even so, getting them in the garden early often pays off. Try direct seeding or planting transplants through slits in black plastic or fabric covering the soil. Always get plastic down at least 2 weeks before planting. If the weather is not stable, protect the plants until it warms up with row covers or cloches. Always remove these once the plants begin to flower. Support row covers to avoid damaging fragile vines. Consider succession planting whether direct seeding or planting transplants. Spread the planting out over 2 to 3 weeks. This way you increase the odds of hitting the correct planting "window."

Problems

Insects

Aphids, cucumber beetles, and, less commonly, squash bugs damage plants and carry disease. Spray off aphids, and remove infested leaves. Use row covers to protect young plants from beetles, borers, and other insect infestations. As mentioned, covers must be removed when flowers bloom and need to be pollinated.

Disease

Alternaria leaf spot (watery spots turning yellow to brown), angular leaf spot (lesions turning gray to tan), anthracnose (spots on leaves and rotting fruit), powdery mildew (whitish powder on foliage), fusarium wilt (plants stunted and yellow), and virus infections (distorted foliage and plants) all can infect watermelons. To prevent disease, buy certified seed, choose varieties resistant to anthracnose and fusarium wilt, and control insects. Plant watermelons in a different place each year. Break down the vines at the end of the year by composting them. Work in the area when it is dry. Remove any diseased leaves or plants immediately. Wash your hands before touching healthy plants again.

Marauders

Deer will eat fruit once it is ripe. Sometimes, they will nibble on the skin, making it unusable or prone to rot. Keep them out with a fence.

Physiological

With adequate foliage cover and proper soil preparation, physiological problems are rare. The main problem is that insects may not pollinate all the flowers. It is frustrating when a vine flowers profusely but produces no fruit. You may have to hand pollinate flowers if no fruit seems to be forming early in the season.

Propagation

Open-pollinated varieties will cross with each other but not with cucumber, muskmelon, pumpkin, or squash. Save seed from open-pollinated (heirloom) varieties by letting the melons mature on the vine. Once they are mature, bring them indoors for 3 weeks. Then cut open, remove the seeds from the pulp, place in bowl of water, swish around removing pulp and any seeds that float to the surface, place in a strainer and wash again, drain, dry on a plate in a single layer, keep seeds apart in a cool, dry place until completely dry, then place in an envelope. Store in a cool, dark place. Watermelon seed may stay viable for up to 4 to 5 years.

Harvesting

The best way to tell whether a watermelon is ripe is to look at the area where the stem connects to the fruit. You will see a tiny tendril there. You won't notice it unless you look for it. This curly "pigtail" tendril is green while the watermelon is ripening. Check the tendril regularly as the melon matures. Once it turns brown and hard or shrivels and dries up, there is a 99 percent chance the watermelon is now ripe and can be harvested. Be patient. You might want to combine this observation with others until you become confident in this single method: as watermelons ripen, their undersides turn from light green or white to yellow or cream. If still pale green or white, then they are not ripe. This color test is the second easiest for the home gardener to use. Or gently lift melons. As they mature, they get heavier. Checking their weight is hard to do without breaking the fruit off the vine. The surface color of the melon can give a clue to ripeness. 'Golden Midget' turns deep gold when mature. So does 'Royal Golden', only the gold has a light-orange tone. 'New Hampshire Midget' turns a faded green. Most melons change from powdery or shiny to a dull color. Some growers squeeze the melon. If it cracks slightly, the melon is ripe. Some gardeners say you can tell when a melon is ripe by thumping it with your knuckles. Immature melons have a metallic ring or "ping" sound. A ripe melon gives off a dull thud or "pong" sound. This method works best early in the morning. There is an old adage about this thumping method that goes something like this: tap your forehead with your knuckles, tap the melon, similar sound, not ripe. Tap your chest, tap the melon, similar sound, ripe. Tap your stomach, tap the melon, similar sound, overripe. I get a headache thinking about it. But under no circumstances should you cut into the melons. Taking out a "plug" to see what is inside opens the melon to infection and rot—don't do it! Pick only ripe melons. If you pick a melon too soon, it will never be as sweet as when mature. Watermelons do not ripen after harvest.

When you have determined that a melon is ripe, snip the stem with a pruners. Only pull it off the vine if it is the last melon to ripen. Avoid damaging the vine if other melons are still maturing. Pick late in the day, when the water content is said to be correct. Yellow varieties must be picked as they first mature. You have more leeway with other watermelons, but you don't want to pick them too early, because they will not get any sweeter with age, as already emphasized.

Storing

Whole watermelons will keep at room temperature for about a week, but once picked they do not ripen further. In the refrigerator whole melons last up to 2 weeks, while sliced melons last only a couple of days. To freeze, cut into pieces, and freeze the flesh with honey or lemon juice.

Culinary Uses

There is an old saying that "eating watermelons is the only way to eat, drink, and wash your face at the same time." Note that some people sprinkle salt lightly on watermelon to make it taste sweeter. If you grow melons with seeds, these can be roasted and salted like pumpkin seeds. After being skinned, watermelon rind is often used for pickles.

Citron melon *(Citrullus lanatus* var. *citroides)* is unique in that it is essentially all rind. Peel and cut into pieces. The firm flesh has a great deal of pectin, which makes it good for candies, pickles, and preserves. The seeds, either green or red depending on the plant's background, are edible and ground into a paste by some.

Varieties

The larger watermelons, which take longer to mature, can be challenging to the cold-climate gardener and even more so to anyone living in the far north. Some are included in the table because they are large and have excellent taste. If you get them in early enough and if the weather cooperates, they may be worth the risk. They do need lots of space to roam.

Choose varieties well suited to cold climates, in short, varieties that mature quickly, certainly less than 85 days. These tend to flower more quickly. Icebox types typically take up less space in the garden, although vines often grow much longer than stated in catalogs. Each plant will produce a few comparatively small fruits with relatively thin skins. These are not as big as the melons produced in the South, but they still have a nice taste.

Seedless types are triploids, crosses between diploids and tetraploids, which simply means they have a different number of chromosomes than a standard watermelon. Seedless have seedlike structures that are relatively inconspicuous and edible. How inconspicuous they end up being seems to depend on environmental conditions. When planting seedless types, you must have one plant of a diploid variety (a pollen donor) for every three plants of the seedless (triploid) varieties. Only the triploid varieties will produce seedless melons. The mature fruit of the diploid variety will have a different appearance from that of the seedless (triploid) varieties.

Some watermelons are sweeter than others. Still, all are enjoyably sweet if allowed to mature fully on the vine. Some catalogs list what is known as a Brix number with the variety. This is a somewhat inexact measurement of the fruits' sweetness. It is a rough guide, but sweetness does vary by location and season. A Brix number of 7.8 to 8.2 means mildly sweet; of 8.3 to 9.0, sweet; and of 9.0 and above, very sweet.

VARIETY	DAYS	RIND/FLESH/FRUIT SHAPE	WEIGHT (POUNDS)
'Baby Doll Hybrid' (icebox)	75	Medium green striped/yellow/oval	10–15
'Blacktail Mountain' (heirloom)*****	70	Darkest green/deep red/round	5–10
'Chris Cross' (heirloom)*****	90	Pale green striped dark green/red/oval	15–20
'Citron' (heirloom)	100	Mottled rind/whitish/round	20–25
'Cream of Saskatchewan' (heirloom)*****	80	Striped green/pale cream yellow/round	4–10
'Crimson Sweet' (heirloom)	95	Striped green/bright red/round to oval	20–25
'Early Moonbean' (heirloom)	80	Pale green striped dark green/yellow/round	5–8
'Faerie Hybrid' (AAS-2012)	75	Cream striped yellow/pink red/oval	4–6
'Festival Hybrid'*****	85	Striped green/dark red/round	10
'Golden Crown Hybrid' (AAS-1991) (icebox)	80	Gold/deep red/oblong	6–8
'Golden Midget' (heirloom)	90	Yellow/pinkish red/oval	4–6
'Gypsy Hybrid' (seedless)	75	Striped green/rich red/oval	13–15
'Jubilee' (heirloom)	95	Mottled striped/deep red/oval	20
'Mickylee' (OP) (icebox)	85	Pale green mottled/red/almost round	6–10
'Moon and Stars' (heirloom)*****	90	Green with yellow dots/pink red/oval	15–20
'Moon and Stars Yellow Flesh' (heirloom)****	95	Green with yellow dots/rich yellow/oval	20–25
'Mountain Sweet Yellow' (heirloom)*****	100	Striped green/deep yellow/elongated	20–35
'New Hampshire Midget' (heirloom) (AAS-1951) (icebox)	75	Slightly striped/pale red/oval	10–15
'New Yellow Baby Hybrid'	75	Green mottled light green/yellow/globe	6
'New Orchid Hybrid' (icebox)	90	Striped green/yellow orange/round oblong	8–10
'New Queen Hybrid' (AAS-1999) (icebox)*****	80	Striped green/orange/oval	6–8
'Orangeglo' (heirloom)*****	85	Striped green/deep orange/elongated oval	15–25
'Osh Kirgizia' (heirloom)*****	100	Mottled/pink red/round	10–15
'Royal Golden' (heirloom)	100	Gold/red/round to oval	10–15
'Sangria Hybrid'*****	100	Striped green/bright red/elongated oval	15–20
'Shiny Boy Hybrid' (AAS-2010)	90	Striped green/dark red/oval	20
'Small Shining Light' (heirloom)*****	90	Dark green/pink red/nearly round	3–5
'Sorbet Swirl Hybrid'	85	Mottled green/yellow pink/round to oval	8–10
'Sugar Baby' (heirloom) (icebox)*****	90	Dark green/bright red/round	5–10
'Sunny's Pride Hybrid'	85	Striped green/red/oblong	20–25
'Sweet Favorite Hybrid' (AAS-1978) (icebox)*****	75	Striped green/red/elongated oblong	10–15
'Sweet Siberian' (heirloom)*****	85	Glossy green/yellow/oblong	8–10
'Tiger Baby Hybrid' (icebox)	80	Striped green/pinkish red/round	7–10
'Yellow Doll Hybrid' (icebox)	75	Striped green/yellow/round	5–8

ACKNOWLEDGMENTS

The author expresses his gratitude to the following people, who helped with the research, writing, and publication of this book: Kathy Allen, Bob Anderson, Erik Anderson, Jim and Dotti Becker, Beth Benjamin, David Benjamin, Sand Bigger, Heron Breen, Larry Chandler, Bob Copeland, Ada Crowl, Christine Cummings, Art Davidson, Ellen and Gary de Casmaker, Mike DeGrandchamp, Louie Diaz, Glenn Drowns, Kevin Falk, Lisa Farnam, Diane Fiebelkorn, Chelsey Fields, Chris Fox, Bruce Frasier, Dave Fuller, Randy Gage, Paul Gallione, Joel and Coleen Girardin, Pam Gregory, Jeff Gunsolus, Dr. J. Erron Haggard, Tom Hauch, Louise Hyde, Trish Imperato, Mary Keirstead, Dave Kellett, Janis Kieft, Mel Knapton, Jacqui and David Krizo, Mike Lilja, Susan Littlefield, the late Robert Henry Lobitz, Kathryn Louis, Jim Luby, Greg Lutovsky, Ellyn Mavalwalla, Monica McCook, Angus Mellish, Liz Milne, Frank and Karen Morton, Ginger Morton, Scott Naegeli, Dan Nagengast, Caitlin Newman, Tim Nourse, Daniel Ochsner, Bev O'Connor, Todd Orjala, Sherry Peace, Ted Pew, Deborah Phillips, Conrad Richter, Mary Rochelle, Victoria Rodriguez, Mary Rogers, Melody Rousseau, Linda Sapp, Laura Schaub, Maya Shiroyama, Dr. Philip W. Simon, Brad Smith, David Stevenson, Sara Straate, Amanda and Mike Straka, Jessica Studeny, Stephanie Turner, Kristian Tvedten, Kristine Uter, David Velasquez, Chuck Vogelsang, Tom Wahlberg, Ron Walden, Scott Walker, Todd C. Weiner, Laura Westlund, Mark Willis, Doug Yates, Don Zeidler, and Macie Zorn.

GLOSSARY

acaricide (miticide): Pesticide that kills mites and ticks.

achene: Fruits with a tough outer coating and seed inside; often mistakenly called seed, as on a strawberry.

acid soil: Soil with pH less than 7.0. Most vegetables thrive in slightly acidic soils.

acidic: Having a pH so low that it stops plants from taking in nutrients and limits the activity of soil microorganisms.

actinomycetes: Major group of soil microorganisms important in decomposition of organic matter; may produce antibiotics in soil.

active ingredient: Material in pesticides with killing effect.

actual nitrogen: Actual amount of nitrogen in fertilizer. A 50-pound bag of 10-0-0 fertilizer is 10 percent nitrogen; actual nitrogen is 5 pounds.

adobe soil: Heavy clay soil.

aeration: The state of having lots of air in well-drained and properly tilled soil; essential for root growth and survival of soil microorganisms.

aerobic bacteria: Bacteria that thrive in the presence of oxygen. These are the best ones in a compost pile because they don't give off any odor.

after-ripening: Changes in seed after harvest that allow it to germinate when conditions are right.

aggregates: Soil particles bound to each other, which are important to provide space for air and water in soil. Soil organisms and earthworms help create aggregates.

agricultural extension service: Government organization in most counties, associated with land grant universities, that educates people about gardening, usually free or at very low cost.

alkali soil: Soil with high pH and sodium, which interferes with plant growth. This condition can be corrected with the application of gypsum leached through the soil with heavy waterings.

alkaline soil: Soil with pH above 7. For a few vegetables prone to clubroot, this can be highly beneficial.

amendment: Anything added to soil to improve its structure and ability to hold moisture and to provide nutrients to plants.

ammonia (NH_3): A strong-smelling gas composed of nitrogen and hydrogen; a main component of many fertilizers.

ammoniacal: Describing any fertilizer containing ammonia, which produces acids in soil. This includes anhydrous ammonia, ammonium nitrate, ammonium sulfate, and urea. These are all considered synthetic and not organic. Replace them with organic fertilizers high in nitrogen.

ammonium (NH_4): A crystalline salt containing nitrogen and hydrogen, often used in fertilizers, especially ammonium sulfate, which acidifies soil. Replace it with an organic fertilizer high in nitrogen along with sulfur to acidify the soil.

ammonium nitrate: Synthetic nitrogen fertilizer with 33 percent nitrogen; not used in organic gardens.

ammonium sulfate: Synthetic nitrogen fertilizer with 21 percent nitrogen; not used in organic gardens.

anaerobic bacteria: Bacteria that thrive without oxygen. These will decompose material in a compost pile but emit an odor.

andromonoecious: Having flowers that contain both female and male organs (perfect flowers).

angiosperm: A plant producing seeds in an enclosed ovary (includes all flowering plants).

anion: A negatively charged ion; important in nutrient exchange.

annual: A plant whose life cycle is over in 1 year, going from seed to plant to seed again.

anther: Upper part of the stamen containing pollen in a flower (the male flower part).

anthracnose: A fungus disease that creates dead areas on fruit, leaves, and stems.

antitranspirant: A spray applied to plants to stop them from drying out.

aphid: Prevalent garden pest that sucks juices from plants and clusters on leaves and growing tips.

apical dominance: Hormonal influence of the growing tip over lateral buds (stops them from growing until the tip is removed). Once the tip is snipped off, side branches grow and make a plant bushier. Tip removal is recommended on some plants but can harm others.

arbor: A structure to support vines.

aromatic: Exuding a strong, pleasant scent (as with mint).

arthropod: The largest group in the animal kingdom, these creatures have an exoskeleton and feed on bacteria, fungi, insects, and plant material in the soil.

asexual propagation (vegetative propagation): Creating a new plant from a plant without seed.

auxin: Plant hormone that promotes growth.

available moisture: Water in soil that can be absorbed by plants.

available nutrient: A nutrient found in soil in a form plants can absorb.

axil: The angle formed by two stems, a branch and a stem, or a leaf and a stem.

azotobacter: Bacteria that are helpful in supplying plants with a usable form of nitrogen.

baby: A term describing the size of a plant's mature fruit (not the size of a plant).

Bacillus thuringiensis (Bt): A biological insecticide (sold as a powder in most nurseries) that infects and kills caterpillars and moths. It must be applied at regular intervals to be effective.

bacteria: Microscopic, generally one-celled organisms, once considered plants but now called prokaryotes.

balanced fertilizer: Fertilizer containing nitrogen, phosphorus, and potassium (N-P-K) in equal amounts. The most common is 10-10-10, which is synthetic. Replace it with a natural fertilizer.

bare-root transplanting: Moving plants without any soil around the roots. Bare-root plants are often half the price of actively growing ones.

basal: Relating to the lowest part of a plant.

base-dressing: Applying fertilizer to the soil before planting seed or transplants.

basket weaving: Supporting plants by tying string or twine tautly between stakes while interweaving these around the plants at varying heights.

bed: Area where many plants are grouped in no specific shape.

berry: A fruit with seeds enclosed within a soft pulp. Blueberries are berries, but raspberries and strawberries are not. The "seeds" (achenes) of strawberries and the "seeds" (drupelets) of raspberries are on the outside of the fruit.

biennial: Any plant that plays out its life over a 2-year period.

biodynamic agriculture: An organic method of growing nutritionally rich produce while protecting the environment, often with ethical and spiritual overtones.

biointensive gardening: A gardening system that tries to maximize yield on a minimum amount of space using materials produced within the garden. John Jeavons is credited with age-old methods to perfect this practice.

biological pest control: Use of bacteria or predator insects to kill off harmful fungus, insects, or mites. The most well-known is *Bacillus thuringiensis,* effective against caterpillars.

biomass: Total amount of organic matter produced by a plant, often used for composting.

blanching (for freezing): Immersing plants in boiling water to prepare them for freezing.

blanching (for whitening): Excluding light from stems or foliage to keep these tender and white.

bleach: Toxic product used to sterilize pots and tools. Many gardeners are switching to rubbing alcohol, hydrogen peroxide, and vinegar—or soap and water with lots of rinsing.

blight: Sudden wilting or death of plant parts.

blocking: Dividing any growing medium of seedling plants into blocks. This prepares the seedlings for transplanting.

blood meal: Dried blood containing approximately 10 percent nitrogen; a good organic fertilizer. Often suggested as rabbit repellent but doesn't work.

bloom stalk: Stem that bears flowers.

blossom end rot: Condition when the flower end of a tomato fruit cracks and develops rot, possibly caused by drought or lack of calcium in the soil.

bolting: Premature flower and seed stalk growth caused by temperatures that are too cool or too hot. Bolting is also related to day length. It destroys many crops, including lettuce and spinach.

bonemeal: Bones pulverized into a fine powder and added to gardens as a source of calcium and phosphorus. Reports about Creutzfeldt-Jakob disease, or mad cow disease, originating from this powder appear unfounded.

botanical pesticide: Any pesticide made from plants, including nicotine, pyrethrum, rotenone, ryania, and sabadilla. Although organic, these can cause damage in the garden.

botrytis: A group of fungi that cause disease, or the name of a specific disease caused by one of these.

bottom heat: Heat applied to the bottom of a bed or container to speed up germination of seeds or encourage root growth from cuttings.

bracts: Leaves around a developing flower, as on an artichoke.

bramble: Usually any wild plant related to blackberries and raspberries. Most have sharp, thorny spikes along the stem.

breaker: A hose attachment that regulates water flow in drip irrigation.

broadcast: To scatter seed or fertilizer over an entire area.

broadleaf: Any plant with wide leaves.

broad-spectrum pesticide: Any pesticide that will kill a wide variety of insects. The most popular is carbaryl (Sevin®), a synthetic product. Replace it with an organic one.

brush cutter: Power tool that cuts through small trees and heavy grass.

brush hog: A power attachment to a tractor that cuts down grass and saplings.

bud: Protrusion on a stem turning into shoot, leaf, or flower.

bulb: A general term describing underground storage parts of many plants. Many roots are called bulbs when they are really corms, rhizomes, tubers, and tuberous roots.

bulbil: A small bulb produced aboveground, as on the end of a stem of an Egyptian onion.

bulblet: A small bulb produced off to the side of an underground bulb.

bush variety: Plant that grows in a compact area, such as a bush variety of squash or bean.

caliche: See **hardpan.**

callus: Healing growth over a plant wound.

calyx: Lower or most-outer flower parts (sepals).

cambium: Cylinder of living cells just under bark.

cane: Hollow or pithy stems.

cane fruit: Fruit of blackberry, boysenberry, currant, dewberry, gooseberry, and raspberry.

canker: Lesion on the stem of a plant.

cap: Hard crust on soil surface.

capsaicin: Substance in peppers that makes them hot; found in the placenta of the fruit.

capsule: Seedpod. Some are delicious, as in radishes.

carbonic acid: The combination of water with carbon dioxide. Helps plants take in nutrients around the root system.

castings: See **worm castings.**

catch crop: Quick-maturing plants interplanted with slower-maturing crops or used between plantings of main crops to maximize use of garden space.

cation: A positively charged ion; important in nutrient exchange.

caution: A signal word on a pesticide indicating slight toxicity.

cell: The smallest living part of any plant or animal.

cellulose: Principal component of cell walls in plants.

certified: Inspected by an accredited third party for verification of a claim being made, such as "organic" or "disease-free."

chelation (key-LAY-shun): The addition of a substance to the soil to prevent loss of chemicals by binding them together. This makes specific nutrients more available to plants.

chemical fertilizer: Any man-made fertilizer; often called artificial fertilizer.

chicon: Swollen white bud on forced chicory roots.

chilling requirement: The number of hours at low temperature required to break dormancy.

chlorophyll: Green pigment in plant cells necessary for photosynthesis.

chlorosis: Lack of chlorophyll indicated by yellowing between veins of leaves.

clay: Very fine soil particles that adhere in moist conditions, causing poor drainage and compacted soil when dry.

cleaning crop: A plant that makes soil easier to work with (for example, potatoes). These break up soil and clear out weeds for other vegetables.

climber: Any plant that shoots out flexible branches that move upward, including many vines.

cloche: Protective cover for seedlings set out in spring and removed when danger of frost is past; now typically made of plastic.

clone: A duplicate plant made from the cell of a parent plant and always identical in all ways to the parent. See also **tissue culture.**

clove: Small portion of a garlic bulb that can be planted to produce a new bulb.

coir: Coconut husks now used as a soil amendment.

cold frame: Any small structure built to protect plants from bad weather.

cold hardiness: Plant tolerance to cold weather.

cole crop: Any member of the cabbage family, including broccoli, Brussels sprouts, cabbage, cauliflower, and kohlrabi.

come true: See **true from seed.**

companion planting: Planting certain plants next to each other for benefits to one or both; a system believed to encourage growth and ward off insects. Also, simply planting different plants together to make full use of available space.

complete (compound) fertilizer: A fertilizer that contains all three major nutrients (nitrogen, phosphorus, and potassium).

compost: Material produced by the collection and decomposition of organic wastes in a pile. In this book it refers to fully, not partially, decomposed material.

compost bin: Any structure or enclosed area that contains organic matter while it breaks down into humus.

compost crop: Plants grown primarily to be added to a compost pile.

compost tea: A mild solution of fertilizer made by soaking compost in water for a period of days.

contact herbicide: Chemical that kills any plant it touches.

cool-season crop: Plants that do well in cool weather and poorly when it gets warm.

copper: Necessary trace element; minute quantities are required in all soil.

corolla: The showy part of a flower made up of many petals.

cotyledons: The first one or two leaves that spring from the seed of a plant. The second leaves to appear are called "true leaves."

cover crop (green manure): A crop grown for its organic matter and nitrogen. Cover crops are turned into the soil as "green manure."

creeper: A plant that vines or trails along the ground, taking root at its nodes (place from which leaves grow).

crop rotation: Planting crops in the same family in different places each year to avoid disease in the soil.

cross-pollination: Transfer of pollen from one plant to another plant with different genetic makeup.

crown: Portion of a plant sticking up from the soil (as with strawberries); the place where stem and root meet; the entire rootstock of asparagus and rhubarb (both planted underground).

crucifer: Any plant in the cabbage family (Brassicaceae). The flowers form a cross with their petals.

CSA: Community-supported agriculture.

cucurbit: Any member of the Cucurbitaceae family, including cucumbers, melons, and squash.

cultivar: In this book, a synonym for variety. Technically, a cultivated variety (one bred by humans) or a mutation of a variety appearing naturally in nature or in the garden but selected and named by a breeder for its unique characteristics.

cultivate: To loosen soil to get rid of weeds and to make carbon dioxide available to roots.

curing: Letting root crops and winter squashes dry prior to storing.

cut and come again: Describing plants that can be sheared but produce new growth for a second crop.

cut flower: Flower that remains beautiful after being cut from the plant; used in flower arrangements.

cutting: Any portion of a plant that can be cut off and grown into a new plant.

cytokinin: A growth-promoting hormone found in seaweed.

damping-off: A fungus disease (or group of diseases) that kills seeds or seedlings. It can be prevented by using sterile potting mix and watering germinating seeds correctly.

danger – poison: Warning on pesticides signaling a highly toxic compound.

day-neutral plants: Plants with no preference for day lengths.

days to maturity: Time required for seed to grow and reach full size; may also refer to time needed to reach maturity from day of planting transplants.

deadheading: Removing all dead flowers from plants.

decomposition: Breakdown of organic material by soil microorganisms.

defoliation: Unnatural loss of leaves from herbicides, insects, or bad weather.

dehiscent: Describing a fruit that opens up once mature to reveal seeds inside, such as a bean.

desiccant: Drying agent; substance that absorbs moisture when storing seeds.

determinate: Having the characteristic of growing only to a certain size and then ceasing to grow.

diatomaceous earth (DE): White powder consisting of skeletal remains of microscopic marine organisms called diatoms; used to kill insects.

dibble: Any pointed instrument to make a hole in soil for planting.

dicot (dicotyledon): Any plant with two leaves (cotyledons) springing from its seed.

dieback: Loss of part of a plant, usually on woody plants exposed to cold winter weather.

dioecious: Bearing male and female flowers on different plants.

diploid: A plant having a full set of chromosomes, one from each of its parents.

direct seeding: Planting seeds in the garden, not in pots.

disease resistance: Ability of a plant to ward off disease or sustain minimal damage.

diurnal: Having flowers that open in day and close at night.

division: Creating two or more plants from a parent plant whose crown and roots are cut into two (or more) pieces with a spade or fork.

dolomitic limestone: Limestone containing magnesium.

dormant: Not actively growing, as plants in an inactive period (as in winter), or seed waiting to spring to life under the right conditions.

dormant spray: Pesticide applied to woody plants before buds appear in spring to kill fungal spores and insect eggs.

double digging: Traditional method for preparing a bed for planting; usually describes a laborious process of loosening soil to a depth of two spade lengths.

double potting: Placing a smaller pot inside a larger pot, typically with material placed between to retain moisture.

drainage: Ability of water to move rapidly through a soil. Poor drainage causes root rot.

draw: A sweet potato sprout planted in a garden to create a new plant.

drill: A shallow furrow for planting seeds.

drip irrigation: Watering plants through soaker hoses or similar systems to cut down on water loss through evaporation and unnecessary watering.

drip line: Imaginary circle around a plant showing where water drops off the leaves. The soil inside that area tends to stay dry.

dust: Extremely fine powder used to apply pesticides to plants.

dust mulching: Stirring up the surface of soil to stop water loss. This now obsolete technique was practiced for decades.

dwarf: A plant that grows much smaller than others of its same kind.

dynamic accumulators: Plants that draw up and collect specific nutrients from the soil. For example, nettle is reported to be rich in iron.

early: Describing the beginning of the growing season, or a variety that matures rapidly.

earthing up: Pulling up soil around a plant, either to blanch it (as with celery), to increase production (as with potatoes), or to support it (as with corn).

earthworm: A burrowing animal that aerates soil, helps drainage, and breaks down organic matter to be used by plants.

edging plant: Low-lying plants placed along edges of lawns or borders. Alpine strawberries are good edging plants.

embryo: The rudimentary plant contained in a seed.

endosperm: Stored food around the plant in a seed.

enzyme: A substance produced by living organisms that acts as a catalyst to biochemical reactions; important in the decomposition of organic materials.

ericaceous: Referring to members of the heath family. Do not lime soil for this group, which includes blueberries.

escapee: See **volunteer**.

esculent: Edible vegetable.

established plant: A plant that has taken root and is growing well.

eudicot: Essentially the same as a dicot for gardening purposes.

everbearing: Producing fruit all season long (usually fruit comes in spurts, not in continuous production).

everlasting flower: A flower that stays beautiful and firm when dried (for example, artichoke flowers, although the artichoke rarely has a long enough season to bloom in cold climates).

eye: A visible bud or growing tip, as on a potato.

eye of seed: The place where a seed was once connected to the ovary wall.

F1 hybrid: First filial, the result of a cross resulting in a hybrid.

family: Classification of plants including broad groups (genera) of similar species.

fertilization: Union of male cell in pollen with the female cell or ovule. Also, the application of nutrients to the soil.

fertilize: To apply nutrients to plants or soil to create growth. Also, to apply pollen to the female part of a plant to create fruit.

fertilizer: Any material that contains plant nutrients.

fertilizer burn: Damage or death to plants after the application of excessive fertilizer. This happens most frequently to seedlings when inorganic fertilizers are used.

fertilizer grade: The analysis of main chemicals on a package of fertilizer expressed in percentages such as 10-10-10 (10 percent nitrogen, 10 percent phosphorus, 10 percent potassium). Replace this common synthetic fertilizer with organic products.

fibrous roots: Root systems with many roots rather than one single root.

filament: The slender stalk that supports the anther, where pollen develops in a male flower.

filler: Inert material mixed in a bag of fertilizer.

fish emulsion: Fish parts processed into liquid fertilizer.

fish meal: Fish parts ground into dry powder.

flat: Any shallow container used for starting seeds.

floating row cover: Light polyester fabric that protects plants from insects and fluctuating temperatures as it "floats" above them.

flocculate: To cause to form clumps (aggregates) of soil; important for pores in soil and proper drainage.

floricane: Two-year-old fruit-bearing cane of brambles, such as raspberries.

flower: Reproductive organ of seed-bearing plants, often colorful.

flower drop: Natural loss of flowers early in the season, but a sign of stress later on.

foliage: Leaves on a plant.

foliar feeding: Application of fertilizer in a fine mist directly to leaves of plants.

forcing: Getting a plant to grow when it normally would not, and excluding light from it at the same time (as with Belgian endive).

forked: Describing root crops that split apart after hitting an object during growth. Roots look like an inverted V.

frass: Sawdust-like material around the stem of a plant produced by boring insects.

friable soil: Soil with a good feel that is easy to crumble in one's hand, indicating excellent texture and lots of organic matter.

frost dates: Approximate time for the last frost in spring and the first frost in fall.

frost lifting: Loosening and lifting of plants from the soil as ground shifts during periods of freeze and thaw. Winter mulches stop this action.

fruit: The part of the plant that develops to protect seeds. Botanically, most vegetables are fruits. Common usage defines fruits more specifically.

full slip: An expression indicating ripeness of melons, which are said to be in "full slip" when they slide right off the vine.

full sun: Six or more hours of direct sun per day. Most vegetables need at least this amount of light to grow well.

fumigation: Gassing soil, plants, or structures with poison to kill pests; not an organic method and rarely done in home gardens. Replace with **solarization**.

fungicide: A pesticide that kills fungi.

fungus (plural, fungi): Formerly classified as plants without chlorophyll that contribute both good (break down organic matter) and bad (cause disease) to the garden. They lack true leaves, roots, and stems. They cannot produce their own food and reproduce by spores. Most are single celled with numerous filaments (hyphae) that gather nutrients for growth. Fungi are now classified as eukaryotes.

furrow: A shallow trench for planting or irrigation.

gall: An abnormal growth on a plant caused by disease or insects.

garden line: String attached to two stakes. Pull the stakes apart, and set them close to the ground to make a straight furrow.

gas or gaseous exchange: Plant process of absorbing carbon dioxide and releasing oxygen into the air through photosynthesis.

genetic engineering: Mechanical transfer of DNA from one organism to another. This is not a natural process. See also **hybridization**.

genus (plural, genera): Plant classification that refers to a group of species, all with similar, but not necessarily identical, characteristics.

germination: Sprouting of seed into active growth.

girdling: Cutting around the stem of a plant by insects or rodents. Cutworms are notorious for this.

glaucous: Having a white to bluish, harmless coating, as on some leaves and fruits.

GMO: Genetically modified organism. See also **genetic engineering**.

graft: To connect one part of a plant (scion) to another plant (rootstock). Most commonly, a scion from an heirloom is attached to a hybrid rootstock for greater hardiness and disease resistance. Often done with tomatoes.

grain: Plants that produce small, hard-shelled fruits on grass-like crops. In most instances, the outside is fused to the inside of the fruit.

granule: Particle of fertilizer or pesticide.

greenhouse: A building with clear sides to control humidity and temperature for plant growth.

greenhouse plant: A plant that grows best in the controlled atmosphere of a greenhouse. Some vegetable varieties are developed primarily for this purpose, such as parthenocarpic cucumbers.

green manure: Any plant grown in the garden to be plowed under for its organic material and nutrients.

greens: Leaves and leaf stems of immature plants that are typically harvested young while tender to be eaten raw or cooked (depending on the vegetable).

ground cover: Any plant grown to stop erosion and weed growth.

growing point: The tip of growing roots or shoots (stems). It can be removed on some plants to encourage branching but should never be removed on others.

growing season: The approximate number of frost-free days in an area.

grow on: To transplant to a larger pot for better development (same as "potting up").

gynoecious: Producing only (mostly) female flowers and thus needing pollination by another plant.

gypsum: Hydrated calcium sulfate; helps the structure of clay soils and with the removal of salt from soils.

habit: The way a plant grows (upright versus spreading, for example); the general shape or outline of a plant.

habitat: A natural area where a plant grows.

half-hardy: Capable of tolerating some cold with limited protection.

hardening off: Placing transplants outdoors for a bit longer each day over a period of 10 days. This allows them to adjust gradually to varying temperatures, humidity, and light conditions. Some gardeners reduce watering as well. Once hardened off, transplants are planted permanently in containers or directly in the garden.

hardiness: The ability of a plant to withstand cold temperatures.

hardpan: A layer of soil that does not allow drainage or root penetration; varies enormously from one area to the next. Some gardeners believe that tilling results in the formation of hardpan in the subsoil.

hardware cloth: Fine wire mesh.

hard water: Water with excessive calcium and magnesium.

hardy: Capable of withstanding excessive cold in winter.

haulm: The stalk or stem of a bean, pea, or potato.

heaving (frost lifting): Lifting of plants from the ground caused by freezing and thawing of soil. Mulch will often prevent this.

heavy soil: Usually a soil with lots of clay.

heeling in: Protecting bare-root plants, usually woody, in a mound of soil or moist sawdust until planting time.

heirloom: A plant that produces seed that when grown, will be essentially identical to the mother plant. Synonymous with *open pollinated,* with the exception that these plants have proven themselves reliable over many decades of use.

herb: Plant whose foliage, flowers, and seed are valued for flavor, medicinal value, or scent.

herbaceous plant: Any plant that dies back to the roots in winter and regrows in spring.

herbicide: Any poison that kills plants.

hill: A spot where several seeds are planted together. Hills can be level or raised into a mound, which provides better drainage and more warmth.

hilling up: Pulling up soil around the stems of plants to increase yield, blanch the base of plants, or keep plants from toppling over in heavy winds (as for potatoes, leeks, and corn).

hoe: A tool used to create furrows, draw up soil, and remove weeds from the garden. Many are designed and shaped for specific purposes.

honeydew: Sweet, sticky substance secreted from insects feeding on plants; very attractive to ants.

hormone: Chemical that affects growth.

horticulture: Cultivation of plants, such as berries, herbs, and vegetables, on a small scale.

host: Any living thing that supports another living organism; usually refers to a plant invaded by disease or insects.

hotbed: A cold frame with an outside source of heat.

HotKaps: Small coverings that protect plants in spring.

houseplant: Any plant well suited to be grown indoors. Some vegetables can be grown indoors, but few are well suited to this.

hull: The outermost covering of a seed, such as a sunflower; also the leafy husk around an ear of corn.

humic acid: Dark-brown, water-soluble substance formed as organic material breaks down. It helps soil release nutrients.

humus: The end product of the breakdown of organic mate-rial in nature. It is rich, dark, and sweet smelling; often called "brown gold" or "black gold" by knowledgeable gardeners.

hybrid: A plant created by crossing plants with different but similar genetic makeups. The seed of these plants rarely pro-duces true (won't re-create itself identically).

hybridization: The process of creating hybrids. This is a natu-ral process, not be confused with genetic engineering.

hybrid vigor: The enhanced vigor plants show as a result of cross-breeding.

hydroponics: Growing plants without soil.

hyphae: Filaments that protrude from fungi.

imperfect flower: A flower with only one sexual organ, either male or female.

indehiscent: Describing a fruit that retains its seeds inside at maturity, such as a parsnip.

indeterminate: Having the characteristic of growing as long as conditions are favorable; having no fixed growth pattern. Many tomatoes will keep vining as long as they are not killed off by cold.

inflorescence: Flower cluster.

inoculant: Bacterial powder dusted on seeds to help nitrogen fixing in legumes.

inorganic: Any chemical not made from animal or vegetable products. Inorganic chemicals come from the earth or are made synthetically.

insecticide: Pesticide that kills insects.

insect vectors: Insects that carry and pass on diseases to plants.

in situ planting: Planting seed directly in the garden.

intensive gardening: Getting the highest yield possible by intercropping and successive planting.

intercropping: Planting two separate crops together to use space efficiently. Usually, one short-season and one long-season crop are planted together. Also called *interplanting.*

internode: Space between two buds (nodes) on a stem.

invasive: Capable of growing quickly and spreading fast; be-coming weed-like.

involucre: Bracts surrounding a central flower (such as edible chrysanthemum).

IPM: Integrated pest management, a term for intelligent pest management.

irrigation: Method of watering through soaker hoses or trenches whenever soil dries out.

jute netting: Biodegradable net of jute fibers used to stop erosion.

kelp: A sea plant pulverized and sold as a fertilizer; often sprayed on leaves of plants to encourage growth.

kitchen garden: Usually a small garden producing herbs, salad greens, and cut flowers for home use.

landscape: The surrounding terrain and its features.

larva (plural, **larvae**): Immature insect (which often damages leafy crops).

lateral branch: Side branch.

lateral bud: Any bud in the axil of a leaf or branch (as opposed to a terminal bud at the tip of the plant).

lattice: Crossed wood strips stapled together as supports for vining plants.

layering: A technique to create roots on branches or stems to propagate new plants. Air layering is done on aboveground stems; ground layering, on stem tissue just above the soil line.

leaching: The removal of dissolved minerals in soil through excessive water.

leader: Main stem of a plant.

leaf: A flattened plant part attached directly to a stem or connected to it with a stalk. If a leaf is divided into separate parts, they are called leaflets.

leaf burn: Spotting on a leaf from high temperature or careless application of fertilizer.

leaf mold: Partially decayed leaves used as a soil amendment or mulch.

leggy: Having grown excessively tall and weak, usually caused by poor light conditions (inside) or overcrowding in the garden (outside).

legume: Any plant belonging to the pea family and able to fix nitrogen from the atmosphere.

lesion: Damaged tissue on a plant, like a wound, most commonly caused by disease or insects.

lifting: Digging a plant to be replanted or stored.

light soil: Loose term for sandy soil.

lignin: Organic substance that helps cells stay rigid and strong; broken down in the composting process.

lime (limestone): Sedimentary rock (calcium or magnesium carbonate) crushed, burned, and ground to a fine powder and applied to gardens to make them more alkaline.

loam: An ideal soil consisting of just the right amount of clay, sand, silt, and organic matter.

lodging: Falling or toppling over, as with corn in heavy winds.

long-day plant: A vegetable that does best in areas where there are many hours of light each day (cold climates). This is important in choosing onion and strawberry varieties.

loose: Having good structure, as a soil that is easy to work, not compacted.

loppers: Long-handled pruning shears for bigger branches.

macronutrients: Chemicals required in larger amounts for optimal growth, including nitrogen, phosphorus, and potassium.

manure: Animal wastes used to improve soil structure and fertility; not as fertile as most people think but critical to soil structure and health.

manure tea: Liquid made by soaking manure in water to make a transplant solution.

margin: The edge of a leaf.

mellow soil: Friable soil that feels great in the hand; loose soil that is easy to work in.

mesclun: Mixture of seed that produces leafy plants (exact types and varieties vary). Create your own mesclun mix from individual packets of seed that produce leafy crops.

microclimate: Any area that is somewhat different in temperature, wind protection, soil, or water moisture. The side of a south-facing fence is different from a north-facing patio. Each microclimate is suited to certain kinds of plants.

microgreens: Leaves or shoots of salad vegetables harvested early in their growth.

micronutrient: Chemical needed in minute quantities by plants to grow well; also called a *trace element.*

microorganisms: Microscopic living organisms, critical to good soil health and the decomposition of organic materials.

mildew: A fungus that often produces a powdery substance on plants.

miniature: Plant bred for its small size for container gardening.

miscible oil: Oil that kills a variety of insects and mites by suffocating victims.

mist: To shower plants with a fine and delicate spray of water; essential for starting plants from seed; also used in foliar feeding.

mite: Spiderlike creature (not an insect) that contributes both good and bad to the garden.

miticide: Pesticide that kills mites.

molluscicide: Pesticide that kills slugs and snails.

monocot (monocotyledon): A plant with only one leaf (cotyledon) springing from its seed, as with corn and grasses.

monoecious: Bearing both male and female flowers.

mosaic: A viral disease that causes mottled leaves. Tobacco mosaic virus (TMV) can be caused by using tobacco in the garden.

mottled: Having light and dark irregular areas on plant tissue; indication of disease.

mucilaginous: Becoming slimy when placed in water, as seeds; a characteristic of interest to people who grow sprouts.

mulch: Material that covers the soil surface.

mycoplasma: Disease-causing microorganism similar to bacteria but lacking a cell wall.

mycorrhiza: A fungus that forms a symbiotic relationship with the roots of some plants.

naked seed: Seeds without hulls, mostly referring to varieties of pumpkins.

native: Any plant that grows naturally in an area.

naturalized: Having been introduced from another area, as a plant, but thriving in its present home.

nematicide: Pesticide that kills nematodes.

nematodes: Microscopic worms in the soil that do both good and bad. They digest microorganisms but can damage plant root hairs.

neonicotinoid: Nicotine-like synthetic insecticides.

neutral soil: Soil with a pH near 7, neither acidic nor alkaline. Almost all of the vegetables in this guide grow well in slightly acidic to neutral soils.

nitrogen-fixing bacteria: Bacteria on the roots of legumes, such as beans and peas, that take nitrogen from the atmosphere and convert it to a form usable by plants.

node: The spot on a stem (usually a little bump) from which a branch or leaf will emerge. Also, a similar bump on a root that can produce a new plant, as with sunchokes.

nonselective herbicide: A chemical that will kill all plants.

no-till farming: A method of growing plants without tilling the soil (also called *natural farming*); proselytized by Masanobu Fukuoka both as a philosophy and farming technique.

N-P-K: Symbols representing nitrogen, phosphorus, and potassium on fertilizer packages.

nut: A hard-shelled fruit. (A peanut is not a nut but rather a legume that forms pods with edible seeds underground.)

nutrient availability: An indication of whether chemicals are in a form that can be assimilated by plants.

nymph: Immature stage of some insects, often resembling adults.

open pollinated: Describing plants whose seeds will grow into plants essentially the same as the mother plant; critical for seed savers.

organic: Derived from plants or animals. All organic materials contain carbon.

organic gardening: A system of gardening using only natural (organic) materials for fertilizing and pest control.

organic seed: Seed produced through strictly organic methods. Seed not available as organic may in some instances be used by organic farmers.

osmosis: Process by which plants take in moisture from the soil and distribute it from cell to cell.

ovary: Part of a flower containing ovules, which once fertilized, produce seed.

overwinter: To remain alive through the winter with or without protection.

ovicide: Pesticide that kills eggs of pests.

ovule: The female cell or egg that becomes a seed when fertilized.

pan: Hard layer beneath soil surface.

parasite: Any creature that lives off another plant or animal at the host's expense.

parthenocarpic: Producing fruit without pollination and without seeds (such as seedless cucumbers).

pathogen: Something that causes a disease in a plant.

peat moss: See **sphagnum peat moss.**

peat pellet: Compressed cube of peat used for starting seeds and cuttings; can be planted directly in the garden without disturbing plant roots.

peat pot: A container made of peat that should break down once planted in the garden.

pelleted seed: Seeds coated with a thin layer of material to make them easier to handle; excellent for sight-impaired gardeners.

perennial: Any plant that lives for more than a few years. Most perennials have to be divided periodically to encourage "everlasting" growth (rhubarb is a good example).

perfect flower: Flower that contains both male and female organs (as with tomatoes).

perianth: The calyx and corolla combined, if present.

perlite: Light, fluffy volcanic material used to aerate soil mixtures; can be used to start seeds if finely ground.

permaculture: Landscapes deliberately designed to mimic nature while striving to take care of human needs, including food. The term was coined by Australians David Holmgren and Bill Mollison.

pesticide: Any chemical used to kill disease pathogens, insects, or mites.

petal: Modified leaf, often colorful to attract pollinators.

pH (potential hydrogen): A number showing how alkaline or acidic the soil is, based on a logarithmic scale.

photosynthesis: The ability of plants to convert water, carbon dioxide, and other compounds into carbohydrates using energy from the sun.

pistil: Female organ in a flower, made up of the stigma, style, and ovary.

pollen: Powder, often yellow, containing male sex cells that fertilize the ovule in a female organ.

pollination: Fertilization of plants as pollen (from male anther) is transferred to the stigma (female part of same or another plant).

pollinator: Bird, insect, or wind that carries pollen to a plant.

porosity (pore space): Space between soil particles; helps to retain air and water at correct levels.

primary nutrients: See **macronutrients.**

primocane: First-year growth of brambles, some of which can produce fruit that year.

propagation: Creating new plants from seed (sexual) or plant parts (asexual).

protoplasm: The clear material making up a cell. The term is considered obsolete but is still used since no word has replaced it.

protozoa: One-celled organisms with the ability to move and eat other organisms. They are considered eukaryotic, with characteristics of plants and animals.

provenance: Origin of plants or seed.

pruning: Cutting off a part of a plant to enhance growth, to reduce disease, or to increase yield.

puddling: Swishing roots of seedlings in mud to cover the roots while planting in the garden; stops them from drying out. It is easier to keep roots in water.

pupa (plural, **pupae**): Nondestructive stage of an insect between larval and adult stages.

race: A group of pathogens of one type within a species (for example, there are many races of fusarium). Plants may be susceptible to one or more, or none.

raised bed: A growing surface higher than the surrounding ground. It can be as simple as a small hill or as complex as a series of permanent beds surrounded by timbers or rocks.

repellent: Any substance that repels insects without killing them.

resistance: Ability of a plant to fight off disease.

respiration: A series of chemical processes that allow a plant to make food.

rhizobium: A type of bacteria on roots of legumes that help fix nitrogen.

rhizome: An underground stem or runner; contains buds or eyes from which stems will emerge.

rhizosphere: The upper portion of soil where most microbial activity occurs around the roots of plants.

rogue: To pull up and destroy diseased or unwanted plants.

root ball: Roots and surrounding soil; best kept intact when planting.

root-bound: Having outgrown available space, creating a mass of roots in the shape of the container or pot.

root crop: Any plant grown for its edible roots.

root cutting: Piece of root used to grow new plants.

root hair: Microscopic roots that take in water and nutrients for the plant.

rooting hormone: Powder or liquid that stimulates root production on cuttings. Honey is often used on hardwood cuttings to replace synthetic products, as is soaking cuttings in willow water or water containing dissolved aspirin.

rootstock: The lower portion of a grafted plant, usually much hardier than the upper portion (scion).

root zone: Area where most roots are found in soil; essentially the same as the rhizosphere.

rose nozzle: Nozzle on a watering can that breaks water into fine streams.

rosette: Circular cluster of leaves at ground level.

rototiller: Machine with revolving blades that dig into and loosen soil to a depth determined by the user.

rototilling: Preparing soil with a rototiller.

row cover: Material set over plants to protect them from cold or insects or to increase heat retention in early spring and late fall.

runner: A plant created to the side of a mother plant (as in strawberries). The runner develops into a new plant.

salad vegetable: An imprecise term referring to vegetables typically eaten raw.

salinity: Saltiness of soil, which inhibits plant growth.

sand: Large soil particles that cannot retain water easily. Organic matter must be added to sand for garden purposes.

sativum: A cultivated plant; term may appear in plant names.

scarification: The scratching or sanding of tough seeds to make them germinate faster.

scion: A branch or shoot grafted onto another plant.

screening: Using plants to block out sound, sun, views, or wind.

secondary nutrients: Chemicals required in moderate amounts for optimal growth, including calcium, magnesium, and sulfur.

secondary pest: Pests that follow the destruction of other pests. Carbaryl (Sevin®), a synthetic pesticide, kills most insects, but not spider mites. The mite population often explodes after its use (a good reason not to use it).

seed: An embryonic plant (fertilized ovule) protected by a thin cover that germinates when planted under the right conditions.

seedbed: An area of soil that the gardener prepares for planting seed.

seed coat: Outer layer of seed that protects the embryo and breaks on growth.

seed leaves: First leaves that appear as a seed sprouts. These are not true leaves.

seedling: Young plant just started from seed; very vulnerable at this stage.

seedpod: Part of maturing plant that holds seed.

seed tapes: Strips embedded with seeds.

selective pesticide: A poison that kills only specific insects.

self-fruitful: Capable of pollinating itself.

self-pollination: The transfer of the pollen of one flower to the stigma of another flower on the same plant.

self-unfruitful: Needing another variety for pollination. Also called *self-incompatible* and *self-infertile.*

sepal: Leaflike structure forming a calyx.

sets: Small onions grown one year for planting the next.

setting: The maturation of fruit from a blossom. When a blossom is pollinated, it sets to form fruit. A fruit sets by maturing.

setting out: Planting seedlings in the garden.

shade plant: A plant that likes to grow in shade.

shatter: To shoot out seeds from a pod as they mature.

sheet composting: Applying materials, including kitchen scraps, directly to the garden rather than composting them in a pile. This is not usually recommended except at the end of the growing season. It is messy, takes nitrogen from soil during decomposition, and attracts animals.

short-day plant: Vegetable that thrives where there are fewer hours of daylight (the South). These do not do well in cold climates.

short-season plant: A plant that develops very quickly from seed to mature plant (such as a radish).

shrub: Any woody perennial plant with numerous stems coming from its base.

side-dressing: Addition of small amounts of fertilizers to the side of plants during the growing season.

siderophores: A molecule specialized in helping plants take in iron.

silt: Soil particles larger than clay but smaller than sand.

skips: Empty spots in a row where seeds did not grow.

slime mold: Ultrasimple organism consisting of protoplasm that appears like jelly and will produce spores (but not considered a fungus).

slip: Any cutting of a soft-stemmed plant that can be rooted in soil or water (as with sweet potatoes).

sludge: Soil amendment made from treated sewage. Milorganite® is widely available but is not considered organic.

sod: Layer of grass.

soil: Mixture of chemicals, particles, water, air, and millions of living plants and animals. Think of soil as a living creature, not an inanimate object.

soil amendment: Anything added to the soil to create better structure.

soil food web: A complex community of living organisms in the soil; the interrelationships of plants, animals, the environment, and the transfer of energy from one to the other.

soilless mix: Mixture of peat, perlite, and vermiculite, but not soil; may contain fertilizer and water-absorbing granules (polymers). The latter are not considered organic.

soil structure: The complicated composition of soil, taking into account all factors, including texture (amounts of clay, sand, and silt), air space, and organic matter.

soil test: An inexact procedure that checks composition, pH, and nutrient levels in a soil sample.

soil texture: A characteristic of soil determined by the relative amounts of clay, sand, and silt in the soil.

solarization: Covering the soil with clear plastic to increase soil temperature in an effort to kill insects, nematodes, and pathogens (disease-causing agents).

sour soil: Soil that is acidic.

species: Plants similar to each other and capable of interbreeding; a hybrid is a cross between two species. Also, plants existing in the wild with similar characteristics. A subdivision of a genus (large plant group). The plural abbreviation is spp.

sphagnum moss: A bog moss used for starting seeds (if screened) and lining hanging pots. It is often stringy and spongy in feel. Always wear gloves and a long-sleeved shirt when working with it to avoid contracting the fungal disease sporotrichosis, which can be serious.

sphagnum peat moss: Partially decomposed wetland matter containing at least 67 percent sphagnum moss; used as a soil amendment and for making soils slightly acidic. This decomposed moss is not linked to any disease.

spike: A tall cluster of flowers along one stem.

spore: Reproductive structure of fungi. Some are windborne and cannot be prevented from carrying disease into the garden.

sprout: A seed with a newly emerging root, often highly nutritious.

spur: A stubby stem on branches that often produces fruit.

staking: Propping up a plant for better growth or ease of picking.

stamen: Male organ of a flower consisting of a filament and an anther that produces pollen.

starting mix: Any solid material used to start seed indoors. Most mixes contain peat, perlite, or vermiculite, all of which are sterile.

stem: Main aboveground portion of a plant.

stem cutting: A piece of stem rooted in soil to create a new plant.

sterile: Unable to bear fruit or viable seed. Also, disease-free.

sterile soil: Soil treated with steam for 20 minutes to kill off pathogens and weed seeds. Soil heated for less time or at a lower temperature is said to be pasteurized.

stigma: Area of the female flower receiving pollen.

stolon: A horizontal stem producing roots and new plants from various nodes at or just under the soil surface, as with grass and some weeds.

stomata: Tiny openings in foliage that allow entry of carbon dioxide and exit of oxygen from the plant.

strain: A group of plants similar to a cultivated variety but grown from seed.

stratification: Storing seeds in cool to freezing temperatures (usually in the refrigerator) to fool them into believing they have passed through a winter. This overcomes their dormancy.

stress: Any condition dangerous to a plant.

style: The slender tube protruding upward from the ovary. The stigma, which traps pollen, is at its tip.

subsoil: Soil underneath the area normally cultivated for planting. It is usually compacted without organic matter present.

subspecies: Naturally occurring variant of a species in a specific area; abbreviated as *ssp.*

succession planting: Creation of an extended harvest by planting short-season plants every few weeks.

succulent: Having leaves that are thick and fleshy, as with Malabar spinach.

sucker: Shoots from the base of the plant, usually growing from roots. Separate these from the mother for new plants. Also, growth from the axil on tomato plants. These can be removed and rooted for new plants (mostly done in warm climates).

sustainable agriculture: Production of food or other plant or animal products using techniques that keep a garden and the surrounding area healthy or more healthy than it was originally; coined by the Australian Gordon McClymont.

sweet soil: Soil that is alkaline.

symbiosis: The living together of organisms with different characteristics to benefit each other in some way.

synthetic: Man-made, as opposed to organic (occurring naturally).

syringe: To wash a plant with a fine spray of water.

systemic pesticide: A pesticide absorbed by a plant. It becomes part of the living organism and cannot be washed off by rain.

tamp: To press lightly or firmly on fresh soil to get rid of air pockets. This can be done by hand or with a flat tool.

taproot: Main root in the soil.

tender plant: Any plant killed or harmed by cold weather.

tendril: Long, curling part of a plant that often twines around any available support.

terminal bud: Bud at the top or tip of the plant. Removal can cause side branching. Also, buds at the end of each branch.

texture: The overall look of contrasting plants in garden design. See also **soil texture.**

thatch: Buildup of dead grass and plant debris on lawns.

thinning (thinning out): Removing part of a crop to give the rest of the plants room to grow.

thongs: Cuttings taken from horseradish roots for propagation of new plants.

till: To work the soil into small fragments; allows soil to absorb water and air.

tilth: The feel of soil, which indicates how it will work and how seeds will grow in it.

tine: Prong of a fork or rake.

tip layering: A method of getting a new plant from an old one by bending a stem to the ground and covering it with soil; used with blackberries.

tissue culture: Using individual cells of plants to create new plants. This can be done by the home gardener, but it is difficult and requires absolutely sterile conditions. Most commonly done by commercial growers on plants highly susceptible to disease.

topdressing: Any fertilizer sprinkled on top of soil but not worked in.

topsoil: Upper part of the soil, filled with living organisms feeding on the heavy concentration of organic matter there; critical area for plant growth.

trace element: See **micronutrient.**

transpiration: Water movement from leaves to air. Plants are constantly cooling themselves through this process, which explains their expanded need for water in hot, dry periods.

transplant: To move a growing plant from one area to another. A plant ready to be moved from a container into the garden.

transplant solution: Mild liquid fertilizer that helps seedlings or young plants survive the ordeal of transplanting.

trap crop: Plants meant to lure pests away from a main crop (rarely works).

treated seed: Seed dusted with chemicals to stop infections caused by pathogens; not considered organic. Seed treatments not requiring prohibited substances are allowed, such as heat treatment.

trellis: Any support for vining plants.

true from seed: Having seed that grow up just like their parent plants.

true leaves: Leaves produced after the seed leaves (first one or two leaves on a seedling). Once true leaves develop, a plant can be transplanted.

tuber: Enlarged portion of an underground stem; has buds for new growth (as with potatoes).

tuberous root: Enlarged portion of a root, such as a sweet potato.

turgid: Being full of water and very firm; opposite of *wilted.*

ultraviolet light: Light waves with short wavelengths; will kill off many damaging soil microorganisms.

urea: Potent nitrogen fertilizer made synthetically or from concentrated urine; not considered organic, because of its high nitrogen content (46 percent).

variety: Technically any plant that occurs naturally in the wild as a variation from the original parent plant (species). Plants that are bred are correctly called *cultivars.*

vegetable: Plant cultivated for edible leaves, roots, flowers, fruits, and seed.

vegetative propagation: Propagating plants using any part of a plant except seeds.

vein: Portion of a leaf that defines its structure and carries food and water.

vermicompost: Organic matter broken down by worms mixed with their excretions (castings).

vermiculite: Mica heated until it pops; used for starting seed and cuttings.

vernalization: Chilling artichoke seedlings to "fool" them into believing it is their second year of growth once they are planted in the garden.

viable: Capable of germinating; still alive.

vine: A plant that grows stems outward or upward on a support.

virus: A disease-causing organism submicroscopic in size that needs to invade a living cell to reproduce.

volunteer: Plant that takes over through seeding or spreading through underground stems (stolons); also known as an *escapee.*

warm-season plant: A plant that thrives in warm weather and will not tolerate cold.

water basin: Ridge around the base of a plant to hold in water.

weed: Any plant growing where you don't want it to.

wettable powder: Pesticide mixed with water and applied to plant surfaces.

whorl: Several leaves all emerging from a single stem or node and encircling it.

wilting: Hanging limply from water loss or disease. Some plants always look limp in the middle of the day (such as vining plants); most do not. Wilting is usually a sign of trouble.

windbreak: Anything that provides protection from the wind.

wind rock: Loosening of a plant from soil by heavy winds.

worm castings: The nutrient-rich excrement of worms.

yellows: Virus disease spread by insects causing stunted growth and yellowed leaves.

INDEX

ABOUT THE AUTHOR

John Whitman is an avid gardener with more than fifty years of gardening experience. Early in his career he was a grower at Bachman's, at that time the largest retail florist and nursery in the United States. His book *Starting from Scratch: A Guide to Indoor Gardening* was chosen as a main selection of the Organic Gardening Book Club and an alternate selection of the Book-of-the-Month Club. He was a contributing writer to the *Better Homes and Gardens New Garden Book* and the writer of the *Better Homes and Gardens* *New Houseplants Book*. He has coauthored several popular books on cold-climate gardening, including *Growing Perennials in Cold Climates, Growing Shrubs and Small Trees in Cold Climates,* and the award-winning *Growing Roses in Cold Climates,* all published by the University of Minnesota Press. He lives in Minnesota and for the past twenty-five years has been growing and field-testing many of the plants featured in this book.